BROADCAST MANAGEMENT IN INDIA

Major Guidelines and Policy Frameworks

BROADCAST MANAGEMENT IN INDIA

Major Guidelines and Policy Frameworks

Angela Wadia

KANISHKA PUBLISHERS, DISTRIBUTORS
NEW DELHI-110 002

KANISHKA PUBLISHERS, DISTRIBUTORS
4697/5-21A, Ansari Road, Daryaganj
New Delhi-110 002
Phones : 2327 0497, 2328 8285
Fax : 011-2328 8285
e-mail: kanishka_publishing@yahoo.co.in

First Published 2007

ISBN 81-7391-911-9

PRINTED IN INDIA

Published by Madan Sachdeva for Kanishka Publishers, Distributors, 4697/5-21A, Ansari Road, Daryaganj, New Delhi-110 002; Typeset by Sunshine Graphics, Delhi, and Printed at Nice Printing Press, Delhi.

Preface

"Broadcast Management in India: Major Guidelines and Policy Frameworks" is a kind of sourcebook on the said subject. It can serve the purpose of a handbook or reference book covering most of the related themes on this issue of contemporary significance. The book provides, in its earlier parts, an international perspective on the subject areas of global broadcasting. Focus lies on the campaign for making public broadcasting available for all. A list of major government broadcasting stations functioning all around the world is given. The details about famous Casablanca Declaration on the subject of public broadcasting is given. An overview of historical account of system of broadcasting in India is provided herein. A detailed account of satellite broadcasting in India in recent decades is outlined, with focus on issues of national significance and kinds of relief given to entertainment industry in recent times. Details about the modern global broadcasting system and the major video formats being used globally is given. Measures required for building bridges between various formats of videos available globally and the standard conversion techniques are dealt in detail. The advent of digital television globally is discussed along with the case study of a multi-standard video equipment from a famous international company. The scene of digital video broadcasting in India is reflected upon with the case study of use of such service of the Indian Meteorological Department. Other Indian achievements in the field of educational satellite broadcasting system as world's first is outlined in brief. A policy perspective on the modern system of educational television broadcasting in India is presented, with a rational perspective on upcoming priorities this field. Success in education through broadcasting is critically analysed at the national level. This book also provides answers regarding worldwide TV standards related questions. It also provides readers with global, cable, radio, television and broadcasting sources list and a glossary of related technical terms.

This book reflects on various dimensions of broadcasting scenario in India. An introduction of Indian news, radio and broadcast media is presented. Prevailing national and global scenario regarding TV Radio, radio and television is discussed. Role of broadcasting in information dissemination. Situations regarding cinema, air network is critically analysed. An introductory overview of Indian radio and television is presented. The elaborate profile, resources and services offered by All India Radio is outlined. The position of Phase II of private FM broadcasting in India and the recommendations of FM Radio Committee is described. The evaluation and popularity of community radio broadcasting in India is dealt in detail and a reality check is conducted on whether it needs a fresh policy in the changing rational scenario. The citizen charter in this regard is discussed in addition to the governmental point of view.

The new radio policy and its broadcasting role for a good society and rural progress is discussed. Television as an instrument of social change in India and abroad is critically analysed. The relationship between television and video flow in India is described and the strategy for making video programme packages is discussed. The recruitment roles of Prasar Bharati is presented. The Indian radio channels, TV channels, and radio network sites are described. The progress of Indian Cinema since independence is briefly analysed and the policy for import of cinematograph films and other films is discussed, in addition to a step-by-step guide for shooting of foreign feature films in India.

This book also presents readers with national broadcasting policies, rules, acts and regulations. Major legal resources included in this regard consists of the Broadcasting Bill (1997), The Prasar Bharati Act (1990), Cable TV Notifications (2003), The Cable TV Networks Acts (1995), Cable Television Network Rules (1994), The Indian Telegraph Act (1885), The Copyright Act (1957), New Telecom Policy (1999), etc. In addition, details regarding the Indian Broadcasting Regulations Forum is provided herein. Concerned government policies, guidelines and reports, in particular with reference to Conditional Access System (CAS), Direct-to-Home (DTH), uplinking and downlinking are dealt in detail. In this regard the governmental foreign investment policy, service tax law and broadcasting codes are also discussed. The historic 1995 judgement on governmental monopoly case on air waves is outlines. The Information Technology Action Plan and the role of Telecom Commission are critically analysed.

The last segment of this book deals with the national broadcast policy, radio communication laws, satellite and cable TV guidelines. Major details listed therein include regarding The Broadband Policy (2004), The Communication Convergence Bill (2001), The National Security Act (1980), etc. The role of the Press Information Bureau is discussed. Policy framework and measures for implementation of internet domain name is provided herein. The Radio Communication laws of Indian is dealt, so is the Citizen Charter of RNI. The relevance of monopolies and restrictive trade practices in this regard is presented. Details of the report of the review committee. On the working of Prasar Bharati is given. The nearly announced norms, guidelines and procedures for satellite communication in India is outlined. The details of the report on the task force on introduction of conditional access system are given. This book also provides readers with the details regarding guidelines for use of SNG/ DSNG, uplinking of news and current affairs TV channels and syndication arrangements by newspapers. In sum, this book comes most of the relevant areas dealing with the subject-matter of broadcasting management in India.

Angela Wadia

Contents

1

Broadcasting: An Introduction

PUBLIC BROADCASTING FOR ALL: A GLOBAL CAMPAIGN

The International Federation of Journalists has launched a worldwide campaign in 2001 to defend public service broadcasting. The campaign aims to promote public service values, editorial independence, quality programmes and democratic and accountable systems of administration.

Globalisation and commercialization in media pose an increasing threat to the future of public service broadcasting.

In developed countries we are already seeing low cost, low quality programming, cuts in editorial budgets and a reduction in employment rights. New technology journalists are expected to film and edit as well as carrying out their journalistic role. There is less quality and less time to investigate and assess information.

In developing countries, international financial institutions or local governments want to privatise former state broadcasters. The IFJ Campaign supports journalists' organisations and civil society in the transformation of state broadcasters in regions such as central Europe, West Africa or South Asia into genuinely public service institutions, not state run or government-controlled, but professional, impartial and high quality networks that serve the public, not private, interest.

The IFJ campaign builds union solidarity. It co-ordinates discussions with international organisations and other global groups dealing with media. This worldwide action programme should lead to the preservation and expansion of broadcasting of high standards and integrity.

MAJOR GOVERNMENT BROADCASTING/TELEVISION STATIONS FROM AROUND THE WORLD

Australia

- ABC (Australian Broadcasting Corporation)
- CBAA (Community Broadcasting Association of Australia)
- Public Radio News (University of Queensland)
- Queer Vision World Wide
- Seven

Austria

- Blue Danube Radio (in English)
- ORF (Austrian Broadcasting Corporation)

Belgium

- BRTN including Teletext
- RTBF

Canada

- Bravo!
- TV for BC (British Columbia Television)
- CBC
- CPAC (Cable Parliamentary Channel)—in English and French
- CTV (Canadian Television)
- CityTV (Toronto)
- ITV
- Know TV (Knowledge Network, Public Ed. TV, British Columbia)
- Showcase Television (fiction network)—updated every hour!
- TSN (The Sports Network)
- TV Ontario (public broadcaster, Toronto) in English and French

Croatia

- Croatian Radio Television—Hrvatske Radio Televizije (HRT, in Croatian language, English soon)

Cuba

- Radio Havana Cuba (In English, French, Portuguese and Spanish)

Czech Republic

- Radio Prague

Denmark

- Danish Broadcasting Corporation (in English and Danish)
- Kabel TV (from Tele Danmark)
- TV2/Danmark (in Danish)

Europe

- ASTRA Satellite System
- Euro TV including TV guide

Finland

- YLE (Finnish Broadcasting Company, mostly in Finnish)

France

- ARTE
- CANAL+
- Ellipse Cabel
- France 2
- France 3

- France Télévision
- La Cinquième (education and knowledge)
- RABELAIS Télévision
- Radio France International (English)
- TF1 (French TV 1, some English)

Germany

- ARD—see regional services: BR, HR, MDR, NDR, SDR, SWF, WDR
- Deutsche Welle Radio and TV International
- Pro-7
- RTL
- RTL2
- SAT1
- SWF
- VOX
- WDR
- ZDF

Greece

- Ant-1
- MEGA Channel
- Sportline

Hong Kong

- Radio HK
- RTHK (Radio Television Hong Kong)

India

- Doordarshan

Ireland

- RTE (Radio Telefs Éireann) including television
- RTE Radio (Internet) News
- RT Cork

Israel

- Israel Broadcasting Authority

Italy

- Mediaset
- Radio Italia (In Italian with Real Audio)
- RAI
- TMC (TeleMonteCarlo, in Italian)

Japan

- TV Asahi Broadcasting Corporation (ANB, Japanese only)
- Kansai Telecasting Corporation (KTV, Japanese only)
- Nagoya Broadcasting Network (NBN)
- Nippon Hoso Kyokai (NHK, Japan Broadcasting Corporation)
    - NHK International TV Broadcasting
    - Radio Japan
- Nippon Television Network Corporation (NTV)
- Tokyo Broadcasting System, Inc. (TBS)

Korea

- KBS (Korea Broadcasting System, in English)

Mongolia

- The Voice of Mongolia

Netherlands

- Dutch Public Broadcasting Companies (in Dutch, with international links in English)
- The Music Factory
- NOS TeleTekst (in Dutch)
- Radio 538
- Radio Netherlands
- SBS 6
- Veronica

New Zealand

- TVNZ (National state-owned network. Television New Zealand)
- Friends of Public Broadcasting
    - Channel 9 Dunedin (Local channel)
- CTV (Canterbury TV—local channel)
- Eastland Television (Gisborne local channel)
- Geyser Television (Rotorua local channel)
- TV3 (National network)
- Saturn Communications (From the Kapiti Coast)
- Sky TV (New Zealand Sky)
- The Juice Music Television (Music channel)
- Triangle Community Television (Non-commercial access television in Auckland)
- 7 am TV Pages (Television listings, reviews, etc.)

Norway

- NRK (Norsk Rikskringkasting, in Norwegan)

Poland

- Radio/TV Merkury Poznan

Russia

- Voice of Russia

South Africa

- South African Broadcasting Corporation

Spain

- Antena 3 TV
- Canal+
- Canal Satelite Digital
- RTVE
- Telecinco
- TVC (Televisió de Catalunya, Barcelona)
- Spanish broadcaster links (in Spanish).

Sri Lanka

- Sirasa FM
- Sri Lanka Broadcasting Corporation (unofficial information)
- TNL Radio

Sweden

- FilmNet
- Kanal5
- Open Channel (Community & Public Access Television)
- SVT (Sveriges Television)
- Sveriges Radio/Radio Sweden
- TV1000
- TV3
- ZTV

United Kingdom

- BBC (British Broadcasting Corporation) including World Service, News, beeb @ the BBC (including the Radio Times and Comedy Zone), BBC Shop and Monitoring Service (summary of world broadcasts).
- Bravo
- Carlton Select (cable)
- Cartoon Network
- Channel 4 including schools and on-line chat
- Channel 5
- Disney Channel
- ITN (Independent Television News)
- ITV (Independent TeleVision). Regions: Anglia, Border, Carlton, Central, Channel, Granada, Grampian, HTV (Wales), LWT (London Weekend Television), Meridian, Scottish, Tyne Tees, Westcountry, Yorkshire.
- Landscape Channel from CableNet

- Live TV (cable)
- London News Network
- NASTA (National Student Television Association)
- The Preview Channel
- S4C (Welsh 4th channel)
- Sky including Sky News and Sky Digital
- Student Radio
- TCC (The Children's Channel)
- Television X (The Fantasy Channel)
- Travel (Landmark Travel Channel)
- Trouble TV

CASABLANCA DECLARATION: PUBLIC BROADCASTING IN THE MEDITERRANEAN REGION

Casablanca, 15-16 November 2001

FINAL DECLARATION

Journalists and news professionals attending the conference on A Voice for the Public: Public Service Broadcasting in the Mediterranean Region (Casablanca, 15-16 November 2001) have adopted the following declaration:

- We reiterate the provisions of the Rabat conference on working together with civil society to create a network of journalists in the Mediterranean region with a view to introducing a strategy of change in the media sector;
- We regret the state monopoly on news media in certain countries in the region and the lack of legal and professional structures to guarantee the economic and political independence of news services;
- We emphasise that editorial independence, freedom of expression, pluralism of opinion and the independence of public broadcasters are essential principles in a democratic society;
- We note that criminal legal provisions—and in particular prison sentences—in the area of freedom of expression are an obstacle to the development of independent broadcasting;
- We note the creation by the International Federation of Journalists, in conjunction with civil society, of a campaign for the establishment and defence of independent public service broadcasting, and we support this campaign in the Mediterranean region;
- We note the development of specific collaborative initiatives involving journalists in the region, such as Mediterraneo and RAI-MED, the latter being a new channel which broadcasts news in Arabic by satellite and over the Internet;
- We call upon journalists and public broadcasting management to support and encourage such initiatives so as to ensure a better dialogue between both sides of the Mediterranean;
- We believe that cooperation with the Permanent Conference of Mediterranean Audiovisual Operators (CoPeAM) is important for the exchange of news and

information programmes between public service broadcasters in the Mediterranean region, and this in conjunction with the EBU's operational structures;

- We recognise the diversity of the public service broadcasting sector and the diversity of relations with the private sector in the region;
- We reiterate the need for high-quality training for journalists, including training in new technologies, ethics, human rights and safety;
- We reiterate the importance of the role played by journalists' trade unions and associations in bolstering editorial independence and forging solidarity between media workers in the region.

We declare that in the countries of the Mediterranean region it is essential to establish and/or protect.

- a legal and financial framework ensuring independent and democratic public broadcasting;
- compliance with or the establishment of an internal democratic decision-making and management process within the public broadcasting sector;
- respect for the role played by supervisory and management bodies, respect for the human rights and obligations of personnel, and respect for the standards set out in editorial statutes, as defined in the International Federation of Journalists' Zagreb Declaration, and the right of personnel to engage in trade union activities;
- the intensification of:
  1. journalists' and media workers' trade union activities.
  2. trade union solidarity.
  3. the activities of the network of journalists in the Mediterranean.
- the intensification of cooperation between journalists and public service broadcasting management with a view to:
  1. improving exchanges of experience and individuals.
  2. developing joint productions. Specific initiatives should be examined for organising training courses and exchanges for this purpose within the broadcasting sector on both sides of the Mediterranean.
- a campaign, in conjunction with civil society, for the defence and/or establishment of democratic, pluralistic public broadcasting.

Casablanca, 16 November 2001

BROADCASTING IN INDIA: A HISTORICAL OVERVIEW

The Indian television system is one of the most extensive systems in the world. Terrestrial broadcasting, which has been the sole preserve of the government, provides television coverage to over 90 per cent of India's 900 million people. By the end of 1996 nearly 50 million households had television sets. International satellite broadcasting, introduced in 1991, has swept across the country because of the rapid proliferation of small scale cable systems. By the end of 1996, Indians could view dozens of foreign and local channels and the competition for audiences and advertising revenues was one of the hottest in the world. In 1995, the Indian Supreme Court held that the government's monopoly over broadcasting was unconstitutional, setting the stage for India to develop into one of the world's largest and most competitive television environments.

Broadcasting began in India with the formation of a private radio service in Chennai in 1924. In the same year, the British colonial government granted a license to a private company, the Indian Broadcasting Company, to open Radio stations in Mumbai and Kolkata. The company went bankrupt in 1930 but the colonial government took over the two transmitters and the Department of Labour and Industries started operating them as the Indian State Broadcasting Corporation. In 1936, the Corporation was renamed All India Radio (AIR) and placed under the Department of Communications. When India became independent in 1947, AIR was made a separate Department under the Ministry of Information and Broadcasting.

The early history of radio broadcasting in independent India is important because it set the parameters for the subsequent role of television in the country. At independence, the Congress government under Jawaharlal Nehru had three major goals: to achieve political integration, economic development and social modernization. Broadcasting was expected to play an important role in all three areas.

The most important challenge the government faced at independence was that of forging a nation out of the diverse political, religious, geographic and lingual entities that composed independent India. In addition to the territories ruled directly by the British, over 500 hundred "independent" princely states had joined the new nation, some quite reluctantly. The country immediately found itself at war with Pakistan over one of those states—Kashmir. The trauma of the partition of the country into India and Pakistan and the violence between Hindus and Muslims had further weekend the political stability of the country.

Broadcasting was harnessed for the task of political nation building. National integration and the development of a "national consciousness" were among the early objectives of All India Radio. Broadcasting was organized as the sole preserve of the chief architect of this process of political integration—the State. The task of broadcasting was to help in overcoming the immediate crisis of political instability that followed Independence and to foster the long-term process of political modernization and nation building that was the dominant ideology of the newly formed state. Broadcasting was also charged with the task of aiding in the process of economic development. The Indian Constitution, adopted in 1950, mandated a strong role for the Indian State in the economic development of the country. The use of broadcasting to further the development process was a natural corollary to this state-led developmental philosophy. Broadcasting, was especially expected to contribute to the process of social modernization, which was considered an important pre-requisite of economic development. The dominant development philosophy of the time identified the problems of development as primarily internal to developing countries. These endogenous causes, to which communication solutions were thought to exist, included traditional value systems, lack of innovation, lack of entrepreneurial ability and lack of a national consciousness. In short, the problem was one of old ideas hindering the process of social change and modernization and the role of broadcasting was to provide an inlet for the flow of modern ideas.

It was in the context of this dominant thinking about the role of broadcasting in India that television was introduced in 1959. The government had been reluctant to invest in television until then because it was felt that a poor country like India could not afford the medium. Television had to prove its role in the development process before it could gain a foot-hold in the country. Television broadcasts started from Delhi in September 1959 as part of All India Radio's services. Programmes were broadcast twice a week for an hour a day on such topics as community health, citizens duties and rights, and traffic and road sense. In 1961 the broadcasts were expanded to include a school educational television project. In time, Indian films and programmes consisting of compilation of musicals from Indian films joined the programme line-up as the first entertainment programmes. A limited number of old US and British shows were also telecast sporadically.

The first major expansion of television in India began in 1972, when a second television station was opened in Mumbai. This was followed by stations in Srinagar and Amritsar (1973), and Kolkata, Chennai and Lucknow in 1975. Relay stations were also set up in a number of cities to extend the coverage of the regional stations. In 1975, the government carried out the first test of the possibilities of satellite based television through the SITE programme. SITE (Satellite Instructional Television Experiment) was designed to test whether satellite based television services could play a role in socio-economic development. Using a US ATS-6 satellite and up-link centers at Ahmedabad and Delhi, television programmes were beamed down for about 4 hours a day to about 2,400 villages in 6 states. The programmes dealt mainly with in- and out-of-school education, agricultural issues, planning and national integration. The programme was fairly successful in demonstrating the effectiveness of satellite based television in India and the lessons learnt from SITE were used by the government in designing and utilizing its own domestic satellite service INSAT, launched in 1982.

In these early years television, like radio, was considered a facilitator of the development process and its introduction was justified by the role it was asked to play in social and economic development. Television was institutionalized as an arm of the government, since the government was the chief architect of political, economic and social development in the country.

By 1976, the government found itself running a television network of eight television stations covering a population of 45 million spread over 75,000 square kilometers. Faced with the difficulty of administering such an extensive television system as part of All India Radio, the government constituted Doordarshan, the national television network, as a separate Department under the Ministry of Information and Broadcasting. Doordarshan was set up as an attached office under the Ministry of Information and Broadcasting—a half-way house between a public corporation and a government department. In practice, however, Doordarshan operated much like a government department, at least as far as critical issues of policy planning and financial decision-making were concerned. Doordarshan was headed by a Director General appointed by the I and B Ministry. The Ministry itself and sometimes the office of the Director General as well, was and continues to be, staffed by members of India's civil services.

In 1982 television began to attain national coverage and develop as the government's pre-eminent media organization. Two events triggered the rapid growth of television that year. INSAT-1A, the first of the country's domestic communications satellites became operational and made possible the networking of all of Doordarshan's regional stations. For the first time Doordarshan originated a nation-wide feed dubbed the "National Programme" which was fed from Delhi to the other stations. In November 1982, the country hosted the Asian Games and the government introduced color broadcasts for the coverage of the games. To increase television's reach, the government launched a crash programme to set up low and high power transmitters that would pick-up the satellite distributed signals and re-transmit them to surrounding areas. In 1983 television signals were available to just 28 per cent of the population, this had doubled by the end of 1985 and by 1990 over 90 per cent of the population had access to television signals.

1976 witnessed a significant event in the history of Indian television, the advent of advertising on Doordarshan. Until that time television had been funded through a combination of television licenses and allocations from the annual budget (licenses were later abolished as advertising revenues began to increase substantially). Advertising began in a very small way with under 1 per cent of Doordarshan's budget coming from advertising revenues in 1976-77. But the possibility of reaching a nationwide audience made television look increasingly attractive to advertisers after the introduction of the "National Programme" in 1982. In turn, Doordarshan began to shift the balance of its programming from educational and informational programmes to entertainment programmes. The commercialization of Doordarshan saw the development of soap operas, situation comedies, dramas, musical programmes, quiz shows and the like. By 1990 Doordarshan's revenues from advertising were about $300 million, accounting for about 70 per cent of its annual expenditure.

By 1991, Doordarshan's earlier mandate to aid in the process of social and economic development had clearly been diluted. Entertainment and commercial programmes had begun to take center stage in the organization's programming strategies and advertising had come to be Doordarshan's main source of funding. However, television in India was still a modest enterprise with most parts of the country getting just one channel except for the major cities which received two channels. But 1991 saw the beginnings of international satellite broadcasting in India and the government launched a major economic liberalization programme. Both these events combined to change the country's television environment dramatically.

International satellite television was introduced in India by CNN through its coverage of the Gulf War in 1991. Three months later Hong Kong based Star TV (now owned by Rupert Murdoch's News Corp.) started broadcasting five channels into India using the ASIASAT-1 satellite. By early 1992, nearly half a million Indian households were receiving Star TV telecasts. A year later the figure was close to 2 million and by the end of 1994, an estimated 12 million households (a little less than one-fourth of all television households) were receiving satellite channels. This increase in viewership was made possible by the 60,000 or so small scale cable system operators who have mushroomed across the country. These systems have redistributed the satellite channels to their customers at rates as low as $5 a month. Taking advantage of the growth of the satellite television audience, a number of Indian satellite based television services were launched between 1991 and 1994, prominent among them Zee TV, the first Hindi satellite channel. By the end of 1994 there were 12 satellite based channels available in India, all of them using a handful of different satellites. This number was expected to double by the end of 1996, with a number of Indian programmers and international media companies like Turner Broadcasting, Time-Warner, ESPN, CANAL 5 and Pearsons PLC, seriously considering the introduction of new satellite television services for India.

The proliferation of channels has put great pressure on the Indian television programming industry. Already the largest producer of motion pictures, India is poised to become a sizable producer of television programmes as well. With Indian audiences clearly preferring locally produced programme over foreign programmes, the new television services are spending heavily on the development of indigenous programmes. The number of hours of television programming produced in India has increased 500 per cent from 1991 to 1996 and is expected to grow at an ever faster rate until the year 2000.

Despite the rapid growth of television channels from 1991 to 1996, television programming continues to be dominated by the Indian film industry. Hindi films are the staple of most national channels and regional channels rely heavily on a mix of Hindi and regional language films to attract audiences. Almost all Indian films are musicals and this allows for the development of inexpensive derivative programmes. One of Doordarshan's most popular programmes, *Chitrahaar,* is a compilation of old film songs and all the private channels, including Zee TV and music video channels like MTV Asia and Channel V, show some variation of *Chitrahaar.* A number of game shows are also based on movie themes. Other genres like soap operas, talk shows and situation comedies are also gaining in popularity, but the production of these programmes has been unable to keep up with demand, hence the continuing reliance on film based programming.

International satellite programming has opened up competition in news and public affairs programming with BBC and CNN International challenging Doordarshan's long-standing monopoly. Most of the other foreign broadcasters, for example, ESPN and the Discovery Channel, are focusing on special interest programming. Only Star TV's STAR Plus channel offers broad-based English language entertainment programmes. Most of its programmes are syndicated US shows, for example soap operas like *The Bold and the Beautiful* and *Santa Barbara* and talk shows like *Donahue* and *Oprah.* However, STAR Plus has a very small share of the audience in India and even this is threatened by the launch of new channels.

A peculiar development in television programming in India has been the use of hybrid English-Hindi programme formats, popularly called "Hinglish" formats, which offer programmes in Hindi and English on the same channel and even have programmes, including news shows, that use both languages within a single telecast. This takes advantage of the audience for television (especially the audience for satellite television) which is largely composed of middle class Indians who have some knowledge of English along with Hindi and colloquially speak a language that is primarily Hindi intermixed with words, phrases and whole sentences in English.

Commercial competition has transformed Doordarshan as well and it is scrambling to cope with the changed competitive environment. Satellite broadcasting has threatened Doordarshan's audiences and self-preservation has spawned a new ideology in the network which is in the process of reinventing itself, co-opting private programmers to recapture viewers and advertising rupees lost to Zee TV and Star TV. In 1994, the government ordered Doordarshan to raise its own revenues for future expansion. This new commercial mandate has gradually begun to change Doordarshan's perception of who are its primary constituents—from politicians to advertisers.

The government's monopoly over television over the years has resulted in Doordarshan being tightly controlled by successive governments. In principle, Doordarshan is answerable only to Parliament. Parliament lays down the guidelines that Doordarshan is expected to adhere to in its programming and Doordarshan's budget is debated and approved by Parliament. But the guidelines established by Parliament to ensure Doordarshan's political neutrality are largely ignored in the face of the majority that ruling parties have held in Parliament. Doordarshan has been subject more to the will of the government than the oversight of Parliament. Successive governments and ruling political parties have used Doordarshan to further their political agendas, weakening its credibility as an neutral participant in the political process. There have been periodic attempts to reconstitute Doordarshan into a BBC-like public corporation, but governments have been reluctant to relinquish their hold on such a powerful medium.

The government drew its right to operate the country's broadcasting services as a monopoly from the Indian Telegraph Act of 1885 which empowers the government with the exclusive right to "establish, maintain and work" wireless services. In addition, the Constitution lists broadcasting as the sole domain of Parliament, effectively shutting out the states from making any laws with regard to television. Within the ambit of these provision it was assumed that media autonomy or liberalization in any form was the prerogative of the government to grant. But the government's monopoly was challenged in the Indian Supreme Court in 1995. The Court held that the government monopoly over broadcasting was unconstitutional and while the government has the right to regulate broadcasting in the public interest, the Constitution forbids monopoly control over any medium by either individuals or the government. The Court directed the government to establish an independent public authority for "controlling and regulating" the use of airwaves. The Court's decision holds out the promise of significant structural changes in Indian broadcasting and the possibility that terrestrial television may finally free itself from governmental control.

It is evident that over time the State's control over television will continue to diminish. As its revenue structure begins to change and Doordarshan begins to respond to increasing commercial pressures, the character of its programming will begin to increasingly reflect the demands and pressures of the market place. In the meantime, caught between the government and the market, Doordarshan continues to struggle to maintain its mandate of public service programming. But the Supreme Court's recent decision ordering the government to establish an independent broadcasting authority to regulate television in the public interest holds the promise of allowing Indian television to escape both the stifling political control of the state and the commercial pressures of the market. There are a number of other constituencies like state governments, educational institutions, non-governmental organizations and social service agencies who can participate in a liberalized broadcast system. The Supreme Court has provided an opportunity to develop a broad based television system. How the country responds to this opportunity in the next few years will determine the future of broadcasting in India in the next century.

Since television was first introduced in India in 1959, the country has emerged as one of the largest TV markets in the world. The type of growth witnessed by the broadcasting sector in the last decade is expected to continue. Television is estimated to reach more than 50 per cent of all individuals (urban and rural) in India. In the last decade the television programming landscape has also been totally transformed. India has one of the largest broadcasting networks in the world. Doordarshan, the Indian National Television Network, was established in 1959. Its terrestrial signals reach more than 90 per cent of the country's population.

SATELLITE BROADCASTING IN INDIA IN RECENT PAST

August 1, 2000 was a historic day in the history of India's communication scene. It was on this day in 1975 that the first satellite broadcasting was started in the country. To mark the 25 years of satellite broadcasting, Development and Educational Communication Unit (DECU) of Indian Space Research Organisation (ISRO) at Ahmedabad organised several events. One of the major events was a one-day seminar on this subject. It was attended by a large number of scientists, media practitioners, managers, social scientists, engineers, television producers and several other interested persons from all over the country. Young students especially of communication also attended it. The seminar was inaugurated by the Minister for Information and Broadcasting. He delivered the keynote address stressing the significance of the event and elaborating on how satellite broadcasting has helped the process of taking the television signals to the remotest areas both for entertainment as well as education and development. The seminar was divided into four major sessions:

1. Broadcasting and Distribution Technology.
2. Educational Broadcasting.
3. Development Broadcasting.
4. Overall discussion titled "Back to the Future".

On this occasion DECU/ISRO brought out two documents:

(*a*) *'Yatra'*—The Journey, dealing with the journey of 25 years of satellite broadcasting in the country.

(*b*) *'Disha'*—The Direction, presenting the case of Jhabua Development Communications Project of DECU/ISRO.

Along with this, exhibitions were also organised. The exhibitions fell into three main categories:

1. Books and Papers.
2. Video Programmes.
3. Photographs.

All the three reflected the major milestones of these 25 significant years of satellite broadcasting. On the previous day, an eminent media personality from a Hindi language private channel gave a public talk on the subject. The proceedings on these events are under preparation and will be published shortly.

The journey of satellite broadcasting was started in the form of the famous Satellite Instructional Television Experiment (SITE) in 1975-76. It used the American satellite ATS-6 and transmitted development programmes through direct reception to 2400 remote villages scattered in six different states of the country. SITE, described as the biggest techno-social communication experiment in the world, is too well-known to be described in detail here. It is sufficient to say that SITE proved India's capability of using advanced technology and adapt to the socio-economic needs of the country. The success was technological, managerial, programme production and research.

Before SITE there was a long gap as far as satellite broadcasting was concerned. The Indian television continued to make steady progress. The small beginning in 1959 was terrestrial transmission in and around Delhi. Post-SITE also the expansion was more based on terrestrial transmission predominantly in the metropolitan and other bigger areas. However, SITE had sown the seeds for expansion of satellite broadcasting in the country. The Indian Space Research Organisation, which was the nodal agency for implementation of SITE, continued to prepare for a national satellite system in the country. Several technical experiments were undertaken by ISRO and eventually INSAT system was launched in 1982.

INSAT provided satellite based national transmission either in the form of direct reception from the satellite or through a hybrid system of receiving it from the satellite and re-transmits it terrestrially through low or high power transmitters. But this provided communication umbrella to the whole country. Operationalisation of INSAT in 1982 coincided with the Asian games held at New Delhi. This initiated a very rapid expansion of transmitters in different parts of the country. There was almost one transmitter a day for over a period of one year during the 1982-83 timeframe. This movement never slackened and today there are well over 1000 transmitters. It would be incomplete to say that the expansion of the television in the country was due only to the technological capability of the INSAT system. The fact that the Asian games were held in New Delhi gave a big boost to the television industry. Around this time government liberalised the import of television sets from other countries and encouraged manufacturing of television sets in the country through a liberal economic policy. This was a big impetus to the increase in the number of television sets in the country. Around this time the political leadership had also grasped the enormous power of the medium. The fact that one could reach out to the entire country was no mean potentiality for the medium. The democratic setup of the country facilitated this entire process. The fact that there was a period of economic liberalisation during this period and commercial viability was being seriously looked at and encouragement went a long way in expanding the satellite based television network in the country.

The Gulf war of 1991 was another very major landmark influencing television scene in the country. CNN was first to beam transnational signals on the war. These transmissions by CNN clearly opened up enormous possibilities. A large number of small enterprising youngsters saw the enormous potentiality of this as a viable business activity. They initiated the present mode of distributing satellite signals through a cable network to individual households. Reception of the satellite channels in India takes place in a unique manner. The cable operator receives the satellite channels and he distributes them through a cable network to the household subscribers for a small fee. Along with CNN many other foreign private satellite channels saw the huge market that was India. Amongst the earliest initiatives came from Rupert Murdoch's Star TV. 1992 was the beginning of Star TV network through the Asiasat-1. They offered a bouquet of free to air channels consisting of soap operas, movies, music, sports, news and so on. Initially all these channels were English language channels. For the first time this gave the Indian audiences—used to the monopoly of Doordarshan—a look at the variety that the television was capable of.

But as things were to prove later expansion through totally English language based channels was not a feasible proposition for a country as diverse, linguistically rich with a unique cultural ethos as India to sustain and certainly not be wholly satisfied on only foreign sourced programmes. Many enterprising Indians saw and seized this opportunity. The earliest being Zee TV network which started a Hindi language channel. It offered programmes produced in India for Indian audiences and transmitted through a foreign satellite. They soon expanded to a bouquet of channels. Indian made soap operas, music; feature film based channels became favourites amongst the large number of middle-class homes in the country. Today, out of 70 million TV households of the country, about 37 million receive satellite channels. The growth in the number of channels has been exponential especially in the Indian regional languages. Southern states of India took a major initiative in this regard. The major initiative came from Sun TV which started a Tamil language channel and soon the channels in other languages like Kannada, Malayalam and Telugu were initiated by many players and almost all of them offering a bouquet of 'niche' channels. Today there are well over 90 channels which an Indian consumer can get in English language as well as Hindi and other regional languages.

Doordarshan now had real competition to face. Gone were the days of monopoly and this national television authority of Government of India had to re-orient itself to face the channels. Doordarshan on its own started several satellite channels. Initially they were all niche channels like news, sports, music, etc. They soon started regional language channels. India has 18 officially recognised languages and the population of these regional languages speakers is scattered all over the country and they are interested in being exposed to programmes in their mother tongue and culture and this has given a big boost to the expansion of the regional language channels.

The period was not only the end of monopoly of Doordarshan or for that matter any other single player, it also meant greater commercialisation and massive growth in all the related cultural as well as hardware industries of the country. Software and content generation has become a major industry. The artistic talent is in great demand. Scriptwriters are in such a heavy demand that they find it difficult to respond to it and this has given a quantum boost to the cultural industries. There has been corporatisation of software industries and this has also given a major growth for the market research agencies. Impact assessment, surveys, formative studies and other research activities are becoming regular practices.

While all this was going on several doubts, questions and concerns started creeping into the national agenda—both political as well as cultural. Does this market-driven expansion mean end of public broadcasting? Is there no place for it? What happens to the educational and development communication? Are the foreign channels adversely affecting the Indian cultural and ethos? Is there a foreign cultural invasion in the country? Is there too much consumerism and encouragement to a hedonistic lifestyle? What shape is the technology taking? What does convergence of technology mean both as hardware and socially? are just some amongst several of the questions which have been raised at different fora both formally and informally. Many of them deliberated upon at the Ahmedabad seminar. I propose to deal with these and some other issues and challenges posed by satellite broadcasting in the next month's article. However, I would like to end once again reiterating the enormous importance and significance of the journey that India has taken in the last 25 years of satellite broadcasting. It has literally changed the face of this country and opened enormous possibilities not only for entertainment and news, but also for education and development. More about it in the next article.

Presenting the union budget for 1999-2000 to Parliament on February 27, Finance Minister Yashwant Sinha acceded to the main demands of the entertainment industry, and announced that it would be accorded similar facilities and tax benefits as are available to the export of goods and merchandise under Section 80HHC of the Income Tax Act. This gives the industry the status of a major export earner and exempts export earnings from income tax.

This, the minister said, would help boost the sector and make the Indian entertainment industry—including films, music and television software—a global leader, and India a media superpower.

The entertainment software industry is expected to register a turnover worth Rs. 10 billion by the year 2002.

The Information and Broadcasting Ministry had suggested bringing the entertainment industry under the purview of Section 80HHC of the Income Tax Act, and additionally proposed a number of fiscal incentives to the entertainment industry, including:

- Rationalisation of the duty structure on entertainment hardware;
- Duty exemption on entertainment software imports; and
- Allowing entertainment software imports on the Open General Licence regime.

In addition, the Indian Broadcasters Society (IBS) had demanded:

- Relief on customs duty for hardware required by cable and satellite TV operators;
- Classification of CDs alongside CD-ROMs for purposes of customs levies; and
- Countervailing duties on raw tapes.

The IBS is a recently formed association of private broadcasters, structured on the same lines as the Indian Newspaper Society.

DTH Policy Still Under Consideration

Even though there is an air of expectancy that the government is about to lift the ban on direct-to-home (DTH) broadcasting services, Union Information and Broadcasting (I&B) Minister Pramod Mahajan said that the government would not act in a hurry. However, ministry officials have been reported as saying that the government is likely to make an announcement in March, permitting private broadcasters to offer DTH services. The decision, which was to have been finalised mid-February, has been delayed because the Group of Ministers (GoM), set up by the government in January to study issues surrounding DTH broadcasting, failed to hold its scheduled February 19 meeting.

Meanwhile, the I&B minister has, on several occasions, spoken in a positive vein about Ku-band and DTH services. But he has announced that the opening up of Ku-band DTH to private broadcasters will be accompanied by a number of "safeguards". For one, the launch of DTH licensing will be followed by a six-month "lock-in" period to allow a maximum number of players to enter the service sector.

In order to regulate the proposed DTH services, the ministry is considering reposing the powers to issue DTH licences in Doordarshan (DD) or with the Prasar Bharati Corporation.

Regulation may also be provided through making it mandatory upon DTH service providers to uplink from India.

The government is also working on a proposed programme and advertising code that will apply to all television broadcasters. At present, a programme and advertising content code applies only to DD channels, while the private broadcasters have voluntarily adopted a code that prohibits them from carrying advertisements related to alcohol and tobacco products during day and prime time hours.

Last month, Mahajan had announced that the code, which will impose a strict content criteria with regards to depiction of violence and explicit sex, would be implemented through post-telecast vetting. The government would vet complaints about violations of the code in programmes and advertisements on air.

The government is also considering whether to set up an independent regulator to deal with complaints and ensure implementation of the code.

However, the I&B ministry is undecided whether to introduce the code as a separate law or as part of the proposed (and long-delayed) Broadcast Bill. Yet another proposal is to amend the Cable Television Networks (Regulation) Act, to bring satellite channels within its purview.

The government is reported to have given up on the proposal that DD itself be allowed to launch DTH services rather than throw this service sector open to private operators.

Union minister of state for I&B M. A. Naqvi has announced that the government is not against private broadcasters being allowed to offer DTH services, but would keep the "remote control" in its hands.

Broadcast Laws to be Amended

The government is considering passing an ordinance to amend the Cable Networks Regulation Act and allow DTH services. Last month, I&B Minister Pramod Mahajan had stated that the Union Government is considering amendments to the Cable Television Networks (Regulation) Act, 1995 to bring it in sync with the proposed policy changes arising out of the imperatives of convergence in the telecom, Information Technology (IT) and broadcasting technologies. The new policy envisages the use of a single conduit for carrying a range of voice, data and video transmission services provided by telecommunications, IT and broadcasting service providers.

Mahajan had also announced that the government proposes to amend the Act to make it mandatory for cable operators to carry at least three DD channels. Currently, DD's terrestrial signals are often 'crowded out' by the satellite signals of private channels.

Legal amendments to make it mandatory on cable operators and broadcasters to observe the provisions of the proposed programming and advertising content code, are also on the cards.

The government would also need to amend—or repeal—the Indian Telegraphs Act, 1885 and the Official Secrets Act, as well as to enact the proposed Freedom to Right to Information Bill.

Cable Operators against Liberalising Communications

The Cable Networks Association of India (CNAI) has petitioned the Government of India and, in particular, the I&B ministry, to stall the proposed permission to broadcasters to commence DTH services. The CNAI has asked that DTH services may be permitted only after the long-pending broadcast law, which was to regulate private broadcasting in the country, is enacted. The association has argued that allowing DTH services without imposing cross-media restrictions, would boost the growth of media monopolies.

The CNAI has also threatened to file a Public Interest Litigation (PIL) in the Supreme Court if DTH services are allowed or if the Cable Networks Regulation Act, 1995, is amended without protecting the existing cable operators.

The proposed DTH policy has also invited opposition from other quarters. Two new Mumbai-based organisations—Save India Society and Society for Advancement of Economic Growth—which are reported to be closely allied with the Zee TV group, have demanded that DTH services should not be permitted until a clear broadcast policy has been legislated. Former I&B Minister S. Jaipal Reddy has also charged the government with attempting to bury the proposed Broadcasting Authority and has demanded that DTH should not be permitted until a clear policy and regulatory authority for the private broadcasting sector are in place.

Cable and satellite networks, which have registered a growth of around 30 per cent in the last four years, have also demanded that the government grant the sector the status of 'industry'.

New Satellite Uplink Policy

The I&B ministry has finalised the rules to govern the modalities of satellite uplinking facilities for foreign channels. Some non-Indian broadcasters will be permitted to uplink from India in the second phase of opening up satellite services.

The new rules are likely to:

- Allow uplink facilities to broadcasting companies not incorporated in India, even with majority foreign shareholding; however, these companies must have a minimum 20 per cent Indian stake;
- Apply only to news and current affairs broadcast companies; and
- Extend permission on the basis of the "track record" of the broadcaster.

In addition, the new policy will permit:

- New broadcast companies to enjoy uplink facilities; currently only existing broadcasters are permitted to apply for uplinking on India-based facilities;
- Broadcasters already uplinking to set up their own uplink facilities; and
- Non-broadcast companies with interest in hardware to uplink if this would help develop a communications infrastructure.

A suggestion that has been put before the Group on Telecommunications (GoT) is that it should be mandatory on broadcasters to lease transponder space on the satellites owned or leased by the Indian Space Research Organisation (ISRO) and that only if such space is unavailable they may be permitted to lease space on foreign-owned transponders. Meanwhile, the Department of Space (DoS) announced that the INSAT 2E launch has been scheduled for April 2.

Currently, private broadcasters do not need government permission to lease space on foreign transponders.

The government is also considering allowing wholly owned foreign companies to set up uplinking infrastructure.

Controlling Prasar Bharati

Even as I&B Minister Mahajan called for a debate on the future of the Prasar Bharati Corporation, board members challenged the genuineness of the invitation. Their objection was echoed by Janata Dal leader and former I&B Minister S. Jaipal Reddy, who described Mahajan's offer as "spurious".

In his response, Mahajan said that he wants a board that will be autonomous, but accountable.

The future of the Prasar Bharati board became uncertain as the I&B ministry postponed scheduled interviews for filling vacancies on it.

Mahajan has also come in for severe criticism on allegations that he is directly controlling and censoring news aired on DD channels and on All India Radio (AIR). Former I&B Minister Reddy, in particular, condemned the present government's attempt to amend the Prasar Bharati Act to bring the Prasar Bharati board under a parliamentary committee, and said that Mahajan is attempting to "saffronise" the public broadcasters. (Saffron is the colour of Hindu fundamentalist groups allied to the leader in the coalition government, the Bharatiya Janata Party (BJP)). Even as Mahajan denied the allegations, the Congress also added its voice to the Janata Dal leader's assertions.

Mahajan, meanwhile, in a thinly veiled attack on the ultra right-wing Maharashtra-based Shiv Sena party, censured attempts by some to act as "moral police". He said that the challenge before broadcasters was from those pretending to "cultural superiority" and not from India's cultural diversity.

DD Targets

Even as the Planning Commission recommended a cut in the Plan budget for DD, I&B Minister Pramod Mahajan has urged the public broadcaster to raise at least Rs. 20 million in advertising revenues in the next financial year. Mahajan has pulled up DD for failing to do better on ad revenues despite its 75 per cent viewership.

The minister also announced that DD and AIR would be switching over to digital technology at their metro centres.

In the States

Andhra Pradesh

The government announced that it plans to provide high bandwidth fibre optic and copper cable networks to IT, basic telecom, and entertainment companies for transmission purposes. Insufficient bandwidth allocation has been cited as one of the major problems of communications networks in the country.

West Bengal

The West Bengal Finance Act, 1998 has prescribed a subscriber-based registration fee for cable networks. If the Bill is passed, cable network operators—especially large ones such as RPG Netcom and SitiCable—are afraid that it may set a precedent for other states and hike their costs considerably.

Corporate Milestones

- The I&B ministry has forwarded a proposal to the Cabinet Committee on Economic Affairs to permit up to 74 per cent foreign equity holding in advertising firms. Former I&B Minister Sushma Swaraj had okayed a policy to allow 74 per cent foreign equity in advertising at the time of her resignation last September. At the time, the I&B Ministry had been asked to call a "temporary halt" to proposals for foreign investment in advertising and cinema.
- Even as the government postponed its decision on DTH services, telecom hardware manufacturer Himachal Futuristic Communications Ltd. (HFCL) announced that it would begin to market set-top boxes for DTH reception in six months. HFCL, which said it is investing in Rs. 1.5 billion in the manufacturing facility, would sell the set-top boxes for Rs. 15,000 each.
- Mumbai-based Sri Bhawani CableTel and Hathway Investments have entered into a joint venture for cable television broadcasting. Under the agreement, Hathway subsidiary, Hathway Cable, and Datacom will pick up a controlling stake in Sri Bhawani.
- Discovery Communications India has expanded its reach to Bangladesh and Nepal. The channel plans to transform itself into a pay channel in India soon.

- Hallmark Entertainment Network, which launched its services early February, has yet to receive government clearance for import of decoders. Modi Entertainment Network, which has tied up with Hallmark for distribution, said that the channel will be a pay channel once import of the decoders has been cleared.
- Alex Kuruvilla, who has been appointed MTV India managing director, will take charge with effect from April 1. Kuruvilla is currently vice-president at Hindustan Thompson.
- Star TV has undergone a major organisational shake-up. Rathikant Basu, the former CEO of the company, has now been appointed as executive chairman of News TV India (NTVI). NTVI has been divided into three divisions, each to be headed by a CEO.
- The entertainment TV division will be handled by Peter Mukherjea, who has been given the post of chief executive. This division will include Star World, Star Plus and Star Movies. In February, two senior officials of the organisation, Vimal Bhalla, executive director, programming, B. Guha, executive director corporate affairs, and two vice-presidents, Basav Raj and Naazish Husseini, were removed from their posts by the management.

GLOBAL BROADCASTING SYSTEM AND MAJOR VIDEO FORMATS USED GLOBALLY

Technical Specifications

Code	*Frames*	*Scan Lines*	*Freq Band*	*Sound Offset*	*Vision Modulation*	*In Use*
Terrestrial Transmission Standards						
A	25	405	VHF	-3.5MHz	Pos	No
B	25	625	VHF	+5.5MHz	Neg	Yes
C	25	625	VHF	+5.5MHz	Pos	Yes
D	25	625	VHF	+6.5MHz	Neg	Yes
E	25	819	VHF	+11MHz	Neg	No
F	25	819	VHF	+5.5MHz	Pos	No
G	25	625	UHF	+5.5MHz	Neg	Yes
H	25	625	UHF	+5.5MHz	Neg	Yes
I	25	625	UHF	+6.0MHz	Neg	Yes
K	25	625	UHF	+6.5MHz	Neg	Yes
KI	25	625	UHF	+6.5MHz	Neg	Yes
L	25	625	UHF	+6.5MHz	Pos	Yes
M	30 (29.97)	525	VHF/UHF	+4.5MHz	Neg	Yes
N	25	625	VHF/UHF	+4.5MHz	Neg	Yes
Satellite Transmission Standards						
Ku-Band	Any	Any	~11GHz	+6.50MHz	Neg	Yes
C-Band	Any	Any	~4GHz	+6.50MHz	Pos	Yes

Additional Features

Stereo Sound

- **MTS**—Used in conjunction with NTSC/525. Consists of two independant carriers each carrying a discrete channel. One channel provides stereo sound by providing left/right channel difference signals relative to transmitted mono audio track. The second carrier carries the Secondary Audio Programme (SAP) which is used for a second language or a descriptive commentary for the blind. Uses a technique based on the dbx noise reduction to improve the frequency response of the audio channel.
- **FM-FM**—Dual carrier FM coded discrete stereo transmissions, analogue. Can be used for bi-lingual operation under user selection, but no auto-selection is available. Audio characteristics better than standard mono soundtrack.
- **NICAM**—(Full name: NICAM 728) Digital two-channel audio transmissions with sub-code selection of bi-lingual operation. Stereo digital signals with specifications approaching those of Compact Disc are possible. NICAM stands for Near Instantaneously Companded Audio Multiplex and uses a 14bit sample at a 32KHz sampling rate which produces a data stream of 728KBits/section.

Subtitling

- **CC**—(Full name: Closed Captioning) Transmitted on line 21 of NTSC/525 transmissions, contains subtitling information only. CC has no support for block graphics or multiple pages but it can support 8-colours and the use of an italic typeface. Frequently found on pre-recorded VHS cassettes and LDs, also used on broadcast. Also found on PAL/625 pre-recorded VHS cassettes in a modified version.
- **TeleText**—An information service of 200-700 "pages" covering a wide range of topics including TV Schedules, News, Financial Market prices, Comment, Reviews, Concert and Theatre information. Subtitles are typically transmitted on page 888 in the UK, on pages 199/299/399 in Belgium and Holland, on page 150 in Germany and on page 777 in Italy. There are a number of variant character sets used, but the encoding is identical and all English alphabet characters plus numbers and most punctuation can be handled by any decoder. Includes support for 8 colours, and limited block graphics, and selective revealing of underlying TV picture. Transmitted on a variable number of lines (specified in header which contains basic information such as time, date and channel), starting on line 12 and continuing for 7-8 lines typically. Found on broadcasts and some LaserDiscs; recording of TeleText signals is marginal on S-VHS, almost impossible on VHS hence the PAL/625 version of CC.

The BBC-designed Teletext system is known in some quarters as World Standard Teletext. There is an enhanced version known as Fastext which defines four links to additional pages that can be followed with one of four coloured buttons on the Teletext receivers remote control. The US "CC" is known widely in technical circles as LITO = LIne Twenty-One! where it lives.

Colour and Broadcasting Systems by Country

Country	*TV*	*Colour*	*Stereo*	*Subtitles*
Albania	B/G	PAL		
Argentina	N	PAL-N		
Australia	B/G	PAL	FM-FM	Teletext
Austria	B/G	PAL	FM-FM	Teletext
Azores (Portugal)	B	PAL		
Bahamas	M	NTSC		
Bahrain	B	PAL		
Barbados	M	NTSC		
Belgium	B/G	PAL	Nicam	Teletext
Bermuda	M	NTSC		
Brazil	M	PAL-M	MTS	
Bulgaria	D	SECAM		
Canada	M	NTSC	MTS	CC
Canary Is	B	PAL		
China	D	PAL		
Colombia	M	NTSC		
Cyprus	B	PAL		
Czechoslovakia	D/K	SECAM/PAL		
Denmark	B	PAL	Nicam	TeleText
Egypt	B	SECAM		
Faroe Islands (DK)	B	PAL		
Finland	B/G	PAL	Nicam	TeleText
France	E/L	SECAM		Teletext
Gambia	I	PAL		
Germany	B/G	PAL	FM-FM	TeleText
Germany (prev East)	B/G	SECAM/PAL		
Gibraltar	B	PAL		
Greece	B/G	PAL (was SECAM)		
Hong Kong	I	PAL	Nicam	
Hungary	B/G & D/K	PAL (was SECAM)	Nicam (Budapest only)	
Iceland	B	PAL		
India	B	PAL		
Indonesia	B	PAL		
Iran	H	SECAM		
Ireland	I	PAL	Nicam	TeleText
Israel	B/G	PAL	Nicam	TeleText
Italy	B/G	PAL	FM/FM	TeleText
Jamaica	N	SECAM		
Japan	M	NTSC	Matrix	
Jordan	B	PAL		
Kenya	B	PAL		
Korea	M	NTSC		
Luxembourg	B/G	PAL	NICAM	TeleText
Madeira	B	PAL		
Madagascar	B	SECAM		
Malaysia	B	PAL		
Malta	B/G	PAL		
Mauritius	B	SECAM		
Mexico	M	NTSC	MTS	CC

(Contd.)

Country	TV	Colour	Stereo	Subtitles
Monaco	L/G	SECAM/PAL		
Morocco	B	SECAM		
Netherlands	B/G	PAL	FM-FM	TeleText
New Zealand	B/G	PAL	Nicam	TeleText
North Korea	D/K?	SECAM		
Norway	B/G	PAL	Nicam	
Pakistan	B	PAL		
Paraguay	N	PAL		
Peru	M	NTSC		
Philipines	M	NTSC		
Poland	D/K	PAL		Teletext
Portugal	B/G	PAL	Nicam	Teletext
Romania	G	PAL		
Russia	D/K	SECAM		
Saudi Arabia	B	SECAM		
Seychelles	I	PAL		
Singapore	B	PAL		
South Africa	I	PAL		
South Korea	M	NTSC		
Spain	B/G	PAL	Nicam	Teletext
Sri Lanka	B/G	PAL		
Sweden	B/G	PAL	Nicam	Teletext
Switzerland	B/G	PAL	FM-FM	TeleText
Tahiti	KI	SECAM		
Taiwan	M	NTSC		
Thailand	B	PAL		
Trinidad	M	NTSC		
Tunisia	B	SECAM		
Turkey	B	PAL	-	TeleText
United Arab Emirates	B/G	PAL		
United Kingdom	I	PAL	Nicam	TeleText
Uruguay	N	PAL	MTS	
USA	M	NTSC	MTS	CC
Venezuela	M	NTSC		
Yugoslavia	B/H	PAL		
Zimbabwe	B	PAL		

Additional TV Systems Used Solely in Video

In addition to the basic TV systems, there are a number of additional hybrid formats which are to be found only in video equipment. These are usually a hybrid signal used to provide compatibility with video material of another TV format without a complete translation. Many of these signals are not symetric in that they cannot be recorded by video recorders that can play them.

Name	Frame/Field Rate	Scan Lines	Colour Systems	Sub-carrier Freq.
NTSC 4.43	29.97/59.94	525	NTSC	4.43MHz
Pseudo-PAL	29.97/59.94	525	PAL	4.43MHz
Pseudo-NTSC	25/50	625	NTSC	3.58MHz

Video Formats—Availability by TV System

For a range of reasons, some of them historical and some of them technical, the main video formats aren't the same in each colour system. There are actually some very dramatic differences in both the availability and maximum running times between the main TV standards. A much more detailed table of video formats including the professional ones is also available—this also includes more technical information on each format. The table below summarises these:

Format	*Scan Lines/Colour*	*Speed*	*Max Playing Time/Tape*
VHS	525/NTSC	SP	160 mins/T-160
		LP	320 mins/T-160
		EP	480 mins/T-160
	625/PAL	SP	300 mins/E-300
		LP	600 mins/E-300
	625/SECAM	SP	300 mins/E-300
		LP	600 mins/E-300
SuperVHS	525/NTSC	SP	160 mins/ST-160
		EP	480 mins/ST-160
	625/PAL	SP	240 mins/SE-240
		LP	480 mins/SE-240
D-VHS	525/NTSC	N/A	Varies
DVC	525/NTSC	miniDV	60 mins
		DVC	180 mins
	625/PAL	miniDV	60 mins
		DVC	180 mins
Video 8	525/NTSC	SP	120 mins/P6-120
		LP	240 mins/P6-120
	625/PAL	SP	90 mins/P5-90
		LP	180 mins/P5-90
	625/SECAM	SP	90 mins/P5-90
		LP	180 mins/P5-90
Hi-8	525/NTSC	SP	120 mins/P6-120ME
		LP	240 mins/P6-120ME
	625/PAL	SP	90 mins/P5-90ME
		LP	180 mins/P5-90ME
LaserDisc	525/NTSC	CAV	30 mins per side
		CLV	60 mins per side
	625/PAL	CAV	37 mins per side
		CLV	72 mins per side
DVD	525/NTSC	Single Layer	Varies (4.7GB)
		Dual Layer	Varies (8.6GB)
	625/NTSC	Single Layer	Varies (4.7GB)
		Dual Layer	Varies (8.6GB)

Notes: SECAM SuperVHS, Hi-8 and LaserDisc are all recorded on tape/disc as PAL signals and are converted to SECAM on playback by those machines sold in SECAM markets.

Comparing Video Tape Lengths

The differences between the running speed of VCRs of the same format in different colour systems has led to some very confusing naming of video tape lengths. Beta is unique in having named the tape after the length rather than it prospective running time, thus making it free of the problems that beset other formats. In the table below, we compare the actual lengths of some standard tape types.

Name	*TV system*	*Actual Length*	*Running time*	
			Own System	*Other System*
		SuperVHS/VHS		
ST/T-120	NTSC/525	250 metres	120 mins	175 mins
SE/E-180	PAL/625	258 metres	180 mins	126 mins
		Hi-8/Video 8		
P6-120	NTSC/525	112 metres	120 mins	90 mins
P5-90	PAL/625	112 metres	90 mins	120 mins

Domestic Analogue Video Formats

This section summarises the domestic video tape formats that exist now and some of the more major historial formats (now obsolete).

Format	*Scan Lines/Colour*	*Speed*	*Max Playing Time/Tape*	*Tape*	
				Width	*Composition*
VHS	525/NTSC	SP LP EP	160 mins/T-160 320 mins/T-160 480 mins/T-160	½" (12.5 mm)	Ferric Oxide
	625/PAL	SP LP	300 mins/E-300 600 mins/E-300		
	625/SECAM	SP LP	300 mins/E-300 600 mins/E-300		
SuperVHS	525/NTSC	SP EP	160 mins/ST-160 480 mins/ST-160	½" (12.5 mm)	Ferric Oxide
	625/PAL	SP LP	240 mins/SE-240 480 mins/SE-240		
Beta	525/NTSC	Beta I Beta II Beta III	100 mins/L-830 200 mins/L-830 300 mins/L-830	½" (12.5 mm)	Ferro-Chrome
	625/PAL	N/A	215 mins/L-830		
	625/SECAM	N/A	215 mins/L-830		
SuperBeta	525/NTSC	Beta I Beta II Beta III	100 mins/L-830 200 mins/L-830 300 mins/L-830	½" (12.5 mm)	Ferro-Chrome
	625/PAL	N/A	215 mins/L-830		
ED-Beta	525/NTSC	Beta II	120 mins/EL-500	½" (12.5 mm)	Metal Particle
		Beta III	180 mins/EL-500		

(*Contd.*)

Video 8	525/NTSC	SP LP	120 mins/P6-120 240 mins/P6-120	8 mm	Metal Particle
	625/PAL	SP LP	90 mins/P5-90 180 mins/P5-90		
	625/SECAM	SP LP	90 mins/P5-90 180 mins/P5-90		
Hi-8	525/NTSC	SP LP	120 mins/P6-120ME 240 mins/P6-120ME	8 mm	Metal Evaporated
	625/PAL	SP LP	90 mins/P5-90ME 180 mins/P5-90ME		
Video 2000	625/PAL	N/A	480 mins/VCC-480	½" (12.5 mm)	Ferric Oxide
LaserDisc	525/NTSC	CAV CLV	30 mins per side 60 mins per side	12" (30 cm) Diameter	PMMA substrate Aluminium
	625/PAL	CAV CLV	37 mins per side 72 mins per side		
LaserVision	625/PAL	CAV CLV	37 mins per side 68 mins per side	12" (30 cm) Diameter	PMMA substrate Aluminium

Notes

- SECAM SuperVHS, Hi-8 and LaserDisc are all recorded on tape/disc as PAL signals and are converted to SECAM on playback by those machines sold in SECAM markets.
- LaserVision (analogue sound) and LaserDisc (digital sound) are different formats in PAL because it was not possible to retain the analogue soundtrack when the digital audio signal was added. Since LaserVision is now considered obsolete, not all PAL or Dual standard LaserDisc players still support the replay of PAL analogue sound LaserVision discs.
- Video 2000 had a Long Play variant that allowed 8 hours per side of a VCC-480 tape.

Professional Analogue Video Formats

Format	*Scan Lines/Colour*	*Tape Size*	*Max Playing Time/Tape*	*Tape*	
				Width	*Composition*
U-Matic	525/NTSC	Large Small	60 minutes (KCA60) 20 minutes (KCS20)	¾" (18.75 mm)	Ferric Oxide
	625/PAL	Large Small	60 minutes (KCA60) 20 minutes (KCS20)		
U-Matic SP	525/NTSC	Large Small	60 minutes (KSP60) 20 minutes (KSP20)	¾" (18.75 mm)	Metal Particle
	625/PAL	Large Small	60 minutes (KSP60) 20 minutes (KSP20)		
Betacam SP	525/NTSC	Large Small	90 minutes (BCT90) 30 minutes (BCT30)	½" (12.5 mm)	Metal Particle
	625/PAL	Large Small	90 minutes (BCT90) 30 minutes (BCT30)		
1" C-Format	525/NTSC 625/PAL	10½" reel	94 minutes	1" (25 mm)	Ferric Oxide
MII	525/NTSC 625/PAL	???	???	½" (12.5 mm)	

Professional Digital Video Formats

Format	*Tape Size*	*Compressor*	*Compression Ratio*	*YUV Sampling*	*Running Time*
DVCAM	6 mm	DV25	5:1	4:1:1 NTSC 4:2:0 PAL	184 mins
DVCPRO	6 mm	DV25	5:1	4:1:1	183 mins
DVCPRO 50	6 mm	DV50	3.1:1	4:2:2	90 mins
Digital S	12.5 mm	DV50	3.1:1	4:2:2	124 mins
Digital Betacam	12.5 mm	Sony	3:1	4:2:2	94 mins

SOLUTIONS
BUILDING BRIDGES BETWEEN THE STANDARDS OF VIDEOS AVAILABLE WORLDWIDE

There are three main approaches to bridging the gaps between the world's many video standards.

The first of these is what I loosely refer to as transcoding. This applies primarily to efforts to replay material from other TV systems using equipment designed with a single particular TV system in mind. Almost all of the solutions based on this technique are replay only and make no provision for the production of material in the *foreign* tv system.

The second approach is that of the true multi-standard equipment. These are pieces of video equipment that can work as fully operational pieces of equipment in any one of a number of TV systems. With a multi-standard video recorder, you expect an NTSC tape to be reproduced as a standard NTSC signal, and the same machine if fed with a PAL tape will reproduce it as a standard PAL signal. A multi-standard VCR can also be expected to make a perfectly normal NTSC recording of an NTSC input signal, and a perfectly normal PAL recording of a PAL input signal.

The third approach is that of standards conversion where the TV signal is actually converted from being a standard signal in one TV system to being a standard signal in another. This is the only way in which material can be sent from one TV system to another with an absolute guarantee of working, and where operations such as recording and copying become possible in the destination TV system.

Transcoding—Pseudo-PAL and Pseudo-NTSC

In this section, we'll look solely at compatibility between NTSC and PAL because that is by far the most common and most difficult of the TV standards barriers to cross. Transcoding is also the newest technique, having only really entered the arena in 1988 with the launch of the Panasonic NV-L28 VHS VCR.

In the early days of television when everything was locked to mains frequency, it was next to impossible to get a TV to accept a signal with even the smallest instability. With the advent of switch mode power supplies and VCRs, there came both the ability and the need to decouple the field timing reference from the mains frequency. The reason for this was that the nature of video recording creates relatively unstable tv signals on replay, and as a result the TV has to follow the fluctuations and variations of the signal in order to reproduce the picture. The down side is that the field timing reference signal now has to be generated by dividing down the *ticks* from a quartz crystal, something that requires an increased component count in the TV receiver.

As time went by TV manufacturers tried to reduce the number of components by producing a dedicated VLSI chipset which did all the work. The majority of designs for these were actually implemented as a single chipset for the world, which would support either 525/60 or 625/50 pictures. It so happens that TV sets based upon such a chipset can actually produce a very acceptable monochrome picture of the other TV system when feed with such a video signal. The chipset will automatically adjust the number of lines in the picture to match those of the incoming signal.

Since PAL and NTSC are not that different in the way they encode colour signals, it's not actually that difficult to modify the signal to achieve a reasonable colour reproduction at the same time. The net effect is that you end up with a signal that has the frame rate/scan line characteristics of the original TV system, but the colour coding and subcarrier characteristics of the local TV system. This hybrid cannot be recorded but does provide a very effective way of *painting over the cracks* and allowing the reproduction of material in the other TV system.

Multi-Standard Equipment

The second way of bridging the gap between the various TV systems is to use true multi-standard equipment. Multi-standard equipment refers to TVs, VCRs, and LaserDisc players that can genuinely work in a number of different TV systems. These machines will typically have switches and indicators to show which TV system they are working in, and when a given TV system has been selected will work exactly the same as a standard single machine in the same system would.

If for example, you had a multi-standard VCR which supported NTSC and PAL, you could record the playback signal of an NTSC camcorder and make a genuine NTSC copy, or record an off-air PAL broadcast and make a genuine PAL VHS recording. What you could not do is to perform any kind of conversion; the VCR changes it's TV system *personality* rather than making any change to the signal. Any signal that is NTSC 525/60 will remain that way, and any signal that is PAL 625/50 will remain PAL 625/50. In order to make effective use of a multi-standard VCR, you will need either a multi-standard TV to display on, or a TV of each TV system you want to watch (as a general rule).

Multi-standard VCRs are not amongst the easiest things to find since they are not a mass-market item. Although most of the major VCR manufacturers do make them, surprisingly few actually distribute them on a world-wide basis. As a result, other than in export markets such as those of countries such as Singapore and Hong Kong, they can only be found at a few specialist dealers and then often only as grey imports. The best advice would normally be to look for adverts in the back of a local video magasine, for example **Video** in the USA or **What Video** in the UK and parts of Europe.

While machines in the transcoding category are only available in a few major colour systems, there will be a multi-standard VCR for every country in the world. This does not mean that all multi-standard VCRs support all the world's TV systems, although some do. There are a number of multi-standard machines that support only the various 625/50 systems such as PAL/SECAM/MESECAM in use in eastern Europe and the

Middle East. There are others that support PAL and NTSC but not SECAM, or maybe only certain versions of SECAM (usually MESECAM). Further complexities are added when you consider the capabilities of the TV tuners and RF adaptors of these machines, many of these support less combinations than the VCR itself can handle as video signals. A common example of this is the French SECAM-L; many multi-standard VCRs can handle this only through the video inputs and outputs, not through the Tuner and RF adaptor. To make a recording of French TV with one of these, you would need to attach it to the video outputs of a French TV and select the TV's tuner to the channel you want to record—not a lot of use if you want to do a timer recording.

In addition to being cautious and making sure that the multi-standard machine supports the TV systems you need, you also need to check for more advanced features, particularly stereo sound systems. Although there are a few exceptions, most stereo (VHS HiFi) multi-standard video recorders can only actually receive stereo broadcasts using one of the techniques, be it NICAM, MTS or FM-FM. In countries using the other systems, you will only be able to receive the mono TV soundtrack with these machines.

Finally, multi-standard machines tend to be fairly basic. Most manufacturers only offer about two models; typically one with only mono sound and one with VHS HiFi sound. Fancy extras like flying erase heads, manual audio record level controls, edit connections, and SuperVHS operation are not available. Neither are multi-standard camcorders. Actually, the last one—the camcorder, seems a bit of a surprise since it is camcorder footage that most often leads people into the morass that is TV system incompatibility in the first place. To be able to buy a camcorder that can record in PAL if you know you're going to send it to relatives in a PAL country, and NTSC if you're going to use it say in the USA would seem quite attractive to many people.

Standards Conversion

Standards Conversion is the most complex, technically difficult and degrading of all of the techniques for building bridges between TV standards. It is also the most desirable since the material actually becomes a genuine signal of the destination TV system, which can be recorded and reproduced by equipment of the destination TV system.

Conversion between TV systems with same frame rate are usually reasonably effective, except of course that the resultant signal usually suffers from the deficiencies of both the source and destination colour system.

Conversion between TV systems with differing frame rates is extremely difficult and there is no perfect solution. With a trained eye, it is possible to spot that any given piece of material has been standards converted within a matter of seconds. The units that perform these conversions are known as Digital Standards Converters. For many years digital standards converters were very expensive indeed and as a result were only used by TV stations and video facilities houses. This all changed in the 1990 with the launch by Panasonic of the NV-W1, a combination VHS deck/digital standards converter at around UK#1,600 (approx US$2300). Since then other manufacturers have also introduced domestic standards converters at even lower prices. Among the manufacturers with standards converters in their range are Panasonic, Aiwa, Sharp and Samsung.

Professional standards converters also exist, many of which can achieve significantly better results, but at a price. One of the best is the DEFT, which costs a cool UK#65,000 (approx US$100,000)!

STANDARDS CONVERSION IN VIDEOS

The Basic Approach

The most fundamental problem when attempting to convert from PAL/625 to NTSC/525 and vice versa is the difference in frame rate. With NTSC/525 fitting 30 frames into a second, and PAL/625 only having 25 frames in the same time period, the frames will only start in the same place in the signal on (at best) five occasions within each second.

The only way to effectively perform such a conversion is to be able to *freeze* a frame and hold it until it's the right time for it to start in the other TV system. The only viable way to hold such a large lump of signal electronically is to digitise it and store into a large block of fast computer memory. This is exactly what a digital standards converter does, with the picture quality of the converter governed by the amount of memory used and the resolution of the digitisation process.

Coping with Movement

The biggest single problem to contend with when doing standards conversion is that of making the motion in the finished image look as smooth as possible. This is an extremely difficult thing to do and there is still no really effective solution to this problem, leading to the purist view that material should always be watched in the TV format it was originally made in. Usually this is only possible for people with multi-standard high end equipment such as multi-standard LaserDisc players and who are prepared to import large amounts of material from other countries.

Even the most advanced standards converters have their problems. While they can usually find any pronounced "edges" in the moving image and predict where it would be half way between the two images; the more indistinct the motion the more likely it will fail to predict the position correctly. With extreme motion such as sporting events, these converters can even sometimes fail to track the object at all. For example, a gymnast's legs can disappear during motion because there is no way of tracking the vectors of the motion between images taken 1/25th of a second appart.

Scanline Artifacts

As ever, the problems don't end there. As well as the problem of dealing with motion, there is also the quest for fine detail in the image. This in itself presents a problem since the differing line structure of NTSC/525 and PAL/625 means that each line of the image is out of proportion in reference to it's neighbour in the other system.

The simpler standards converters merely drop or repeat every fifth line or so in the output picture, resulting in some slightly strange effects particularly on text, but retaining much of the definition. The median approach is to mix the appropriate lines together, often on a proportional basis, as illustrated in the diagram. The extreme top end approach is to try and detect edges of objects within each scan line by areas of rapid transition and to predict where the exact position would be based upon the position of the edge in the scan line above and the scan line below.

This area in particular is made much worse by the *two field to a frame* interlace used by all the world's TV systems. The idea is that to keep the flicker of the screen down, each TV frame is drawn onto the screen in two halfs. The first trip down all the odd-numbered lines of the TV picture are drawn, the second time down the even-numbered lines are drawn. This means that a low end converter with only a field store will only be able to do comparisons between adjacent lines from the field, rather than adjacent lines from the full frame. This means that the lines being compared will in fact have a missing (even if the pair are odd) line that should have gone between them.

DIGITAL TELEVISION

The Fundamental Basis

Digital Television systems are now being deployed in various parts of the world, but unfortunately they are even more diversified and different than the old analogue systems. They do have some things in common. Almost all are based on the MPEG-2 (Motion Picture Experts Group) high compression video encoding system. This system is also used on DVDs and some web streaming video applications. Sometimes the picture quality achieveable with MPEG-2 can be absolutely astounding; much of the time bandwidth and related financial constraints result in some truely appalling artifacts.

The majority of broadcast TV applications, known as DVB (Digital Video Broadcasting), use MPEG-2 at lower quality levels or "bit rates". These bit rates are expressed in megabits per second or Mb/sec—Note that the b is lower case—MB/sec would mean megaBYTES per second which would be a wholly different measurement. DVDs typically use bitrates of between 2 Mb/sec and 10 Mb/sec (the maximum allowed). Some digital TV applications fall below even 2 Mb/sec, unfortunately. Further the process of encoding video into MPEG-2 for broadcast/DVD is a technically complex procedure. The majority of DVDs are encoded "non-real-time", in other words, they are analysed by a computer frame by frame over the course of several hours before the final result is available. This results in a much better quality picture at a lower bitrate than could be achieved if the MPEG-2 encoding has been done "in real time". Unfortunately most DVB systems do not use any material already coded into MPEG-2 (from the DVD master for instance)—most are coded "on the fly" in real time. This again makes for inferior results.

DVB systems also use the slightly inferior 4:2:0 method of colour encoding (in common with DVD), although there is a variant of MPEG-2 for broadcast use that uses the industry standard 4:2:2 method of coding. This encoding method reduces the amount of detail in the colour information part of the picture. Many of the worlds DVB systems also include some form of scrambling technology to allow for subscription and pay-per-view broadcasting, and these again differ between various countries, territories and suppliers. Others also include facilities for *Interactive Television* which tries them to running a specific "environment" on which the computer code for these services runs.

SDTV

The term SDTV (Standard Definition Television) refers to the use of a digital broadcast to carry TV pictures of the same physical parameters as today's existing systems. These are interlaced signals (i.e., each frame is divided into two fields) and the only new feature they add over existing analogue TV distribution from a picture viewpoint is automatic support for both 4:3 and 16:9 aspect ratio operation.

CASE STUDY: MULTI-STANDARD VIDEO EQUIPMENT

VHS Video Cassette Recorders

SLV-X830

Key Features

- Multi-standard—PAL, SECAM, MESECAM, NTSC3.58 and NTSC4.43
- HiFi stereo with Tuner equiped for NICAM (B/G & I) and German Stereo
- On-screen display
- Shuttle equiped remote control

Also available is the mono-only version, the SLV-X 730

LaserDisc Players

MDP-850

Key Features

- Dual Standard—PAL and NTSC3.58
- Two side play
- Bitstream D/A convertor
- NTSC can be output as RGB for PAL TVs with SCART sockets

DIGITAL VIDEO BROADCASTING IN INDIA

India chose the DVB-T standard for Terrestrial Digital Broadcasting in July 1999 after 18 months of study and testing.

The state broadcaster Doordarshan started a pilot trial in Delhi during 2002 which is extending to Kolkata, Mumbai and Chennai.

General

DVB-T adopted	8th July 1999
Pilot Trials	2000
Soft launch	2002 Delhi
Analogue switch off	no date announced

Data

Population	1 billion (UN 2003)
TV households	70 million (2000)
Cable penetration	29 million (2002)

CASE STUDY: DIGITAL BROADCASTING SERVICE OF INDIA METEOROLOGICAL DEPARTMENT

Introduction

As part of Global Data Communication under the World Weather Watch programme of WMO, India Meteorological Department is committed to provide Meteorological data, analysed weather charts, weather warnings and satellite imageries to ships and neighbouring countries within a radius of 6000 km around New Delhi.

This document reflects towards improvement in broadcast of GTS data, Weather charts, Output models and Satellite imageries using internet and commercial satellite system as a cost-effective means benefiting end users in Central South Asia, Middle East and Far East countries. India Meteorological Department has started new meteorological data and processed products broadcasting service from 1st July 2003 using World Space "Asia Star" satellite.

Broadcasting

Traditional broadcast through HF are being replaced worldwide by commercial digital radio and data casting. In the same directions India Meteorological Department has replaced HF broadcast services by utilizing commercial data casting services from a company named "World Space".

At RTH level (Analog and binary) files are automatically uploaded in a server scheduled on hourly basis through FTP and graphics (analysed weather charts, output models and satellite imageries) are loaded at scheduled intervals through digital scanner or through IMD's web site. The products are uploaded to uplinking facility at Singapore through Internet. The uplinking site broadcasts these products on hourly basis through World Space satellite "Asia Star".

Receiving System

The receiving system needs a very small L-band antenna, a commercially available small and portable inexpensive digital satellite receiver and a Digital Data Adopter (DDA) at approximate cost of US $150 and a Windows PC. The output of the receiver is fed to the DDA connected to a Data acquisition and Visualization Work Station. The customized Software can be used to visualize the data, satellite images, Weather charts, Automatic plotting of data, analysis and manipulation of data for the benefit of weather forecasters and other users. Printing of selective satellite images and meteorological data and products is also possible.

The reception is in downlink frequency 1467 to 1492 MHz and downlink speed of data is 128 kbps. For receiving the products no human intervention is required. The data can also be received at mobile platforms such as ships. The cost of uplinking is very nominal appox. US 10$ per MB. With data compression, the broadcast is much more cost-effective. Most important aspect is that receiving system is not affected by natural disasters and terrestrial disturbances, ensuring that the signal reaches its destination in even the most adverse conditions. The use of proprietary encryption ensures that only authorised recipients have access to such information. The beneficiaries are recipients covered under the footprints of the World Space satellite Asia Star.

Setup at RTH New Delhi

Half hourly GTS files are generated at RTH computer and two consecutive files are kept in a folder in a server (for digital broadcasting) automatically through ftp process ten minutes before the full hour UTC. Within ten minutes slot these files are uploaded through scheduler on the uplinking server at Singapore through Internet link. The graphics (processed weather charts, output models and satellite imageries) are either scanned through digital scanner or directly from IMD's web site are kept on the server at RTH and through scheduler are uploaded to uplinking server through Internet link. The products are broadcast at full hour UTC.

Meteorological Products

(*i*) GTS data (SYNOP, PILOT, TEMP, METAR, TAF, Weather warnings etc.) of India and neighbouring countries.

(*ii*) Satellite images of INSAT and KALPNA are now being broadcast for wider coverage which, earlier was not possible due to limitation of the footprint of these satellites.
Indian Satellite Images such as three hourly Visible, Infrared, Colour and Water Vapour images.

(*iii*) Analysed Weather charts and model outputs.

Service Plan

In the initial phase data receiving sets have been installed at national centers and the reception is satisfactory. In the second phase the service will be extended by increasing facilities at more national centers as well as to neighbouring countries.

Note: Digital data casting through internet and satellite broadcast is cost-effective and reliable, noise free communication solution as a replacement to obsolete HF broadcast service. Implementation of the satellites "Amri Star"
And "Afri Star" will give worldwide coverage.

INDIA LAUNCHES WORLD'S FIRST EDUCATION SATELLITE

Millions of illiterate people in remote, rural India could soon have access to an education, as a satellite devoted exclusively to long distance learning was launched on Monday. It is the world's first dedicated educational satellite, according to the Indian Space Research Organisation (ISRO).

India launched the $20 million, 2-tonne EDUSAT from the Satish Dhawan Space Centre at Sriharikota, a tiny island in the Bay of Bengal. The satellite is the heaviest ever launched by an Indian-made rocket—the new Geosynchronous Satellite Launch Vehicle (GSLV), which cost $33 million.

About 35 per cent of the country's billion-plus population are illiterate, a 2001 government census showed. "India will require 10,000 new schools each year and meeting the teaching needs on such a scale [by conventional methods] will be impossible," Madhavan Nair, chairman of ISRO, told New Scientist.

To date, India has used both of its multi-purpose INSAT satellites to provide long-distance education information alongside their telecommunications, broadcasting and weather-forecasting functions.

But EDUSAT's dedicated function will substantially improve the service provided. It will use the virtual classroom concept to offer education to children in remote villages, quality higher education to students in areas without access to good technical institutes, adult literacy programmes and training modules for teachers.

"It is a unique mission and we are happy to have achieved it," Nair says. H.P. Dixit, vice-chancellor of Indira Gandhi Open University, added: "It will revolutionise education in our country."

EDUSAT carries six KU-band transponders and six extended C-band transponders. All but one of the KU-band transponders will be dedicated to specific regions of India, while the rest of the transponders will provide blanket coverage for the country.

The satellite will utilise an antenna with a 1.2-metre reflector to direct the KU-band spot beams towards their intended regions. This will enable information to be broadcast in relevant local languages—India has 18 official languages and over 400 dialects. The educational programmes can be viewed on any television set through a simple low-cost receiver costing about $65, Nair says.

Once EDUSAT is commissioned in two months' time it will initially provide one satellite link per beam, with each link catering for up to 200 classrooms. When fully operational, 25 to 30 satellite links will broadcast to about 5000 remote terminals.

Monday's launch marks several firsts for India's space programme, says Nair. EDUSAT is India's first satellite dedicated for education. Others being planned include AGRISAT, to address the country's agricultural needs, and HEALTHSAT, for providing telemedicine services.

It is also GSLV's first operational flight. India will no longer depend on Europe's Ariane rockets to launch satellites of up to 2 tonnes, though it will continue to use them for heavier spacecraft.

EDUCATIONAL TELEVISION BROADCASTING IN INDIA: A POLICY PERSPECTIVE

With the introduction of satellite technology and its convergence with the new information technologies at the global level, satellite television broadcasting is increasingly used for distance education and training. There is considerable optimism about the potential of educational television to harness educational development in developing countries. For solving the educational problems of access, equity and polity, how policies in education and broadcast media in India have responded to new developments in communication and information technology.

The use of educational television in India is guided more by technological development than by thorough and systematic educational planning based on educational needs and priorities. Development planners in India have not yet come up with a clear-cut policy on the use of communication technology in the educational system. The emerging broadcasting policy also has not addressed the issue of making available new communication technologies for education and training on a wider and sustained basis. In the absence of a policy, growing commercialisation of education and television is likely to dilute the broader concerns for equity and equality in education and accentuate existing educational disparities.

EDUCATIONAL BROADCASTING: THE NATIONAL PERSPECTIVES AND PRIORITIES

Importance of educational broadcasting cannot be over-emphasised for accelerating the pace of national development in general and for bringing about qualitative as well as quantitative improvement of education in particular. This is felt more significant in developing countries like India where socio-economic condition is yet to reach a take-off stage and universalisation of elementary education is still to be realised as per the constitutional directive. Therefore, there has been an imperative need for furthering national development in all facets of life and for providing increased access to education both through formal and non-formal system and reducing the massive wastage and stagnation at all stages of education. Educational broadcasting is required to be a potential instrument of educational advancement and an integral component of educational inputs in traditional as well as distance education or other alternative learning systems for different categories of learners.

Attempts of the APEID at the Continental Level

The Asian Programme of Educational Innovation for Development Technical Working Group in its Draft Final Report in the context of formulating guidelines for the development of educational broadcasting services has laid down the following for consideration:

(*a*) guidelines should have application to the universalisation of education and the special needs of rural communities,

(*b*) there is a great variety of administrative patterns and in the stages of development in educational broadcasting among member countries,

(*c*) advice should be practical for implementation and should have a proper regard for limits of financial and other resources,

(*d*) radio is a cheaper form of broadcasting than television, both in the production and transmission of programmes and in the facilities required for reception. It has the advantage of greater penetration of the general population, and

(*e*) notwithstanding the previous statement, television is a powerful educational tool and must be given full consideration by governments and ministry policy makers when determining priorities for the allocation of resources.

Consideration at the National Level

In view of the above considerations, the APEID Group was rightly conscious of its limitations and has aptly observed that the guidelines that were laid down by it are either general principles or specific statements that are not applicable to any one country or educational system. Therefore, it was felt necessary to discuss and spell out these guidelines in further details of specificity in National Seminars or Workshops of various Asian countries. In India, such a National Workshop was held at New Delhi from December 1 to 6, 1980, under the joint collaboration of the Ministry of Education and Culture as well as the UNESCO's Asian Programme of Educational Innovation for

Development (APEID). This workshop in the fitness of things specifically viewed educational broadcasting including both radio and TV programmes:

(*a*) as a means of motivation by informing and encouraging people to participate in national development,
(*b*) as a major component of the non-formal education system by providing an alternative approach to the education of out of school children, youth and adult,
(*c*) as a direct instructional medium dispensing with the need for an intermediary,
(*d*) as an enrichment of the formal system of education where it can fill instruction gaps, up-to-date knowledge and bring in new learning experiences,
(*e*) as a training component for teachers (instructors) and supervisors,
(*f*) as a means of imparting vocational (agricultural and industrial) and professional (medical and engineering) skills.

Nature of Education Broadcasting

The National Workshop thus wished that educational broadcasting would be multi-purpose and sought to make multi-pronged efforts for educational advancement. It would not only move away from narrow syllabus based approaches, but also would try to reach the learners directly. It would aim at reduction of load and drudgery in the classroom and making teaching-learning process interesting and effective. Both radio and television programmes would serve all categories of learners and provide all kinds of learning experiences—knowledge, understanding, appreciation, attitude and skills. The new curriculum with emphasis on SUPW, citizenship training and national integration could be better realised with the help of educational broadcasting.

National Priorities

In planning and production of programmes both the media—radio and television would emphasise the following national priorities at least during the next ten years.

(*a*) universalisation of elementary education both formal and non-formal,
(*b*) non-formal education for adults, linking education to economic and social tasks,
(*c*) development of vocational and professional skills,
(*d*) training for citizenship,
(*e*) popularising science with a view to developing a scientific outlook,
(*f*) promoting national integration,
(*g*) providing information about themes of national importance—population education, energy conservation, preservation of wildlife, environmental sanitation, nutrition and health.

Planning and Management

With a view to realising the above national objectives and priorities, it has been decided that educational broadcasting should form an integral part of the total educational system. It means that the responsibility for policy and management of educational broadcasting should be with the educational authority. It has been suggested that Advisory Bodies and Educational Technology Institutes should be set up at the national and State levels for extending advice from time to time and taking up the management.

These advisory and executive bodies should take up responsibility for all kinds of educational media. This responsibility must include formulation of policy, programme planning, production, utilisation, evaluation and feedback, training of personnel, providing support materials and publicity. This must also comprise administration and accounting of the organisation. Although these institutions would be part of the educational infrastructure, they should have operational freedom.

Educational broadcasting by its very nature must address itself to mass audience. It must serve the national interests and goals. But it is also necessary that it should take cognizance of local needs, language differences, cultural variety and other similar factors. Therefore, besides national framework within which the priorities, broad areas, themes, objectives, utilisation and evaluation procedures of educational broadcasting should be spelt out, similar action should also be taken up at regional, State and even local levels. Planning, production and evaluation should be a collaborative venture involving curriculum developers, subject experts, teachers, scriptwriters, social scientists and producers. Even audience would be involved in planning, production and evaluation for ensuring credo and reality in programmes.

Utilisation and Feedback

In order to ensure optimum and effective utilisation of educational broadcasts, the National Workshop has suggested that all schools and learning centres should be adequately equipped with listening and viewing facilities. Although government should take up the main responsibility for this, public funding participation of the community and national as well as international voluntary agencies may also be explored. Adequate steps should be taken for maintenance and operation of the receivers. Even necessary incentives may be made available to teachers for bringing their own radio sets for enabling pupils to hear broadcasts. Educational broadcasting should also form an integral part of teacher-education programme. Besides, in-service training courses should be organised for orienting the teachers and supervisors with the effective use and techniques of media; various kind of support materials should also be provided to teachers and students by the educational authorities. Research and evaluation should form a significant part of the total process of educational broadcasting. Both short-term as well as long-term, formative and summative research studies should be conducted for better utilisation, evaluation and feedback.

In View of the INSAT

All steps were taken both at the National and State levels for making the ETV Programmes a great success with the help of INSAT. The experts in the Working Groups for Hardware and Manpower as well as Software submitted their detailed suggestions for implementing the project more effectively and efficiently. These documents were considered along with other relevant papers in the National Workshop at New Delhi and after minute discussion and deliberation resolutions were taken for facing the unique challenge successfully. It was felt by all concerned that educational broadcasting has to be made meaningful and efficacious if education is to be "an instrument of human progress and a condition for human survival."

With the availability of INSAT-1A, new types of ETV Programmes were telecast for primary schools from August 15, 1982. But unfortunately the said INSAT had some mechanical disorders and failed to function properly. Even then ETV Programmes have continued to be telecast through the terrestrial transmission stations in Andhra Pradesh and Orissa. "It is hoped that the INSAT-IB which has successfully been launched on the 30th August, 1983, will help promoting expansion and utilisation of ETV Programmes in the country."

In an under-developed society it is only proper that an important role should be assigned to communication in the campaign for modernisation and economic development, and, in a country in which most people are illiterate, the role of broadcasting would be must more important than that of the printed media. From its earliest years AIR has accepted this role and several of its programmes are devised to fulfil it, whether they are intended for the general listener or for specific groups like farmers, women students, teachers and workers.

The accent in all such programmes is on education and instruction, in the broad sense, and the purpose is to achieve through these programmes certain constructive goals of national endeavour. In the broadcasts for the general listener, the educational and instructive element is subordinated to the need to attract the listener's attention while in the programmes for specific audiences the educational approach is more direct. That is not to say that such programmes are intended to be, or are in fact, entirely didactic. Each of them includes entertainment, in some measure, but it is incidental to the main object.

The broadcast of such programmes is among the most important of AIR's activities, yet it would be impossible, in one chapter, to discuss each of them with the attention they deserve. Though they vary in content, and possess some distinctive characteristics they also share certain features in their organisation, propagation and reception. This review is confined to educational broadcasts for schools and university students and those for rural listeners.

Both radio and TV are used for such programmes. In an earlier chapter the development of TV in India was discussed in relation to its distinctive technology, programming, and other aspects. Its use for national development will be discussed in this chapter along with that of radio because the two media have to be used to complement each other and it is always necessary to determine which is most appropriate for any given objective.

School Broadcasting

Even before All India Radio came into existence there were broadcasts for schools from Mumbai and Kolkata. These were occasional in character. It was only in 1937 that organised school broadcasting started in Kolkata because both the University and the Department of Education of Bengal asked for it. Even so the broadcasts were only bi-weekly and for half an hour at a time.

Meanwhile, encouraged by the interest shown by the educational authorities in Bengal, AIR wrote to a number of educationists asking for their views and suggestions for starting regular broadcasts for schools from all AIR stations. The response led AIR to believe that the time was ripe for introducing programmes for schools because the educational authorities indicated that they would cooperate in drawing up the programmes and allot funds for schools to buy radio sets.

Carried away by their enthusiasm, the AIR authorities embarked on school programmes from Delhi, Kolkata, Chennai and Mumbai without waiting for schools to acquire radio sets. They hoped that starting of the programmes would induce schools to buy sets. The duration of the programmes ranged from half-an-hour to one hour and the frequency from two days a week at Kolkata to six days a week at Delhi.

Pamphlets; distributed free of charge to schools which had radio sets, gave details of the broadcasts for each school term.

In retrospect, it was unwise to start such broadcasts without commitments from the educational authorities to make schools buy radio sets and to provide in their time-tables for regular listening to the programmes. In the absence of any such commitment AIR soon found that the number of schools which acquired radio sets was very small. Even today only about 60,000 out of almost 5,00,000 schools have them, and more than half the schools with sets are in Tamil Nadu.

Considering the financial condition of the majority of our schools it would be unrealistic to expect all of them to have radio sets when many of them do not even have furniture and equipment but a suitable radio set costs about Rs. 350 and it is difficult to imagine that only 60,000 schools can afford it. No one knows how many of these are actually used. The Verghese Group's Report mentions that a survey by the National Council for Educational Research. No teachers have been represented on the Panels though they serve on Subjects Committees which assist the Panels in drawing up the programmes. This apart, the Panels are set up by AIR and educationists are invited to serve on them for specific periods. Educational authorities in the States and teachers in schools do not consider School Broadcasting as their activity; it is AIR's responsibility and they render such assistance as they have time and inclination to provide. This is the basic weakness. If, from the start, AIR had offered to place its facilities and expertise and the disposal of the States' education departments, thus making them responsible for planning the programmes, formulating the policy and organising the listening arrangements, the broadcasts would certainly have been far more fruitful, at least in the States which are administratively efficient.

Listening arrangements have been left entirely to the schools. Appeals are made, from time to time, to the Departments of Education to persuade schools to buy sets and to make the broadcasts an integral part of the school time-table. These are sympathetically received but the effect is negligible.

On the other hand, the TV broadcasts from Delhi, being planned with the active participation of teachers and being based on the school syllabi, replace the teachers in the sense that the same subject does not have to be taught by the teacher in the classroom. Scripts of broadcasts are also examined by teachers before broadcast. The Delhi Directorate of Education is responsible for the planning of the broadcasts and ensures that they fit into the school time-table.

The quality of programmes on radio has been very uneven. As far back as 1938, Fielden has stated, in his report to government, that there was a dearth of qualified speakers. Not all teachers are good broadcasters. Because of the multiplicity of languages it is not possible to ask an outstanding broadcaster in one language to broadcast in another, and the funds available for programmes in general are so inadequate that for school programmes only very limited amounts can be spent. Thus AIR programmes are restricted to talks and can seldom introduce topics in the form of stories of drama which have a much greater appeal.

Even though posts of producers for School Broadcasts have been created at several stations, they lie vacant for years on end because educationists are not attracted either by the salaries offered by AIR or by the prospects of achieving something worthwhile through these broadcasts.

The staff of AIR concerned with planning, editing and producing the programmer belonged, for the greater part, to the Programme cadre of AIR and did not possess the intimate knowledge of schools and school children which is necessary. Also, the number of persons detailed to attend these broadcasts has always been inadequate.

Under all these handicaps it is not surprising that school broadcasts on radio never caught on. AIR was well aware of the poor response but apart from making appeals to schools and to educational authorities it had no authority to force schools to take its broadcasts. It would have been worthwhile, in the circumstances, to discontinue to programmes except in those States like Tamil Nadu and Maharashtra, in which there was some interest, and to concentrate staff and funds at those stations to see whether at least at one or two centres the scheme could not be made to work. But a government department lacks the incentives to cut its losses. Government was reluctant to discontinue an activity which was supposed to raise the prestige of the organisation. So for more than thirty years the broadcasts have continued with few listeners. For it must be remembered that all the 60,000 sets are not being used to listen to the programmes. Random visits to schools in different parts of the country from time to time revealed that often the set was out of order or it was locked up for safety in the headmaster's office, or it was installed at the headmaster's residence, or there was not time to listen to the programmes. Only a thorough countrywide survey would reveal how many children actually listen.

But undeterred by this rather disappointing outcome of AIR's broadcasts for schools, some educationists and many non-educationists have, in the past few years, made rather tall claims for what radio and TV can do in the field of formal education. They maintain that the Indian educational system is grinding to a halt. By conventional means it has not been possible to fulfil the constitutional directive to provide free, compulsory, primary education to all out children. Nor has it been possible to reduce the drop-outs at middle-school age. There are 450 million people living in our villages and most of them are very poor. If school education was universal, even upto the primary stage, the role of broadcasting would not be so important but with 70 per cent illiteracy, it is argued, radio and TV must be used to supplement the schools' to eradicate it. Villages without schools can be served by TV sets with teaching assistants so that at least a fundamental education can be provided to children even before schools can be built in their village.

It is also argued that only half the primary school teachers in India possess a high school diploma. The village TV set could be used to improve the standard of classroom teaching.

Moreover, the population explosion makes it impossible to satisfy the demand for education with existing facilities. In other countries formal school and university courses on radio TV help students to pass high school and university examinations without attending school or college.

Radio and TV can impart vocational training, technical and agricultural skills, and so forth. They can reach the entire population, even illiterates. If the demand for trained manpower is not met, the development of India will be retarded. Examples are given of countries in which radio and TV have been used to overcome the shortage of teachers and school buildings.

There is a consensus among teachers that the percentage of know-how absorbed by school children from electronic media outside the classroom is, in many developing societies, greater than that absorbed in the class. A good teacher on TV can achieve results comparable with those of the good teacher in the classroom but better than those of the mediocre or weak teacher.

But there are certain difficulties which have to be faced and solved in using the media for formal education. So far they have been wished away or ignored altogether.

Radio and TV sets can only be used in electrified areas. If installed in unelectrified villages it has to be ensured that battery operated sets are available and can be maintained satisfactory.

The technical problem of proper maintenance of the receivers and the satisfactory reception of the programme in the schools is very important and cannot be tackled after the project is started as AIR's experience shows.

The integration of the instruction to be imparted through the media and that reserved for the classroom presents great difficulty and requires much advance planning and preparation. The media can only be part of the whole system and cannot possibly assume an independent role. Experts differ as to the relative importance of the elements in the multi-media system.

It has been found in experiments elsewhere that the use of radio and TV for education has involved a re-structuring of the entire educational system. It requires co-operation between media personnel and educationists. It also needs sufficient qualified personnel and above all it needs evaluation at every stage.

While radio alone has never been successfully used for formal education and has always been regarded as an aid for teachers, it has sometimes been argued that lessons on TV can replace classroom lessons. This point is vigorously disputed by many educationists.

Professor Wilbur Schramm, an acknowledged authority on instructional TV and radio, gives several reasons for being wary about accepting all the claims made for TV.

First of all it is a one-way channel and unless it is combined with correspondence, or some special arrangements in the classroom, it is impossible to tell how much a student has got out of a lesson. The student cannot control the pace of the lesson to fit his needs. This is a formidable handicap. For this reason TV lessons cannot cover all areas of learning. The development of critical or analytical reasoning and the encouragement of creative expression require very close interplay between student and teacher that TV can never provide.

Experience so far suggests that TV stimulates teachers more than students and can thus be of immense help in improving a teacher's performance but it has yet to be proved that it can teach without a teacher present to guide the student.

Secondly, TV lessons for schools must be made locally about particular subjects, directed at a particular class, in a particular State. It is not possible to plan TV lessons centrally for broadcast all over the country. Thus numerous production and transmitting centres would be necessary.

Thirdly, there is yet no concrete evidence of the success of educational TV for schools, whether broadcast by satellite or by conventional TV transmitters, except as an aid to teaching. In the absence of evidence of success it is highly risky to build our whole school educational system on the assumption that many millions of our children would be educated by TV. Satellites cannot be real teaching instruments in places where the post is unreliable because test-papers and work sheets, have to be sent by post.

Finally, educational TV is very expensive and can never be a cost-saving device. Good programmes cost enormous sums of money and poor ones are of no use. Professor Schramm says that he has never seen a major programme introduced in a developing country without ample funds being donated by an international organisation or a donor country.

In view of these difficulties and limitation the question is how radio and TV can best serve our educational system. Radio and TV can be used to supplement the teaching in the classroom. This is what AIR's programmes have done so far. Or they can be used to teach the basic core of the subject while the teacher guides the students in following the broadcast and in supervising the exercises they do. The teacher in the broadcast studio provides the expertise in the subject taught and the classroom teacher discusses the subject with the students, answers their questions, and helps them in the activity of learning.

Broadcasts can also be used to extend learning outside the school. Where there are no schools or where children cannot go to schools or where those who have had to leave school to work can only study in non-working hours, where certain skills have to be taught, radio and TV, combined with correspondence study, or group study under the supervision of a relatively untrained teachers of leader, can be effective.

Obviously supplementary broadcasts are an extra charge and should not be considered at all in our situation where, if funds for such broadcasts were available, they would be better spent on opening more schools. Supplementary broadcasts, such as those of the BBC and NHK of Japan, are very effective in societies where every child goes to school and the educational standard is fairly good.

Broadcasting for core teaching is very expensive. The entire curriculum has to be revised, and every teacher has to be trained. Moreover, such broadcasts are economical only if millions of students can take them. With our linguistic diversity and the diversity and the differences in syllabi from State to State we cannot use such teaching except at vary heavy cost.

So we are left with the use of the media for extending education to areas and for groups which we cannot serve with schools and institutions. This is a substitute, though an inferior one, for schools and teachers and though primary, secondary and university education cannot be imparted in this way at least some education can be provided for those who would otherwise be deprived of it. Some urgent needs for informal education of this type for adults and for children can be met by the media.

For this type of educational broadcasting which would we use—radio or TV? Again, Professor Schramm, in a pamphlet entitled "TV Reconsidered", issued by the Asian Mass Communication Research and Information Centres, asks whether we have passed too quickly by radio. Radio is much cheaper and demands much less sophistication in programming and production. The technology requires much less maintenance and it is within the capability of developing countries. Even a TV set requires far more attention than a radio set. Of course, the potential of radio as a teaching medium is not so great as that of TV. There are some teaching situations in which both sound and sight are needed but research has shown that there is only a slight difference in the effectiveness of instructional radio and instructional TV. In some fields such as music, languages, and mathematics radio is better than TV. This is why Australia, for example, uses radio rather than TV to combine with correspondence study. Japan uses both as does Britain. The indications are that students who listen to radio programmes do as well as those who view TV. This raises the question whether it would not be better to take education and information to ten times as many people in the villages than to invest the money in TV since the cost radio is ten to one.

The potential audience for radio is much larger—there are three times are many radio sets in the world as TV sets and in India the radio is much higher. Besides, as the low-cost radio set is within the means of farmers, artisans, domestic servants and all except the very poor, students in towns and villages can listen to broadcasts in their own homes or in neighbours' homes. But it will be a generation or more before TV sets can be purchased by any save the very rich and even informal education for children or adults will require an organisation in each district for the installation and maintenance of community TV sets with all the attendant uncertainties of their regular and satisfactory functioning.

For all these reasons it seems worthwhile to use radio, to the extent possible, for all such informal education. Even in the case of broadcasts intended to be heard in schools the visual element can be supplied by slides which can be sent by post to illustrate radio programmes. This would be much cheaper than broadcasting TV programmes for schools through satellites, and supplying and maintaining TV sets. Again cost-benefit studies need to be made before deciding which medium would yield the greatest benefit.

In view of the limitations of the TV medium discussed above, what is the relevance of satellite broadcasting/in so far as educational broadcasts are concerned?

INSAT-IB will broadcast a 45 minute programme daily for 340 villages to start with. As only $1^1/_2$ per cent hours are available on the Satellite, only two languages can be served. What about other languages?

As the broadcasts cover children in Classes I to V they cannot possibly follow the syllabus but try to achieve two things. Firstly, it is claimed, they would make school more interesting than it is at present with the poor quality of teaching available in our primary schools. Thus children would not drop out of school as much as they do. Secondly, the broadcasts would improve the children's basic concepts and skills, promote aesthetic sensitivity, instill habits of hygiene and healthy living, bring awareness of modernisation of life and society. So we are back to the policy of "enrichment" which has failed so far to persuade teachers and educationists to respond to educational broadcasts on radio.

However, the priority given to primary schools is correct and if the programmes are planned by the NCERT, as has been decided, they may be effective. But if the programmes are not well-planned and presented children may stop taking any interest in them after the initial novelty wears off. If listening arrangements are satisfactory and if evaluation is done systematically it is possible that programmes may be useful but the problem remains that school lessons through the satellite must necessarily be highly centralised whereas our schools need lessons planned specifically for limited areas. Consider the numerous languages and dialects in which children must be taught. INSAT would have only two channels. How can India be covered with two programmes?

Has a representative body of educationists, as distinct from the officials of the Ministry of Education, had an opportunity to examine the kind of education to be provided through the satellite and whether that is what we need? And what about the cost? Has anyone bothered to work out how much it would cost to broadcast similar lessons for the same number of schools through terrestrial transmitters which could very the lessons according to the needs of the areas.

Assuming that all the problems of using radio and TV for education are solved, the question remains how educational broadcasting should be organised.

From the experience gained by AIR in forty-four years of radio broadcasts for schools and twenty-one years of educational TV, and from the experience of other broadcasting organisations, it is quite clear that without the support of the educational authorities and the goodwill of teachers the broadcasts cannot be effective. The Ministry of Education must play an important part in laying down the policy for educational broadcasting, teachers must have a say, through their representatives, in determining the general character of the broadcasts, and the detailed planning and production of the broadcasts must be entrusted to men and women who are firmly grounded in education but are trained and equipped with a high degree of skill in radio and TV production techniques. This is difficult but it can be done.

It has not been possible for AIR and Doordarshan over the years, to obtain the effective support of the educational authorities either from the Ministry of Education at the Centre, or from the education departments in the States. Nor it is likely ever to mobilise the required degree of support as long as educational broadcasts remain under AIR's exclusive control.

The direct control of the Ministry of Education would also be inappropriate for an activity in which broadcasting personnel and policies are involved. A national council for school broadcasting for the country as a whole, with councils for each State, may provide the right institutional frame for the collaboration necessary between educationists and broadcasters.

The State councils must have representatives of every major educational body—the department of education, professional associations off teachers, university departments, colleges of education, and off course of AIR and Doordarshan. They should not be merely advisory bodies but must be delegated certain powers. They should not be merely advisory bodies but must be delegated certain powers. They should consider all plans for programmes for schools and for children who cannot attend school in their State. They must have the authority to determine the aims and character of each programmes series. Programme sub-committees to assist the councils should have representatives of practising teachers and producers and radio and TV programmes. They must consider the training of scriptwriters and teachers who are asked to broadcast.

The councils must also decide on the time of broadcasts so that they are fitted into the school time-table and they must organise suitable valuation procedures through inspection of listening schools during listening hours to study the impact of the broadcasts on teachers and students.

The national council for school broadcasts, with representatives of AIR and Doordarshan and of the Ministry of Education, the National Council for Educational Research and Training, and of associations of teachers should lay down the policy for school broadcasts for the country as a whole.

Among the most important of its functions would be the determination of priorities for the use of radio and TV, taking into account the resources available, the cost involved, and the educational goals which the county wants to attain. The council must decide whether composite programmes for children of primary Classes I-V, as INSAT (1A) was planning to provide, will serve any purpose. Can we afford the "enrichment" which such broadcasts can provide while millions of children remain illiterate? If not, the council may advise that satellite TV is not suited to our needs.

It must also commission detailed cost-benefit studies to help it to decide between the various means of education available to us and between radio and TV.

The national council should also be responsible for advising on the type of radio and TV sets to be installed in schools and to take up with the government questions relating to the production and sale of such sets to make them available as cheaply as possible.

The training of staff in educational broadcasting would be one of the most important tasks before the national council. The NCERT and other institutions would have to be equipped for the purpose.

While the State councils would organise regular inspection of schools for evaluating the impact of specific lessons on students and teachers, the national council should undertake research, through appropriate bodies, on the quality of broadcasts, and the short-and long-term results of school broadcasts in general for the progress of education. For example, it is necessary to know how many schools, what kind of schools and in what areas in the country as a whole take school broadcasts. If in certain States the organisation of broadcasts is defective and the listening is limited the national council may advise that school broadcasts should be discontinued in those States.

Finally, the national council should be provided with adequate funds to meet the goals it sets out to achieve. In view of the vast variations between the States it might be best for the Union Government to allocate funds for school broadcasting all over the country so that they may be spent to achieve optimum results. States very too much in their resources and efficiency.

Broadcasts for Universities

Radio talks on subjects of academic interest have been broadcast from AIR stations from the very beginning of organised broadcasting. Advisory panels were set up at Stations to suggest subjects and talkers. The talks were broadcast once a week or less frequently from some stations. When in 1964, an attempt was made to assess the impact of these broadcasts on students in six cities it was found that there was little interest in them. In the absence of any organisation to plan group listening, students listened to such talks as sporadically as they listened to any other talks. University authorities obviously did not find the broadcasts sufficiently useful to make any effort to organise listening.

Meanwhile the idea of correspondence courses for university students has been discussed in the past ten years and from experience in India and elsewhere it is likely that such courses will be popular provided they are organised efficiently.

Our desire to spread higher education as widely as possible among the different strata of society combined with our need for engineers, teachers, technicians, and other skilled personnel demand an expansion of educational facilities which has already strained our resources and it is not possible any more to meet the growing demand for more and more places and other institutions of higher education. Obviously social justice requires that such courses should be available to all who are qualified to pursue them.

Faced by the same problem other societies have considered the ways in which radio and TV can contribute to formal and systematic study and their experience and research show that the media are effective only when supported by other modes of teaching and so organised as to evoke regular and active response from the learner. Broadcasting is a one-way medium; teaching is a two-way process and the broadcast of talks cannot serve the purpose. It was in these circumstances that correspondence courses with the help of radio and TV were started.

Some of the most successful of these have provided opportunities to young people to continue their education even though they cannot attend schools or colleges either because they cannot afford to or because of geographical isolation. In Japan such courses serve 150,000 students to pass their high school examinations. Radio NHK provides TV and radio programmes for every grade of the course, in every subject, according to text-books approved by the Ministry of Education. Several other countries have also started such courses of high school students.

In the field of university broadcasts also Japan has given the lead. Nine universities and six junior colleges offer courses by correspondence. NHK works with them, transmitting regular broadcasts by lectures and producing text-books. In the USA, the Chicago Board of Education has, for more than a decade, offered on TV the whole curriculum of its City Junior College. Students are allotted to "Section Teachers". These not only mark exercises sent in by students but are also available during weekend telephone "conferences". About 10,000 students take advantage of this course Post-graduate credit courses, including one leading to a diploma in industrial engineering, are offered by radio and TV in Australia in association with seminars and laboratory work at the University of New South Wales. In the Soviet Union too more than half of all higher education students are studying by correspondence.

The experiment that appears to have most excited our educationists is the Open University of Britain. Correspondence tuition has long been used in Britain for students of a variety of subjects. Such teaching allows for a two-way traffic of ideas. The printed word is far more effective than TV pictures or the spoken word on radio in posing a problem to be solved at the student's pace and time. Also, for the response from the student the printed word alone is available as also for the individual attention which his exercises and essays demand from his tutors. Radio and TV can only aid this process and the student of Britain's Open University finds that the main part of his course lies in the packaged material which he receives by post and which assigns the written work he has to do for a correspondence tutor to whom he must send it. He is also advised on the text-books he must read. The material includes slides, gramophone records and apparatus for scientific experiments. In fact only about ten per cent of the whole curriculum is carries by radio and TV.

One TV and one radio programme per week supplement the written material for students of the basic university course. The shortage of air-time makes it impossible to give so many broadcasts for students of advanced courses. Since the use of the media is expensive, they are used only for those functions which they are best equipped to carry out, such as the initial presentation of a series of topics, or highlighting and illustrating points of difficulty, or stimulating interest in the course. They can also bring the students in to touch with first-rate minds. They help to reduce the "fall-out" rate which is generally high in adult education. Moreover, such broadcasts, since they go out on the public broadcast channels, can be heard by anyone who is interested, even if he is not enrolled for the course, and thus help to spread knowledge and understanding to a wider audience.

TV is ten times as expensive as radio and is used mainly for subjects which demand a visual element such as scientific demonstrations but radio is just as good for subjects which demand verbal symbols. Full scale notes on the broadcast programmes are sent to the students in advance so that the programmes form an integrated part of the course.

For students who find it difficult to listen to such broadcasts at home, Study Centres have been established throughout the UK. All are equipped for direct reception and for tape-recording the programmes so that students can hear them or view them at their convenience.

At these Study Centres the students also receive tutorial services. They are situated, usually, in technical colleges or other institutions which allow the use of their libraries, laboratories and recreation facilities to the students of the correspondence course.

Even in Britain it was not easy to find time on the BBC's radio and TV channels for the broadcasts. In Japan there are special educational channels for such courses and Britain is considering a separate radio channel. There has been very close coordination between the academic staff of the Open University and the BBC producers of the radio and TV programmes. The latter, while remaining operationally a part of the BBC, have become, in effect, a part of the Open University.

The authorities of the Open University have detailed the conditions for the success of the project. Firstly, a sufficient number of persons, capable of higher education, who cannot obtain it through conventional institutions; secondly, an efficient distribution network, including postal, radio and TV distribution; thirdly an adequate pool of qualified part-time teachers. One might add that the efficient coordination of the different media of instruction to make a coherent system is most important.

If even highly industrialised countries need to use radio and TV to extend education it is argued that developing societies must do so too. But can we, in India, meet all the conditions necessary for success?

To start with, TV must be ruled out because for a long time to come only the very rich can afford TV sets. University courses cannot be followed on community TV receivers unless these are located in institutions of higher education where the student can view and listen without disturbance. Such institutions are already working to capacity and can hardly accommodate students of correspondence courses. Besides, they are concentrated in big cities and would be of no help to students in small towns and rural areas who most need the correspondence courses.

We have, therefore, to depend on radio, as AIR has done, to aid the correspondence courses of the Delhi University, the Punjab University (Chandigarh), Punjabi University (Patiala) and the Kashmir and Madurai Universities. Some other Universities have asked AIR broadcasting support for their correspondence courses but so far no others have been started. AIR cannot afford this activity from its own limited resources and is asking the University Grants Commission to make funds available for such broadcasts. Universities charge approximately Rs. 200 to 250 per annum from students of their correspondence courses and part of this collection should be made available to AIR.

Responsibility for planning the courses rests entirely with the universities. For example, in Delhi the Correspondence School of Delhi University works out the details in committees on which AIR is represented only to provide information of the possibilities of using radio for certain purposes.

As mentioned in earlier chapters, most stations of AIR have only one broadcast channel and unless a special channel for educational broadcasts is available it is difficult to see how AIR could provide radio support for such courses from its various stations. Delhi is exceptional in having four medium-wave channels at its disposal. Even so, the time and duration of broadcasts are confined to the early morning hours on the Yuva Vani channel. Students would find the evening hours more convenient but there is no time for them.

The absence of any organised group-listening is a very serious obstacle; individual students cannot be expected to organise systematic listening.

The Verghese group examined these questions in its report and felt that there were several weak points. "The lecturers are paid no more than Rs. 50 per lesson by Akashvani. Of this perhaps 40 per cent goes in typing and transport. Not all the lecturers are of high quality. Owing to shortage of tapes the lectures are not preserved and sometimes even the scripts are not maintained, with the result that whole effort is repeated the following year at considerable cost. This would appear to be a huge waste of talent since it should be possible to engage lecturers at better fees and to build up a rich cassette library related to a standard curriculum for correspondence courses throughout the country and also to print and circulate the scripts, if necessary as supplementary reading mater."

Even without a separate channel stations could provide an hour's broadcast daily provided the different universities in a State coordinate their courses so that a single broadcast service can serve them all. But the range of most AIR stations is limited to about 80 km or so and the really needy students in isolated areas would not be able to benefit from the broadcasts.

Above all, the capacity of the university authorities to organise correspondence courses into which broadcasts are suitably integrated is doubtful. AIR's experience with schools and educational authorities in the States is not encouraging.

A National Institute of Correspondence Courses is now being set up to advise universities on such courses and also to finance them. This may help in designing courses to use radio for maximum effect. A special educational channel would be found inescapable if correspondence courses are to proliferate.

The quality of the radio support to be given is also of importance. The Delhi experiment is now wholly reassuring on this point. If the broadcasts are dull and merely repeat the contents of text-books they are not worth broadcasting. An audience survey in 1973 revealed that on the whole students' reactions are favourable.

As far as TV is concerned, its role, for many years, would be to provide adult education for teleclubs in urban and rural areas, including some measure of vocational training.

WORDWIDE TV STANDARDS

Q.1. I have some camcorder recordings I want to send to relatives in another country—I live in a country with NTSC, they live in a country with PAL/SECAM

This may well be easier than you think. The ability to replay NTSC VHS tapes is quite common amongst PAL VCRs—not all can do it, but there are a lot that can. At the very least, they should be able to buy a new VCR that can play NTSC tapes for the equivalent of around US $300; this is a lot cheaper than any of the conversion alternatives. Do be aware however that not all TVs will work with these VCRs, but most built in the last ten years should be able to.

Q.2. I have some camcorder recordings I want to send to relatives in another country—I live in a country with PAL/SECAM, they live in a country with NTSC

This is much harder. You are basically going to need to have the recordings standards converted from PAL/SECAM into NTSC as almost no NTSC VCRs are capable of playing PAL/SECAM tapes. This is a service that can be offered by some photographic shops and by most professional video dealers. Expect to be asked to confirm that there is no copyrighted material within the source tape you supply to them for conversion—most companies will not handle conversion of commercially available movies, videos, etc. Rates can be anything up to US $25 per hour.

The alternatives, particularly if there is likely to be a continuing flow of such tapes, are to either equip the recipient of your tapes to play PAL/SECAM or to purchase a standards converting VCR yourself and do your own conversions. Standards converting VCRs are available at around US $700 upwards from manufacturers such as Samsung and Panasonic, and from specialist dealers such as Lektropacks. To equip your recipient with playback equipment, the cheapest option is often to export a simple combined 14" TV/VCR unit after having checked that it will work on 110 volts AC as well as 220/240 volts. Alternatively a low cost PAL/SECAM VCR can be sent out, and either a video projector (most are multistandard, even in the US (but do check first)) or a professional video monitor sourced locally. In the USA, 14" professional video monitors start from around US $400 and are about the only TV like units available in the US that can handle a PAL playback signal. They are only available through specialist professional dealers.

Q.3. I've been looking for High Band (Hi-8/SVHS/DV) multi-standard equipment and I can't seem find any

There are now a couple of models of SVHS deck available which are multi-standard, from at least JVC and Philips. I know of no Hi-8 equipment that is multi-standard. For DV, there are three of the Sony Professional DVCAM decks that can playback and record at SP speed on DV and mini-DV tapes in both PAL and NTSC. These units are the DSR-11, DSR-25 and DSR-45. The DSR-11 starts at around US $2,000.

GLOBAL CABLE, RADIO, TELEVISION AND BROADCASTING SOURCES

- Antique Radio Classified ("The National Publication for Buyers and Sellers of Old Radios and Related Items").
- Arbitron (ratings).
- Airwaves Radio Journal.
- Americans for Radio Diversity.
- ASCAP (The American Society of Composers, Authors and Publishers. They license music for broadcast)
- Association for Local Television Stations.
- BROADCASTNET.
- BEA (Broadcast Education Association)
- BMI (Broadcast Music, Inc.).
- Broadcast FAQ (frequently asked questions) Broadcast FAQ at an Alternate location.
- Broadcast Net (products and services for the broadcast industry).
- Buchanan High School Jazz Band Clearinghouse for Jazz.
- Bry's Pirate Radio Page.
- CPB (Corporation for Public Broadcasting)
- Current Online (News about Public Broadcasting)
- Doug Lung's R.F. Page.
- The Gallup Organization (consulting, research, selection, training, polling).
- Opinion from the libertarian CATO Institute: With Friends Like These: Why Community Radio Does Not Need the Corporation for Public Broadcasting.
- Recording Technology History from Mcmix Production Services.
- International Listening Guide.
- Internet Guide to International Broadcasters from Thorsten Koch in Germany.
- InterNetwork Radio Listener Page.
- iRADIO (A Newsleter and Resource for the Radio and Broadcast Industry)
- ITN (television production and transmission)
- Jazz Clearinghouse.
- Journal of Radio Studies.
- KZSU at Stanford University has a broad selection of radio information.
- Macromedia (home of Shockwave Audio).
- Museum of Radio and Technology.
- Museum of Television and Radio.
- NAB (The National Association of Broadcasters)
- New Dimsenions Radio.

- NFCB (National Federation of Community Broadcasters)
- A.C. Nielsen (ratings).
- Non-Commercial Radio Stations.
- Pacifica—Related Stuff.
  - Free Pacifica.
  - Save Pacifica.
  - R. Paul Martin's Page (has a show on WBAI).
  - KPFA (Berkeley).
  - KPFA History.
  - Pacifica Radio.
  - WBAI (New York).
  - The Union at WBAI.
- LiveEvents from Pennwell Publishing.
- MIT List of Radio Stations on the Internet.
- National Public Broadcasting Archives at the University of Maryland.
- Pharis-Video.com (Chuck Pharis' Web page about video, history of cameras...).
- Play (makers of Trinity—computer based audio & video switching & effects).
- Professional Audio Resources.
- Quantel.
- Radio Havana Cuba.
- Radioinfo and their list of Other Radio Sites.
- Radiospace from Newsdirect (US News and World Report)
- RNTDA (Radio-Television News Directors Association)
- Radio Archive of the University of Memphis.
- R&R Radio & Records.
- Larry Dowell's Radiodaze.
- Radio List from MIT.
- RadioNet Talk Radio.
- Radio Networks.
  - ABC Radio National (Australian Broadcasting System)
  - ABC RadioNet (American Broadcasting System)
  - American Indian Radio on Satellite.
  - AudioNet (broadcasting on the Internet)
  - BBC (British Broadcasting Corporation)
  - CBC (Canadian Broadcasting Corporation)
  - CBS Radio (Columbia Broadcasting System)
  - Earthwatch Radio.
  - Learfield Communications (regional news & sports networks).
  - NHK (Japan Broadcasting Corporation)
  - NPR (National Public Radio)
  - Pacifica Radio.
  - PRI (Public Radio International)
  - Swiss Broadcasting Corporation.
  - Westwood One (NBC Radio, Mutual Broadcasting, CNN Radio)
  - WPR (Wisconsin Public Radio)

    - WRN (World Radio Network) (on the Internet)
- Radio Online.
- Radio Resistors League.
- Radio Stations.
    - WFMT—Chicago's Fine Arts Radio Station—(one of) the best classical radio stations in the US.
    - WOJB—Owned and operated by the Lac Courte Oreilles Ojibwe Tribe in Northwest Wisconsin.
    - WORT—Madison's Community Radio Station at 89.9 MHz.
    - The History of WORT by Dave Devereaux-Weber.
- RadioSpace (news and programming sponsored by corporations agencies and associations).
- RealAudio.
- Usenet: rec.radio.broadcasting.
- SBE: Society of Broadcast Engineers.
    - SBE Madison Chapter.
- Taylor Subscription Talk (fee-based Internet Radio Broadcasting).
- US Marconi Museum.
- Virtual Media Resources—A consulting firm serving ad agencies, retailers, media; site includes media research, demographics…
- VYVX (Video Transmission Over Fiber Optics)
- World Wide Web Virtual Library: Audio.
- Worldwide Television Standards (from School of EEITM, University of Surrey, UK).
- Worldwide Television Standards (from Telsat™ Communications Ltd).
- Web-Radio. FM—Radio Stations on the Net (note the interesting use of the top-level domain FM, which actually belongs to the Federated States of Micronesia).
- Wisconsin Broadcasters Association.
- The Wisconsin Idea—In Broadcasting.
- Xing Technology (digital audio and video)

GLOSSARY OF TECHNICAL TERMS

Compact Disc

Compact Disc is a stereo digital audio system based upon a 12 cm single sided disc made from a polycarbonate material with an internal reflective layer of aluminium or occasionally gold. The information is read by sensing the presence or absense of reflected light from a tightly focused Laser beam pointing at the pits and bumps in the reflective surface within the disc. The digital audio signal is sampled to 16 bits per channel at a rate of 44.1 KHz. The major developers were Philips electronics of Holland and Sony of Japan; it was largely based upon optical disc technology developed for Philip's VLP video disc system which later became LaserDisc, and the digital Pulse Code Modulation (PCM) work done by Sony.

CCIR

The CCIR is a standards body that originally defined the 625 line 25 frames per second TV standard used in many parts of the world. The CCIR standard defines only the monochrome picture component, and there are two major colour encoding techniques used with it, PAL and SECAM. The CCIR standard uses 1:2 interlace which means that each 625 line TV image is composed from 2 video fields, each consisting of 312 lines of picture information. The first video field contains just the odd numbered lines from the 625 line picture, the second field contains just the even ones.

EIA

The EIA (Electronic Industry Association) is the standards body that originally defined the 525 line 30 frame per second TV standard used in North America, Japan, and a few other parts of the world. The EIA standard, also defined under US standard RS-170A, defines only the monochrome picture component but is mainly used with the NTSC colour encoding standard, although a version which uses the PAL colour encoding standard does also exist. It is similar to the CCIR TV system in that it uses 1:2 interlace and has two fields per video frame.

LaserDisc

LaserDisc is a laser read optical disc system used for the reproduction of video and audio signals. The system reproduces a full bandwidth analogue video signal with around 7 MHz response, along with dual FM coded analogue audio signals. Subsequent revisions have seen the addition of two 44.1 KHz 16 bit digital audio channels in the NTSC version, and the replacement of the two analogue channels with digital ones in the PAL version. Originally developed by Philips as the Video Long Player (VLP) during the 1970s, it eventually reached the NTSC video market in 1978 as DiscoVision. By the time it reached the European market in 1981, it was appearing under the name LaserVision. LaserDisc was adopted as the current format name in 1990 when Pioneer offered the use of its trademark to allievate the confusion created by the move to digital soundtracks in the PAL markets.

NTSC

NTSC is a colour encoding system named after the US National Television Standards Committee which developed it. NTSC colour is usually used on top of the EIA TV standard. It has received a nickname of 'Never Twice the Same Colour' due to problems it has with colour errors caused by phase shifts in the transmitted signal. These problems do not occur in a cable TV or video environment.

PAL

PAL stands for Phase Alternate Lines. It is an enhanced version of the NTSC colour encoding method which reverses the phase of the colour signal every other line to ensure that any phase errors are immediately countered by an equal and oposite phase error. PAL is usually used in conjunction with the CCIR TV standard, but is used in a few countries (notably Brazil) in conjunction with the EIA TV standard.

RGB

Literally, Red Green Blue. RGB is used to describe the transfer of colour video signals as three separate picture signals, one for each of the primary colours of the TV picture tube. It is a raw, decoded form of the TV picture used internally within the TV set immediately prior to display. The SCART connector allows for future TV system changes by allowing the TV to display a pre-decoded RGB signal; originally intended for text display applications, it has also been used to allow for S-Video style input to non S-Video connector equiped TV sets.

SCART

The SCART is a 20-pin rectangular connector fitted to the vast majority of PAL market TV receivers. It provides composite video inputs and outputs, stereo audio in and out, and RGB input. Modified versions can also support S-Video style Y/C operation on some sets. It is also known as Euro-connector and PERI-tel.

SECAM

SECAM stands for Seqential Couleur Avec Memoire. It was developed in France as an alternative colour encoding system to PAL, and was adopted extensively throughout eastern Europe to ensure incompatibility with nearby western European PAL transmissions. It is always used in conjunction with the CCIR TV standard.

2

Broadcasting in India: Various Dimensions

INDIAN NEWS, RADIO AND BROADCAST MEDIA: AN INTRODUCTION

India News, India radio & broadcast media: The Indian national television (Doordarshan) and radio (All India Radio, or Akashwani) networks are state-owned and managed by the Ministry of Information and Broadcasting. Their news reporting customarily presents the government's point of view. For example, coverage of the 1989 election campaign blatantly favoured the government of Rajiv Gandhi, and autonomy of the electronic media became a political issue. V.P. Singh's National Front government sponsored the Prasar Bharati (Indian Broadcasting) Act, which Parliament considered in 1990, to provide greater autonomy to Doordarshan and All India Radio. The changes that resulted were limited. The bill provided for the establishment of an autonomous corporation to run Doordarshan and All India Radio. The corporation was to operate under a board of governors to be in charge of appointments and policy and a broadcasting council to respond to complaints. However, the legislation required that the corporation prepare and submit its budget within the framework of the central budget and stipulated that the personnel of the new broadcasting corporation be career civil servants to facilitate continued government control. In the early 1990s, increasing competition from television broadcasts transmitted via satellite appeared the most effective manner of limiting the progovernment bias of the government-controlled electronic media.

Since the 1980s, India has experienced a rapid proliferation of television broadcasting that has helped shape popular culture and the course of politics. Although the first television programme was broadcast in 1959, the expansion of television did not begin in earnest until the extremely popular telecast of the Ninth Asian Games, which were held in New Delhi in 1982. Realizing the popular appeal and consequent influence of television broadcasting, the government undertook an expansion that by 1990 was planned to provide television access to 90 per cent of the population. In 1993, about 169 million people were estimated to have watched Indian television each week, and, by 1994, it was reported that there were some 47 million households with televisions. There also is a growing selection of satellite transmission and cable services available.

Television programming was initially kept tightly under the control of the government, which embarked on a self-conscious effort to construct and propagate a cultural idea of the Indian nation. This goal is especially clear in the broadcasts of such megaseries as the Hindu epics *Ramayana* and *Mahabharata*. In addition to the effort at nation-building, the politicians of India's ruling party have not hesitated to use television to build political support. In fact, the political abuse of Indian television led to demands to increase the autonomy of Doordarshan; these demands ultimately resulted in support for the Prasar Bharati Act.

The 1990s have brought a radical transformation of television in India. Transnational satellite broadcasting made its debut in January 1991, when owners of satellite dishes—initially mostly at major hotels—began receiving Cable News Network (CNN) coverage of the Persian Gulf War. Three months later, Star TV began broadcasting via satellite. Its fare initially included serials such as "The Bold and the Beautiful" and MTV programmes. Satellite broadcasting spread rapidly through India's cities as local entrepreneurs erected dishes to receive signals and transmitted them through local cable systems. After its October 1992 launch, Zee TV offered stiff competition to Star TV. However, the future of Star TV was bolstered by billionaire Rupert Murdock, who acquired the network for US $525 million in July 1993. CNN International, part of the Turner Broadcasting System, was slated to start broadcasting entertainment programmes, including top Hollywood films, in 1995.

Competition from the satellite stations in India brought radical change to Doordarshan by cutting its audience and threatening its advertising revenues at a time when the government was pressuring it to pay for expenditures from internal revenues. In response, Doordarshan decided in 1993 to start five new channels in addition to its original National Channel. Programming was radically transformed, and controversial news shows, soap operas, and coverage of high-fashion events proliferated. Of the new Doordarshan channels, however, only the Metro Channel, which carries MTV music videos and other popular shows, has survived in the face of the new trend for talk programmes that engage in a potpourri of racy topics.

TV RADIO, RADIO AND TELEVISION: NATIONAL AND GLOBAL SCENARIO

Broadcasting

Governmental Broadcasting Agencies

- *DD-Doordarshan India*: India's national, regional, local, and cable networks, government controlled.
- Ministry of Information and Broadcasting.

News Agencies

- Antara.
- Reuters India.

Industry News

- Exchange4media.com.

Television

National Television Networks

- *India*: Television Broadcasting.

Television Broadcasting Services

- Siti Cable.

Television Related Web Sites

- *Indian Cable TV*: Online community for cable tv operators in India.
- *IndianTelevision.com*: An online information resource on the Indian television industry. Provides information, news and market research.
- *Satellite and Cable TV India.*

Radio

National Radio Networks

- *AIR (All India Radio) (Akashvani)*: India's main radio broadcasting network, government operated, with one national service, 100+ regional, and 70+ local stations.

Radio Broadcasting Parent Companies

- *Prasar Bharati (Broadcasting Corporation of India)*: Autonomous parent corporation of All India Radio and Doordarshan.

Radio Stations on the Web

- *India*: Local Radio/Television Stations on the Web.

Shortwave Broadcasters

- All India Radio External Service: AIR's shortwave external service in several languages.
- BBC—Hindi Service.
- BBC—Tamil Service.
- *DD India*: International Service of Doordarshan.

RADIO, TELEVISION AND CINEMA

In the United States of America, the beginning of radio was made as early as in 1909. A station in San Jose, California, started broadcasting announcements and phonograph music. But regular and systematic broadcasting began only in 1920. Thereafter, the expansion was fast in the USA and other countries. Before long there was a huge network of radio broadcasting almost in every country. In India, like in many other countries, amateurs were the first to start broadcasting. The Radio club of Mumbai, broadcast its first programme in June, 1923. In November 1923, the Kolkata Club went on the air. The Chennai Radio Club started broadcasting on 31 July, 1924 with a 40 watt transmitter. Later, it broadcast with a 200 watt transmitter, for 2½ hours very evening. But it closed down due to financial difficulties. The Chennai Corporation re-started the broadcast service in 1930.

Organised broadcasting in India was started by the Indian Broadcasting Company (IBC) in 1927. Mumbai and Kolkata stations were inaugurated in July and August, 1927. The first radio programme journal India Radio Times was started on July 15, 1927. Its name was later changed to The India Listener and again to Akashvani.

IBC was a financial failure in spite of a loan from the government. It went into liquidation and was closed down in March, 1930. Under pressure from the radio-set declares, programmers and the general public, the government took over the Mumbai and Kolkata stations in April, 1930. The Indian Broadcasting Service was formed. Those were the days of worldwide depression. The government too faced financial difficulties. Even otherwise, it was not very enthusiastic about broadcasting. So, it ordered the closure of the Indian Broadcasting Service on October 10, 1931. Representations and agitations compelled the government to reverse the orders of November 23, 1931. The Government doubled the duty on radio sets.

In 1932, the British Broadcasting Corporation (BBC) started an Empire Service. The number of receiving sets, which were all imported doubled in less than two years. This resulted in an increase in the Government's income from license fees. The increase in import duty on radio sets and components of the radio sets also enhanced the government's revenue. Broadcasting now become financially viable. It was decided to start a radio station in Delhi. It actually went on the air on January 1, 1936. The BBC loaned the services of Lionel Fielden who became the Controller of Broadcasting. (Today the radio chief is called Director General). He persuaded the government to realise the potential of broadcasting and allot more money to the service. In his autobiography. The Natural Bent, he writes about financial problem and red-tapism. He also gives an interesting account of how he could persuade the then Viceroy to adopt the name All India for the broadcasting service. The name was adopted from June 8, 1936.

Fielden got together a group of devoted young people. With the help of these and of Goyder, his Chief Engineer, he started short-wave service in 1938, to cover the entire country. Lucknow station went on air on April 2, 1938, and Chennai on June 16, 1938. In 1939, the Tiruchi station into being. The same year the External Service Division at Delhi started.

A.S. Bokhari, another dynamic administrator, took over from Fielden to become the first Indian Director General. He was the chief during all the war years and thereafter till the partition. A new Broadcasting House was built on Parliament Street, New Delhi. On June 3, 1947, Lord Mountbatten (the Viceroy), Jawaharlal Nehru and Mohd. Ali Jinnah made historic broadcasts on the partition of India. In the midnight on August 14-15, Nehru broadcast his famous speech "Tryst with Destiny". It is preserved in the AIR archives.

Following the country's partition, six radio stations came to the share of India (Mumbai, Kolkata, Delhi, Tiruchi, Lucknow and Chennai). When the princely states become a part of India, five more stations (Hyderabad, Aurangabad, Baroda, Mysore and Trivandrum) were taken over by AIR. During the First Five Year Plan (1951-56) much development of broadcasting took place. In 1952, the first National Orchestra was set up with Pundit Ravi Shankar as its conductor. Regional news bulletins in Hindi and Marathi were started in 1953 from Lucknow and Nagpur respectively. The first National programme of Talks too went on the air in 1953. In 1955 the first Radio Sangeet Sammelan was broadcast.

Dr. B.V. Keskar, the Minister for Information and Broadcasting (1953-61), did a lot for Indian classical music. He also brought eminent writers, poets, musicians and playwrights on contract as Producers. Finances for broadcasting for the Second Plan (1956-61) were creased four times against finances in the First Plan. In 1957, Vividh Bharati, an All India Radio Variety Programme Service, was started at Mumbai. It provided light entertainment with a generous dose of film music. Over the years, it has become a very popular service. The service was started to cataract the increasing popularity of Radio Ceylon's commercial service. It has succeeded very well in its aim.

1957 also saw the start of an Inter-station Programme Exchange unit at Delhi. An annual folk music festival, "Songs of National Builders", was started in 1958 but it was short-live. The scheme of Radio Rural forums was implemented in 1959, for two-way communication with rural listeners. In 1960, Jawaharlal Nehru's speech at the UN was directly relayed from New York. By 1961, radio covered 55 per cent of the population and 37 per cent of the area. The Third Five Year Plan (1962-66) saw much expansion of medium wave broadcasting. As many as 26 transmitters were added to Air stations for broadcasting Vividh Bharati Programmes. In addition, two independent transmitters were installed at Chandigarh and Kanpur. By 1966, 54 station covered 70 per cent of the population and 52 per cent area.

A committee on Broadcasting and Information Media was set up in 1964 under the Chairmanship of A.K. Chanda. It gave its report in 1966. It recommended separation of radio and television with the two independent corporations. It was not accepted by the government then. The separation ultimately came about 1976 and the TV setup was called Doordarshan. Another recommendation was for the starting of a commercial service was started from Vividh Bharati in 1967.

A 9-point code for broadcasters, introduced in 1969, prohibits the following: criticism of friendly countries; attack on religion or communities; anything obscene or defamatory; incitement to violence or anything against maintenance of law and order; aspersions against the integrity of the President, Governors and Judiciary; attack on a political party by name; anything amounting to contempt of court; hostile criticism of any state of the Centre; anything showing disrespect to the constitution or advocating change in the constitution by violent means, but advocating changes in a constitutional way should not be debarred.

In 1969, a new channel "Yuva Vani" was started at Delhi. The sponsored programmes on the commercial service were introduced in 1970 and the Sanskrit news bulletins were introduced in 1974. Earlier, in 1971, the highest AIR station was set up at Leh. In the same year, the first satellite link was established.

In 1977, the Janata government appointed a Working Group headed by B.G. Verghese, to suggest an autonomous setup for AIR and Doordarshan. The Group recommended in 1978 the creation of a National Broadcast Trust or Akash Bharati to look after both radio and TV. A bill to create the recommended Trust, was introduced in 1979. The recommendations of the Working Group, however were much diluted in the Bill. Eventually the bill lapsed when the Janata government went out of power.

The Janata government also introduced party election broadcasts for the first time in 1977, on the eve of assembly election in several states.

By 1980, radio covered about 90 per cent of the population and over 78 per cent of the area in the country. Expenditure on radio broadcasting in the First Plan (1951-56) was just over 2 crores. By the 7th Plan (1985-90) it increased to 700 crores. In 1991, we had 102 full-fledged radio stations which were production centres. The number of broadcasting centres, which included relay centre, was 205. The population covered was 97.5 per cent. Area covered was 91 per cent. The number of transmitters was over 300. This number included short wave and VHP (very high frequency) or FM (frequency modulation) transmitters. National AIR channel via satellite was started in May, 1988.

Vividh Bharati programmes are broadcast from 32 centres including two short wave transmitters at Mumbai and Chennai. They are relay Centre with low-power transmitters. They broadcast taped or prerecorded programmes. The tapes are sent to the various centre much in advances.

The External Services Division broadcasts programmes in 24 languages (17 foreign and 7 Indian) for a total of 75 hours daily. A special weekly programme is prepared and is broadcast through foreign radio stations in UK, USA and Canada. These programmes are meant for a large number of Indians living in these countries.

Several stations broadcast educational programmes for schools (schools broadcasts), twice or thrice a week. The duration generally is 30 minutes. Unfortunately one about 20 thousand schools out of 7 lac schools have their own radio sets. Only about 40 per cent schools actually listen to school broadcasts. They too do not have the listen period in their regular time-table.

Some stations help the Directorates of Correspondence Courses with University broadcasts. "Yuv Vani" provides the youth (15-30 years) with a channel to express themselves and for their talents to blossom.

Communication process is a two-way process. Unless there is feedback, the quality of effectiveness of broadcasts cannot be known. For this purpose AIR started an Audience Research Wing in 1946. But in 1952, after six years, the wing was closed. Some critics say that it was closed because the finding of the Research Wing were not very pleasant for the bosses. In mid-sixties the Audience Research cell was set up again. Unfortunately it does not have adequate staff. The staff is also not very well trained. Some other means of getting feedback are letters from the listeners, staff meetings (daily) of stations and newspaper media columns.

Radio now covers almost the entire population of India. It has a great ability to inform, educate and entertain the people. It can be made effective as an agent for development, especially in the rural areas. Rural areas do not have as many facilities for information, education and communication as the urban areas have. It remains a very relevant medium in India, like in other developing countries. This is so because about 40 per cent people in India are below the poverty line. Many are able to afford only a radio set or a transistors. TV sets are out of their reach. That is why, in a poor country like India, TV is called an elite medium which only the rich can afford.

Here, about half the populations is illiterate, Radio, being a medium of the spoken word uses conversational, simple and direct language. This can be easily understood even by illiterate folks. The effectiveness of radio can be gauged from the fact that its Rural Programme has been able to help the farmers in agricultural work. Varieties of grain or fertilizer popularized by the radio are commonly known as "radio seeds" or "radio Khad".

But to be fully effective, radio must come out with new categories of programmes and new styles of presentation. It should encourage the formulation of Radio Forums or

Clubs. Through these, radio should associate the people, the target audience with very aspect of programmes. In this way, there will be audience participation which surely leads to the success and effectiveness of radio. Radio stations should also go local. There should be at least one radio station in each district. The station should take care of the felt needs of the local communities. Small stations can involve the local communities in the total production process. That way the local people will have a sense of belonging to the radio and its broadcasts.

FM (frequency modulation) should be strengthened to provide reception without noise and disturbance. Feedback needs to be strengthened. Fair systematic research along can yield truthful findings. Feedback for external services broadcasts should be obtained in a more meaningful way. These services are important for our nationals sitting far away from home. Their thirst for home news and cultural needs to be adequately satisfied. External services are also important for projecting the Indian culture and situation correctly and effectively in foreign countries.

Experiments in TV broadcasting started in the USA in the twenties of this century. But the available equipment did not scan the picture effectively. In the next five years came certain inventions like the picture tube, electronics camera and TV sets. They made it possible for NBC (National Broadcasting Co.) in the thirties to set up a TV station in New York. BBC too started a TV station in London.

The Second World War halted the expansion of TV. But immediately after the war TV broadcasting started expanding in the USA and other Western countries. By 1948, there were 48 TV stations in 25 cities and two million TV sets in the USA. Within 10 years, 512 stations were sending programmes to 5 crore sets, Canada, Japan and European countries were also making brisk progress. Satellite revolutionised TV broadcasting from 1962. In that year appeared the first satellite called the Early Bird. In 1965 came Intelsat, a big international communication system. Another such system, Intersputnik was added in 1971. Today, more than 125 countries have their earth stations linked to satellites. Thirty-five satellite systems have brought the people and nations of the world much nearer. In the seventies, computer technology made possible a 2-way communication between the transmitting stations and receiving households. Then came audio visual cassettes and the video tape recorder and player. They were followed by closed-circuit TV, cable TV, pay-phone TV and now Direct Broadcasting System (DBS). In DBS broadcasting, you do not need even a receiving station. Programmes can be transmitted direct to the TV sets.

The latest broadcasting technology has not yet reached several Third World countries in Asia, Africa and Latin America. There is a gap between the rich and the poor countries in this respect. That is why UN observed 1983 as the World Communications Year, to narrow down this gap.

Television came to India rather late, on September 15, 1959. For years the debate went on whether a poor country like India could afford TV. It was feared that TV might alienate us from our cultural roots, that it might spread a consumerist culture. Consumerism would increase the hunger for comforts and luxuries. It might increase frustration and lead to social conflict between the rich and the poor. But manufactures, businessmen, educational institutions continued to make strong demands for TV in India. UNESCO offered a grant of twenty thousand dollars to buy community sets. The

USA also offered some equipments. Philips India offered a transmitter at a low price. Ultimately, the Government yielded. It set up a TV station at Delhi on an experimental basis. The declared aim was to discover what TV could achieve in community development and formal education.

The transmission could cover an area of 40 km in and around Delhi. Programmes were beamed twice a week. Each programme was of 20 minutes duration. The viewers were members of 180 tele-club. These club were provided free TV sets for community viewing by UNESCO. Programmes were beamed from an improvised studio at Delhi. UNESCO conducted a survey in 1961 and its conclusion was that TV did make "some impact". On pressure from public and TV set manufacturers, internment programmes were started on August 15, 1965.

The first rural programme "Krishi Darshan" was started from Delhi on the Republic Day, January 26, 1967. This programme was received by farmer-members of 180 village tele-club in Delhi, U.P. and Haryana.

Daily TV transmission was increased from one to one and half hours and to two hours on Sundays on August 15, 1968, On 3rd December 1971, the first English news bulletin was introduced. In 1972 (October) the inauguration of the Mumbai TV centre came about. In 1973, Srinagar and Amritsar Kendras started relaying programmes from Mumbai that year. Kolkata, Chennai and Lucknow TV centre were set up in 1975. So, we can see that the real expansion of TV in India came about in the seventies. For example, the number of TV sets, all of which were imported was 22,000 in 1975. In 1975, the number shot to over one lakh. What is even more important is that now the Indian sets are available in the market.

In 1975, the Satellite Instructional Television Experiment (SITE) was conducted. It made a deep impact on the country and the world. The one year SITE exercise proved to India itself that it was ready for the satellite television. In 1967, a UNESCO study was conducted in India on satellite TV's use in the country. The study concluded that India can and should use satellite for national development. Accordingly, our Department of Atomic energy entered into an agreement with the National Aeronautic and Space Administration (NASA) of USA for the loan of a satellite for one year. The satellite called ATS 6 was provided free of cost from August 1, 1975, to July 31, 1976, for SITE.

Educational programmes were broadcast direct from a satellite to the TV sets for the first time. Direct satellite transmission means that it does not pass through the relay station. The SITE programmes were revived by 2400 villages in six states—Andhra Pradesh, Bihar, Karnataka, Madhya Pradesh, Orissa and Rajasthan. An additional 25000 villages and towns in these states received these programmes through earth transmitters.

The daily 4 hours programmes were on education, agriculture, health and family planning. The satellite provided for two video channel and two audio channels, so that various programmes could be telecast only in two languages at one time. According to surveys conducted by the Indian Space Research Organisation (ISRO) and others, the experiment had a fair though not complete success. Commercial service on TV was started on January 1, 1976. Advertisers had to be allowed in because TV is a "Supreme Salesman". But a code for Advertisers was framed. Every advertisement had to be in accordance with the code. It could not be offensive. It could not hurt the normal, aesthetic and religious sentiments of the people. It could not be obscene and could not encourage violence or social conflict.

On April 6, Doordarshan was separated from All India Radio or Akashvani. Now Doordarshan, like AIR, got a directorate of its own, with its own Director General as the chief. But both AIR and Doordarshan continued to be under the Ministry of Information and Broadcasting. There had been great demand from the opposition parties to be given time on the electronic media. They strongly criticised the ruling party for using these powerful media of mass communication for their own political ends. It was for the first time in 1977 that the opposition shared time with the ruling party for election campaign. It was a step forward for the growth of a healthy democracy.

The Janata Party was the first non-Congress party to come into power at the centre in 1977. It appointed a Working Group to find out how best Doordarshan and AIR could be freed from the government control and made autonomous. Opposition parties has always been against the government control of the electronic media. So now that they were in power, they wanted to show their commitment to his conviction. They did so by appointing the Working Group. The Group is popularly called the Verghese Group since the Chairman of the 12-member group was B.G. Verghese.

The Group submitted its reports in March 1978. It recommended a single autonomous National Broadcast Trust (NBT). It suggest that such an independent, impartial and autonomous Trust could be made by an Act of Parliament, National Broadcast Trust or Akash Bharati would look after the working of the both AIR and Doordarshan. It did not recommend two separate corporations for radio and TV. Because of their different nature, they would be two unit no doubt, but at the apex level these two units would be integrated under the care of a single Trust.

There would be Licensing Board to issue License to franchise stations for institutions like the universities. These franchise stations could have their own transmitters for specific proposes. No commercial advertising would be allowed on the educational channel. Their license would be renewable every three years. The Group also recommended the setting up of a Complaints Boards, selected by the Chief Justice of India. This Board would deal with the complaints of unfair treatment of persons, subjects, events etc., by AIR or Doordarshan.

The Trust would be responsible to the Parliament through its budget, annual reports, auditor's reports, reports of the Complaints Board and the Licensing Board.

The Controller General of Broadcasting (CGB), the chief of radio and TV broadcasting would provide a link between the trustees and the entire broadcasting organisation.

The year 1980 saw the start of the National Programmes of Music and Dance. The basic aims of radio and TV are to provide information, education and entertainment. It is also their responsibility to preserve and promote our culture and heritage. It is to fulfill this aim that Doordarshan started these National Programmes. The idea of National Programmes was already existing at AIR. The National Programme for the whole of India began on TV on August 15, 1982. In 1982, Doordarshan took to colour transmission August 15. Then occurred two significant events in the development of Indian TV. In November 1982, the Asian Games were efficiently covered through colour transmission. The way the TV personnel handled this huge task was appreciated widely in India and abroad. In March 1983, Doordarshan covered the Non-aligned Meet (NAM) held in Delhi. This was another feather in the cap of Doordarshan.

The first domestic satellite was launched in 1982. This satellite, INSAT 1-A, was placed in orbit but it could not become operational. India's second satellite, INSAT 1-B, was launched in August 1983. This made TV programmes available to much larger segment of our population, it also improved the quality of broadcasts. The year 1984 was very important for our TV. The first sponsored serial, Humlong went on the air in July. Higher Education TV (HETV), produced by the University Grants Commission, was started. Doordarshan celebrated its silver jubilee and Delhi Kendra's second channel started.

Before our own Humlong, we imported serials, sitcoms (situation comedies), soap operas and similar other programmes. The name soap opera is given to sentimental, sob-and-sigh dramatic serials. Such serials first appeared on the radio in 1920s in America. They were sponsored by soap sellers and their sentimental stuff was mainly meant for women. Broadcasts like 'The Fox' 'Sorry', 'I Love Lucy', and 'Star Trek' were all imported. The imports came mainly from the USA and Germany. Our Indian soap operas took their inspiration from Mexico and achieved great success with its soap operas like 'Come With Me' and 'Come Along with Me'. The first was meant to encourage adult literacy. The later attempted to popularise family planning. The project of Humlong was inspired by these Mexican soap operas. The serial was on the air for 156 weeks. It became very popular with the viewers. Actors become TV personalities. This soap opera was sponsored by Food Specialities that launched Maggi noodles in the market. The sales of noodles increased enormously, especially in urban India. Educational TV (ETV) was started in 1961 from Delhi. The broadcasts, to start with were, for science teachers and students of Delhi Schools. Later, they covered larger areas and more subjects. ETV was then extended to other kendras like Mumbai, Kolkata, Chennai and Srinagar. The service was also made available to higher secondary schools.

We have already noted that the Verghese Group recommended franchise stations for the University to prepare and broadcast their own programmes. Such programmes for higher education were started by the University Grants Commission (UGC) in 1984, UGC set up an ISAT Cell at Jamia Millia Islamia, New Delhi, to co-ordinate programmes prepared at different university. The UGC transmission for higher education was called Countrywide Classroom.

Several Audio-Visual-Research Centres (ADRCs) and Educational Media Research Centres (EMRCs) were set up in different parts to produce programmes. The programmes are meant to supplement the old and old formal process of education. They also try to promote the interest of students in seeking knowledge outside the syllabi. The morning Transmission was introduced in 1987. The late night feature film project was also introduced that year. Besides a weekly news bulletin for the deaf and dumb was launched. In 1988, Kolkata and Chennai got a second channel, INSAT-IC was also launched. In 1989 came the Afternoon transmission. In 1990, INSAT-ID was launched. In 1993, Doordarshan started five Metro Channel, including music, sports, entertainment channels. They were started under pressure from the foreign channels like the Hong Kong based Star TV and the US based CNN. We must acknowledge three important things that happened in the 1980s eight is. One was the Joshi Report on TV. The second was the video boom and the third was the appearance of Cable TV.

The Joshi Committee on Software for TV set up under the Chairmanship of P.C. Joshi, gave its report in 1985. The report is called "An Indian Personality for Television". The report criticised Doordarshan for concentrating mostly on the North for its programme content. It also criticised TV's attitude to made broadcasts predominantly in Hindi. The Committee said that Doordarshan has not been able to achieve its aim of becoming a medium of public service and social education. The reason was that it did not have functional freedom.

The Joshi Committee recommended the setting up of a National Doordarshan Council. Its aim would be (1) to review and guide Doordarshan's performances, (2) to act as a guardian of functional and professional autonomy, (3) to act like Press Council to examine complaints of unfairness against the medium. The committee also recommended decentralisation of Doordarshan. Local stations at district level should be set up to involve the local communities in the process of programme production. Every village must have at least one community viewing set, and the Audience Research Unit should be strengthened. Viewers should be encouraged to give views freely so that the organisation becomes democratic in its programming.

The Committee did not ask for an autonomous corporation for Doordarshan. But it asked the organisation to find its roots in the rich Indian heritage and develop a strong Indian personality. Only then shall we be able to fight the foreign invasion of the Indian Skies.

When you go around any city or town, you find that many individuals possess Video Cassette Records (VCR) or Video Cassette Players (VCP). It appears like a situations of a video boom. Why only in cities and towns, even comparatively well off villages in many states like Punjab, Karnataka, Kerala, Maharashtra seem to have a situation of that kind. Even the northeastern states have not been left behind. The video seems to be even more active when you come across video parlours, video clubs, video restaurants and video buses. Video has become a profitable business proposition. It is shown to a fair number of people who are charged tickets. And this activity of video playing and watching activity continue till late in the night.

Video boom in India came in the early eighties, especially after the Asiad in 1982. No confirmed figures are available for the number of video players in India. Similarly, correct figures are not available for the number of people who watch video daily. Figures for players very from one to four million and for watchers from one to two million daily. Estimates and surveys have been made by advertisement agencies, cinema organisation and individuals. They have used different methods. So naturally the figures differ. For example, the number of video parlours ranges between 50,000 and two lakhs, according to different estimates.

Films are transferred to the tapes or cassettes illegally. Several "blue" (absence or not in good taste) film are also obtained in this manner. Cassettes are also obtained illegally from Dubai an Hong Kong. The government amended the Cinematograph Act. It was made illegal to screen or show films without a certificate from the Central Board of Film Certification. In spite of the amendment, the video business continued. It is rather difficult to catch hold of very video criminal.

One reason why people gather in video restaurants and parlours that cinema theatres are not enough even in towns and several cities. Villages have only mobile make-shift in cinema theatres. Video parlours cash in the hunger of the people for watching films. Another reason is that people do not have to stand for long in queues to buy tickets. It is quality convenient to a parlour and buy a ticket easily. Also the price of entry into the parlour is reasonable.

For the parlour owners too, things seem convenient. They do not have to contract a theatre for showing films. They can screen films at their shop or in a room of their house. And the cost of the video is fast recovered. They can also rent out the video players at fairly high rates at night till the early hours of the morning or till they themselves will require it for their group of customers.

The cassettes are not very costly for the businessmen. One cassette costs anywhere between 100 and 150 rupees, depending on its quality. All sorts of cassettes are today available from T-series and Gold to the National Film Development Corporation cassettes. The NFDDC cassettes have foreign film prints too. The video owner uses one cassette several times. Many a times a film is copied from a copy. That is why many video cassettes are poor in quality.

Video has affected the film producers and theatre owners. People, who can see a movie on video, have stopped going to the cinema theatre. Illegal screening of films on video without paying any royalty to the producer or distributor means a loss to the latter. That is why cinema producers, film makers, distributors and exhibitors have joined hands to demand laws and action against illegal video operators. Cable TV is another significant development. It has spread in a big way, especially during the 1990s, cable was there earlier too, in metro cities like Mumbai. Cable has been operating in Mumbai and other metres for almost ten years. But in the past two years cable TV has invaded much smaller cities.

Cable TV is operated by linking the viewers' TV sets through cables to a common antenna. It is operated trough a dish antenna and from a control room. The dish antenna, placed in a particular angle, can catch signal from broadcasting services like Doordarshan or foreign services like Star TV, CNN, BBC, MTV, Prime Sports, Pakistan TV etc. These broadcasts can be relayed through cable to individual customers of a cable TV operator. He also provides what is generally called 'domestic service or TV'. In this service, he shown films or other programmes like Pakistani tele-play, according to the demands of his customers. The Customers are charged installation fee to lay-cable. After this they are charged a monthly fee. This fee, generally various from Rs. 50 to 200 per month the fee or the rent would depend on the cost or providing the services, quality of the service, number of channels made available to customers and the customers capacity to pay. Cable TV is fast becoming popular. By paying say, one hundred rupees a month you can get five to eight or even more channels. On the top of it you also get one or two movies in the domestic service provided by the operator. And these movies the customers can get on demand. Video and cable TV are now increasingly being used by political parties, especially during elections. Industrialists, businessmen and professionals like doctors, architects and consultants have also started using these media. Several video news magazines like India Today's News Track, Stardust's Starbuzz and former Union Minister, Harmohan Dhawan's Third Eye give a round-up of even news.

Their cameras go when Doordarshan's cameras do not go. These magazines probe subjects which are nor taken up by Doordarshan. Their coverage and comments tend to be bolder and deeper. Sometimes, of course, they can indulge in what is called "yellow" journalism (cheap, Sentimental).

Our TV, like all TV services abroad, offers a wide variety of programmes. These programmes are generally divided into general audience and special audience broadcasts. In the first category are included programmes of general interest like news, current affairs, films, light music, film songs, Chitrahaar, tele-plays, serials, soap operas. In the second category are included broadcasts for particular section of the population. For example, youth programmes, women's broadcasts, children's films and other children's telecasts, quiz shows, interviews, discussion, documentaries on particular subjects, features, docu-features, sports educational TV (ETV), Countrywide classroom, classical music etc. We have also now Intent Service, which was introduced in Delhi in 1985. It now broadcasts information on airlines, transport, railway services, stock exchange, cultural engagements, tourist services, current affairs, sports. This information is made available from the Second Channel of Delhi Kendra. Our TV has made some contribution no doubt but there is much left to be desired. It has provided internment to the viewers. It has brought films in their drawing rooms. It has served the farmers by informing them of new methods and techniques of agriculture, horticulture, poultry and villages industry. It has also traded to spread awareness about our great epics, about women's condition and role, about political processes like elections. It has made people aware of what is happening beyond India. ETV (educational TV) and HETV (Higher Education) have also imparted education to schools, college and university students in an informal way.

But our TV has not been able to do several other important things. It has not been impartial and fearless in reporting political developments. Its current affair programmes could have been an important platform for political education for the general public. It also not been as efficient as required in reporting the national and international news—in respect of neither speed nor of analysis. It is too much dependent on news agencies. After all it is a medium of immediacy, of "here and now". TV in Indian not proved to be an effective medium for social change, and development. TV has a great potential to change a traditional society into a modern society. It has been contented to be a medium for internment. There has been a great predominance of film-based programmes on its screen. Its failure to promote and popularise our cultural heritage can be clearly seen. It has not been able to develop for itself what could be called a unique Indian personality. In short, it has not been able to change the traditional attitudes of people. Nor has it been able to change its own attitude of moving leisurely, behaving like a government organisation. It has been much too loyal to the government, forgetting its responsibility towards the people as a medium of mass communication.

THE AIR NETWORK

It is hardly possible to exaggerate the role which radio can play in our society. With seventy per cent of our people illiterate and with most of them living in rural areas, radio has been the most important and most effective medium for providing information and stimulating new attitudes wherever it has reached. Communication by word of mouth alone had been possible until radio was used to spread the word. The difficulties faced by All India Radio were formidable; a vast country, with a huge population speaking numerous languages, and a varied pattern of social and economic development, living in villages, some of which are isolated for months on account of geographical, climatic and other reasons. Besides, the chronic inadequacy of capital resources, of equipment and manpower posed the kind of challenge which could only be met by zeal and enthusiasm, both were available in plenty in AIR's pioneering days.

But forty-four years after the start of organised broadcasting, radio listening is still very restricted in spite of the extension of the radio network. Why? Because the zeal and enthusiasm have been weakened by the absence of a long-term communication policy on the basis of which the extension of the network could be properly planned. Such a policy, taking into account the priorities and the available resources, would have provided the guidelines for development appropriate to the country's needs. In the absence of such policy, the expansion has been hesitant, short-sighted and out of step with listeners' demands and requirements. Impromptu decisions, often taken in haste, have led to the present stagnation and lack of balance in the network.

The first plan of development, drawn up in 1945, was quite correctly based on a medium-wave service for the entire country. This involved putting up one or more fairly powerful transmitters in each linguistic and cultural area which had not, until then, been adequately served by AIR's medium-wave service. But because the cost of the installations was rather high, and because political considerations demanded that stations should be completed more or less simultaneously, to avoid charges of neglect of some areas and partiality towards others, the government decided to instal 'pilot' stations with transmitters of one kilowatt or even less power and make-shift studios with the minimum of staff and equipment. It was decided that once these were all installed they would gradually be replaced by more powerful transmitters and permanent studio and, offices.

In 1951, at the start of the First Five Year Plan, a primary service on medium-wave was available to about twenty per cent of the population. By the end of the Second Plan, by 1960, fifty-six per cent of the population and thirty-seven per cent of the country's area was covered by a medium-wave service. In the rest of the country, people had to make-do with a short-wave service from a few centres or with a poor grade medium-wave service from a distant transmitter.

The rate of growth has continued to be slow. Even in 1984 a reliable medium-wave service can reach only ninety per cent of the population and seventy-eight per cent of the area of India. This is in spite of 85 broadcasting centres, but there are only 25,000,000 radio sets of which only about 5,000,000 are in the countryside where 450,000,000 people live. So, in fact, radio serves not more than 20 per cent of the people and most of them live in the cities.

There are still considerable parts of the country which get no service at all or a very unreliable short-wave service. But as all radio sets do not have short-wave bands those who cannot afford these more expensive sets are, in fact, denied a service of any kind.

When to this limitation is added the restriction of language, the reach of AIR's services is still further reduced for there are large linguistic minorities in most States of the Indian Union who are not content to listen to programmes from their regional centre in the language of the majority. Their demand for a service, or at least a partial service in their own language, cannot be met without many more transmitters to provide alternative channels for the different languages.

It is not as though AIR has not heeded the demand for such services. At some stations where more than one channel is available it provides programmes in more than one language, as in the case of Delhi, Mumbai, Chennai and a few others, even if there is only a nominal service in some of the languages. Dialects, even those spoken by millions of people, can also be served only nominally. In Awadhi and Bhojpuri, to take two major dialects of Hindi, there are just a few programmes of music from Lucknow; in Kumaoni and Maithili there are programmes of less than there hours per week from Lucknow and Patna.

This incomplete coverage in terms of area, population and language has retarded the growth of listening in the country. After 1968 the annual rate of increase in licences has fallen steadily. We have only twenty-five million households with radios in the country.

The production figures of radio receivers tell the same story. Between 1960 and 1970 or so the demand for sets was greater than the supply but since 1970 the annual increase in the sales of radio sets, which was between forty per cent and fifty per cent in 1968 and 1969, was reduced to thirty per cent in 1970 and seven per cent in 1971. Even the cheaper single-band medium-wave receivers are not much in demand. This is disappointing because the green revolution had inspired hopes that there would be a spurt in the demand for sets from rural areas and manufactures had expanded their capacity to meet it. There are only about five million domestic receivers outside the towns and about ninety thousand community receivers for eight per cent of the population. Even according to the out of date UNESCO standard, there should be 110,00,000 receivers in India for a population of six hundred and fifty million. There is therefore a vast potential market for sets; why does it not materialise?

To set things right, the first and most urgent need is to decide the nature and extent of the service to be provided in the next ten years. As a poor country, beset with numerous problems crying out for solution, we cannot afford to give the people the variety and quality of broadcasting which more affluent countries can afford. With limited resources we can only hope to fulfil targets over a period of time according to well-considered priorities. While there can be no unanimity on such priorities and it would be impossible to satisfy all the different competing demands, it should be possible for a group of professional broadcasters and persons experienced in communication to advise and assist the Planning Commission and the Government to draw up a plan for development which would be professional in content. Several ideas aired in the past few years require to be examined on the basis of reliable data and research. The National Council for Mass Communication, which is discussed in a later chapter, would be an appropriate body to take up this assignment.

Whatever the policy prescribed, certain, ingredients are essential in any plan forr AIR's development. Firstly, it must be accompanied by plans for the production of a cheap radio set. It is quite clear that there will be no increase in listening in the towns unless a set is available for less than Rs. 120 which is the price of the cheapest reliable set today.

Such a set is also required for growth of listening in rural areas because it is now admitted that the scheme for community listening has outlived its utility and there is talk of subsidising the sale of low-cost receivers to increase and popularise domestic listening in the countryside. In the present economic conditions it would hardly be possible to subsidise millions of receivers. The solution lies in allowing the manufacture of a cheap set which would be within the means of even a family of landless labourers. How this can be done was discussed in the Report of the Committee on Broadcasting and Information Media.

Increase in listening also depends on an expansion of the services in regional languages from the regional transmitters of AIR. These must, in as short a time as possible, cover the entire population. This may require the installation of some more transmitters but, as far as possible, it should be achieved by strengthening the existing transmitters. A smaller number of powerful transmitters is easier and more economical to manage than a lager number of low-power ones. Besides, powerful transmitters would ensure that the signal is strong enough to provide satisfactory reception on low-priced sets.

The regional services of AIR can only use the language of the majority of people in the State. Any attempt to broadcast programmes for linguistic minorities would lead to fragmentation of the programme pattern which can satisfy no one. For some years we cannot afford to serve those who live in a State in which their mother-tongue is not the language of the majority.

The regional service should be a comprehensive service of entertainment and information catering for all the different groups of listeners who can be reached in the language of the State. Thus programmes for children, women, students and youth should find a place in each day's programme plan.

A policy plan for development must decide on whether the rural or the urban community must take precedence. Till now, the urban listener has received far more attention although in the cities people have access to other media, such as the press and the cinema. It seems only proper that the present urban bias in the planning of programmes should give place to more attention and resources being devoted to programmes for rural listeners. The limited time, one to two hours per day, for which such programmes are broadcast is only one of the problems. Still more unsatisfactory is the content of the programmes. Broadcasting can only help in development if radio and TV are accessible to the people. Instead of local broadcasts of immediate concern to the rural community in local languages and dialects, the programmes are broadcast from one centre for a whole State as large and variegated as Andhra Pradesh or Uttar Pradesh. Such programmes are often irrelevant for large areas of the State and cannot attract any listening. The only solution is a local radio service. Even in countries in which the gulf between the city and the village is not as wide as in India, local radio stations are being set up where they did not exist earlier. The regional service such as we have at present, or such as could be organised around one transmitter in a State, neglects the needs of our vast agricultural population. Though the music, news, talks and other items broadcast in the regional service would be available to all listeners, the agriculturist needs programmes of education and instruction which cannot be broadcast from one centre in a State in which climate, soil, crops, and other conditions vary from district to district. The local transmitter would also put out programmes of interest to rural women and youth and for part of the time could relay news and light entertainment from the Vividh Bharati or regional service. Unfortunately, the Planning Commission has provided for only 6 local stations in the 6th Plan whereas there should be at least 300.

The Vividh Bharati service of light entertainment should continue though it needs to be reorganised to constitute a proper service instead of being mainly based on film music. Listening in the countryside would increase if the Vividh Bharati service could be made available on medium wave. At present it is broadcast on short wave to cover a substantial area of the country, and on low-power medium-wave transmitters, located in thirty-one towns, each of which serves a limited area of about 16 km radius. It has been noticed that the demand for sets in a rural area increases as soon as it comes within the range of a medium-wave Vividh Bharati transmitter. The present thirty-one low-power medium-wave transmitters need to be replaced by a few of higher power, so located as to serve the entire country. The low-power transmitters can then be used to carry classical music, talks and discussions in English, serious radio features and other programmes for which there is a small but articulate audience mainly in the towns. These transmitters can also be used for the programmes for industrial workers and other groups living in cities. Some of these transmitters can also be moved to form art of the local radio service for agriculturists.

The lack of foreign exchange and resources in general has prevented the setting up of as many studios, transmitters, auxiliary centres and Vividh Bharati centres as are required to provide a good service. For every Five Year Plan the funds sanctioned for AIR have been much less than AIR asked for. This is partly because broadcasting is not given a high priority and, more so, because the decisions are not taken by professional broadcasters but the generalist civil servants of the government. It is also a measure of the failure of AIR to convince the Government of India of the importance of broadcasting in the process of development.

The Planning Commission has provided approximately 0.25 per cent of the total outlay for broadcasting. It has been argued that at least one per cent of the total should be made available for the development of broadcasting. But even the allocations are not spent to achieve the best possible results. This is because until recently the plans were made for each five-years period. This is far too short a span. Considering the time taken to implement many of the projects and to take into account the progressive changes in the needs of listeners, the time span of fifteen to twenty years would be more appropriate. Only long-term policies would make such planning possible.

AIR and the other authorities concerned have been much too easily satisfied with token achievements. For example, to provide a worthwhile service for each of the tribes on our north-east frontier may require many more studios and transmitters than we can afford. The choice, then, is to have no service at all, or a satisfactory service in English,

Hindi, and one or two of the major dialects. But this requires a firm decision on the part of the political leadership which is not available because whatever the decision it would be unpopular with some of the tribes; so, the compromise of broadcasting in five dialects from Gauhati, eight from Dibrugarh, ten from Imphal and thirteen from Kohima for ten minutes in each tribal dialect once or twice a week. The service does not and cannot attract any listening and scarce funds are thus wasted merely to sustain a claim that there is broadcasting to most of the tribes in the region.

Incorrect decisions of this kind were sometimes the result of haste to meet the deadlines laid down by the Planning Commission. AIR was sometimes given a week in which to revise its proposals to reduce the total outlay by half. This could not allow careful thought or the collection of relevant information or sufficient consultation between engineers, programme officers and such audience research personnel as AIR has. But incorrect decisions were also the result of a wrong approach to planning on the part of non-professional civil servants in AIR and in the Ministry of Information and Broadcasting. The Minister of the day would direct the thinking about the nature of the development plans for the next five years along the lines he desired. Every time with the change of Minister there was a change in policy and a re-allotment of priorities. Thus a scheme given top priority by one minister might be downgraded to such an extent that it might not be taken up for ten years after it was officially approved. Likewise, top priority would be given to a scheme which had not even been considered before a particular Minister expressed interest in it.

The awkward and irrational location of certain AIR transmitters is the result of such non-professional zeal to bestow favours on certain areas or cities. For example, when the coverage for Kerala was under examination it was suggested that transmitters in Trivandrum and Calicut would not serve the entire State adequately but political considerations demanded that Calicut must have a transmitter. When many listeners complained that they could not hear the programmes from either centre a third transmitter had to be installed hurriedly at Trichur.

Planning under such conditions was bound to be erratic. The development of technical resources such as the installation of a transmitter became a matter of patronage and so the programme output had to be fitted to the technical facilities available instead of first considering the requirements of listeners and then providing the technical facilities to meet their needs. Such non-professional interference in making and implementing plans for development was the outcome of the absence of a communication policy.

Certain wasteful procedures and practices can also be traced back to the absence of long-term policies and plans, such as the use of high-power short-wave transmitters for the broadcast of news from Delhi. Thus news in Oriya, for example, goes out on two high-power transmitters just for the Cuttack transmitter to relay it for listeners in Orissa. Correct planning would have given priority to the laying of permanent telephone lines between Delhi and all AIR centres so that all news bulletins and programmes like 'Spotlight' and 'Current Affairs', nation-wide broadcasts by the President or Prime Minister, and national programmes of music and talks could be fed on such lines to the stations concerned. This would also have ensured satisfactory reception all over the country. The present short-wave radio link makes listening difficult in several areas.

Or, to take another example, if a satisfactory medium-wave coverage for Vividh Bharati required the installation of a small number of high-power transmitters which had to be imported, because we did not make them, and if foreign exchange was not available, the decision was to set up many low-power (one kilowatt) transmitters which were available locally but which could serve only a small part of the country. Worse still, since AIR does not have a network of transmitters for the Vividh Bharati service, the thirty-one individual centres have to be fed with tape-recordings of the entire day's programmes of about $12^1/_2$ hours per day made several days in advance at the Vividh Bharati headquarters. The labour involved in making so many copies, in dispatching them by post, in collecting them at the other end, in returning the tapes to headquarters so that they may be used again, add up to an exorbitant expense which must by now have exceeded the cost, which seemed prohibitive in 1957, of installing a few high-power transmitters to make the service available all over the country. Economy can only be measured in the long-term but a department of government is bound by the rigidity of the annual budget.

The basic plan I am suggesting for the next few years would provide:

A comprehensive regional service of information and entertainment for the entire population of a State;

A Vividh Bharati service available to the entire population on medium wave;

A 'local' radio service on about two hundred-and-fifty low-power medium-wave transmitters for the rural areas in which programmes of education and information, planned and produced locally, would be supplemented by programmes of entertainment relayed from the regional or Vividh Bharati services.

A 'city' service on a few low-power medium-wave transmitters providing classical music, serious talks and discussions in English and other languages for educated listeners in some of the bigger cities. These transmitters could also be used for programmes for other urban groups such as the industrial workers.

The expense involved in providing a minimum service on these lines can be spread over some years. The regional service is already well provided and only a few pockets require additional or higher-power transmitters. The present twenty-five auxiliary centres can be used for the local radio service but at least two hundred more would be necessary to serve the entire agricultural population. Some Vividh Bharati transmitters can be shifted for the local service but, in any case, low-power transmitters made in India cost only Rs. 1,50,000. The expensive part of this package plan is the installation of high-power medium-wave to be imported and installed at a cost of about Rs. 40,00,000 each. Since the commercial service, which already earns Rs. 18 crores per annum, would, as an all-India service, earn much more, the expense could be met.

With this basic service every listener will have what he needs for entertainment and for instruction and information. In course of time alternative channels at stations can be considered provided that by then TV does not make radio expendable.

Once a plan of development to meet the essential needs of listeners is drawn up, it would be necessary for a committee or body of experts in electronics engineering to advise on the equipment to be used; the power of the medium-wave transmitters needed for the Vividh Bharati service and the nature of the transmitters best suited for local broadcasting, whether AM (amplitude modulation) or FM (frequency modulation), VHF (very high frequency) or UHF (ultra high frequency), taking into account the costs not only of the equipment but also of the different types of radio receivers which may be required to receive signals from the transmitters. The expected development of TV would also have to be kept in minds as certain transmitters can be used for TV signals as well as radio.

Ultimately there is no substitute for clear thinking to make a satisfactory plan of development. Expert committees may suggest what they think best but if the government, that is the Planning Commission, the Ministry of Information and Broadcasting and the Cabinet as a whole, which in theory is responsible for each plan, does not give the correct lead the plans will continue to be patchy, fulfilling short-term objectives at the expense of long-term goals. The aims and objectives of broadcasting should be the guiding factor and not the ways and means position at any given time. If resources are wanting the development can be spread over a longer period but it is wasteful, in the extreme, to adopt temporary palliatives which have to be scrapped entirely in due course. The government's hesitation in making long-term commitments has already cost us dear and retarded the growth of radio and TV. And when government does, occasionally, commit itself, the inadequate delegation of powers to the Director-General of All India Radio prevents the implementation of the schemes.

INDIAN RADIO: AN INTRODUCTORY OVERVIEW

Radio broadcasting is a Government of India monopoly under the Directorate General of All India Radio—established in 1936 and since 1957 also known as Akashvani—a government-owned, semicommercial operation of the Ministry of Information and Broadcasting. From only six stations at the time of independence, All India Radio's network had expanded by the mid-1990s to 146 AM stations plus a National Channel, the Integrated North-East Service (aimed at tribal groups in northeast India), and the External Service. There are five regional headquarters for All India Radio: the North Zone in New Delhi; the North-East Zone in Guwahati, Assam; the East Zone in Kolkata; the West Zone in Mumbai; and the South Zone in Chennai.

The government-owned network provides both national and local programmes in Hindi, English, and sixteen regional languages. Commercial Radio services in India, which were inaugurated in 1967, are provided by Vividh Bharati Service, headquartered in Mumbai. Vividh Bharati, which accepts advertisements, broadcasts from thirty-one AM and FM stations in the mid-1990s.

India has an extensive network of medium wave and shortwave stations. In 1994 there were eighty-five FM stations and seventy-three shortwave stations that covered the entire country. The broadcasting equipment is mostly Indian made and reaches special audiences, such as farmers needing agroclimatic, plant protection, and other agriculture-related information. The number of radio receivers increased almost fivefold between

1970 and 1994, from around 14 million to nearly 65 million. Most radios are also produced within India.

The foreign broadcast service is a function of the External Services Division of All India Radio. In 1994 seventy hours of news, features, and entertainment programmes were broadcast daily in twenty-five languages using thirty-two shortwave transmitters. The principal target audiences are listeners in neighbouring countries and the large overseas Indian community.

Terrestrial Radio, India

FM Radio

91.0 Radio City Bangalore—Bangalore (Karnataka) IN
91.9 Gyan Vani—Coimbatore (Tamil Nadu) IN
91.9 Radio Mirchi—Ahmedabad (Gujarat) IN
92.5 Go 92.5—Mumbai (Maharashtra) IN
93.9 Radio Mirchi—Pune (Maharashtra) IN
98.3 Radio Mirchi—Delhi (Delhi) IN
98.3 Radio Mirchi— Mumbai (Mumbai) (Maharashtra) IN
98.3 Radio Mirchi—Chennai (Chennai) (Tamil Nadu) IN
98.3 Radio Mirchi—Kolkata (Kolkata) (West Bengal) IN
98.4 Radio Mirchi—Indore (Madhya Pradesh) IN
102.6 AIR FM Rainbow—Delhi (Delhi) IN
105.6 Gyan Vani—Delhi (Delhi) IN.. *educational*
105.6 Gyan Vani—Mumbai (Mumbai) (Maharashtra) IN.. *educational*
105.6 Gyan Vani—Lucknow (Uttar Pradesh) IN.. *educational*
105.8 Suryan FM—Chennai (Chennai) (Tamil Nadu) IN
105.8 Suryan FM—Coimbatore (Tamil Nadu) IN
106.4 AIR FM Gold—Delhi (Delhi) IN
106.8 Suryan FM—Tirunelveli (Tamil Nadu) IN
107.4 Gyan Vani—Allahabad (Uttar Pradesh) IN.. *educational*
107.6 Gyan Vani—Bangalore (Karnataka) IN.. *educational*

AM Radio

666 100kW AIR Radio Delhi A—Delhi (Delhi) IN
819 200kW AIR Radio Delhi B—Delhi (Delhi) IN
1215 AIR National Channel I rep.—Delhi (Delhi) IN
1368 10kW AIR Radio Delhi C—Delhi (Delhi) IN
1566 1000kW AIR National Channel—Nagpur (Maharashtra) IN

Internet Radio, India

Internet Radio

Web Radio DD India
Web Radio Dishant.Com Radio
Web Radio EBC Radio

Web Radio	India Radio
Web Radio	IndiaStereo.. hindi/Pakistani music
Web Radio	Mehfil Remixes.. Bollywood remixes
Web Radio	Nazrana Radio
Web Radio	Radio of India
Web Radio	Radio Xiaos Hits.. Bollywood hits
Web Radio	Radio Xiaos Remixes.. Bollywood remixes
Web Radio	Rza Radio.. Hindi Bhangra remixes
Web Radio	TeluguFM. Hindi music
Web Radio	Thenisai—Ar Rahman.. CHR-Tamil movie hits Tamil
Web Radio	Thenisai—Ilaiyaraja.. CHR-Tamil movie hits Tamil
Web Radio	Thenisai—Oldies.. oldies Tamil
Web Radio	Thenisai—Tamil FM.. CHR-Tamil pop Tamil
Web Radio	Vishwabharti.. news/talk/info

Shortwave Radio, India

Shortwave Radio

(Swave.)	BBC Aajkal Service
(Swave.)	BBC Hindi Service
(Swave.)	BBC Tamil Service
(Swave.)	BBC Vivechna Service

TELEVISION

Television service is available throughout the country. Broadcasting is a central government monopoly under the Ministry of Information and Broadcasting, but the only network system, Doordarshan, also known as TV1, accepts advertisements for some programmes. Doordarshan, established in 1959 and a part of All India Radio until 1976, consists of one national network and seven regional networks. In 1992 there were sixty-three high-power television transmitters, 369 medium-power transmitters, seventy-six low-power transmitters, and twenty-three transposers. Regular satellite transmissions began in 1982 (the same year color transmission began).

By 1994 some 6 million people were receiving television broadcasts via satellite, and the number was expected to increase rapidly throughout the rest of the decade. Cable television was even more prolific, with an estimated 12 to 15 million subscribers in 1994. Besides Doordarshan, Zee TV—an independent station broadcasting from Mumbai since 1992—uses satellite transmissions. In fact, because Doordarshan is the only network that is permitted to broadcast television signals domestically, Zee TV and other entrepreneurs broadcast their Indian-made videotapes via foreign transmitters. Other networks joining the fray are Cable News Network (CNN—starting in 1990); Asia Television Network (1991); Hong Kong-based Star TV (1991); Jain TV, near Mumbai (1994); EL TV, a spinoff of Zee TV in Mumbai (1994); HTV, an affiliate of the *Hindustan Times* in New Delhi (1994); and Sun TV, a Tamil-language service in Chennai (1994). In a communications breakthrough in July 1995,

Doordarshan agreed, for a US $1.5 million annual fee and 50 per cent of advertising revenue when it exceeds US $1.5 million, to allow CNN to broadcast twenty-four hours a day via an Indian satellite.

Doordarshan offers national, regional, and local service. The number of television sets increased from around 500,000 in 1976 to 9 million in early 1987 and to around 47 million in 1994; increases are expected to continue at around 6 million sets per year. More than 75 per cent of television sets were black and white models in 1992, but the proportion of color sets is increasing annually. Most television sets are produced in India.

ALL INDIA RADIO: PROFILE, RESOURCES AND SERVICE OFFERED

- *AIR* Resources—a Technology Centre under AIR for marketing the vast resources of *Prasar Bharati* (The Broadcasting Corporation of India).
- *Prasar Bharati* one of the largest broadcast facilities setup in its two organisations—All India Radio (AIR) and Doordarshan (DD) catering to one billion people.
- *AIR Resources* provides total solution for Broadcasting, audio, video and telecommunication needs by pooling from *Prasar Bharati's* vast reservoir of resources in the form of Infrastructure, Human Resources and Technical Expertise in the field of broadcasting and related areas.
- *AIR Resources* is open to commercial opportunities and Revenue Earning ventures in the field of broadcasting covering planning, installation, operation and maintenance of broadcast facilities.

Achievements

- Signed an agreement on 2nd August 2001 with IGNOU to provide turn-key solutions for setting up 40 FM stations for Gyan Vani Channels in the country (consultancy, implementation, maintenance and operation).
- IGNOU's Gyan Vani Stations in Allahabad and Coimbatore became operational on 7th November 2001 and 14th January 2002.
- AIR time on Bangalore station of AIR was given on licence fee basis to IGNOU.
- Another 12 stations are in various stages of commissioning.
- Signed an agreement on 9th October 2001 with M/s. Music Broadcast Pvt. Ltd. for sharing Prasar Bharati Infrastructure at AIR, Lucknow.
- MBPL's City Radio became operational in December 2001.
- Harness inner strengths of the organisation to identify, develop and consolidate its resource base.
- Generate revenue by taking profitable venture in the field of broadcasting, computers and communications.
- To provide world class consultancy services and undertake turn key jobs in the specialised field of broadcast engineering and related areas.
- To facilitate growth of Indian Broadcasting sector by optimal utilization of Broadcasting facilities and resources.
- To become premier national and global provider of broadcast transmission infrastructure and related services.

- To initiate appropriate measures and develop business opportunities to undertake profitable projects and activities in broadcasting sector.
- To allow other broadcasters/telecom providers to use Prasar Bharati hardware/software infrastructure by charging licence fee/usage fee.
- To provide consultancy and services to various broadcasting organizations, private companies, telecom service providers, ISPs etc.
- To undertake system design, integration with existing infrastructure, drawing of specifications, costing, formulation of proposals and other related works for the clients.
- To undertake installation, operation and maintenance of broadcasting facilities.

Infrastructure: Studio set-ups, transmitters, Terrestrial & Satellite Linking system, lands & buildings.

Manpower: Core team to do basic work of consultancy, soliciting business, technical design. Draws the staff from *Prasar Bharati* to execute projects and activities.

Prasar Bharati Technical Infrastructure

Radio and TV—Broadcasting Facilities

All India Radio

Broadcast Centres	207
Transmitters	321
External Services Transmitting Centres	19
Studios	193
Studio to Transmitter Links	122
Satellite Uplinking Captive Earth Stations	20
Receive Radio/TV Networking Ferminals	350

Doordarshan

Programme Production Centre	49
Transmitters	1223
Satellite uplink stations Mobile uplink and News Gathering Vans	21

Management

- *AIR Resources'* set up and managed on the lines of profit centres in a corporate entity under AIR.
- At apex level CEO, *Prasar Bharati* assisted by an empowered committee consisting of Engineer-in-Chief (AIR), Financial Advisor, Head AIR Resources.
- Head AIR Resources, responsible for implementation of projects and fulfilling commitments to the clients.

Achievements

- Taken up the job of providing turn-key solution to Indira Gandhi National Open University (IGNOU) in setting up FM transmitter at 40 places in the country.

This included planning, system design, formulation of specifications and installation of the transmitters at 40 locations.

- The Prasar Bharati has signed an agreement with M/s. Music Broadcast Pvt. Ltd. for sharing Prasar Bharati's infrastructure viz. Land, building and tower at AIR, Lucknow on licence fee basis.
- AIR Resources is in consultation with Bureau of Police Research and Development, Ministry of Home Affairs to enhance the standards of Police performance by providing training support through AIR's Broadcast media.
- AIR Resources is in consultation with other private broadcasters to provide consultancy and use of Prasar Bharati infrastructure for setting up their FM transmitters in metro and other cities.

Use of Prasar Bharati hardware/software infrastructure by charging licence fee/ usage charges.

Consultancy services including feasibility studies, turn-key jobs and operations and maintenance in the specialised fields of:

- *Terrestrial Broadcasting for Radio and Television*: This includes the frequency planning, coverage planning, system design, installation and commissioning, operation and maintenance of terrestrial broadcast networks.
- *Satellite Broadcasting*: This includes planning and system design, execution of operation of fixed and mobile (SNG) uplink and down-link systems using both analogue and digital technologies.
- Studio systems including interior design, acoustics, state-of-the-art, studio and post-production equipment.
- Data Broadcasting and Internet broadcasting.
- Acoustics and audio video system for theatres, auditoriums and conference halls:
  - Selling of Air time on broadcast transmitters.
  - Availability of programmes from its large and rich archives.
  - Production services and software generation.
  - On site and institutional training in various disciplines of broadcasting.
- Software development and content packaging.

Key objectives in every project undertaken are:

- Flexible, state-of-the-art and cost effective solution to every customers unique requirement.
- Emphasis on total professional approach, on schedule completion of projects and customer satisfaction.
- High quality and cost-effective operation and maintenance support.
- Consultancy and advice in selection of appropriate equipment in customers best interest.

PRIVATE FM BROADCASTING

Report of the Radio Broadcast Policy Committee
Executive Summary of the Recommendations of FM Radio Committee
Public Notice Committee for FM—Phase II

No. 212/94/2003-B(D)/FM
Ministry of Information and Broadcasting
'A' Wing, Shastri Bhawan, New Delhi-110001

Dated: 24-07-2003

ORDER

The Government is pleased to constitute a "Committee" to make recommendations for Radio Broadcasting for Phase-II. The Committee will consist of the following:

S/Shri

1. Amit Mitra (Chair Person) — FICCI
2. Dilip Chennoy — CII
3. Kiran Karnik — NASCOM
4. Ameen Sayani — Radio Personality
5. P.K. Garg. Wireless Adviser — WPC
6. K.M. Paul, E-in-C — AIR
7. K.R.P. Verma, CMD — BECIL
8. Shardul Shroff — Amirchand Mangal Das
9. Ms. Noreen Naqvi, DDG (Prog) — AIR
10. Ms. Mahua Pal, Director — Ministry of I & B

The Committee may co-opt experts in the field as may be considered necessary from time to time, to obtain advice/inputs.

The Terms of Reference of the Committee will, inter-alia, include the following:

(*i*) Determining a transparent and effective bidding/auction process to be adopted for allotment of frequencies.

(*ii*) Assessment of a viable licencee fee structure for the various cities (one time entry fee, fixed licence fees, revenue sharing etc.) to be based on clearly defined parameters.

(*iii*) Suggestions regarding extent of foreign equity participation in private FM in order to make them economically more viable/sustainable while also keeping in mind regimes in other sectors and requirements of national security.

(*iv*) Study the desirability and legal implications of making modifications in licensing regime of Phase-I licencees and a different licensing regime be proposed for phase-II.

(*v*) Suggestions for improvement in content being broadcast and considering the inclusion of news.

(*vi*) Examining the possibility of having non-commercial, non-advertisement driven channels, to be operated/licenced by the same commercial broadcasters; terms and conditions thereof; consideration of whether type of content of these channels could include subjects related to the heritage and culture of India.

(*vii*) Recommendations for a code of conduct in programming matters and method of strict enforcement for violations thereof.

(*viii*) Assessment of whether co-location is necessary and desirable and if found otherwise, approach to be adopted in the metros, where co-located setups involving huge investments stand operationalised.

(*ix*) Determining the legal implications of the regime which may be proposed vis-à-vis the existing one.

(*x*) Formulating draft bidding documents and contract/licence.

(*xi*) Other matters as may be referred to the Committee from time to time.

The Members of the Committee would participate and contribute on a voluntary basis and no Travelling/Daily Allowance or other incidental expenses would be payable by the Government.

The Committee will submit its report by the 30th September, 2003.

(Mahua Pal)
Director (BP&L)

RECOMMENDATIONS OF FM RADIO COMMITTEE

Licensing Process

The Committee is of the view that the open auction bid process was not suitable for auctioning of the frequencies and it did not yield the desired results. Various legal challenges were raised in connection with the open auction bid process followed in case of Phase I of the liberalization of FM broadcasting. The Committee recommends that adoption of tender process for radio licenses is more suitable for the following reasons:

1. It is a standard and simple process followed by the Government in numerous sectors whereby sufficient experience has been garnered. The process is also judicially well-recognised.
2. It is an internationally well-accepted process[1].
3. It is the preferred process, specifically for broadcast licenses. It is one of the prescribed processes in case of auction of spectrum licenses in Australia and is also followed in the United Kingdom. The European Community recommendation on Independent Broadcast Regulator also envisages a tender process for broadcast licenses.

The License process shall consist of the following rounds:

(*a*) The first round should be the prequalification round and only bidders complying with the financial and technical eligibility criteria specified in the tender documents and as certified through a viability/sensitivity study by an Eligible Financial Institution/Bank should qualify for the next round. The security for participating in this stage should be the earnest money deposit as specified in the tender document. The security amount should be in line with Phase I tender document.

1. It is the standard process in international competitive bidding recognized and elaborated upon in a number of International Instruments like the WTO Agreement of Government Procurement, UNCITRAL Model Law on the Procurement of Goods (Under Article 18 tendering is the preferred mode of procurement), World Bank Guidelines on Procurement etc.

(*b*) After the pre-qualification stage, the financial bids of the qualified applicants should be opened at a notified time and place to determine the Entry Fees.

The bid license amount must be based on the business plan and the security for the same should be in the form of an irrevocable, unconditional and confirmed bank guarantee for the full amount of the quoted license fees. The bank guarantee shall be the security for the period from the date of application till the date of payment in full of the entry fees (i.e., the date of allocation of frequency).

In the tender process the entry fees could naturally be different for each bidder. The number of highest bidders that equal the number of frequencies available, would automatically win the frequencies at each center (e.g., if there are seven frequencies available at a center, the seven highest bidders would be allotted the frequencies).

Immediately upon award of the bid, 25 per cent of the entry fees should be payable and the frequency should be allocated only upon payment of the balance amount of the entry fees.

License Fees

The fixed annual license fee (that escalates annually at the rate of 15 per cent) determined by the auction procedure in Phase-I of FM Licenses for Private Broadcasters has proved to be unviable. In such a scenario, migration to a one-time entry fees plus revenue sharing model, as in the case of cellular licenses (Telecom) in India, is the most suitable option.

Entry fees: The Committee recommends that the entry fees should be determined by a competitive bid process that will reflect the true market value of the frequency.

Revenue Share: In light of the fact that:

- The Tenth Plan has also envisaged a revenue share mechanism in radio.
- The revenue sharing arrangement has been tried in a number of instances in India (like Telephones/Major ports etc.) and in the media sector as well (in case of DTH).
- Revenue understatement may be a cause of concern in the case of large public utilities. But radio is comparatively a small local industry with much smaller capital investment and revenue flows. The only form of revenue in the radio industry is in the nature of advertising and opportunities of revenue understatement are therefore much less in comparison to an infrastructure industry like electricity or oil.
- Detailed guidelines have been formulated in relation to related party transactions in Accounting Standard 18 of the Institute of Chartered Accountants of India.
- Internationally the revenue share model is used in spectrum allocation (as in Australia) and broadcast licenses.

The Committee recommends a revenue share of 4 per cent of gross revenue.[1] This revenue share shall be subject to review by a committee every five years and may be

1. The revenue share percentage suggested by industry players varies in the range of 2-3 per cent of gross revenue. On the other hand, the revenue share percentage suggested in Ernst & Young Report is in the range of 3-5 per cent.

increased/decreased, depending on the then prevailing market conditions. Such revision, covered under the agreement, will not be considered as a change in law.

Duration of License

The duration of the licenses in Phase-I of the award of FM broadcast licenses was fixed at ten years and no extensions were permissible on any grounds whatsoever. Internationally, the initial period of license is lower (e.g., in Canada the period is seven years,[1] in UK it is eight years). However, in most countries, renewal of the licenses is permitted, which taken together with the original license period, would mean that the term of the license extends more than 10 years (e.g., in Canada renewals of license for terms not exceeding seven years is permitted[2] while in UK licenses are renewable for one term not exceeding eight years, after the completion of the first eight years of license).

The Committee recommends that the license would be valid for a period of 10 years from the date of grant of operational license by WPC, as in the case of Phase-I. The Committee also recommends that the renewal of license be permitted, for a further period of five years, subject to satisfactory performance by the licensee and provided that no default has occurred during the license period. This assessment and recommendation for renewal of license will be made by the independent regulator to the Government, once the regulator is in place.

Multiple Licenses in a City

In Phase-I the licensees were not permitted to own multiple frequencies in the same city. The recent trend internationally is towards abolition of such restrictions, as evident in (say) the Canadian Commercial Radio Policy, 1998. Due to non-viability of market in the Indian context, the restriction on multiple licenses in the same center needs to be reviewed, without loosing sight of the potential for monopolies/oligopolies.

Therefore, the Committee recommends that:

(*a*) The number of frequencies that an entity, directly or indirectly, may hold in a particular center be restricted to 3 or 33 per cent of the total licenses available in the center, whichever is less.

(*b*) No entity shall hold more than one frequency (license) for news and current affairs in any one center.

(*c*) Further, such additional licenses should be permitted only if the total number of frequencies available in a center to establish a broadcast station (including frequencies in Phase-I) is equal to or more than six.

Total Number of Frequencies that an Entity May Hold: Containing Monopoly

The total number of frequencies that an entity may hold, directly or indirectly, nationally in each phase should not be more than 25 per cent of the total number of frequencies being tendered during the phase.[3] The bidder should at the time of submitting a bid

1. Section 9 (b) of the Broadcasting Act, 1991.
2. Section 9 (d) of the Broadcasting Act, 1991.
3. Similar restrictions obtain internationally e.g., in UK.

furnish a declaration to the effect that it shall not accept bids for more than 25 per cent of the frequencies offered in any phase.

An undertaking should be said to be in a dominant position, if it holds more than 25 per cent of the total operationalised licenses in the country and in the event of abuse of dominance by such dominant undertakings, the Government or the regulator, as the case may be, should have the power to order the sale of the licenses, through a tender process, to other undertakings that are not connected in any manner whatsoever, with any dominant undertaking. This condition of reserving the right of the Government or the regulator (as the case may be) to break up a monopoly, should be part of the tender documents so as to minimize the chances of litigation.

The content plan for each separate frequency at the same center being bid for, by the same bidder must be different to ensure wider availability of choices to the listeners.

The licensees would neither be permitted to network among the multiple channels in one center, nor would they be allowed to network with another licensee in the same center.

Each license should constitute a separate undertaking and licensees should maintain separate accounts for each frequency allocated to them. It should be the endeavour of each licensee to properly segment the expenditure with reference to each license in accordance with the applicable accounting standards or guidelines issued by Institute of Chartered Accountants of India.

Networking

Networking or chain broadcasts means simultaneous transmission of programmes by various broadcast stations (transmitters). Licensees in Phase I were not permitted to Network except on important occasions with the prior permission of the Government.

In light of the fact that networking can significantly reduce the Capital Expenditure and Operating Expenditure of a broadcast station (especially in small cities), we recommend that networking be permitted. We believe that the market mechanism will ensure differentiation of content reflecting listener's choice.

Please note that Networking be permitted only amongst the broadcast stations of the same entity and not across the licensees. Furthermore, networking should not be permitted in the same city.

News and Current Affairs

Phase-I licensees were not permitted to broadcast news and current affairs. The Committee recommends that the restriction on news and current affairs should be lifted and the committee strongly recommends that the AIR Code of Conduct and the applicable industry codes should be strictly followed. The violation of any aspects of these codes would result in the immediate revocation of the license.

Co-location

Co-location, in this particular context, is the term used to mean locating the transmitting setups of various broadcasters of a particular city in the same premises and sharing the common tower. This term gathers more significance in the situations of lesser frequency separation between the channels allotted for the same city. The basic idea behind co-location is that the Effective Radiated Power (ERP) of all the channels would be nearly the same and since they are located at the same site, they will be attenuated similarly with the distance thus maintaining the same protection between the channels.

In this context, following observations are made:

(*i*) Co-location in metro cities was mandatory in Phase-I. The objective was to increase the availability of frequencies by spacing them 400 kHz instead of 800 kHz.

(*ii*) Most of the representations received by the Committee have opposed co-location due to the following reasons:

(*a*) For co-location purpose, it is necessary for private broadcasters to form a consortium.

(*b*) It is very difficult to form a consortium of private broadcasters competing with each other.

(*c*) If a Private broadcaster backs out, his share of cost on common infrastructure would have to be borne by the remaining ones.

(*d*) Private broadcasters have to bear substantial cost on studio-transmitter link as in co-location case, the studio setup would mostly be at a different location.

(*e*) There are number of other operational difficulties.

In view of the above difficulties expressed by the private broadcasters, it is recommended that co-location may not be made mandatory in Phase-II.

Reserve Entry Fees

In Phase-I the Government divided the centers (cities where frequencies were offered to private bidders) in five categories for the purposes of license fee: A+ (reserved license fee Rs. 125 lacs), A (reserved license fee Rs. 100 lacs), B (reserved license fee Rs. 75 lacs), C (reserved license fee Rs. 50 lacs) and D (reserved license fee Rs. 20 lacs).[1]

In light of the following:

Internationally (e.g., in case of Spectrum Allocation in Australia) the Government is free to determine a reserve price in case of scarce resources like frequencies so that due to imperfections, the market does not grossly undervalue the frequencies. In Phase I also, some licenses were granted to the bidders at the reserve price, as there were no other applicants. Even internationally, instances wherein there is only one bidder for a particular frequency are quite common.

However, the purpose of such reserve price is again not meant for revenue maximization but only to prevent gross undervaluation. Reserve price must be objectively calculated on pre-published criteria in the light of alternate and probable uses of the frequency. It should necessarily reflect the lowest permissible price.

The Committee recommends that the historical reserve price of Phase I be followed. The Government can consider revising the reserve price in subsequent regimes.

1. Section 1 of the Tender Documents.

Foreign Investment

The Committee is in favour of a simplified foreign investment regime for radio.

We recommend that the following safeguards be introduced in the license agreement:

(*a*) FDI up to 26 per cent should be permitted in FM broadcasting (news as well as entertainment).

(*b*) While calculating the 26 per cent limit on FDI, the foreign holding component, if any, in the equity of the Indian shareholder companies of the licensee should be duly factored in on a pro rata basis to determine the total foreign holding in the licensee.[1] The equity held by the largest Indian shareholder group should be at least 51 per cent of the equity excluding equity held by public sector banks and public financial institutions.

(*c*) 75 per cent of the directors of the licensee, the Chief Executive Officer of the licensee and/or head of the channel and all key executives and editorial staff of the channel must be resident Indians appointed by the licensee without any reference on or from any other company for all news channels. For all entertainment channels exception to the above could be made for 'People of Indian Origin' cardholders/NRIs for the position of key executives and editorial staff. This facility will not be available to channels providing any kind of news. It should be obligatory on the part of the licensee to inform the Ministry in writing before effecting any alteration in the foreign shareholding pattern or in the shareholding of the largest Indian shareholder and/or in the CEO/Board of Directors. Further, the licensee should be liable to intimate the Ministry the details of any foreigners/NRIs employed/engaged by it for a period exceeding 60 days. Further, there should be a bar on direct/indirect outsourcing of content to foreign parties.

(*d*) The licensee should be required to make disclosures of any shareholders agreements, loan agreements and such other agreements that are finalized or proposed to be entered into. Subsequent changes to the said agreements should be permitted only with the prior approval of the Ministry. Further, the licensee should not be permitted to raise loans from foreign entities for all news channels beyond the proportion of foreign equity allowed. (In other words, for Licensees putting out news, up to 26 per cent of their total equity can be taken as loans from foreign sources and no more).

(*e*) In the light of the aforementioned changes to the FDI policy, in respect of FM broadcasting, the existing licensees should be required to effect the necessary amendments to their Memorandum of Association and Articles of Association and relevant agreements no later than two months from the date of migration of their licenses from Phase I to Phase II.

Increase in Number of Frequencies for Private FM Broadcasts

Committee is of the view that the released frequencies for Phase II of liberalization of FM transmission will include unutilized spectrum in Phase I after migration.

1. See revised eligibility criteria Clause (b) and (d).

The spectrum being a scarce resource has to be used rationally, efficiently and optimally by all.

The committee strongly recommends that as the market develops and gathers the required momentum, Government should release additional frequencies in subsequent phases of liberalization, so as to boost further growth of the market.

The Committee is of the opinion that some other available frequencies may be more effectively utilized for the purposes of educational broadcasts by IGNOU. It has been brought to the notice of the Committee that during the last few years AIR is in the process of migrating high quality music programmes like Vividh Bharati from MW to FM. The possibility of availing these MW transmitters from AIR for the purposes of educational broadcasts by IGNOU requires serious consideration. This would address the issue of costs as IGNOU will not have to incur heavy expenditure on building broadcast infrastructure because AIR facilities could be used by IGNOU at a reasonable cost. This arrangement would lead to the best possible use of spectrum and release of additional frequencies.

Non-Commercial Channels

The PBS (Public Broadcast Service in the USA) model and the BBC model for non-commercial channels are widely followed abroad, where the programmes are funded by various organisations.

The Committee proposes a similar model wherein, out of the 4 per cent revenue share that the Government would receive from the FM broadcasters, 1 per cent point of the revenue share should be set apart as a separate fund dedicated for the purpose of developing the non-commercial channels (related to a wide range of areas such as culture and heritage of India, public health etc.). The resources which will accumulate in this fund will be sought by private broadcasters to develop non-commercial channels and programmes, in accordance with the directions of a Committee of eminent personalities of the nation formed by the Government. The funds should be disbursed through transparent rules and regulations framed for this purpose by the esteemed Committee. There would be a yearly audit of the broadcaster and the audit report would be presented to the Committee.

Such non-commercial channels will be initially required in all A+, A and B category towns, followed by its expansion in other cities in the future.

Considering the fact that the number of commercial channels are already limited, it is suggested that additional frequencies be released at the earliest for the above non-commercial channels.

Niche Channels Through Fiscal Incentives

The Committee is of the view that it is possible to help the market process in the direction of development of niche channels. In this respect the Committee recommends the following:

In every city, certain frequencies should be reserved for niche channels to be tendered separately with a low reserve fee and low revenue share percentage. Detailed terms and conditions may be prescribed to ensure that such channels are exclusively developed for niche programming and no partial niche programming be allowed.

The Committee feels that such niche channels will be initially required in A+, A and B category towns, followed by its expansion in other cities in future. The Committee also strongly urges the Government to consider releasing additional frequencies to encourage such niche channels.

Foreign Satellite Broadcast

Presently, Government of India has a policy on uplinking of TV channels. The following two major benefits have accrued from this policy:

(*a*) Outflow of foreign exchange has been curtailed since the uplinking is done from the Indian soil instead of foreign countries.

(*b*) Government is able to enforce a code of conduct for the TV channels.

In the absence of similar policy on the uplinking of Radio channels in the country, valuable foreign exchange outflow is taking place and the Government is unable to enforce any code of conduct on Satellite radio channels.

In view of the above, it is recommended that Government should come out with a policy on uplinking of satellite radio channels and downlinking process, so that the forex outflow could be curtailed and a code of conduct could be enforced.

Migration

For the purposes of migration to the new regime, 24th July 2003 (the day of appointment of this Radio Broadcast Policy Committee) shall be taken as the "Cut-off Date" from which the rights and obligations under the new regime will be applicable to the players. Rights accrued and Liabilities incurred till the Cut-off Date shall be governed by the old regime.

The Committee is of the opinion that operationalisation of license or at least a serious attempt at operationalisation should be the criterion for distinguishing between serious licensees and not so serious ones. Therefore, the following should be entitled to migrate to the new regime:

(*a*) Successful bidders that have operationalised the license and have paid the license fees till date. From the cut off date all fees paid shall be adjusted (but not refunded) against the new system of revenue share.

(*b*) Successful bidders that operationalised the license but later due to non-viability of business defaulted in payment of license fees.

(*i*) They will have to pay the original license fees due till the Cut off Date.

(*ii*) Defaults in the original license fee that was to be due, after the cut off date, are to be ignored.

(*iii*) Payment will be treated as one time entry fee.

(*c*) In case of delay in operationalisation due to co-location, those who are operating under "deemed operationalisation", should be granted a revised deadline, either to co-locate by say December 31, 2003 or set up independent facilities by say March 31, 2004. On completing either of the above, they shall be entitled to migrate to the Phase II licensing system. Till the point of operationalisation, they will be governed by the old regime.

The Committee strongly recommends that there should not be any blacklisting of bidders for new licenses on the basis of their default in Phase-I, as the Phase-I was characterized by acute market and regulatory imperfections that rendered the market unviable. Also, the Committee appeals to all bidders who have gone to court to withdraw their litigations and take advantage of the new Phase-II regime.

Import Duty

In this sector, almost all the broadcasting equipments are imported and none of them are manufactured domestically. To make the economics more viable, the Committee suggests that the import duty on the broadcast equipment be brought in line with that of the Telecom sector.

Code of Conduct

The Committee suggests that broadcast by private broadcasters must not, inter alia contain the following (as per the AIR code):

- Criticism of friendly countries.
- Attack on religion or communities.
- Anything obscene or defamatory.
- Incitement to violence or anything against maintenance of law and order.
- Anything amounting to contempt of court.
- Aspersions against the integrity of the President, Governors and Judiciary.
- Attack on political party by name.
- Hostile criticism of any State or the Centre.
- Anything showing disrespect to the Constitution or advocating change in the Constitution by violent means, but advocating changes in the constitutional way should not be debarred.

AIR code and the advertising code to be looked at as per current scenario and appropriate changes can be made, if required.

Shift of IGNOU (Educational Broadcast) to Medium Wave and Availing of MW Transmitters from AIR

In Phase-I of liberalization of FM broadcasting one frequency in each of the forty cities was reserved for educat ional broadcast by IGNOU. However, so far IGNOU has been able to operationalise only 10 FM stations. It appears that due to limits on availability of funds IGNOU may not be in a position to operationalise all these frequencies. On account of paucity of spectrum it is not advisable to allocate FM frequencies for educational broadcasts.

The Committee is of the opinion that some other available frequencies (like medium wave) may be more effectively utilized for the purposes of educational broadcasts by IGNOU. It has been brought to the notice of the Committee that during the last few years AIR is in the process of migrating high quality music programmes like Vividh Bharati from MW to FM. The possibility of availing these MW transmitters from AIR for the purposes of educational broadcasts by IGNOU requires serious consideration. This would address the issue of costs as IGNOU will not have to incur heavy expenditure on building broadcast infrastructure because AIR facilities could be used by IGNOU at a reasonable cost. This arrangement would lead to the best possible use of spectrum.

Broadcast Regulator

The radio industry in India is in a nascent stage of growth. However, as the market develops a number of legal and social issues (like content regulation, networking regulation etc.) as well as technological issues [like digital radio broadcasting (terrestrial/satellite) subscription radio channels etc.] are likely to arise in relation to radio. The market competitive forces may not always work in harmony and sometimes may require reconciliation of competing interests. Therefore, as the industry develops it will require maintenance of an appropriate regulatory environment through an autonomous regulator.

The Committee in this respect shares the views and the concerns of the Hon'ble Supreme Court as reflected in the case of *Secretary, Ministry of Information and Broadcasting vs. Cricket Association of Bengal,*[1] wherein it was observed that the Central Government should establish an independent autonomous public authority representative of all sections and interests in the society to control and regulate the use of airwaves.

The Committee therefore, recommends the constitution of an independent broadcast regulator.

The Committee would like to clarify that the Broadcast Regulator should provide and maintain appropriate regulatory environment to foster market led growth rather than seek to supplant and substitute market forces through regulation. The main objective of the Broadcast Regulator should be to seek proper enforcement of rules and regulations and its actions should primarily be complaint driven.

We suggest to the Ministry of Information & Broadcasting that pending the creation of a Regulator (which is likely to take time, requiring Parliamentary approval), a non-statutory Committee be set up which has Terms of Reference similar to what the Regulator would have. (We understand that the formal creation of SEBI was preceded by such a Committee).

Penalty for Non-Operationalisation of Awarded Licenses

The Committee strongly recommends that after being awarded the license, it is mandatory for Licensee to operationalise the license within a maximum period of one year. If the licensee does not operationalise the license within one year from the date of the award, the Government, as a condition of the license, will forfeit the license and re-tender it in public interest.

COMMUNITY RADIO BROADCASTING IN INDIA

With the advent of community broadcasting, a whole new exciting world awaits listeners in far-flung areas where radio listening revolves around community centres. The proposed community radio serves to bring small groups together through their own

1. (1995) 2 SCC 161.

participation to reflect their day-to-day concerns. The community will participate by creating contents of the programmes for its own people. This narrow broadcasting does not require big transmitters. Community radio of the future will strive to bring people together through interaction. Like teleconferencing, the listeners will be able to talk to each other through the radio network using small wireless sets. This will help in business activities of the particular district or a village where the artisan will know his prospective buyer for his wares.

At present, however, programmes will be created for the listeners in the community and reflect what is relevant for their needs and aspirations. The community in these areas is well-knit. There is always a collective response to all radio programmes as the listeners generally assemble at one place where they listen to radio programmes, discuss and react. This turns into public service broadcast because it is here that the aspirations of the people can be fulfilled. To achieve this, the programmes have to be drawn up with a foresight keeping in mind the priorities of varied areas so that people can easily identify themselves with the programmes.

Out of the existing network of All India Radio, the Frequency Modulation, commonly known as the FM, technique of the radio wave has a distinct advantage. The Medium Wave and Short Wave suffer from the disadvantage of deteriorating sound quality with the increase in distance. The FM provides stereo quality and is ideal for short-range broadcasts. In the far-flung rural areas where the availability of power supply is unreliable, the FM is ideally suited for community broadcast for dissemination of information, education and entertainment. The Working Group on the 10th Plan has recommended future expansion of radio, primarily in the FM mode. To supplement the broadcasting by All India Radio, the Government, in July 1999, approved private participation in FM broadcasting.

After offering licences to private FM broadcasting in 40 cities through 110 channels for commercial broadcasting, the Government has decided to offer private licences to the established educational institutions and organizations having their own campus and residential schools. At present, AIR has 133 FM transmitters covering more than 21 per cent of area and about 31 per cent population of the country. Private licences for FM broadcasting have been offered in 40 cities for 110 channels for setting up 10 KW radio transmitters, except in four metro cities where the capacity could be between 10 to 20 KW. These private channels are already operating in Delhi, Mumbai, Kolkata, Chennai, Bangalore, Indore, Ahmedabad, Pune and Lucknow. Next in the line are Patna, Bhuvaneswar, Cuttack, Jabalpur, Coimbatore, Tirunelveli and Vishakhapatnam. The number of channels will provide plurality of choice to the listeners leading to improvement in the quality of programmes.

To start with, programmes on the community radio service will focus on issues relating to education, health, environment, agriculture and rural and community development. The Government expects these programmes to be popular if done innovatively done to sustain the listeners' interest.

This service is expected to provide a platform for students and teachers to give expression to their creative talent in producing programmes and in socio-cultural cohesion of the masses at the local level. The licencees will not be allowed to broadcast any news, current affairs programmes, election and political broadcasts. They will also not be allowed to air any advertisement of sponsored programmes.

The Government is aware of the need to safeguard the radio stations from being misused for undesirable propaganda against national interest and safety and security of the country. Therefore, in the first phase, the Government has given licenses to only the selected and established educational institutions in the country for community broadcasts. For the sake of credibility, the licensees will ensure that nothing is included in the programme that goes against good taste and decency. The code of conduct rules out anything obscene, defamatory and innuendos. The licencees will also ensure that there is nothing that amounts to contempt of court or by casting aspersions on the integrity of the President or the judiciary.

The programme code will almost be the same as for All India Radio. It would strive to promote national integration, religious harmony, scientific temper and Indian culture.

The applicant will be permitted only one licence valid for three years and the licencee will provide service on free-to-air basis. No channel will be permitted for commercial purposes. The Government will have the right to inspect broadcast facilities and reserve the right to take over the entire services or network or revoke or suspend the licence in the interest of national security.

The licensee will ensure that all foreign personnel likely to be appointed as employees or consultants obtain security clearance from the Government. The licensee will be expected to furnish a bank guarantee to ensure timely performance of the licensee agreement and failure to start the services within the stipulated period can result in cancellation of licence and forfeiture of the bank guarantee.

The people are likely to immensely benefit from community radio because of its inter-active nature and low costs of broadcasting.

Radio as a communication medium plays an important role in the nation's socio-cultural, political and economic development. It has the unique advantage of being receivable through low cost, battery operated, and mobile receiving sets, affordable for almost everyone, even in the rural areas. With appropriate strategies, radio can expand its reach to sparsely populated areas and remote corners of the country.

Concept

There are three options for expansion of radio network viz: (*i*) the commercial broadcast model, (*ii*) public service broadcast route and (*iii*) the community radio. While each of these modes helps in enhancing coverage, there could be clashes of interest particularly in the share of target audience and content. A commercial radio station is market driven and therefore its objective is to gain as much market share as possible, expand business and take competitive initiatives in the public service domain. Public service broadcasting, on the other hand, concentrates on content for education, information and entertainment with the broad objective to address the concerns of a large and varied listener group and it generally accords lower priority to commercial considerations. Community radio, as distinct from public service broadcasting, serves to bring small communities together, focuses on the common man's day-to-day concerns and helps in realizing local aspirations. In this sense, it aims to contribute to the lives of the local community by creation of content by the people and for the people of that community.

Policy on Community Radio Broadcasting

In December 2002, the Government announced a policy for the Grant of Community Radio Licenses to educational institutions and organizations to be identified/selected, in accordance with the prescribed eligibility conditions and on the terms and conditions given in the Guidelines for the grant of licenses for Community Radio Stations.

Under the terms of this policy, Community Broadcasting Licenses can be granted to well-established educational institutions/organizations, recognized by the Central Government or the State Government. These will include the Universities and institutes of technology/management and residential schools.

Community Radio is expected to focus on issues relating to education, health, environment, agriculture, rural and community development. The contents are to be confined to social, cultural and local issues and the format, subject, presentation and language must reflect and exude the local flavour and fragrance.

Period of Licence

License will be granted for 3 years.

Fees

Since community radio broadcasting has to operate on non-commercial basis, no license fee is being charged. The licensee will be required to furnish a Bank Guarantee for a sum of Rs. 50,000 only, to ensure performance of the license agreement. The licensee will, however, be required to pay spectrum usage fee, as determined by the Wireless Advisor in WPC Wing of Ministry of Communications.

Benefits

(*i*) Enhancing participation of the people in the development process
(*ii*) Capacity building in rural areas, through education.
(*iii*) Providing opportunities to the people to upgrade their skills and enhance their creative talents.
(*iv*) Preserving and promoting the traditional wisdom, knowledge and skills, thereby helping to promote and project the local language, arts, craft, culture and traditions.
(*v*) Bring within easy reach of the rural population, topical information in areas of agriculture, social welfare, education, health and environment.
(*vi*) Help in creating rural networks for the rural cottage and village industry.

Selection Procedure

Through open advertisement in a transparent manner from eligible educational institutions/organizations. The intending educational institutions need to apply for licence, in the prescribed application form, in accordance with the guidelines for grant of licenses for Community Radio Stations.

Power and Cost of Community Radio

Maximum 50 watt transmitter power permitted with an antenna height of 30 meters above ground covering an area of about 5-10 KM radius. One-time capital investment is estimated at around Rs. 8-10 lakhs.

Execution of Project

Educational institutions can set up the Radio Station on their own or with the help of All India Radio or BECIL (Broadcast Engineering Consultants India Ltd.), a wholly owned PSU of this Ministry.

Inter-Ministerial Clearances Prior to Grant of Letter of Intent/License

- Ministry of Home Affairs.
- Wireless Planning and Coordination (WPC), Ministry of Communications & Information Technology.
- Ministry of Human Resource Development.

Safeguards

1. Adherence to programme code of All India Radio. News and Current Affairs, election and political broadcasts are prohibited.
2. Government can revoke/terminate/suspend license, in case of violation of the terms and conditions of license.
3. Bank Guarantee of Rs. 50,000 to ensure timely performance.
4. To prevent overlap with private FM, the community radio stations will be non-commercial ventures—advertisements or sponsored programmes prohibited.
5. Preservation of records for 6 months, by the licensee.

Frequency

Licence will be issued in the shared frequency band from 87.5 to 100 MHz. However, in the event of frequency not being available in this band, the exclusive broadcast band of 104 to 108 MHz may also be considered, as in case of private FM broadcasters. The frequency band from 100 to 104 MHz, earmarked exclusively for the use of AIR, Prasar Bharati, will not be disturbed.

Implementation of the Decision on Community Radio

(*i*) A public notice, inviting applications for grant of licences for setting up Community Radio Stations has been issued, which has appeared in various daily newspapers, in the first fortnight of February, 2003.

(*ii*) The Ministry has received 55 applications from various educational institutions including universities, which are under active consideration in consultation with other Ministries.

(*iii*) WPC, Ministry of Communications and IT has earmarked frequencies to 17 applicants and accordingly letter of intent has been issued to 12 applicants whose applications have been cleared by Ministry of Home Affairs and Human Resource Development.

(*iv*) Country's first Community Radio Station has become operational since 1st February 2004 at Anna University, Chennai, after grant of licence by Ministry of Information and Broadcasting.

The Constraints

Though the idea was holistic and the approach positive, yet there were some apprehensions. One apprehension was regarding the ability and willingness of the educational institutions to come forward for the social cause of upliftment of the society and the communities at large. Another area of concern was in the context of the present security scenario of the country and the pluristic nature of our society. The issues of sustainability and the arithmetic of cost economics are equally important. The technical issues like efficient spectrum management; proper bandwidth usage and the receiver technologies hold the key to the growth of community radio in India. Last, but not the least is the need for the self-regulation and observance of the code of conduct for the content of the programmes to be broadcast.

Need for Policy Reforms

Incidentally, the present policy on community radio contained the element of mid-term course correction. To address the above issues, it is logical to attempt such a mid-term correction now. A Workshop on Community Radio provides a platform to share the experiences of other countries and organizations and to come out with a policy framework that takes into account all the issues raised above.

Ministry of Information and Broadcasting therefore proposes to organize a workshop on Community Radio in collaboration with UNDP and UNESCO, who can bring in the perspective of international experience in tackling such issues.

Purpose of the Workshop

To study and share the experience of other key stakeholders about successful community radio frameworks and practices as well as to identify and brainstorm on key issues of concern while formulating a national policy framework on Community Radio in India.

Organisers

Ministry of Information & Broadcasting with the support of UNDP, UNESCO, AIR, BECIL and PRIA.

Key Objectives

Effective policy instruments and regulatory mechanisms for India.

Issues to be Addressed

- Eligibility criteria—Broad basing the existing policy beyond educational institutions to other well established social organizations working in the field of community development.
- Technical Issues—spectrum usage, band width, receiver technologies and value added services like radio browsing and convergence of technology etc.

- Procedures to ensure public notice and intervention concerning licenses and systems of public accountability.
- Programme content.
- Capacity Building for content generation.
- Linkage to local development planning.
- Security—the present day scenario and the possible safeguards.
- Sustainability and costs—various business models including sponsorship etc.
- Self-regulation/code of conduct—the need for self-restraint and shouldering the responsibility for self-regulation.

Participants

- Government of India: Ministry of Home Affairs, Ministry of Information and Broadcasting, Ministry of Defence, Ministry of External Affairs, Ministry of Environment & Forests, Ministry of Human Resource Development, Ministry of Communication & Information Technology, Ministry of Rural Development, Ministry of Agriculture, Ministry of Health and Family Welfare, Ministry of Social Justice & Empowerment, Ministry of Tribal Affairs.
- All India Radio, Prasar Bharati, IIMC.
- Multilateral and bilateral organizations: UNESCO, UNDP, UNICEF, UNFPA, DfID, World Bank.
- NGOs: Population Foundation of India, PRIA, KMVS, NFI, VOICES, Kalpvriksh, DDS, SWRC.
- Academics and experts working on CR.

Resource Persons

- Legal and policy experts—policy instruments and modalities of regulation.
- Practitioners—different models, addressing key concerns.

CITIZENS' CHARTER

This Charter is a declaration of our mission, values and standards and our commitment to achieve excellence in formulation and implementation of policies and procedures of this Ministry in order to strike a balance between the commercial needs and benefit of the public at large.

Our Services/Activities

- We play an effective role in empowerment of people by providing free flow of information through the mass communication media consisting of radio, television, films, press, publication, advertising and traditional modes of dance and drama.
- We cater to the vital needs of communication and entertainment of all sections of the Society.
- We are responsible for formulation of policies, rules, regulations and laws relating to information, broadcasting and film sectors.
- We interact with our foreign counterparts with a view to further international co-operation in the fields of broadcasting, films and print media.

Our Commitment

- Carry out tasks with integrity and judiciousness, courtesy and understanding, objectivity and transparency, promptness and efficiency.
- All officers/staff available during office hours.
- Speedy and timely redressal of grievances by creating friendly environment.
- Simplification and rationalization of the system for the beneficiaries under various welfare schemes.
- Transparency in working by creating an Internet based system.
- Simplification of procedure for reports and returns.
- Progressive increase in use of e-governance as a measure for improving efficiency of the Ministry.

Our Expectations

We expect Media Units, Attached and Subordinate Offices, PSUs under the control of the Ministry of Information and Broadcasting to be prompt and reasonable in discharging their duties and to be true and honest in furnishing information to us.

Media Units, Autonomous Organisations and Public Sector Undertakings

Media Units

Press Information Bureau (PIB)

- Acts as a nodal agency of the Government for disseminating information to the print/electronic media on government policies, programmes, initiatives and achievements through press releases, photographs, press conferences, interviews, press tours etc.
- Provides accreditation facility to media persons to enable them easy access to information from the Government sources.

Research Reference and Training Division (RR&TD)

- Functions as an information-serving agency for Ministry of Information and Broadcasting, its media units and their field offices.
- Serves as an information bank as well as an information feeder service to the media units to help in their programming and publicity campaigns.
- Studies trends in Mass Communication Media and maintains a reference and documentation service of Mass Communication.
- Provides background, reference and research materials and other relevant facilities relating to mass communication.
- Looks after the training aspect of the Indian Information Service (IIS) officers in collaboration with the Indian Institute of Mass Communication.
- It publishes annually "Reference Annual India".

Publications Division (PD)

- Publishes and sells books and journals at affordable prices on India's art and culture, land and people, biography, flora and fauna, ancient wisdom, works of reference, books for children.

- Some of the important journals published by the Division include Yojana, Kurukshetra, Employment News, Aajkal, Bal Bharati etc.
- Publishes speeches of prominent leaders.
- Published the largest series on Father of our Nation—"The Collected Works of Mahatma Gandhi"—in 100 volumes in English, out of which 87 volumes have been published in Hindi.
- Publishes the biographies of personalities in Hindi, English and Regional languages under Builders of Modern India (BMI) series who contributed to the growth and development of Modern India.

Photo Division

- Prepares photographs both in black and white and colour on the subjects pertaining to the growth and social changes in the country for documentation and for internal and external publicity on behalf of the Government of India.
- Supplies photographs on payment to non-publicity organisations and general public under Competitive pricing scheme.

Registrar of Newspapers for India (RNI)

- Verifies and approves titles of newspapers, registers them, checks and establishes circulation claims.
- Circulation claims of individual papers and Journals are also taken up on demand.
- Publishes *PRESS IN INDIA* containing detailed information on print media.
- Issues eligibility certificates for import of foreign and purchase of indigenous newsprint from specified mills as well as essentiality certificates for import of printing machinery etc., for use by registered publications.

Directorate of Field Publicity (DFP)

- Plays pivotal role in national cohesion and development with the active involvement of people belonging to different strata of society, especially the weaker sections by using a variety of communication modes including group discussions, public meetings, seminars, symposia and competitions of various kinds.
- Organizes publicity campaign on women's empowerment, healthcare, prevention of diseases, awareness of AIDS, Population hazards, promotion of blood donation etc.

Song and Drama Division (S&DD)

- Organises Information Communication Techonology activities in hilly, tribal, desert, sensitive and border areas.
- Organises sound and light shows and presenting theatrical shows on national/social themes in consultation with nodal Ministry.
- Caters entertainment requirements of the Armed Forces in most inhospitable and remote border areas.

Directorate of Advertising and Visual Publicity (DAVP)

- Acts as the primary multi-media advertising agency of the central government.
- Caters information and education to the people, both rural and urban, about the government's policies and programmes and motivates them to participate in development activities.
- Endeavours to make aware the common mass about the national integration and communal harmony, rural development programmes, health and family welfare, women empowerment, girl child upliftment, population control, new economic measures, small savings, consumer affairs, literacy, employment, AIDS, Income Tax, Defence, Environment, energy conservation, handicraft etc.

Films Division

- Educates and motivates people for their active support and participation in the implementation of national programmes to uplift the national image and to project the national heritage.
- Produces documentaries, short films, animation films and newsmagazines having significance in the field of information, communication and integration.

Directorate of Film Festivals (DFF)

- Provides platform for the best in Indian cinema by organizing the National Film Awards, the Indian Panorama and the International Film Festivals of India every year.
- Promotes cultural understanding and friendship at international level.
- Makes latest trends in world cinema accessible to the public within the country.

National Film Archive of India (NFAI)

- Traces, acquires and preserves for posterity, the heritage of Indian cinema.
- Classifies documents data and undertakes research relating to films.
- Acts as a center for dissemination of film culture.

Central Board of Film Certification (CBFC)

- Responsible for certifying the films produced in India as well as outside the country suitable for public exhibition.
- Gives four categories of certificates "U" for unrestricted public exhibition, "A" for public exhibition restricted to adults only, "UA" for unrestricted public exhibition with parental guidance for children below the age of 12 and "S" for exhibition to restricted audience such as doctors etc. These certificates are issued through the Regional Offices of the Board located at Bangalore, Kolkata, Chennai, Cuttack, Guwahati, Hyderabad, Mumbai, New Delhi and Thiruvananthapuram.
- Appeal against the decision of the Board lies with the Film Certification Appellate Tribunal.

Autonomous Organisations: Prasar Bharati

All India Radio (AIR)

- AIR's network provides radio coverage to 97.3 per cent of the population and reaches 90 per cent of the total area of the country. It comprises the National Channel, Regional Stations, Local Radio Stations, Vividh Bharati Centres, FM Stereo Service, External Services and North-Eastern Services.
- Educates, entertains and provides information for enrichment of lives of the people.
- Provides information through news and current affairs programmes and entertainment through Music—devotional, classical (Indian & Western) Folk/Pop/Light, Film songs etc.
- Provides live service on the Internet on a regular 24 hours basis for coverage of AIR programmes to all parts of the world including USA and Canada, where signals of AIR External Service are not received adequately.

Doordarshan (DD)

- One of the largest broadcasting organsiations in the world in terms of the infrastructure of studios and transmitters, the variety of software and the vastness of the viewership.
- Accessible to more than 87 per cent of population of the country through a network of nearly 1044 terrestrial transmitters and 19 channels—two All India Channels, 11 Regional Languages Satellite Channels (RLSC), four State Networks (SN), an International channel and a Sports Channel. About 46 Doordarshan Studios are producing TV software.
- On DD-1 National programmes, Regional programmes and Local programmes are carried on time-sharing basis. Metro Entertainment channel carries Network programmes from Delhi and also Single-Metro Programmes from the four metro cities.
- The Regional Languages Satellite channels have two components—The Regional service for the particular state relayed by all terrestrial transmitters in the state and additional programmes in the Regional Language in prime time and non-prime time available only through cable operators.

Press Council of India (PCI)

- A statutory autonomous body established for the purpose of preserving the freedom of the press, and of maintaining and improving the standards of newspapers and news agencies in India.
- Deliberates on the complaints received either by the press or against the press and is empowered to make observation in respect of conduct of any authority including the Government.
- If it is considered necessary, it can warn, admonish or censure the newspaper, news agency, the editor or the journalist or disapprove the conduct of the editor or the journalist. The decision of the Council cannot be questioned in any court of law.

Film and Television Institute of India (FTII)

- Member of the International Liaison Centre of Cinema and TV School (CILECT).
- Provides latest education and technological experience in the art and technique of film-making and television production.
- Provides in-service training to officers of all grades of Doordarshan.
- Provides excellent exposure to the faculty and students of film and television with the latest digital and broadcast grade production set up.

Satyajit Ray Film and Television Institute (SRFTI)

- Imparts practical and theoretical training in all aspects of film and television programme conception and production including introduction to allied fields.
- Grants certificates, diplomas, honours diplomas and such other certificates, advanced diplomas as may be instituted by the Governing Council to the trainees on successful completion of prescribed courses of study.
- Co-ordinates the activities of education and skill development in the field of film and television programme conception and production.

Indian Institute of Mass Communication (IIMC)

- Runs courses with the objective to produce well-equipped communication professionals sensitive to needs of changing mass communication scenario.
- Conducts short-term specialized courses to meet the professional training needs of media personnel working in the Central/State Governments and Public Sector Organisations.
- Organizes seminars, symposia and conferences on various themes of communication with a view to contributing better understanding of communication in the context of India and other developing countries.
- Provides consultancy services on request to Central/State Government Departments and Public Sector Undertakings, and helps in designing and organizing training and research programmes related to Development communication.
- Publishes seminar reports, research studies, teaching material and books related to various aspects of communication.
- Publishes the quarterly journals like *Communicator in English & Sanchar Madhyam in Hindi* based on the Institute's academic works as well as on major issues in the field of communication.

Children's Film Society, India (CFSI)

- Provides value-based entertainment to the children and young people through the medium of films.
- Organizes Mini Film Festivals and CFSI's International Children's Film Festivals.

Public Sector Undertakings

Nation Film Development Corporation Limited (NFDC)

- Plans, promotes and organizes an integrated and efficient development of the Indian Film Industry keeping in view the economic policy and objectives laid down by the Government from time to time.
- Encourages the concept of low-budget films, quality contents and thematic values by funding/producing.

Broadcast Engineering Consultants India Limited (BECIL)

- Provides consultancy services in the field of Acoustics, Audio, Video, MMDS, Digital Satellite Contribution links etc.
- Executes several turn key jobs such as design/installation of Sound Reinforcement System, Audio Announcement Management System for Airports, integration and supply of Satellite Receiving Terminal, design and installation of Video Compression System for satellite uplink in India as well as abroad.
- At present, the company is run by a Board of Directors.

Prominent Schemes/Services Meant for Citizens Provided by the Various Media Units of Ministry of Information and Broadcasting are Given in the Following Table:

Name of the Media Unit/Organisation Under Ministry of Information and Broadcasting	*Schemes/Services Provided to the Citizens*
(1)	*(2)*
Film and Television Institute of India	Teaching/Training Courses in Film and Television
Indian Institute of Mass Communication	Teaching Courses in Jornalism, Advertising and Public Relation
Children's Film Society of India	Production of feature films, TV Serials and Short Films Purchase of Films Dubbing and subtitling of films
Prasar Bharati (Doordarshan)	Commercial Bookings, Sponsered Programmes and Commissioned Programmes
National Film Development Corporation	Film Finance and Production Import and Distribution of Films in India Export of Films Technical Services for Pre/Post-Production of Films Cine Artist Welfare Fund Panorama Films
Press Information Bureau	Accredition to Media Representatives

Name of the Media Unit/Organisation Under Ministry of Information and Broadcasting	*Schemes/Services Provided to the Citizens*
(1)	*(2)*
Publications Division	Production and Sale of Books on Art, History, Culture etc. Publication and Sale of Journals viz. Employment News: Yojna, Kurukshetra, Aajkal and Bal Bharati Production and Sale of CDs on Collected Works of Mahatma Gandhi
Registrar of Newspapers for India	Title Verification Registration of Newspapers Verification of Circulation Claims Issue of eligibility certificate for import of Newsprint Issue of essentiality certificate for import of printing machinery and allied material.
Directorate of Advertising and Visual Publicity	Empanelment of Printers Empanelment of Producers for Audio Video productions Empanelment of Newspapers/Periodicals for the purpose of release of advertisements. Empanelment of Outdoor Publicity Agencies
Films Division	Sale of Stock Shots Sale of Video Cassettes of Films Produced by Films Division Entering of Agreements with the Theatre Owner for Screening of Approved Films Lending of Video Theatres and Premises of Gulshan Mahal on Rental Basis. Conducting of Biennial International Film Festival for Documentary, Short and Animation Films Hiring of Equipments at Prescribed Rates Loaning of Print Films Made by Films Division to Schools/Colleges, Societies for Non-Commercial Exhibitions
Directorate of Film Festivals	Participation of Film Makers in the India Panorama Section of Internation Film Festival of India Participation of Film Makers in the National Film Awards Hiring of Sirifort Auditoria for the public on rental basis for events

(Contd.)

Name of the Media Unit/Organisation Under Ministry of Information and Broadcasting	Schemes/Services Provided to the Citizens
(1)	(2)
Song and Drama Division	Registration of Private Cultural Troupe and Empanelment of Performing and Back Stage Artistes.

Redressal of Grievances

This Ministry is sensitized to redress grievances received from public and employees directly or through Department of Administrative Reforms and Public Grievances in a responsible and effective manner through the following:

- A Grievance Cell under the chairmanship of Joint Secretary (Administration) has been set in the Main Ministry.
- Complaint Committee has been constituted to deal with the complaints of sexual harassment of female employees in the Ministry of Information and Broadcasting.
- Similar Cells have been set up in all the attached and subordinate offices.
- Citizen's Charter has been formulated by all the Media Units/Autonomous Organisation/Public Sector Undertakings under the control of this Ministry.
- E-mail address of the Grievances Cell of the Ministry has already been registered for grievance monitoring. The e-mail address of the Public Grievance Cell is: jsp@sb.nic.in.

The Citizen's Charter will be reviewed annually for further improving our response to the public.

Time Frame of Redressal of the Grievances

Sl.No.	Subject	Time
1.	Issue of acknowledgement/interim reply to the petitioner	2 weeks
2.	Forwarding of the grievances/petition to the concerned authority	2 weeks
3.	Final disposal of transferred/referred cases by the concerned Ministry/Department/State and time limit for informing the position of the outcome.	3 months
4.	Cases referred to Complaint Committee on "Sexual Harassment of Women at workplace"	3 months

Information Facilitation Counter

An Information Facilitation Centre has been set up for providing the following services to the public:

- Receive the public, reply to their queries and direct them to concerned Officer/Section.

- Provide information regarding various schemes and procedures through brochures, booklets, reports etc.
- Forms that are to be utilised for various procedures are made available.
- Provide information regarding the functioning of the Ministry.

Ministry of Information and Broadcasting—Important Telephone Numbers

Main Secretariat

1.	Minister of Information and Broadcasting, 'A' Wing, Shastri Bhawan, New Delhi–110001.	011-2338 4782/2338 4340/ 2338 6892
2.	Minister of State, Information and Broadcasting, 'A' Wing, Shastri Bhawan, New Delhi–110001.	011-23381074/2338 4894
3.	Secretary, 'A' Wing, Shastri Bhawan, New Delhi–110001.	011-2338 2639
4.	Joint Secretary (Admn. & PG), Room No. 657, 'A' Wing, Shastri Bhawan, New Delhi–110001.	011-2338 3857
5.	Director (C) & Chairperson of Complaint Committee on "Sexual Harassment of Women at workplace", Room No. 556, 'A' Wing, Shastri Bhawan, New Delhi–110001.	011-2338 4484
6.	Deputy Secretary (Admn) & Liaison Officer for SC/ST, Room No. 553, 'A' Wing, Shastri Bhawan, New Delhi–110001.	011-2338 5592

Grievance Officers of Media Units, Autonomous Organisations and PSUs

1.	Director of Programmes (PP&D), Directorate General: All India Radio, Room No.115, Akashwani Bhawan, Sansad Marg, New Delhi–110001.	011-2342 1542
2.	Deputy Director General (Admn.), Directorate General: Doordarshan, Room No. 510, Doordarshan Bhawan, Mandi House, New Delhi–110001.	011-2338 2093
3.	Additional Principal Information Officer, Press Information Bureau, Room No. 113(a), 'A' Wing, Shastri Bhawan, Dr. Rajendra Prasad Marg, New Delhi–110001.	011-2338 2127
4.	Regional Director, Directorate of Advertising and Visual Publicity, Room No. 16, 3rd Floor, PTI Building, Sansad Marg, New Delhi–110001.	011-2371 787
5.	Joint Director (Admn), Publications Division (DPD), Room No. 122, Patiala House, Tilak Marg, New Delhi–110001.	011-2307 3015
6.	Deputy Press Registrar, Office of the Registrar of Newspapers for India, West Block-8, Wing No. 2, R.K. Puram, New Delhi–110066.	011-2610 6251
7.	Joint Director (M), Directorate of Field Publicity, East Block IV, Level III, R.K. Puram, New Delhi–110066.	011-2610 4475
8.	Deputy Director (S&L), Song & Drama Division, Room No. 929, Soochna Bhawan, C.G.O. Complex, Lodi Road, New Delhi–110003.	011-2436 3509
9.	Joint Director, Research, Reference and Training Division, Room No. 402, 'B' Wing, Shastri Bhawan, Dr. Rajendra Prasad Marg, New Delhi–110001.	011-2338 4844
10.	Director, Photo Division, Soochna Bhawan, C.G.O. Complex, Lodi Road, New Delhi–110003	011-2436 2384
11.	Chief Producer, Films Division, Films Bhawan, 24 Dr. Gopalrao Deshmukh Marg, Mumbai–400026.	022-2386 4633
12.	Chairman, Central Board of Film Certification, Bharat Bhavan, 91E, Walkeshwar Road, Mumbai–400006.	022-2363 1048

13.	Deputy Director (Admn), Directorate of Film Festival, Siri Fort Cultural Complex, August Kranti Marg, New Delhi–110049.	011-2649 9370
14.	Deputy Director-cum-Curator, National Films Archive of India, Law College Road, Pune–411 004.	0952-5659487
15.	Professor of Music, Film and Television Institute of India, Law College Road, Pune–411 004.	020-543 0416 Extn. 277
16.	Administrative Officer, Children's Film Society, India, Films Division Complex, 24, Dr. Gopalrao Deshmukh Marg, Mumbai–400026.	022-2380 8592
17.	Manager, National Film Development Corporation Limited, "Discovery of India", Nehru Centre, Dr. Anne Besant Road, Worli, Mumbai–400018.	022-2492 9096
18.	Registrar, Indian Institute of Mass Communication, Aruna Asaf Ali Marg, JNU New Campus, New Delhi–110007.	011-2610 9268/ 2618 9925
19.	Deputy Secretary, Press Council of India, Faridkot House (Ground Floor), Copernicus Marg, New Delhi–110001.	011-238 1726
20.	Registrar, Satyajit Ray Film & Television Institute, E.M. Bye Pass Road, P.O. Panchsayar, Kolkata–700094.	033-2432 8355
21.	Controller of Accounts, Principal Accounts Office, Tropical Building, Connaught Circus, New Delhi–110001.	011-23323151
22.	Director (Operation & Marketing), Broadcast Engineering Consultants India Limited, B-1, Sector-31, Noida–201301 (UP).	0120-245 8034

MINISTRY OF INFORMATION AND BROADCASTING

Subject: Revised draft Seniority List in respect of Indian Information Service, Group 'A' as on 31.3.2000.

In compliance with judgement dated 17/7/2002 of Hon'ble Principal Bench of CAT, New Delhi in O.A.No. 1963/2000 filed by *Shri Y.S.R. Murthy & Others* Vs. *Union of India* and O.A.No. 2685/2000 filed by *Shri D. Satpathy & Others* Vs. *Union of India,* draft Seniority/Civil List of II S Group 'A' officers as on 31/3/2000 was circulated vide this Ministry's I.D.No. C-17011/20/2002-IIS dated 30/9/2002. Objections were invited on the same by 31/10/2002. Objections received in response thereto were duly considered and after considering the objections, final seniority list in respect of Higher Grade, Selection Grade and Senior Administrative Grade was circulated vide this Ministry's ID dated 16/12/2002.

The objections relating to the seniority list from officers in the other grades have also been examined in consultation with DOP&T. DOP&T have, inter-alia, advised adoption of the following criteria while finalizing the seniority list:

(*i*) For the period 1/1/74 to 31/12/80, 58 regular DPs of 1978 DPC and 22 regular DPs of 1980 DPC should be made enbloc senior to the DRs of CSE-1981 onwards as per amendment dated 25/1/82 under CIS (Amendment) Rule, 1982;

(*ii*) For the period of CSE-1981 to CSE-1986, 61 "officiating" DPs of 1980 DPC and 102 "officiating" DPs of 1981 DPC should be interpolated with DRs of CSE-1981 onwards on 1:1 basis in accordance with DOP&T's OM No. 9/1/55-RPF dated 22/12/59 (slot system). The promotee officers should be bunched only to the extent of shortfall in direct recruitment for the above period below the DRs of CSE-1986;

(*iii*) For the period CSE-1987 onwards, the inter-se-seniority should be determined in accordance with DOP&T's OM dated 7/2/86 (bunching system);
(*iv*) After refixing inter-se-seniority, if there are any excess (beyond quota) promotee officers in Grade-II, they should be dealt with as per the extant rules;
(*v*) All IIS officers whether retired or in service should be reflected in the revised seniority list; and
(*vi*) Post-based roster in DOP&T OM No.36012/2/96 are only an aid to determine the entitlement of different categories (SC/ST/OBC) with regard to quota reserved for them. They are not to be used for determining the seniority.

The above mentioned advice of DOP&T has necessitated that a fresh draft seniority list be prepared, since there is a change in the principles followed while formulating the draft seniority list circulated vide ID of even number dated 30/9/02 and the principles followed now as per the advice of DOP&T. The fresh draft seniority list is hereby circulated in keeping with the principles of natural justice to provide an opportunity to the concerned officers to file objections if they so desire. Objections, if any, to this fresh draft seniority list may be sent by the concerned officers to this Ministry at the earliest and not later than 3 October, 2003. Objections received after the stipulated date are liable to be rejected straightaway.

Sd/-
(G.S. Pundir)
Under Secretary (IIS)
Tel. No. 338 1941

Broadcasting Policy and Administration

All matters relating to radio and television broadcasting within the Union including regulation of the use of All India Radio and Doordarshan by recognised national and regional political parties during elections to the Lok Sabha and State Assemblies and procedure to be followed by the official electronic media during periods of national mourning on the demise of a high dignitary.

The enunciation and implementation of the law relating to radio and television broadcasting in India by private Indian companies or Indian nationals.

Broadcast Monitoring and Administration of the Prasar Bharati (Broadcasting Corporation of India) Act, 1990 (25 of 1990).

All matters relating to the Indian Broadcasting (Programme) Service and the Indian Broadcasting (Engineering) Service until they are handed over to Prasar Bharati.

Cable Television Policy

Cable Television Networks (Regulation) Act, 1995 (7 of 1995).

Radio

All business connected with All India Radio embracing news services in the home programmes, programmes for the foreign countries and Indians overseas, radio journals, research in the field of broadcasting engineering, monitoring of foreign broadcasts, programme exchange and transcription services, supply of community receiving sets to State Governments under the community listening scheme, etc.

Development of Radio Broadcasting throughout the Union, installation and maintenance of Radio Stations and Transmitters and operation of broadcasting services.

Doordarshan

Exchange including cultural exchange of television programmes.

Development of television throughout the Union, including installation, maintenance and operation of television Programme Production Centres and Transmitters, and operation of television services.

Promotion of production of television programmes outside Doordarshan.

Films

Legislation under entry 60 of the Union List, viz., 'Sanctioning of Cinematograph films for exhibition'.

Administration of the Cinematograph Act, 1952 (37 of 1952).

Import of feature and short films for theatrical and non-theatrical viewing.

Export of Indian films, both feature and short films.

Import of unexposed cinematograph films and various types of equipment required by the film industry.

All matters relating to film industry, including developmental and promotional activities thereto.

Promotion of good cinema by institution of State awards for films produced in India and assistance through the National Film Development Coporation Limited.

Production and distribution of documentaries and newsreels and other films and film strips for internal and external publicity.

Preservation of films and filmic materials.

Organisation of International Film Festivals in India and participation of India in International Film Festivals abroad.

Organisation of Film Festivals under Cultural Exchange Programmes.

Film society movement.

Advertising and Visual Publicity

Production and release of advertisements on behalf of the Government of India.

Press

Presentation and interpretation of the policies and activities of the Government of India through the medium of the press.

Advising Government on information problems relating to the Press, keeping Government informed of the main trends of public opinion as reflected in the Press and liaison between Government and the Press.

Publicity to and for the Armed Forces.

General conduct of Government relations with the Press excluding the administration of Sections 95 and 96 of the Code of Criminal Procedure, 1973 (2 of 1974).

Administration of the Press and Registration of Books Act, 1867 (25 of 1867) relating to Newspapers.

Administration of the Press Council Act, 1978 (37 of 1978).

Allocation of Newsprint to Newspapers.

Publications

Production, sale and distribution of popular pamphlets, books and journals on matters of national importance for internal as well as external publicity, with a view to imparting to the general public at home and abroad upto date and correct information about India.

Research and Reference

To assist the Media Units of the Ministry of Information and Broadcasting in collection, compilation and preparation of material involving research into published works, etc.

Building up of a compendium of knowledge on important subjects and to prepare guidance and background notes on current and other topics for the use of the Media Units of the Ministry.

Miscellaneous

Publicity for the policies and programmes of Government of India.

Administration of Journalists Welfare Fund.

Financial assistance to distinguished musicians, both vocal and instrumental, dancers and dramatists who have contributed substantially to the success of All India Radio and other units of the Ministry or their survivors in indigent circumstances.

All matters relating to the Asia-Pacific Broadcasting Union, Commonwealth Broadcasting Association and the Non-Aligned News Agency Pool.

Cadre management of the Indian Information Service (Groups 'a' and 'b').

Attached and Subordinate Organisations

(*a*) All India Radio.
(*b*) Doordarshan.
(*c*) Press Information Bureau.
(*d*) Directorate of Advertising and Visual Publicity.
(*e*) Publications Division.
(*f*) Office of the Registrar of Newspapers for India.
(*g*) Central Board of Film Certification.
(*h*) Films Division.
(*i*) Directorate of Film Festivals.
(*j*) National Film Archives of India.
(*k*) Directorate of Field Publicity.
(*l*) Song and Drama Division.
(*m*) Research, Reference and Training Division.
(*n*) Photo Division.
(*o*) Principal Accounts Office.
(*p*) Central Monitoring Service.

Autonomous Organisations

(*a*) Film and Television Institute of India, Pune.
(*b*) Satyajit Ray Film and Television Institute, Kolkata.
(*c*) Children Film Society of India.

(*d*) Indian Institute of Mass Communication.
(*e*) Press Council of India.
(*f*) Federation of Film Society of India.

Public Sector Undertaking

National Film Development Corporation Limited.
Broadcast Engineers Consultants (India) Limited.

BROADCASTING FOR RURAL PROGRESS

The role of television and radio in education has been discussed in the previous section in so far as school children and university students are concerned. Similar claims are made for the part the electronic media can play in adult education though, in recent years, there is a growing awareness that broadcasting by itself can achieve little.

Social science has shown that broadcasting and other mass media can provide information, and affect listeners' tastes but by themselves they cannot change attitudes which lead to positive action. The mass media cannot win against traditional attitudes unless they are reinforced by personal influence. In all developing societies where traditions die hard broadcasting, controlled and run by educated, urban people has been less important in communications information and ideas to the villages than traditional village leaders and even bazaar gossip.

If broadcasting is used to support inter-personal communication it proves very effective, and, in several cases, man-to-man communication must have the help of broadcasting to be effective.

The media can bring timely information directly to people; they can inform them of new methods and devices and give them incentives to act in new ways. In the sphere of social reform, radio and television programmes can encourage socially progressive practices and attitudes in respect of marriage, child rearing, health and hygiene. They can also create the urge for a higher standard of living which can lead, firstly, to greater productivity, by the employment of modern techniques in agriculture and home industries, and, secondly, to more favourable attitudes to saving and investment in productive items and a reduction in wasteful expenditure on traditional ceremonies. So though broadcasting cannot do any of the essential tasks of village level workers, agriculture extension officers, malaria spraying teams or family planning and medical personnel, without it development plans and programmes would continue to suffer delays caused by lack of basic knowledge in the villages.

In the course of the last forty years, since rural broadcasting began, many farmers and their families scattered over the entire country have come to depend on AIR for information and entertainment. In some parts of the country the broadcasts have succeeded in changing agricultural practices to the advantage of the individual farmer and the country's agricultural production. Such success encourages one to hope that radio can be an agent for change and progress if properly used.

But while, in theory, the claims of broadcasters are valid it is in practice that the lofty aims are unfulfilled because of a variety of factors. From our own experience and that of other societies which have attempted to use radio and television for purposes other than entertainment, it is now acknowledged that certain conditions must be met if such broadcasts are not to fail.

The very first of these is that priorities must be clearly laid down. With scarce resources it is essential to concentrate on the most important targets and ignore others until such time as they can be considered. The primary consideration is to ensure that the benefits of whatever investment the community makes flow to the section of people who need them most. In this respect AIR's rural programmes have not been effective. Women and Harijans have not been allowed in many villages to be present when the community listening set is on. Studies show that it is only the middle-level farmers who derive benefit from the programmes. The illiterate find them too difficult to follow.

Perhaps the most important condition for success is the proper organisation of listening. When AIR started rural broadcasting radio sets were too expensive for individual farmers to own and listening at community sets alone was possible. Even today though one-band sets are available for about Rs. 120 they are well beyond the means of landless labourers and poor artisans.

As at present, State Governments buy, instal and maintain community receivers with the help of grants from the Union Government. Local communities also pay a small share of the cost. There are about 70,000 community receivers in all. Apart from the limited number of villages provided with sets there is the problem of maintenance. Most villages are unelectrified and battery operated sets have to be installed. The replacement of batteries and other repairs require on organisation which most States have not been able to achieve. In the States which have managed to set up a fairly efficient organisation the cost is extremely heavy as may be expected when government undertakes such an operation. The Vidyalankar Committee found that as many as 50 per cent of the total number of sets were not functioning on any given day.

It is not only the malfunctioning of sets that has made the scheme unworkable. People in the villages find it irksome to go to the *Panchayatghar* or the *Chaupal*, or wherever the set is installed, after a day's hard work to listen to the rather dull programmes to which the community sets are pretuned. They would rather listen on a neighbour's private set to Vividh Bharati.

The failure of community listening has been evident for a long time but AIR has been unable to scrap it and replace it with some more effective way of reaching the villages. The only alternative is to allow farmers and their families to listen in their homes to programmes of entertainment and education. This would be possible if the price of a radio set were within the means of the average farmer. The Report of the Committee on Broadcasting and Information Media has discussed at length the reasons for the high cost of radio sets in India and suggested how it can be brought down by reducing or abolishing taxes and duties now levied by government.

Experience has shown that broadcast programmes must be used in coordination with other media of communication to get results. Whether in adopting new agricultural practices or in accepting the idea of family planning, the broadcasts have to be reinforced by personal contacts with local opinion leaders and those who have accepted and adopted the new ideas and practices. Such contacts must be institutionalised by forming groups or forums in which new ideas can be discussed. But coordination of this kind requires great flexibility. Rigid institutions and organisations which cannot experiments with a variety of methods of reaching a desired goal cannot hope to succeed in using new technological devices.

In 1959 AIR started Radio Forums. It was felt that with the organisation of such Forums the rural programme would have a greater impact. The Forums were modelled on the Farm Radio Forums of Canada. They are organised listening groups of fifteen to twenty persons who listen together at a community set to bi-weekly programmes, directed specially to them, as part of the Rural Programme. After the broadcast the farmers are expected to discuss the information and suggestions contained in the programmes and to decide on a plan of action. It was believed that such action oriented discussion in the villages would result in many innovations being accepted which, otherwise, would not.

But the Forums too have become moribund. After the first flush of enthusiasm the collective listening has dwindled and with it the plans for action. No one knows how many are active though each State has a chief organiser of Forums to organise its activities in collaboration with the district officials.

The reasons for the failure of the Forums are not far to seek. AIR lacked the resources to operate so ambitious a programme covering the whole country. The villages lacked the leadership to conduct the discussions intelligently and effectively and AIR could not be expected to provide. The machinery for carrying the reactions of the Forums to the programme planners was weak. In Canada the Forums were the joint responsibility of the Canadian Broadcasting Corporation, the Canadian Broadcasting Federation of Agriculture and the Canadian Association for Adult Education. While the broadcasts were the responsibility of the broadcasting organisation, the other two provided the money for running offices to look after the Forums. A very elaborate system was evolved of planning the broadcast discussions and for reporting the findings. Unfortunately AIR could not afford anything like this organisation. Without a close contact between the radio station and the Forums their success was only partial at best.

Besides, it has been found that only forums with a homogenous membership can be successful. It is the farmers in the age-group 30-50 with a middle-school level education who are most keen on listening to radio programmes which would help them to improve their productivity and thus their standard of living. The poor and illiterate farmer fails to derive any benefit from the broadcasts. For him personal contact with the village level worker is the only effective medium for changing his ideas, attitudes and practices.

With the growth of TV, programmes for rural viewers around the TV centres have been started. They go out for thirty minutes or so twice or thrice a week. What has been their impact? The introduction of Krishidarshan in 1967 from Delhi for eighty villages around the capital was mentioned in the chapter on the growth of TV. It contains agricultural instruction for fifteen minutes thrice a week. There is also some suitable entertainment.

The first point of interest is that from the start of the programme only half the members of the teleclubs turned up to watch it and since then the number has steadily declined. Non-members also watch the programmes in limited numbers. In all there is an audience of ten to twenty persons. About a third of the total number of farmers in the village never watch Krishidarshan. Yet as many as four hundred people turn up to watch films and 'Chitrahar'. Why? The surveys indicate that the programmes are unsuitable. While some viewers understand technical language, English words and metric measures as many as 90 per cent of the women said they could not follow them. Secondly, TV sets are not kept in working order. A study in 1970 by ISRO found that on 13 per cent of the days when Krishi Darshan is broadcast the sets were not working because of electric failure, minor flaws which could not be repaired, the operator was not available, and so forth. On the question of persuading farmers to adopt new techniques the studies are inconclusive.

Another study in Maharashtra produced similar findings. Out of about 250 villages with TV sets in the Pune district, fifty were visited during a period of one-and-a-half years from 1977-79. Most of them were revisited at least once during the same period to see if there was any change. It was found that TV sets were put on Sundays, Saturdays and Thursdays, on which dates film based programmes are telecast. Monday, Wednesdays and Fridays a special rural programme is telecast, but does not reach the villagers, as the sets are not put on. The rural chunk from Pune is rarely seen or heard by the community viewers. On the other hand 'Chhaya Geet' and feature films are never missed.

When the custodians of the sets were asked why there was such poor attendance, they blamed the Gram Panchayats. But the plain fact is that no one is interested in the TV programmes meant for development. It can be assumed that the same pattern prevails in all the villages in the Pune district.

Obviously the custodians are not playing their part. They should inform Doordarshan why the rural programmes is not popular. It is not difficult to guess why.

Rural programmes have a very low priority in the output of a TV centre. Out of the entire programme in the month only 4 per cent is devoted to the rural viewer. All the rest are programmes for urban viewers. While the policy declared by the government is to make TV a rural medium, 96 per cent of the programmes are for the urban rich in languages which rural people cannot understand.

Even the 4 per cent broadcast for rural viewers are of agricultural achievements by the big farmers. There is very little of such topics as health, nutrition, sanitation, which would greatly help in improving life in the villages. Moreover, the programmes are all in the from of talks and discussions. Drama, folk music, folk dance, which would sustain interest are never attempted because they would cost money and would involve too much time being spent on them. In view of this, it is not surprising that the village viewer finds the programmes dull and irrelevant, and the TV set is turned off.

Obviously, the potential of TV could be realised only if the programmes are based on the needs of those they profess to serve in language which the people can understand.

It is also obvious that if TV is to be used as a medium for education and instruction, the custodians of community sets must be given a course in the mode of using the TV programmes. There should also be weekly briefs sent to the custodians about programmes to be telecast in the coming week or two. These could be inserted between some film based programmes so as to ensure that the custodians would be watching the screen.

Adequate investment of funds is essential for the success of broadcasts for education and development. If funds are spread too thinly over a variety of projects none is likely to succeed. Because technical equipment is more or less a fixed charge, the danger is that programme material will be starved of funds, but the best technical devices are of no avail of the messages they carry are vague, dull and ineffective.

The greatest weakness, in trying to manage with inadequate funds, arises in respect of personnel. Underdeveloped societies suffer from a shortage of qualified people in almost all fields. If inadequate remuneration keeps out the best qualified people, programme planning, production and presentation will be dull and therefore unsuccessful. Training of personnel assumes considerable importance in these circumstances, and the training cannot be of a general nature. It has to be related to the specific programme activity involved, because the requirements for educating children are not the same as those for instructing village women or farmers. Besides technicians it is necessary to train TV instructors and monitors for villages, field representatives versed in the techniques employed in the programmes, staff experts to recruit people, and research working and evaluators.

Continuous audience research is necessary to ensure the success of such programmes. Before they are launched there must be some form of pre-testing to ensure that the language, the format, the time, the duration, are appropriate. After they are launched the reactions of the audience have to be assessed periodically and regularly. If this had been done by AIR, the results of several of its educational and instructive programmes would have been far more rewarding. Research and evaluation are usually starved of funds. This is false economy in every sense.

Although rural broadcasts have been put out since 1936 there has been no systematic evaluation because AIR has no funds for such research. A few limited studies here and there are all there is to go on.

TV programmes for rural viewers have received more attention—the impetus came from SITE and the glamour of TV attracts many students of social science, communication and so forth.

It is now recognised the world over that educational broadcasts must use the local language and idiom and must be planned to meet local needs. It is not possible to centralise, even at the State capital, the planning and preparation of instructional material, whether for adults of children, if it is to be relevant in terms of the listeners' linguistic, cultural, social and religious background. The careful preparation of such material is one of the most important conditions for the success of the project. Without an interested, responsive human receiver at the other end no message can be learned or accepted. Nothing is less effective and more boring than a poorly produced educational programme.

Unfortunately, AIR has not, for a variety of reasons, been able to broadcast programmes for the rural community which are of local interest and this, combined with the weaknesses of the community listening scheme, is mainly responsible for the limited impact of its programmes.

From the start of rural broadcasting, programmes have been broadcast from the regional stations of AIR to cover an entire State or large areas in a State. Starting with broadcasts from Peshawar for the N-WFP, the Delhi station introduced in 1936.

As new station came up the same pattern was repeated and continues more or less unchanged to this day. The programmes contain news and the broadcasts are, for many in the rural areas, the only source of news, market and weather reports, which are useful for the farming community. Entertainment in the form of folk music and film music and plays are popular. But it is difficult to say how effective the instructional content of the programmers has been. Research has been haphazard and very limited. Such findings as are available indicate that radio is behind other media in influencing farmers to adopt new techniques of farming. Demonstration and personal contact with village level workers are far more important than listening to the radio.

To some extent this because the programmes are not always very lovely even though some of them are very good; to some extent, because in the absence of satisfactory organisation and coordination, the broadcasts are not accompanied by or followed up by personal visits by village level workers or agricultural extension workers; and to some extent because the content of most programmes is of general interest and not related specifically to the needs of the farming community.

Realising this in 1966, AIR initiated Farm and Home broadcasts. At AIR headquarters and at several station Farm and Home Units have been formed to provide information and advice on fertilisers, pesticides, implements, seeds and other items of interest to farmers through the rural programmes of stations located in the intensive agricultural development areas.

It was necessary to give farmers intensive education and assistance in adopting the improved practices in their own fields. The broadcasts differed from the earlier ones because they gave technical information, for day-to-day farming operations, which was supplied by specialists and extension workers and was related to the needs of small farming communities in the vicinity of the stations. The Units were also required to record discussions and interviews with farmers for broadcast in the rural programmes and to obtain from them suggestion for the future planning of the broadcasts.

As a result of staff shortages the intention of broadcasting programmes which were mostly field-based has not been fulfilled. The high cost of petrol makes it still more difficult to collect recordings from the villages and so the programmes will continue to be mainly studio-based, consisting of talks by "experts". All the same, some studies reveal that the Farm and Home Broadcasts are popular with semi-educated farmers who listen to the agricultural advice they obtain as it helps them to increase productivity and earn more from their farms.

The title "Farm and Home" would imply that the Units must give some thought to the home in urban and rural areas and to the women who run these homes but, in fact, this side of their activity has been neglected. The broadcast of programmes in health and hygiene in the rural programme can of course be heard by women as well as men but it has been noticed that women do not go to the community listening sets when the men are collected there and they find the evening hour inconvenient. Special programmes for rural women are broadcast once or twice a week during the rural programme for thirty minutes from some stations but not from all. There are no funds either to increase their frequency or to extend the broadcast to every station.

With "Farm and Home" broadcasts it could be said that AIR has taken the first step towards broadcasting material of local interest to small farming communities in place of the omnibus programmes it has broadcast hitherto, but unless the broadcast of programmes shifts to the districts the programmes cannot be "local" in the proper sense.

Even countries which do not have to make a massive effort for development are turning to local radio. The UK started some years ago but the USA has had local broadcasting for many years. Every small town has its own station. It is an Australia that such local station have been set up with the primary aim of serving the rural community. The new station were "expected to combine popular programming with fostering a greater public awareness of local affairs and involvement in the community."

Ordinary citizens were expected to acquire a new and effective channel for their views, demands and grievances. The stream of local news would keep people informed about the issues and policies affecting their lives, supplemented by special investigations into particular matters of local concern. There would be a permanent arena for discussion and debate about local issues. Its local news service, always seen as a key element in its output, would contribute greatly progress towards local democracy.

Everywhere it is now recognised that the development of centralised systems of mass communication is useless unless regional and local systems of communication are developed. Such local systems have to reflect local life but also show how local problems are connected with events in the community of the State, the country and even the world.

In India we have found that programmes broadcast from regional stations in the language or dialect most widely spoken by rural people in that State leaves many listeners unapproached. With the diversity of languages in our country there may have to be programmers in half a dozen languages or dialects in any one State.

One centralised programme is irrelevant to the needs of many parts of the State. Farmers like programmes which tell them what to do and how to do it in the form of informal conversations or questions and answers. Such broadcasts can only be planned and transmitted locally for each homogeneous agricultural region with a common language, common crop, similar weather conditions, marketing facilities and so forth. The farmers' preference for field-based programmes has been noted earlier. This cannot be met from the studios of the regional station. Nor can the stations afford the transport for covering all the distracts for such field-based programmes. A local radio station could get farmers and others to come to it for recording their views, suggestions and questions.

Small-scale television has become possible in technological terms with the development of VTR Portapak units and time-base correctors which enable language video to be used for making programmes away from a studio, for editing and transmission at minimum cost.

On the other hand, the technical standards adopted nationally and internationally tend towards ever higher technical and production standards. These call for high-cost sophisticated equipment, which implies a minimum capital cost per station, and reliance on network programming. The service area has to be large enough to justify the station's existence or make a profit. But the resulting service area is too large to allow a station adequately to reflect the needs of small communities within it.

Fifteen years ago, the Committee on Information and Broadcasting popularly known as the Chanda Committee, studied the failure of communication with the rural people. It found that there were few listeners for the rural programmes and this was mainly because the local needs of the vast audience of about 450 million people, living in 550 thousand villages, had not and could not be met by a conventional urban based, professionally staffed broadcasting system. It concluded that two important, radical changes were needed in the reception and broadcast of programmes for the rural people.

First, the community listening scheme must be abandoned as Governments in the various States of the Indian Union had failed to organise and operate the scheme satisfactorily. Listening in rural areas should move from the community set to the village home through one-band radio receivers which could be made much cheaper by adopting the correct industrial and fiscal policies.

Secondly, the broadcast of the programmes must be over low-power transmitters located in the countryside at the headquarters of each of India's 400 districts, each serving about one or two million people. This would ensure that the programmes would be relevant to the specific problems of people in comparatively small areas. Such station would allow centrally planned messages about development to be modified or added to as may be appropriate for each community. They would provide for local inputs without which centrally-planned messages fail to evoke the desired response.

The duration of the daily service would depend on local needs but if programmes for farmers and their families are to be meaningful they must be for at least three or four hours a day, at times most convenient for the community, and should provide information and advice relevant to the needs. Programmes would vary from district to district but some massage would be common to all. The Government's plans for promoting family planning, for improving sanitation and health, for increasing agricultural productivity, for non-formal education for adults, for literacy and basic education for children, for stimulating innovation and enterprise in traditional and new crafts, for discouraging custom and attitudes which hinder economic and social progress, all these and others would find a place in the broadcasts.

News could be prepared specially at each local station to satisfy local interest. The present news bulletins in the rural services of AIR are not tailored to rural requirements either in terms of language or content. Operators of small town radio stations in the USA, Australia and elsewhere find that comprehensive local news coverage is the single most attractive programme which makes listeners forsake the national networks in favour of their local station. Village folk are interested in district developments and the activities of the Taluka Panchayat Samiti and not in those of the remote Legislative Assemblies and the even remoter Lok Sabha. They want news of development work in co-operation, rural industries, irrigation, the construction of village roads, a new bus service, personalised stories of achievements of individual farmers, problems of land-holders and agricultural labourers, irrigation rates, and all those things that affect their lives. A local station can collect such news from district officials, panchayats, social workers, teachers, traders, and others and also give timely warning of flooding of roads, breakdowns in the bus service, and so forth.

Local broadcasting alone can ensure co-ordination with district authorities and with extension services to guarantee follow-up action and to make available the inputs discussed in the programmes. It is hardly possible, at the State capital, for AIR to plan programmes in consultation with extension workers and to effect coordination with district personnel in the veterinary, agriculture, forestry, health and other departments.

The local station must appeal to voluntary effort. In place of professional standards and bureaucratic rules and regulations there has to be a unofficial atmosphere and a spirit of experimentation. The programmes should be initiated by the community and the staff has to be small and flexible as it used to be even in the old established broadcasting stations in their pioneering days. This would make it possible for one or two professional broadcasters to run a station with the help of local volunteers. Village extension workers, young people, women, the elderly, those with little or no formal education, could all be employed as volunteers with, possibly, a small honorarium. The main duty of the professional staff would be to train the volunteers and coordinate their work.

When rural people begin to communicate within their community they acquire self-confidence which encourages them to articulate their own needs and those of their community.

It would be unrealistic to expect that community stations could be run by the established broadcasting organisation which caters for the population as a whole. The objectives and methods are so different that any attempt to combine the services will most certainly hinder the growth of the community stations.

These would have to be quite different from the conventional broadcasting station in India and elsewhere with its sophisticated and expensive equipment. The technology employed has to be the simplest and most economical: a low-power transmitter; one or two improvised studios, without complicated equipment; mobile, light-weight type-recorders and playback equipment; a bicycle or two to supplement public transport; a good radio receiver to receive news and programmes of entertainment to be relayed from one of the urban centres. High technical standards would have to be abandoned. Who, then, should be responsible for community radio?

The ownership and control of each station by the local community, as in the United States or Canada, may not be possible in India and other developing societies for some time because of the poverty of the people. But if local stations are to yield results, decisions on programmes and policies must be made by the listeners and the volunteers, assisted by the professional staff, while the ownership of the stations may be diversified. Such stations can be set up by any group or institution and can be licensed by the government on certain conditions. These would ensure that the station is to be used in the community's interest, that it would provided a certain amount of educational and instructive programming and so forth. A local authority, an agricultural university, a co-operative society, a band of social workers or educationists, and many other such groups of citizens could be allowed to operate community stations. At present the Government of India, like many other governments, has a monopoly of broadcasting and refuses permission to start even closed-circuit radio and television services.

The question of finance is difficult. Some funds could be obtained from advertising appropriate items of rural consumption such as bicycles, tortures, radio sets, clothing, soap, detergents, disinfectants, nutritious food stuffs, simple drugs and so forth. As the stations would help to achieve several national goals in education, health, family planning, and economic development, it would be quite appropriate for government to provide funds at least for the capital investment in transmitters and equipment. If such funds are made available through a properly constituted authority it could supervise their use. To prevent government interference in the work of the authority and of the community stations the funds would have to be allotted to the authority for several years at a time, through the Finance Commission or some such body. The authority itself should not interfere in the day-to-day working of the stations.

If the community radio station is to be a community effort the authority should not establish stations without a demand from the community and a promise of its active involvement; it can stimulate such interest and guide the efforts of the local community or suitable organisations to set up a station; it can help to obtain the required capital and the professional staff but, for the rest, it should be responsible only for the overall performance of the station which can be reviewed at the time of renewing the license.

This is looking too far in to the future. The immediate need is to encourage the starting of independent local stations wherever some individuals or organisations are capable of doing so with some financial assistance. Experiments with different kinds of control, staffing and financing should be allowed to find out which mix would be the most rewarding. All India Radio is going in for local stations—six have been sanctioned by the Planning Commission during the Sixth Plan—these should co-exist with a few independent ones until, after some years' experience, all the local stations can be brought under one authority which could then organise the extension of the service to every district in India where the people are willing to give voluntary service for their community station.

It is a question of priorities. If the Government of India is convinced that communication with the people and their willing cooperation is essential for progress and national development, the money and the equipment can be found to take radio to the people.

Finally, the relative merits of radio and TV must be assessed in respect of every programme of this type. There is a growing feeling in India and outside that radio is being neglected even for tasks it can perform as well as if not better than TV, and at considerably lower cost. Nearly 80 per cent of our population can be served by radio if an abundant number of cheap radio sets is made available. While there are already over 200 million radio receivers, we produce about two million each year. There are already 70,000 community receivers and 20,000 schools sets, too few for a country of our size but certainly far more than the TV sets and service we can expect to provide for some years to come.

A telecommunication system to serve the less developed countries effectively must be cheap and reliable and should not require highly sophisticated maintenance and operating personnel. It should function even without an elaborate infrastructure of a stable electric supply, good roads and a network of microwave cable. We have the infrastructure for radio technology; we do not have it for TV and will not have it for decades. In other developing countries TV has remained an entertainment for the rich. Experience in Algeria, Brazil and other Third World countries shows that when sophisticated technology is introduced into a static tradition-bound social environment, it does not work.

Of course, there are some things TV can do better but surely the cost factor is important for a poor country like ours. The point is that serious cost-benefit studies must be undertaken before it is decided which medium to use for any purpose.

Without attempting any such studies the Government of India has decided that TV would be more effective than radio. If 500,000 villages are to be provided with TV sets how much will it cost? Radio sets on the other hand, which cost ten times less, can be provided in every village though the proper thing to do is to reduce their cost or subsidise their sale so that private sets can spread throughout the village homes.

To provide radio programmes for village we need about 400 low-power district transmitters—all of which can be produced in India. Local TV transmitters would cost a fortune. But, say the protagonists of TV, we do not need local TV transmitters—the satellite will take TV programmes everywhere. And that brings us up against the question whether, where TV is to be used, it should be through satellite or through terrestrial stations.

Although INSAT (1A) is no longer available, INSAT (1B) has become operative from August 1983 and presumably the plans for the use of INSAT (1A) will be carried forward. In the chapter on the Growth of TV, the use of satellite technology has been discussed in general. Here its utility for broadcasts for the rural community is assessed. According to the plans announced by the Minister for Information and broadcasting, a one hour programme will be broadcast daily for a few hundred direct receiving sets which will be increased to 2,000 by the end of the 6th Plan. There would be 2,000 community viewing sets.

To begin with, the Ministry of I & B had intended to provide 1,00,000 DRS—the least required to justify the claim that the satellite would revolutionise life in the village of India but financial constraints reduced the number of 8,000 by the end of the Sixth Plan 8,000 out of 500,000 villages.

There are far more serious problems, first of all, the difficulty of providing suitable and effective programmes for rural audiences through a satellite have to be examined. Apart from experience in other parts of the world, our own SITE showed up certain glaring shortcomings of satellite communication.

Due to the extremely limited time available for TV programmes and with only two channels, the rural programmes, even for only a few villages, can only be of half-an-hour's duration per day in the language of the area. The remaining half hour is in Hindi. Hardly sufficient to sustain interest.

"Secondly, the programmes made at two or three centres at Hyderabad, Cuttack and Nagpur for six villages in six different States could not cater to the special needs of the different groups of villages. During SITE it was found that programmes prepared in Delhi in Hindi for villages in Rajasthan, Bihar and Madhya Pradesh failed to make any impact. This is because our village folk speak in dialect and not the language of the city.

Thirdly, the cost of satellite communication cannot be justified if the village audience finds the programmes irrelevant.

Fourthly, there was the difficulty of maintenance of the Direct Reception TV sets. Although the Indian Space Research Organisation was responsible for their maintenance, there were frequent breakdowns. What will the position be when the State Governments or local bodies are made responsible for the maintenance of the sets? AIR's experience of the very poor maintenance of community radio receivers, much simpler to maintain, should cause concern but such difficult questions are brushed aside in the hope that they will disappear!

And finally, programmes of local interest and relevance cannot possibly be transmitted through a satellite. The multiplicity of languages and cultural patterns makes locally relevant programming for a satisfactory duration an imperative. To say a satellite can illuminate the whole of India does not mean satisfying programmes in all languages. Only programmes centrally planned and produced can be fed to the satellite. Therefore, it has to be decided in advance how many terrestrial stations Doordarshan must necessarily have regardless of the satellite.

For all these reasons professional broadcasters consider such technology entirely unsuitable for India's communication needs. Local radio stations and possibly some local TV stations are what we require. Some students or the subject have suggested that the failure of INSAT (IA) should be turned to our advantage by using the terrestrial transmitters for local broadcasts. They also feel that the acquisition of a third satellite INSAT (1C) would be totally indefensible because in a country of India's size, a hook-up programme is about all that the satellite can provide. If government can be brought to give up its satellite mania, it would realise that low-power TV transmitters which cost less than Rs. 20 lakhs, can cover 300-500 sq kms. One Direct Reception Set (DRS) costs Rs. 30,000. One local transmitter would cost only as much as about sixty-five DRS which can serve only sixty-five villages with all the disadvantages mentioned above.

A hundred ordinary TV receivers cost about Rs. 30,00,000. So the cost of a local station serving 100 villages or so would be only Rs. 50 lakhs. Moreover, local terrestrial transmitters would enable individual homes in urban and rural areas within the range to have TV receivers of their own to pick up the programmes. It is still not too late to reconsider the question afresh.

Two things stand out in this brief review and analysis of rural broadcasting. Firstly, unless listening on radio and TV is extended to many millions more of the people who live in our rural areas the impact of rural broadcasting will be limited. Secondly, unless the programmes are made meaningful to small rural communities by dealing with their specific conditions and problems, ascertained through continuous research, they will continue to be regarded as something imposed from above and will not become a vital force in the regeneration of rural life.

TELEVISION AS AN INSTRUMENT OF SOCIAL CHANGE IN INDIA AND ABROAD

The antennas on the roof tops are increasing day by day all over the world. Today there is scarcely a country which is not utilising television with a view to achieving its cultural, social, political and economic development. TV gives information by transmitting programmes through space satellites to and from people all over the world. Media men often view TV as an electronic magic carpet, the 20th Century's creation of the technological revolution, the great instrument of persuasion, and the most powerful weapon for social change. Things which were considered as luxuries in the past have become sheer necessities today. TV is treated as their constant companion by people in advanced countries. This indicates the tremendous mark it has made on world civilization. A unique combination of commercial, political, academic and cultural programmes is the main characteristic feature of TV. The scope of TV programmes can be broadly visualised from three angles, *i.e.*, information, education and entertainment. With communication satellites the task of realising its basic functions has become much easier and the purpose more effective.

Men of many lands contributed to the development of TV. TV was made possible by electronic discoveries in the late 19th century and early 20th century. In 1884 Paul Njpkow, a German, patented a scanning disc for transmitting pictures by wireless. Charles F. Jenkins a German again began his study of the subject around 1880. The English physicist, E.E. Fournier d'Albe conducted experiments in the 1900s. In 1915, Marconi predicted "visible telephone." In 1923 physicist Vladimir Zworykin, a Russian-born American, applied for a patent on the iconoscope camera tube. In the years that followed, there were more experiments by E.F.W. Alexanderson and Philo T. Famsworth of Russia and by John L. Baird in England. An experimental TV programme was sent by wire between New York and Washington by the Bell Telephone Laboratories in 1927. The next year Bell experimentally televised outdoor programmes. The Federal Radio Commission reported that "a few" broadcast stations were experimenting with video in 1923. In the same year WGY Schenectady, N.Y., broadcast the first TV drama. A large screen TV was demonstrated by Radio Corporation of America, at a New York theater in the year 1930. Radio Corporation of America (RCA) tested outdoor TV pickup at Camden, N.J., in 1936. By 1937 there were 17 experimental TV stations operating.

Many advanced countries in the world have tried to fully utilise the potentialities of TV for their political and socio-economic development. Extensive research has been conducted to assess the impact of TV on the minds of the people. In the light of these studies, many developing countries have realised the need for a sophisticated technology like TV which could bring revolutionary changes especially among illiterate masses. Presently, many countries are utilising the satellite facility for live telecasts. Satellite communication system is effectively binding the World with its threads of sight and sound. Today, one can sit at home and simultaneously watch the events that are taking place even in very remote corners of the world. Applying space technology in the communication system is one of the world's recent developments. It strengthens the social, political and economic fabric of the world. Mere invention of technology will not accomplish the task of effective communication. Its value is decided on the way it utilised. In spite of technological development, a major portion of the population in underdeveloped countries is not fully aware of the events that are taking place, and are also deprived of effective enjoyment of their right to information. For example, a poor Indian peasant knows little or nothing about his counterpart in a foreign country. Unless this gap is bridged, development of any sort is not possible. These facts have lead to the idea of using satellites for the purpose of broadcasting. Mass communication technology accelerates the interaction among various cultures of the world. Especially in countries with high population the majority of which being illiterates, this technology can bring about certain radical and imperative changes.

Population, illiteracy and poverty are the three major problems faced by a developing country today. Television, which has shown a tremendous result in advanced countries, can be used as a major instrument in solving these problems and bring about changes in the long run. Considering these possibilities, a worldwide satellite Television experiment called SITE (Satellite Instructional Television Experiment) was initiated for the upliftment of the rural masses. In September 1969, a memorandum of understanding was signed between ISRO (Indian Space Research Organisation) and the NASA (National Aeronautical and Space Authority) of the United States of America. This memorandum lead to the development of the satellite instructional TV experiment (SITE). It is an agreement between the two countries to co-operate in undertaking an experiment in instructional Television via satellite. The USA had the responsibility of providing an application technology satellite (ATS) and placing it in orbit in such a way that it would be available to India for a whole year. India had the responsibility of production of earth stations, receiving stations, microwave transmitters—and receiving sets, of programmes for education, instruction and entertainment. The social benefit of satellite television was expected to break all barriers between nations and also to help promote an understanding among them. There is a relationship between the economic development and social change in a country. Communication plays an important role in bringing social change. Hence a country which needs to develop itself requires the assistance of communication system.

India is a developing country. Therefore, the significance of mass media in this country needs no exaggeration. It can have great impact. Government of India has been taking several steps in educating the masses and bringing awareness through modern media. A majority of our population is living in rural areas. According to the provisional totals of 1981 census, 2331 per cent of the 685 million people live in urban areas and the remaining 76.68 per cent in rural areas. While the urban population is concentrated in 4029 towns, the rural population is spread over 6.05 lakh villages (including 48,087 uninhabitated villages).

In spite of tremendous strides in urbanization, industrialization and mechanization India is still for behind in many aspects. If it has to compete with other countries of the world in economic development and overall progress, India has to start from the village level in its nation building programme. The backwardness of our rural folk chiefly lies in their poverty, innocence, ignorance, illiteracy and inhibitions. The planners desire to give them higher aspirations, with the intention of individual self-development that ultimately leads to national development. The existing formal education system is not able to cater to the needs of the present situation. Hence a medium like television should be made thoroughly extensive in its use for mass educational programmes. Here it may be questioned why TV when there are more formal institutions and other media? The major problem here is that the rural folk is too poor to engage their grown up children in long years of schooling which in their opinion fetches nothing in the end. Being ignorant of the advantages of the small family system, the poor have many children and undergo several hardships to even feed them. This may be due to the feeling that daily labour gives them daily bread and is by far the best solution to their problem. Coming to the print media, it appeals to people who can read and understand and as such it is popular only among a limited sections of the people. Next, the radio is more popular even among illiterates including women and children. Though Radio is still very popular among the villagers, the TV with its additional quality of colour vision is attracting the masses. Here it can be said that the audio and visual combination of TV is a capable medium if the programmes of rural mass education are to be meaningful. The broadcast media provides an opportunity for rural participation in their programmes. The kind of individual participation which brings the media to the masses may be more interesting way of presentation than the monotony of listening to routine talks and lectures. Then, if the broadcast media, especially the TV, is so powerful as to give our poor village rural folk individual self-recognition, then why not exploit it more fully for their own benefit?

The invention of communication satellites has given us a chance to experiment on this basis. Utilization of TV for socially purposive programmes is not limited to India alone. It was experimented even in some advanced countries also. The ATS-6 satellite in USA and Anik Satellite in Canada are used to provide programmes for isolated communities and for tribal people. The Communist countries score in promoting the widest access to media like Radio and TV. The most extensive test of TV as a vehicle of literacy teaching has been made in Italy. Illiteracy is a major obstacle for the fast growth and development of a nation. Countries like Japan and Russia have promptly recognised this as a serious problem and have taken it as a challenge to completely eradicate illiteracy in order to build up a new society. In Japan within less than 40 years of Meiji restoration the transformation of an illiterate mass into literate and enlightened people was achieved. Similarly, the Soviet Union after the Socialist revolution mobilized all the instruments of state and society for eradication of illiteracy in the shortest period of time. In the light of the experience of other countries and in of the dangers ahead by neglecting the issue, the Government of India has recognised the magnitude of the problem and accordingly formulated various schemes to educate the masses. A comparative study with other nations reveals that our efforts are not enough for the magnitude of the problem. Use of sophisticated technology like TV has already been introduced in different fields like agriculture, education etc., but, we are still far behind.

The development of a country sometimes depends on the type or system of the government it adopts. The requirements of a democratic country may differ from a communist country or a totalitarian state. Public opinion is the basis for the democratic form of government. When people are involved in the formation of the government and its policy making, an awareness of the rights and responsibilities and duties of citizens becomes the first and foremost necessity. The role of political parties and their leaders is as important as the role of citizens, for the effective functioning of a democratic society. Formal and non-formal political education that is being imparted by institutions must be supplemented by political leaders from time to time. In a democracy it is upto the elected leaders to provide an environment which makes every common man feel that he is an important citizen. A basic knowledge about politics becomes imperative when it comes to the people choosing a leader. The right understanding of the body politic helps to choose good and efficient leaders without any pressure or influence. Political education teaches what is democracy, the difference between democracy and totalitarianism, the rights and principles of democratic citizens and also the purpose of national policies. Communication researchers observed TV as a potent medium in forming public opinion and illuminating the political fabric of a nation. Describing how politicians can effectively reach the unknown voters through this channel, they say that when a particular medium is popular among the public there is little chance of their accepting a political leader who is not well-acquainted to them through that media. A politician can impress a majority of people with a TV speech than going round the comer of every village and explaining his policies.

The power of the mass media in familiarising and enhancing the personal charisma of a leader is another aspect to be considered. As Wilbur Schramm argues, in a developing country where the media are relatively scarce and the stream of the names in the news is smaller, this power of the media may be even greater than it is in economically developed countries and may provide a way to build leadership. Development of TV has facilitated many political leaders to reach millions of voters without moving from their place. It is evident from the history that they have gained access to the public through televised political campaigns. President Kennedy used live televised conferences and debates in American presidential elections. Many political observers believe that his performance in the campaign debates on TV with Richard Nixon was the decisive factor in his election to the Presidency. Subsequently, Carter and Reagan also concentrated on their TV programmes to impress the public. Considering the role of TV in political affairs, especially in a developing country where the rural population is more, the present study attempts to know the influence of TV on villagers with reference to their levels of political awareness. To convert the ignorant village folk into intelligent thinking citizens the first step should be to provide them an atmosphere of social and political awareness. Especially in a democracy where the policies of the government are the needs of the people, a basic knowledge of this system becomes necessary. To educate the mass of population in this area must naturally start with political education. This is already being done by formal institutions as well as by mass-media. In view of the effectiveness of TV when compared to other media in shaping public opinion it was intended to study the impact of television on the rural masses and the role it plays in creating political consciousness among them. Ten villages in Andhra Pradesh have been selected as the sample and the political programmes telecast over Hyderabad TV were taken to study the impact. Before proceeding to the details of the study a brief account of TV in the world as well in India and a few aspects pertaining to TV may need to be mentioned here.

Impact of Television Worldwide

At present many countries in the world are trying to project their profile through TV. In doing this, they are not only having a common medium but are also having common objectives and definite goals. Nations like Sri Lanka that have hesitated to introduce TV in the beginning are now utilizing the services of TV. However, there are countries like Tanzania which did not go for TV since it has other priorities like health and universal literacy. In 1975 UNESCO reported that 30 countries of Africa and Asia had no TV. During the past decade there was a rapid expansion of TV in the world.

An examination of the broadcasting systems in a global perspective reveals the following features:

Except in a few countries all advanced countries enjoy autonomy in broadcasting. But even while full autonomy exists, commissions and special committees restrict superfluous expression and misuse of the media. In developed countries, while a few channels are continuously engaged in educating the public, a few others orient them on matters of home and foreign policies. Regarding entertainment, a twenty-four hour up-to-date multiform service is being made available by private broadcasting corporations. In developing countries due to lack of funds and a limited channel system there is comparatively less effective transmission; non-availability of multiple channel system has over burdened the programme planners with much to do under severe limitation. As AED (Academy for Educational Development) reports, the programmes in these countries are largely imported, much of it from the United States.

The report notices a trend towards the emergence of National TV production centres such as in Egypt and Mexico which produce programmes of increasing appeal to neighbouring countries. It further states that few nations can invest the money required to produce entertaining TV programming. The appetite of TV system for new programming requires a market of many millions to finance production. Therefore, for most countries TV will continue to be an international medium with a high degree of foreign cultural influence.

The revenue for this medium comes in three ways, the licence fee, the commercial revenue and the government aid. The form of revenue varies from one country to another. Commercial advertising brings in the bulk of the income in most of the countries, except where advertizing is limited or totally banned. For example, Indonesia had discontinued commercials on its Television in 1981 after finding that they were having a destablizing effect on Indonesian society by promoting wants in the form of luxury goods and services which the common people have no means to acquire. It is observed that TV has dominated the other media in some of the countries. The circulation of newspapers, Radio listening and movie going have been heavily affected due to TV in advanced countries including Japan. The results of a comparative study done between India and Japan in 1970 are presented in Table 2.1. In Colombo a drastic drop in movie house attendance for locally produced films has been reported by the presidential committee of inquiry. According to the report the decline which began in 1980 has registered a loss of 20 million seats for Simhala films. This trend shows that TV may superceds all the other media when it becomes available to each and every person. However, the high cost of TV set may be an obstacle in this direction. Considering the fact that TV is a costly medium, it is doubtful in the first place, that the common man, a poor villager can afford to purchase himself a set and feel the desired impact of TV. With growing demand for entertainment among urban viewers, there is a possibility of programmes following a commercial pattern. It is also observed that the present day programmes are in-keeping with this trend.

Table 2.1: Comparative Study of Growth of Different Media in India and Japan

Sl. No.	*Newspaper Circulation*		*Film Audience*		*Number of Radios*		*Number of Television Sets*	
	India	*Japan*	*India*	*Japan*	*India*	*Japan*	*India*	*Japan*
1.	21.7 crores (1965)	4.4 crores (1965)	310 crores (1971)	73 crores (1946)	15.59 lakhs (1958)	57 lakhs (1945)	6.2 thousand (1962)	91 lakh (1958)
2.	29.3 crores (1970)	5.3 crores (1970)	372 crores (1975)	112.7 crores (1958)	53.99 lakhs (1965)	91.6 lakhs (1950)	37 thousand (1971)	68.6 lakhs (1961)
3.	37.4 crores (1977)	5.86 crores (1975)	420 crores (1979)	86 crores (1961)	64.84 lakhs (1966)	1.46 crores (1958)	6.77 lakhs (1977)	2.28 crores (1971)
4.		21.6 crores (1970)	2.06 crores (1979)	22 lakhs (1967)				

Note: Figures in respect of Radio subscribers of Japan are not available after 1971.
Source: Mass media in India 1980-81, Published by Ministry of Information and Broadcasting, New Delhi, 1982, p. 78.

Then why should the developing countries invest crores of rupees on this luxury entertainment when there are other immediate problems of urgent priority to be tackled? Similar doubt was expressed when Radio programmes were started in India. But now, the Radio has reached even the remotest areas of our country. This is largely due to the transistor revolution. But the cost of TV is not comparable to the transistor Radio. Due to the above facts providing TV sets to rural areas has been undertaken by the governments as a part of development of TV. For example, China could achieve progress in supplying TV sets in its programme of rural mass education.

It is evident from the above discussion that the organization of TV medium is not an easy task especially in developing countries. However, with all the difficulties TV continues to grow in all these countries including India.

History of Television in India

TV transmission started in India (1959) long before SITE was even thought of. The major aim and objective in introducing TV in India was rural development. In view of its backwardness it was intended to utilize TV for the upliftment of rural masses by creating social awareness among them. For doing this India faced, and is still facing, a unique obstacle. The uniqueness of our country's problem lies in the multilingual nature of its people. We do not have enough financial strength to counteract this problem. Though the hardware technology was readily available in the market, introduction of TV in India was not possible because of lack of trained personnel and knowledge in the software aspects and also due to the huge financial implications. In 1959 with the help of UNESCO's grant, a study was conducted in India to test the use of TV, as a medium of education, rural uplift, and community development. The result of the study conducted after an year's transmission of special educational programmes proving positive and encouraging, the next stage of educational programmes for Delhi schools was taken up in 1961. Six years later *i.e.,* in 1967 came the pilot project of agricultural communication initiated by late Dr. Vikram Sarabhai which was primarily aimed at demonstrating the effectiveness of TV as a medium for propagating improved farming practices. With the introduction of agricultural programmes a number of telecasts were organized in rural areas. Earlier from 15th August 1965 onwards, a daily one hour transmission was introduced in the evening. The second TV centre in the country was commissioned in Mumbai in 1972. The Srinagar and Amritsar centres were inaugurated in 1973 while Kolkata, Chennai and Lucknow found place on the TV map two years later, making it a network of seven centres including the relay station at Pune. In the meanwhile, at international forums on space communication, suggestions were being made for pilot project for assessing the practical uses of space communication technology. India was selected for the experiment. SITE transmissions were inaugurated on August 15, 1975 reaching 2,400 villages in the backward areas in Andhra Pradesh, Bihar, Karnataka, M.P., Orissa and Rajasthan representing a wide range of linguistic, cultural, climatic and agricultural regions of the country. The growth of TV in India was slow in the beginning. Since the necessary technology was at the stretch of the hand and due to the experience gained during SITE, the development of Indian TV was rapid after SITE.

The significant events that took place in the history of TV in India and the other information such, as number of TV transmitters etc., is as below:

Introduction of commercials in TV	:	1st January 1976
TV separated from All India Radio	:	1st April 1976
Operationalisation of INSAT (1A) and inauguration of National programmes and colour telecast	:	1st August 1982
INSAT (1A) abandoned	:	8th September 1981
Launching of INSAT (1B)	:	30 August 1983
Operationalization of INSAT (1B)	:	15th October 1983
Inauguration of 2nd Channel in Delhi	:	17th September 1984
Morning transmission inaugurated	:	23rd February 1987
News bulletins for hearing impaired	:	15th October 1987

Number of TV Transmitters

Total TV transmitters	:	221
Main centres	:	12
Relay centres	:	8
INSAT centres	:	6
HPTs/LPTs linked with Delhi	:	153
HPTs/LPTs linked with Mumbai	:	25
HPTs/LPTs linked with Hyderabad	:	17

Coverage

Total population in lakhs	:	4843 (72%)
Total area (in '000 sq. kms)	:	1519 (48%)

TV Sets: The first indigenous black and white TV receiver was produced in India in 1969. From a production level of a few thousand sets in 1970, the industry had grown to produce 3 million sets in 1986. Of this, 21,50,000 were black and white and 8,50,000 colour sets. This is expected to go upto 29.2 million by 1990 and 45.6 million by 1992.

Policy Guidelines

The Television medium is based on psychological principles. According to the mass communication theories, people take the assistance of mass-media to confirm their ideas, beliefs and convictions. The psychological effects may be positive or negative depending on the individuality of the viewer. Hence, the Ministry of Information and Broadcasting has formulated certain policy guidelines for the proper functioning of radio and TV.

Coverage to government's programmes, publicity to developmental programmes, importance to rural population programmes to eradicate social evils, balanced coverage of news and other features and coordination between different media units are some of the important guidelines. While giving free hand in its programming the policy guidelines imposed certain restrictions and also make it clear that the broadcast media has to operate very cautiously. The AIR Code, which also applies to Doordarshan, was adopted in 1968 and revised in 1970 states that Broadcasts on All India Radio by individuals will not permit:

1. Criticism of friendly countries.
2. Attack on religion or communities.

3. Anything obscene; or defamatory.
4. Incitement to violence or anything against maintenance of law and order.
5. Anything amounting to contempt of court.
6. Aspersions against the integrity of the President, Governors and Judiciary.
7. Attack on political party by name.
8. Hostile criticism of any state or the centre.
9. Anything showing disrespect to the Constitution or advocating change in the Constitution by violence; but advocating changes in a constitutional way should not be debarred.

Committees—Recommendations

The media under government's control is certain to face a lot of problems and complications. The discharge of functions may not be so efficient with limited resources and multiple restrictions. Keeping in view the possibility of probable difficulties in the functioning, the government has constituted different advisory committees under the chairmanship of eminent people and experts in the field of broadcast media. Accordingly, in 1964 the government appointed a committee on information and broadcasting under the chairmanship of Sri Ashok K. Chanda. This was the first enquiry committee appointed at the initiative of Late Smt. Indira Gandhi the then minister for Information and Broadcasting who felt that Broadcasting needed a fresh look. The Chanda Committee made three major recommendations in its report which was published in 1966. It suggested that AIR be converted into a corporation run by a Board of Governors on the BBC model: that television be separated from Radio and given a twenty-year development plan; and that the Vividh Bharati channel be commercialised and its profits ploughed back into radio for the improvement of programmes. After four years, the government rejected the first recommendation on the ground that the time was not ripe for AIR to be converted into a corporation. While Government did not prepare a long-range plan for the development of TV, it did agree that the country needed TV and that it should be expanded within the available resources. Separation was affected only a decade later. The Chanda Committee's proposal to commercialise the Vividh Bharati channel was accepted and brought into effect in 1967, though here also it took nearly ten years before the profits were actually made available to AIR. In 1978 the Verghese Committee submitted its report on autonomy. The recommendations of the above committee will be discussed under 'AUTONOMY'. With the increase in the number of transmitters all over the country, the necessity for the software development of Doordarshan has grown. So the government appointed a committee under the Chairmanship of Dr. P.C. Joshi to give recommendations on the software aspects of our television. In a report submitted in 1985 the Committee expressed doubt about the rural orientation of the present TV programming. Criticizing the commercial attitude adopted by TV, the committee advised the restructuring of its programme pattern. As observed by P.C. Chatterji, the three enquiry committee reports are comprehensive documents which have made on an average two hundred and thirty recommendations each covering almost every aspect of broadcasting. They are spaced over a period of nearly twenty years and it is remarkable that they agree on several of their recommendations.

Advisory Committees

Doordarshan gets guidance from various advisory committees consisting of eminent non-officials and experts in the field. There are eight Advisory Committees functioning for the benefit of Doordarshan which includes the Media Advisory Committee at the Centre, the Central Advisory Committee for the utilisation of INSAT, Programme Advisory Committees at the Doordarshan Kendras, Advisory Committees on various categories of programmes such as family, welfare programmes, science programme and the like. Special attention is paid to maintaining contact with agricultural universities, and in certain cases programmes are produced jointly by stations and universities. Though Doordarshan maintain contact with a large number of non-official bodies such as academic institutions, social welfare groups etc., such contacts are informal and no official procedure has been laid down for maintaining them.

Autonomy

Invention of modem technology has changed our life pattern to a great extent. The impact of modern technology on our lives has been seriously viewed by the futurologists. Along with the research and development in scientific areas, man has to follow some ethics and code of conduct for his own welfare. The full use of modern technology had to become restricted for the sake of peaceful living. This may be applicable to communication system also where the usage of modern technology is increasing day by day. History says that from the beginning the political systems have invented communication structure to meet their needs such as getting support to their policies etc. Starting from smoke signals, drummers and runners to present day television, the communication system is being utilized to get backing to the purposes and policies of the government. The exploitation of media is also observed from the beginning such as giving selected information to the people. The United Nations Commission on Human Rights has called information as one of the basic rights. One cannot deny the right to information. Knowledge has to be communicated from one person to another. But at the same time the media cannot be used without considering the evil effects. To quote Nehru "Freedom from ignorance is as essential as freedom from hunger. The mass-media which are very useful have an element of danger in them in that they may be distorted for private gain. The rich group or the rich nation can flood the country and the world through the mass-media with its own view of things which may or may not be the correct one".

The electronic media are highly powerful. Autonomy to electronic media has been under debate since broadcasting started in India. The issue has been viewed from different angles. According to the Indian Constitution Broadcasting together with Posts and Telegraphs, Telephones, Wireless and other like forms of communication are in the union list and, therefore, are the exclusive responsibility of the Union or Central Government. According to K.S. Duggal:

"When Radio was introduced in India in the late thirties the then rulers tried as far as possible to keep the radio free from political controversy. The media advisors Lionel Fielden and Ahmed Shah Bokhari have convinced their masters that once Radio loses its credibility with the listeners it would cease to have any meaning."

"When India became independent, Nehru seriously considered according of autonomy to AIR on the lines of BBC. However, he could take no concrete steps towards relaxing the control over the media. Mrs. Gandhi when she came into power as Information and Broadcasting Minister and later as Prime Minister announced that the old practice would continue. She said 'It is important that the channels should not be subject to political and economic control which could constrain the flow of information.'"

The Chanda Committee recommended among other things the setting up of two autonomous corporations for Radio and Television. This, however, was not acceptable to the government. It was argued that as the press and films were in the private sector, Radio and TV must remain with the government to build its image.

Submitting it's report on autonomy, the Verghese Committee recommended a single National Broadcast Trust instead of autonomous regional corporations or even a federation of state government corporations. There will be a large measure of power delegated to the regional and local levels, so that the organisation enjoys the advantages of quick decision-making, sensitivity to local problems, familiarity with local customs and taste, and close linkages with various governments and institutions. As K.S. Duggal further observes:

"The Verghese Committee recommended that the freedom of the Press and Broadcasting is derived from Article 19(1)(a) of the Constitution which guarantees freedom of speech and expression to every citizen. Accordingly the National Broadcasting Trust has proposed it to be a national trustee of the collective right of the Indian people to freedom of speech and expression through the broadcast media. To this end it suggested that the proposed corporation be defined as 'a corporate citizen of India' so that it might exercise and enjoy all the fundamental rights and obligations given to individual citizens.

The Prasara Bharathi bill that was introduced in Parliament by the Janata Government diluted the recommendations made by the group, while rejecting the proposed constitutional amendment altogether. With the collapse of the Janata Government, even this bill lapsed.

When the Congress (I) came into power again, one of the earliest announcements it made was that Radio and TV would continue to function as departments of government. They would however, have functional autonomy."

But many political thinkers and media experts view government's control as monopoly over the media. In this connection Ashok Mitra says that the constitution gives the centre the right to control, but not the right to monopoly over the media. In a country of India's diversities and complexities. Television and Radio offer the quickest and widest reach. The monopoly of the media is the most precious weapon which the ruling party possesses in the battle for winning the people's mind. Explaining the unsatisfactory performance of TV and the problems it has under government's control. Ramesh Thaper states that "The tasks of transformation, of building the alternative vision, are too complex for bureaucratic communication. The freeing of the electronic media will free the mind of India."

Autonomy (for broadcasting is a critical issue. In countries where illiteracy is not a problem, people can receive information through the media with objectivity. But in our country the condition is quite contrary, especially in the rural areas, which are backward in all aspects. It is easy to influence the rudimentary thoughts of the people with a powerful medium and this is the kind of exploitation that is taking place today in the fields of free press and movies. Political and business motives have dominated our free press and films giving room to perversion. Hence it is unthinkable to leave the electronic media in the hands of a vested few in the name of autonomy. At the same time free flow of correct information cannot be arrested in the name of control. A judicious method has to be identified and adopted while using this sophisticated technology. Eventhough full autonomy was given to broadcast media in some advanced countries, there is a constant check on their functioning from time to time. For example, the BBC which is considered as impartial and independent broadcasting authority is also under fire from its government. Thatcher herself has in the past publicly criticized the BBC for corrupting, the morals of the young by broadcasting too much sex and violence. Keeping the above arguments and practical implications in mind the government must formulate a policy where both the programmes of the government as also the public views are given a due place.

Economics of Television

Financing for Broadcasting is wholly made from the consolidated fund of India. The budget for AIR and Doordarshan is presented as part of the expenditure of the Ministry of Information and Broadcasting. A major portion of the revenue for television comes from the commercials. The Revenue from commercials continues to increase over the years. There is substantial increase in revenue from 77 lakhs during 1976-77 to 74 crores during 1987-88 (*i.e.,* up to October 87 only). The yearly licence fee has been abolished since March 85. Now only one time excise duty of Rs. 100 per TV set is levied at the time of purchase.

The growth of television is very high during Sixth Five Year Plan period. The expansion was so rapid that from July 84 onwards till the end of the year almost every day one transmitter was commissioned in some corner or other of the country. This shows that the expenditure was more on hardware side than on software. This fact has been recognised in the Seventh Five Year Plan and the policy makers have therefore placed greater emphasis on the development of software facilities.

Seventh Plan Schemes

An outlay of Rs. 700 crores has been approved in the Seventh Plan for the developmental schemes of Television in the country. The plan includes replacement of all black and white equipment which has completed its useful life, establishment of regular studio centres at 12 places and programme, generation facilities at 12 more places. Coupled with the proposed extension of microwave network, Doordarshan will be able to provide primary service in each state in the local language. The total number of production facilities would be 47 and the coverage would extend to 80 per cent of the population.

The long-term objective of television is that the largest number of people in the country should have access to three TV programmes.

1. The primary service in the language of the state and originating within the state.

2. The national service available on domestic receivers to all viewers in addition to the primary service.
3. The educational service which again has to be available on all domestic receivers and ultimately provide educational programmes on various subjects at primary, secondary and university levels at times convenient to the target audience and in the language in which education is being imparted in that area.

Besides the above it is also desirable that programmes for special audiences be made available but these need not be on domestic receivers nor necessarily in the language of the state.

Programme Pattern

Education, information and entertainment are the three major aims of TV programming. Sometimes entertainment is mixed with information *i.e.,* humour is used wherever possible to drive home a point. Dialogues, discussions, playlets and other folk forms like Burra Katha are use to present the programmes which involves the participation of the villagers. Music is a part and parcel of every programme. Sometimes a small beat of the drum or a flick of a string may convey much more than words. Scripts for the programmes are prepared by experts in the particular fields and presented by trained artists. As far as possible visual aspect is given importance in the programmes. Sometimes suitable pictures with commentry are substituted whenever films are not available. Though the format of the programmes on Television is fixed, it varies depending upon the occasional, seasonal and other special programmes. For example, major sports events, political conventions etc.

At present the following three types of programmes are available on TV.

(*i*) *Regional Programme*: This is transmitted in local languages from the respective programme production centres generally between 6.00 PM and 8.40 PM. These include programmes of information, education inbuilt with entertainment addressed to general and specific audiences including farmers, women, children, youth, industrial workers and others.

(*ii*) *National Programme*: A common national programme for a duration of 155 minutes between 8.40 PM and 11.15 PM on all days of the week except Saturdays when it goes upto midnight is telecast from Delhi which is carried by all the transmitters in the country. The national programme is relayed after the regional telecast. However, Chennai receives the National from 9.00 PM. This programme aims at fostering social, economic and cultural awareness, promoting the spirit of national integration and projecting the progress made by the country in various fields. Besides, two news bulletins—one in Hindi and another in English—are also telecast. Other items in the national programmes include art, music, dance and programme based on literary work in various Indian languages and important features/discussions on Current Events. Programmes of entertainment sponsored privately and produced by eminent producers are also telecast.

In addition to National programme, Network programme is also being organised on Saturday afternoons and Sunday-full day. Saturday afternoon service is mainly meant for the housewives and children. The service is on the air from 1.45 PM. On Sundays from 9.00 a.m. to 12.15 p.m. a number of sponsored serials and Doordarshan's own programmes are telecast for the entertainment of viewers. From 1.15 p.m. to 4.00 p.m. a feature film in regional language is telecast. In its Sunday network, Doordarshan has recently introduced a 15 minutes news bulletin in sign language with narration in English under the title News for the Hearing Impaired.

Morning Transmission is also being aired on the entire network for a duration of 45 minutes, starting from 7.30 a.m. Besides, two news bulletins—one each in Hindi and English—the programme includes visual presentation of 'Vande Mataram' followed by items of physical exercise and entertainment. The transmission also includes programmes like 'Money matters' providing information on the latest trends in economy. Important personalities are also interviewed.

(*iii*) *Area specific and development oriented programmes* for the INSAT clusters are telecast for a duration of 35 to 40 minutes. Programmes on National Integration and Communal Harmony are telecast both in National Network as well as by the various programme producing Kendras in the local languages. These programmes are telecast in various entertaining formats, including mushairas, quawalis, documentaries, sponsored programmes, plays and quiz programmes.

INSAT based Doordarshan Kendras make programmes in a different way. For programmes intended for rural people via satellite it conducts research in the beginning known as formative research. The plan of the programme is first given to the viewers. Opinions are called for and then the programmes are prepared. Sometimes the programmes are prepared in advance keeping in view the requirements of the viewers and the feedback is analysed.

Objectives of the Programmes

Agriculture

Programmes on agriculture, animal husbandry, forestry irrigation, cottage and small scale industries, health, hygiene and sanitation etc., of varying duration bard core items pertaining to these aspects are telecast supported by suitable visuals of film in order to promote greater agricultural production. In respect of these programmes special chunks are assigned taking into account the viewing habits of the rural audience. The entertainment aspect is not neglected. For making these programmes more palatable folk songs, folk dances, playlets and special features on festive occasions are also in the day to day programmes. Family welfare has been one of the important themes where the thrust has been for limiting the size of the family and bringing about qualitative changes in the standard of life of the people. These programmes received promotional publicity in various forms and formats. Doordarshan utilized the funds provided by the Ministry of Health and Family Welfare for the production of documentaries on the advantages of FP of varying durations and in different languages to make an impact on the people.

Special Audience Programmes

Children, adolescents, youth, women, industrial workers, intellectuals, elderly persons, and the general citizens at large—A large number of programmes keeping in view the varied interests and need of these audience groups are produced with their involvement and participation.

Music and Dance

To reflect cultural heritage, tradition and to entertain people a substantial percentage of transmission is devoted to music programmes. These include, vocal and instrumental music (classical, folk and modern).

The dances of India also find a place of pride in the Doordarshan's programmes. Folk and modern dance are also encouraged and their votaries invited to perform.

Drama

Produce and telecast drama on various social themes almost every week.

Feature Films

A number of good feature films in Hindi and other regional languages are telecast. Since TV is a family medium the suitability of films for family viewing is taken into consideration for selection of films.

Sports

Cultivation of interest in and promotion of sports has been one of the major objectives of Doordarshan.

News and Current Affairs: The aim and objective of the news and current affairs programmes telecast from Doordarshan are to widen the awareness of the people about the major events and developments within and outside the country and to deepen their understanding of current social, economic and political events and issues.

Audience Research

Doordarshan in it's approach for progressive planning relies heavily on the feedback received from the people, by way of letters, views individual or collective expressed in meetings or critical reviews made in the press. In addition, through the scientific system of surveys, audiences reactions are analysed by the Audience Research Units which are in-built in the Doordarshan organisational setup. The Audience Research Unit of All India Radio conducts over 120 field surveys and nearly 1,000 panel surveys during the course of a year. In the field surveys some 44,000 radio and TV households are contacted to assess the quantum of listening/viewing and to determine demographic and other characteristics. Doordarshan has fourteen units attached to its main Kendras and post-SITE centres. They attempt to monitor the quantitative viewing of programmes through field surveys, panel surveys, analysis of viewers' letters and the like. Some studies conducted by them have been on subjects such as the impact of TV on children, surveys on Family serials etc. The Indian Institute of Mass Communication (IIMC) functions in New Delhi as an autonomous body under the Ministry of Information and Broadcasting. Among other things it conducts studies on the impact of media on audiences. Some studies have concerned themselves with AIR/Doordarshan programmes. The two departments co-operate with the IIMC and take note of its findings. Research work has also been conducted by private organisations such as the Operations Research Group (Baroda), the Public Opinion Quarterly and some university departments of communication.

Commercial Service

Commercial service of Doordarshan was started in January 1976 from seven Kendras and later extended through more Kendras. The scheme of sponsored programmes was introduced in 1983 enabling various organizations, business houses etc., to sponsor either programmes produced by them or imported programmes or programmes produced by Doordarshan. The advertisements are telecast as per the provisions of the code for commercial advertising. The code prohibits advertising of tobacco, liquor and gambling, including betting on horse-racing and other sports. The booking of commercials, static or film spots and the sponsored programmes is done through the advertising agencies and in some cases directly by the advertisers. As a matter of policy upto 10 per cent of the total transmission duration can be utilised for commercial advertisements.

The revenues from commercials increased to Rs. 74 crores (upto October 87) from a meagre Rs. 77 lakhs in 1976-77. The steady increase in the revenues is evident from the following:

Year	*Revenue Earnings (in crores)*
1976-77	Rs. 0.77
1977-78	Rs. 2.20
1978-79	Rs. 4.97
1979-80	Rs. 6.16
1980-81	Rs. 8.09
1981-82	Rs. 11.60
1982-83	Rs. 15.89
1983-84	Rs. 19.79
1984-85	Rs. 31.43
1985-86	Rs. 60.20
1986-87	Rs. 93.31
1987-88 (Upto Oct. 87)	Rs. 74.49

International Relations

In accordance with the policy of the Government of India cultural agreements have been signed with some 20 countries which include Yugoslavia, France, USSR, Hungary and Czechoslovakia. These agreements include a section which deals with broadcasting. Exchange of programmes, co-operation in the field of technology, assistance to visiting news correspondents of other countries, and training and exchange of personnel are included in the agreements. Programme exchange has been largely confined to music but AIR and Doordarshan have also supplied scripts of plays (in English translation) to foreign organisations. There is programme exchange and co-operation in different fields, though no cultural agreement has been signed with USA. In the area of training AIR and Doordarshan have both benefited from and made considerable contributions to the Asian Institute of Broadcast Development (AIBD) in Kuala Lumpur.

Training

In service training for Television staff is provided at the Film and Television Institute of India at Pune. The Institute was set up initially for films in 1960 and a television section was added in 1974. Courses at the FTII have varied between six and four months depending on the pressure to open new TV centres.

Annual Awards for TV Programmes

Awards for TV programmes are given annually for the best programmes produced and telecast by Doordarshan during each calendar year. The aim of these awards is to promote the art of TV as a medium of communication and means of self-expression and to raise the standards of Doordarshan production. The awards are of two types: best production Awards and individual excellence Awards. Television being a central government organisation its distribution system and functioning is uniform throughout the country. Doordarshan, Hyderabad (the sample district selected is located around the city of Hyderabad) which is part and parcel of central TV network is also functioning on the similar lines as discussed earlier. However, some specific aspects about Hyderabad TV needs to be mentioned here since the same was choosen for the present study.

History of Television in Andhra Pradesh

In Andhra Pradesh, Television transmission commenced from the Capital city of Hyderabad in 1977. Earlier in 1975-76, Andhra Pradesh was one of the states which benefitted by the SITE experiment. The role played by Hyderabad TV as a part of the experiment is worth mentioning. Since the software aspects and other arrangements have to be looked after by India, every state here was fully prepared for the experiment. The SITE programme was so organized that it would be received simultaneously by 24,000 villages located in six different states in India each with its own regional language. These states were selected partly for technological reasons based upon satellite location and partly for reasons of relative economic backwardness. Approximately 400 villages were selected for SITE in each state. Rangareddy, Medak and Mahaboobnagar districts in Telangana area and Kurnool district in Rayalaseema area of Andhra Pradesh are covered under the above scheme. A Total of five hundred and fifty-five community TV sets (VHF sets) have been installed under Hyderabad Transmitter Range out of which 407 sets are installed by the Government of India and the remaining by Andhra Pradesh Government. Under INSAT direct reception scheme in Mahaboobnagar and Kurnool districts the Government of India installed 375 community TV sets. Audience (men, women and children) on a daily-average are in the range of 200-400 per community TV set. It is understood that this figure usually more than doubles on feature film days. The SITE is a historical event. For the first time a satellite has been used for transmitting TV programmes at international level. The findings of the research done after the experiment says that the rural masses of A.P. have responded with enthusiasm and motivation and in some areas people showed more interest compared to other states. The regional programmes for the evening broadcast were produced mainly at the base production centres located in 4 cites of Hyderabad, Cuttack, Ahmedabad and Delhi which took responsibility for 4 days in a week. The research and development work for hardware was done primarily at ISRO at Ahmedabad and the ECIL at Hyderabad. Three years were spent on planning by ISRO. The satellite was lifted into the space in May 1974. A few endings given in UNESCO report about Andhra Pradesh during SITE experience are worth looking before proceeding to know the structure of TV in the state.

Audience Size

A comparison of the audience size in the six clusters shows that except in the states of Andhra Pradesh and Orissa, in all other states the audience tended to decrease as the programme proceeded. However, in the states of Andhra and Madhya Pradesh the programme continued to draw a steady number of viewers. The Hyderabad programmes were broadcast in two states Andhra Pradesh and Karnataka. With regard to presentation and comprehension the most frequently occurring comment was that the programme presentation was interesting and good.

Regularity in Attendance

Between adults and children the latter were found to be more regular in attendance in Andhra Pradesh and in Madhya Pradesh. The response was highest in AP with 71 per cent return of cards and, the lowest in Bihar with only 28. The response from the other states was around 60 per cent. The above information speaks that the television impact on the villagers of Andhra Pradesh is satisfactory. With the provision of TV service all over the state recently, people of Andhra Pradesh both urban and rural are enjoying the programmes.

Area and Population

The area of A.P. is 2,75,068 sq. kms. The population of the state as per the 1981 census provisional figures is 5,35,49,673. The state has a rural population of 410.62 lakhs and urban of 124.87 lakhs—Andhra Pradesh is the fifth largest state in the country both in area and population. There are 23 districts in the state. A.P. is primarily an agricultural state.

Capital	Hyderabad
Principal languages	Telugu and Urdu
Literacy	29.94 per cent
Number of Newspapers	1071 (dailies 62)
Radio Stations	Hyderabad, Vijayawada, Vishakhapatnam Cuddapah and Adilabad.

Hyderabad Television (Upagraha Doordarshan Kendra, Hyderabad) is primarily a rural centre catering to community TV villages in the surrounding districts. It has been doing so since 1975 when the SITE programmes commenced. It was in October 1977 that Hyderabad transmitters became operational. Andhra Pradesh is the second states where in all the relay centres were linked with the regional Kendra via INSAT B. Maharashtra being the first one. Since the SITE covered only Telangana and Rayala-Seema areas the Andhra area was totally deprived of the enjoyment of TV for a long time. With the installation of transmittrers and satellite relays this deficiency was covered to some extent from 14th January 1986. The programmes that are telecast from Hyderabad are now feeded throughout A.P. The total area covered by Hyderabad Doordarshan Kendra is approximately 95,009 sq. kms. The total population covered is 254.63 lakhs, out of which 95.29 lakhs is urban population and 159.34 lakhs is rural. Andhra Pradesh like many other states is noted for diversities in culture. In addition to Telugu which is the main language, Urdu is also widely spoken especially in Telangana areas. This calls for special attention on the part of the programme makers to satisfy the needs of the programme viewers. It is very difficult to satisfy the different tastes of people at one and the same time. The massiveness of the medium poses a challenge to the broadcasters. Before trying to teach a concept through projection the programme makers attempt to create an interest for leading in the minds of the viewers. The medium has to maintain a balance between urban demand and the rural needs. Hence, the task is not an easy one in practical terms with limited technical resources, inadequate training in software aspects and financial drawbacks. An overall view of the TV was discussed hitherto with a sociological perspective. TV, like a tree, has various branches related to different subjects. Each branch needs detailed study. Political broadcasting which is concerned with the present study is one among them. This area has some background which requires special attention. The next chapter has been devoted for the main focus of the study *i.e.,* political broadcasting and the research work done in the field of political communication.

The television networks, which can sell everything from soap to automobiles to a complacent public in large quantities, have had their troubles in establishing equal acceptance for news and public affairs. A fairly convincing case can be made out against some of the elements in top management for not having tried very hard, but the same accusation can scarcely be documented against the zealots of broadcast journalism. They have tried, sometimes at excessive cost to themselves. But on the whole they have not been too successful.

The Federal Communications Commission, which is supposed to worry about such things, has scarcely been noted in its history for taking bold and forthright positions in support of the need for stronger, larger, and more independent broadcast journalism services. "Public service programming, particularly in the entertainment and news fields, is often the most expensive and the least profitable. It is not much of an excuse, particularly when it is put forward by a federal regulatory agency. Since when has public service been supposed to show a profit?

It is not lack of talent or ideas in broadcast journalism, but an almost continual carnival atmosphere on television that has caused a substantial proportion of local stations to reject some well-intentioned network news specials on major topics. There should be no surprise, consequently, over the decline during much of the 1960s in the network offerings of scheduled public affairs material. Thus, particularly in foreign affairs, the same kind of a news blackout that has existed for years in areas serviced by the purely local-minded daily press has spread to a large section of the local electronic media. Under such circumstances, a mass audience does not often have an alternative between show business and the news except for all but most of the compelling events. But in the current atmosphere of television, it takes very real journalistic statesmanship to embark on such ventures.

The Scope of Television News

True, the all-sponsored major network Monday—Friday news programmes have had wide acceptance on local stations, primarily because the early evening news has no fixed commercial competitors in most areas. However, the principal network commentators have generally been the first to concede that they are obliged to deal with bulletin-type news, supplemented by filmed reports when available, and can neither explain nor interpret for more than a minute or two at a time on a scheduled programme.

Thus, news coverage in depth is seldom possible during one of the regularly scheduled network programmes of news. For this, there is no substitute today except a good newspaper but these, too, are in short supply. Confronted with what amounts to a considerable local radio, television, and newspaper censorship of world and even national news in some parts of the nation, the serious-minded citizen who wants to keep informed has no alternative but to wait for the news magazines, a responsible Sunday newspaper, or specialized publications. And this in a nation that so often boasts it is the best-informed in the world.

It is a dangerous illusion, moreover, that the networks, for all their vast expenditures and claims of large editorial staffs, originate a great deal of their own news. Even at the time of the escalation of the Vietnam War in early 1966, when American bombers were ordered to blast North Vietnam for the first time, the indifference of the irresponsible part of the local electronic media was matched only by the supine performance of an important segment of the strongly local daily press. Six days later, the use of another Vietnam War news special was only a little better. In other words, approximately half of the network affiliates of each chain refused to break into the evening's routine entertainment (and advertising) to show the American public a vitally necessary programme. These were superior jobs by television correspondents and cameramen, covering their first war, and merited full-scale public attention instead of a selfish and self-serving local censorship.

Just as is the case with the daily press, television has its stalwarts in the area of public affairs who make up in part for the negligence of the majority. All the network news and public affairs programmes in the 1966 survey showed fewer than half such programmes that were being offered. It is clear that advertising on sponsored programmes counts for far more with many local stations, regardless of merit, than public interest on unsponsored programmes.

This was the background for the widely publicized internal argument in CBS that led to the resignation of Fred W. Friendly as president of CBS News. No mere local station was the issue here, but a great national network with a major responsibility to the public that transcended considerations of advertising and entertainment.

The new president of CBS Television, who also had been made responsible for news policy, was John A. Schneider, who had previously been a local station manager and was schooled in the value of dollars and cents. He had been interposed between the CBS top management, William S. Paley and Frank Stanton, and the volatile and dedicated Friendly. To newspaper reporters, Schneider made various explanations for curtailing the marathon coverage of the Senate hearings. "We just didn't feel it was the kind of thing to carry," he told one newspaperwoman. "Nobody's looking at it, not even housewives." Another reporter quoted Schneider as saying that the CBS-TV audience had fallen 50 per cent on two previous days, although NBC for the same programmes reported an audience of 27 million. In effect, what Schneider had decided to do was condense the whole business for showing in compact form later in the day, or in the evening.

It was undoubtedly a source of dour satisfaction that the three networks cancelled all regular entertainment programmes and commercial announcements for more than four hours of prime time on the night of June 6, 1967 to carry the United Nations Security Council debate on the six-day Middle East war. If it cost television millions of dollars in revenue, it also did much to make up for the instances of negligence that have cost the electronic media dearly in public confidence in the past. For this is what television public service is really all about and this is television's job; no other medium can bring national and world issues before a mass public with such immediacy and impact.

Public Television

The nationwide discussion of public television, which Friendly among others has helped to stimulate, undoubtedly has played a part in the willingness of network television as a whole to pay more attention to its responsibilities to the nation. It would, of course, be both uncharitable and unfair, and very probably untrue, to ascribe the motivation for the pooled United Nations coverage to such pressures on commercial television. However, it cannot help but play a part in the thinking of the principal television proprietors as they contemplate the situation in which they find themselves today.

They have control of what is without doubt the most powerful of all instruments of mass communications, properly used, and a source of income of consistently high potential because it is a business with a limited possibility for competitive entry. Unlike published material, which in theory anybody with the means and the desire can issue in the United States, the number of usable broadcasting signals that can be transmitted in any given area at a particular time is now limited; moreover, there are competing uses for the radio spectrum. Thus, while Congress under the Bill of Rights may make no law restricting the freedom of the press, it has in effect subscribed to some sharp limitations on the electronic media that have been imposed by the Federal Communications Commission. In many populous areas of the country, the number of television signals that may be decently received is restricted to as few as two or three, and sometimes only one; in other places, such as the Los Angeles area, for example, a dozen television stations are authorized.

"Although this same physical limitation and governmental restraint does not make networking... necessarily oligopolistic," the FCC has pointed out, "the economies of scale in programme distribution have conspired with the restraints on numbers of stations to produce only three national television networks and four national radio networks. While the importance of networking to radio has declined greatly since the rise of television, the networks have continued to dominate television production and distribution. This has meant that three large corporations are responsible for the bulk of the television programming which goes into American homes."

It was inevitable that such power in private hands would be challenged, particularly after a period of rising complaints against inadequate public service programming. A number of ingenious ideas were put forward, the first being the McGeorge Bundy—Fred

Friendly proposal for the Ford Foundation which would have financed non-commercial television out of the partial proceeds of a system of domestic satellites to cut the costs of commercial television. Friendly also provided the inspiration, and the Ford Foundation put up the money, for an experimental series of Sunday night programmes over National Educational Television, the Public Broadcast Laboratory, which got off to an indifferent start late in 1967. But it remained for the Carnegie Commission on Educational Television to take the big leap away from private television and propose to put the government behind what it called public television. This has since become the generic term for educational and all other forms of non-commercial television.

Conceivably, both commercial and public television may be radically altered in the foreseeable future by the swift pace of technological innovation. The growth of Cable Television (CATV), and the enormous power that it places in the hands of private operators to offer or shut out whatever programmes they wish regardless of the desires of subscribers, is one facet of television that requires constant surveillance. Another is the increase in satellite transmission with its promise of greater efficiency and scope for television as well as the prospect that it will reduce operating costs eventually. Just what the broadening of ultrahigh frequency transmission and reception will do to television can only be guesswork at this stage in its development. Beyond that lies the imponderable influence of the laser (light beam) and other techniques that are now in the laboratory stage. Certainly, the electronic media are poised on the threshold of an age of monumental change that will add immeasurably to their opportunities as well as their problems.

Toward a Better Operating Standard

What the public therefore has a right to expect from commercial as well as public television is a manifest of good intentions, not merely in the form of a single programme of public service or even a group of programmes, but an operating philosophy that puts the public interest ahead of every other consideration. It is easy to take the pledge, particularly for public television which has nothing to lose, but to carry it out faithfully is something else again. Consequently, it is heartening to find individual television stations scattered throughout the country that do not have to be prodded into the practice of public service journalism. While they are still comparatively few in number, they are creating a new standard for the electronic media—one that approaches and sometimes matches the work of a superior public service newspaper.

It is worth noting that the leaders in local television are trying to move into the area so long pre-empted by the press. Moreover, they are doing it for the most part with skill, spirit, and courage. But just as the laggards in the daily press trade on the reputations of their public-spirited leaders, the even larger number of commercially minded electronic managers merely cheer the pace-setters but do as little as possible themselves.

The responsible ones of television, conscious of the increasingly critical attitude of the better educated segment of the population, know perfectly well what is wrong. Dick Pinkham, of the Ted Bates Advertising Agency, argues that the direction and thrust of television programmes—including news and public affairs—have been outside the mainstream of American society for a considerable time. "We are, after all, an increasingly educated nation," he said. "And yet, television—in the direction it is going now with programmes like 'Batman'—is exactly counter to this." An even more obvious ailment has been diagnosed as follows by Howard K. Smith, the ABC news commentator:

"Balancing each thought or statement with its opposite is the order of the day. If you find a man who says the world is round, you'd better find a man who says the world is flat." There is no hope for television in a sterile objectivity; long ago, the better newspapers decided that a basic honesty and a devotion to the "on the other hand" objectivity are not necessarily synonymous.

Television's problem with the top level of its audience was summed up as follows by Senator Robert F. Kennedy of New York in a taped interview with David Susskind:

Q. Do you watch television very much?

A. No, I don't.

Q. That's discouraging. The evening programmes aside from news and public affairs—do you have any appetite for that at all?

A. No, not really. I don't watch it. I don't think I really watch it hardly at all.

Q. Well, is that because you find it not worth to watch?

A. Well, the times I've watched it. I thought it was awfully boring, so I didn't watch it any more.

Q. Do your children watch it very much?

A. I think the ones that are getting older watch it less. They started to watch it and then I think they're getting bored with it, too.

But the political uses of television, like its undoubted power as an advertising medium, can scarcely excuse the generally lack-luster quality of many of its programmes and its failings in the general area of news and public service. Of course, there are first-rate institutional sponsors like Hallmark cards, Xerox. Others who insist on quality when they can get it, as do the networks themselves. But years after Newton N. Minow's devastating criticism of much of television as a "vast wasteland," the term is still generally applicable.

Minow said "You will see," a procession of game shows, violence, audience participation shows, formula comedies about totally unbelievable families, blood and thunder, mayhem, violence, sadism, murder, Western badmen, Western goodmen, private eyes, gangsters, more violence and cartoons. And endlessly, commercials—many screaming, cajoling and offending. And most of all, boredom. True, you will see a few things you will enjoy. But they will be very, very few. And if you think I exaggerate, try it".

Few among the proprietors of television have paid much attention to Minow and their other critics. One of the latest trends is a tendency to increase the number of advertising spots in nighttime television in order to boost revenues. With the cost of network television programmes estimated at a low of about $100,000 an hour for production alone, the supposed justification is obvious. For example, NBC has increased the number of spot commercial announcements in its feature-length films from 14 to 16. It may not seem like much until a little elementary calculation shows that the cost of each spot to advertisers is $57,000, which means an increase in gross revenue of $228,000 a week or more than $11.8 million a year for a single network. And the end is not yet.

Station breaks may be extended, second by second, and still other ingenious ways may be found to crowd in additional advertising. Rising expenses, of course, add to the pressure for more revenue, but the increasing investment of the television companies in diversified interests creates the impression that cost is neither the only reason nor even the main reason for expanded advertising content.

Conflicts of Interest

No sensible person will argue that television companies should not diversify; nor can it be contended that newspapers or news magazines should have no outside financial interests whatever. That is flying in the face of reality. What does matter very much, however, is that any proprietor who deals in news and opinion must realize his outside investments will be carefully scrutinized by a discerning public to determine if they are influencing the quality or presentation of his news. The big objection to government operation of, or substantial power over, the news media is precisely the fear that it will slant, twist, or directly change the quality of news reporting to suit its own ends. The danger is no less grave in the privately operated news media when proprietors, either innocently or willfully, let their financial interests sway their responsibilities to the public.

In the diversification process in television, some very large questions have been raised over the sponsorship within the electronic media of various amateur and professional sports, particularly big money football. The practice of having-sports announcers paid by sponsoring television interests has also led to considerable criticism, as has the television "time out" to permit the insertion, of. But it is part of a pattern that has scarcely added to the stature of television.

If public suspicions of journalistic probity are thus confirmed in so seemingly innocent a field as sports, the work of television in the far more complicated areas of labor relations, civil rights, national affairs, and foreign policy is also likely to be questioned from time to time. It is no answer to point to polls that show the particular respondents are impressed by the basic fairness of television in covering the news, presumably, they are a part of the audience that can also be sold cigarettes in ever larger quantities despite the federally imposed warnings that are stamped on each package. Moreover, it should never be forgotten that the pressures for regulating news that arise within journalism are very small compared to the tremendous influence that is so often brought to bear from outside the profession.

There is still another source of difficulty in television's handling of the news that is somewhat more common to the news media as a whole. These are the cases of conflict of interest, which very often differ in intent from the rather pitiable efforts to promote rather than report sports. A Wolper production entitled "Wall Street: Where The Money Is" shows the embarrassment that can result in television, even when those involved are people of unquestioned integrity.

In defense of the networks, it may be said in such cases that they are doing no more—and probably not really as much—as the newspaper that puts out a special section for an advertiser and stuffs it with editorial matter about the company's interests. However, the ills that newspapers have developed over two centuries can scarcely justify the practices that have been adapted to television in a little more than two decades. Both the special puff section and the puff documentary are commercial ventures, undertaken primarily to benefit an advertiser, and are morally indefensible as journalism.

TV and Editorial Opinion

The electronic media, however, have done something more than merely pick up bad habits from their older contemporaries. As a primary force in the development of public service, the slow and careful evolution of editorialization in broadcast journalism provides the basis for hope and promise of better things to come. For example, the editorial leadership of WMCA Radio in New York as a champion of such causes as better housing and legislative reapportionment has been outstanding. Stimson Bullitt, operator of several Pacific Northwest television stations, did not hesitate to broadcast editorial criticism of the conduct of the Vietnam War when he thought it justified.

This is still just a trend and not a movement, for the broadcast editorialist has many built-in handicaps that do not affect his associates in print. While the FCC encourages the broadcast of opinion in theory, it actually inhibits such work in practice under the equal opportunities provision of Section 315 of the Communications Act. What this means, in effect, is that time must be given to opposing opinions if a station takes an editorial position that arouses controversy. Consequently, at regular intervals, any station with strong editorial opinions has no choice but to provide time for rebuttal, whether the opposition is qualified or not.

In recognition of this troublesome situation. Congress partially suspended Section 315 in the 1960 Presidential campaign but only 62 stations broadcast editorials for or against candidates. In the next national election, in 1962, the total rose to 148 and it has been slowly increasing since despite the continual threat that someone will have to be granted equal time for response. The FCC in effect has held to its position "that licensees devote a reasonable percentage of their broadcasting time to the discussion of public issues of interest in the community... and that such programmes be designed so that the public has a reasonable opportunity to hear different opposing positions on the public issues of interest and importance to the community."

Without doubt there is wisdom in the continued insistence on time for rebuttal in the electronic media, where the power to influence public opinion may be more easily abused than in the press. But what constitutes a "reasonable opportunity" is something that defies precise definition. This is the heart of the controversy over Section 315 and it is not likely to be settled very quickly. It does not excuse the sanctimonious TV editorial, picked up from a spineless section of the press, that comes out four-square against dope addicts, prostitution, and crime, and celebrates the virtues of home, mother, and the flag. But it also scarcely justifies a position of neutrality in broadcast journalism toward the issues of the day. The licensing authority of the FCC is, of course, a constant threat to the freedom of expression of the electronic media in cases involving the interest of the government, but it should not be permitted to cow" the broadcast journalist into abject silence when the public interest is involved.

Radio, which exerted a tremendous influence on American public opinion during the campaign for intervention preceding World War II, may well do as much as television—and perhaps even more—in developing the potential of the electronic media for broadcasting news and opinion. The FCC rule, which requires commonly owned AM and FM stations in large cities to offer different programmes at least 50 per cent of the broadcast day, places more pressure on radio to delve into public service journalism on both the fact-finding and opinion levels. In addition, despite the boredom of the "grind" all-day news programmes of some of the pioneering radio stations, it has proved a ready source for the dissemination of news in capsule form. The steady training of radio news staffs and the efforts of editors to diversify the news "grind" have yielded some improvements, though not many. For as long as proprietors and advertisers are willing to support the "all news" station experiment, it is bound to be a laboratory for the trial of all manner of electronic innovations in public service journalism. The pity is that so few of the "all news" stations are trying to grasp the opportunity.

Neither radio nor television is consigned indefinitely to a diet of news and entertainment geared for the most part to the lowest intelligence. The strength of broadcast journalism is growing in the United States. The need for it is demonstrable. What remains to be supplied is the determination to broaden and deepen current practice, particularly among local stations in television, and provide the public at all times with the news, opinion, and relevant background it must have if self-government is to be anything more than a carefully nurtured delusion in the United States.

TELEVISION AND VIDEO FLOW INTO INDIA

Background

The main purpose of conducting the studies of international television flows is the assumption that these flows imply cultural and economic effects on countries, regions or groups of viewers (Sepstrup, 1990). Several terms like 'international,' 'transnational' 'internationalisation' and 'transnationalisation' are used by different researchers. The terms are often used interchangeably and without being defined properly. Mowlana's (1984) definition as quoted by Sepstrup (1990), 'International flow of information is defined here as the movement of message across national boundaries between and among two or more national and cultural systems' is favoured by the author.

Channels of Flow

The international flow of "supply" of foreign television programmes is possible in three different ways:

1. Imported programmes shown over the national television network, e.g. Doordarshan telecasting 'I Love Lucky' or 'The Vanity Fair' or the Agatha Christie serials.
2. Foreign programmes telecast through foreign satellites and beamed towards a specific country or countries, e.g. programme of STAR TV and CNN seen in India.
3. Foreign programmes seen in a country because of 'spillover' in the neighbouring country, e.g., Pakistan or Bangladesh television programmes seen in some parts of India or vice versa.

This 'supply' is a necessary condition for viewing the programmes, but it is not a sufficient condition for 'consumption' of these programmes. The term 'consumption' refers to the actual viewing of the supplies programmes by the viewers. The viewing behaviour is dependent on several factors other than the supply of the availability of the programmes. Whether the 'supply' and 'consumption' have a social, cultural or political impact is a more interesting issue but is a 'second' level study. The 'first' level study is to empirically find out the extent of international programme supply, the pattern of supply, the channels of supply and the consumption thereof. This is tedious, less 'glamorous' out necessary step before studying the 'substantial' effects of the 'second' level (Sepstrup, 1990). This paper focuses only on the 'first' level.

International TV and Video Flow Study

It is in the light of this background that a study of the international flow of television programmes was conducted in four Asia-Pacific countries. A similar study was earlier conducted in Western Europe. The study used a common research agenda and a common strategy. It covered three aspects:

- Television landscape—Viewers' actual and technical access to content and households' access to television sets/programmes.
- Programme supply—analysis of programmes actually transmitted in terms of duration, classification of programmes according to subject/format, proportion of national and foreign programmes transmitted per day per channel.
- Programme consumption—analysis of programmes actually viewed in terms of duration, subject/format/national vs. foreign programmes by age, education, sex and the level of urbanisation.

Television Landscape

The experimental transmission of television programmes in India started in 1959. In 1975-76 India conducted the Satellite Instructional Television Experiment (SITE), the world's largest techno-social experiment in direct satellite broadcasting. However, the expansion of television continued to be slow and halting till 1982. A phenomenal growth in the number of both television sets and television viewers was observed thereafter (see Table 2.2 and Table 2.3). The major reason for this was the operationalisation of India's INSAT system.

Table 2.2: Percentage Expansion of Doordarshan Area and Population Covered between 1959-91

Year	*Area in sq. kms*	*Total no. of transmitters*	*Percentage Expansion*	*Population covered in Millions*
1959-1964	14,300	1	0	10.0
1964-1969	14,300	1	0	10.0
1969-1974	37,700	5	400	25.9
1974-1979	1,60,400	16	225	118.8
1979-1984	4,71,000	180	1,025	348.6
1984-1991	18,70,000	523	290	663.0

Note: Data are taken at mid-points of the year.
The percentage growth has been calculated using the previous year's figure as a base.

Source: Modified from the earlier table of Agrawal (1987: 3).

Table 2.3: Decennial Distribution of Television Sets in India between 1962-1992

Sl. No.	*Year*	*Total Television Sets**
1.	1962	41
2.	1972	84,114
3.	1982	20,95,537
4.	1992	3,00,00,000

* Figure upto 1984 are based on the actual licences issued by Post and Telegraph Department. Thereafter the system of licensing has been abolished. Rest are estimated figures.

Source: Television India 1991 (1991: 36).

The growth was phenomenal in terms of the absolute number as well as the rate of growth. However, it is small in terms of the percentage of the total population having access to television sets. Only about 20 per cent of India's population has actual access to television. Compared to the other three countries included in the study, India was poorest in terms of access provided (see Table 2.4). Ninety-nine per cent or more households in Australia and South Korea had access to television; in the Philippines 51 per cent of the households had access.

Table 2.4: Description of Countries According to Population and TV Households

Country	*Total Population*		*Total TV Household*	
	Household	*Persons*	*Household*	*Persons*
Australia	53,43,000	1,72,10,800	52,89,570 (99% of total)	1,70,38,692 (99% of total)
India	17,00,00,000	84,39,30,861	3,40,00,000 (20% of total)	17,00,00,000 (20% of total)
Philippines	1,07,73,300	6,14,39,000	54,94,383 (51% of total)	3,13,33,890 (51% of total)
Korea	1,13,57,160	4,35,20,000	1,13,54,80 (99% of total)	4,34,76,480 (99% of total)

Source: Based on A Survey of Transnationalisation of Television in Four Asian Countries, Goonasekera (1992).

A more recent phenomenon has changed the television landscape of the country both qualitatively and quantitatively. There has been a spurt in satellite-based international television transmission. It began with the CNN channel telecasting during the 1990 Gulf War. But it really grew at a remarkable rate with the launch of STAR TV. The Hong Kong based STAR television—giving 24 hour television fare of five channels, in addition to the limited duration Hindi service channel—has been the most noticeable development in recent times. It is estimated that 400,000 Indian households are already hooked on to STAR TV (*Times of India*, February 21, 1992).

The spread of Video Cassette Recorders (VCRs) in India has also been significant. Binod C. Agrawal (1989) estimated that there were about two million VCRs in the country. The number has gone up significantly since then. It is estimated that two per cent of Indian households have a VCR. But the actual access to the video programmes is much greater, due to the prevalence of 'cable television.' The term cable television in India means distribution of video programmes from a centrally located VCR in a residential complex.

The same 'cable television's is now used for the distribution of television programmes received directly from satellites through a dish antenna. The channel selection very often rests not with the subscriber but with the cable operator who controls the centrally-operated dish antenna and VCR. There has been a manifold increase in the number of dish antenna and cable television subscribers but the precise number is not known. In a small sample survey, S.R. Joshi (1991) found that out of 54 television viewing households in Ahmedabad 14 subscribed to cable television, while none of the 54 rural households in two villages near Ahmedabad subscribed to cable television. In another nation-wide study S.R. Joshi and K.M. Parma (1992) found that out of 483 respondents 59 respondents subscribed to cable television and that all of them resided in metropolitan or urban areas. In short, one can say that, in spite of a substantial growth in the number of television sets and cable subscribers, a large majority of India's population does not have access to television and that the dish or cable television is largely an urban semi-urban phenomenon.

Television Programme Supply

The mode of programme transmission in India is different from that of the other countries have multiple channels and very often there are specialised channels. For example, there is an entertainment channel a music channel, a sports channel, a new and current affairs channel and so on. In India, there are only two channels, both managed by Doordarshan. The 'second' channel is restricted to the four metros. The 'first' channel is the primary channel in the sense that it is a nation-wide channel. This channel is utilised for different purposes of a time-sharing basis. The same channel is used for local, regional and national transmission and for entertainment, new education/sports, etc., all on a time-sharing basis.

Since the four countries differed in the number of channels, the data were normalised on the basis of minutes transmitted per day per channel to make cross-country comparison possible. Data regarding the programmes actually transmitted were gathered for two randomly selected two-week periods—that is, for 28 days of transmission. The data were analysed to see, among other things, the proportion of national to foreign programmes. A programme was defined as 'foreign programme' when it originated in a foreign country and it was transmitted without any change in its content of video or audio. Table 2.5 shows that over 90 per cent of the programmes transmitted by Doordarshan were Indian programmes. The Indian situation was very similar to the Korean one but it was very different from the situation in Australia and the Philippines, where the foreign programme component was 54 per cent and 67 per cent respectively.

Table 2.6 gives the breakup of national and foreign programmes in the different countries according to UNESCO-defined programme categories. An earlier UNESCO study conducted in Europe had shown that the drama/movie programme category totally dominated the foreign programmes shown on national television. The situation is

Table 2.5: Internationalisation of National Programme Supply (Per Day Per Channel)

Country	*Australia*		*India*		*Philippines*		*Korea*	
	Minutes	*%*	*Minutes*	*%*	*Minutes*	*%*	*Minutes*	*%*
Domestic Supply	549	46	722	91.7	634	67.3	687	91.1
Foreign Supply	649	54	65	8.3	311	32.7	67	8.9
Total Supply	1198	100	787	100	945	100	754	100

Source: Based on Survey of Transnationalisation of Television in Four Asian Countries, Goonasekera (1992).

somewhat different in the Asia-Pacific countries. In Australia and South Korea drama and movies dominate, with 66.8 per cent and 51.3 per cent of foreign programme respectively. In India the figure is 31.1 per cent and in the Philippines it is 44.3 per cent, sports (54.9%) and educational programmes (0.9%) are the other two categories with significant foreign programme inputs. While making comparisons between different countries one should keep in mind than the total component of foreign programmes varied a great deal. It was less than nine per cent in India and Korea, but it was more than 50 per cent in Australia and Philippines.

Table 2.6: National Supply, Foreign Supply, Total Supply on National Channel by Programme Categories

Programme Category	*Australia*			*India*			*Philippines*			*Korea*		
	Nat. %	*For.* %	*Total* %	*Nat.* %	*For.* %	*Total* %	*Nat.* %	*For.* %	*Total* %	*Nat.* %	*For.* %	*Total* %
Dramamovies	8.2	66.8	40	24.9	31.1	25.4	22.2	44.3	29.4	12.5	51.3	15.8
Light Enter	22.3	13.4	17.5	2.2	0.0	2.0	26.0	26.0	25.9	14.3	21.2	14.9
Music	10.4	0.9	5.5	9.9	0.0	9.1	3.5	5.4	4.1	0.7	0.0	0.7
Sports	16.5	3.5	9.5	9.2	54.9	13.0	6.4	1.4	4.8	12.0	1.5	11.1
News	8.9	5.5	7.1	14.6	0.0	13.4	10.5	2.0	8.0	16.8	6.0	15.9
Information	21.2	0.0	9.7	20.1	3.1	18.7	11.9	10.2	11.2	27.9	2.4	25.6
Arts	3.2	0.7	1.9	0.7	0.0	0.6	0.3	3.0	1.1	3.2	17.6	4.5
Education	7.6	9.0	8.4	12.9	10.9	12.7	5.1	0.6	3.6	12.1	0.0	11.0
Religious	1.5	0.0	0.7	0.0	0.0	0.0	10.6	7.5	9.6	0.2	0.0	0.2
Others	0.0	0.0	0.0	5.5	0.0	5.1	3.1	0.0	2.3	0.4	0.0	0.4
Total (%)	100	100	100	100	100	100	100	100	100	100	100	100
PR Channel	549	787	1198	722	65	787	634	311	945	687	67	754
All Channels	2745	3245	5990	722	65	787	3170	1555	4725	3433	335	3768

Source: Based on A Survey of Transnationalisation of Television in Four Asian Countries, Goonasekera (1992).

It is clear that the proportion of foreign programmes supply in India has been very small. However, one should remember that when this study was conducted, STAR TV had barely made its entry through the Indian sky and there was hardly the proliferation of dish antennae that one sees today. The study was primarily based on Doordarshan supply since that was practically the only source of programme supply. The situation has definitely changed today.

Programme Consumption

The pattern of consumption of the programmes also varies from country to country. Table 2.7 gives the country-wise break up. It is lowest in India (1.9 %). It may be recalled that while the supply of foreign programmes was almost the same in India and South Korea, the consumption was much higher in South Korea (11.7 %). But in Australia and Philippines, where more than half the programme supply was foreign, more than one-third of the programmes consumed were foreign programmes.

Table 2.7: Internationalisation of Consumption of National Programme Supply (Per Person Per Day)

Country	*Australia*		*India*		*Philippines*		*Korea*	
	Minutes	%	*Minutes*	%	*Minutes*	%	*Minutes*	%
Domestic	108	62.9	87	98.1	62	60.8	132	88.3
Foreign	66	37.1	2	1.9	40	39.2	18	11.7
Total Consumption	178	100	89	100	102	100	150	100

Source: Based on A Survey of Transnationalisation of Television in Four Asian Countries, Goonasekera (1992).

The consumption of foreign programmes varies according to sex age, education and the level of urbanisation of the viewers. If one were to draw the profile of the Indian viewer who watches more foreign in programmes, the profile would be that of a young, educated, male residing in a metropolitan area. The consumption of foreign programmes is almost negligible amongst children, females and those residing in rural areas and those having minimal education. Language ability seems to be playing an important role in determining whether a person would watch a foreign programme or not.

Table 2.8 indicates that in India, the maximum consumption of foreign programmes falls in the category of sports and the rest is equally distributed in drama, light entertainment and information-related programmes. It is of interest to note that while a little over 10 per cent of the total foreign programmes supplied consisted of educational programmes, there is no consumption of the same. The pattern for consumption of national programmes was quite different. The maximum consumption fell in the drama/ movies category followed by news and music programmes.

Table 2.8: Internationalisation of Total Consumption of National Programme Supply by 10 Programme Categories (Per Person Per Day)

Programme Category	*Natioinal*	*Foreign*	*Total Consumption*	*As % of Programme Category*
1. Drama/Movie	67.8	8.3	66.6	0.2
2. Light Enter.	2.1	8.3	2.3	7.1
3. Music	11.3	0.0	11.1	0.0
4. Sports	1.3	75.0	2.7	52.9

5. News	12.5	0.0	12.3	0.0
6. Information	3.9	8.3	4.0	4.0
7. Arts	0.8	0.0	0.0	0.0
8. Education	0.2	0.0	0.0	0.0
9. Religious	0.0	0.0	0.0	0.0
10. Others	0.0	0.0	0.0	0.0
Total	100	100	100	1.9
Total Minutes	87	2	89	*

Note: NAT= National Origin FOR = Foreign Origin
Foreign as % of Total = Foreign Origin Consumption Minutes/Total Consumption Minutes (For One Programme Category)

Source: Based on A Survey of Transnationalisation of Television in Four Asian Countries, Goonasekera (1992).

Coefficient of Utilisation

Table 2.9 presents data on coefficients of utilisation of programmes in different countries. The coefficient is calculated according to the following formula:

$$\text{Coefficient} = \frac{\text{Consumption per person per day}}{\text{Supply of all channels per day}} \times 100$$

Table 2.9: Coefficients of Utilisation of National Programme Supply

Origin	*Australia* %	*India* %	*Philippines* %	*Korea* %
Domestic	3.9	12.0	1.9	3.8
Foreign	2.0	3.1	2.6	5.4
Total Supply	3.0	11.3	2.2	4.0

Formula coefficient (Consumption per person per day/supply all channels per day)

Source: Based on A Survey of Transnationalisation of Television in Four Asian Countries, Goonasekera (1992).

The coefficient is the ratio of supply to consumption stated in percentage terms. It was seen that India had the highest coefficient of utilisation. It was also observed that the coefficient of utilisation was much higher for Indian programmes as compared to the foreign programmes. It was observed that in India the highest coefficient of utilisation was in the category of information (7.1 %) followed by sports (3.6 %).

Analysis of cable television and video programme viewing also indicated that there was very little viewing of foreign programmes in India. As mentioned earlier, out of 483 respondents, only 59 respondents subscribed to cable television and all of them resided in the metropolitan or urban areas. These 59 respondents reported viewing of 153 programmes in a one week period. Of these, 57 programmes (37.2 %) were foreign programme, mostly transmitted through foreign satellites. Significantly, out of 483 respondents, only 22 or 4.55 per cent respondents watched these foreign programmes. The most predominant use of cable television was to watch Indian movies or other film-based programmes.

Conclusions

While the number of television sets has increased enormously in the last 10 years, there is still a long way to go for providing the Indian population with access to television. At present only 20 per cent of households in India has access to television.

- Indian television shows a very small percentage of foreign programmes and the consumption of foreign programmes is also very low.
- The use of foreign satellites is mainly restricted to upper middle class, young, educated persons residing in urban or metropolitan areas. However, the situation appears to be changing fast.
- The main use of television as well as cable television is entertainment. However, there is also a significant use of television for news and information.
- The coefficient of utilisation is highest in India.

A great deal of anxiety is often expressed about the onslaught of foreign satellites and programmes. The anxiety is about the cultural, social, political and economic impact of these. There is also the anxiety that viewers will be lured away from Doordarshan. My view is that there is no reason to take a negative or pessimistic view of the situation. There are certain technological developments which cannot be wished away. There is no reason to believe that Indians will mainly view foreign programmes. On the contrary, many foreign satellite channels, like Zee TV and ATN have started showing Indian programmes. This will only mean more Indian programmes, even if they are on a foreign satellite channel. Competition will increase, foreign programmes will be watched, but most Indians will continue to watch Indian programmes.

The Crucial Question

Since the Sixth Plan there is a definite move on the part of the government to give higher funding to the Communication Sector. Now the question arises whether in its enthusiasm to expand the communication network, there has been a reshuffling of priorities by the government. Has the higher allocation, to this sector been achieved at the cost of other basic sectors, such as health, education, water and sanitation? The fundamental issue is whether the government is morally justified in diverting huge funds to the communication sector in the face of growing poverty in the country. The Seventh Plan clearly states that over 300 million people in India live below the poverty line. It is a sad irony that over Rs. 12,000 crores have been earmarked to develop a network, which benefits less than 25 per cent of the population, thus depriving hundreds of millions of people of their basic right to food, clothing and shelter. (Media Development, 1989).

STRATEGY FOR MAKING VIDEO PROGRAMME PACKAGES

Television holds tremendous potential as a means of educating and making the viewers conscientious about problems pertaining to their own health, in particular, and the environmental wholesomeness, in general. It is pertinent to recognise, however, that health and nutrition, important ingredients of life as they are, cannot be looked at in isolation from the socio-cultural and economic aspects of the human populace, urban and rural, both. Dealing with health problems piecemeal, devoid of the interacting process of life, minimises, the effectiveness of such programmes in generating a positive, rationalistic and scientific attitude towards solving these problems. Such a fragmentary approach becomes a dilutory effort leading to vague generalities, inconsequential in mobilising the viewers to desired action.

Before starting with the more concrete process of producing these programmes, it is important to arrive at a more in-depth analysis and understanding of the interlinkages in human affairs as well as the underlying causes at the root of diseases, both social and physiological in nature. Consequential upon a whole lot of factors, the changes (subtle and obvious) that have occurred in the social situation in as far as the lifestyle, level of consciousness and value systems of the people are concerned, require to be studied to enable use to view and deal with these issues in a wider perspective. The technological developments, more specifically in the area of medicine and surgery, the effects and influences they have on the well-being or otherwise of the people, cannot be ignored. The potentials and limitations of the on-going medical systems, availability of an accessibility to the resources of care and good health for the average population, are other factors that need to be pondered over and taken into account. The ever-increasing gap between the growing infrastructural facility on the one side and constantly multiplying numbers that need them on the other, makes in imperative to arrive at alternatives that can help maintain a reasonable balance between the two.

Besides, the commercialisation of medical system renders the proper use of such facilities beyond the means and reach of the larger chunk of our population. The culture of over-dependence on the modern and more sophisticated techniques of medical process have almost wiped out the localised systems of curing—even the most common and conventionally manageable ailments; notwithstanding the hazards of potentially dangerous drugs when used more frequently and without proper medical guidance and supervision. In such a state of affairs identifying the local resources and means, educating the viewers regarding the advantages of preventive measures, emphasising the need for proper nutrition and planned family size, and demonstrating the possibilities of domestic cure, can lessen dependence on outside assistance and supplies, and go a long way in providing answers to the general health problems of the people who themselves happen to be the most valuable resource for their own health.

With this backdrop we may now proceed to work out a strategy for preparing video-programme packages—both for transmission as well as non-transmission use.

Scope and Objectives

The general objectives of such a programme-package should be to:

(*i*) Sensitise the viewers towards the problems and needs pertaining to their health, nutrition, family size and their inter-relationship with the environmental realities—with a view to generate a more scientific and rationalistic attitude and approach in dealing with these problems (both immediate as well as long-term) and finding practically manageable solutions to tackle them effectively.

(*ii*) Stressing on self-help as one of the best ways to good health and helping the viewers to develop a sense of collectiveness and responsibility towards one another and encouraging them to be involved in the decisions about health.

The specific objectives would be as under:

(*i*) To apprise the viewers about the hazards of over-dependence and blind faith in any of the prevailing medical systems, emphasising the damage that indiscriminate use of drugs can do.

(*ii*) To sensitise the viewers about the environmental influences on their health, and the need for a clean and healthy environment.

(*iii*) To demonstrate the positive advantages of preventive measures as well as suggesting simple and effective means of coping with common, symptomatic ailments like diarrhoea, cold, indigestion etc.

(*iv*) Giving the viewers skills to promote good health and to treat minor illness and injuries by themselves.

(*v*) To make the viewers conscious about the maladies of mal-nutrition and unhygienic diet and suggest a more balanced diet system, possible within the average income-status.

(*vi*) To educate the audience about the possible ill-effects of some of the taboos and superstitions pertaining to prenatal as well as post-natal problems among women and also the process of child-rearing (this shall be done in such a manner that their deep-rooted cultural feelings do not get hurt) and suggest scientific means of dealing with these issues.

Note: It may be emphasised that children and women shall form the core attention-group in as far as the priorities in the selection of diseases and problems as also some practically possible suggestions regarding health and well being, are concerned.

The Pedagogical and Communications Approach

In order to attain the set objectives to the optimum possible level, we may adopt what can be termed as the integrated approach.

The integrated approach is the total approach, wherein the varied aspects of life that influence the human situation, are taken into account. "Too often health professionals and governments have tried to tell the people what was wrong, rather than encouraging the people to be involved in the decisions about health" (Lowell Levin, *World Health*).

On the media side, our experience shows that when it comes to making health programmes, it is generally the diseases, their symptoms, their causes and effects, possible remedies and preventive measures, that are taken up. Such single-slot disease centred approach does perhaps have its meaning, but it only scratches the surface. While the need for specific and detailed information cannot be overemphasised, by itself it does not suffice the cognitive requirements of the viewers in as far as their active involvement is concerned. The disease lies much deeper.

"There are social causes for much sickness and death, not just biological ones" (Lowell Levin). Focus on symptomatic aspects of diseases keep the human element in the background, reducing it to the secondary status, which in effect alienates the viewers from their problems. The viewer response to such programmes is only casual. While they gain information, the will to take to new ideas, and apply the acquired knowledge in practice is not sufficiently stimulated. The gains as opposed to media efforts made as such are only peripheral. Not without reasons though. The practical difficulties of treading on non-conventional paths are manifold and it becomes easier to stick to tested routes, however, inadequate they might be.

While it becomes necessary to evoke the need for change, it is equally important to work out the modalities for such desired change within the framework of real situations as they exist, the pre-occupations of the people that are being addressed, and practically of the suggestions put forward through these programmes. Some of the traditional values that are detrimental to development and change have to be cautiously and carefully questioned, taking the sensitivities of the viewers pertaining to their beliefs and customs into full cognisance. The approach should be such as can generate confidence among the viewers inasfar as their personal security (physical as well as psychological) *vis-à-vis* the subject-matter and presentation of these programmes is concerned.

Emphasising self-dependence and help, should form the main thrust inasfar as the pedagogical aspects of these programmes are concerned.

As for the portrayal of characters and the events associated with them, the overall approach will have to be of positive attitude-building taking up both negative and positive elements that happen to be a part of the existent realities. The purpose is not showing, things, just as they are but also showing how they ought to be, or could be. The ultimate goal is not to frighten the viewers about the grimness of the situation, but letting them realise that grim and different though the situation is, it is possible to find ways of improving it to our benefit within the resources at our disposal as of now. One may call it an idealistic approach, but it is required as a part of the pedagogical process to make people more confident in themselves, in their own potentials. There is no Utopia, but there are pragmatic practical possibilities within the reach of human effort. The totality of the situation when taken care of in the process of designing, planning, executing and transmitting these programmes will go a long way in optimising positive viewer response and helping them to acquire the status of "praxis" the process of reflection and action—each leading to other.

As is evident, the integrated approach implies a wider canvas, a broader frame of reference. Our emphasis is on the people—their lives with its sweet and bitter experiences, their dreams and aspirations, their potentials and shortcomings, their varied day-to-day as well as long term problems. Blended with all these will be the problems of their health—their minor and major ailments, an analysis of the clinical and underlying causes of these diseases and the pros and cons of the current practices that they follow tackling these problems. All this will be coupled with suggestions regarding the possibilities of approaching these problems and seeking solutions in a scientific and rationalistic manner.

Social life in terms of events, interactions between people at different levels, concerns caused by historical as well as the ongoing influences and also the philosophic content of each individual life have a certain continuity; physical and abstract. It is therefore, necessary that the spirit of these linkages and continuity gets reflected through these programmes.

PRASAR BHARATI RECRUITMENT RULES

Public broadcaster Prasar Bharati is in the process of finalising recruitment rules and service conditions of its employees, Rajya Sabha was told today.

The finalisation of the recruitment rules and service conditions will give the option to the employees of Prasar Bharati for absorption as per the provisions of Prasar Bharati Act 1990, S. Jaipal Reddy, the Minister for Information and Broadcasting, told Rajya Sabha in written reply to a question.

The government had allowed deemed deputation status to the employees working in the Prasar Bharati Corporation and this was done to clarify the state of the government servants in the Corporation and enable Prasar Bharati to exercise necessary powers of a borrowing authority, he said.

Reddy said National Federation of Akashwani and Doordarshan Employees had submitted a memorandum in September 2004 urging upon the government to ensure proper funding of Prasar Bharati through the grants-in-aid and ensure that they continue to receive the facilities to which they are entitled as government employees.

BECIL

Broadcast Engineering Consultants India Limited (BECIL), a Government of India enterprise, established in the year 1995, provides consultancy services and also undertakes turnkey jobs in the specialised fields of Broadcast Engineering and Information Technology. BECIL has a vast reservoir of experts who come from the premier broadcasting organizations of the country.

BECIL Strength

BECIL provides rapid response to customer needs with quality-driven, attractively priced propositions. It has flexible, tailor-made solutions to every customer's unique requirements. A total quality approach with frequent reviews and monitoring facilitates efficient and cost-effective completion of every project on schedule.

BECIL Field of Activities

BECIL provides consultancy services including turnkey jobs in the specialized fields like Acoustics, Audio-Video Systems (SRS/conferencing/recording/production and post-production systems), Terrestrial & Satellite Broadcasting, Data Broadcasting, MMDS and CATV Network.

BECIL Services

BECIL consultancy and turnkey services range from system design, planning, specifications, site selection, installation and commissioning to projecting running costs, staffing and in service operations regardless of location.

INDIAN RADIO AND TV CHANNELS

- AVS TV—Telecasts Indian movies and songs in USA.
- Adhikari Brothers Television Network—TV programme production.

- All India Radio—Sound broadcasting service operated by Government of India.
- Asian Entertainment TV—Entertainment channel catering Asian community.
- Asianet TV—Asian channel on cable TV network in the United Kingdom.
- Broadcast Engineering Society—Dissemination of Radio and Television broadcast knowledge.
- DD India—News, live telecast, programme schedule and more.
- Delhi FM—Online radio and music channel.
- DesiGrooveRadio—Internet radio channel for Hindi and Bhangra music.
- Doordarshan—Major TV channel in India.
- Doordarshan Jaipur—Rajasthan state television channel.
- Gemini TV—Telugu satellite channel.
- ITBC Radio—Canadian International Tamil radio.
- Ilaignan.com—Tamil Internet radio.
- India Guide—Guide on Indian TV programmes & channels.

RADIO NETWORKS

Site Listings

Most Popular

- Voice of America@.
- National Public Radio (NPR) (46).
- BBC Radio@.
- Radio France Internationale (RFI)—variety of frequencies and programmes on cable, FM, and short wave.
- Radio Free Europe/Radio Liberty—US government funded network with multilingual broadcasts on shortwave, AM and FM bands.
- Air America Radio (13).
- Pacifica Radio (6).

Alphabetical

- ABC Radio Networks (2).
- Air America Radio (13).
- BBC Radio@.
- Birach Broadcasting—operates a network of radio stations encompassing the midwest, northeast portions of the United States and Ontario.
- Caracol Cadena Basica—Colombian radio network.
- CNNRadio—provides news, sports, business, and feature reports to affiliate radio stations worldwide.
- Emmis Communications (Nasdaq: EMMS).
- ESPN Radio Network@.
- Great Lakes Radio Consortium—produces environmentally focused radio and news features heard on more than 100 public radio stations.
- Islamic Broadcasting Network—IBN—offers family programmes, news, and current affairs. Aims to meet the religious and cultural needs of American

Muslim youth, as well as dispel myths and stereotypes about Islam and Muslims.

- Learfield Communications. Inc.
- Michigan Radio Network—programmed daily news service for commercial radio stations, including both data and audio news properties.
- Minnesota Public Radio@.
- Monitor Radio—Monitor Radio programming is heard on countless Public Radio International stations and by shortwave listeners worldwide. Now, Monitor Radio is available via the global Internet computer network.
- National Public Radio (NPR) (46).
- New Dimensions Broadcasting Network—in-depth dialogues seeking positive ways to meet personal, social, spiritual, and cultural challenges.
- North Carolina News Network—news, hurricane tracking and sports.
- Pacifica Radio (6).
- Prairie Public Broadcasting—providing free information and discussion throughout North Dakota and northwestern Minnesota.
- Premiere Radio Networks—features programming covering sports, health, politics, music, entertainment and more.
- Public Radio International (PRI) (6).
- Radio America—the 24-hour conservative radio network.
- Radio Bakwaas—Indian talk and music radio network.
- Radio Disney.
- Radio France Internationale (RFI)—variety of frequencies and programmes on cable, FM, and short wave.
- Radio Free Europe/Radio Liberty—US government funded network with multilingual broadcasts on shortwave, AM and FM bands.
- Radio Left—the Anti-Rush, Anti-GOP Antidote. Driving the right wing nuts.
- Radio Sawa—communicating directly in Arabic with the peoples of the Middle East by radio.
- Red River Radio Network—public radio network offering programming information, community information and more.
- TARBS—World TV—Television and Radio Broadcasting Services. Operates within Australia and internationally as a multicultural subscription TV and radio broadcaster.
- Tribune Radio Networks—carries agribusiness programming and Chicago Cubs broadcasts.
- Voice of America@.
- WestStar TalkRadio Network—broadcast syndicator produces The Kim Komando Radio Show, An American Christmas, and The Komando Computer Minute.
- Westwood One (NYSE:WON)—provides news, sports, weather, traffic, video news services, and other local content to the radio and television industries.
- Yellowstone Public Radio—listener supported public radio in Montana and northern Wyoming.

India Television

- Doordarshan India—Doordarshan India network.

Hindi Entertainment

- Zee Television—One of India's prime Hindi Channels.
- Sony Entertainment Television—Another mainly Hindi Channel' shows dubbed English serials and some Hindi programmes.

Movie Channels

- Star Movies.
- Zee Cinema—The official website of the different Zee Cinema around the globe from Asia to the Americas.

Guides

- Indian television—India's cable, satellite terrestrial broadcasting portal.
- Indian television dot com is the online destination of all professionals wanting to be in touch with the Indian television industry, television news, information, research, programming and profession databases, and E-commerce related to the television business.
- theindiaguide.com is India's first website for personalized TV.

Music

- Channel V—Star Networks Music channel.
- MTV Asia—Asia transmission of MTV.
- Music Asia—Music Asia Hindi Songs.

News

- British Broadcasting Corporation.
- CNN—Cable News Network. The News channel.
- Star News Channel—A new 24 hour channel on Star, guided famous political analyst Prannoy Roy.

Sports

- 10 Sports.
- DD Sports—Cricket A Doordarshan site that hosts cricket related information. Occasionally broadcasts live games as well.
- ESPN-Star.

Others

- CNBC Asia—The Asian version of the American CNBC channel.
- Pakistan Television.
- Siti Cable.
- Star Television—The TV network that kind of started the satellite revolution in India.

Radio

- AIR—All India Radio.
  This is the official website of All India Radio. Yeh Aakashwani hai.
- India Network Radio.
- Radio of India—Website that broadcasts Songs and other programmes in numerous languages such as Hindi, Tamil and Telugu.
- Radio Mirchi—Radio Mirchi is an organization that broadcasts programmes over FM from different cities in India such as Mumbai, Delhi, Ahmedabad, Pune and Indore.

INDIAN CINEMA

If India attained a pre-eminent position in any single visual art after Independence it was film making. It shot up to become the top in the world and still retains that pinnacled position. In 1983, over 800 feature films were certified for public exhibition mostly in colour and a few in black and white. This number was nearly four times what India was producing immediately after Independence. Language-wise, Telugu topped the list followed by films in Hindi and Malayalam. Trailing behind were films in Bengali, Gujarati and Marathi. Within the film industry the most significant development that has taken place during this period is the acceleration of film making in south India. Both in terms of the number of cinema halls, and in respect of the number of pictures produced, the south has forged ahead to take the lead from the well-entrenched traditional centre of Mumbai. Over the years more than 17,000 films have been produced in India. More than 13 million Indians go to the movies everyday, sometimes trudging miles to the nearest movie hall.

Yet this enormous structure caters essentially for urban and suburban people, who represent only one-fifth of the total population. The number of cinema houses where films can be screened are 11,682 including the touring talkies. These cinema houses are unevenly distributed and obviously well below the world average.

Milestones in the Growth of Cinema

Many milestones marked the overall growth of cinema in the country since Independence. The government showed concern about the balanced development of the cinema which had become a money bag and multi-star industry. To this end, it appointed the Film Enquiry Committee whose recommendations resulted in the foundation of some basic institutions like Films Division of India, Film Finance Corporation and Children's Film Society in the sixties. In their own way these institutions including a growing number of talented producers and directors have cumulatively given a shot in the arm to the film industry.

The Films Division set up by the Ministry of Information and Broadcasting in 1948 gave a boost to documentary films and upgraded it professionally and technically. In 1975 the National Films Development Corporation was constituted, which was activated in 1980 and the Film Finance Corporation and the Indian Motion Picture Export Corporation were amalgamated with it. The Corporation plays a vital role. Its function is to plan, promote and organise an integrated and efficient development of the industry in accordance with the national economic policy and objectives. Its broad range of activities covers the handling of the import and export of feature films, allocation and distribution of raw stock and equipment used by the industry, distribution and exhibition of films through the existing network, and undertaking a programme of construction of a chain of national theatres, promotion of quality films, research and development in film equipment and raw stock. Recently the Corporation has taken an innovative step in deciding to finance the production of featurettes, *i.e.*, films of approximately half an hour to one hour duration. These can be shown on TV networks in India and abroad.

Film as a Change Agent

The film is motion, picture, sound, theatre and school all packed in one. That is why it can communicate effectively, create better impact than other mass media and draw hundreds and thousands of viewers including the illiterates, workers and villagers. Even the elite and urbanites swarm cine halls or glue to their seats at home near video-cum-TV sets. The film being visual reality and a universal language cutting across cultural barriers, film exponents advocate that a socially relevant cinema can prove to be the best activist. Taking the example of India as a developing country where less than five per cent of the population buy or read newspapers and books, the talkie film is perhaps the only popular form of culture available to a large number of the common people. The contact of most of the people with prose is the dialogue that they hear in pictures, the only poetry that enriches their lives is the poetry of film lyrics, and their models for style, fashion and mannerisms are the celluloid heroes. Many experts therefore think that the film can educate and inspire, motivate and change their attitudes. To use the communication language, the film in the hands of good script writers and directors can function not only to spread a common filmy language but act as a social monitor and a gatekeeper as well. Like any magazine or newspaper, it can be effectively investigatory and expository. More than any other media it can tellingly project social angularities and injustices, forcibly portray the moods and attitudes of alienated and wayward youngsters, emotionally and incisively depict what poverty is and how farmers/workers, woman and the poor and down-trodden eke out their existence. Recent feature and TV films show that given wise direction, the film without becoming didactive or ceasing to be an entertainer, can expose the black marketeer, the corrupt politician, the anti-social, industrialist or a trade union *dada*, the 'yes minister' bureaucrat, eve teaser and social parasite. Not only in this respect but positively it can stimulate values of good life and citizenship as also participatory virtues of developmental activities. Through characterisation, demonstration and depiction of scenes and situations, it can even directly help to sell the concepts and norms of national or emotional integration, dignity of labour, the bare-foot doctor or engineer, an understanding spouse and the pulls of extra-marital relations. Documentary experts say that within the constraints of creative reality, even these films can reflect their country's development aspirations and strivings and even the failings and achievements of its people.

In some African, Asian or communist countries there are few individual film makers classified as new-wave film makers, who have set in motion the movement for the socially relevant cinema. This indicate the effort to use the power of the film medium not only to entertain, but to educate and influence the life pattern of viewers. As a change agent its potentiality has started manifesting to reach wider audience, to persuade them and to get their acceptance. The commercial cinema has also started reflecting some of these new trends and offbeat themes of great social significance.

Commercial Cinema

The cinema after Independence in India was predominantly commercial so far as feature films were concerned. The star system, high budgets, escapism, concoction of popular entertainment ingredients, and abundance of music, song and dance were generally the characteristics of this cinema. Circumstances like inflation, overcrowding, dislocated life, social tension, rampant unemployment, disillusionment and youth alienation encouraged film makers to resort to fantasies and escapist or entertaining themes for their pictures. Starting with *Sholay* and graduating from certain films like *Kache Dhage* and *Reshma Aur Shera,* Indian heroes started having an image of a Robin Hood, Garth or Tarzan. The films had revenge as the theme with accompanying attributes of fighting violence. As one critic points out "the dividing lines between art and industry, between north and south, between the moghul and the maverick became hazier than before, movies more than any of the arts provided a spectacle that enthralled, exasperated and appalled in excess." Multi-crore budgeting registered ascendance in *Naseeb* and *Kranti* and reached its culmination in *Razia Sultan,* which also sought to outdo any other picture in respect of grandiose of set and costumes.

Reaction to this trend however found a manifestation both in the form of the evolution of a new wave or art cinema and the appearance of new directions in commercial cinema itself.

A new trend in film making was born first in Kolkata and then in sporadic waves in other centres of film production in the south. The impact of international film festivals, the institution of film awards, documentary cinema, and the influence of famous film makers from abroad like Jean Renoir (France), Frank Capra (Hollywood), V.I. Pudovkin (USSR) were some of the forces which contributed to the quest for an alternative cinema. These new trend films were made at low costs, outside the mainstream of commercial cinema. Their dominant characteristics were their social concern, purposefulness, realism, narrative style, exclusion of unrelated song and dance routines and fights and other familiar devices of the commercial package. Their acceptance by the intelligent and cultivated audiences in the country and the high praise which some of the really good new trend films won abroad brought a much needed self-confidence to adventurous or innovative film makers. The Film Finance Corporation and its successor the National Films Development Corporation provided institutional aid to the otherwise individualistic trend among young film makers. Some notable proponents of this new wave cinema, also called socially relevant cinema or alternative cinema, were Satyajit Ray, K.A. Abbas, Balraj Sahni, Raj Kapoor, Shyam Benegal, Mrinal Sen, Basu Chatterjee, M.S. Sathyu, Utpalendu Chakraborty, Pattabhi Rama Reddy, Adoor Gopahlakrishnan, Govind Nihalani, Girish Karnad and B.V. Karanth. This trend was, however beset with difficulties. Important among these were lack of finance and exhibition halls, direct confrontation with influential commercial cinema and their monopoly distributors, and extreme individualism in communication appeals and entertainment techniques by sophisticated aesthetics. Yet, with assistance from Film Finance Corporation and other means, some prize winning films like *Ghare Baire* and *Paar* have been produced. Mrinal

Sen, who is regarded as one of the Third World's most experienced and internationally renowned radical film makers, has produced new films that win prize after prize. From *Ek Din Pratidin to Khandar* is a saga of laurel winning in film making. He himself says that cinema should not hibernate and many a film maker with his way of thinking besides India's film wizard Satyajit Ray, have been experimenting with the medium to find a new analysis on the growing explosive social situations around them. The films *Chokh* by Utpalendu Chakraborty and *Damul* by Prakash Jha are described as models of possible alternative cinema, for it is cinema of hope. It is advocated that a good film is one that should depict the odds against the best of life and yet seek to transcend them and affirm that these odds should not choke the indomitable spirit of the men, women and children of a society. *Ardh Satya* is considered the new cinema's biggest hit. It deals with the inequitous system of justice through the story of a sadistic policeman. It is heartening that old masters of new cinema continue to work with increasing maturity and younger film makers are exploring newer subjects and styles with growing confidence.

While the movement for the new cinema in India is still on, though with different intensity and dimensions in different regions, there are some discernible new directions manifested in the commercial cinema itself. Reaction against high budgeting was visible when Hrishikesh Mukherjee carried on the New Theatres tradition with some success. The films of Basu Chatteriee, *Rajnigandha* and *Chhotisi Baat* with their humorous insights into the ordinary daily life of people, proved that such movies could also attract crowds. Films like *Love Story* and *Ek Dujje Ke Liye,* costing one-tenth of the high price-tagged pictures, almost shattered the concept that multi-crore and multi-star pictures would essentially be box-office hits. A change in acting style seemed to be obvious. A new line of heroes and heroines have started emerging who seek to play their roles as actors and actresses and not just stars. Another thing that has emerged is the return of love stories and adoption of offbeat themes including women's lib, extra-marital relations, estrangement between parents and children and the lives of coal miners. Pictures like *Arth, Souten, Dard Ka Rista, Talaq, Mandi, Do Dishayen, Devta, Mayuri* and *Kalka* have proved that such pictures have started having more appeal to the changing tastes and moods of cine goers. Film makers have stopped depicting women as objects of sex exploitation or male chauvinism. A set of films dubbed as feminine genre are gaining popularity. These films present women as equal citizens and individuals in their own right. In *Arth,* two women, a wife and a lover, move from emotional dependence on a man to the freedom of rebuilding their lives on their own. *Subha* sought to find justification for a woman to seek fulfilment in her career even at the cost of her marital security. The movie *Mujhe Insaf Chahiye* depicts the story of a liberated woman in all her trials and turbulations, including her angry cry for justice.

Yet another trend visible in the commercial cinema is an occasional effort at light comedies like *Chupke Chupke, Khatta Mitha, Naram Garam* and *Kissi se na Kehna.* These efforts only show that reasonable thematic experimentation or innovativeness in film-making in India can be tried without box-office debacle.

The taste of cinema goers seems to be changing also in respect of over padding of chaotic song and dance sequences. This is discernible in cinema halls when viewers walk out when such scenes are being shown.

Some of the film critics today maintain that the real trend centres in the commercial cinemas are the regional films. While the previous monopoly of artistic Bengali films and of the commercial Hindi films has gone down, the regional cinema in Malayalam, Kannada, Telugu and other southern languages is coming into its own. Young directors and new stars are emerging in these regions. Even in competitions the winners are dominantly from regional cinema. However, a recent avalanche of semi-pornographic and blue films from the south, adroitly side-stepping the censor's regulations, constitute an alarming trend.

Documentary in India

India is forging ahead even in the field of documentary films, news reels, cartoon films and quickies which are all different visual instruments of public information, education and instruction, motivation and attitude changes. Defined originally as creative treatment of actuality, today documentary and information films include those which deal with significant historical, social, scientific or economic subjects, photographed in actual occurrence or reenacted, and the emphasis is more on factual content than on entertainment. These films record contemporary history and present filmic reports on the social and economic progress of a country.

Starting modestly when the Films Division of the Ministry of Information and Broadcasting was set up in 1948, India is currently having an annual production of 104 short films. In 1983-84 the Films Division produced 143 documentary films including 40 produced by independent producers.

In India the State governments, public undertakings and private enterprises can also produce documentaries. If they are within the maximum length of 2000 feet, these films can be released on theatrical circuits only through the Films Division. Production assignments can be also given to independent producers, and annually about 40 to 50 films are produced that way.

India has many well-known documentary film makers both in the public and private sectors. They have made both individually and collectively, significant contributions to the development of Indian documentatries and animated films. Produced by Films Division many of these films have obtained international and national awards. Many independent producers outside Films Division have also made documentary films of merit and received awards for their films.

Documentaries and news reels are exhibited in all cinema houses and at each performance; the rental is one per cent of the average weekly collections. Every week one news reel and two short films are released at all important centres. The Films Division also supplies prints on loan to government departments, semi-government educational and charitable institutions, hospitals, social welfare organisations and individuals. This is done through its distribution branch offices as well as through the regional and field publicity units of the Directorate of Field Publicity. For non-commercial shows films are loaned free of charge.

The documentary film movement has a bright future in India. Other than the number of good film makers in the country, there are also sponsoring organisations which realise the importance of documentary films as a powerful and effective visual medium for depicting creative actuality of our changing social scenes and ecology. The government on its own part is looking forward to having more such films on technology, science, environment, ecology, places of pilgrimage, hill stations, sports, folk music, folk dances and other varieties of art and culture from various parts of the country.

Many Miles to Go

Whatever may be the quality of our motion pictures, they continue to be popular. The video and TV boom has further-boosted their importance and craze. TV films have added a new dimension and it is significant that the first TV film *(Sadgati)* was made by Satyajit Ray and more such films are being produced by other eminent film makers. Good films for children is another branch which needs to be further activised and diversified. To this end, the Children's Film Society, the main producing agency, is being keyed up.

India is an exporter of films especially to those areas where Indians or Asians live in fairly large numbers. It is heartening that package marketing interests and tastes of the internal audience has started being reflected in the widening range of current themes and their improving treatments. Participation in various national and international film festivals is helping to infuse new trends and techniques among the more professionally alert film makers, actors and technicians. Yet, some communication experts still believe that apart from popular entertainment ingredients, creativity and aesthetics, Indian films should become more socially purposeful. They should rid of their irrelevant paddings or trappings and professionally unedifying constituents to have a more ennobling impact on the youth and illiterate persons, without becoming pedantic or shedding individual creativity or professional merit.

At present there are, however, some inbuilt handicaps in the films industry. Apart from the firmness of censors and the new danger from video piracy, the most important hurdle in the way of this popular visual medium reaching a vast majority of people is scarcity of cinema houses and exhibition facilities. Very few of the existing cinema theatres have proximity. Very few of the existing cinema theatres have proximity to deep and distant places of rural India. Although Field Publicity units of the Central and State Governments do try to fill in the gap, the total number of cinema seats is much less than 2/5th of UNESCO's minimum norm. From the point of view of adequate and sophisticated technology the 16 mm, 8 mm super and wide screen technologies need to be improved. The position in respect of raw material and studio equipment also needs to be further geared up. Government activisation and the efforts of the National Films Development Corporation and other media organisations as also innovative film makers both in the field of commercial and new cinema, have pushed the medium and industry well ahead. But our films have many miles to go as yet in the direction of professional, communication and technical excellence, creative visual impact, wholesome entertainment, aesthetics and international marketability.

This task of the Indian cinema, in becoming a booming industry, a more persuasive and socially relevant change agent, technically well-equipped and a decent package offering wholesome entertainment and good music, places at tremendous responsibility upon the industry and on those who operate and direct it, as also on the governing media institutions and censors.

POLICY FOR IMPORT OF CINEMATOGRAPH FILMS AND OTHER FILMS

In exercise of powers conferred under Paragraph 4.11 of the Export and Import Policy 1997-2002, as notified in the Gazette of India extraordinary, Part II, Section 3, sub-section (ii) vide S.O. No. 283(E) dated 31.3.1997 and in supersession of Public Notice No. 4(PN)/9702 dated 31.3.1997, as amended from time to time, the Director General of Foreign Trade hereby notifies the policy for import of cinematograph films and other films (including film on video tape, compact video disc, laser video disc or digital video disc).

(*i*) Import of cinematograph feature films and other films (including film on video tape, compact video disc, laser video disc or digital video disc) shall be allowed without a licence.

(*ii*) The importer of the film shall comply with the provisions of all applicable Indian laws governing the distribution and exhibition of films, including the requirement of obtaining a certificate of public exhibition prescribed under the Cinematograph Act, 1952.

(*iii*) Import of any unauthorized/pirated films shall be prohibited.

(*iv*) import of foreign reprints of Indian films shall not be permitted without the prior permission in writing from the Ministry of Information and Broadcasting, Government of India.

(*v*) The Ministry of Information and Broadcasting, Government of India, on being satisfied that it is necessary or expedient in public interest to do so, may waive or relax the above requirements.

This issues in the public interest.

SHOOTING OF FOREIGN FEATURE FILMS IN INDIA

The Government of India invites foreign film teams to shoot their films in India—a country with locations of untold beauty. We have also simplified the procedure for shooting of films by foreigners in India and the ensuing paragraphs, we hope, will answer all your questions regarding the procedure to apply for shooting permission.

What should Accompany your Application?

- You need to send us a simple letter, telling us of your intention to shoot in India, mentioning the dates of shooting, particulars of the cast and crew, and you chosen locations. Please address your letter to the relevant address a month before your planned shooting schedule, and enclose four copies of the final, detailed shooting script, a draft/cheque for US $200 drawn in favour of Pay & Accounts Officer, Ministry of I&B, (MS), New Delhi (that is a fee for scrutiny of the script), detailed shooting locations and particulars regarding the cast and crew coming to India. *No fee is required for shooting documentaries in India.*
- Should you wish to bring your own shooting equipment, please send us a list of the equipment to be temporarily imported. This will enable us to make a recommendation to the customs authorities to exempt the temporary import from customs duty.

- Your permission to shoot will normally not take more than three weeks to process. The permission letter issued by the Government of India will facilitate your permission from other local authorities, which may, in some cases, need to be obtained directly from these authorities.
- In case any living personality is portrayed in the film as a Character, we suggest that you share the script with that personality or his/her legal heirs, before beginning the shooting, and obtain a 'No Objection Letter'. This letter will expedite the clearance of your application, and also guard against the possibility of any defamation or libel suits.
- If you propose to shoot your film as a co-production, a copy of the agreement between your company and the Indian party, indicating the role of each party, its responsibilities and liabilities, must accompany the application.
- If your film requires shooting in the scenic but sensitive areas of Jammu & Kashmir, the North Eastern India or border belts, and your application will be considered for specific approval in consultation with the Ministry of Home Affairs. In such cases, you would need to allow more time to process your application.

What the Indian Mission in your Country will do for you?

- Do submit the detailed particulars of all the members of the shooting team, to the Indian Mission in the country from which they would be departing for India at the time, indicating your intention to shoot in India. Our mission will issue them visas in the normal course.

Other Things that you may Want to Know

- An expert from a panel constituted by us for this purpose will scrutinize your script. If considered necessary, to facilitate the shooting, a *liaison officer may be attached to a film shooting team*. This officer will help you to get local clearances, and provide an interface with any local institutions. Where a liaison officer is so attached to the shooting team, the Government of India will bear his expenses. In exceptional cases you may need to show the completed film to a representative of the Government of India, in India or in an Indian Mission abroad, before its release anywhere in the world. This requirement will apply only to films made on subjects of political, religious or socio-cultural sensitivity, and is focused on ensuring that the film has been shot in accordance with the scrutinized script and that the film has nothing objectionable from the point of view of presentation of a correct and balanced perspective on the topic covered.
- During the shooting of the film if it is felt that any material changes or deviation from the approved script is necessary, permission may be taken from this Ministry before shooting these scenes.

Send Applications for Shooting Feature Films/Telefilms in India to:

The Ministry of Information and Broadcasting
Government of India
'A' Wing, Shastri Bhavan
New Delhi–110 001

Send Applications for Shooting Documentaries in India to:

The Ministry of External Affairs

(External Publicity Division)
Government of India
'A' Wing, Shastri Bhavan
New Delhi–110 001

To

The Secretary,
Ministry of Information and Broadcasting
Government of India,
New Delhi

Sub:

Sir,

With reference to the Ministry of Information and Broadcasting's letter No...................... dated .... we hereby give the following undertakings:

(*i*) Shooting of the film will be done in locations in India in accordance with the script as approved by the Government of India. If we consider any material changes are necessary in the script, we shall obtain, the prior approval of the Government of India for such changes.

(*ii*) We shall furnish the detailed particulars of the members of the shooting team and the exact locations where the shooting would take place in India at least one month in advance of the arrival of the team in India. We note that prior approval of the Government of India is necessary for the fixing of locations for shooting in certain areas.

(*iii*) We note that in the case of assistance to be obtained from other Ministries such as Defence, Education etc., separate agreements as stipulated by these Ministries, are required to be signed with them.

(*iv*) We shall shoot the film only in the presence of a Liaison Officer where attached to the team by the Ministry of Information and Broadcasting.

(*v*) We accept that part of the Liaison Officer's duty will be to ensure that nothing detrimental in the depiction of India or the Indian people shall be shot or included in the film. In the event of any disagreement arising between the team and the Liaison Officer in this respect, the matter will be immediately referred to the Ministry of Information and Broadcasting whose decision will be final. We shall ensure that India's security interests are not compromised in any manner.

(*vi*) We undertake to show our completed film to the representative of the Government of India/the Indian Mission in.................. for scrutiny if recommended by the Ministry of I&B and we further undertake to delete and destroy the portions of the film that may be found objectionable on such scrutiny by the Government of India, before the film is utilized for public exhibition anywhere in the world.

(*vii*) After the shooting of the film is completed in India we shall provide, in duplicate, to the Ministry of Information and Broadcasting a narrative report about the details of shooting done in India.

Yours truly,
(XYZ)

3

National Broadcasting Policy, Rules, Acts and Related Regulations

MAJOR LEGAL RESOURCES

(*a*) TRAI Consultation Paper on Issues related to Broadcasting and distribution of TV channels—CP No. 9/2004.

(*b*) Report of the task force on introduction of conditional access system.

(*c*) The Indian Broadcasting Regulations Forum.

Goverment Rules and Policies

(*d*)	The New Telecom Policy [NTP 1999] announced by the Government.	New Telecom Policy...
(*e*)	The Media Policy announced by the BJP government as a part of their Election manifesto for the forthcoming Lok Sabha elections.	Media Policy
(*f*)	National Task Force on Information Technology and Software Development Information Technology Action Plan.	Information Technology Action Plan

Acts and Regulations for Cable and Television in India

(*g*)	The Cable Television Networks Rules, 1994	The Cable Television Networks Rules, 1994
(*h*)	The National Security Act, 1980	The National Security Act, 1980
(*i*)	Almost everybody in the country is familiar with the cable television. It has been spreading its wings from the initial urban cities, right to the remote villages. There has been a haphazard mushrooming of cable television networks all over the country due to the availability of signals of foreign television networks via satellites. To check the screening of undesirable programmes and advertisements which are screened on these channels and to regulate the operation of the cable television networks in the country, so as to bring uniformity in their functioning, the Cable Television Networks (Regulation) Act was passed in both the Houses of the Parliament.	The Cable Television Networks (Regulation) Act

(*j*)	The Prasar Bharati Act, 1990 was passed to provide for the establishment of a Broadcasting Corporation for India, to be known as Prasar Bharati. It says that it shall be the primary duty of the Corporation to organize and conduct public broadcasting services to inform, educate and entertain the public and to ensure a balanced development of broadcasting on radio and television.	The Prasar Bharati Act, 1990
(*k*)	The Bill is to provide for an independent authority to be known as the Broadcasting Authority of India which is for the purpose of facilitating and regulating broadcasting services in India.	The Broadcasting Bill, 1997
(*l*)	The Indian Telegraph Act, 1885 came into force on 1st October, 1885. "Telegraph" means any appliance, instrument, material or apparatus used or capable of use for transmission or reception of signs, signals, writing, images, and sounds or intelligence of any nature by wire, visual or other electro-magnetic emissions, Radio waves or Hertzian waves, galvanic, electric or magnetic means. The Indian Telegraphic Act, 1885 was an Act to amend the law relating to Telegraphs in India.	The Indian Telegraph Act, 1885
(*m*)	"The importance of copyright was recognized after the invention of the printing press which enabled the reproduction of books in large quantity. The Indian Copyright Act was thus passed in 1914. But, during the last four decades, modern and advanced means of communications like broadcasting, litho-photography, television, etc made inroads in the Indian economy. It necessitated the fulfillment of international obligations in the field of Copyright. A comprehensive legislation had to be introduced to completely revise the Copyright law. This was achieved by the introduction of a Copyright Bill, 1957 in the Parliament."	The Copyright Act...
(*n*)	"The Union Government has taken a decision on 25th July, 2000 to further liberalise its Uplinking Policy and permit the Indian private companies to set up uplinking hub/teleports for licensing/hiring out to other broadcasters. The new policy also permits uplinking of any television channel from India. It also allows the Indian news agencies to have their own uplinking facilities for purposes of newsgathering and its further distribution."	Guidelines for up-linking from India.
(*o*)	The Cable Televison Network Regulation Amendment Bill, 2002	Latest CAS amend-ments of the Cable Television Act
(*p*)	The proceedings in the Rajya Sabha regarding the passage of The Cable Television Networks (Regulation) Amendment Bill, 2002	What the speakers had to say.

Important Judgements and Committee Reports

■ Excerpts from the historic judgment in 1995 which stated that the Air Waves are not the monopoly of the Indian Government.	Judgement for ownership of Air Waves
■ The Nitesh Sengupta Committee was set up to review the provisions of Prasar Bharati (Broadcasting Corporation of India) Act, 1990 and to make recommendations regarding the restructuring of Prasar Bharati. Read the contents of the report submitted by The Nitesh Sengupta Committee.	The Nitesh Sengupta Committee Report
■ Excerpts from 'Major Recommendations' of Shri B.G. Verghese Working Group on Autonomy for Akashvani and Doordarshan, February 1978.	Recommendations of Verghese Working Group
■ "We envisage an autonomous national trust as the authority under which Akashvani and Doordarshan should grow. This we are naming Akash Bharati—the National Broadcast Trust."	
■ Summary of the recommendations given by the Ram Vilas Paswan Consultative Committee on National Media Policy for the Information and Broadcasting Ministry, 1996.	Recommendations by Ram Vilas Paswan Consultative Comittee.
■ "9.1—The broadcasting should observe a greater degree of responsibility and sensitivity to Indian culture and ethos and cater to the developmental requirement of the country. It should achieve an Indian personality in telecasting/broadcasting." (para 6.4.1.1)	
■ Summary of the recommendations of the interdepartmental committee on electronic media under the chairmanship of Shri K.A. Varadan, Additional Secretary in the Ministry of Information and Broadcasting.	Varadan Committee Report
■ India's dream of becoming a super-power in Information Technology. India is in a competitive race for investment and it is believed that investment in this new millenium will flow to countries where there is visible evidence of a strong policy framework, supported by clear and precise laws facilitating growth of business in a converged environment.	Interim Report of the Sub-group on convergence
■ A complete report presented by Fali Nariman Committee to Cabinet.	Final Report of the Sub-group on convergence
■ Draft Communication Convergence Bill, 2000.	Draft Communication Convergence Bill, 2000
■ Incorporating Comments/suggestions received from interested organisations and individuals on the Draft Bill prepared by the Sub-group on Convergence in January 2001.	Revised Draft Communication Convergence Bill, 2001
■ The Communication Convergence Bill, 2001 which was introduced in Parliament on 31 August, 2001 by Former Communications minister Ram Vilas Paswan.	Communication Convergence Bill 2001

Policies for Doordarshan

■ The DD Notice	The DD Notice
■ The DD Advertising Code	
■ The Code for commercial advertising on Doordarshan.	The DD Advertising Code
■ Guidelines for Commissioning of Programmes in Doordarshan	DD Press release

THE INDIAN BROADCASTING REGULATIONS FORUM

The Indian Government has announced that it wants a Broadcasting Act enacted within the next six months. It has the old broadcasting bill draft and the report of the Sharad Pawar Committee which reviewed the draft as reference points. But it is seeking the opinion of the satellite channels and cable TV industry once again later this month. You, as a television or media executive, can share your opinions on what shape Indian broadcasting regulations should take by posting them in Indian television.com's Indian Broadcasting Regulations Forum. Feel free to air your views on:

- The limits for foreign equity in Indian broadcasting and on cross-media holdings. On what should these restrictions be based.
- Whether DTH television should be allowed and in what form.
- Whether a broadcasting regulator is needed or not and what shape should it take, what powers should it have.
- Whether a television licence fee is needed.
- Whether a Prasar Bharati is needed and should it be autonomous or government-controlled.
- Whether the current unorganised nature of the cable TV business should be allowed to continue or whether licensing should be brought in and in what form.
- Whether uplinking from India should be made mandatory for all channels including foreign ones.
- Whether wireless cable should be permitted.
- Whether private firms should be allowed to enter terrestrial television broadcasting.

Inclusion of Community Broadcasting in the Broadcasting Bill, 1997: Recommendations to the Ministry of Information and Broadcasting on non-profit community broadcasting. Prepared by VOICES in consultation with broadcasting and development professionals and the National Law School of India, Bangalore. VOICES is a development communication organization. One of our key thrust area is Community Radio and we have been working in this issue for the past four years. This includes, Bangalore Declaration on Radio, Airing community related programmes from AIRs Chitradurga FM station, and lobbying for promotion of CR at ministerial and local level. Respected H'nble Minister with the ongoing technological revolution, information plays a crucial role in bringing people together and enables them to make informed choices. The right of free speech and expression includes the right to receive and impart information. For ensuring the Indian citizens' right to free speech and information, it is necessary that they have the benefit of plurality of views and access to range of options to public issues. The national goals of an Indian broadcasting policy have to be unique keeping in mind the diverse citizenary and the need for the peoples participation in a democracy. The Joshi Commission (1982) recommended a decentralized system of broadcasting, stressing upon the need for access, participation, local autonomy and control training and public service as the basis for broadcasting future of India. Thus any broadcasting policy must carry with it the onus to safeguard the citizen's right be informed, transmit varied programmes to awaken, inform, enlighten, educate, enrich and entertain all sections of the people and serve the rural and urban illiterate and underprivileged populations, keeping in mind the special needs and interests of the young women, social and cultural minorities, the tribal populations and those residing in the backward areas. The Broadcasting Bill, 1997 must be analyzed in this light to see if it fulfils these national objectives. Analysis of the Provisions of the Broadcasting Bill Section 16(2) talks about granting licensee to institutions which provide, education, environment protection and community service under a restricted bid system as notified by the regulations. There is some ambiguity in the terms used here: What type of institutes can be considered eligible? Private institutions, non-profit institutions or community broadcasting services. The South African Independent Broadcasting Authority Act 153 of 1993 defines a community broadcasting service as—one which is fully controlled by non-profit entity and operated for non-profitable purposes: serves a particular community:. encourages members of the community served by it to participate in the selection and provisions of the programmes to be broadcast: may be funded buy donations, grants, sponsorship or advertising or membership fees. This kind of clarity of definition is required. There must be cogent differentiation between a private broadcasting service operated for profit and non-profit community broadcasting which can fall under Section 16(2).

Suggested Amendments to Clauses

DEFINATIONS

Section 2 of the Bill should therefore include of both running thus: 2(zt) "Private Broadcasting Service" means a broadcasting service operated for profit and controlled by an entity which is not a public broadcasting licensee. 2(zu) "Community Broadcasting Service" means a non-profit broadcasting service which caters to the needs of geographically bounded group of persons having a definite ascertainable common interest, subject to Section 25(2) and which is permitted to raise funds to meet operational costs through donations, grants, sponsorships, membership fees, advertising or a combination of aforementioned.

FUNCTIONS OF THE AUTHORITY

Section 7 of the Bill deals with the Functions of the Authority. This section lays no positive obligation on the Authority to promote a diverse range of services on national, local, and regional level which would cater to the different cultural language groups and communities. It must be seen that a healthy balance is maintained between the different electronic media so that it does not lead to the marginalization of radio which is the only medium of information for 70 per cent of rural India and covers 90 per cent of the geographical area. Promotion of community-based non-profit developmental radio, which is characterized by active participation of the community the process of creating news, information, entertainment, and culturally relevant material with emphasis on local issues and concerns, should be one of the responsibilities of the Authority. An addition should be included under Section 7, to come after 7(*iii*) to read as: 7(*iv*) To promote broadcasting through low cost terrestrial radio and protect the interests and concerns of local communities.

GRANT OF LICENSES

Section 16(2) may read as: Notwithstanding anything contained in sub-section (1), the Authority may grant licences to such institutions as may be notified for terrestrial broadcasting services through restricted bids or on payment of nominal fee that may be determined by the regulations. The proviso 16(2) should be broadened in the public interest, to read: Provided that no institution shall be notified under this sub-section unless the object of such institutions is to promote education, community service, environment protection, health awareness, women's empowerment or cultural expression.

RESTRICTIONS ON HOLDING LISCENCES

Part I, Clause 4 of the schedule disqualifies publicly funded bodies from obtaining licence. This brings under its purview universities and other educational institutions as well as co-operatives. These should be exempt, bearing in mind the need for youth participation in media and deployment of media for promoting education. The Varadan Report (1991) had in fact enunciated that preference to be given to public bodies like universities, co-operative institutions etc., if they apply for licences. The proviso to Clause 4 here should read as: Provided that this disqualification does not apply to the universities and other educational institutions and co-operatives. Provided that the disqualified under this clause shall not apply to the community broadcasting service.

STATEMENT OF OBJECTS AND REASONS

One of the objects of this Bill is to meet the challenges proposed by the invasion of the skies by direct satellite broadcasting by foreign entities and it has addressed this issue. However, the main object remains to keep India's democratic traditions alive and keep its diverse citizens well-informed and this issue needs a closer look. For instance deregulation in the USA is not synonymous with the total abrogation of government regulation: media laws can liberate this neo-liberal communication policy initiative by not ignoring matters vital to public interest and community participation in India. The last sentence of the statement number 3 of this section should read as: This can be provided by facilitating private broadcasting and broadcasting services which enable access and participation by the citizens of the Country. The role of broadcasting is all the more important in providing information and access to media so that people can participate in the process of nation building. In the unique conditions of India, terrestrial radio has the widest audience. Thus the Bill seeks to encourage and create conditions for the development of community radio.

SIGNATORIES

Ms. Sucharita Eashwar, Ex-Director-VOICES, Bangalore; Dr. K.E. Eapen, International Communication Expert and Scholar; Mr. N. Kalayan Raman, ASC Enterprises, New Delhi; Dr. Michael Traber, United Theological College, Bangalore; Mr. A.R. Pasha, Cinematics, Bangalore; Ms. Ammu Joseph, Freelance Journalist, Bangalore; Ms. M.T. Rukhmini, Family Planning Association of India, Bangalore; Ms. N. Lakshmi, Concerned for Working Children, Bangalore; Ms. N. Bhatia, Indian Express, Bangalore; Ms. Amula Seethanaman, Indian Express, Bangalore; Ms. Raji Reddy, Bangalore; Ms. Vijayashree Rajaram, Jyothi Nivas College, Bangalore; Ms. Preetha Mount, Carmel College, Bangalore; Ms. Udaya Mount Carmel, Bangalore; Ms. Vinaya Mount Carmel, Bangalore; Ms Puja Mount Carmel, Bangalore; Ms. Bhavana Thakur, National Law School of India, Bangalore; Mr. M.A.S. Rajan, IAS (Retd.), Formerly Add. Chief Secretary, Karnataka; Ms. Indubai Ramesh, Director of Commercial Broadcasting, (Retd.), AIR, Bangalore; Ms. K.E. Eapen, Bangalore; Mr. Chandra Mouli, AIR, Bangalore; Mr. Sam Emmanuel, Media Centre, Bangalore; Mr. T.N. Munniswamy, FPAI, Gauribidanur; Mr. Prem James, FEBA, Bangalore; Mr. Simon, Verghese Deccan Herald, Bangalore; Ms. Prachi Bhuchar, Indian Express, Bangalore; Mr. Sowmya Bharadwaj, Jyothi Nivas College, Bangalore; Ms. Neerja, Mount Carmel College, Bangalore; Ms. Shalini, Mount Carmel College, Bangalore; Ms. Winnie, Mount Carmel College, Bangalore; Ms. Mayura, Mount Carmel College, Bangalore.

VOICES is Bangalore based non-profit development communication organization. One of our key thrust area is promoting community radio and have been into it for the past four and half years now. We came up with Bangalore Declearation on radio in 1996. We also aired programmes exclusively on local issues on FM in Chitradurga.

Courtesy: AIR, in 1999 and plan to set up a CR in Kolar, 165, 9th Cross, Stage-I, Indiranagar, Bangalore-650 038.

THE BROADCASTING BILL

The Bill is to provide for an independent authority to be known as the Broadcasting Authority of India for the purpose of facilitating and regulating broadcasting services in India. The authority will have a perpetual succession and a common seal with powers to enter into a contract and can sue and can be sued in its name.

It consists of a chairperson who will be appointed by the President of India on recommendation from the chairman of the states who will be the chairman of the committee, the information and broadcasting minister and the Press Council of India. It will also consist of a maximum of 11 part-time members to be appointed by the central government, a secretary to the government in charge of the department of telecommunications and a secretary general.

The chairperson will be a whole-time member and will hold office for a term of five years. He will be appointed from amongst the persons of eminence with more than 15 years of experience in administration, law, broadcasting and public relations. The functions of authority will be:

1. To carry out frequency planning of such frequencies or band of frequencies assigned to it by the wireless adviser to the government for the purpose of ING services.
2. To grant licences for broadcasting services.
3. To ensure that a wide range of broadcasting services are available throughout India.
4. To ensure services of high quality and offer a wide range of programmes to appeal to a variety of tastes and interests.
5. To determine the programme code and standard.
6. To take necessary action for violation of code, violation of condition of licence.
7. To set technical and other quality standards to ensure a reasonable quality of reception.

The authority can appoint a committee of experts to advise on:

1. Practices to be followed in connection with unjust and unfair treatment to any person in programmes, unwarranted infringement of privacy included in programmes.
2. Practices to be followed in connection to portrayal of violence, sexual conduct in the programmes, *i.e.*, to set standards of decency for programmes, with regard to the attitude of the public at large.

Licences

No person is entitled to provide broadcasting services without obtaining a licence, after commencement of this act. The authority can grant licences for the following broadcasting services, namely:

1. Terrestrial radio broadcasting.
2. Terrestrial television broadcasting.
3. Satellite radio broadcasting.
4. Satellite television broadcasting.
5. Direct-to-home broadcasting.
6. Local delivery sevices.
7. Such other services as may be prescribed.

The terrestrial broadcasting services can be further categeorised into analogue and digital and also into national, regional, local, restricted local services or any other similar service for the purposes of the licences and prevention of their accumulation.

The licence shall be provided subject to following conditions:

1. The person granted the licence will ensure that nothing is included in the programmes of the licensee which is likely to encourage crime or lead to disorder or will be offensive to public feeling.
2. The licensee will ensure that news given in the programme will be presented with due accuracy and impartiality.

3. The licensee has to ensure that due impartiality is maintained with respect to social or political issues or matters relating to public policy.
4. The licensee will ensure that due responsibility is exercised with respect to religious programmes with a view to avoiding improper exploition of religious susceptibilities and offence to the religious views and beliefs of those belonging to a particular religion.
5. The licensee will ensure that due emphasis is given to promote national integration, Indian culture in his programmes.
6. The licensee will have to ensure that time, determined by the authority, is earmarked for broadcasting of—children's programmes, educational programmes, programmes of Indian origin, a range of diversity of independent production.
7. The licensee will have to follow the programme codes and standards and codes set by the authority.
8. The licensee will pay the licence fees in the same manner as may be determined by the regulations.
9. The licensee will not carry out networking of local or regional broadcasting services without prior approval of the authority.
10. The conditions of the licence can be changed by the authority after giving to the licensee a reasonable opportunity of being heard.

The licence granted for direct-to-home service or local delivery service shall be subject to the following conditions in addition to the conditions referred above:

1. The licensee will have to provide a tier basic service which may include a number and type of terrestrial broadcasting for every permitted service and also of the public service broadcaster.
2. The licensee will include only licensed services or permitted services in his delivery package for the purpose of distribution and also he will not use more than that number of channels as determined by the authority out of the total channel capacity of the system for providing his own programming.

The period of licence for each category will be for a period not exceeding 10 years.

The licence is not transferable and it will lapse prior to its normal expiry in case of insolvency or death of the licensee. No person will be given the number of licences for a category of service. There are restrictions on cross media ownership between the newspaper and the broadcasting service. The government can modify any limit on interest or equity holding in the body corporate or companies by notification in the official gazette.

Grant of Licence for Satellite Broadcasting Services

1. Any person desirous of obtaining a satellite broadcasting licence will have to apply to the authority.

2. If the authority is satisfied that the applicant: (*a*) has acquired transponder on an Indian satellite system or on a foreign satellite system, (*b*) has obtained technical clearance for transponders from the wireless adviser, (*c*) has fulfilled all other conditions laid down in the act; the authority may grant a licence to such person on payment of fees; if the authority refuses to grant a licence it will have to give the applicant an opportunity to be heard. Provide further that such a person providing his broadcasting services immediately before the commencement of the act may continue to do so without a licence for a period of one month from such commencement.

Grant of Licence for Direct-to-Home Service

The authority will invite bids for grant of licence and it will be granted to the highest bidder if he fulfils all the conditions for the grant of such licence. The authority grants such number of licences (not less than two) as may be prescribed.

Special Provisions for Satellite Broadcasting and Direct-to-Home Services

The wireless adviser will give technical clearance for licensing (the clearance can be refused on technical or security reasons). In cases where operations of the services are permitted with foreign satellite system, while giving technical clearance for relicensing or renewal of such services, give priority for their operation with Indian satellite system.

The licensee shall carry out the uplinking of satellite broadcasting services or direct-to-home will grant two licences for local delivery service for each telecom circle as identified by the Central Government. The authority will invite bids and licence will be granted to the highest bidder. The wireless adviser shall assign frequencies for MMDS for providing local delivery service, wherever it is required.

The authority may exempt the non-commercial establishments under common ownership from obtaining a licence for the purpose of providing cable television services for the exclusive use of their members. The Government can by notification confer upon the licensee of the local delivery services, such rights and obligations as it may consider necessary in respect of the placing and maintaining of his cable networks as available to the telegraph authority.

Enforcement of Licences

The authority can take any of the following actions in case of breach of any terms of the licence:

1. Direct licensing to correction or apology or not to repeat a programme.
2. To impose a penalty which may extend up to Rs. 50 lakh.
3. Suspend the licence for a specified period.
4. Curtail the period of the licence.
5. Revoke the licence.

Any aggrieved person may prefer an appeal and action of the authority in the high court having jurisdiction within 30 days of such action.

The proceeds of the licence fee will be credited to the consolidated fund of India. The authority will have its own fund and all receipts of the authority will be credited to the fund and all payments by the authority will be from them. The authority will submit a report at the end of each financial year to the Central Government.

Offence and Punishments

A person who provides, distributes or receives any broadcasting service which is neither a licensed service nor a permitted service or abets or assists transmission of such service in any manner which may include collection of subscription for his principal, issuing of advertisements to such service, dealing in or distribution of decoders or dish antennas, shall be guilty of committing an offence of illegal broadcasting and on conviction, shall be punishable with imprisonment which may extend up to five years, or with fine which may extend up to Rs. 10 lakh and in subsequent offence such fine may extend to rupees Rs. 50 lakh, or with both.

Special Provisions for Certain Foreign Satellite Broadcasting Services

The authority after receiving a request in this regard, may grant permission for reception of an unlicensed foreign satellite broadcasting service in India, if such broadcasting is service:

1. Is free to air broadcasting service.
2. Does not carry any advertisements; or carries advertisements for the duration as may be fixed by the authority and the service is devoted solely to sports or international news and current affairs.
3. Fulfils the programme standard with respect to permitted service. Provided that the authority may revoke such permission, if it feels that the service has contravened any of the above conditions.

No licensee shall carry a live broadcast of any sporting or other event of national or international interest held in India, without the consent of the authority unless the public service broadcasters have also been given the broadcasting right for carrying the same.

Procedure and Powers of the Authority

1. The authority will be guided by principles of natural justice and subject to the other provisions of this act and of any rules, the authority will have powers to regulate its own procedure including the fixing of places and times of its inquiry.
2. The authority will have for the purpose of discharging its functions under this act, the same powers as are vested in a civil court under the code of civil procedure, while trying a suit, in respect of the following matters, namely:
   (*a*) Summoning and enforcing the attendance of any person and examining him on oath.
   (*b*) Receiving evidence on affidavits.
   (*c*) Issuing commissions for the examination of witnesses or documents.
   (*d*) Any other matter which may be prescribed.

In event of any war or a natural calamity of national magnitude, the Central Government may, in public interest, take over the control and management of any broadcasting service or any facility connected therewith, suspend its operation or entrust the public service broadcaster to manage it in the manner directed by the Government for such period as it deems fit.

The government, if it considers necessary or expedient to do so, may, in public interest, at any time require the authority to direct any licensee to:

1. Transmit in his broadcasting service such announcement in such a manner as may be considered necessary.
2. Stop any broadcasting service which is considered prejudicial to friendly relations with a foreign country, public order, security of state, or communal harmony. The Central Government may in public interest, issue such other directions, to the authority, from time to time as considered necessary.

Powers of the authority to seek information conduct enquires, take evidence, etc.

1. The licensee will have to start his service within the period specified by the authority and maintain documents, records and transmission schedules as may be specified and allow inspection of such records to the authority.
2. The authority can call for information from the licensee which it considers in the public interest and necessary for the transparency and ascertaining the true ownership of the licensee. The authority will have all the powers of an inspecting officer. If the licensee defaults with any conditions, the authority can cancel the licence. The application of this law is in addition to and not in derogation of the provisions of any other law.

Power to Make Rules

The Central Government can by notification make rules for carrying out provisions of this Act. The rules will provide for all or any of the following matter:

1. Provide for circumstances for communication.
2. Salaries and allowances payable to the chairperson and other part-time members.
3. The functions to be performed by the authority.
4. Number of licences more than which can't be given.

Power to Make Regulations

The authority can make regulations and rules made thereunder by notification. The rules will provide for all or any of the following matter:

1. The time and place of the meetings, the procedure of transaction of business.
2. The manner of appointment of officers and employees and their salary.
3. The quality of reception and the programme code and standard.
4. The manner in which the licence fee should be paid by the licensee and the conditions of granting licence.
5. The minimum number and type of ING service of public service broadcaster and of terrestrial broadcasting services for every permitted service.
6. The number of channels to be used and the period of licence to the licensee.

7. The criteria subject to which the uplinking from outside India will be permitted in respect of these services for coverage of live events taking place outside India.
8. Restricted area under which permission may be granted.
9. Any sporting or other event of national or international interest of which live telecast shall be carried out without the authority's permission.
10. The documentary record and transmission schedule to be maintained.

Every rule and regulation is to be laid before the parliament. The Central Government can make provisions in the act within three years of commencement of this bill and not after that, to remove any difficulties that arise.

Repeal and Saving

The Cable Television Networks (Regulation) Act, 1995 is repealed. The cable operators registered under this Act can make an application to the authority for grant of licence within six months of commencement of this act. The authority may grant or refuse the licence to the operator. No licence will be granted to any cable TV network which provides such service to more than 5000 households and from more than one location.

No refusal can be made unless the applicant has a chance to present the case. The authority will authorise a district magistrate to look in to the complaints of the public, give notice to the operators, make enquiries and take necessary action.

THE PRASAR BHARATI (BROADCASTING CORPORATION OF INDIA) ACT

An Act to provide for the establishment of a Broadcasting Corporation for India, to be known as Prasar Bharati, to define its composition, functions and powers and to provide for matters connected therewith or incidental thereto.

CHAPTER I
PRELIMINARY

1. Short Title, Extent and Commencement: (1) This Act may be called the Prasar Bharati (Broadcasting Corporation of India) Act, 1990.

(2) It extends to the whole of India.

(3) It shall come into force on such date as the Central Government may, by notification, appoint.

2. Definitions: In this Act, unless the context otherwise requires,—

(*a*) "Akashvani" means the offices, stations and other establishments, by whatever name called, which, immediately before the appointed day, formed part of or were under the Director-General, All India Radio of the Union Ministry of Information and Broadcasting;

(*b*) "appointed day" means the date appointed under Section 3;

(*c*) "broadcasting" means the dissemination of any form of communication like signs, signals, writing, pictures, images and sounds of all kinds by transmission of electro-magnetic waves through space or through cables intended to be received by the general public either directly or indirectly through the medium of relay stations and all its grammatical variations and cognate expression shall be constructed accordingly;

(*d*) "Board" means the Prasar Bharati Board;

(*e*) "Broadcasting Council" means the Council established under Section 14;

(*f*) "Chairman" means the Chairman of the Corporation appointed under Section 4;

(*g*) "Corporation" means the Prasar Bharati (Broadcasting Corporation of India) established under Section 3;

(*h*) "Doordarshan" means the offices, kendras and other establishments, by whatever name called, which, immediately before the appointed day, formed part of or were under the Directorate-General, Doordarshan of the Union Ministry of Information and Broadcasting;

(*i*) "Elected Member" means a Member elected under Section 3;

(*j*) "Executive Member" means the Executive Member appointed under Section 4;

(*k*) "kendra" means telecasting centre with studios or transmitters or both and includes a relay station;

(*l*) "Member" means a Member of the Board;

(*m*) "Member (Finance)" means the Member (Finance) appointed under Section 4;

(*n*) "Member (Personnel)" means the Member (Personnel) appointed under Section 4;

(*o*) "Nominated Member" means the Member nominated by the Union Ministry of Information and Broadcasting under Section 3;

(*p*) "Non-lapsable Fund" means the Fund created from the commercial revenues of Akashvani and Doordarshan to meet expenditure on certain schemes;

(*q*) "notification" means a notification published in the official Gazette;

(*r*) "Part-Time Member" means a Part-Time Member of the Board appointed under Section 4, but does not include an Ex-Officio Member, the Nominated Member or an Elected Member;

(*s*) "prescribed" means prescribed by rules made under this Act;

(*t*) "Recruitment Board" means a board established under sub-section (1) of Section 10;

(*u*) "Regulations" means regulations made by the Corporation under this Act;

(*v*) "Station" means any broadcasting station with studios or transmitters or both and includes a relay station;

(*w*) "Whole-Time Member" means the Executive Member, Member (Finance) or Member (Personnel);

(*x*) "year" means the financial year.

CHAPTER II
PRASAR BHARATI
(BROADCASTING CORPORATION OF INDIA)

3. Establishment and Composition of Corporation: (1) With effect from such date as the Central Government may by notification appoint in this behalf, there shall be established for the purposes of this Act a Corporation, to be known as the Prasar Bharati (Broadcasting Corporation of India).

(2) The Corporation shall be a body corporate by the name aforesaid, having perpetual succession and a common seal with power to acquire, hold and dispose of property, both movable and immovable, and to contract, and shall by the said name sue and be sued.

(3) The Headquarters of the Corporation shall be at New Delhi and the Corporation may establish offices, kendras or stations at other places in India and, with the previous approval of the Central Government, outside India.

(4) The General Superintendence, direction and management of the affairs of the Corporation shall vest in the Prasar Bharati Board which may exercise all such powers and do all such acts and things as may be exercised or done by the Corporation under this Act.

(5) The Board shall consist of—

(*a*) a Chairman;

(*b*) one Executive Member;

(*c*) one Member (Finance);

(*d*) one Member (Personnel);

(*e*) six Part-Time Members;

(*f*) Director-General (Akashvani), ex-officio;

(*g*) Director-General (Doordarshan), ex-officio;

(*h*) one representative of the Union Ministry of Information and Broadcasting, to be nominated by that Ministry; and

(*i*) two representatives of the employees of the Corporation, of whom one shall be elected by the Engineering Staff from amongst themselves and one shall be elected by the other employee from amongst themselves.

(6) The Corporation may appoint such committees as may be necessary for the efficient performance, exercise and discharge of its functions, powers and duties:

Provided that all or a majority of the members of each committee shall be Members and a member of any such committee who is not a Member shall have only the right to attend meetings of the committee and take part in the proceedings thereof, but shall not have the right to vote.

(7) The Corporation may associate with itself, in such manner and for such purposes as may be provided by regulations, any person whose assistance or advice it may need in complying with any of the provisions of this Act and a person so associated shall have the right to take part in the discussions of the Board relevant to the purposes for which he has been associated, but shall not have the right to vote.

(8) No act or proceeding of the Board or of any committee appointed by it under sub-section (6) shall be invalidated merely by reason of—

(*a*) any vacancy in, or any defect in the constitution of, the Board or such committee; or

(*b*) any defect in the appointment of a person acting as a Member or a member of such committee; or

(*c*) any irregularity in the procedure of the Board or such committee not affecting the merits of the case.

4. Appointment of Chairman and other Members: (1) The Chairman and the other Members, except the ex-officio Members, the Nominated Member and the elected

Members shall be appointed by the President of India on the recommendation of a committee consisting of—

(*a*) the Chairman of the Council of States, who shall be the Chairman of the Committee;

(*b*) the Chairman of the Press Council of India established under Section 4 of the Press Council Act, 1978; and

(*c*) one nominee of the President of India.

(2) No appointment of a Member shall be invalidated merely by reason of any vacancy in, or any defect in the constitution of, the committee appointed under sub-section (1).

(3) The Chairman and the Part-time Members shall be persons of eminence in Public life; the Executive Member shall be a person having special knowledge or practical experience in respect of such matters as administration, management, broadcasting, education, literature, culture, arts, music, dramatics or journalism; the Member (Finance) shall be person having special knowledge or practical experience in respect of financial matters and the Member (Personnel) shall be a person having special knowledge or practical experience in respect of personnel management and administration.

(4) The recommendations made by the committee constituted under sub-section (1) shall be binding for the purposes of appointments under this section.

5. Powers and Functions of Executive Member: (1) The Executive Member shall be the Chief Executive of the Corporation and shall, subject to the control and supervision of the Board, exercise such power and discharge such functions of the Board as it may delegate to him.

6. Terms of Office, Conditions of Service, etc., of Chairman and Other Members: (1) The Chairman shall be Part-Time Member and shall hold office for a term of six years from the date on which he enters upon his office.

(2) The Executive Member, the Member (Finance) and Member (Personnel) shall be Whole-Time Members and every such Member shall hold office for a term of six years from the date on which he enters upon his office or until he attains the age of sixty-two years whichever is earlier.

(3) The Term of office of Part-Time Members shall be six years, but one-third of such Members shall retire on the expiration of every second year.

(4) The term of office of an elected Member shall be two years or till he ceases to be an employee of the Corporation, whichever is earlier.

(5) As soon as may be after the establishment of the Corporation, the President of India may, by order, make such provision as he thinks fit for curtailing the term of office of some of the Part-Time Member then appointed in order that one-third of the Members holding office as such Part-Time Members shall retire in every second year thereafter.

(6) Where before the expiry of the term of office of a person holding the office of Chairman, or any other Member, a vacancy arises, for any reason whatsoever, such vacancy shall be deemed to be casual vacancy and the person appointed or elected to fill such vacancy shall hold office for the unexpired period of the term for which his predecessor in office would have held office if such vacancy had not arisen.

(7) The Whole-Time Members shall be the employees of the Corporation and as such shall be entitled to such salaries and allowances and shall be subject to such conditions of

service in respect of leave, pension (if any), provident fund and other matters as may be prescribed:

Provided that the salaries and allowances and the conditions of service shall not be varied to their disadvantage after their appointment.

(8) The Chairman and Part-Time Members shall be entitled to such allowances as may be prescribed.

7. **Removal and Suspension of Chairman and Members:** (1) Subject to the provisions of sub-section (3), the Chairman or any other Member, except an ex-officio Member, the Nominated Member and an elected Member shall only be removed from his office by order of the President of India on the ground of misbehaviour after the Supreme Court, on a reference being made to it by the President, has, on inquiry held in accordance with such procedure as the Supreme Court may by rules provide, reported that the Chairman or such other member, as the case may be, ought, on such ground, be removed.

(2) The President may suspend from office the Chairman or other Member, except an ex-officio Member, the Nominated Member or an elected Member, in respect of whom a reference has been made to the Supreme Court under sub-section (1) until the President has passed orders on receipt of the report of the Superme Court on such reference.

(3) Notwithstanding anything contained in sub-section (1), the President may, by order, remove the Chairman or any Wholetime Member from his office if such Chairman or such Wholetime Member—

(*a*) ceases to be a citizen of India; or

(*b*) is adjudged an insolvent; or

(*c*) engages during his term of office in any paid employment outside the duties of his office; or

(*d*) is convicted of any offence involving moral turpitude; or

(*e*) is, in the opinion of the President, unfit to continue in office by reason of infirmity of body or mind:

Provided that the President may, by order, remove any Part-Time Member from his office if he adjudged an insolvent or is convicted of any offence involving moral turpitude or where he is, in the opinion of the President, unfit to continue in office by reason of infirmity of body or mind.

(4) If the Chairman or any Wholetime Member, except any ex-officio Member, the Nominated Member or any elected Member, is, or becomes in any way concerned or interested in any contract or agreement made by or on behalf of the Corporation of the Government of India or the Government of a State, participates in any way in the profit thereof, or in any benefit or emolument arising therefrom than as a member, and in common with other members of an incorporated company, he shall, for the purposes of sub-section (1), be deemed to be guilty of misbehaviour.

(5) If a Part-time Member is, or becomes in any way concerned, or interested in any contract, or agreement made by or on behalf of the Corporation, he shall, for the purposes of sub-section (1), be deemed to be guilty of misbehaviour.

(6) The Chairman or any other Member may resign his office by giving notice thereof in writing to the President of India and on such resignation being accepted, the Chairman or other Member shall be deemed to have vacated his office.

8. Meetings of Board: (1) The Board shall meet at such times and places and shall observe such rules of procedure in regard to the transaction of business at its meetings (including the quorum at meetings) as may be provided by regulations:

Provided that there shall not be less than six meetings every year but three months shall not intervene between one meeting and the next meeting.

(2) A Member shall be deemed to have vacated his office if he absents himself for three consecutive meetings of the Board without the leave of the Chairman.

(3) The Chairman shall preside at the meetings of the Board and if for any reason he is unable to attend any meeting, the Executive Member and in the absence of both, any other Member elected by the Members present at such meeting, shall preside at the meeting.

(4) All questions which come up before any meeting of the Board shall be decided by a majority of the votes of the Members present and voting and, in the event of an equality of votes, the Chairman, or in his absence, the person presiding, shall have and exercise a second, or casting vote.

9. Officers and Other Employees of Corporation: (1) Subject to such control, restrictions and conditions as may be prescribed, the Corporation may appoint, after consultation with the Recruitment Board, the Director-General (Akashvani), the Director-General (Doordarshan) and such other officers and other employees as may be necessary.

(2) The method of recruitment of such officers and employees and all other matters connected therewith and the conditions of service of such officers and other employees shall be such as may be provided by regulations.

10. Establishment of Recruitment Boards: (1) The Corporation shall, as soon as may be, after the appointed day and in such manner and subject to such conditions and restrictions as may be prescribed, establish for the purpose of Section 9, one or more Recruitment Boards consisting wholly of persons other than the Members, Officers and other Employees of the Corporation:

Provided that for the purposes of Appointment to the posts carrying scales of pay which are not less than that of a Joint Secretary to the Central Government, the Recruitment Board shall consist of the Chairman, other Members, the Ex-officio Members, the Nominated Members and the elected Members.

(2) The qualifications and other conditions of service of the members constituting the Recruitment Board and the period for which such members shall hold office, shall be such as may be prescribed.

11. Transfer of Service of Existing Employees to Corporation: (1) Where the Central Government has ceased to perform any functions which under Section 12 are the function of the Corporation, it shall be lawful for the Central Government to transfer, by order and with effect from such date or dates as may be specified in the order, to the Corporation any of the officers or other employees serving in the Akashvani or Doordarshan and engaged in the performance of those functions:

Provided that no order under this sub-section shall be made in relation to any officer or other employee in the Akashvani or Doordarshan who has, in respect of the proposal of the Central Government to transfer such officer or other employee to the Corporation, intimated within such time as may be specified in this behalf by the Central Government, his intention of not becoming an employee of the Corporation.

(2) The provisions of sub-section (1) shall also apply to the members of the Indian Information Service, the Central Secretariat Service or any other service or to persons borne on cadres outside Akashvani and Doordarshan who have been working in Akashvani or Doordarshan immediately before the appointed day:

Provided that where any such member intimated, within the time specified in sub-section (1), his intention of not becoming an employee of the Corporation but to continue on deputation, he may be allowed to continue on deputation in accordance with such terms and conditions as may be prescribed.

(3) In making an order under sub-section (1), the Central Government shall, as far as may be, take into consideration the functions which the Akashvani or, as the case may be, Doordarshan has ceased or ceases to perform and the area in which such functions have been or are performed.

(4) An officer or other employee transferred by an order under sub-section (1) shall, on and from the date of transfer, cease to be an employee of the Central Government and become an employee of the Corporation with such designation as the Corporation may determine and shall, subject to the provisions of sub-sections (5) and (6), be governed by such regulations as may be made as respects remuneration and other conditions of service including pension, leave and provident fund and shall continue to be an officer or other employee of the Corporation unless and until his employment is terminated by the Corporation.

(5) Every officer or other employee transferred by an order made under sub-section (1) shall, within six months from the date of transfer, exercise his option, in writing, to be governed—

(*a*) by the scale of pay applicable to the post held by him in the Akashvani or Doordarshan immediately before the date of transfer or by the scale applicable to the post under the Corporation to which he is transferred;

(*b*) by the leave, provident fund, retirement or other terminal benefits admissible to employees of the Central Government in accordance with the rules or orders of the Central Government, as amended from time to time, or leave, provident fund or other terminal benefits admissible to the employees of the Corporation under the regulation, and such option once exercised under this Act shall be final:

Provided that the option exercised under clause (a) by an officer or other employee shall be applicable only in respect of the post under the Corporation to which such officer or other employee is transferred and on appointment to a higher post under the Corporation he shall be eligible only for the scale of pay applicable to such higher post:

Provided further that if immediately before the date of his transfer any such officer or other employee is officiating in a higher post under the Government either in a leave vacancy or any other vacancy of a specified duration, his pay on transfer shall be protected for the unexpired period of such vacancy and thereafter he shall be entitled to the scale of pay applicable to the post under the Government to which he would have reverted or to the scale of pay applicable to the post under the Corporation to which he is transferred, whichever he may opt:

Provided also that when an officer or other employee serving in the Union Ministry of Information and Broadcasting or in any of its attached or subordinate officers is promoted to officiate in a higher post in the Ministry or office subsequent to the transfer to the Corporation of any other officer or employee senior to him in that Ministry or office before such transfer, the officer or other employee who is promoted to officiate in such higher post shall, on transfer to the Corporation, be entitled only to the scale of pay applicable to the post he would have held but for such promotion or the scale of pay applicable to the post under the Corporation to which he is transferred, whichever he may opt.

(6) No officer or other employee transferred by an order made under sub-section (1) or sub-section (2),—

(*a*) shall be dismissed or removed by an authority subordinate to that competent to make a similar or equivalent appointment under the Corporation as may be specified in the regulations;

(*b*) shall be dismissed or removed or reduced in rank except after an inquiry in which he has been informed of the charges against him and given a reasonable opportunity of being heard in respect of those charges:

Provided that where it is proposed after such inquiry to impose upon him any such penalty, such penalty may be imposed on the basis of evidence adduced during such inquiry and it shall not be necessary to give such person an opportunity of making representation on the proposed penalty:

Provided further that clause (b) shall not apply where an officer or other employee is dismissed or removed or reduced in rank on the ground of conduct which has led to his conviction on a criminal charge.

12. Functions and Powers of Corporation: (1) Subject to the provisions of this Act, it shall be the primary duty of the Corporation to organise and conduct public broadcasting services to inform, educate and entertain the public and to ensure a balanced development of broadcasting on radio and television.

Explanation: For the removal of doubts, it is hereby declared that the provisions of this section shall be in addition to, and not in derogation, of the provisions of the Indian Telegraph Act, 1885.

(2) The Corporation shall, in the discharge of its functions, be guided by the following objectives, namely—

(*a*) upholding the unity and integrity of the country and the values enshrined in the Constitution;

(*b*) safeguarding the citizen's right to be informed freely, truthfully and objectively on all matters of public interest, national or international, and presenting a fair and balanced flow of information including contrasting views without advocating any opinion or ideology of its own;

(*c*) paying special attention to the fields of education and spread of literacy, agriculture, rural development, environment, health and family welfare and science and technology;

(*d*) providing adequate coverage to the diverse cultures and languages of the various regions of the country by broadcasting appropriate programmes;

(*e*) providing adequate coverage to sports and games so as to encourage healthy competition and the spirit of sportsmanship;

(*f*) providing appropriate programmes keeping in view the special needs of the youth;

(*g*) informing and stimulating the national consciousness in regard to the status and problems of women and paying special attention to the upliftment of women;

(*h*) promoting social justice and combating exploitation, inequality and such evils as untouchability and advancing the welfare of the weaker sections of the society;

(*i*) safeguarding the rights of the working classes and advancing their welfare;

(*j*) serving the rural and weaker sections of the people and those residing in border regions, backward or remote areas;

(*k*) providing suitable programmes keeping in view the special needs of the minorities and tribal communities;

(*l*) taking special steps to protect the interests of children, the blind, the aged, the handicapped and other vulnerable sections of the people;

(*m*) promoting national integration by broadcasting in a manner that facilitates communication in the languages in India; and facilitating the distribution of regional broadcasting services in every State in the languages of that State;

(*n*) providing comprehensive broadcast coverage through the choice of appropriate technology and the best utilisation of the broadcast frequencies available and ensuring high quality reception;

(*o*) promoting research and development activities in order to ensure that radio and television broadcast technology are constantly updated; and

(*p*) expanding broadcasting facilities by establishing additional channels of transmission at various levels.

(3) In particular, and without prejudice to the generality of the foregoing provisions, the Corporation may take such steps as it thinks fit—

(*a*) to ensure that broadcasting is conducted as a public service to provide and produce programmes;

(*b*) to establish a system for the gathering of news for radio and television;

(*c*) to negotiate for purchase of, or otherwise acquire, programmes and rights or privileges in respect of sports and other events, films, serials, occasions, meetings, functions or incidents of public interest, for broadcasting and to establish procedures for the allocation of such programmes, rights or privileges to the services;

(*d*) to establish and maintain a library or libraries of radio, television and other materials;

(*e*) to conduct or commission, from time to time, programmes, audience research, market or technical service, which may be released to such persons and in such manner and subject to such terms and conditions as the Corporation may think fit;

(*f*) to provide such other services as may be specified by regulations.

(4) Nothing in sub-sections (2) and (3) shall prevent the Corporation from managing on behalf of the Central Government and in accordance with such terms and conditions as may be specified by that Government the broadcasting of External Services and monitoring of broadcasts made by organisations outside India on the basis of arrangements made for reimbursement of expenses by the Central Government.

(5) For the purposes of ensuring that adequate time is made available for the promotion of the objectives set out in this section, the Central Government shall have the power to determine the maximum limit of broadcast time in respect of the advertisement.

(6) The Corporation shall be subject to no civil liability on the ground merely that it failed to comply with any of the provisions of this section.

(7) The Corporation shall have power to determine and levy fees and other service charges for or in respect of the advertisements and such programmes as may be specified by regulations:

Provided that the fees and other service charges levied and collected under this sub-section shall not exceed such limits as may be determined by the Central Government, from time to time.

13. Parliamentary Committee: (1) There shall be constituted a Committee consisting of twenty-two Members of Parliament, of whom fifteen from the House of the People to be elected by the Members thereof and seven from the Council of States to be elected by the Members thereof in accordance with the system of proportional representation by means of the single transferable vote, to oversee that the Corporation discharges its functions in accordance with the provision of this Act and, in particular, the objectives set out in Section 12 and submit a report thereon to Parliament.

(2) The Committee shall function in accordance with such rules as may be made by the Speaker of the House of the People.

14. Establishment of Broadcasting Council, Term of Office and Removal, etc., of Members Thereof: (1) There shall be established, by notification, as soon as may be after the appointed day, a Council, to be known as the Broadcasting Council, to receive and consider complaints referred to in Section 15 and to advise the Corporation in the discharge of its functions in accordance with the objectives set out in Section 12.

(2) The Broadcasting Council shall consist of—

(*i*) a President and ten other members to be appointed by the President of India from amongst persons of eminence in public life;

(*ii*) four Members of Parliament, of whom two from the House of the People to be nominated by the Speaker thereof and two from the Council of States to be nominated by the Chairman thereof.

(3) The President of the Broadcasting Council shall be a wholetime member and every other member shall be a part-time member and the President or the part-time member shall hold office as such for a term of three years from the date on which he enters upon his office.

(4) The Broadcasting Council may constitute such number of Regional Councils as it may deem necessary to aid and assist the Council in the discharge of its functions.

(5) The President of the Broadcasting Council shall be entitled to such salary and allowances and shall be subject to such conditions of service in respect of leave, pension (if any), provident fund and other matters as may be prescribed.

Provided that the salary and allowances and the conditions of service shall not be varied to the disadvantage of the President of the Broadcasting Council after his appointment.

(6) The other members of the Broadcasting Council and the members of the Regional Councils constituted under sub-section (4) shall be entitled to such allowances as may be prescribed.

15. Jurisdiction of, and the Procedure to be Followed by, Broadcasting Council: (1) The Broadcasting Council shall receive and consider complaints from—

(*i*) any person or group of persons alleging that a certain programme or broadcast or the functioning of the Corporation in specific cases or in general is not in accordance with the objective for which the Corporation is established;

(*ii*) any person (other than officer or employee of the Corporation) claiming himself to have been treated unjustly or unfairly in any manner (including unwarranted invasion of privacy, misrepresentation, distortion or lack of objectivity) in connection with any programme broadcast by the Corporation.

(2) A complaint under sub-section (1) shall be made in such manner and within such period as may be specified by regulations.

(3) The Broadcasting Council shall follow such procedure as it thinks fit for the disposal of complaints received by it.

(4) If the complaint is found to be justified either wholly or in part, the Broadcasting Council shall advise the Executive Member to take appropriate action.

(5) If the Executive Member is unable to accept the recommendation of the Broadcasting Council, he shall place such recommendation before the Board for its decision thereon.

(6) If the Board is also unable to accept the recommendation of the Broadcasting Council, it shall record its reasons therefore and inform the Broadcasting Council accordingly.

(7) Notwithstanding anything contained in sub-sections (5) and (6), where the Broadcasting Council deems it appropriate, it may, for reasons to be recorded in writing, require the Corporation to broadcast its recommendations with respect to a complaint in such manner as the Council may deem fit.

CHAPTER III
ASSETS, FINANCES AND ACCOUNTS

16. Transfer of Certain Assets, Liabilities, etc., of Central Government to Corporation: As from the appointed day—

(*a*) all property and assets (including the Non-lapsable Fund) which immediately before that day vested in the Central Government for the purpose of Akashvani or Doordarshan or both shall stand transferred to the Corporation on such terms and conditions as may be determined by the Central Government and the book value of all such property and assets shall be treated as the capital provided by the Central Government to the Corporation;

(*b*) all debts, obligations and liabilities incurred, all contracts entered into and all matters and things engaged to be done by, with or for the Central Government immediately before such day for or in connection with the purposes of Akashvani or Doordarshan or both shall be deemed to have been incurred, entered into and engaged to be done by, with or for the Corporation;

(*c*) all sums of money due to the Central Government in relation to the Akashvani or Doordarshan or both immediately before such day shall be deemed to be due to the Corporation;

(*d*) all suits and other legal proceedings instituted or which could have been instituted by or against Central Government immediately before such day for any matter in relation to the Akashvani or Doordarshan or both may be continued or instituted by or against the Corporation.

17. Grants, etc., by Central Government: For the purposes of enabling the Corporation to discharge its functions efficiently under this Act, the Central Government may, after due appropriation made by Parliament by law in this behalf, pay to the Corporation in each financial year—

(*i*) the proceeds of the broadcast receiver licence fees, if any, as reduced by the collection charges; and

(*ii*) such other sums of money as that Government considers necessary, by way of equity, grant-in-aid or loan.

18. Fund of Corporation: (1) The Corporation shall have its own Fund and all the receipts of the Corporation (including the amounts which stand transferred to the Corporation under Section 16) shall be credited to the Fund and all payments by the Corporation shall be made therefrom.

(2) All moneys belonging to the Fund shall be deposited in one or more nationalised banks in such manner as the Corporation may decide.

(3) The Corporation may spend such sums as it thinks fit for performing its functions under this Act and such sums shall be treated as expenditure payable out of the Fund of the Corporation.

Explanation: For the purposes of the section, "nationalised bank" means a corresponding new bank specified in the First Schedule to the Banking Companies (Acquisition and Transfer of Undertakings) Act, 1970 or a corresponding new bank specified in the First Schedule to the Banking Companies (Acquisition and Transfer of Undertakings) Act, 1980.

19. Investment of Moneys: The Corporation may invest its moneys in the securities of the Central Government or any State Government or in such other manner as may be prescribed.

20. Annual Financial Statement of the Corporation: (1) The Corporation shall prepare, in each financial year, an Annual Financial Statement for the next financial year showing separately—

(*a*) the expenditure which is proposed to be met from the internal resources of the Corporation; and (*b*) the sums required from the Central Government to meet other expenses and distinguishing—

(*i*) revenue expenditure from other expenditure; and

(*ii*) non-plan expenditure from plan expenditure.

(2) The Annual Financial Statement shall be prepared in such form and forwarded at such time to the Central Government for its approval as may be agreed to by that Government and the Corporation.

21. Accounts and Audit of Corporation: (1) The Corporation shall maintain proper accounts and other relevant records and prepare an annual statement of accounts in such form and in such manner as may be prescribed.

(2) The accounts of the Corporation shall be audited by the Comptroller and Auditor General of India at such intervals as may be specified by him and any expenditure incurred in connection with such audit shall be payable by the Corporation to the Comptroller and Auditor-General.

(3) The Comptroller and Auditor-General and any person appointed by him in connection with the audit of the accounts of the Corporation shall have the same rights and privileges and authority in connection with such audit as the Comptroller and Auditor-General has in connection with the audit of Government accounts and, in particular, shall have the right to demand the production of books, accounts, connected vouchers and other documents and papers and to inspect any of the offices of the Corporation.

(4) The accounts of the Corporation as certified by the Comptroller and Auditor-General of India or any other person appointed by him in this behalf together with the audit report thereon shall be forwarded annually to the Central Government and that Government shall cause the same to be laid before each House of Parliament.

22. Corporation not Liable to be Taxed: Notwithstanding anything contained in the Income-Tax Act, 1961, or any other enactment for the time being in force relating to income-tax or any other tax on income, profits or gains, the Corporation shall not be liable to pay any income-tax or any other tax in respect of—

(*a*) any income, profit or gains, accruing or arising out of the Fund of the Corporation or any amount received in that Fund; and

(*b*) any income, profits or gains derived or any amount received, by the Corporation.

CHAPTER IV
MISCELLANEOUS

23. Power of Central Government to Give Directions: (1) The Central Government may, from time to time as and when occasion arises, issue to the Corporation such directions as it may think necessary in the interests of the sovereignty, unity and integrity of India or the security of the State or preservation of public order requiring it not to make a broadcast on a matter specified in the direction or to make a broadcast on any matter of public importance specified in the direction.

(2) Where the corporation makes a broadcast in pursuance of the direction issued under sub-section (1), the fact that such broadcast has been made in pursuance of such direction may also be announced along with such broadcast, if the Corporation so desires.

(3) A copy of every direction issued under sub-section (1) shall be laid before each House of Parliament.

24. Power of Central Government to Obtain Information: The Central Government may require the Corporation to furnish such information as that Government may consider necessary.

25. Report to Parliament in Certain Matters and Recommendations as to Action Against the Board: (1) Where the Board persistently makes default in complying with any directions issued under Section 23 or fails to supply the information required under Section 24, the Central Government may prepare a report thereof and lay it before each House of Parliament for any recommendation thereof as to any action (including supersession of the Board) which may be taken against the Board.

(2) On the recommendation of the Parliament, the President may by notification supersede the Board for such period not exceeding six month, as may be specified in the notification:

Provided that before issuing the notification under this sub-section, the President shall give a reasonable opportunity to the Board to show cause as to why it should not be superseded and shall consider the explanations and objections, if any, of the Board.

(3) Upon the publication of the notification under sub-section (2)—

(*a*) all the Members shall, as from the date supersession, vacate their offices as such;

(*b*) all the powers, functions and duties which may, by or under the provision of this Act be exercised or discharged by or on behalf of the Board, shall, until the Board is reconstituted under this Act, be exercised and discharged by such person or persons as the President may direct.

(4) On the expiration of the period of supersession specified in the notification issued under sub-section (2), the President may reconstitute the Board by fresh appointments, and in such a case any person who had vacated his office under clause (a) of sub-section (3) shall not be disqualified for appointment:

Provided that the President may, at any time before the expiration of the period of supersession, take action under this sub-section.

(5) The Central Government shall cause the notification issued under sub-section (2) and a full report of the action taken under this section to be laid before each House of Parliament.

26. Office of Member not to Disqualify a Member of Parliament: It is hereby declared that the office of the member of the Broadcasting Council or of the Committee constituted under Section 13 shall not disqualify its holder for being chosen as or for being a member of either House of Parliament.

27. Chairman, Members, etc., to be Public Servants: The Chairman and every other Member, every officer or other employee of the Corporation and every member of a Committee thereof, the President and every member of the Broadcasting Council or every member of a Regional Council or a Recruitment Board shall be deemed to be a public servant within the meaning of Section 21 of the Indian Penal Code.

28. Protection of Action Taken in Good Faith: No suit or other legal proceeding shall lie against the Corporation, the Chairman or any Member or officer or other employee thereof or the President or a member of the Broadcasting Council or a member of a Regional Council or a Recruitment Board for anything which is in good faith done or intended to be done in pursuance of this Act or of any rules or regulations made thereunder.

29. Authentication of Orders and Other Instruments of Corporation: All orders and decisions of the Corporation shall be authenticated by the signature of the Chairman or any other Member authorised by the Corporation in this behalf and all other instruments executed by the Corporation shall be authenticated by the signature of the Executive Member or by any officer of the Corporation authorised by him in this behalf.

30. Delegation of Powers: The Corporation may, by general or special order, delegate to the Chairman or any other Member or to any officer of the Corporation, subject to such conditions and limitations, if any, as may be specified therein, such of its powers and duties under this Act as it may deem fit.

31. Annual Report: (1) The Corporation shall prepare once in every calendar year, in such form and within such times as may be prescribed, an annual report giving a full account of its activities (including the recommendations and suggestions made by the Broadcasting Council and the action taken thereon) during the previous year and copies thereof shall be forwarded to the Central Government and that Government shall cause the same to be laid before each House of Parliament.

(2) The Broadcasting Council shall prepare once in every calendar year, in such form and within such time as may be prescribed, an annual report giving a full account of its activities during the previous year and copies thereof shall be forwarded to the Central Government and that Government shall cause the same to be laid before each House of Parliament.

32. Power to Make Rules: (1) The Central Government may, by notification, make rules for carrying out the provisions of this Act.

(2) In particular, and without prejudice to generality of the foregoing power, such rules may provide for all or any of the following matters, namely—

(*a*) the salaries and allowances and conditions of service in respect of leave, pension (if any), provident fund and other matters in relation to the Wholetime Members under sub-section (7) of Section 6;

(*b*) the allowances payable to the Chairman and Part-time Members under sub-section (8) of Section 6;

(*c*) the control, restrictions and conditions subject to which the Corporation may appoint officers and other employees under sub-section (1) of Section 9;

(*d*) the manner in which and the conditions and restrictions subject to which a Recruitment Board may be established under sub-section (1) of Section 10;

(*e*) the qualification and other conditions of service of the members of a Recruitment Board and their period of office under sub-section (2) of Section 10;

(*f*) the terms and conditions in accordance with which the deputation may be regulated under sub-section (2) of Section 11;

(*g*) the salary and allowances and conditions of service in respect of leave, pension (if any), provident fund and other matters in relation to the President of the Broadcasting Council under sub-section (5) of Section 14;

(*h*) the allowances payable to other members of the Broadcasting Council and the members of the Regional Councils, under sub-section (6) of Section 14;

(*i*) the manner in which the Corporation may invest its moneys under Section 19;

(*j*) the form and the manner in which the annual statement of accounts shall be prepared under sub-section (1) of Section 21;

(*k*) the form in which, and the time within which the Corporation and the Broadcasting Council shall prepare their annual report under Section 31;

(*l*) any other matter which is required to be, or may be, prescribed.

33. Power to Make Regulations: (1) the Corporation may, by notification, make regulations not inconsistent with this Act and the rules made thereunder for enabling it to perform its functions under this Act.

(2) Without prejudice to the generality of the foregoing power such regulations may provide for all or/any of the following matters, namely—

(*a*) the manner in which and the purposes for which the Corporation may associate with itself any person under sub-section (7) of Section 3;

(*b*) the times and places at which meetings of Board shall be held and, the procedure to be followed thereat, and the quorum necessary for the transaction of the business at a meeting of the Board under sub-section (1) of Section 8;

(*c*) the methods of recruitment and conditions of service of officers and other employees of the Corporation under sub-section (2) of Section 9;

(*d*) the remuneration and other conditions of service, including pension, leave and provident fund in relation to an officer or other employee of the Corporation under sub-section (4) of Section 11;

(*e*) the authority competent to make certain appointments referred to in clause (a) of sub-section (6) of Section 11;

(*f*) the services which may be provided by the Corporation under clause (f) of sub-section (3) of Section 12;

(*g*) the determination and levy of fees and other service charges in respect of advertisements and other programmes under sub-section (7) of Section 12;

(*h*) the manner in which and the period within which complaints may be made under sub-section (2) of Section 15;

(*i*) any other matter in respect of which provision is, in the opinion of the Corporation, necessary for the performance of its functions under this Act:

Provided that the regulations under clause (c) or clause (d) shall be made only with the prior approval of the Central Government.

34. Rules and Regulations to be Laid before Parliament: Every rule and every regulation made under this Act shall be laid as soon as may be after it is made, before each House of Parliament, while it is in session for a total period of thirty days which may be comprised in one session or in two or more successive sessions, and if, before the expiry of the session immediately following the session or the successive session aforesaid, both Houses agree in making any modification in the rule or regulation, or both Houses agree that the rule or regulation should not be made, the rule or regulation shall thereafter have effect only in such modified form or be of no effect, as the case may be; so, however, that any such modification or annulment shall be without prejudice to the validity of anything previously done under that rule or regulation.

35. Power to Remove Difficulties: If any difficulty arises in giving effect to provisions of this Act, the Central Government may, by order, publish in the official Gazette, make such provisions, not inconsistent with the provisions of this Act, as it may deem necessary, for the removal of the difficulty:

Provided that no such order shall be made after the expiry of a period of three years from the appointed day.

NOTIFICATIONS UNDER CABLE TV ACT

[To be Published in Part II, Section 3, sub-section (ii) of the Gazette of India (extraordinary)]

Government of India
Ministry of Information and Broadcasting
(New Delhi, the 7th May, 2003)

Notification

S.O. 503(E)—In exercise of the powers conferred by sub-sections (2) and (3) of Section 4A of the Cable Television Networks (Regulation) Act, 1995 [7 of 1995] (hereinafter referred to as the "Act"), and in pursuance of the notification of the Government of India in the Ministry of Information and Broadcasting number S.O. 39(E) dated 14th January, 2003, the Central Government hereby specifies the minimum number of free-to-air channels to be included in the package of channels forming the basic service tier as thirty, in the areas specified below, namely:

1. Chennai Metropolitan area.
2. Municipal Council of Greater Mumbai area.
3. Kolkata Metropolitan area.
4. National Capital Territory of Delhi.

2. The package of channels forming the basic service tier must include the compulsory transmission of three Doordarshan channels notified under Section 8 of the said Act and the genres of entertainment, news, sports, children's programmes and music and must be in English, Hindi and the regional language, depending on the availability of such channels in the areas afore-mentioned.

3. Further, in exercise of the powers conferred by sub-section (4) of Section 4A of the said Act, the Central Government, having been satisfied that it is necessary so to do, in public interest, hereby specifies the maximum amount which a cable operator in the aforementioned areas may demand from a subscriber for receiving the programmes transmitted in the basic service tier provided by such cable operator to be Rs. 72 (Rupees

seventy-two) only. Free-to-air channels, over and above the basic service tier, would also be made available to the subscribers within the maximum amount mentioned above.

[*Footnote*: The Notification S.O. 39(E) dated the 14th January, 2003 was published in the Gazette of India (Extraordinary) dated 14th January, 2003 in Part II, Section 3, sub-section (ii)]

(SUDHIR SHARMA)
Joint Secretary to the Government of India

[To be Published in the Gazette of India (Extraordinary)
Part II, Section 3, sub-section (ii)]

Government of India
Ministry of Information and Broadcasting
(New Delhi, the 10th July, 2003)

Notification

S.O……..(E)—In exercise of the powers conferred by sub-section (1) of Section 4A, read with Section 9 of the Cable Television Networks (Regulation) Act, 1995 (7 of 1995) the Central Government having been satisfied that it is necessary in public interest so to do, and in supersession of notification S.O.39(E), dated 14th January, 2003, hereby notifies the 1st day of March 2003 as the date within six months from which it shall be obligatory for every cable operator to transmit/retransmit programmes of every pay channel through an addressable system in the areas specified below, namely:

(*i*) In the Municipal Council of Greater Mumbai, the area to the West of the main line of Central Railway between Chatrapathi Shivaji Terminus (CST) station and Sion Railway Station, including the area from Navy Nagar (in the south) upto the CST Railway Station (in the north), including Ballard Estate, bound by the Sion-Bandra Link Road and the Mahim Causeway on the northern side and includes the areas Colaba, RC Church, World Trade Centre, Maker Towers, Nariman Point, Cuffe Prade, Fort, Fountain, Mumbai Stock Market, Prince of Wales Museum, CIDCO, Marine Drive Gateway of India, Horniman Circle, Reserve Bank of India, Churchgate, Ballard Estate, Town Hall, Shahid Bhagat Singh Road, Madam Cama Road, Veer Nariman Road, Mahatma Gandhi Road, Dr. Dadabhai Nauroji Marg, Marine Lines, Charni Road, Kalbadevi, Thakurdwar, Girgaum, Walkeshwar Road, Nepensea Road, Cumbala Hill, Malabar Hill, Grant Road, Khetwadi, Breach Candy, Peddar Road, Hajiali, Mahalaxmi, Worli, Tardeo, Altomout Road, Dr. Dadasheb Bhadkamkar Marg, Sardar Vallabhai Patel Road, Saat Rasta, Lala Lajpatrai Marg, Mahalakshmi Race Course, Dr. Annie Besant Marg, N.M. Joshi Marg, Gokhale Road, Dr. Moses Road, Prabhadevi, Dadar (West), Shivaji Park, Cadell Road, Lady Jamshedji Road, Sitladevi Road, Mahim, Gen Arunkumar Vidya Marg.

(*ii*) In the National Capital Territory of Delhi, the area covering Chanakyapuri, Motibagh, Vasant Vihar, Safderjung, Vasantkunj, Chattarpur, Madangir, Kalkaji, Sarita Vihar, Maharani Bagh; bounded in the East by Yamuna River (from Delhi-Haryana border near Badarpur to Bhairon Marg; bounded in the West by Wellington Crescent, Sardar Patel Marg, NH8 (from Dhaulakuan to Gurgaon

Border); bounded in the South by Delhi-Haryana border (from Gurgaon to Badarpur and Yamuna river); bounded in the North by Bhairon Marg, Rajpath (from National Stadium to Vijay Chowk), Parliament House, Talkatora Road upto Ram Manohar Lohia Hospital.

(*iii*) In the Kolkata Metropolitan Area, the areas whose northern boundary is the eastern bank of the river Hooghly up to the confluence with Tolly's Nalla on the right; eastern boundary is the line along the western bank of Tolly's Nalla starting from its confluence with river Hooghly in the north, running south down along the Tolly's Nalla/Kaorapukur Khal to the mouzas of Magurkhali; Southern Boundary is along the line following the southern boundaries of mouzas Magurkhali, Ramjibanpur, Sajnaberia, Gopalnagar, Kalua, Hanspukuria area within Police Station Behala proceeding towards the southern boundaries of mouzas Kalagachhia, Sankharipota, Naoabad, Khanberia, Chandigar, Shibhugli and Rameshwarpur within Police Station Maheshtola.

Thereafter the same line following the southern boundaries of mouzas Betuabi Rajarampur, Santoshpur, Uttar Raipur, Benjan Haria Charial, Eastern and southern mouzas of Nischintapur and southern boundaries of mouzas of Uttar Ramchandrapur, Raghunathpur, Rajarampur, Achhipur within Police Station Budge Budge.

And then proceeding further westward in a straight line and meeting the western boundary-line of District 24 Parganas in the river Hooghly; and western boundary is the line along the east bank of river Hooghly starting from the confluence of Tolly's Nalla running south-south-west where it meets the line of District 24 Parganas in the river Hooghly.

(*iv*) Chennai Metropolitan area.

[*Footnote*: The Notification S.O. 39(E) dated 14th January, 2003 was published in the Gazette of India (Extraordinary) dated 14th January, 2003 in Part II, Section 3, sub-section (ii)]

(RAKESH MOHAN)
Joint Secretary to the Government of India

CONCERNED GOVERNMENT POLICIES

- Consultation paper on issues relating to Broadcasting and Distribution of TV Channels
- The Register of Interconnect Agreements (First Amendment) Regulations 2004 (2 of 2004)
- The Telecommunication (Broadcasting and Cable) Services Tariff Order 2004 (1 of 2004)
- TRAI Consultation Note
- TRAI Order
- TRAI Notification
- The Cable Television Networks (Regulation) Amendment Bill, 2002
- CAS Notification—Dated 14th Jan 2003
- CAS Notification—Dated 7th May 2003
- CAS Notification—Dated 6th June 2003
- CAS Notification—Dated 10th July 2003

- The Cable Television Networks (Regulation) Act, 1996
- Digital Set Top Box—Specification
- Analog Set Top Box—Specification
- Guidelines for Obtaining License for Providing Direct-to-Home (DTH) Broadcasting Service in India
- BIS Specs for DTH Set Top Boxes
- Uplinking of News & Current Affairs TV Channels from India
- The Indian Telegraph Act, 1885
- Guidelines for Uplinking from India
- I & B Foreign Investment Policy
- Broadcasting Code for AIR & Doordarshan
- The Indian Copyright Act
- Excerpts from the Supreme Court Judgement: "AIR Waves are Public Property"
- National Task Force on Information Technology and Software Development
- New Telecom Policy
- ISP Guidelines
- BJP (Ruling Party) Media Manifesto
- Citizen Charter of RNI
- Nariman Committee Report on Convergence
- National Security Act, 1980
- Monopolies and Restrictive Practices
- Report of the Review Committee on the Working of Prasar Bharati
- Norms, Guidelines and Procedures for Satellite Communications Announced
- The Prasar Bharti (Broadcasting Corporation of India) Act, 1990
- Report of the Task Force on Introduction of Conditional Access System
- Guidelines for use of SNG/DSNG
- Guidelines for Uplinking of News and Current Affairs TV Channels from India—Eligibility Criteria
- Guidelines for Uplinking of News and Current Affairs TV Channels from India
- Guidelines for Syndication Arrangements by Newspapers

THE CABLE TELEVISION NETWORKS (REGULATION) ACT

(Act No. 7 of 1995)

[*25th March, 1995*]

Promulgated by the President in the Forty-fifth Year of the Republic of India.

An Act to regulate the operation of cable television networks in the country and for matters connected therewith or incidental thereto.

Be it enacted by Parliament in the Forty-sixth year of the Republic of India as follows:

CHAPTER I
PRELIMINARY

1. Short Title, Extent and Commencement: (1) This Act may be called the Cable Television Networks (Regulation) Act, 1995.

(2) It extends to the whole of India.

(3) It shall be deemed to have come into force on the 29th day of September, 1994.

2. Definitions: In this Act, unless the context otherwise requires—

[1][(*a*) "authorised officer" means, within his local limits of jurisdiction—

(*i*) a District Magistrate, or

(*ii*) a Sub-divisional Magistrate, or

(*iii*) a Commissioner of Police,

and includes any other officer notified in the Official Gazette, by the Central Government or the State Government, to be an authorised officer for such local limits of jurisdiction as may be determined by that Government;]

[2][(*aa*)] "cable operator" means any person who provides cable service through a cable television network or otherwise controls or is responsible for the management and operation of a cable television network;

(*b*) "cable service" means the transmission by cables of programmes including retransmission by cables of any broadcast television signals;

(*c*) "cable television network" means any system consisting of a set of closed transmission paths and associated signal generation, control and distribution equipment, designed to provide cable service for reception by multiple subscribers;

(*d*) "company" means a company as defined in Section 3 of the Companies Act, 1956 (1 of 1956);

(*e*) "person" means—

(*i*) an individual who is a citizen of India;

(*ii*) an association of individuals or body of individuals, whether incorporated or not, whose members are citizens of India;

(*iii*) a company in which not less than fifty-one per cent of the paid-up share capital is held by the citizens of India;

(*f*) "prescribed" means prescribed by rules made under this Act;

(*g*) "programme" means any television broadcast and includes—

(*i*) exhibition of films, features, dramas, advertisement and serials through video cassette recorders or video cassette players;

(*ii*) any audio or visual or audio-visual live performance or presentation, and the expression "programming service" shall be construed accordingly;

(*h*) "registering authority" means such authority as the Central Government may, by notification [3]in the Official Gazette, specify to perform the functions of the registering authority under this Act;

(*i*) "subscriber" means a person who receives the signals of cable television network at a place indicated by him to the cable operator, without further transmitting it to any other person.

---

1. Inserted by Act No. 36 of 2000 (w.e.f. 1-9-2000).
2. Renumbered as (aa) from (a) by Act No. 36 of 2000 (w.e.f. 1-9-2000).
3. Vide Notification No. S.O. 718(E) dated 29-9-1994, the Post Master of a Head Post Office, of the area within whose jurisdiction the office of Cable operator is situated notified to be registering authority.

CHAPTER II
REGULATION OF CABLE TELEVISION NETWORK

3. Cable Television Network not to be Operated Except after Registration: No person shall operate a cable television network unless he is registered as a cable operator under this Act:

Provided that a person operating a cable television network, immediately before the commencement of this Act, may continue to do so for a period of ninety days from such commencement; and if he has made an application for registration as a cable operator under Section 4 within the said period, till he is registered under that section or the registering authority refuses to grant registration to him under that section.

Programmes of foreign satellite channels which can be received without the use of any specialised gadgets or decoder are exempt from the operation of this section.

4. Registration as Cable Operator: (1) Any person who is operating or is desirous of operating a cable television network may apply for registration as a cable operator to the registering authority.

(2) An application under sub-section (1) shall be made in such form and be accompanied by such fee as may be prescribed.

(3) On receipt of the application, the registering authority shall satisfy itself that the applicant has furnished all the required information and on being so satisfied, register the applicant as a cable operator and grant to him a certificate of such registration:

Provided that the registering authority may, for reasons to be recorded in writing and communicated to the applicant, refuse to grant registration to him if it is satisfied that he does not fulfil the conditions specified in clause (e) of Section 2.

[1]**[4A. Transmission of Programmes through Addressable System, etc.:** (1) Where the Central Government is satisfied that it is necessary in the public interest to do so, it may, by notification in the Official Gazette, make it obligatory for every cable operator to transmit or retransmit programme of any pay channel through an addressable system with effect from such date as may be specified in the notification and different dates may be specified for different States, cities, towns or areas, as the case may be.

(2) If the Central Government is satisfied that it is necessary in the public interest so to do, it may, by notification in the Official Gazette, specify one or more free-to-air channels to be included in the package of channels forming basic service tier and any or more such channels may be specified, in the notification, *genre-wise* for providing a programme mix of entertainment, information, education and such other programmes.

(3) The Central Government may specify in the notification referred to in sub-section (2), the number of free-to-air channels to be included in the package of channels forming basic service tier for the purposes of that sub-section and different numbers may be specified for different States, cities, towns or areas, as the case may be.

(4) If the Central Government is satisfied that it is necessary in the public interest so to do, it may, by notification in the Official Gazette, specify the maximum amount which a cable operator may demand from the subscriber for receiving the programmes transmitted in the basic service tier provided by such cable operator.

1. Inserted by Act No. 2 of 2003 (w.e.f. 1-1-2003).

(5) Notwithstanding anything contained in sub-section (4), the Central Government may, for the purposes of that sub-section, specify in the notification referred to in that sub-section different maximum amounts for different States, cities, towns or areas, as the case may be.

(6) Notwithstanding anything contained in this section, programmes of basic service tier shall be receivable by any subscriber on the receiver set of a type existing immediately before the commencement of the Cable Television Networks (Regulation) Amendment Act, 2002 without any addressable system attached with such receiver set in any manner.

(7) Every cable operator shall publicise, in the prescribed manner, to the subscribers the subscription rates and the periodic intervals at which such subscriptions are payable for receiving each pay channel provided by such cable operator.

(8) The cable operator shall not require any subscriber to have a receiver set of a particular type to receive signals of cable television network:

Provided that the subscriber shall use an addressable system to be attached to his receiver set for receiving programmes transmitted on pay channel.

(9) Every cable operator shall submit a report to the Central Government in the prescribed form and manner containing the information regarding—

(*i*) the number of total subscribers;

(*ii*) subscription rates;

(*iii*) number of subscribers receiving programmes transmitted in basic service tier or particular programme or set of programmes transmitted on pay channel.

in respect of cable services provided by such cable operator through a cable television network, and such report shall be submitted periodically at such intervals as may be prescribed and shall also contain the rate of amount, if any, payable by the cable operator to any broadcaster.

Explanation: For the purposes of this section—

(*a*) "addressable system" means an electronic device or more than one electronic devices put in an integrated system through which signals of cable television network can be sent in encrypted or unencrypted form, which can be decoded by the device or devices at the premises of the subscriber within the limits of authorisation made, on the choice and request of such subscriber, by the cable operator to the subscriber;

(*b*) "basic service tier" means a package of free-to-air channels provided by a cable operator, for a single price to the subscribers of the area in which his cable television network is providing service and such channels are receivable for viewing by the subscribers on the receiver set of a type existing immediately before the commencement of the Cable Television Networks (Regulation) Amendment Act, 2002 without any addressable system attached to such receiver set in any manner;

(*c*) "channel" means a set of frequencies used for transmission of a programme;

(*d*) "encrypted", in respect of a signal of cable television network, means the changing of such signal in a systematic way so that the signal would be unintelligible without a suitable receiving equipment and the expression "unencrypted" shall be construed accordingly;

(*e*) "free-to-air channel", in respect of a cable television network, means a channel, the reception of which would not require the use of any addressable system to be attached with the receiver set of a subscriber;

(*f*) "pay channel", in respect of a cable television network, means a channel the reception of which by the subscriber would require the use of an addressable system to be attached to his receiver set.].

5. Programme Code: No person shall transmit or re-transmit through a cable service any programme unless such programme is in conformity with the prescribed programme code:

[1][x x x x x]

6. Advertisement Code: No person shall transmit or re-transmit through a cable service any advertisement unless such advertisement is in conformity with the prescribed advertisement code:

[2][x x x x x]

7. Maintenance of Register: Every cable operator shall maintain a register in the prescribed form indicating therein in brief the programmes transmitted or re-transmitted through the cable service during a month and such register shall be maintained by the cable operator for a period of one year after the actual transmission or re-transmission of the said programmes.

[3]**[8. Compulsory Transmission of Doordarshan Channels:** (1) Every cable operator shall, from the Commencement of the Cable Television Networks (Regulation) Amendment Act, 2000, re-transmit at least two Doordarshan territorial channels and one regional language channel of a State in the prime band; in satellite mode on frequencies other than those carrying terrestrial frequencies.

(2) The Doordarshan channels referred to in sub-section (1) shall be transmitted without any deletion or alteration of any programme transmitted on such channels.

(3) The Prasar Bharati (Broadcasting Corporation of India) established under sub-section (1) of Section 3 of the Prasar Bharati (Broadcasting Corporation of India) Act, 1990 may, by notification in the Official Gazette, specify the number and name of every Doordarshan channel to be re-transmitted by cable operators in their cable service and the manner of reception and re-transmission of such channels.]

9. Use of Standard Equipment in Cable Television Network: No cable operator shall, on and from the date of the expiry of a period of three years from the date of the establishment and publication of the Indian Standard by the Bureau of Indian Standards in accordance with the provisions of the Bureau of Indian Standards Act, 1986 (63 of 1986), use any equipment in his cable television network unless such equipment conforms to the said Indian Standard.

---

1. Proviso to Section 5 omitted by Act No. 36 of 2000. (w.e.f. 1-9-2000).
2. Proviso to Section 6 omitted by Act No. 36 of 2000. (w.e.f. 1-9-2000).
3. Subs. by Act No. 36 of 2000 (w.e.f. 1-9-2000).

[1][Provided that the equipment required for the purposes of Section 4A shall be inserted by Cable operator in his cable television network within six months from the date, specified in the notification issued under sub-section (1) of that section, in accordance with the provision of the said Act for said purposes.]

10. Cable Television Network not to Interfere with any Telecommunication System: Every cable operator shall ensure that the cable television network being operated by him does not interfere, in any way, with the functioning of the authorised telecommunication systems.

CHAPTER III
SEIZURE AND CONFISCATION OF CERTAIN EQUIPMENT

11. Power to Seize Equipment used for Operating the Cable Television Network: [2][(1) If any authorised officer has reason to believe that the provisions of [3][Sections 3, 4A] 5, 6 or 8 have been or are being contravened by any cable operator, he may seize the equipment being used by such cable operator for operating the cable television network.]

(2) No such equipment shall be retained by the authorised officer for a period exceeding ten days from the date of its seizure unless the approval of the District Judge, within the local limits of whose jurisdiction such seizure has been made, has been obtained for such retention.

12. Confiscation: The equipment seized under sub-section (1) of Section 11 shall be liable to confiscation unless the cable operator from whom the equipment has been seized registers himself as a cable operator under Section 4 within a period of thirty days from the date of seizure of the said equipment.

13. Seizure or Confiscation of Equipment not to Interfere with Other Punishment: No seizure or confiscation of equipment referred to in Section 11 or Section 12 shall prevent the infliction of any punishment to which the person affected thereby is liable under the provisions of this Act.

14. Giving of Opportunity to the Cable Operator of Seized Equipment: (1) No order adjudicating confiscation of the equipment referred to in Section 12 shall be made unless the cable operator has been given a notice in writing informing him of the grounds on which it is proposed to confiscate such equipment and giving him a reasonable opportunity of making a representation in writing, within such reasonable time as may be specified in the notice against the confiscation and if he so desires of being heard in the matter:

Provided that where no such notice is given within a period of ten days from the date of the seizure of the equipment, such equipment shall be returned after the expiry of that period to the cable operator from whose possession it was seized.

(2) Save as otherwise provided in sub-section (1), the provisions of the Code of Civil Procedure, 1908 (5 of 1908) shall, so far as may be, apply to every proceeding referred to in sub-section (1).

---

1. Inserted by Act No. 2 of 2003 (w.e.f. 1-1-2003).
2. Substituted by Act No. 36 of 2000 (w. e. f.1-9-2000).
3. Substituted for "Section 3" by Act No. 2 of 2003 (w.e.f. 1-1-2003).

15. Appeal: (1) Any person aggrieved by any decision of the court adjudicating a confiscation of the equipment may prefer an appeal to the court to which an appeal lies from the decision of such court.

(2) The appellate court may, after giving the appellant an opportunity of being heard, pass such order as it thinks fit confirming, modifying or revising the decision appealed against or may send back the case with such directions as it may think fit for a fresh decision or adjudication, as the case may be, after taking additional evidence if necessary.

(3) No further appeal shall lie against the order of the court made under sub-section (2).

CHAPTER IV
OFFENCES AND PENALTIES

16. Punishment for Contravention of Provisions of this Act: [1][(1)] Whoever contravenes any of the provisions of this Act shall be punishable—

(*a*) for the first offence, with imprisonment for a term which may extend to two years or with fine which may extend to one thousand rupees or with both;

(*b*) for every subsequent offence, with imprisonment for a term which may extend to five years and with fine which may extend to five thousand rupees.

[2][(2) Notwithstanding anything contained in the Code of Criminal Procedure, 1973 the contravention of Section 4A shall be cognizable offence under this Section.]

17. Offences by Companies: (1) Where an offence under this Act has been committed by a company, every person who, at the time the offence was committed, was in-charge of, and was responsible to the company for the conduct of the business of the company, as well as the company, shall be deemed to be guilty of the offence and shall be liable to be proceeded against and punished accordingly:

Provided that nothing contained in this sub-section shall render any such person liable to any punishment, if he proves that the offence was committed without his knowledge or that he had exercised all due diligence to prevent the commission of such offence.

(2) Notwithstanding anything contained in sub-section (1), where any offence under this Act has been committed by a company and it is proved that the offence has been committed with the consent or connivance of, or is attributable to any negligence on the part of, any director, manager, secretary or other officer of the company, such director, manager, secretary or other officer shall also be deemed to be guilty of that offence and shall be liable to be proceeded against and punished accordingly.

Explanation: For the purposes of this section—

(*a*) "company" means any body corporate and includes a firm or other association of individuals; and

(*b*) "director" in relation to a firm, means a partner in the firm.

18. Cognizance Offences: No court shall take cognizance of any offence punishable under this Act except upon a complaint in writing made [3][by any authorised officer].

---

1. Section 16 renumbered as sub-section (1) by Act No. 2 of 2003 (w.e.f. 1-1-2003).
2. Sub-section (2) inserted by Act No. 2 of 2003 (w.e.f. 1-1-2003).
3. Subs. for certain words by Act No. 36 of 2000 (w.e.f. 1-9-2000).

CHAPTER V
MISCELLANEOUS

19. Power to Prohibit Transmission of Certain Programmes in Public Interest: Where [1][any authorised officer], thinks it necessary or expedient so to do in the public interest, he may, by order, prohibit any cable operator from transmitting or retransmitting [1][any programme or channel if, it is not in conformity with the prescribed programme code referred to in Section 5 and advertisement code referred to in Section 6 or if it is] likely to promote, on grounds of religion, race, language, caste or community or any other ground whatsoever, disharmony or feelings of enmity, hatred or ill-will between different religious, racial, linguistic or regional groups or castes or communities or which is likely to disturb the public tranquillity.

20. Power to Prohibit Operation of Cable Television Network in Public Interest: [1][(1)] Where the Central Government thinks it necessary or expedient so to do in public interest, it may prohibit the operation of any cable television network in such areas as it may, by notification in the Official Gazette, specify in this behalf.

[2][(2) Where the Central Government thinks it necessary or expedient so to do in the interest of the—

(*i*) sovereignty or integrity of India; or

(*ii*) security of India; or

(*iii*) friendly relations of India with any foreign State; or

(*iv*) public order, decency or morality,

it may, by order, regulate or prohibit the transmission or re-transmission of any channel or programme.

(3) Where the Central Government considers that any programme of any channel is not in conformity with the prescribed programme code referred to in Section 5 or the prescribed advertisement code referred to in Section 6, it may by order, regulate or prohibit the transmission or re-transmission of such programme].

21. Application of Other Laws not Barred: The provisions of this Act shall be in addition to, and not in derogation of, the Drugs and Cosmetics Act, 1940 (23 of 1940), the Pharmacy Act, 1948 (8 of 1948), the Emblems and Names (Prevention of Improper Use) Act, 1950 (12 of 1950), the Drugs (Control) Act, 1950 (26 of 1950), the Cinematograph Act, 1952 (37 of 1952), the Drugs and Magic Remedies (Objectionable Advertisements) Act, 1954 (21 of 1954), the Prevention of Food Adulteration Act, 1954 (37 of 1954), The Prize Competitions Act, 1955 (42 of 1955), the Copyright Act 1957 (14 of 1957), the Trade and Merchandise Marks Act, 1958 (43 of 1958), the Indecent Representation of Women (Prohibition) Act, 1986 (60 of 1986) and the Consumer Protection Act, 1986 (68 of 1986).

22. Power to Make Rules: (1) The Central Government may, by notification in the Official Gazette, make rules to carry out the provisions of this Act.

(2) In particular, and without prejudice to the generality of the foregoing power, such rules may provide for all or any of the following matters, namely:

(a) the form of application and the fee payable under sub-section (2) of Section 4;

---

1. Renumbered as sub-section (1) by Act No. 36 of 2000 (w.e.f. 1-9-2000).
2. Sub-sections (2) and (3) inserted by Act No. 36 of 2000 (w.e.f. 1-9-2000).

[1][(aa) the manner of publicising the subscription rates and the periodical intervals at which such subscriptions are payable under sub-section (7) of Section 4A;

(aaa) the form and manner of submitting report under sub-section (9) of Section 4A and the interval at which such report shall be submitted periodically under that sub-section.]

(*b*) the programme code under Section 5;

(*c*) the advertisement code under Section 6;

(*d*) the form of register to be maintained by a cable operator under Section 7;

(*e*) any other matter which is required to be, or may be, prescribed.

(3) Every rule made under this Act shall be laid, as soon as may be after it is made, before each House of Parliament, while it is in session, for a total period of thirty days which may be comprised in one session or in two or more successive sessions, and if, before the expiry of the session immediately following the session or the successive sessions aforesaid, both Houses agree in making any modification in the rule or both Houses agree that the rule should not be made, the rule shall thereafter have effect only in such modified form or be of no effect, as the case may be; so, however, that any such modification or annulment shall be without prejudice to the validity of anything previously done under that rule.

23. Repeal and Savings: (1) The Cable Television Networks (Regulation) Ordinance, 1995 (3 of 1995) is hereby repealed.

(2) Notwithstanding such repeal, anything done or any action taken under the said Ordinance, shall be deemed to have been done or taken under the corresponding provisions of this Act.

CABLE TELEVISION NETWORKS RULES

(as Amended upto 8.9.2000)
To be Published in the Gazette of India
(Extraordinary) Part II, Section 3, sub-section (i)

Government of India
Ministry of Information and Broadcasting

New Delhi, the 29th September, 1994

Notification

G.S.R. 729 (E)—In exercise of the powers conferred by sub-section (1) of Section 22 of the Cable Television Networks (Regulation) Ordinance, 1994 (Ordinance No. 9 of 1994) the Central Government makes the following Rules namely:

1. Short Title and Commencement: (1) These rules may be called the Cable Television Networks Rules, 1994.

(2) They shall come into force on the date of their publication in the Official Gazette.

2. Definitions: In these rules unless the context otherwise requires—

1. Clauses (aa) and (aaa) inserted by Act No. 2 of 2003 (w.e.f. 1-1-2003).

(*a*) "cable operator" means any person who provides cable service through a cable television network or otherwise control or is responsible for the management and operation of a cable television network;

(*b*) "cable service" means the transmission by cables of programmes including re-transmission by cables of any broadcast television signals;

(*c*) "cable television network" means any system consisting of a set of closed transmission paths and associated signals generation, control and distribution equipment, designed to provide cable service for reception by multiple subscribers;

(*d*) "company" means a company defined in Section 3 of the Companies Act, 1956;

(*e*) "form" means form appended to these rules;

(*f*) "person" means—

(*i*) an individual who is a citizen of India;

(*ii*) an association of individuals or body of individuals, whether incorporated or not, whose members are citizens of India;

(*iii*) a company in which not less than fifty-one per cent of the paid-up share capital is held by the citizens of India;

(*g*) "programme" means any television broadcast and includes;

(*i*) exhibition of films, features, dramas, advertisements and serials through video cassette recorders or video cassette players;

(*ii*) any audio or visual or audio-visual live performance or presentation; and the expression "programming service" shall be construed accordingly;

(*h*) "registering authority" means the registering authority notified under clause (h) of Section 2 of the Cable Television Networks (Regulation) Ordinance, 1994;

(*i*) "subscriber" means a person who receives the signal of cable television network at a place indicated by him to the cable operator, without further transmitting it to any other person.

3. Application for Registration as a Cable Television Network in India: (1) Every application for registration as a cable television network in India shall be made in writing in Form I and shall be renewable after every twelve months.

(2) The application shall be addressed to the Registering Authority and delivered to his office in Form 1.

[1](3) (*a*) Every application for registration or renewal of registration shall be accompanied by—

(*i*) a fee of rupees five hundred only; and

(*ii*) the requisite documents mentioned in Form 1 and Form 2.

(*b*) Every application for issue of duplicate certificate of registration shall be accompanied by—

(*i*) a fee of rupees two hundred and fifty only; and

(*ii*) the requisite documents mentioned in Form 1.

[2](4) The amount of fee shall be deposited in the Head Post Office where the application for registration or renewal of registration or issue of duplicate certificate of registration is being made.

1. Inserted by G.S.R. 459(E) dated 8-10-96.
2. Inserted by G.S.R. 459(E) dated 8-10-96.

[1](5) The amount of the fees shall be deposited under the Head 'Un-Classified Receipts (U.C.R.)'.

4. Examination of Applications: (1) On receipt of an application under rule 3, the registering authority shall examine the application having regard to the provisions of Section 4 of the Ordinance.

5. Registration: (1) On being satisfied that the applicant fulfills the provisions of the Ordinance, the registering authority shall issue a registration certificate in Form 3:

Provided that where the registering authority is satisfied that the registration cannot be granted to the applicant, he shall inform the applicant in Form 4.

[2](2) On receipt of an application under clause (b) of sub-rule (3) of rule 3 for issue of duplicate certificate the Registering Authority shall examine the application having regard to the provisions of rule 3 and shall issue a duplicate Registration Certificate in Form 3 A.

6. Programme Code: (1) No programme should be carried in the cable service which—

(*a*) Offends against good taste or decency;

(*b*) Contains criticism of friendly countries;

(*c*) Contains attack on religions or communities or visuals or words contemptuous of religious groups or which promote communal attitudes;

(*d*) Contains anything obscene, defamatory, deliberate, false and suggestive innuendos and half truths;

(*e*) Is likely to encourage or incite violence or contains anything against maintenance of law and order or which promote anti-national attitudes;

(*f*) Contains anything amounting to contempt of court;

(*g*) Contains aspersions against the integrity of the President and Judiciary;

(*h*) Contains anything affecting the integrity of the Nation;

(*i*) Criticises, maligns or slanders any individual in person or certain groups, segments of social, public and moral life of the country;

(*j*) Encourages superstition or blind belief;

(*k*) Denigrates women through the depiction in any manner of the figure of a women, her form or body or any part thereof in such a way as to have the effect of being indecent, or derogatory to women, or is likely to deprave, corrupt or injure the public morality or morals;

(*l*) Denigrates children;

(*m*) Contains visuals or words which reflect a slandering, ironical and snobbish attitude in the portrayal of certain ethnic, linguistic and regional groups;

(*n*) Contravenes the provisions of the Cinematograph Act, 1952;

[3](*o*) is not suitable for unrestricted public exhibition.

Explanation: For the purpose of this clause, the expression "unrestricted public exhibition" shall have the same meaning as assigned to it in the Cinematograph Act, 1952 (37 of 1952);

---

1. Inserted by G.S.R. 459(E) dated 8-10-96.
2. Inserted by G.S.R. 459(E) dated 8-10-96.
3. Inserted vide GSR 710(E) dated 8-9-2000.

(2) The Cable operator should strive to carry programmes in his cable service which project women in a positive, leadership role of sobriety, moral and character building qualities.

[1](3) No Cable operator shall carry or include in his cable service any programme in respect of which copyright subsists under the Copyright Act, 1972 (14 of 1972) unless he has been granted a licence by owners of copyright under the Act in rest of such programme.

(4) Care should be taken to ensure that programmes meant for children do not contain any bad language or explicit scenes of violence.

(5) Programmes unsuitable for children must not be carried in the cable service at times when the largest numbers of children are viewing.

7. Advertising Code: (1) Advertising carried in the cable service shall be so designed as to conform to the laws of the country and should not offend morality, decency and religious susceptibilities of the subscribers.

(2) No advertisement shall be permitted which—

(*i*) derides any race, caste, colour, creed and nationality;

(*ii*) is against any provision of the Constitution of India;

(*iii*) tends to incite people to crime, cause disorder or violence, or breach of law or glorifies violence or obscenity in any way;

(*iv*) presents criminality as desirable;

(*v*) exploits the national emblem, or any part of the Constitution or the person or personality of a national leader or a State dignitary;

(*vi*) in its depiction of women violates the constitutional guarantees to all citizens. In particular, no advertisement shall be permitted which projects a derogatory image of women. Women must not be portrayed in a manner that emphasises passive, submissive qualities and encourages them to play a subordinate, secondary role in the family and society. The Cable operator shall ensure that the portrayal of the female form, in the programmes carried in his cable service, is tasteful and aesthetic, and is within the well-established norms of good taste and decency;

(*vii*) exploits social evils like dowry, child marriage;

[2](*viii*) promotes directly or indirectly production, sale or consumption of—

(*a*) cigarettes, tobacco products, wine, alcohol, liquor or other intoxicants;

(*b*) infant milk substitutes, feeding bottle or infant food.

(3) No advertisement shall be permitted, the objects whereof, are wholly or mainly of a religious or political nature; advertisements must not be directed towards any religious or political end.

[3](3A) No advertisement shall contain references which hurt religious sentiments.

(4) The goods or services advertised shall not suffer from any defect or deficiency as mentioned in Consumer Protection Act, 1986.

---

1. Substituted vide GSR 710(E) dated 8-9-2000.
2. Inserted vide GSR 710(E) dated 8-9-2000.
3. Inserted vide GSR 710(E) dated 8-9-2000.

(5) No advertisement shall contain references which are likely to lead the public to infer that the product advertised or any of its ingredients has some special or miraculous or super-natural property or quality, which is difficult of being proved.

(6) The picture and the audible matter of the advertisement shall not be excessively loud;

(7) No advertisement which endangers the safety of children or creates in them any interest in unhealthy practices or shows them begging or in an undignified or indecent manner shall not be carried in the cable service.

(8) Indecent, vulgar, suggestive, repulsive or offensive themes or treatment shall be avoided in all advertisements.

(9) No advertisement which violates the standards of practice for advertising agencies as approved by the Advertising Agencies Association of India, Mumbai, from time to time shall be carried in the cable service.

(10) All advertisement should be clearly distinguishable from the programme and should not in any manner interfere with the programme viz., use of lower part of screen to carry captions, static or moving alongside the programme.

8. Register: Each cable operator shall maintain a register in Form 5 for each month of the year for which the registration is granted.

[1]FORM 1

[See Rule 3 (1)]

(To be Submitted in Duplicate)

Form of application for *registration/renewal of registration/issue of duplicate certificate of registration as a cable operator.

To

The Head Postmaster
Head Post Office

Application for *registration/renewal of registration/issue of duplicate certificate of registration as a cable operator.

1. (*a*) Name of Applicant (individual/firm/company/association of persons/body of individuals)*
   (*b*) *Age/Date of establishment/Date of incorporation.
2. (*a*) Address (office)
   (*b*) Telephone number (if any)
3. (*a*) Nationality (for individual applicants/body of individuals)
   (*b*) By birth/domicile.
4. (*a*) Amount of fee paid for *registration/renewal/issue of duplicate certificate Rs....................
   (*b*) Name of Head Post Office....................
   (Attach copy of challan vide which the fees have been deposited)

---

1. Substituted by GSR 459(E) dated 8-9-96.

5. Area in which cable television network is working/proposed to be set up..............
6. Date from which the cable television network is operating/proposed to be set up .....
7. Number of channels being provided/proposed to be provided (with names) ....
8. (a) Whether using Television Receive Only (TVRO) Yes/No
   (b) If yes, number and size of TVRO....................
   (c) Location....................
9. Names of Doordarshan satellite channels included in cable service....................
10. Copy of earlier registration certificate enclosed. Yes/No
    (To be filled in only for renewal of registration).
11. (a) State reasons for issue of duplicate certificate of registration....................
    (Attach mutilated or defaced original certificate of registration/copy of report made to the police in case of theft or loss of the original certificate)
    (b) Period of validity of the original Registration Certificate for which the duplicate Registration Certificate is being sought..........
    (To be filled in only for issue of duplicate Registration Certificate)
12. Declaration in Form 2 enclosed. Yes/No
    (To be filled in for *registration/renewal of registration only)

I/We.............................the applicant(s)

*(Individual/firm/company/association of persons/body of individuals) do hereby declare that the above facts are correct in all respects.

Signature of Applicant

*(Individual/firm/company/association of persons/body of individuals)

Place:................. Name ....

Date:.................. Address ....

* Score out the word or words which are not applicable.

FORM 2
[See Rule 3(1-3)]

I/We.............................the applicant(s) *(individual/firm/company/association of person/body of individuals) for registration as a cable operator/renewal of registration as a cable operator do hereby declare that:

(i) I/We shall ensure that my/our television network shall be run in accordance with the provisions of the Cable Television Networks (Regulation) Ordinance 1994 at all times.

(ii) I/We shall not permit/associate any person who is not eligible to run a cable television network under the Cable Television Networks (Regulation) Ordinance 1994 to run/with the running of my/our cable television network.

(*iii*) I/We shall strive to the best of my/our ability to provide cable service to the satisfaction of the subscriber(s) of my/our cable television network.

(*iv*) I/We shall strive to the best of my/our ability to ensure that my/our cable television network is not used for any unlawful purpose.

(*v*) I/We shall obtain the necessary approval/clearance from the relevant authority for the running of my/our cable television network.

(*vi*) I/We shall abide by any direction issued by the Central Government in respect of the running of a cable television network within India.

Signature of Applicant

*(Individual/firm/company/association of persons/body of individuals)

Place:............. Name ....

Date:.............. Address.......................

* Score out the word or words which are not applicable

FORM 3

[See Rule 5]

Government of India

Head Post Office

Registration Certificate Number

1. Shri/Shrimati/M/s.......................resident of.......................... is registered as a cable operator (individual, firm,*Company, association of persons or body of individuals) for running a cable television network at the following address.....................in the city/town of.....................for a period of twelve months with effect from.....................

   His Registration Number is ....
2. This Certificate is only valid for the premises stated above.
3. This Registration Certificate is not transferable.
4. The Certificate shall remain valid for the period indicated above or till the holder carries on the cable service or where the surrender of the certificate is accepted by the competent authority.

Head Postmaster

Head Post Office

(town/city)

Place:..................

Date:...................

To be displayed prominently on the premises of the cable operator.

* Tick whichever is appropriate.

---

[1]FORM 3A

[See Rule 5(2)]

Government of India

Head Post Office

Duplicate Registration Certificate

1. Shri/Shrimati/M/s......................resident of............................is registered as a cable operator *(individual/firm/company/association of persons or body of individuals) for running a cable television network at the following address............................in the city/town of............................for a period of twelve months with effect from......................(date from which the Original Registration Certificate was valid).
   His Registration number is ....
2. This Certificate is valid only for the premises stated above.
3. This Registration Certificate is not transferable.
4. The Certificate shall remain valid for the period indicated above or till the holder carries on the cable service or where the surrender of the certificate is accepted by the competent authority.

Head Postmaster
Head Post Office
...... (town/city)

Place:...............
Date:...............

To be Displayed Prominently on the Premises of the Cable Operator.

*Tick whichever is appropriate

FORM 4

[See Proviso to Rule 5 (1)]

To

Sir,

Reference your application dated..................for registration as a cable operator. The necessary registration cannot be granted to you for the following reason (s):

(*i*) Application is incomplete.
(*ii*) Registration fee has not been tendered.
(*iii*) Applicant is not a citizen of India.
(*iv*) Less than fifty-one per cent of the paid-up share capital of the applicant company is held by citizens of India.

Head Postmaster
Head Post Office

Place:................
Date:................ .

---

1. Inserted by GSR 459(E) dated 8-10-96.

FORM 5
[See Rule 8]

Form of Register to be maintained by each Cable Operator.

SI. No.	Encrypted 1.	Duration 2.	Date 3.	Month 4.	Year 5.	Channel/Programme 6.	From to 7.

Signature of Cable Operator

[To be published in the Gazette of India Extraordinary Part II, Section 3, sub-section (ii)]

Government of India
Ministry of Information and Broadcasting

New Delhi, 29th September, 1994

Notification

S.O. 718(E)—In exercise of the powers conferred by clause (h) of Section 2 of the Cable Television Networks (Regulation) Ordinance, 94, the Central Government hereby notifies the Head Post Master of a Head Post Office, of the area within whose territorial jurisdiction of office of the cable operator is situated, as the Registering Authority for registering cable television networks in the said area for the purposes of the said ordinance.

REPORT ON INTRODUCTION OF CONDITIONAL ACCESS SYSTEM

Introduction

The issue of introduction of an addressability system has been engaging the attention of the Government for sometime, keeping in view the problems being highlighted by sections of the broadcasting industry, including Cable operators, MSO's and Content Providers. A large number of complaints had also been received from subscribers, protesting unwarranted and frequent increase in subscription rates by Cable operators. With almost 38 million cable and satellite households in the country and with a household paying on an average Rs. 125 per month, as subscription charges, the revenue generated in the sector is close to Rs. 5,700 crores. Of this, there have been reports of substantial underreporting by different sections depriving the different players of the industry of their entitled revenue/collection and reportage of transparent viewership figures and the Government of Tax.

To deliberate and decide upon various issues on this topic, it was decided to set up a Task Force, under Joint Secretary (Broadcasting) in the Ministry of Information and Broadcasting, with representations from the cross section of the industry. The objective, inter-alia, was to deliberate in the need for introducing a Conditional Access System for viewing channels through the cable network and to determine the modalities for doing so.

Constitution of Task Force and Terms of Reference

The Task Force was constituted by an order dated 25th September, 2001 and it consists of representatives from Indian Broadcasting Federation, MSOs Content Creators, Cable Operators, Broadcasters, Infrastructure Providers, nominee from the Ministry of Consumer Affairs, representative of Consumer activists and technical experts. The order constituting the Committee, with its Terms of Reference, is annexed.

The Committee was empowered to invite experts and to broad base the representation on the Task Force, technical experts were co-opted from the industry. Other participants who desired to contribute were also invited to attend. The primary issue of concern for the Committee was to establish the need for introducing Conditional Access System in order to provide a choice to the consumer and to examine the feasibility of doing so, to protect the interests of the consumer from additional costs on replacement of the TV receiver or on purchase of the Conditional Access System, and to debate technology issues relating to standardization and performance.

Meetings

The Task Force held three meetings, one each in the month of October, November and December 2001. At each meeting specific issues were identified for discussion and deliberation and decisions were taken thereon, at the same meeting. Since the technology issues were more complex and required extensive consultations, a Subcommittee was constituted under Director (BD), I&B with representations from the industry, equipment manufacturers and technical experts to go into those aspects. This Subcommittee held separate meetings and their recommendations were considered by the Task Force in its last meeting held on 26th December, 2001. At each stage the members were encouraged to send further comments/observations in writing for the consideration of the Task Force.

After each meeting of the Task Force, the minutes were circulated to the members by post as well as over Internet. Members of the Task Force as well as other representatives of the industry have provided inputs, which were also considered by the Task Force. This included comments, which were received from National Cable and Telecommunications Associations, Cable Operators etc.

Summary of Discussions

It was acknowledged that Cable Television in India was a technology, which had entered in an unbridled manner and had become a reality totally through private investment. A connectivity of over 35 million homes had been achieved in this syndrome. The MSOs were later entrants. Cable and Satellite Television had gradually become an irresistible force in the process of transformation of communication technology and the perceived potential of Cable TV, DTH, DTT etc., was immense. The Cable Operators observed that since demand of content was driving ad revenue and viewership, the Broadcasters and the Content Creators were whimsically levying exorbitant charges for programmes, channels and for bouquets. Arbitrary increases in subscription rates were creating a problem because Cable Operators were left with no option but to pass on this burden frequently to the subscribers.

The Group discussed the problems and alternatives available and was of the view that the consumer needed to exercise a choice of watching what he chose, and that the viewer should be made aware of what it would cost to view 'Pay' Channels. Addressability is a technique, where signals are sent in an encoded form and an equipment, placed at the subscriber's end, decodes the signals, in accordance with the choice exercised by the Consumer, Authorized and the Service Provider, specifically on the subscriber's request. The Task Force considered it desirable that the Conditional Access System should be introduced to provide the consumer choice of viewing and an option to pay for what he chose to watch. The Consumer should also not be expected to pay unreasonably for the 'Free-to-Air' channels and must be able to receive the 'Free-to-Air' channels without any Set Top Box or any need to change the existing receiver.

The Task Force acknowledged the existence of the value chain starting from the Content Maker, to the Content Provider (Broadcaster) to the main Content Distributor, to the last mile Content Distributor (Cable Operator) and finally the consumer household. In the existing arrangement the consumer was paying for all the channels, irrespective of what he actually watched or desired to watch. There was now need to make the system transparent in respect of the Pay Channels/Pay programmes, which can be watched by selective subscribers. The subscribership of all 'Pay' channels should be fully determinable.

This transparency would allow entitled revenue to accrue to the different links in the chain, permit the consumer to have programming of his choice and watch channels according to their affordability, hopefully at a lower cost, and provide realistic and authentic viewership data. The Task Force was unanimous that the Conditional Access System is necessary to bring transparency at different levels, but that it should not add to the financial burden of the consumer. It was decided that the Government should mandate it by law.

The Set Top Box, allowing addressability, should be required only for 'Pay' channels; for subscribers who opt to view only 'Free-to-Air' channels, there would be no requirement of a Set Top Box. The Set Top Box shall be supported by the MSOs/Cable Operators through installation of necessary infrastructure like Subscriber Management System etc. It was considered desirable that the Government must be empowered to enter and inspect the premises and operations of the MSOs and Cable Operators to ensure enforcement of the requirements of the Set Top Box, of transparent recording of viewership figures, display of channel rates etc.

The Task Force saw a presentation on the system introduced by M/s. Ortel Communications, in Bhubaneshwar, on experimental basis. It is using 'Dalvi', a low cost conditional access scrambling system, which combines security and multi-tiered addressability. It encrypts analogue signals and the system is compatible with any video transmission system. The system has the potential to address 80,000 customers with a subscriber Management System. A total of 4 channels-mix of 'Free-to-Air' and 'Pay'—are presently being routed through the Set Top Box. The cost of the Set Top Box is approximately Rs. 3,500. The system is one way and not interactive. It was informed that the start up costs, for investment in equipment at Head-end Level, was approximately Rs. 50,000 for each channel. The financial implications of introducing the Set Top Box and addressability system, at each level, were discussed against this background. The need to keep the present system intact, at least for those viewers who prefer to watch only 'Free-to-Air' channels, was favoured.

The Task Force felt that the Set Top Box should be mandated only for "Premium Tier"; 'Free-to-Air' channels being taken in a "Basic Tier", receivable by all viewers at a standard subscription rate. The Task Force debated other issues emerging out of the presentation and felt that the price of channels/content for the Cable Operators should be fixed in a transparent manner, by Content Providers and Channel owners, for all operators.

The Task Force was unanimous in its view that there was need for an enabling provision in the legislation for Government to prescribe certain basic minimum standards for the equipment and its performance. In order to consider all issues relating to prescriptions of Standards and Performance Parameters, for the Set Top Box/Conditional Access System, a Sub-Committee made recommendations on the standards and the specifications for Digital Cable TV and Analogue Cable TV, as well as for Digital/Analogue Set Top Boxes.

It also recommended that the Cable Operator/Equipment Provider should declare, in a transparent manner, the capability of the Set Top Box and its inter-operability with other networks. It also recommended that unauthorized viewing/redistribution of the signal should be made a cognizable offence. The packaging of services, including Value Added Services, should be left to the Operators who should be free to choose the middleware/software/hardware provided that it conformed to basic minimum performance standards. It further recommended that the subscriber management system should provide transparent information to all the players.

The Task Force was of a strong view that there was urgent need to educate the subscribers, by all the stake holders, on the operation of Cable Television and the cost of various services, including the operation and cost of Set Top Boxes. The Task Force accepted the recommendation of the Sub-Committee, for an enabling provision in the Act to prescribe basic minimum technical standards and performance parameters, through the Bureau of Indian Standards (BIS). The manufacturers of the equipment must provide full information on the capability of the hardware.

It was also considered desirable that BIS may invite comments from the industry and examine internationally acceptable standards before prescribing standards for India. The Task Force was of the view that eventually the Set Top Box would permit migration, by the subscriber, across various delivery media-Satellite, Cable and Terrestrial. The user will thus have the capability to migrate to various delivery media, simply by changing the "Network Interface Module".

The members of the Task Force debated the need for a Conditional Access System base on DVB simulcrypt technology or any other currently acceptable technology but eventually felt it appropriate to leave the issue of technological specifications to the Bureau of Indian Standards, who would ensure that the technology is not proprietary in nature. In order to ensure transparency in the interface between MSOs and the Cable operators, it was decided that the Government be empowered to obtain monthly reports from the MSOs, Broadcasters and Cable operators in the manner prescribed.

The Task Force also debated the issue of "must carry" provision for the content of the Public Service Broadcaster and the pricing of the "Basic Tier" of service and the Set Top

Box. The Group felt that the consumer should not be burdened with the cost of changing his television sets on purchasing a Set Top Box, if he wanted to view only Free-to-Air channels. The Subscriber should exercise choice of viewing the 'Pay' channels through a Set Top Box. However, there was no need to prescribe the cost price of either the Set Top Box or the 'Pay' channels.

It was however, considered desirable that the pricing of various channel bouquets, by the Broadcasters, MSOs should be done in a transparent manner. The Group was unanimous that the Government should fix the price of the 'Basic Tier' and therefore legislation should enable the determination of the 'Basic Tier' price, from time to time by the Government. The Pricing/subsidy of the Set Top Boxes, by any player should be left to market forces, as long as the consumer was made fully aware of the availability and capability of the equipment. The equipment suppliers were confident that with larger volume, market forces would drive down the price of Set Top Boxes. The Group also felt that the Broadcasters, MSOs and Cable Operators should be allowed the freedom to work out their individual business plans to subsidise the Set Top Boxes, in accordance with their own marketing strategy.

The Group acknowledged the fact that with progressive introduction of Digital Video Broadcasting technology, its combination with interactive return path, between the user and the Service operator, will pave the way for other Services, for which the subscriber should be prepared to pay on the basis of charges fixed.

Recommendations

The Conditional Access System and the supportive Subscriber Management System should be mandated under the Cable Television Networks (Regulation) Act, 1995.

The Set Top Box shall be required only for "Pay" Channels and the "Free-to-Air" channels shall be receivable by the subscribers in the current mode, without Set Top Box. The encrypted channel should be defined as "Subscription based Channel".

The Technical parameters of the Set Top Box shall conform to the Indian standards, to be prescribed by the Bureau of Indian Standards, in accordance with the provisions of the Bureau of Indian Standards Act, 1986. While doing so, the Bureau of Indian Standards may take into account the internationally acceptable standards and obtain recommendations from technologists and manufacturers of equipment.

It shall be mandatory for the Equipment Provider/Manufacturer to declare, in a transparent manner, the capability of the Set Top Box and its interoperability on other networks.

In order to ensure transparency in the operations between MSOs, Cable Operators etc., the Government must be empowered to obtain detailed information, on regular basis, from each level of operation. This may include information on total subscriber base, on individual programmers, viewership of independence channels, subscription rates, charges fixed by the Broadcasters, Content Creators for each channel etc. Each subscriber shall be keep informed in a transparent manner of the subscription rates for each individual 'Pay' channel.

Unauthorised viewing/distribution/redistribution of the broadcast signal should be made a cognizable offence.

The Government should regulate the price of 'Basic Tier' of the 'Free-to-Air' channels. The Government should also be enabled to revise the cost of the 'Basic Tier', from time to time. The Government will also make a special provision for the channels of the Public Services Broadcaster. No government intervention was considered necessary with regard to the cost of the Set Top Box or the rates of the individual 'Pay' channel.

There should be no requirement for change of the receiving set, irrespective of whether the consumer chooses to watch 'Free-to-Air' channels and/or 'Pay' channels.

There was an immediate need to educate the consumer on the operation of cable television, on the cost of content creation and its distribution upto the households. The Broadcasters, Content Creators and MSOs should not enhance the charges of the 'Pay' channels arbitrarily, it should be done in a transparent manner.

The packaging of services, includes Value Added Services, as well as the pricing of the paid bouquets would be left to market forces. However, consumer interest needed to be protected by providing efficient and responsive service and through a transparent and accurate billing and collection system. This will also ensure that the revenue accruable to the Government is determined in a fair manner.

GUIDELINES FOR OBTAINING LICENSE FOR PROVIDING DIRECT-TO-HOME (DTH)

The Union Government has decided to permit Direct-to-Home (DTH) TV service in Ku Band in India. The prohibition on the reception and distribution of television signal in Ku Band has been withdrawn by the Government vide notification No. GSR 18(E) dated 9th January, 2001 of the Department of Telecommunications.

The salient features of eligibility criteria, basic conditions/obligations and procedure for obtaining the license to set up and operate DTH service are briefly described below. For further details, reference should be made to the Ministry of Information and Broadcasting. Direct-to-Home (DTH) Broadcasting Service, refers to distribution of multi channel TV programmes in Ku Band by using a satellite system by providing TV signals direct to subscribers' premises without passing through an intermediary such as cable operator.

Following are the eligibility criteria for applicants, conditions which will apply to DTH license and procedural details:

Eligibility Criteria: Applicant Company to be an Indian Company registered under Indian Company's Act, 1956.

Total foreign equity holding including FDI/NRI/OCB/FII in the applicant company not to exceed 49 per cent.

Within the foreign equity, the FDI component not to exceed 20 per cent.

The quantum represented by that proportion of the paid up equity share capital to the total issued equity capital of the Indian Promoter Company, held or controlled by the foreign investors through FDI/NRI/OCB investments, shall form part of the above said FDI limit of 20 per cent.

The applicant company must have Indian Management Control with majority representatives on the board as well as the Chief Executive of the company being a resident Indian.

Broadcasting companies and/or cable network companies shall not be eligible to collectively own more than 20 per cent of the total equity of applicant company at any time during the license period. Similarly, the applicant company not to have more than 20 per cent equity share in a broadcasting and/or cable network company.

The Licensee shall be required to submit the equity distribution of the Company in the prescribed Proforma once within one month of start of every financial year.

Number of Licensees: There will be no restrictions on the total number of DTH licenses and these will be issued to any person who fulfils the necessary terms and conditions and subject to the security and technical clearances by the appropriate authorities of the Govt. Period of license.

License will be valid for a period of 10 years from the date of issue of wireless operational license by Wireless Planning and Coordination Wing of Ministry of Communications. However, the license can be cancelled/suspended by the Licensor at any time in the interest of Union of India.

Basic Conditions/Obligations: The license will be subject to terms and conditions contained in the agreement and its schedule. Procedure for application and grant of licenses: To apply to the Secretary, Ministry of I&B, in triplicate, in the prescribed proforma. On the basis of information furnished in the application form, if the applicant is found eligible for setting up of DTH platform in India, the application will be subjected to security clearance in consultations with the Ministry of Home Affairs and for clearance of satellite use with the Department of Space.

After these clearances are obtained, the applicant would be required to pay an initial non-refundable entry-fee of Rs. 10 crores to the Ministry of Information and Broadcasting. After such payment of entry-fee, the applicant would be informed of intent of Ministry of I & B to issue license and requested to approach WPC for SACFA clearance.

After obtaining SACFA clearance, within one month of the same, the Licensee will have to submit a Bank guarantee from any Scheduled Bank to the Ministry of Information and Broadcasting for an amount of Rs. 40 crores valid for the duration of the license. After submission of this Bank Guarantee, the applicant would be required to sign a licensing agreement with the Ministry of Information and Broadcasting as per prescribed proforma. After signing of such licensing agreement with the Ministry of Information and Broadcasting, the applicant will have to apply to the Wireless Planning and Coordination (WPC) Wing of the Ministry of Communications for seeking Wireless Operational License for establishment, maintenance and operation of DTH platform. The Licensee shall pay an annual fee equivalent to 10 per cent of its gross revenue as reflected in the audited accounts of the Company for that particular financial year, within one month of the end of that financial year.

The Licensee shall also, in addition, pay the license fee and royalty for the spectrum used as prescribed by Wireless Planning and Coordination Authority (WPC), under the Department of Telecommunications.

Arbitration Clause: In case of any dispute, matter will be referred to the sole Arbitration of the Secretary, Department of Legal Affairs, Government of India or his nominee, for adjudication. The award of the Arbitrator shall be binding on the parties. The Arbitration proceedings will be governed by the law of Indian arbitration in force at the point of time. Venue of Arbitration shall be India.

GUIDELINES FOR UPLINKING OF NEW AND CURRENT AFFAIRS TV CHANNELS FROM INDIA

Preamble

The Union Government has revised the policy for uplinking of TV channels from India, insofar it relates to the News and Current Affairs channels. Accordingly, the guidelines for permission/approval for uplinking of News and Current Affairs TV channels from India, have been framed for immediate compliance.

Channels which do not have any news and current affairs content will, however, continue to be eligible to uplink from India, irrespective of ownership, equity structure or management control.

The use of all equipment/platforms for collection of footage/news by channels uplinked from outside for specific programme(s)/event(s) of temporary duration will be entertained on recommendation from the PIB and permitted on a case to case basis, in consultation with the Ministry of Home Affairs and other Ministries/Departments concerned.

Applicability

- These guidelines will apply to existing News and Current Affairs TV channels uplinked from India as well as to those proposing to uplink from India.
- For the purposes of these guidelines (*i*) News and Current Affairs channel means a channel which has any element of news and current affairs in its programme content; and (*ii*) an existing channel means any channel which has been permitted by the Ministry of Information and Broadcasting to uplink from India. Existing channels will be required to conform to these guidelines within a period of one year from the date of issue of these guidelines.

Eligibility Criteria

An applicant company desirous of uplinking news and current affairs TV channel(s) from India will be considered eligible, if it fulfils the following criteria:

It is registered/incorporated in India under the Companies Act, 1956,

Foreign equity holding in the applicant company does not exceed 26 per cent of the total paid up capital,

Majority of its Board of Directors are Resident Indians,

CEO of the applicant company, known by any designation, and/or Head of the channel is a Resident Indian,

News Editor(s) or authority(ies) exercising editorial control over news and current affairs programme(s) of the channel(s) are Resident Indians.

Period of Approval/Permission

Ten (10) years.

Basic Conditions/Obligations

- Permission for usage of facilities/infrastructure for live news/footage collection and transmission, irrespective of the technology used, will be given to only those channels which are uplinked from India. To ensure compliance of this policy in respect of permissions/licences given/to be given for utilization of VSAT/RTTS/Satellite Video Phone and similar other infrastructure, which lends itself for use in uplinking/point to point transfer of content for broadcast purposes, separate guidelines will be issued by the Ministry of Communications and Information Technology.

- The channel/company will ensure that its news and current affairs content provider(s), if any, are accredited with the Press Information Bureau. Such accredited content provider(s) only can use equipment/platform for collection/transmission of news/footage.
- The company/channel should ensure that it uses equipment which is duly authorised and permitted by the competent authority, or its content provider(s), if any, use equipment duly authorised by the competent authority.
- It will be obligatory on the part of the company to take prior permission from the Ministry of Information and Broadcasting, before effecting any alteration in the foreign shareholding pattern and/or in the CEO/Board of Directors.
- The company/channel will be liable to intimate to the Ministry of Information and Broadcasting the details of any foreigners/NRIs employed/engaged by it for a period exceeding 60 days.
- The company/channel shall undertake to comply with the Programme and Advertising Codes, as laid down in the Cable Television Networks (Regulation) Act, 1995 and the Rules framed thereunder.
- It shall keep record of the content uplinked for a period of 90 days and produce the same before any agency of the Government, as and when required.
- It shall furnish such information, as may be required by the Ministry of Information and Broadcasting, from time to time.
- The company/channel shall provide for the necessary monitoring facility, at its own cost, for monitoring of programmes or content by the representatives of the Ministry of Information and Broadcasting or any other Government agency as and when so required.
- The applicant company should use transponder on a satellite in C-Band only and the same should have been co-ordinated with INSAT system.
- The applicant company/channel shall comply with all the terms and conditions of the permission/approval prescribed by the Ministry of Information and Broadcasting and failure to comply with any of the terms and conditions will result in withdrawal of such permission/approval and suspension/cancellation of the wireless operating licence issued by the WPC.

Procedure

- The applicant company shall apply to the Secretary, Ministry of Information and Broadcasting in triplicate in the prescribed proforma (Form 2.1) along with affidavits in Form 2A and 2B and shareholding pattern of the company as per annexures.
- On receipt of the applications and the affidavit as mentioned above, if the applicant company is found eligible, its request will be sent for security clearance

to the Ministry of Home Affairs and for clearance of usage of satellite to the Department of Space.

- On receipt of these clearances, the applicant company will be permitted by the Ministry of Information and Broadcasting to uplink its channel(s) through an authorised hub/teleport.

Transitory Arrangements

- Content Providers/Channels who are currently using VSAT/RTTS/Satellite Video Phone and similar other infrastructure, which lends itself for use for uplinking/point-to-point transfer of content for broadcast purposes, will be allowed a maximum period of three months to come within the framework of these guidelines.

THE INDIAN TELEGRAPH ACT

A backgrounder—The Indian Telegraph Act was passed by the Legislature in 1885 and it came into force on 1st October, 1885. It extended to the whole of India but by the A.O. 1950 its extension to the State of Hyderabad was withdrawn by inserting the words "except the State of Hyderabad".

Later by Section 3 and schedule of the Part B State (Laws) Act, 1951 (3 of 1951) the words "except the State of Hyderabad" were omitted and now it extends to the whole of India. By the definition given in the Act "Telegraph" means any appliance, instrument, material or apparatus used or capable of use for transmission or reception of signs, signals, writing, images and sounds or intelligence of any nature by wire, visual or other electric-magnetic emissions, radio waves or Hertzian waves, galvanic, electric or magnetic means. 'Telegraph' which expression by the definition would include a telephone and FAX also. A Video and Television both fall within the definition of "telegraph". A telegraph wireless receiving station is a "telegraph" as defined in the Act.

List of Amending Acts and Adoptation Orders

1. Act 11 of 1888
2. Act 7 of 1914
3. Act 14 of 1914
4. Act 27 of 1930
5. A.O. 1937
6. Act 45 of 1948
7. A.O. 1950
8. The Part B States (Laws) Act, 1951 (3 of 1951)
9. The Indian Telegraph (Amendment) Act, 1957 (47 of 1957)
10. The Telegraph Laws (Amendment) Act, 1961 (15 of 1961)
11. The Indian Telegraph (Amendment) Act, 1971 (33 of 1971)
12. The Indian Telegraph (Amendment) Act, 1972 (38 of 1972)
13. The Indian Telegraph (Amendment) Act, 1974 (48 of 1974)

The Indian Telegraph Act, 1885 (13 of 1885) [22nd July, 1885] An Act to amend the law relating to Telegraphs in India WHEREAS it is expedient to amend the law relating to telegraphs in India. It is hereby enacted as follows: Part I Preliminary.

PART I
PRELIMINARY

1. Short Title, Local Extent and Commencement: (1) This Act may be called the Indian telegraph Act, 1885.

[(2) It extends to the whole of India.]

(3) It shall come into force on the first day of October, 1885.

2. Repeal and Savings: [Rep. By the Repealing Act, 1938 (1 of 1938,) Section 2 and Schedule]

3. Definitions: In this Act, unless there is something repugnant in the subject or context,—

[(1) "telegraph" means any appliance, instrument, material or apparatus used or capable of use for transmission or reception of signs, signals, writing, images and sounds or intelligence of any nature by wire, visual or other electro-magnetic emissions, Radio waves or Hertzian waves, galvanic, electric or magnetic means.

Explanation: "Radio waves" or "Hertzian waves" means electro-magnetic waves of frequencies lower than 3,000 giga-cycles per second propagated in space without artificial guide;]

(2) "telegraph officer" means any person employed either permanently or temporarily in connection with a telegraph established, maintained or worked by [the Central Government] or by a person licensed under this Act;

(3) "message" means any communication sent by telegraph, or given to telegraph officer to be sent by telegraph or to be delivered;

(4) "telegraph line" means a wire or wires used for the purpose of a telegraph, with any casing, coating, tube or pipe enclosing the same, and any appliances and apparatus connected therewith for the purpose of fixing or insulating the same;

(5) "post" means a post, pole, standard, stay, strut or other above ground contrivance for carrying, suspending or supporting a telegraph line;

(6) "telegraph authority" means the Director General of [Posts and Telegraphs], and includes any officer empowered by him to perform all or any of the functions of the telegraph authority under this Act;

(7) "local authority" means any municipal committee, district board, body of port commissioner or other authority legally entitled to, or entrusted by the Central or any State Government with, the control, management of any municipal or local fund.

PART II
PRIVILEGES AND POWERS OF THE GOVERNMENT

4. Exclusive Privilege in Respect of Telegraphs, and Power to Grant Licenses: (1) Within [India], the Central Government shall have exclusive privilege of establishing, maintaining and working telegraphs:

Provided that the Central Government may grant a license, on such conditions and in consideration of such payments as it thinks fit, to any person to establish, maintain or work a telegraph within any part of [India]:

Provided further that the Central Government may, by rules made under this Act and published in the Official Gazette, permit, subject to such restrictions and conditions as it thinks fit, the establishment, maintenance and working—

(*a*) of wireless telegraphs on ships within Indian territorial waters and on aircraft within or above [India], or Indian territorial waters], and

(*b*) of telegraphs other than wireless telegraphs within any part of [India].

(2) The Central Government may, by notification in the Official Gazette, delegate to the telegraph authority all or any of its powers under the first proviso to sub-section (1).

The exercise by the telegraph authority of any power so delegated shall be subject to such restrictions and conditions as the Central Government may, by the notification, think fit to impose.]

5. Power for Government to Take Possession of Licensed Telegraphs and to Order Interception of Messages: (1) On the occurrence of any public emergency, or in the interest of the public safety, the Central Government or a State Government or any officer specially authorized in this behalf by the Central Government or a State Government may, if satisfied that it is necessary or expedient so to do, take temporary possession (for so long as the public emergency exists or the interest of the public safety requires the taking of such action) of any telegraph established, maintained or worked by any person licensed under this Act.

(2) On the occurrence of any public emergency, or in the interest of the public safety, the Central Government or a State Government or any officer specially authorized in this behalf by the Central Government or a State Government may, if satisfied that it is necessary or expedient so to do in the interests of the sovereignty and integrity of India, the security of the State, friendly relations with foreign States or public order or for preventing incitement to the commission of an offence, for reasons to be recorded in writing, by order, direct that any message or class of messages to or from any person or class of persons, or relating to any particular subject, brought for transmission by or transmitted or received by any telegraph, shall not be transmitted, or shall be intercepted or detained, or shall be disclosed to the Government making the order or an officer thereof mentioned in the order:

Provided that press messages intended to be published in India of correspondents accredited to the Central Government or a State Government shall not be intercepted or detained, unless their transmission has been prohibited under this sub-section.

6. Power to Establish Telegraph on Land of Railway Company: Any Railway company, on being required so to do by the Central Government, shall permit the Government to establish and maintain a telegraph upon any part of the lank of the Company, and shall give every reasonable facility for working the same.

[6A. Power to Notify Rates for Transmission of Messages to Countries Outside India: (1) The Central Government may, from time to time, by order, notify the rates at which, and the other conditions and restrictions subject to which messages shall be transmitted to any country outside India.

(2) In notifying the rates under sub-section (1), the Central Government shall have due regard to all or any of the following factors, namely—

(*a*) the rates for the time being in force, for transmission of messages, in countries outside India;

(*b*) the foreign exchange rates for the time being in force;

(*c*) the rates for the time being in force for transmission of messages within India;

(*d*) such other relevant factors as the Central Government may think fit in the circumstances of the case.]

7. Power to Make Rules for the Conduct of Telegraphs: (1) The Central Government may, from time to time, by notification in the Official Gazette, make rules consistent with this Act for the conduct of all or any telegraphs established, maintained or worked by the Government or by persons licensed under this Act.

(2) Rules under this section may provide for all or any of the following among other matters, that is to say—

(*a*) the rates at which, and the other conditions and restrictions subject to which, messages shall be transmitted [within India];

(*b*) the precautions to be taken for preventing the improper interception or disclosure of messages;

(*c*) the period for which, and the conditions subject to which, telegrams and other documents belonging to, or being in the custody of, telegraph officers shall be preserved;

(*d*) the fees to be charged for searching for telegrams or other documents in the custody of any telegraph officer;

(*e*) the conditions and restrictions subject to which any telegraph line, appliance of apparatus for telegraphic communication shall be established, maintained, worked, repaired, transferred, shifted, withdrawn or disconnected;

[(*ee*) the charges in respect of any application for providing any telegraph line, appliance or apparatus;]

(*f*) the charges in respect of—

(*i*) the establishment, maintenance, working, repair, transfer or shifting of any telegraph line, appliance or apparatus;

(*ii*) the services of operators operating such line, appliance or apparatus;

(*g*) the matters in connection with the transition from a system where under rights and obligations relating to the establishment, maintenance, working repair, transfer of shifting of any telegraph line, appliance or apparatus for telegraphic communication attach by virtue of any agreement to a system where under such rights and obligations attach by virtue of rules made under this section;

(*h*) the time at which, the manner in which, the conditions under which and the persons by whom the rates, charges and fees mentioned in this sub-section shall be paid and the furnishing of security for the payment of such rates, charges and fees;

(*i*) the payment of compensation to the Central Government for any loss incurred in connection with the provision of any telegraph line, appliance or apparatus for the benefit of any person—

(*a*) where the line, appliance or apparatus is, after it has been connected for use, given up by that person before the expiration of the period fixed by these rules, or

(*b*) where the work done for the purpose of providing the line, appliance or apparatus is, before it is connected for use, rendered abortive by some act or omission on the part of that person;

(*j*) the principles according to which and the authority by whom the compensation referred to clause (*i*) shall be assessed;

[(*jj*) the qualifications to be possessed and the examinations, if any, to be passed by the persons employed for the establishment, maintenance or working of any telegraph and the fees to be charges for admission to such examinations;] and

(*k*) any other matter for which provision is necessary for the proper and efficient conduct of all or any telegraphs under this Act.

(3) When making rules for the conduct of any telegraph established, maintained or worked by any person licensed under this Act, the Central Government may by the rules prescribe fines for any breach of the same:

Provided that the fines so prescribed shall not exceed the following limits, namely—

(*i*) When the person licensed under this Act is punishable for the breach, one thousand rupees, and in the case of a continuing breach a further fine of two hundred rupees for everyday after the first during the whole or any part of which the breach continues.

(*ii*) When a servant of the person so licensed, or any other person, is punishable for the breach, one-fourth of the amounts specified in clause (i).

[(4) Nothing in this section or in any rules made hereunder shall be construed as—

(*a*) precluding the Central Government from entering into an agreement with a person for the establishment, maintenance and working by that Government on terms and conditions specified in the agreement of any telegraph line, appliance or apparatus for the purpose of affording means of telegraphic communication, where having regard to the number of the lines, appliance or apparatus required by that person for telegraphic communication, it is necessary or expedient to enter into such agreement with him, or

(*b*) subjecting the Central Government to any obligation to provide any telegraph line appliance or apparatus for the purpose of affording means of telegraphic communication.]

[(5) Every rule made under this section shall be laid as soon as may be after it is made before each House of Parliament while it is in session for a total period of thirty days [which may be comprised in one session or in two or more successive sessions, and it, before the expiry of the session immediately following the session or the successive sessions aforesaid] both Houses agree in making any modification in the rule or both Houses agree that the rule should not be made, the rule shall thereafter have effect only in such modified form or be of no effect as the case may be; so, however, that any such modification or annulment shall be without prejudice to the validity of anything previously done under that rule.]]

[7A. Saving of Existing Agreements: Nothing in Section 7 shall authorize the making of any rules determining any agreement entered into by the Central Government with any person before the commencement of the Indian Telegraph (Amendment) Act, 1957 (47 of 1957), relating to the establishment, maintenance or working of any telegraph line, appliance or apparatus for telegraphic communication; and all rights and obligations thereunder relating to such establishment, maintenance or working hall be determined in accordance with the terms and conditions of such agreement.

7B. Arbitration of Disputes: (1) Except as otherwise expressly provided in this Act, if any dispute concerning any telegraph line, appliance or apparatus arises between the telegraph authority and the person for whose benefit the line, appliance or apparatus is, or has been provided, the dispute shall be determined by arbitration and shall, for the purposes of such determination, be referred to an arbitrator appointed by the Central Government either specially for the determination of that dispute or generally for the determination of disputes under this section.

(2) The award of the arbitrator appointed under sub-section (1) shall be conclusive between the parties to the dispute and shall not be questioned in any court.]

8. Revocation of Licenses: The Central Government may, at any time, revoke any license granted under Section 4, on the breach of any of the conditions therein contained, or in default of payment of any consideration payable thereunder.

9. Government not Responsible for Loss or Damage: The Government shall not be responsible for any loss or damage which may occur in consequence of any telegraph officer failing in his duty with respect to the receipt, transmission or delivery of any message; and no such officer shall be responsible for any such loss or damage, unless he causes the same negligently, maliciously or fraudulently.

PART III
POWER TO PLACE TELEGRAPH LINES AND POSTS

10. Power for Telegraph Authority to Place and Maintain Telegraph Lines and Posts: The telegraph authority may, from time to time, place and maintain a telegraph line under, over, along, or across, and posts in or upon any immovable property:

Provided that—

(*a*) the telegraph authority shall not exercise the powers conferred by this section except for the purposes of a telegraph established or maintained by the [Central Government], or to be so established or maintained;

(*b*) the [Central Government] shall not acquire any right other than that of user only in the property under, over, along, across in or upon which the telegraph authority places any telegraph line or post; and

(*c*) except as hereinafter provided, the telegraph authority shall not exercise those powers in respect of any property vested in or under the control or management of any local authority, without the permission of that authority; and

(*d*) in the exercise of the powers conferred by this section, the telegraph authority shall do as little damage as possible, and, when it has exercised those powers in respect of any property other than that referred to in clause (c), shall pay full compensation to all persons interested for any damage sustained by them by reason of the exercise of those powers.

11. Power to Enter on Property in Order to Repair or Remove Telegraph Lines or Posts: The telegraph authority may, at any time, for the purpose of examining, repairing, altering or removing any telegraph line or post, enter on the property under, over, along, across, in or upon which the line or post has been placed:

PROVISIONS APPLICABLE TO PROPERTY VESTED IN OR UNDER THE CONTROL OR MANAGEMENT OF LOCAL AUTHORITIES

12. Power for Local Authority to Give Permission Under Section 10, Clause (c), Subject to Conditions: Any permission given by a local authority under Section 10, clause (c), may be given subject to such reasonable conditions as that authority thinks fit to impose, as to the payment of any expenses to which the authority will necessarily be put in consequence of the exercise of the powers conferred by that section, or as to the time or mode of execution of any work, or as to any other think connected with or relative to any work undertaken by the telegraph authority under those powers.

13. Power for Local Authority to Require Removal or Alteration of Telegraph Line or Post: When, under the foregoing provisions of this Act, a telegraph line or post has been placed by the telegraph authority under, over, along, across, in or upon any property vested in or under the control or management of a local authority, and the local authority, having regard to circumstances which have arisen since the telegraph line or post was so placed, considers it expedient that it should be removed or that its position should be altered, the local authority may require the telegraph authority to remove it or alter its position, as the case may be.

14. Power to Alter Position of Gas or Water Pipes or Drains: The telegraph authority may, for the purpose of exercising the powers conferred upon it by this Act in respect of any property vested in or under the control or management of a local authority, alter the position thereunder of any pipe (not being a main) for the supply of gas or water, or of any drain (not being a main drain):

Provided that—

(*a*) when the telegraph authority desires to alter the position of any such pipe or drain it shall give reasonable notice of its intention to do so, specifying the time at which it will begin to do so, to the local authority, and, when the pipe or drain is not under the control of the local authority, to the person under whose control the pipe or drain is;

(*b*) a local authority or person receiving notice under clause (a) may send a person to superintend the work, and the telegraph authority shall execute the work to the reasonable satisfaction of the person so sent.

15. Disputes between Telegraph Authority and Local Authority: (1) If any dispute arises between the telegraph authority and a local authority in consequence of the local authority refusing the permission referred to in Section 10, clause (c), or prescribing any condition under Section 12, or in consequence of the telegraph authority omitting to comply with a requisition made under Section 13, or otherwise in respect of the exercise of the powers conferred by this Act, it shall be determine by such officer as the [Central Government] may appoint either generally or specially in this behalf.

(2) An appeal from the determination of the officer so appointed shall lie to the [Central Government]; and the order of the [Central Government] shall be final.

PROVISIONS APPLICABLE TO OTHER PROPERTY

16. Exercise of Powers Conferred by Section 10, and Disputes as to Compensation, in Case of Property Other than that of a Local Authority: (1) In the exercise of the powers mentioned in Section 10 in respect of property referred to in clause (d) of that section is resisted or obstructed, the District Magistrate may, in his discretion, order that the telegraph authority shall be permitted to exercise them.

(2) If, after the making of an order under sub-section (1), any person resists the exercise of those powers, or, having control over the property, does not give all facilities for this being exercised, he shall be deemed to have committed an offence under Section 188 of the Indian Penal Code (45 of 1860).

(3) If any dispute arises concerning the sufficiency of the compensation to be paid under Section 10, clause (d), it shall, on application for that purpose by either of the disputing parties to the District Judge within whose jurisdiction the property is situate, be determined by him.

(4) If any dispute arises as to the persons entitled to receive compensation, or as to the proportions in which the persons interested are entitled to share in it, the telegraph authority may pay into the Court of the District Judge such amount as he deems sufficient or, where all the disputing parties have in writing admitted the amount tendered to be sufficient or the amount has been determined under sub-section (3), that amount; and the District Judge, after giving notice to the parties and hearing such of them as desire to be heard, shall determine the persons entitled to receive the compensation or, as the case may be, the proportions in which the persons interested are entitled to share in it.

(5) Every determination of a dispute by a District Judge under sub-section (3) or sub-section (4) shall be final:

Provided that nothing in this sub-section shall affect the right of any person to recover by suit the whole or any part of any compensation paid by the telegraph authority, from the person who has received the same.

17. Removal or Alteration of Telegraph Line or Post on Property Other than that of a Local Authority: (1) When, under the foregoing provisions of this Act, a telegraph line or post has been placed by the telegraph authority under, over, along, across, in or upon any property, not being property vested in or under the control or management of a local authority, and any person entitled to do so desires to deal with that property in such a manner as to render it necessary or convenient that the telegraph line or post should be removed to another part thereof or to a higher or lower level or altered in form, he may require the telegraph authority to remove or alter the line or post accordingly:

Provided that, if compensation has been paid under Section 10, clause (d) he shall, when making the requisition, tender to the telegraph authority the amount requisite to defray the expense of the removal or alteration, or half of the amount paid as compensation, whichever may be the smaller sum.

(2) If the telegraph authority omits to comply with the requisition, the person making it may apply to the District Magistrate within whose jurisdiction the property is situated to order the removal or alteration.

(3) A District Magistrate receiving an application under sub-section (2) may, in his discretion reject the same or make an order, absolutely or subject to conditions, for the removal of the telegraph line post to any other part of the property or to higher or lower level or for the alteration of its form; and the order so made shall be final:

PROVISIONS APPLICABLE TO ALL PROPERTY

18. Removal of Trees Interrupting Telegraphic Communication: (1) If any tree standing or lying near a telegraph line interrupts, or is likely to interrupt, telegraphic communication, a Magistrate of the first or second class may, on the application of the telegraph authority, cause the tree to be removed or dealt with in such other way as he deems fit.

(2) When disposing of an application under sub-section (1), the Magistrate shall, in the case of any tree in existence before the telegraph line was placed, award to the

persons interested in the tree such compensation as he thinks reasonable, and shall be final.

19. Telegraph Lines and Posts Placed before Passing of this Act: Every telegraph line or post placed before the passing of this Act under, over, along, across, in or upon any property, for the purposes of a telegraph established or maintained by the [Central Government], shall be deemed to have been placed in exercise of the powers conferred by, and after observance of all the requirement of, this Act.

[19A. Person Exercising Legal Right Likely to Damage Telegraph or Interfere with Telegraphic Communication to Give Notice: (1) Any person desiring to deal in the legal exercise of a right with any property in such a manner as is likely to cause damage to a telegraph line or post which has been duly placed in accordance with the provisions of this Act, or to interrupt or interfere with telegraphic communication, shall give not less than one month's notice in writing of the intended exercise of such right to the telegraph authority, or to any telegraph officer whom the telegraph authority may empower in this behalf.

(2) If any such person without having complied with the provisions of sub-section (1) deals with any property in such a manner as is likely to cause damage to any telegraph line or post, or to interrupt or interfere with telegraphic communication, a Magistrate of the first or second class may, on the application of the telegraph authority, order such person to abstain from dealing with such property in such manner for a period not exceeding one month from the date of his order and forthwith to take such action with regard to such property as may be in the opinion of the Magistrate necessary to remedy or prevent such damage, interruption or interference during such period.

(3) A person dealing with any property in the manner referred to in sub-section (1) with the bona fide intention of averting imminent danger of personal injury to himself or any other human being shall be deemed to have complied with the provisions of the said sub-section if he gives such notice of the intended exercise of the right as is in the circumstances possible, or where no such previous notice can be given without incurring the imminent danger referred to above, if he forth with gives notice of the actual exercise of such right to the authority of officer specified in the said sub-section.

19B. Power to Confer Upon Licensee Powers of Telegraph Authority Under this Part: The Central Government may, by notification in the Official Gazette, confer upon any licensee under Section 4, in respect of the extent of his license and subject to any conditions and restrictions which the Central Government may think fit to impose and to the provisions of this Part, all or any of the powers which the telegraph authority possesses under this Part with regard to a telegraph established or maintained by the Government or to be so established or maintained:

Provided that the notice prescribed in Section 19A shall always be given to the telegraph authority or officer empowered to receive notice under Section 19A(1).

PART IV
PENALTIES

[20. Establishing, Maintaining or Working Unauthorized Telegraph: (1) If any person establishes, maintains or works a telegraph within [India] in contravention of the provisions of Section 4 or otherwise than as permitted by rules made under that section, he shall be punished, if the telegraph is a wireless telegraph, with imprisonment which may extend to three years, or with fine, or with both, and in any other case, with a fine which may extend to one thousand rupees.

(2) Notwithstanding anything contained in the Code of Criminal Procedure, 1898 (5 of 1898), offences under this section in respect of a wireless telegraph shall, for the purposes of the said Code, be bailable and non-cognizable.

(3) When any person is convicted of an offence punishable under this section, the Court before which he is convicted may direct that the telegraph in respect of which the offence has been committed, or any part of such telegraph, be forfeited to Government.]

[20A. Breach of Condition of License: If the holder of a license granted under Section 4 contravenes any condition contained in his license, he shall be punished with fine which may extend to one thousand rupees, and with a further fine which may extend to five hundred rupees for every week during which the breach of the condition continues.]

21. Using Unauthorized Telegraphs: If any person, knowing or having reason to believe that a telegraph has been established or is maintained or worked in contravention of this Act, transmits or receives any message by such telegraph, or performs any service incidental thereto, or delivers any message for transmission by such telegraph or accepts delivery of any message sent thereby, he shall be punished with fine which may extend to fifty rupees.

22. Opposing Establishment of Telegraphs on Railway Land: If a Railway Company, or an officer of a Railway Company, neglects or refuses to comply with the provisions of Section 6, it or he shall be punished with fine which may extend to one thousand rupees for everyday during which the neglect or refusal continues.

23. Intrusion into Signal-room, Trespass in Telegraph Office or Obstruction: If any person—

(*a*) without permission of competent authority, enters the signal-room of a telegraph office of the Government, or of a person licensed under this Act, or

(*b*) enters a fenced enclosure round such a telegraph office in contravention of any rule or notice not to do so, or

(*c*) refuses to quit such room or enclosure on being requested to do so by any officer or servant employed therein, or

(*d*) willfully obstructs or impedes any such officer or servant in the performance of his duty,

(e) he shall be punished with fine which may extend to five hundred rupees.

24. Unlawfully Attempting to Learning the Contents of Messages: If any person does any of the acts mentioned in Section 23 with the intention of unlawfully learning the contents of any message, or of committing any offence punishable under this Act, he may (in addition to the fine with which he is punishable under Section 23) be punished with imprisonment for a term which may extend to one year.

25. Intentionally Damaging or Tampering with Telegraphs: If any person, intending—

(*a*) to prevent or obstruct the transmission or delivery of any message, or

(*b*) to intercept or to acquaint himself with the contents of any message, or

(*c*) to commit mischief,

(*d*) damages, removes, tampers with or touches any battery, machinery, telegraph line, post or other thing whatever, being part of or used in or about any telegraph or in the working thereof,

(*e*) he shall be punished with imprisonment for a term which may extend to three years, or with fine or with both.

[25A. Injury to or Interference with a Telegraph Line or Post: If, in any case not provided for by Section 25, any person deals with any property and thereby willfully or negligently damages any telegraph line or post duly placed on such property in accordance with the provisions of this Act, he shall be liable to pay the telegraph authority such expenses (if any) as may be incurred in making good such damage, and shall also, if the telegraphic communication is by reason of the damage so caused interrupted, be punishable with a fine which may extend to one thousand rupees:

Provided that the provisions of this section shall not apply where such damage or interruption is caused by a person dealing with any property in the legal exercise of a right if he has complied with the provisions of Section 19A (1).]

26. Telegraph Officer or Other Official Making away with or Altering, or Unlawfully Intercepting or Disclosing, Messages, or Divulging Purport of Signals: If any telegraph officer, or any person, not being a telegraph officer but having official duties connected with any office which is used as a telegraph office.

(*a*) willfully, secrets, makes away with or alters any message which he has received for transmission or delivery, or

(*b*) willfully, and otherwise than in obedience to an order of the Central Government or of a State Government, or of an officer specially authorized [by the Central or a State Government] to make the order, omits to transmit, or intercepts or detains, any message or any part thereof, or otherwise than in pursuance of his official duty or in obedience to the direction of a competent Court, discloses the contents or any part the contents of any message, to any person not entitled to receive the same, or

(*c*) divulges the purport of any telegraphic signal to any person not entitled to become acquainted with the same,

(*d*) he shall be punished with imprisonment for a term which may extend to three years, or with fine, or with both.

27. Telegraph Officer Fraudulently Sending Messages without Payment: If any telegraph officer transmits by telegraph any message on which the charge prescribed by the [Central Government], or by a person licensed under this Act, as the case may be, has not been paid, intending thereby to defraud the [Central Government], or that person, he shall be punished with imprisonment for a term which may extend to three years, or with fine, or with both.

28. Misconduct: If any telegraph officer, or any person not being a telegraph officer but having official duties connected with any office which is used as a telegraph office is guilty of any of drunkenness, carelessness of other misconduct whereby the correct transmission or the delivery of any message is impeded or delayed or if telegraph officer loiters or delays in the transmission or delivery of any message, he shall be punished with imprisonment for a term which may extend to three months, or with fine which may extend to one hundred rupees, or with both.

29. [Sending Fabricated Messages]: Rep. By the Indian Telegraph (Amendment) Act, 1971 (33 of 1971), Section 4.

[29A. Penalty: If any person, without due authority—

(*a*) makes or issues any document of a nature reasonably calculated to cause it to be believed that the document has been issued by, or under the authority of, the Director-General of [Posts and Telegraphs], or

(*b*) makes on any document any mark in imitation of, or similar to, or purporting to be, any stamp or mark of any Telegraph Office under the Director-General of [Posts and Telegraph], or a mark of a nature reasonably calculated to cause it to be believed that the documents so marked has been issued by, or under authority of, the Director-General of [Posts and Telegraphs],

he shall be punished with fine which may extend to fifty rupees.]

30. Retaining a Message Delivered by Mistake.—If any person fraudulently retains, or willfully secretes, makes away with or detains a message which ought to have been delivered to some other person, or, being required by a telegraph officer to deliver up any such message, neglects or refuses to do so, he shall be punished with imprisonment for a term which may extend to two years, or with fine, or with both.

31. Bribery: A telegraph officer shall be deemed a public servant within the meaning of Sections 161, 162, 163, 164 and 165 of the Indian Penal Code (45 of 1860); and in the definition of "legal remuneration" contained in the said Section 161, the word "Government" shall, for the purposes of this Act, be deemed to include a person licensed under this Act.

32. Attempts to Commit Offences: Whoever attempts to commit any offence punishable under this Act shall be punished with the punishment herein provided for the offence.

PART V
SUPPLEMENTAL PROVISION

33. Power to Employ Additional Police in Places Where Mischief to Telegraphs is Repeatedly Committed: (1) Whenever it appears to the State Government that any act causing or likely to cause wrongful damage to any telegraph is repeatedly and maliciously committed in any place, and that the employment of an additional police force in that place is thereby rendered necessary, the State Government may send such additional police force as it thinks fit to the place, and employ the same therein so long as, in the opinion of that Government, the necessity of doing so continues.

(2) The inhabitants of the place shall be charged with the cost of the additional police force, and the District Magistrate shall, subject to the orders of the State Government, assess the proportion in which the cost shall be paid by the inhabitants according to his judgment of their respective means.

(3) All moneys payable under sub-section (2) shall be recoverable either under the warrant of a Magistrate by distress and sale of the movable property of the defaulter within the local limits of his jurisdiction, or by suit in any competent Court.

(4) The State Government may, by order in writing, define the limits of any place for the purposes of this section.

[34A. Application of Act to Presidency-towns: (1) This Act, in its application to the Presidency-towns, shall be read as if for the words "District Magistrate" in Section 16, sub-section (1), and Section 17, sub-sections (2) and (3), for the words "Magistrate of the first or second class" in Section 18, sub-section (1), [and Section 19A, sub-section (2),] and for the word "Magistrate" in Section 18, sub-section (2), there had been enacted the words "Commissioner of Police", and for the "District Judge" in Section 16, sub-sections (3), (4) and (5), the words "Chief Judge of the Court of Small Causes".

(2) Omitted.

(3) The fee in respect of an application to the Chief Judge of a Presidency Court of Small Causes under sub-section (3) of Section 16 shall be the same as would be payable under the Court-fees Act, 1870 (7 of 1870), in respect of such an application to a District Judge beyond the limits of a Presidency-town, and fees for summonses and other processes in proceedings before the Chief Judge under sub-section (3) or sub-section (4) of that section shall be payable according the scale set forth in the Fourth Schedule to the Presidency Small Cause Courts Act, 1882.

35. Reference to Certain Laws of Part B States: [Rep. by Part B States (Laws) Act 1951 (Act 3 of 1951), Section 3 and Schedule].

GUIDELINES FOR UPLINKING FROM INDIA

Uplinking of TV Signals from Indian soil has been envisaged in three phases. In the first phase, uplinking from Indian soil and through VSNL was permitted to those Indian broadcasters who had been taking foreign exchange release for this purpose for uplinking from abroad.

In the second phase, uplinking has been permitted to all Indian companies who are broadcasters, without making it mandatory to uplink through VSNL.

In the third phase (yet to be implemented) uplinking would be mandatory from Indian soil for all broadcasters. As per present policy, the facility to uplink from India is provided on case to case basis subject to certain parameters and criteria, the main ones being as follows: The applicant should be an Indian satellite channel with resident Indian equity holding of not less than 80 per cent and effective management control being with resident Indians.

The channels would be required to abide by the Programme and Advertising Codes, as are presently applicable to Doordarshan. The uplinking facility would be available either through VSNL or with effect from 1.8.99, through own uplink earth station for own TV channels only.

The facility would be available only to ITU coordinated satellites—which would mean successful completion of national and international coordination as appropriate, within the coordinated technical parameters. Applicants would have to be in possession of a transponder on such satellite as enumerated in point 5 above. The approvals would be subject to the siting clearance from Standing Advisory Committee for Frequency Assignment (SACFA) of Ministry of Communications and clearance from the Department of Space as per their SATCOM policy.

The transmission would be in C Band (not above 4800 MHz for downlink frequency) for Television signals only. The uplinking permission would be granted for a period of one year in the first instance.

In terms of procedure, the applications would need to be made to the Ministry of Information and Broadcasting. On the basis of a No Objection Certificate issued by this

Ministry the final approval and licence would be given by the Wireless Planning Adviser (WPA) in the Department of Telecommunications, subject to the usual terms and conditions, and payment of licence fee and royalty etc.

MINISTRY OF INFORMATION AND BROADCASTING FOREIGN INVESTMENT POLICY

Ministry of Information and Broadcasting is the nodal Ministry for formulation of policies on foreign investment in broadcasting, film, print and advertising sector. It invites foreign investment and frames laws keeping an eye on the widest national interest.

Advertising Sector

Following guidelines for foreign direct investment in advertising sector is being pursued: There should not be any cap on the percentage of foreign investment in a new or greenfield project. Where the proposal is for a new joint venture or enhancing foreign direct investment in an existing joint venture, foreign direct investment should be limited to 74 per cent. In exceptional cases, the 74 per cent limit could be relaxed to go up to 100 per cent with the consent of the Indian partner/partners and subject to the justification being established to the satisfaction of the Government. Where a foreign company/ investor already has a joint venture in this sector, a new wholly owned subsidiary shall normally not be permitted, unless there are strong reasons to make such an exception. Foreign Direct Investment would include all repatriable investment, irrespective of who or what the investor is. Such investment would be permitted through the automatic approval route.

Electronic Sector

Foreign investment proposals directly linked to Broadcasting will be kept pending till Broadcasting Law comes into effect. Presently, companies with 80 per cent Indian equity may be allowed to uplink for satellite channels. The proposals related to production of software and marketing of TV rights, airtime, advertisements, etc., may be recommended with the condition that all future laws on Broadcasting will be applicable to them and they will not claim any privilege or protection by virtue of this approval.

Print Media

Foreign ownership of newspapers and periodicals in India and publication of their Indian editions is guided by the Cabinet decision of 13th Sept., 1955. The relevant extracts of the decision are:

- No foreign owned newspapers and periodicals should, in future, be permitted to be published in India. Foreign newspapers and periodicals which deal mainly with news and current affairs should not be allowed to bring out Indian editions.
- Above decision was taken on recommendation of the First Press Commission, which inter alia had observed that proprietorial interest in the daily and weekly newspapers should predominantly vest in Indian hands. It also

considered Indianisation of both capital and staff desirable, especially at the higher level.

It was felt that newspapers should not be viewed similar to an industry since their true function was to influence working of democracy by shaping public opinion. Foreign participation in ownership or control of newspapers could be used for purpose of influencing Indian opinion in support of foreign interest and in some cases such participation could be at the instance of a foreign Government as well.

In pursuance of the above decision, this Ministry has since 1955, consistently denied permission for any foreign equity holding in print media or publication of Indian editions of foreign newspapers and periodicals. Due to many developments taken since then in the overall media scenario in the country and grant of Open General Licence to foreign newspapers and magazines, which resulted in their easy availability in the market, efforts are being made to review the 1955 Cabinet decision.

Foreign Ownership of News Agencies

The existing policy of foreign ownership of news agencies in India is governed by the Cabinet decision of 1956 which was also based on the recommendation of the first Press Commission.

The relevant extracts of the decision is reproduced below:

> Communication facilities should be granted to foreign news agencies only where the distribution of news within the country is to be effected through an Indian news agency owned and managed by Indians, which would have full and final authority in the selection of foreign news for distribution and which would also be in a position to supply Indian news in a reasonable volume to the foreign news agency with whom they have a working arrangement.

This decision has been the yardstick for examining requests of foreign news agencies to operate in India. Direct distribution of financial news by foreign news agencies is not violative of the 1956 Cabinet decision. Subsequent to this decision, this Ministry conveyed to its no objection to the permission accorded by RBI to M/s Reutors, subject to the condition that their financial services would be only for selected Indian non-media clients for their own use and not for reproduction and public distribution.

BROADCASTING CODE FOR AIR AND DOORDARSHAN

Advertising Code

The Prasar Bharati Corporation consists of two wings namely All India Radio and Doordarshan Commercials were introduced on AIR on 1st November, 1967 and on Doordarshan on 1st January, 1976.

Both AIR and Doordarshan have served as an effective instrument for advertisers to publicise their goods and services. As a public service broadcasting organisation, AIR and Doordarshan has responsibility to ensure that the advertisements either in terms of contents, tone or treatment, do not mislead the listeners and viewers as well as the consumers or are not repugnant to good taste.

The earning of commercial revenue is not the sole criteria of the Prasar Bharati. Thus the code has stricter provisions and the main features of the code are as follows:

(*i*) Tobacco products including 'Pan Masala' and liquors are not permitted.
(*ii*) The goods and services advertised should be in consonance with the laws of the country enacted to protect the rights of the consumers.
(*iii*) The commercial should never project a derogatory image of women and should not endanger the safety of children

Programme code: The General Broadcasting Code which is otherwise called Programme Code for both AIR and Doordarshan prohibits the following:

(*a*) Criticism of friendly countries;
(*b*) Attack on religions or communities.
(*c*) Anything obscene or defamatory.
(*d*) Incitement to violence or anything against maintenance of law and order.
(*e*) Anything amounting to contempt of court.
(*f*) Aspersions against the integrity of the President and Judiciary.
(*g*) Anything affecting the integrity of the Nation, and criticism by name of any person.

THE COPYRIGHT ACT

Introduction

In ancient days creative persons like artists, musicians and writers made, composed or wrote their works for fame and recognition rather than to earn a living, thus, the question of copyright never arose. The importance of copyright was recognised only after the invention of printing press which enabled the reproduction of books in large quantity practicable. In India the first legislation of its kind the Indian Copyright Act was passed in 1914 which was mainly based on the UK Copyright Act, 1911.

During the last four decades modern and advanced means of communications like broadcasting, litho-photography, television, etc., have made inroads in the Indian economy with the result that it became essential to fulfil international obligations in the field of copyright. This necessitated that a comprehensive legislation may be introduced to completely revise the copyright law. To this effect a Copyright Bill, 1957 was introduced in the Parliament.

Statement of Objects and Reasons

The existing law relating to copyright is contained in the Copyright Act, 1911 of the United Kingdom (hereinafter referred to as the United Kingdom Act) as modified by the Indian Copyright Act, 1914. Apart from the fact that the United Kingdom Act does not fit in with the changed constitutional status of India, it is necessary to enact an independent self-contained law on the subject of copyright in the light of growing public consciousness of the rights and obligations of authors and in the light of experience gained in the working of the existing law during the last forty years. New and advanced means of communications like broadcasting, lithophotography, etc., also call for certain amendments in the existing law. Adequate provision has also to be made for fulfilment of international obligations in the field of copyright which India might accept. A complete revision of law of copyright, therefore, seemed inevitable, and the Bill attempts such a revision.

Though the draft Bill follows generally, in a re-arranged form the main principles of the existing law, it has introduced several new features which are briefly indicated below:

1. A Copyright Office is sought to be established under the immediate control of a Registrar of Copyrights who shall act under the superintendence and direction of the Central Government. The principal function of the Copyright Office will be to maintain Register of Copyrights in which may be entered, at the option of the authors, the names and addresses of authors and owners of copyright for the time being, and other relevant particulars. Such Register will easily make available useful information to interested members of public in regard to copyrighted works. In order to encourage registration of copyrights, provision is made that no proceeding regarding infringement of copyright shall be instituted unless copyright is registered in the Copyright Office. In addition to being in charge of the Copyright Office, the duties of the Registrar of Copyrights will be to entertain and dispose of applications for compulsory licences and to inquire into complaints of importation of infringing copies. An appeal to the Copyright Board is provided for against the orders of the Registrar of Copyrights.
2. Provision is made for setting up a Copyright Board which will determine the reasonableness of the rates of fees, charges or royalties claimed by Performing rights societies, consider applications for general licences for public performances of works and will assess compensation payable under the Bill in certain circumstances. An appeal will lie to the High Court against the decisions of the Copyright Board.
3. The definition of "copyright" is enlarged to include the exclusive right to communicate works by radio-diffusion.
4. A cinematograph film will have a separate copyright apart from its various components, namely, story, music, etc.
5. An author assigning copyright in his work is allowed the option to re-acquire the copyright after seven years but before ten years of the assignment on the condition that he returns the amount received by him at the time of the assignment with interest thereon.
6. The normal term of the copyright is fixed to be the life of the author and a period of 25 years after his death as against the existing term of the life of the author, and a period of 50 years after his death. Shorter terms are fixed for anonymous or pseudonymous works, cinematograph films, mechanical contrivances, photographs, etc.
7. Under the existing law, the sole right to produce a translation of a work first published in India is extinguished after ten years, unless a translation thereof is produced within that period. The Draft Bill makes the right co-extensive with other rights arising out of copyright.
8. Provision is made for the issue of a general or special licence for public performances of any work by means of a radio-receiving set or a mechanical contrivance.

9. A licence may be issued to any library to make or cause to be made one copy of any book in which copyright subsists and which is not available for sale.
10. Provision is made for regulating the activities of performing rights societies and also for controlling the fees, charges or royalties to be collected by them.
11. Certain rights akin to copyright are conferred on Broadcasting authorities in respect of programmes broadcast by them.
12. International copyright relations which are based on international treaties will be regulated by specific orders to be made by the Central Government.
13. A fair dealing with any work for the purposes of radio summary or judicial proceeding will not hereafter constitute an infringement of copyright.

In preparing the Bill, the British Copyright Report, 1952, the suggestions of various Ministries of the Government of India, the State Governments, the Indian Universities and certain interested industries and associations, who were invited to send their comments on the subject, have been taken into consideration.

Act 14 of 1957

The Copyright Bill, 1957 as passed by both the Houses of Parliament received the Assent of the President on 4th June, 1957 and came into the Statute Book as The Copyright Act, 1957 (14 of 1957). However, this Act came into force on the 21st January, 1958.

List of Ammending Acts

1. The Copyright (Ammendment) Act, 1983 (23 of 1983) *(w.e.f. 9.8.1884).*
2. The Copyright (Ammendment) Act, 1984 (65 of 1984) *(w.e.f. 9.10.1984).*
3. The Copyright (Ammendment) Act, 1992 (13 of 1992) *(w.e.f. 29.12.1991).*
4. The Copyright (Ammendment) Act, 1994 (38 of 1994) *(w.e.f. 10.5.1995).*

CHAPTER I
PRELIMINARY

1. Short Title, Extent and Commencement; (1) This Act may be called the Copyright Act, 1957.

(2) It extends to the whole of India.

(3) It shall come into force on such date [21st January, 1958, vide Notification No. 269 dated 21-1-58 Gazette of India, Extraordinary, Part II, Section 3, p. 167] as the Central Government may, by notification in the Official Gazette, appoint.

2. Interpretation: In this Act, unless the context otherwise requires—

(*a*) "adaptation" means—

(*i*) in relation to a dramatic work, the conversion of the work into a non-dramatic work;

(*ii*) in relation to a literary work or an artistic work, the conversion of the work into a dramatic work by way of performance in public or otherwise;

(*iii*) in relation to a literary or dramatic work, any abridgement of the work or any version of the work in which the story or action is conveyed wholly or mainly by means of pictures in a form suitable for reproduction in a book, or in a newspaper, magazine or similar periodical; and

(*iv*) in relation to a musical work, any arrangement or transcription of the work;

(*b*) "architectural work of art" means any building or structure having an artistic character or design, or any model for such building or structure;

(*c*) "artistic work" means—

(*i*) a painting, a sculpture, a drawing (including a diagram, map, chart or plan), an engraving or a photograph, whether or not any such work possesses artistic quality;

(*ii*) an architectural work of art; and

(*iii*) any other work of artistic craftsmanship;

(*d*) "author" means,—

(*i*) in relation to literary or dramatic work, the author of the work;

(*ii*) in relation to a musical work, the composer;

(*iii*) in relation to an artistic work other than a photograph, the artist;

(*iv*) in relation to a photograph, the person taking the photograph;

(*v*) in relation to a cinematograph film, the owner of the film at the time of its completion; and

(*vi*) in relation to a record, the owner of the original plate from which the record is made, at the time of the making of the plate;

(*e*) "calendar year" means the year commencing on the 1st day of January;

(*f*) "cinematograph film" includes the sound track, if any, and "cinematograph" shall be construed as including any work produced by any mechanical instrument or by radio-diffusion;

(*g*) "delivery", in relation to a lecture, includes delivery by means of any mechanical instrument or by radio-diffusion;

(*h*) "dramatic work" includes any piece for recitation, choregraphic work or entertainment in dumb show, the scenic arrangement or acting form of which is fixed in writing or otherwise but does not include a cinematograph film;

(*i*) "engravings" include etchings, lithographs, wood-cuts, prints and other similar works, not being photographs;

(*j*) "exclusive licence" means a licence which confers on the licensee or on the licenses and persons authorised by him, to the exclusion of all other persons (including the owner of the copy right), any right comprised in the copyright in a work, and "exclusive licensee" shall be construed accordingly;

(*k*) "Government work" means a work which is made or published by or under the direction or control of—

(*i*) the government or any department of the Government;

(*ii*) any Legislature in India;

(*iii*) any court, tribunal or other judicial authority in India;

(*l*) "Indian work" means a literary, dramatic or musical work, the author of which is a citizen of India;

(*m*) "infringing copy" means,—

(*i*) in relation to a literary, dramatic, musical or artistic work, a reproduction thereof otherwise than in the form of a cinematograph film;

(*ii*) in relation to a cinematograph film, a copy of the film or a record embodying the recording in any part of the sound track associated with the film;

(*iii*) in relation to a record, any such record embodying the same recording; and (*iv*) in relation to a programme in which a broadcast reproduction right subsists under Section 37, a record recording the programme,

if such reproduction, copy or record is made or imported in contravention of the provisions of this Act;

(*n*) "lecture" includes address, speech and sermon;

(*o*) "literary work" includes tables and compilations;

(*p*) "musical work" means any combination of melody and harmony or either of them, printed, reduced to writing or otherwise graphically produced or reproduced;

(*q*) "performance" includes any mode of visual or accoustic presentation, including any such presentation by the exhibition of a cinematograph film, or by means of radio-diffusion, or by the use of a record, or by any other means and, in relation to a lecture, includes the delivery of such lecture;

(*r*) "performing rights society" means a society, association or other body, whether incorporated or not, which carries on business in India of issuing or granting licences for the performance in India of any works in which copyright subsists;

(*s*) "photograph" includes photo-lithograph and any work produced by any process analogous to photography but does not include any part of a cinematograph film;

(*t*) "plate" includes any stereotype or other plate, stone, block, mould, matrix, transfer, negative or other device used or intended to be used for printing or reproducing copies of any work, and any matrix or other appliance by which records for the acoustic presentation of the work are or are intended to be made;

(*u*) "prescribed" means prescribed by rules made under this Act;

(*v*) "radio-diffusion" includes communication to the public by any means of wireless diffusion whether in the form of sounds or visual images or both;

(*w*) "record" means any disc, tape, perforated roll or other device in which sounds are embodied so as to be capable of being reproduced therefrom, other than a sound track associated with a cinematograph film;

(*x*) "recording" means the aggregate of the sounds embodied in and capable of being reproduced by means of a record;

(*y*) "work" means any of the following works, namely—

(*i*) a literary, dramatic, musical or artistic work;

(*ii*) a cinematograph film;

(*iii*) a record;

(*z*) "work of joint authorship" means a work produced by the collaboration of two or more authors in which the contribution of one authors in which the contribution of one author is not distinct from the contribution of the other author or authors;

(*za*) "work of sculpture" includes casts and models.

3. **Meaning of Publication:** For the purposes of this Act, "publication" means—

(*a*) in the case of a literary, dramatic, musical or artistic work, the issue of copies of the work to the public in sufficient quantities;

(*b*) in the case of a cinematograph film, the sale or hire or offer for sale or hire of the film or copies thereof to the public;

(*c*) in the case of a record, the issue of records to the public in sufficient quantities;

but does not, except as otherwise expressly provided in this Act, includes—

(*i*) in the case of a literary, dramatic or musical work, the issue of any recording such work;

(*ii*) in the case of a work of sculpture or an architectural work of art, the issue of photographs and engravings of such work.

4. When Work not Deemed to be Published or Performed in Public: Except in relation to infringement of copyright, a work shall not be deemed to be published or performed in public, if published, or performed in public, without the licence of the owner of the copyright.

5. When Work Deemed to be First Published in India: For the purposes of this Act, a work published in India shall be deemed to be first published in India, notwithstanding that it has been published simultaneously in some other country, unless such other country provides a shorter term of copyright for such work; and a work shall be deemed to be published simultaneously in India and in another country if the time between the publication in India and the publication in such other country does not exceed thirty days or such other period as the Central Government may, in relation to any specified country, determine.

6. Certain Disputes to be Decided by Copyright Board: If any question arises—

(*a*) Whether for the purposes of Section 3, copies of any literary, dramatic, musical or artistic work, or records are issued to the public in sufficient quantities; or

(*b*) Whether for the purposes of Section 5, the term of copyright for any work is shorter in any other country than that provided in respect of that work under this Act;

it shall be referred to the Copyright Board constituted under Section 11 whose decision thereon shall be final.

7. Nationality of Author Where the Making of Unpublished Work is Extended Over Considerable Period: Where, in the case of an unpublished work, the making of the work is extended over a considerable period, the author of the work shall, for the purposes of this Act, be deemed to be a citizen of, or domiciled in, that country of which he was a citizen or wherein he was domiciled during any substantial part of that period.

8. Domicile of corporations.—For the purposes of this Act, a body corporate shall be deemed to be domiciled in India if it is incorporated under any law in force in India.

CHAPTER II
COPYRIGHT OFFICE AND COPYRIGHT BOARD

9. Copyright Office: (1) There shall be established for the purposes of this Act an office to be called the Copyright Office.

(2) The Copyright Office shall be under the immediate control of 639 M. of Law...7 the Registrar of Copyrights who shall act under the superintendance and direction of the Central Government.

(3) There shall be a seal for the Copyright Office.

10. Registrar and Deputy Registrars of Copyrights: (1) The Central Government shall appoint a Registrar of Copyrights and may appoint one or more Deputy Registrars of Copyrights.

(2) A Deputy Registrar of Copyrights shall discharge under the Superintendence and direction of the Registrar of Copyrights such functions of the Registrar under this Act as

the Registrar may, from time to time, assign to him; and any reference in this Act to the Registrar of Copyrights shall include a reference to a Deputy Registrar of Copyrights when so discharging any such functions.

11. Copyright Board: (1) As soon as may be after the commencement of this Act, the Central Government shall constitute a Board to be called the Copyright Board which shall consist of a Chairman and not less than two nor more than eight other members.

(2) The Chairman and other members of the Copyright Board shall hold office for such period and on such terms and conditions as may be prescribed.

(3) The Chairman of the Copyright Board shall be a person who is, or has been, a Judge of the Supreme Court or a High Court or is qualified for appointment as a Judge of a High Court.

(4) The Registrar of Copyrights shall be the Secretary of the Copyright Board and shall perform such functions as may be prescribed.

12. Powers and Procedure of Copyright Board: (1) The Copyright Board shall, subject to any rules that may be made under this Act, have power to regulate its own procedure, including the fixing of places and times of its sittings:

Provided that the Copyright Board shall ordinarily hear any proceeding instituted before it under this Act within the zone in which at the time of the institution of the proceeding, the person instituting the proceeding actually and voluntarily resides or carries on business or personally works for gain.

Explanation: In this sub-section "zone" means a zone specified in (37 of 1956) Section 15 of the States Reorganisation Act, 1956.

(2) The Copyright Board may exercise and discharge its powers and functions through Benches constituted by the Chairman of the Copyright Board from amongst its members, each Bench consisting of not less than three members.

(3) If there is a difference of opinion among the members of the Copyright Board or any Bench thereof in respect of any matter coming before it for decision under this Act, the opinion of the majority shall prevail:

Provided that where there is no such majority—

(*i*) if the Chairman was one of the members who heard the matter, the opinion of the Chairman shall prevail;

(*ii*) if the Chairman was not one of the members who heard the matter, the matter shall be referred to him for his opinion and that opinion shall prevail.

(4) The Copyright Board may authorize any of its members to exercise any of the powers conferred on it by Section 74 and any order made or act done in exercise of those powers by the member so authorized shall be deemed to be the order or act, as the case may be, of the Board.

(5) No member of the Copyright Board shall take part in any proceedings before the Board in respect of any matter in which he has a personal interest.

(6) No act done or proceeding taken by the Copyright Board under this Act shall be questioned on the ground merely of the existence of any vacancy in, or defect in the constitution of, the Board.

(7) The Copyright Board shall be deemed to be a civil for the purposes of Sections 480 and 482 of the Code of Criminal Procedure, 1898 (5 of 1898), and all proceedings before

the Board shall deemed to be judicial proceedings within the meaning of Sections 193 and 228 of the Indian Penal Code (45 of 1860).

CHAPTER III

13. Works in Which Copyright Subsists: (1) Subject top the provisions of this section and the other provisions of this Act, copyright shall subsist throughout India in the following classes of works, that is to say—

(*a*) original literary, dramatic, musical and artistic works;
(*b*) cinematograph films; and
(*c*) records.

(2) Copyright shall not subsist in any work specified in sub-section (1), other than a work to which the provisions of Section 40 or Section 41 apply, unless—

(*i*) in the case of a published work, the work is first published in India, or where the work is at the date of such publication, or in a case where the author was deed at that date, was at the time of his death, a citizen of India;
(*ii*) in the case of an unpublished work other than an architectural work of art, the author is at the date of the making of the work a citizen of India or domiciled in India; and
(*iii*) in the case of an architectural work of art, the work is located in India.

Explanation: In the case of a work of joint authorship, the conditions conferring copyright specified in this sub-section shall be satisfied by all the authors of the work.

(3) Copyright shall not subsist—

(*a*) in any cinematograph film if a substantial part of the film is an infringement of the copyright in any other work;
(*b*) in any record made in respect of a literary, dramatic or musical work, if in making the record, copyright in such work has been infringed.

(4) The copyright in a cinematograph film or a record shall not affect the separate copyright in any work in respect of which or a substantial part of which, the film, or as the case may be, the record is made.

(5) In the case of an architectural work of art, copyright shall subsist only in the artistic character and design and shall not extend to processes or methods of construction.

14. Meaning of Copyright: (1) For the purposes of this Act, "copyright" means the exclusive right, by virtue of and subject to the provisions of, this Act—

(*a*) in the case of a literary, dramatic or musical work, to do and authorize the doing of any of the following acts, namely—
  (*i*) to reproduce the work in any material form;
  (*ii*) to publish the work;
  (*iii*) to perform the work in public;
  (*iv*) to produce, reproduce, perform or publish any translation of the work;
  (*v*) to communicate the work by radio-diffusion or to communicate to the public by a loud-speaker or any other similar instrument the radio-diffusion of the work;
  (*vi*) to make any adaptation of the work;
  (*vii*) to do in relation to a translation or an adaptation of the work any of the acts specified in relation to the work in clauses (i) to (vi);

(*b*) in the case of an artistic work, to do or authorise the doing of any of the following acts, namely—
 (*i*) to reproduce the work in any material form;
 (*ii*) to publish the work;
 (*iii*) to include the work in any cinematograph film;
 (*iv*) to make any adaptation of the work;
 (*v*) to do in relation to an adaptation of the work any of the acts specified in relation to the work in clauses (i) to (iii).

(*c*) in the case of a cinematograph film, to do or authorise the doing of any of the following acts, namely—
 (*i*) to make a copy of the film;
 (*ii*) to cause the film, insofar as it consists of visual images, to be seen in public and, insofar as it consists of sounds, to be heard in public;
 (*iii*) to make any record embodying the recording in any part of the sound track associated with the film by utilising such sound track;
 (*iv*) to communicate the film by radio-diffusion;

(*d*) in the case of a record, to do or authorise the doing of any of the following acts by utilising the record, namely—
 (*i*) to make any other record embodying the same recording;
 (*ii*) to cause the recording embodied in the record to be heard in public;
 (*iii*) to communicate the recording embodied in the record by radio-diffusion.

(2) Any reference in sub-section (1) to the doing of any act in relation to a work or a translation or an adaptation thereof shall include a reference to the doing of that act in relation to a substantial part thereof.

15. Special Provision Regarding Copyright in Designs registered or Capable of being Registered under the Indian Patents and Designs Act, 1911: (1) Copyright shall not subsist under this Act in any design which is registered under the Indian Patents and Designs Act, 1911 (5 of 1911).

(2) Copyright in any design, which is capable of being registered under the Indian Patents and Designs Act, 1911 (2 of 1911), but which has not been so registered, shall cease as soon as any article to which the design has been applied has been produced more than fifty times by an industrial process by the owner of the copyright or, with his licence, by any other person.

16. No Copyright Except as Provided in this Act: No person shall be entitled to copyright or any similar right in any work, whether published or unpublished, otherwise than under and in accordance with the provisions of this Act or of any other law for the time being in force, but nothing in this section shall be construed as abrogating any right or jurisdiction to restrain a breach of trust or confidence.

CHAPTER IV
OWNERSHIP OF COPYRIGHT AND THE RIGHTS OF THE OWNER

17. First Owner of Copyright: Subject to the provisions of this Act, the author of a work shall be the first owner of the copyright therein:

Provided that—

(*a*) in the case of a literary, dramatic or artistic work made by the author in the course of his employment by the proprietor of a newspaper, magazine or similar periodical under a contract of service or apprenticeship, for the purpose of publication in a newspaper, magazine or similar periodical, the said proprietor shall, in the absence of any agreement to the contrary, be the first owner of the copyright in the work insofar as the copyright relates to the publication of the work in any newspaper, magazine or similar periodical, or to the reproduction of the work for the purpose of its being so published, but in all other respects the author shall be the first owner of the copyright in the work;

(*b*) Subject to the provisions of clause (a), in case of a photograph taken, or a painting or portrait drawn, or an engraving or a cinematograph film made, for valuable consideration at the instance of any person, such person shall, in the absence of any agreement to the contrary, be the first owner of the copyright therein;

(*c*) in the case of a work made in the course of the author's employment under a contract of service or apprenticeship, to which clause (a) or clause (b) does not apply, the employer shall, in the absence of any agreement to the contrary, be the first owner of the copyright therein;

(*d*) in the case of the Government work, Government shall, in the absence of any agreement to the contrary, be the first owner of the copyright therein;

(*e*) in the case of a work to which the provisions of Section 41 apply, the international organisation concerned shall be the first owner of the copyright therein.

18. Assignment of Copyright: (1) The owner of the copyright in an existing work or the prospective owner of the copyright in a future work may assign to any person the copyright either wholly or partially and either generally or subject to limitations and either for the whole term of the copyright or any part thereof:

Provided that in the case of the assignment of copyright in any future work, the assignment shall take effect only when the work comes into existence.

(2) Where the assignee of a copyright becomes entitled to any right comprised in the copyright, the assignee as respects the rights so assigned, and the assignor as respects the rights not assigned, shall be treated for the purposes of this Act as the owner of copyright and the provisions of this Act shall have effect accordingly.

(3) In this section, the expression "assignee" as respects the assignment of the copyright in any future work includes the legal representatives of the assignee, if the assignee dies before the work comes into existence.

19. Mode of Assignment: No assignment of the copyright in any work shall be valid unless it is in writing signed by the assignor or by his duly authorised agent.

20. Transmission of Copyright in Manuscript by Testamentary Disposition: Where under a bequest a person is entitled to the manuscript of a literary, dramatic or musical work, or to an artistic work, and the work was not published before the death of the testator, the bequest shall, unless the contrary intention is indicated in the testator's will or any codicil thereto, be construed as including the copyright in the work insofar as the testator was the owner of the copyright immediately before his death.

Explanation: In this section, the expression "manuscript" means the original document embodying the work, whether written by hand or not.

21. Right of Author to Relinquish Copyright: (1) The author of a work may relinquish all or any of the rights comprised in the copyright in the work by giving notice in the prescribed form to the Registrar of Copyrights and thereupon such rights shall, subject to the provisions of sub-section (3), cease to exist from the date of the notice.

(2) On receipt of a notice under sub-section (1), the Registrar of Copyrights shall cause it to be published in the Official Gazette and in such other manner as he may deem fit.

(3) The relinquishment of all or any of the rights comprised in the copyright in a work shall not affect any rights subsisting in favour of any person on the date of the notice referred to in sub-section (1).

CHAPTER V
TERM OF COPYRIGHT

22. Term of Copyright in Published Literary, Dramatic, Musical and Artistic Works: Except as otherwise hereinafter provided, copyright shall subsist in any literary, dramatic, musical or artistic work (other than a photograph) published within the lifetime of the author until fifty years from the beginning of the calendar year next following the year in which the author dies.

Explanation: In this section the reference to the author shall, in the case of a work of joint authorship, be construed as a reference to the author who dies last.

23. Term of Copyright in Anonymous and Pseudonymous Works: (1) In the case of a literary, dramatic, musical or artistic work (other than a photograph), which is published anonymously or pseudonymously, copyright shall subsist until fifty years from the beginning of the calendar year next following the year in which the work is first published:

(2) In sub-section (1), references to the author shall, in the case of an anonymous work of joint authorship, be construed—

(*a*) where the identity of one of the authors is disclosed, as references to that author;

(*b*) where the identity of more authors than one is disclosed, as references to the author who dies last from amongst such authors.

(3) In sub-section (1), references to the author shall, in the case of a pseudonymous work of joint authorship, be construed—

(*a*) where the names of one or more (but not all) of the authors are pseudonyms and his or their identity is not disclosed, as references to the author whose name is not a pseudonym, or, if the names of two or more of the authors are not pseudonyms, as references to such of those authors who dies last;

(*b*) where the names of one or more (but not all) of the authors are pseudonyms and the identity of one or more of them is disclosed, as references to the author who dies last from amongst the authors whose names are not pseudonyms and the authors whose names are pseudonyms and are disclosed; and

(*c*) where the names of all the authors are pseudonyms and the identity of one of them is disclosed, as references to the author whose identity is disclosed or if the identity of two or more of such authors is disclosed, as references to such of those authors who dies last.

Explanation: For the purposes of this section, the identity of an author shall be deemed to have been disclosed, if either the identity of the author is disclosed publicly by both the author and the publisher or is otherwise established to the satisfaction of the Copyright Board by that author.

24. Term of Copyright in Posthumous Work: (1) In the case of literary, dramatic or musical work or an engraving, in which copyright subsists at the date of the death of the author or, in the case of any such work of joint authorship, at or immediately before the date of the death of the author who dies last, but which, or any adaptation of which, has not been published before that date, copyright shall subsist until fifty years from the beginning of the calendar year next following the year in which the work is first published or, where an adaptation of the work is published in any earlier year, from the beginning of the calendar year next following that year.

(2) For the purposes of this section a literary, dramatic or musical work or an adaptation of any such work shall be deemed to have been published, if it has been performed in public or if any records made in respect of the work have been sold to the public or have been offered for sale to the public.

25. Term of Copyright in Photographs: In the case of a photograph, copyright shall subsist until fifty years from the beginning of the calendar year next following the year in which the photograph is published.

26. Term of Copyright in Cinematograph Films: In the case of a cinematograph film, copyright shall subsist until fifty years from the beginning of the calendar year next following the year in which the film is published.

27. Term of Copyright in Records: In the case of a record, copyright shall subsist until fifty years from the beginning of the calendar year next following the year in which the record is published.

28. Term of Copyright Government Works: In the case of Government work, where Government is the first owner of the copyright therein, copyright shall subsist until fifty years from the beginning of the calendar year next following the year in which the work is first published.

29. Term of Copyright in Works of International Organisation: In the case of a work of an international organisation to which the provisions of Section 41 apply, copyright shall subsist until fifty years from the beginning of the calendar year next following the year in which the work is first published.

CHAPTER VI
LICENCES

30. Licences by Owners of Copyright: The owner of the copyright in any existing work or the prospective owner of the copyright in any future work may grant any interest in the right by license in writing signed by him or by his duly authorized agent:

Provided that in the case of a license relating to copyright in any future work, the license shall take effect only when the work comes into existence.

Explanation: Where a person to whom a license relating to copyright in any future work is granted under this section dies before the work comes into existence, his legal representatives shall, in the absence of any provision to the contrary in the license, be entitled to the benefit of the license.

31. Compulsory License in Works Withheld from Public: (1) If at any time during the term of copyright in any Indian work which has been published or performed in public, a complaint is made to the Copyright Board that the owner of copyright in the work—

(*a*) has refused to republish or allow the republication of the work or has refused to allow the performance in public of the work, and by reason of such refusal the work is withheld from the public; or

(*b*) has refused to allow communication to the public by radio-diffusion of such work or in the case of a record the work recorded in such record, on terms which the complaint considers reasonable;

the Copyright Board, after giving to the owner of the copyright in the work a reasonable opportunity of being heard and after holding such inquiry as it may deem necessary, may, if it is satisfied that the grounds for such refusal are not reasonable, direct the Registrar of Copyrights to grant to the complainant a licence to republish the work, perform the work in public or communicate the work to the public by radio-diffusion, as the case may be, subject to payment to the owner of the copyright of such compensation and subject to such other terms and conditions as the Copyright Board may determine; and thereupon the Registrar of Copyright shall grant the lincence to the complainant in accordance with the directions of the Copyright Board, on payment of such fee as may be prescribed.

Explanation: In this sub-section, the expression "Indian work" includes—

(*i*) an artistic work, the author of which is a citizen of India; and

(*ii*) a cinematograph film or a record made or manufactured in India.

(2) Where two or more persons have made a complaint under sub-section (1), the licence shall be granted to the complainant who in the opinion of the Copyright Board would best serve the interest of the general public.

32. Licence to Produce and Publish Translations: (1) Any person may apply to the Copyright Board for a licence to produce and publish a translation of a literary or dramatic work in any language.

(2) Every such application shall be made in such form as may be prescribed and shall state the proposed retail price of a copy of the translation of the work.

(3) Every applicant for a licence under this section shall, along with his application, deposit with the Registrar of Copyrights such fee as may be prescribed.

(4) Where an application is made to the Copyright Board under this section, it may, after holding such inquiry as may be prescribed, grant to the applicant a licence, not being an exclusive licence, to produce and publish a translation of the work in the language mentioned in the application, on condition that the applicant shall pay to the owner of the copyright in the work royalties in respect of copies of the translation of the work sold to the public, calculated at such rate as the Copyright Board may, in the circumstances of each case, determine in the prescribed manner:

Provided that no such licence shall be granted, unless—

(*a*) a translation of the work in the language mentioned in the application has not been published by the owner of the copyright in the work or any person authorised by him, within seven years of the first publication of the work, or if a translation has been so published, it has been out of print;

(*b*) the applicant has proved to the satisfaction of the Copyright Board that he had requested and had been denied authorisation by the owner of the copyright to produce and publish such translation, or that he was unable to find the owner of the copyright;

(*c*) where the applicant was unable to find the owner of the copyright, he had sent a copy of his request for such authorisation to the publisher whose name appears from the work, not less than two months before the application for the licence;

(*d*) the Copyright Board is satisfied that the applicant is competent to produce and publish a correct translation of the work and possesses the means to pay to the owner of the copyright the royalties payable to him under this section;

(*e*) the author has not withdrawn from circulation copies of the work; and

(*f*) an opportunity of being heard is given, wherever practicable, to the owner of the copyright in the work.

CHAPTER VII
PERFORMING RIGHTS SOCIETIES

33. Performing Rights Society to File Statements of Fees, Charges and Royalties: (1) Every performing rights society shall, within the prescribed time and in the prescribed manner, prepare, publish and file with the Registrar of Copyrights, statements of all fees, charges or royalties which it proposes to collect for the grant of licences for performance in public of works in respect of which it has authority to grant such licences.

(2) If any such society fails to prepare, publish or file with the Registrar of Copyrights the statements referred to in sub-section (1) in relation to any work in accordance with the provisions of that sub-section, no action or other proceeding to enforce any remedy, civil or criminal, for infringement of the performing rights in that work shall be commenced except with the consent of the Registrar of Copyrights.

34. Objections Relating to Published Statements: Any person having any objections to any fees, charges or royalties or other particulars included in any statement referred to in Section 33 may at any time lodge such objections in writing at the Copyright Office.

35. Determination of Objections: (1) Every objection lodged at the Copyright Office under Section 34 shall, as soon as may be, be referred to the Copyright Board and the Copyright Board shall decide objection in the manner hereinafter provided.

(2) The Copyright Board shall, in respect of every such objection, gave notice thereof to the performing rights society concerned.

(3) The Copyright Board shall, after giving such society and the person who lodged the objection a reasonable opportunity of being heard and after making such further inquiry as may be prescribed, make such alterations in the statements as it may think fit, and shall transmit the alterations made by it to the Registrar of Copyrights, who shall thereupon, as soon as practicable after the receipt of such alterations, publish them in the Official Gazette and furnish the performing rights society concerned and the person who lodged the objection with a copy thereof.

(4) The fees, charges or royalties as altered by the Copyright Board shall be the fees, charges or royalties which the performing rights society concerned may respectively

lawfully sue for or collect in respect of the grant by it of licences for the performance in public of works to which such fees, charges or royalties relate.

(5) No performing rights society shall have any right of action or any right to enforce any civil or other remedy for infringement of the performing rights in any work against any person who has tendered or paid to such society the fees, charges or royalties specified in respect of that work in a statement published by that society under sub-section (1) of Section 33 or where such statement has been altered by the Copyright Board under this section in the statement so altered.

(6) Where any person has lodged an objection at the Copyright Office regarding the fees, charges or royalties in request of any work included in a statement published under Section 33, that person or any other person, on depositing such fees, charges or royalties at the Copyright Office, may, pending the final decision of such objection by the Copyright Board or the High Court, as the case may be, perform that work without infringing the copyright therein.

(7) The fees, charges or royalties deposited at the Copyright Office under sub-section (6) shall be paid to the performing rights society concerned or to the person who made the deposit, or partly to such society and partly to such person, in accordance with the final decision on the objection as aforesaid.

36. Existing Rights not Affected: Nothing in this Chapter shall be deemed to affect—

(*a*) any rights or liabilities in relation to the performing rights in any work accrued or incurred before the commencement of this Act;

(*b*) any legal proceedings in respect of such rights or liabilities pending at such commencement.

CHAPTER VIII
RIGHTS OF BROADCASTING AUTHORITIES

37. Broadcast Reproduction Right: (1) Where any programme is broadcast by radio-diffusion by the Government or any other broadcasting authority, a special right to be known as "broadcast reproduction right" shall subsist in such programme.

(2) The Government or other broadcasting authority, as the case may be, shall be the owner of the broadcast reproduction right and such right shall subsist until twenty-five years from the beginning of the calendar year next following year in which the programme is first broadcast.

(3) During the continuance of a broadcast reproduction right in relation to any programme, any person who—

(*a*) without the licence of the owner of the right—

(*i*) rebroadcasts the programme in question or any substantial part thereof; or

(*ii*) causes the programme in question or any substantial part thereof to be heard in public; or

(*b*) without the licence of the owner of the right to utilise the broadcast for the purpose of making a record recording the programme in question or any substantial part thereof, makes any such record,

shall be deemed to infringe that broadcast reproduction right.

38. Other Provisions of this Act to Supply to Broadcast Reproduction Rights: Sections 18, 19, 30, 53, 55, 58, 64, 65 and 66 shall, with any necessary adaptations and modifications, apply in relation to the broadcast reproduction right in any programme as they apply in relation of the copyright in a work:

Provided that a license to utilize a broadcast for the purpose of making a record recording a programme in which broadcast reproduction right subsists or any substantial part of such programme, shall not take effect unless the person to whom such license is granted has also obtained a license to make records recording the work embodied in such programme from the owner of the copyright in such work.

39. Other Rights not Affected: For the removal of doubts, it is hereby declared that the broadcast reproduction right conferred upon a broadcasting authority under this Chapter shall not affect copyright—

(*a*) in any literary, dramatic or musical work which is broadcast by that authority; or

(*b*) in any record recording any such work.

CHAPTER IX
INTERNATIONAL COPYRIGHT

40. Power to Extend Copyright to Foreign Works: The Central Government may, by order published in the Official Gazette, direct that all or any provisions of this Act shall apply—

(*a*) to works first published in any territory outside India to which the order relates in like manner as if they were first published within India;

(*b*) to unpublished works, or any class thereof, the authors whereof were at the time of the making of the work, subjects or citizens of a foreign country to which the order relates, in like manner as if the authors were citizens of India;

(*c*) in respect of domicile in any territory outside India to which the order relates in like manner as if such domicile were in India;

(*d*) to any work of which the author was at the date of the first publication thereof, or, in a case where the author was dead at that date, was at the time of his death, a subject or citizen of a foreign country to which the order relates in like manner as if the author was a citizen of India at that date or time;

and thereupon, subject to the provisions of this Chapter and of the order, this Act shall apply accordingly:

Provided that—

(*i*) before making an order under this section in respect of any foreign country (other than a country with which India has entered into a treaty or which is a party to a convention relating to copyright to which India is also a party), the Central Government shall be satisfied that that foreign country has made, or has undertaken to make, such provisions, if any, as it appears to the Central Government expedient to require for the protection in that country of works entitled to copyright under the provisions of this Act;

(*ii*) the order may provide that the provisions of this Act shall apply either generally or in relation to such classes of works or such classes of cases as may be specified in the order;

(*iii*) the order may provide that the term of copyright in India shall not exceed that conferred by the law of the country to which the order relates;

(*iv*) the order may provide that the enjoyment of the rights conferred by this Act shall be subject to the accomplishment of such conditions and formalities, if any, as may be prescribed by the order;

(*v*) in applying the provisions of this Act as to ownership of copyright, the order may make exceptions and modifications as appear necessary, having regard to the law of the foreign country.

(*vi*) the order may provide that this Act or any part thereof shall not apply to works made before the commencement of the order or that this Act or any part thereof shall not apply to works first published before the commencement of the order.

41. Provisions as to Works of Certain International Organisations: (1) Where—

(*a*) any work is made or first published by or under the direction or control of any organisation to which this section applies, and

(*b*) there would, apart from this section, be no copyright in the work in India at the time of the making or, as the case may be, of the first publication thereof, and

(*c*) either—

(*i*) the work is published as aforesaid in pursuance of an agreement in that behalf with the author, being an agreement which does not reserve to the author the copyright, if any, in the work, or

(*ii*) under Section 17 any copyright in the work would belong to the organisation;

there shall, by virtue of this section, be copyright in the work throughout India.

(2) Any organisation to which this section applies which at the material time had not the legal capacity of a body corporate shall have and be deemed at all material times to have had the legal capacity of a body corporate for the purpose of holding, dealing with, and enforcing copyright and in connection with all legal proceedings relating to copyright.

(3) The organisation to which this section applies are such organisations as the Central Government may, by order published in the Official Gazette, declare to be organisations of which one or more sovereign powers or the Government or Governments thereof are members to which it is expedient that this section shall apply.

42. Power to Restrict Rights in Works of Foreign Authors first Published in India: If it appears to the Central Government that a foreign country does not give or has not undertaken to give adequate protection to the works of Indian authors, the Central Government may, by order published in the Official Gazette, direct that such of the provisions of this Act as confer copyright on works first published in India shall not apply to works, published after the date specified in the order, the authors whereof are subjects or citizens of such foreign country and are not domiciled in India, and thereupon those provisions shall not apply to such works.

43. Orders Under this Chapter to be Laid before Parliament: Every order made by the Central Government under this Chapter shall, as soon as may be after it is made, be laid before both Houses of Parliament and shall be subject to such modifications as Parliament may make during the session in which it is so laid or the session immediately following.

CHAPTER X
REGISTRATION OF COPYRIGHT

44. Register of Copyrights: There shall be kept at the Copyright Office a register in the prescribed form to be called the Register of Copyrights in which may be entered the names or title of works and the names and addresses of authors, publishers and owners of copyright and such other particulars as may be prescribed.

45. Entries in Register of Copyrights: (1) The author or publisher of, or the owner of or other person interested in the copyright in, any work may make an application in the prescribed form accompanied by the prescribed fee to the Register of Copyrights for entering particulars of the work in the Register of Copyrights.

(2) On receipt of an application in respect of any work under sub-section (1), the Register of Copyrights may, after holding with inquiry as he may deem fit, enter the particulars of the work in the Register of Copyrights.

46. Indexes: There shall be also kept at the Copyright Office such indexes of the Register of copyrights as may be prescribed.

47. Form and Inspection of Register: The Register of Copyrights and indexes thereof kept under this Act shall at all reasonable times be open to inspection, and any person shall be entitled to take copies of, or make extracts from, such register or indexes on payment of such fee and subject to such conditions as may be prescribed.

48. Register of Copyrights to be Prima Facie Evidence of Particulars Entered Therein: The Register of Copyrights shall be prima facie evidence of the particulars entered therein and documents purporting to be copies of any entries therein, or extracts therefrom certified by the Registrar of Copyrights and sealed with the seal of the Copyright Office shall be admissible in evidence in all courts without further proof or production of the original.

49. Correction of Entries in the Register of Copyrights: The Registrar of Copyrights may, in the prescribed cases and subject to the prescribed conditions, amend or later the Register of Copyrights by—

(*a*) correcting any error in any name, address or particulars; or

(*b*) correcting any other error which may have arisen therein by accidental slip or omission.

50. Rectification of Register by Copyright Board: The Copyright Board, on application of the Registrar of Copyrights or of any person aggrieved, shall order the rectification of the Register of Copyrights by—

(*a*) the making of any entry wrongly omitted to be made in the register, or

(*b*) the expunging of any entry wrongly made in, or remaining on, the register, or

(*c*) the correction of any error or defect in the register. .

CHAPTER XI
INFRINGEMENT OF COPYRIGHT

51. When Copyright Infringed: Copyright in a work shall be deemed to be infringed—

(*a*) when any person, without a licence granted by the owner of the Copyright or the Registrar of Copyrights under this Act or in contravention of the conditions of a licence so granted or of any condition imposed by a competent authority under this Act—

(*i*) does anything, the exclusive right to do which is by this Act conferred upon the owner of the copyright, or

(*ii*) permits for profit any place to be used for the performance of the work in public where such performance constitutes an infringement of the copyright in the work unless he was not aware and had no reasonable ground for believing that such performance would be an infringement of copyright, or

(*b*) when any person—

(*i*) make for sale or hire, or sells or lets for hire, or by way of trade displays or offers for sale or hire, or

(*ii*) distributes either for the purpose of trade or to such an extent as to affect prejudicially the owner of the copyright, or

(*iii*) by way of trade exhibits in public, or

(*iv*) imports (except for the private and domestic use of the importer) into India, any infringing copies of the work.

Explanation: For the purposes of this section, the reproduction of a literary, dramatic, musical or artistic work in the form of a cinematograph film shall be deemed to be an "infringing copy".

52. Certain Acts not to Infringement of: (1) The following acts shall not constitute an infringement of copyright, namely—

(*a*) a fair dealing with a literary, dramatic, musical or artistic work for the purposes of—

(*i*) research or private study;

(*ii*) criticism or review, whether of that work or of any other work;

(*b*) a fair dealing with a literary, dramatic, musical or artistic work for the purpose of reporting current events—

(*i*) in a newspaper, magazine or similar periodical, or

(*ii*) by radio-diffusion or in a cinematograph film or by means of photographs;

(*c*) the reproduction of a literary, dramatic, musical or artistic work for the purpose of a judicial proceeding or for the purpose of a report of a judicial proceeding;

(*d*) the reproduction or publication of a literary, dramatic, musical or artistic work in any work prepared by the Secretariat of a Legislature or, where the Legislature consists of two Houses, by the Secretariat of either House of the Legislature, exclusively for the use of the members of that Legislature;

(*e*) the reproduction of any literary, dramatic or musical work in a certified copy made or supplied in accordance with any law for the time being in force;

(*f*) the reading or recitation in public of any reasonable extract from a published literary or dramatic work;

(*g*) the publication in a collection, mainly composed of non-copyright matter, bona fide intended for the use of educational institutions, and so described in the title and in any advertisement issued by or on behalf of the publisher, of short passages from published literary or dramatic works, not themselves published for the use of educational institutions, in which copyright subsists:

Provided that not more than two such passages from works by the same author are published by the same publisher during any period of five years.

Explanation: In the case of a work of joint authorship, references in this clause to passages from works shall include references to passages from works by any one or more of the authors of those passages or by any one or more of those authors in collaboration with any other person;

(*h*) the reproduction of a literary, dramatic, musical or artistic work—

(*i*) by a teacher or a pupil in the course of instruction; or

(*ii*) as part of the questions to be answered in an examination; or

(*iii*) in answers to such questions;

(*i*) the performance in the course of the activities of an educational institution, of a literary, dramatic or musical work by the staff and students of the institution, or of a cinematograph film or a record, if the audience is limited to such staff and students, the parents and guardians of the students and persons directly connected with the activities of the institution;

(*j*) the making of records in respect of any literary dramatic or musical work, if—

(*i*) records recording that work have previously been made by, or with the licence or consent of, the owner of the copyright in the work; and

(*ii*) the person making the records has given the prescribed notice of his intention to make the records, and has paid in the prescribed manner to the owner of the copyright in the work royalties in respect of all such records to be made by him, at the rate fixed by the Copyright Board in this behalf:

Provided that in making the records such person shall not make any alternations in, or omission from, the work, unless records recording the work subject to similar alterations and omissions have been previously made by, or with the licence or consent of, the owner of the copyright or unless such alterations and omissions are reasonably necessary for the adaptation of the work to the records in question;

(*k*) the causing of a recording embodied in a record to be heard in public by utilising the record,—

(*i*) at any premises where persons reside, as part of the amenities provided exclusively or mainly for residents therein, or

(*ii*) as part of the activities of a club, society or other organisation which is not established or conducted for profit;

(*l*) the performance of a literary, dramatic or musical work by an amateur club or society, if the performance is given to a non-paying audience, or for the benefit of a religious institution;

(*m*) the reproduction in a newspaper, magazine or other periodical of an article on current economic, political, social or religious topics, unless the author of such article has expressly reserved to himself the right of such reproduction;

(*n*) the publication in a newspaper, magazine or other periodical of a report of a lecture delivered in public;

(*o*) the making of not more than three copies of a book (including a pamphlet, sheet of music, map, chart or plan) by or under the direction of the person in charge of a public library for the use of the library if such books is not available for sale in India;

(*p*) the reproduction, for the purpose of research or private study or with a view to publication, of an unpublished literary, dramatic or musical work kept in a library, museum or other institution to which the public has access:

Provided that where the identity of the author of any such work or, in the case of a work of joint authorship, of any of the authors is known to the library, museum or other institution, as the case may be, the provisions of this clause shall apply only if such reproduction is made at a time more than fifty years from the date of the death of the author or, in the case of a work of joint authorship, from the death of the author whose identity is known or, if the identity of more authors than one is known from the death of such of those authors who dies last;

(*q*) the reproduction or publication of—

(*i*) any matter which has been published in any Official Gazette except an Act of a Legislature;

(*ii*) any Act of a Legislature subject to the condition that such Act is reproduced or published together with any commentary thereon or any other original matter;

(*iii*) the report of any committee, commission, council, board or other like body appointed by the Government if such report has been laid on the Table of the Legislature, unless the reproduction or publication of such report is prohibited by the Government;

(*iv*) any judgement or order of a court, tribunal or other judicial authority, unless the reproduction or publication of such judgement or order is prohibited by the court, the tribunal or other judicial authority, as the case may be;

(*r*) the production or publication of a translation in any Indian language of an Act of a Legislature and of any rules or orders made thereunder—

(*i*) if no translation of such Act or rules or orders in that language has previously been produced or published by the Government; or

(*ii*) where a translation of such Act or rules or orders in that language has been produced or published by the Government, if the translation is not available for sale to the public:

Provided that such translation contains a statement at a prominent place to the effect that the translation has not been authorised or accepted an authentic by the Government;

(*s*) the making or publishing of a painting, drawing, engraving or photograph of an architectural work of art;

(*t*) the making or publishing of a painting, drawing, engraving or photograph of a sculpture, or other artistic work falling under sub-clause (iii) of clause (c) of Section 2, if such work is permanently situate in a public place or any premises to which the public has access;

(*u*) the inclusion in a cinematograph film of—

(*i*) any artistic work permanently situate in a public place or any premises to which the public has access; or (*ii*) any other artistic work, if such inclusion is only by way of background or is otherwise incidental to the principal matters presented in the film.

(*v*) the use by the author of an artistic work, where the author of such work is not the owner of the copyright therein, of any mould, cast, sketch, plan, model or study made by him for the purpose of the work:
Provided that he does not thereby repeat or imitate the main design of the work;

(*w*) the making of an object of any description in three dimensions of an artistic work in two dimensions, if the object would not appear, to persons who are not experts in relation to objects of that description, to be a reproduction of the artistic work;

(*x*) the reconstruction of a building or structure in accordance with the architectural drawings or plans by reference to which the building or structure was originally constructed:
Provided that the original construction was made with the consent or licence of the owner of the copyright in such drawings and plans;

(*y*) in relation to literary, dramatic, or musical work recorded or reproduced in any cinematograph film, the exhibition of such film after the expiration of the term of copyright therein:
Provided that the provisions of sub-clause (ii) of clause (a), sub-clause (i) of clause (b) and clauses (d), (f), (g), (m) and (p) shall not apply as respects any act unless that act is accompanied by an acknowledgement—

(*i*) identifying the work by its title or other description; and

(*ii*) unless the work is anonymous or the author of the work has previously agreed or required that no acknowledgement of his name should be made, also identifying the author.

(2) The provisions of sub-section (1) shall apply to the doing of any act in relation to the translation of a literary, dramatic or musical work or the adaptation of a literary, dramatic, musical or artistic work as they apply in relation to the work itself.

53. **Importation of Infringing Copies:** (1) The Registrar of Copyrights, on application by the owner of the copyright in any work or by his duty authorised agent and on payment of the prescribed fee, may, after making such inquiry as he deems fit, order that copies made out of India of the work which if made in India would infringe copyright shall not be imported.

(2) Subject to any rules made under this Act, the Registrar of Copyrights or any person authorised by him in this behalf may enter any ship, dock or premises where any such copies as are referred to in sub-section (1) may be found and may examine such copies.

(3) All copies to which any order made under sub-section (1) applies shall be deemed to be goods of which the import has been prohibited or restricted under Section 19 of the Sea Customs Act, 1878, and all the provisions of that Act shall have effect accordingly:

(3 of 1878)

Provided that such copies confiscated under the provisions of the said Act shall not vest in the Government but shall be delivered to the owner of the copyright in the work.

CHAPTER XII
CIVIL REMEDIES

54. Definition: For the purposes of this Chapter, unless the context otherwise requires, the expression "owner of copyright" shall include—

(*a*) an exclusive licensee;

(*b*) in the case of an anonymous or pseudonymous literary, dramatic, musical or artistic work, the publisher of the work, until the identity of the author or, in the case of an anonymous work of joint authorship, or a work of joint authorship published under names all of which are pseudonyms, the identity of any of the authors, is disclosed publicly by the author and the publisher or is otherwise established to the satisfaction of the Copyright Board by that author or his legal representatives.

55. Civil Remedies for Infringement of Copyright: (1) Where copyright in any work has been infringed, the owner of the copyright shall, except as otherwise provided by this Act, be entitled to all such remedies by way of injunction, damages, accounts and otherwise as are or may be conferred by law for the infringement of a right:

Provided that if the defendant proves that at the date of the infringement he was not aware and had no reasonable ground for believing that copyright subsisted in the work, the plaintiff shall not be entitled to any remedy other than an injunction in respect of the infringement and a decree for the whole or part of the profits made by the defendant by the sale of the infringing copies as the court may in circumstances deem responsible.

(2) Where, in the case of a literary, dramatic, musical or artistic work, a name purporting to be that of the author or the publisher, as the case may be, appears on copies of the work as published or in the case of an artistic work, appeared on the work when it was made, the person whose name so appears or appeared shall, in any proceeding in respect of infringement of copyright in such work, be presumed, unless the contrary is proved, to be the author or the publisher of the work, as the case may be.

(3) The costs of all parties in any proceedings in respect of the infringement of copyright shall be in the direction of the court.

56. Protection of Separate Rights: Subject to the provisions of this Act, where the several rights comprising the copyright in any work are owned by different persons, the owner of any such right shall, to the extent of that right, be entitled to the remedies provided by this Act and may individually enforce such right by means of any suit, action or other proceeding without making the owner of any other right a party to such suit, action or proceeding.

57. Authors Special Rights: (1) Independently of the author's copyright and even after the assignment either wholly or partially of the said copyright, the author of a work shall have the right to claim the authorship of the work as well as the right to restrain, or claim damages in respect of—

(*a*) any distortion, mutilation or other modification of the said work; or

(*b*) any other action in relation to the said work which would be prejudicial to his honour or reputation.

(2) The right conferred upon an author of a work by sub-section (1), other than the right to claim authorship of the work, may be exercised by the legal representative of the author.

58. Rights of Owner Against Persons Possessing or Dealing with Infringing Copies: All infringing copies of any work in which copyright subsists, and all plates used or intended to be used for the production of such infringing copies, shall be deemed to be the property of the owner of the copyright, who accordingly may take proceedings for the recover of possession thereof or in respect of the conversion thereof:

Provided that the owner of the copyright shall not be entitled to any remedy in respect of the conversion of any infringing copies, if the opponent proves—

(*a*) that he was not aware and had not reasonable ground to believe that copyright subsisted in the work of which such copies are alleged to be infringing copies; or

(*b*) that he had reasonable grounds for believing that such copies or plates do not involve infringement of the copyright in any work.

59. Restriction on Remedies in the Case of Works of Architecture: (1) Notwithstanding anything contained in the Specific Relief Act, 1877 (1 of 1877), where the construction of a building or other structure which infringes or which, if completed, would infringe the copyright in some other work has been commenced, the owner of the copyright shall not be entitled to obtain an injunction to restrain the construction of such building or structure or to order its demolition.

(2) Nothing in Section 58 shall apply in respect of the construction of a building or other structures which infringe or which, if completed, would infringe the copyright in some other work.

60. Remedy in the Case of Groundless Threat of Legal Proceedings: Where any person claiming to be the owner of the copyright in any work, by circulars, advertisements or otherwise, threatens any other person with any legal proceedings or liability in respect of an alleged infringement of the copyright, any person aggrieved thereby may, notwithstanding anything contained in Section 42 of the Specific Relief Act, 1877 (1 of 1877), institute a declaratory suit that the alleged infringement to which the threats related was not in fact an infringement of any legal rights of the person making such threats and may in any such suit—

(*a*) obtain an injunction against the continuance of such threats; and

(*b*) recover such damages, if any, as he has sustained by reason of such threats:

Provided that this section shall not apply if the person making such threats, with due diligence, commences and prosecutes an action for infringement of the copyright claimed by him.

61. Owner of Copyright to be Party to the Proceeding: (1) In every civil suit or other proceeding regarding infringement of copyright instituted by an exclusive licensee, the owner of the copyright shall, unless the court otherwise directs, be made a defendant and where such owner is made a defendant, he shall have the right to dispute the claim of the exclusive licensee.

(2) Where any civil suit or other proceeding regarding infringement of copyright instituted by an exclusive licensee is successful, no fresh suit or other proceeding in respect of the same cause of action shall lie at the instance of the owner of the copyright.

62. Jurisdiction of Court over Matters Arising Under this Chapter: (1) Every suit or other civil proceeding arising under this Chapter in respect of the infringement of copyright in any work or the infringement of any other right conferred by this Act shall be instituted in the direct court having jurisdiction.

(2) For the purpose of sub-section (1), a "district court having jurisdiction" shall, notwithstanding anything contained in the Code of Civil Procedure, 1908 (5 of 1908), or any other law for the time being in force include a direct court within the local limits of whose jurisdiction, at the time of the institution of the suit or other proceedings, the person instituting the suit or other proceeding or, where there are more than one such persons, any of them actually and voluntarily resides or carries on business or personally works for gain. (5 of 1908)

CHAPTER XIII
OFFENCES

63. Offence of Infringement of Ccopyright or Other Rights Conferred by this Act: Any person who knowingly infringes or abets the infringement of—

(*a*) the copyright in a work, or

(*b*) any other right conferred by this Act,

shall be punishable with imprisonment which may extend to one year, or with fine, or with both.

Explanation: Construction of a building or other structure which infringes or which, if completed, would infringe the copyright in some other work shall not be an offence under this section.

64. Power of Police to Seize Infringing Copies: (1) Where a magistrate has taken cognizance of any offence under Section 63 in respect of the infringement of copyright in any work, it shall be lawful for any police officer, not below the rank of sub-inspector, to seize without any warrant from the magistrate, all copies of the work wherever found, which appear to him to be infringing copies of the work and all copies so seized shall, as soon as practicable, be produced before the magistrate.

(2) Any person having an interest in any copies of a work seized under sub-section (1) may, within fifteen days of such seizure, make an application to the magistrate for such copies being restored to him and the magistrate, after hearing the applicant and the complainant and making such further inquiry as may be necessary, shall make such order on the application as he may deem fit.

65. Possession of Plates for Purposes of Making Infringing Copies: Any person who knowingly makes, or has in his possession, any plate for the purpose of making infringing copies of any work in which copyright subsists shall be punishable with imprisonment which may extend to one year, or with fine, or with both.

66. Disposal of Infringing Copies or Plates for Purpose of Making Infringing Copies: The court trying any offence under this Act may, whether the alleged offender is convicted or not, order that all copies of the work or all plates in the possession of the alleged offender, which appear to it to be infringing copies, or plates for the purpose of making infringing copies, be delivered up to the owner of the copyright.

67. Penalty for Making False Entries in Register, etc., for Production or Tendering False Entries: Any person who—

(*a*) makes or causes to be made a false entry in the Register of Copyrights kept under this Act, or

(*b*) makes or causes to be make writing falsely purporting to be a copy of any entry in such register, or (*c*) produces or tenders or causes to be produced or tendered as evidence any such entry or writing, knowing the same to be false,

shall be punishable with imprisonment which may extend to one year, or with fine, or with both.

68. Penalty for Making False Statements for the Purpose of Deceiving or Influencing any Authority or Officer: Any person who—

(*a*) with a view to deceiving any authority or officer in the execution of the provisions of this Act, or

(*b*) with a view to procuring or influencing the doing of omission of anything in relation to this Act or any matter thereunder, makes a false statement or representation knowing the same to be false, shall be punishable with imprisonment which may extend to one year, or with fine, or with both.

69. Offences by Companies: (1) Where any offence under this Act has been committed by a company, every person who at the time the offence was committed was in charge of, and was responsible to the company for, the conduct of the business of the company, as well as the company shall be deemed to be guilty of such offence and shall be liable to be proceeded against and punished accordingly:

Provided that nothing contained in this sub-section shall render any person liable to any punishment, if he proves that the offence was committed without his knowledge or that he exercised all due diligence to prevent the commission of such offence.

(2) Notwithstanding anything contained in sub-section (1), where an offence under this Act has been committed by a Company, and it is proved that the offence was committed with the consent or connivance of, or is attributable to any negligence on the part of, any director, manager, secretary or other officer of the company, such director, manager, secretary or other officer shall also be deemed to be guilty of that offence and shall be liable to be proceeded against and punished accordingly.

Explanation: For the purpose of this section—

(*a*) "company" means any body corporate and includes a firm or other association of persons; and

(*b*) "director" in relation to a firm means a partner in the firm.

70. Cognizance of Offences: No court inferior to that of a presidency magistrate or a magistrate of the first class shall try any offence under this Act.

CHAPTER XIV
APPEALS

71. Appeals Against Certain Orders of Magistrate: Any person aggrieved by an order under sub-section (2) of Section 64 or Section 66 may, within thirty days of the date of such order, appeal to the court to which appeals from the court making the order ordinarily lie, and such appellate court may direct that execution of the order be stayed pending disposal of the appeal.

72. Appeals Against Orders of Registrar of Copyrights and Copyright Board: (1) Any person aggrieved by any final decision or order of the Registrar of Copyrights may, within three months from the date of the order or decision, appeal to the Copyright Board.

(2) Any person aggrieved by any final decision or order of the Copyright Board, not being a decision or order made in an appeal under sub-section (1), may, within three months from the date of such decision or order, appeal to the High Court within whose jurisdiction the appellant actually and voluntarily resides or carries on business or personally works for gain:

Provided that no such appeal shall lie against a decision of the Copyright Board under Section 6.

(3) In calculating the period of three months provided for an appeal under this section, the time taken in granting a certified copy of the order or record of the decision appealed against shall be excluded.

73. Procedure for Appeals: The High Court may make rules consistent with this Act as to the procedure to be followed in respect of appeals made to it under Section 72.

CHAPTER XV
MISCELLANEOUS

74. Registrar of Copyrights and Copyright Board to Possess Certain Powers of Civil Courts: The Registrar of Copyrights and the Copyright Board shall have the powers of a civil court when trying a suit under the Code of Civil Procedure, 1908 (5 of 1908), in respect of the following matters, namely—

(*a*) summoning and enforcing the attendance of any person and examining him on oath;
(*b*) requiring the discovery and production of any document;
(*c*) receiving evidence on affidavits;
(*d*) issuing commissions for the examination of witnesses or documents;
(*e*) requisitioning any public record or copy thereof from any court or office;
(*f*) any other matter which may be prescribed.

Explanation: For the purpose of enforcing the attendance of witnesses, the local limits of the jurisdiction of the Registrar of Copyrights or the Copyright Board, as the case may be, shall be the limits of the territory of India.

75. Order for Payment of Money Passed by Registrar of Copyrights and Copyright Board not to be Executable as a Decree: Every order made by the Registrar of Copyrights or the Copyright Board under this Act for the payment of any money or by the High Court in any appeal against any such order of the Copyright Board shall, on a certificate issued by the Registrar of Copyrights, the Copyright Board or the Registrar of the High Court, as the case may be, be deemed to be a decree of a civil court and shall be executable in the same manner as a decree of such court.

76. Protection of Action Taken in Good Faith: No suit or other legal proceeding shall lie against any person in respect of anything which is in good faith done or intended to be done in pursuance of this Act.

77. Certain Persons to be Public Servants: Every officer appointed under this Act and every member of the Copyright Board shall be deemed to be a public servant within the meaning of Section 21 of the Indian Penal Code (45 of 1860).

78. Power to Make Rules: (1) The Central Government may, by notification in the Official Gazette, make rules [For the Copyright Rules, 1958, see Gazette of India, Extraordinary, Part II, Section 3, Page 167] for carrying out the purposes of this Act.

(2) In particular, and without prejudice to the generality of the foregoing power, the Central Government may make rules to provide for all or any of the following matters, namely—

(*a*) the term of office and conditions of service of the Chairman and other members of the Copyright Board;

(*b*) the form of complaints and applications to be made, and the licences to be granted, under this Act;

(*c*) the procedure to be followed in connection with any proceeding before the Registrar of Copyrights;

(*d*) the manner of determining any royalties payable under this Act, and the security to be taken for the payment of such royalties;

(*e*) the form of Register of Copyrights to be kept under this Act and the particulars to be entered therein;

(*f*) the matters in respect of which the Registrar of Copyrights and the Copyright Board shall have powers of a civil court;

(*g*) the fees which may be payable under this Act;

(*h*) the regulation of business of the Copyright Office and of all things by this Act placed under the direction or control of the Registrar of Copyrights.

(3) All rules made under this section shall, as soon as may be after they are made, be laid before both Houses or Parliament for not less than thirty days and shall be subject to such modifications as Parliament may make during the session in which they are so laid or the session immediately following.

79. Repeals, Savings and Transitional Provisions: (1) The Indian Copyright Act, 1914 (3 of 1914), and the Copyright Act of 1911 passed by the Parliament of the United Kingdom as modified in its application to India by the Indian Copyright Act, 1914 (3 of 1914), are hereby repealed.

(2) Where any person has, before the commencement of this Act, taken any action whereby he has incurred any expenditure or liabilities in connection with the reproduction or performance of any work in a manner which at the time was lawful or for the purpose of or with a view to the reproduction or performance of a work at a time when such reproduction or performance would, but for the coming into force of this Act, have been lawful, nothing in this section shall diminish or prejudice any rights or interests arising from or in connection with such action which are subsisting and valuable at the said date, unless the person who, by virtue of this Act, become entitled to restrain such reproduction or performance agrees to pay such compensation as, falling agreement, may be determined by the Copyright Board.

(3) Copyright shall not subsist by virtue of this Act in any work in which copyright did not subsist immediately before the commencement of this Act under any Act repealed by sub-section (1).

(4) Where copyright subsisted in any work immediately before the commencement of this Act, the rights comprising such copyright shall, as from the date of such commencement, be the rights specified in Section 14 in relation to the class of works to which such work belongs, and where any new rights are conferred by that section, the owner of such rights shall be—

(*a*) in any case where copyright in the work was wholly assigned before the commencement of this Act, the assignee or his successor-in-interest;

(*b*) in any other case, the person who was the first owner of the copyright in the work under any Act repealed by sub-section (1) or his legal representatives.

(5) Except as otherwise provided in this Act, where any person is entitled immediately before the commencement of this Act to copyright in any work or any right in such copyright or to an interest in any such right, he shall continue to be entitled to such right or interest for the period for which he would have been entitled thereto if this Act had not come into force.

(6) Nothing contained in this Act shall be deemed to render any act done before its commencement in infringement of copyright if that act would not otherwise have constituted such an infringement.

(7) Save as otherwise provided in this section, nothing in this section shall be deemed to affect the application of the General Clauses Act, 1897 (10 of 1897), with respect to the effect of repeals.

HISTORIC JUDGEMENT ON THE AIR WAVES Vs CRICKET ASSOCIATION OF BENGAL (REDDY, J., CONCURRING)*

While I agree with the conclusion arrived at by my learned Brother Sawant**, J. in para 122 of his judgement, I propose to record my views and conclusions on the issues arising in these matters in view of their far-reaching importance.

Airwaves constitute public property and must be utilized for advancing public good. No individual has a right to utilize them at his choice and pleasure and for the purposes of his choice including profit. The right of free speech guaranteed by Article 19(1)(a) does not include the right to use airwaves, which are public property.

The airwaves can be used by a citizen for the purpose of broadcasting only when allowed to do so by a statute and in accordance with such statute. Airwaves being public property, it is the duty of the State to see that airwaves are so utilized as to plurality and diversity of views, opinions and ideas.

This is imperative in every democracy where freedom of speech is assured. The free speech right guaranteed to every citizen of this country does not encompass the right to use these airwaves at his choosing. Conceding such a right would be detrimental to the free speech rights of the body of citizens in as much as only a privileged few—powerful economic, commercial and political interests—would come to dominate the media. By manipulating the news, views and information, by indulging in misinformation and disinformation, to suit their commercial or other interests, they would be harming—and not serving—the principle of plurality and diversity of views, news, ideas and opinions.

This has been the experience of Italy where a limited right, *i.e.*, at the local level but not at the national level was recognized. It is also not possible to imply or infer a right from the guarantee of free speech, which only a few can enjoy.

(*a*) Broadcasting media is inherently different from press or other means of communication/information. The analogy of press is misleading and inappropriate. This is also the view expressed by several constitutional courts including that of the United States of America.

(*b*) I must clarify what I say; it is that the right claimed by the petitioners (CAB and BCCI)—which in effect is no different in principle from a right to establish and operate a private TV station does not flow from Article 19(1)(a); such that a right is not implicit in it. The question whether such right should be given to the citizens of this country is a matter of policy for Parliament. Having regard to the revolution in information technology and the developments all around, Parliament may, or may not, decide to confer such right. If it wishes to confer such a right, it can only be by way of an Act made by Parliament.

The Act made should be consistent with the right of free speech of the citizens and must have to contain a strict programme and other controls, as has been provided, for example, in the Broadcasting Act, 1991 in the United Kingdom. This is the implicit command of Article 19(1): (a) and is essential to preserve and promote plurality and diversity of views, news, opinions and ideas.

(*c*) There is an inseparable interconnection between freedom of speech and the stability of the society, *i.e.*, stability of a nation-State. They contribute to each other. Ours is a nascent republic. We are yet to achieve the goal of a stable society. This country cannot afford to read into Article 19(1)(a) an unrestricted right to listening (right of broadcasting) as claimed by the petitioners herein.

(*d*) In the case before us, both the petitioners have sold their right to telecast the matches to a foreign agency. They have parted with the right. The right to telecast the matches, including the right to import, install and operate the requisite equipment, is thus really sought by the foreign agencies and not by the petitioners.

Hence, the question of violation of their right under Article 19(1)(a) resulting from refusal of licence/permission to such foreign agencies does not arise.

2. The Government monopoly of broadcasting media in this country is the result of historical and other factors. This is true of every other country, to start with.

That India was not a free country till 1947 and its citizens did not have constitutionally guaranteed fundamental freedom till 1950 coupled with the fact that our Constitution is just about forty-five years into operation explains the Government monopoly.

As pointed out in the body of the judgement, broadcasting media was a monopoly of the Government, to start with, in every country except the United States where a conscious decision was taken at the very beginning not to have State monopoly over the medium. Until recently, the broadcasting media has been in the hands of the public/statutory corporations in most of the West European countries. Private broadcasting is comparatively a recent phenomenon.

The experience in Italy of allowing private broadcasting at local level (while prohibiting it at a national level) has left much to be desired. It has given rise to powerful media empires not conducive to free speech right of the citizens.

3.(*a*) It has been held by this court—and rightly—that broadcasting media is affected by the free speech right to the citizens guaranteed by Article 19(1)(a). This is also the view expressed by all the constitutional courts whose opinions have been referred to in the body of the judgement.

Once this is so, monopoly of this medium (broadcasting media), whether by Government or by an individual, body or organisation is unacceptable. Clause (2) of the Article 19 does not permit a monopoly in the matter of freedom of speech and expression as it is permitted by clause (6) of Article 19 vis-à-vis the right guaranteed by Article 19(1)(g).

(*b*) The right of free speech and expression includes the right to receive and impart information. For ensuring the free speech right of the citizens of this country, it is necessary that the citizens have the benefit of plurality of views and a range of opinions on all public issues.

A successful democracy posits an aware citizenry. Diversity of opinions, views, ideas and ideologies is essential to enable the citizens to arrive at informed judgement on all issues touching them. This cannot be provided by a medium controlled by a monopoly—whether the monopoly is of the State or of any other individual, group or organization. As a matter of fact, private broadcasting stations may perhaps be more prejudicial to free speech rights of the citizens than the government controlled media, as explained in the body of the judgement.

The broadcasting media should be under the control of the public as distinct from Government. This is the command implicit in Article 19(1)(a).

5. The CAB did not ever apply for a license under the first proviso to Section 4 of the Telegraphic Act nor did its agents ever make such an application.

The permissions, clearances or exemption obtained by it from the several departments (mentioned in judgement) are no substitute for a license under Section 4 (1) proviso. In the absence of such a license, the CAB had no right in law to have its matches telecast by an agency of its choice. The legality or validity of the orders passed by Shri N. Vithal, Secretary to the Government of India, Telecommunications Department need not be gone into since it has become academic.

In the facts and circumstances of the case, the charge of mala fides or of arbitrary and authoritarian conduct attributed to Doordarshan and Ministry of Information and Broadcasting is not acceptable. No opinion need be expressed on the allegations made in the Interlocutory Application filed by BCCI in these matters. Its intervention was confined to legal questions only.

6. Now the question arises, what is the position till the Central Government or the Parliament takes steps as contemplated in para 4 of the summary, *i.e.*, if any sporting event or other event is to be telecast from the Indian soil?

The obvious answer flowing from the judgement (and paras 1 and 4 of this summary) is that the organizer of such event has to approach the nodal ministry as specified in the decision of the Meeting of the Committee of Secretaries held on 12-11-1993. I have no reason to doubt that such a request would be considered by the nodal ministry and AIR and Doordarshan on its merits, keeping in view the public interest.

In case of any difference of opinion or dispute regarding the monetary terms on which such telecast is to be made, matter can always be referred to an arbitrator or panel of arbitrators. In case, the nodal ministry or AIR and Doordarshan find such broadcast/telecast not feasible, then they may consider the grant of permission to the organizers to engage an agency in addition to AIR/Doordarshan, if they are of the opinion that such a course is called for in the circumstances.

For the above reasons, the appeals, writ petition and applications are disposed of in the aboove terms. No costs.

Notes *(1995) 2 S.C.C. 161, 252, 298-301. **

Justice Sawant stated:

2. We, therefore, hold as follows:

(*a*) The airwaves or frequencies are a public property. Their use has to be controlled and regulated by a public authority in the interests of the public and to prevent the invasion of their rights. Since the electronic media involves the use of the airwaves, this factor creates an inbuilt restriction on its use as in the case of any other public property.

(*b*) The right to impart and receive information is a species of the right to freedom of speech and expression guaranteed by Article 19(1)(a) of the Constitution. A citizen has a fundamental right to use the best of means of imparting and receiving information and as such to have an access to telecasting for the purpose.
However, this right to have an access to telecasting has limitations on account of the use of the public property, viz., the airwaves, involved in the exercise of the right and can be controlled and regulated by the public authority. This limitation imposed upon the nature of the public property involved in the use of the electronic media is in addition to the restrictions imposed on the right to freedom of speech and expression under Article 19(2) of the Constitution.

(*c*) The Central Government shall take immediate steps to establish an independent autonomous public authority representative of all sections and interests in the society to control and regulate the use of the airwaves.

(*d*) Since the matches have been telecast pursuant to the impugned order of the High Court, it is not necessary to decide the correctness of the said order.

(*e*) The High Court will now apportion between the CAB and DD the revenues generated by the advertisements on TV during the telecasting of both the series of the cricket matches, viz., the Hero Cup, and the International Cricket Matches played in India from October to December 1994, after hearing the parties on the subject.

The civil appeals are disposed off accordingly in view of the disposal of the civil appeals, the writ petition filed by the Cricket Association of Bengal also stands disposed off accordingly.

Secretary, Ministry of Info. and Broadcasting Vs. Ass'n of Bengal (1995) 2 S.C.C. at 251-52.

INFORMATION TECHNOLOGY ACTION PLAN

Preamble

In the history of civilisation, no work of science has so comprehensively impacted on the course of human development as Information Technology (IT). Undoubtedly, IT has been the greatest change agent of this century and promises to play this role even more dramatically in the coming decades. IT is changing every aspect of human life—communications, trade, manufacturing, services, culture, entertainment, education, research, national defence and global security. IT is breaking old barriers and building new interconnections in the emerging Global Village. IT has also become the chief determinant of the progress of nations, communities and individuals.

For India, the rise of Information Technology is an opportunity to overcome historical disabilities and once again become the master of one's own national destiny. IT is a tool that will enable India to achieve the goal of becoming a strong, prosperous and self-confident nation. In doing so, IT promises to compress the time it would otherwise take for India to advance rapidly in the march of development and occupy a position of honor and pride in the comity of nations.

The Government of India has recognised the potential of Information Technology for rapid and all-round national development. The National Agenda for Governance, which is the Government's policy blueprint, has taken due note of the Information and Communication Revolution that is sweeping the globe. Accordingly,it has mandated the Government to take necessary policy and programmatic initiatives that would facilitate India's emergence as an Information Technology Superpower in the shortest possible time.

This commitment to Information and Communication Technology in the National Agenda for Governance has been forcefully articulated by Prime Minister Shri Atal Bihari Vajpayee on a number of occasions.

In his speech at the CII Annual Session on April 28, 1998, the Prime Minister said: "This is one area where India can quickly establish global dominance. India can be fully competitive in this area with tremendous pay-offs in terms of wealth creation and generation of high quality employment".

The Prime Minister announced at the CII Annual Session the Government's resolve to set up, within 30 days, a National Task Force on Information Technology, which would formulate the draft National Informatics Policy.

Accordingly, the Office of the Prime Minister issued a Notification on 22nd May, 1998 constituting a National Task Force on Information Technology and Software Development. This Task Force is chaired by Shri Jaswant Singh, Deputy Chairman, Planning Commission and co-chaired by Shri N. Chandrababu Naidu, Chief Minister of Andhra Pradesh and Dr. M.G.K. Menon, Former Minister of State for Science and Technology. Its members include eminent representatives from the Government, industry and academia.

The Prime Minister has given five main tasks and 15 terms of reference to the IT Task Force (see Annexure). The tasks include recommending, within one month, immediate steps that the Government needs to take to remove bottlenecks in the path of rapid development of IT in India and give a big boost to Indian IT and software industry.

The Task Force has completed its deliberations on this immediate task and is pleased to submit its first report to the Prime Minister. This report, called the Information Technology Action Plan, contains 108 recommendations covering both bottleneck areas and broad promotional measures that are crucial for boosting IT in India.

These recommendations cover a wide spectrum of issues relating to telecommunications, finance, banking, revenue, commerce, electronics, human resource development, defence and rural development. They address critical national needs in the areas of information infrastructure, Internet access, software development and exports, hardware manufacture, electronic commerce, R&D in IT, manpower training and education.

Software exports has received much attention of the Task Force. Recognising India's competitive advantage in this area, the Action Plan has made many recommendations aimed at enabling Indian exporters to capture a large share of the global software market in a short time.

A unique promotional campaign suggested in the report is OPERATION KNOWLEDGE, which aims at universalising IT and IT-based education at all levels of the education pyramid in India.

A notable feature of these recommendations is the conscious effort of the Task Force to give Information Technology a pro-people and pro-development thrust. These recommendations flow from a perspective that India can become a strong IT power only if information technology reaches out to the masses in rural areas and in small towns and if its use in Indian languages can also be given major encouragement.

Taken together, the recommendations in the Information Technology Action Plan significantly broaden and deepen the process of economic reforms by encouraging competition, entrepreneurship and innovation—the three priniciples which are cardinal for India's progress in the emerging knowledge-driven global economy.

The Task Force is confident that the implementation of these recommendations will send a strong signal to people within India and abroad that India can swiftly ride on the Information Superhighway.

Activities of the Task Force till Date

The Office of the Prime Minister issued a Notification on 22nd May, 1998 constituting a National Task Force on Information Technology and Software Development. Dr. M.G.K. Menon, Co-Chairperson of the Task Force, Dr. N. Seshagiri, Member-Convener, and Shri Sudheendra Kulkarni of the PMO met Shri Jaswant Singh, Deputy Chairman, Planning Commission and Chairperson of the Task Force on 26th May, 1998 for finalising the guidelines regarding the deliberations of the Task Force.

The Task Force created a Web Site on the Internet, with a web-letter from the Chairman, inviting suggestions from IT professionals around the world. On the basis of a number of useful reports on the topic prepared earlier by various organisations like the Planning Commission, Ministry of Commerce, Department of Electronics, NIC, Government of Andhra Pradesh, as well as industry associations like NASSCOM, MAIT and ESC and the suggestions given by the various members of the Task Force, the Member-Convener prepared a Basic Background Report (BR-1) and hoisted the same on the Web. More than 3,000 suggestions have been received on the Web from IT professionals around the world.

The Task Force held a number of preparatory meetings, and several formal and informal meetings with the Ministers concerned and their Secretaries and senior officials as per the following schedule:

26 May, 1998	:	Meeting with the Deputy Chairman, Planning Commission & Chair-person of the Task Force
12, 13 & 15 June, 1998		Preparatory meetings in New Delhi under the Chairmanship of Professor M.G.K. Menon, Co-Chairperson of the Task Force
16 June, 1998	:	Meeting in the Department of Telecommunication
18 June, 1998	:	Meeting with the Chief Minister of Maharashtra, senior officials of the State Government and scientists and academicians and industry representatives in Mumbai
20 June, 1998	:	Meeting with the Wireless Adviser, Government of India
22, 23 June, 1998	:	Meeting with the Minister for Communications
23 June, 1998	:	Meeting with Chairman, Telecom Commission
24 June, 1998	:	Meeting with Scientific Adviser to Raksha Mantri & Secretary, Defence (Research)
25 June, 1998	:	Meeting with Finance Minister
25 June, 1998	:	Meeting with Chief Minister of Andhra Pradesh & Co-Chairperson of the Task Force
26 June, 1998	:	Meeting with Finance Secretary
27 June, 1998	:	Meeting with Finance Secretary
29 June, 1998	:	Meeting with Finance Secretary
1 July, 1998	:	Meeting with Finance Minister
1 July, 1998	:	Meeting with Wireless Adviser & Defence Ministry officials

This is the first time in India that representatives of so many ministries, departments, industry associations, business houses, educational institutions and State Governments interacted so intensively and in such a short period of time to cover so many bottleneck and promotional areas in Information Technology. It is also the first time that agreement was reached and concurrence received on most of the points in the Action Plan. This, the Task Force believes, augurs well for its early and effective implementation.

Future Activities

After submission of the first report on bottleneck and immediate promotional issues, the Task Force will begin work on the more substantive work of formulating the draft National Informatics Policy. Towards this end, it will soon set up Working Groups on various specific subjects, on which representatives from Government, industry, academia and other sections of society from across the country will be represented. A few of the Working Groups have already started their work.

The Task Force also plans to identify a large number of national missions which will be so designed as to make visible and catalytic impact on the use of IT in India.

In order to broadbase its consultations, the Task Force has drawn up a plan to visit Bangalore, Hyderabad, Kolkata and Guwahati in the coming weeks. It has already held one such meeting in Mumbai on June 18, 1998.

Within the next ten days, the Task Force will prepare a Vision Statement whose aim will be to excite and energize the people of India, creating the faith in them that Information Technology vitally aids personal growth and national growth. It will also embark on an awareness creation strategy for the effective articulation and dissemination of that Vision.

OVERVIEW OF INFORMATION TECHNOLOGY ACTION PLAN

The Government of India, recognising that the impressive growth the country has achieved since the mid-Eighties in Information Technology is still a small proportion of the potential to achieve, has resolved to make India a Global IT Superpower and a front-runner in the age of Information Revolution. The Government of India considers IT as an agent of transformation of every facet of human life which will bring about a knowledge based society in the twenty-first century. As a first step in that direction, the following revisions and additions are made to the existing Policy and Procedures for removing bottlenecks and achieving such a pre-eminent status for India.

The revisions and additions are aimed at accomplishing the following basic objectives:

(*i*) *Info-Infrastructure Drive*: Accelerate the drive for setting up a World class Info Infrastructure with an extensive spread of Fibre Optic Networks, Satcom Networks and Wireless Networks for seamlessly interconnecting the Local Informatics Infrastructure (LII), National Informatics Infrastructure (NII) and the Global Informatics Infrastructure (GII) to ensure a fast nation-wide onset of the INTERNET, EXTRANETs and INTRANETs.

(*ii*) *Target ITEX-50*: With a potential 2 trillion dollar Global IT industry by the year 2008, policy ambiance will be created for the Indian IT industry to target for a $ 50 billion annual export of IT Software and IT Services (including IT-enabled services) by this year, over a commensurately large domestic IT market spread all over the country.

(*iii*) *IT for all by 2008*: Accelerate the rate of PC/set-top-box penetration in the country from the 1998 level of one per 500 to one per 50 people along with a universal access to Internet/Extranets/Intranets by the year 2008, with a flood of IT applications encompassing every walk of economic and social life of the country. The existing over 600,000 Public Telephones/Public Call Offices (PCOs) will be transformed into public tele-info-centres offering a variety of multimedia Information services. Towards the goal of IT for all by 2008, policies are provided for setting the base for a rapid spread of IT awareness among the citizens, propagation of IT literacy, networked Government, IT-led economic development, rural penetration of IT applications, training citizens in the use of day-to-day IT services like tele-banking, tele-medicine, tele-education, tele-documents transfer, tele-library, tele-info-centres, electronic commerce, Public Call Centres, among others; and training, qualitatively and quantitatively, world Class IT professionals.

Info-Infrastructure Drive

With a target of 30 per cent of annual growth rate from the 1998 level of Fibre Optic backbone of 75,000 route kilometers, VSATs of aggregate capacity of over 300 Megabit per Second, Satellite Transponders of aggregate capacity of more than 3000 Megahertz and in the corresponding 'last mile' Wireless Communication as well as Data Communication based value added services, the Data and Multimedia Info-Infrastructure Policies are liberalised as under:

1. INTERNET access nodes will be opened by DoT and authorised ISPs at all District Headquarters and local charging areas by 26th January 2000. As an interim measure, and till nodes are provided in all local charging areas, access to nearest INTERNET access nodes will be on local call rates with effect from 15th August, 1998. ISPs will be responsible for ensuring that this facility is not misused for telephone traffic.

2. Voice & Data Communication is permitted for IT Software Development and IT Services on dedicated or leased circuits, but no telephone traffic is permitted. Surcharge on 64 Kbps and higher capacity circuits for voice-cum-data applications is withdrawn with effect from 15th August, 1998.

3. Doubling of the lease rental charged by DoT for high speed data circuits leased by Closed User Group (CUG), Licensees of Basic Service, Cellular Service and other Value Added Services and users shall be reduced to single normal lease rental charge.

4. Requests made by public sector Software Technology Park (STPs) or Private Sector STPs or IT promotional organisations approved by the Government for release of bandwidth shall be acted upon by the VSNL by intimating INTELSAT within two weeks of receipt.

5. Setting up of Central call centres by IT Service Providers shall be permitted for which DoT and other Basic Telecom Service Providers will make available bandwidth.

6. Intelligent Network (IN) Services including free phone and premium Service (e.g. 1-800 and 1-900) Services shall be introduced by DoT by 31 December, 1998 in several cities over an Intelligent Network (IN) Platform.

7. For setting up ISP Operations by companies, there shall be no license fee for first five years and after five years a nominal license fee of one rupee will be charged.

8. The monopoly of the VSNL on International Gateway for INTERNET shall be withdrawn and authorised public/government organisations will be allowed to provide INTERNET Gateway access directly without going through VSNL Gateways. Private ISPs are allowed to provide such Gateways after obtaining Defence clearance. Suitable monitoring mechanisms will be put in place to take care of security considerations.

9. The Railways, Defence, State Electricity Boards, National Power Grid Corporation as well as organisations like ONGC, GAIL and SAIL who have rights of way shall be allowed to host fibre optic backbone. These organisations shall be allowed to provide service to the public based on this backbone by having an interface with the existing or new public networks, but without necessarily having to go through DoT network.

10. Networks such as NICNET, STPs, as well as private networks shall be allowed inter-connectivity without necessarily having to go through the DoT's INET network.

11. Providing access to INTERNET through authorised Cable TV shall be permitted to any service provider without additional licensing.

12. The 'last mile' linkages shall be freely permitted either by fibre optic or radio communication for IT application enterprises, IT promotional organisations and ISPs. In case of radio linkages, coordination by the Wireless Adviser will be observed to avoid frequency interference.

13. The radio frequency band in the range of 2.4–2.483 GHz shall be open as 'public wireless' for any Government organisation or PSU or Private Sector Company to set up

Spread Spectrum based non-interference type Wireless data/multimedia communication equipment subject to a maximum of 4 Watt EIRP; WPC will periodically issue a district-wise directory of two or three selected subbands of 10 MHz each for each of the districts on the criteria of least congestion and reserve these subbands maximally for the exclusive use of Spread Spectrum Communication as above. The use of the band will be on the basis of non-interference, non-protection and non-exclusiveness. Private sector, Public sector and Government operators shall bilaterally obtain Defence Clearance for location, the area covered and the frequency sub-band: The Private Sector Units will be required to obtain MHA clearance directly. The security agencies shall convey their decision within 30 days of application failing which the application would be deemed to have been cleared from the security angle. If cleared, the Private and Public Sector operators shall be required to obtain a registration and automatic license directly from WPC by producing the copies of security clearances; the Government operators will directly register with WPC; WPC will be empowered to monitor the violation of the above conditions and impose penalties on defaulters in three stages: Written warning, monetary penalty and debarring for two years. A Public Wireless Technical Audit Unit comprising a representative each from the Defence, DoT, NIC and from NASSCOM for the limited purpose of representing private user interests, shall monitor the implementation of the above policy

14. Data communication requirements for Electronic Commerce (EC/EDI) shall be met by DoT in a liberal framework by assigning the highest priority under their priority classification if the EC/EDI requirement is certified by authorities in Government authorised by the Ministry of Commerce.

15. Public TeleInfo Centres (PTIC) having multimedia capability specially ISDN Services, Remote Database Access, Government and Community Information systems, Market Information, Desk Top Videoconferencing, TeleInfo and INTERNET/Web Access Services shall be permitted and encouraged by the Government. DoT and other Basic Service Providers, Value Added Service Providers and authorised IT promotional organisations shall be permitted to promote these services on non-exclusive basis. No license fee will be charged for operating these services and the usual tariff, where applicable, will be payable by the PTIC Service providers/franchisees. Efforts will be made by DoT and other Service Providers to upgrade STD/ISD PCOs to convert them into these powerful PTICs for which ISDN or other digital facilities shall be provided on priority without necessarily having to make additional investment on this account.

16. DoT shall take suitable action to delicense Multimedia services, including FAX, provided by PCOs.

17. To enhance the pace of PC and INTERNET penetration in remote and far flung areas in the country, the Defence Services shall enable provisions of connectivity for civilian applications to their communication backbone.

18. Existing Software Centres by themselves may not be able to fulfill the high targets now set for the IT industry by the year 2008. International experience has shown that hi-tech industries flourish essentially in the rural hinterland adjacent to cities with modern telecom and communication infrastructure and top class hi-tech educational/research institutions. India will promote such 'Hi-tech Habitats' in the rural hinterland adjacent to suitable cities. For this purpose suitable autonomous structures will be designed and

progressive regulations will be framed to facilitate infrastructurally self-contained self-financed Hi-Tech Habitats of high quality. Initially, five such Hi-Tech Habitats shall be planned and implemented in the rural hinterland of the cities: Bangalore, Hyderabad, Pune, Delhi and Bhubaneswar. It is estimated that progressively 50 such Hi-Tech Habitats can be viably set up by empowering the State Governments to autonomously nucleate them within a technologically progressive and administratively liberal set of guidelines to be prepared by a Special Working Group on Hi-Tech IT Habitats to be set up by the Task Force.

Target ITEX-50

For creating a congenial ambiance for exporters of IT Software and IT Services (including IT enabled services) to reach the export target of US $50 billion by the year 2008, the following incentives shall be provided:

19. (*a*) *Definition*: "IT Software" means any representation of instructions, data, sound or image, including source code and object code, recorded in a machine readable form, and capable of being manipulated or providing interactivity to a user, by means of an automatic data processing machine falling under heading 'IT Products', but does not include 'non-IT products'. 'IT service' is defined as any service which results from the use of any IT software over a system of IT products for realising value addition. The term 'IT Industry' shall cover development, production and services related to IT Products. The term 'IT Software' shall be substituted in place of 'Computer Software' in all notifications.

(*b*) Finance Ministry (CBEC) shall introduce a new classification called, 'Information Technology (IT) Products' including Computer, Digital/Data communication and Digital/Data Broadcasting products, by recognising the progressive technological convergence of these three categories and in line with the classification list in Attachment A (Sections I and II) of the WTO (ITA) Agreement and, additionally, Data Communication equipment.

(*c*) IT Software shall be entitled for zero customs duty and zero excise duty.

20. A revised Notification giving the following new schedule for the Government of India acceding to the WTO-ITA Ministerial Declaration of 13 December, 1996 at Singapore shall be issued by the Ministry of Finance:

In Attachment A, Sections I and II of WTO-ITA:

(*a*) Duty shall be brought down to zero by 1 January, 1999 on the following items: Parts and components excluding populated PCBs in HSN 8473.30, all storage devices in HSN 8471.70, ICs above Rs. 1000 in HSN 8542, Stepper Motors in HSN 8501.10, Colour Graphic Display Tube in HSN 8540.40 and Deflective components for Colour monitor in HSN 8504.

(*b*) Out of the 217 items listed in ITA-I, 94 items which were proposed earlier for zero duty by 1st January 2000 shall now be advanced to 1st January, 1999.

(*c*) The remaining items earlier proposed for zero duty by the 1st January 2003/2004/2005 shall now be advanced to 1 January, 2002.

Concomitantly, the following schedule will be adopted:

- Duty on Capital Goods for the manufacture of items in (c), wherever applicable, becomes zero by 1 January, 2000.
- Inputs/raw materials for the manufacture of the items in (c), wherever applicable, becomes zero by 1 January, 2001.
- Dual purpose items will be taken care of, wherever applicable, by allowing duty drawback benefits or by treating the supplies to the IT industry as deemed export.
- Zero excise duty is concomitant with zero Customs duty with in-phase reduction.

Additionally, other suitable supportive measures shall be taken to encourage Indian hardware industry to become globally competitive in the light of the revised WTO-ITA schedule.

21. Customs duty on import of CD-ROMs or Optical Disc Media or Magnetic Media containing text, data or multimedia as content shall be charged only on the media and not on the contents.

22. Imported IT Products shall be permitted to be taken out of bonded offices or out of Electronics/IT Units under EOU/EPZ/STP/EHTP Schemes after a period of 2 years from the date of import if these are donated to recognised educational institutions, Government organisations and registered charitable hospitals, etc., as defined in the clause 9.19 of the Handbook of Procedures (Volume I) of the EXIM Policy through a customs notification.

23. IT Software and IT Services companies, being constituents of the knowledge industry, shall be exempted from inspection by Inspectors like those for Factory, Boiler, Excise, Labour, Pollution/Environment etc.

24. With technological advancements in Wide Area Computer-Communication networks, which have brought about 'Virtual Technology Parks' in which IT Software and IT services are developed through online integration of software and services subsystems from widely separated locations in the country, the concept of physical bonding has become obsolete. Accordingly, Software developers/exporters are exempted from Customs bonding at various export promotion schemes including STP/EOU/EPZ, etc. The export obligation shall be the same value as given under the EPCG Scheme. Existing bonded units under the various Software Export Promotion schemes will also be considered under the above scheme.

25. A clarification shall be issued by CBEC that Service Tax is not applicable on computer software development industry.

26. The Ministry of Civil Aviation shall issue the following notifications/amendments in the regulations:

- Export shipment time for air cargo will be reduced to less than 24 hours.
- "Known Shipper" will be introduced to avoid delays on account of cooling off period.
- Cargo companies and other associated agencies to allow consolidation of export air cargo.

27. Section 80 HHE of the Income Tax Act provides for income tax exemption to profits derived from software and services exports. This section shall be amended as follows:

- The existing formula will be so changed that tax on profits shall not have any relation to domestic turnover.
- The definition of software and export turnover will be changed so as to include IT services exports.
- The benefits of this section for income tax exemption to profits from exports will be extended to supporting IT Software and IT Services developers.

28. IT software and IT services shall be deemed as manufacturing activity for the limited purpose of applicability of Section 10 (15) (iv) of the Income Tax Act.

29. IT Software and IT Services shall be exempted from withholding tax through amendments in the 'explanation' of Section 9 of the Income Tax Act.

30. For individuals buying IT products including computer, the expenditure shall be deductible under Section 88 of the Income Tax Act.

31. No gift tax shall be charged for the giver or Income Tax for the receiver on PCs upto Rs. 30,000 of the original purchase price.

32. For any investment made in IT products and IT software 100 per cent depreciation shall be allowed in two years for which Ministry of Finance shall take suitable action.

33. As the traditional method of asset-based funding of working capital would not meet the adequate and timely requirements of fund of the software sector, a differential and flexible approach shall be adopted by giving special dispensation towards working capital requirements of this sector in view of the unique nature of the industry. Accordingly, RBI shall issue, by 15th August, 1998, new guidelines with regard to working capital requirements for the IT software and services sector which would be based on simple criteria such as turnover. Banks shall be advised to give 25 per cent of the contract value for 18 months, with the first six months as term loan (without collaterals) and from the 7th month onwards annualized Cash Flow Statements shall be accepted instead of collaterals.

34. IT software and services industry shall be treated as a Priority Sector by banks for the next five years. This would help to meet the requirements of IT software and services exports, and also the IT industry and applications within the country. Major banks will be advised to create specialised IT financing cells in important branches, where IT Software and Services units are sufficiently large in number. Performance in this dimension will be monitored by the Ministry of Finance.

35. Against the present estimate of Rs. 400 crores of working capital for the industry, the amount shall be increased to around Rs. 1200 crores by the year 2000 subject to the broad criteria of pro-rata increase for the prospective requirements 24 months ahead as compared to the actuals of the current requirements at any given time. As quantitative targeting is not appropriate, a system will be put in place which would enable substantial increase in working capital provided by the banks.

36. Bank lending to IT Software and Services exporters shall be made eligible for RBI refinancing with sufficiently low interest rates.

37. The banks shall be allowed to invest in the form of equity in dedicated venture capital funds meant for IT industry as part of the 5 per cent of increment in deposits currently allowed for shares.

38. Banks/FIs like ICICI, IDBI, UTI and SBI shall set up joint ventures with Indian or foreign companies for setting up of at least four different venture capital dedicated funds of a corpus of not less than Rs. 50 crores each to cater to the credit need of the industry. Such venture capitalists may be allowed to set off losses in one invested company and profit in another invested company during the block of years for the purpose of income tax.

39. The Company's Act shall be amended to facilitate issuance of Sweat Equity to employees. A new definition No. (66) will be added after definition No. (65) in clause 2 as under:

"(66) Sweat Equity means equity allotted to promoters, Directors or employees for providing any intellectual property or value addition to the Company".

40. Ministry of Finance shall include IT software and IT service sector while issuing general guidelines for dual listing of companies, as well as while considering two-way fungability for ADRs/GDRs.

41. Dollar Linked Stock Options to employees of Indian Software companies were announced in the 1998 Budget and detailed guidelines on this have been issued by DEA, Ministry of Finance. This shall be modified in accordance with the definition of IT Software and IT Services given under (19)(a) and (b) above.

- Employee Stock option schemes for stock listed in India would also be encouraged. Also, clarification shall be issued that income tax is applicable only at the time of sale and not at the time of excise of option.

42. Recognising the high velocity of business, high degree of competition and fast technological obsolescence faced by the IT software and IT service exporters, RBI shall be maximally accommodate the following:

(*a*) A blanket approval for overseas investment for acquisition of software/IT companies across the board for software exporters with previous three years cumulative actual export realisation in excess of US$ 25 million to be given up to 50 per cent or US$ 25 million, whichever is lower, out of the cumulative actual export earning of the previous three years. This is subject to submission of a certificate of software industry by appropriate authorities.

(*b*) For FERA approvals beyond this limit, RBI would set up a mechanism for expeditious processing of applications from this sector. This shall be announced by 15 August, 1998.

(*c*) For overseas ventures, a dispensation shall be given for allowing the capitalisation of both goods and services; RBI shall accordingly notify this in consultation with Commerce Ministry by 15 August, 1998.

(*d*) As the present allowable limit of 70 per cent of the contract amount for expenditure abroad does not provide flexibility for utilisation for the purpose of general corporate objectives or for business growth purposes, RBI shall permit IT exporters to freely spend upto 5 per cent of the export proceeds abroad (out of the total 70 %) for miscellaneous/sundry purposes to give full flexibility. Also, a new list of allowable expenses under the 70 per cent limit would be worked out by RBI in consultation with NASSCOM.

(*e*) RBI shall issue revised EEFC guidelines to eliminate restrictions on staggered remittance, second and higher generation subsidiaries and also to allow 20 per cent of the EEFC balances for the use on the following:

(*i*) Advance remittances for downloading software (upto US$ 1 lakh per transaction).

(*ii*) Purchase of equipment and related expenditure.

(*iii*) Miscellaneous expenses not detailed in EEFC guidelines (upto 5%) of EEFC balances. Such EEFC accounts shall be permitted for making payments from offshore branches of Indian banks directly.

(*f*) Use of International Credit Cards (ICC) abroad for a variety of purposes required by the IT Software and IT Services sector shall be permitted, the detailing of which will be carried out by RBI and notified by 15 August, 1998, in particular:

(*i*) All payments currently made under Exchange Earnings Foreign Currency (EEFC) Account shall also be allowed to made through International Credit Cards (ICC). Advance payment for IT software and IT services shall be permitted to be done through ICC for which RBI will issue a notification. Notification shall be issued that ICC may also be used for paying for IT Software and IT services purchased over INTERNET or EXTRANET and also for registering domain names.

(*ii*) RBI shall issue a modified and simplified SOFTEX form required for IT Software and IT Services export by 15 August 1998.

43. In the EPCG scheme a system of self-declaration shall be introduced with 100 per cent post-checking subject to punitive penalty for default.

44. The value limit for import of IT Products including personal computers shall be reduced from Rs. 1.50 lakhs (c.i.f.) to Rs. 70,000 (c.i.f.).

45. Private and public organisations providing IT infrastructure shall be included for duty exemption for importing capital goods. Such service providers, in view of such capital goods imported, shall undertake the export obligations as provided for import of capital goods in the EPCG scheme.

46. The India Brand Equity Fund Scheme operated by the Ministry of Commerce shall be made available for Software companies with lower interest and longer interval.

47. On-site IT Services should be made easier by combating Visa regulations of the recipient countries through a planned diplomatic strategy by the Ministry of External Affairs and the Indian Missions abroad for which MEA will create a suitable dedicated structure. This will also include signing of totalisation agreements, wherever necessary so as to maintain the competitive advantage of Indian companies.

48. Returns from package software development shall be increased by enabling Indian Marketing companies to set up wholesale companies abroad. They shall also be given maximum flexibility in organising the marketing of package software from India through INTERNET.

49. For benchmarking our country with our emerging competitors, a study shall be conducted at Government cost once in two years by internationally reputed consultancy companies.

50. Restrictions on the location of IT software and IT Services (including IT training) companies in residential areas shall be removed.

51. To enable organisations and companies to identify, explore and plan strategies for Large Niche Markets like Y2K and Euro, nationally and corporatewise, all applicable provisions shall be made applicable on higher priority basis. Through MOC and DOE funds 'India Pavilions' shall be set up in several major IT exhibitions around the world through the initiative and coordination of ESC and NASSCOM.

52. Recognising the catastrophic effect of the Y2K problem for solving which a few hundred billion dollars are being spent around the world, an immediate investment of Rs. 700 crore as corpus funds shall be mobilised to control the crisis in critical Government, Public and Private organisations and services; efforts to sensitise such organisations in the country facing the crisis shall be taken up by the Government immediately including issuance of Government orders for strict compliance in a time-bound manner; a High level empowered Task Force with representatives from the Government, Industry Associations, Banks and Financial Institutions, Defence Services, Utility and other Public Service organisations, Railways, among others, shall be constituted by the Government of India.

53. 'Mega Websites' shall be created on INTERNET for promoting marketing and encouraging Indian Software products and packages under multiple initiatives.

- Creation and hosting of websites on servers located in India will be encouraged.

54. Under DEPB Rupee trade arrangement, IT Software, IT Services and IT product export to Russia shall be permitted with promotional support given by the Electronics and Software Export Promotion Council (ESC), STP, etc.

55. All promotional and liberalisation policy instruments available to IT Software and IT Services shall be made available to IT enabled services including the Information Content Industry by classifying IT enabled Services as tantamount to IT Software and IT Services.

56. For promoting Indian Software Packages (system as well as application software) users shall be given fiscal incentives for buying Indian packages. A special screening mechanism will be worked out for identifying the more promising packages developed in India and giving consistent support by the Government as well as the industry for ensuring acceptance in international markets.

57. Private STPs shall be encouraged to be set up by combining the provisions under (4), (7), (8), (12), (13), (24), (43), (45), (54) and (55), among others.

IT for All by 2008

For enabling a proactive drive for 'IT for all by 2008', the following new policy instruments shall be devised and activated.

Operation Knowledge

Recognising Information Technology to be a frontier area of knowledge, and also a critical enabling tool for assimilating, processing and productivising all other spheres of knowledge, the Government shall launch 'OPERATION KNOWLEDGE'. The aim of this national campaign will be to universalise computer literacy and also to spread the use of computers and IT in education. 'OPERATION KNOWLEDGE' shall be developed into a comprehensive policy within the next three months. However, the following initiatives shall be taken for the immediate implementation of some of its key objectives:

58. The Government shall soon launch three schemes—Vidyarthi Computer Scheme, Shikshak Computer Scheme and School Computer Scheme—to enable every student, teacher or school respectively desirous of buying computers to do so under attractive financial packages. These schemes will be supported by a suite of initiatives such as lowering the cost of PCs, easy-instalment bank loans, computer donations by IT companies and other business houses, bulk donations of computers by NRI organisations, large-volume bargain price imports, multi-lateral funding, etc.

59. Computers and Internet shall be made available in every school, polytechnic, college, university and public hospital in the country by the year 2003.

60. All universities, engineering colleges, medical colleges and other institutions of higher learning in the country as well as Research and Development Organisations shall be networked for a supplementary programme of distance education for improving the quality of education before year 2000.

61. The seven national level institutions (IITs, IISc.) shall be encouraged to triple their output of students in IT by suitably restructuring the programme.

62. A National Council of IT Education comprising experts from both the industry and the academicia, shall be set up for defining courses and their content in the light of rapid developments taking place in Information Technology. The Council will also initiate a 'Teach the Teachers' (3T) programme for upgrading on a regular basis the IT knowledge and skills of teachers.

63. An IT Course Module shall be made a compulsory component of all Degree Courses within a short period.

64. The setting up of Indian Institutes of Information Technology (IIIT) shall be implemented with urgency to make up for the lost time. Hi-tech institutions like the Indian Institute of Information Technology (IIIT) will be given the Deemed University status without insisting upon the mandatory three-year stipulation.

65. The Government shall promote the pairing of our Universities with centres of excellence in IT in developed countries.

66. Specific courses shall be launched in association with the Software Industry and IIMs to provide Project Management skills and develop specialised courses on Software Marketing.

67. The concept of SMART Schools where the emphasis is not only on Information Technology in Schools, but also on the use of skills and values that will be important in the next millennium, shall be started on a pilot demonstrative basis in each State.

68. An Institute for Computer Professionals of India shall be set up on the pattern of the Institute of Chartered Accountants of India; the Institute will be nucleated by NASSCOM with initial financial support from the industry and the Government. The Institute will be given the responsibility as an Accreditation Body for IT Education and Training Programmes with full Government recognition in addition to the DOEACC Programme of the Department of Electronics.

69. To enhance the knowledge base of IT related education at all levels the Government shall establish Information Technology, System Engineering and IT Security Institutes from within existing manpower of the Armed Forces. The Centres of Excellence in IT Software and System Engineering in the Defence Services will be utilised to the national advantage.

70. Virtual Institutes in different parts of the country shall be set up to achieve excellence in distance education.

71. The talent and expertise of IT-trained ex-servicemen shall be utilised for IT penetration in rural India and Government will fully support this offer of the Armed Forces. A Plan will be prepared and implemented for utilising the services of the large number of IT literate defence personnel retiring every year for propagating the IT culture at sub-district levels.

72. A 'National Qualification Framework' shall be established for computerised online objective system of knowledge acquisition. An 'Educational Credit Bank' shall be implemented for giving flexibility to integrate credits earned in different institutions/ systems towards the eligibility for diplomas and degrees.

73. A specialised sub-committee of this Task Force shall coordinate the setting up of National and State level Digital Libraries Projects.

74. A pilot project under the aegis of the National Task Force on Information Technology shall be launched in some lead districts which have already attained universal literacy, with the aim of achieving universal computer literacy in all the secondary schools in these districts. Alongside, the network of educational institutions in these districts will be assisted to maximise the induction of IT in order to create world-class talent at the top-end of the education pyramid. These pilot projects will be joint initiatives of the local educational institutions, respective State Governments and the Centre. In the first instance, such a pilot project will be launched in Dakshin Kannada and Udupi Districts in Karnataka on a substantive self-financing basis. Within a short time, the same will be extended to suitable districts in other States.

75. In view of the lower-than-national-average levels of technical and IT education facilities in Uttar Pradesh, Bihar, Madhya Pradesh and Rajasthan, several educational centres will be identified with a view to making them models for IT-based education and training at all levels. The aim of this initiative will be to promote IT education and awareness in Hindi-speaking States and thereby revitalise the Hindi heartland in all the fields of knowledge and knowledge-based enterprises. Allahabad shall be developed as the first such model IT-based education-cum-business centre. Within a short time, this initiative will be extended to other States which are underdeveloped in IT.

IT Penetration and IT Awareness

76. Government shall encourage the setting up of value-added network services including ATMs, Electronic Kiosks, Telephones, Smart Cards, etc., for providing a 'One-Stop Non-Stop' service to the public.

77. To make IT a mass movement, an awareness creation strategy shall be worked out within two months and the structures for implementing the same shall be put in place.

78. A major promotional campaign shall soon be launched to boost IT in Indian languages. This campaign will be based on a multi-pronged approach, involving fiscal and other incentives for R&D, production, marketing and popularisation of IT products in Indian languages. This recommendation addresses the reality that India can become a major IT power only if IT penetration in the country deepens and widens—which in turn, is dependent on large-scale use of IT in Indian languages.

79. The Government shall take all the necessary steps to boost IT for agricultural and integrated rural development. Towards this end, a number of demonstration projects will be devised in each State taking into account the specific strengths and needs at the local

level. A unique 'WIRED VILLAGES' pilot project has been launched under the aegis of the National Information Technology Task Force on Information Technology at the Warananagar Cooperative Complex in Kolhapur District in Maharashtra. Efforts will be made to quickly replicate such projects in other states.

80. The Government shall take necessary measures to develop, productivise and use, in domestic and global markets, indigenous technologies in wireless telecommunication such as CorDECT, remote access switch, etc., to achieve the national objective of rapid, low-cost expansion of telephone and Internet connectivity in rural and remote areas. Similarly, promotional measures shall be taken to encourage technologies that bring IT and Internet to the masses through the vast network of Cable TV houses.

81. For promoting electronic commerce in a time-bound manner, a strict directive shall be given to Sea Ports, Airports Authority of India, DGFT, Banks, Container Services, Customs and Indian Railways in accordance with the programme approved in the tenth Export Promotion Board meeting.

82. Bar Coding of every item sold in the country shall be made compulsory within a five-year period.

83. The Armed Forces shall integrate far-flung and remote areas (Ladakh, North-East, Andaman & Nicobar Islands, Kutch, Lakshadweep and Minicoy Islands, border areas of Himachal and Rajasthan) with mainstream India, through IT penetration as part of their Civic Action Programme. The funds for this initiative shall be provided through the Government/Venture/Seed Capital.

Citizen IT Interface

84. The Cabinet has approved NIC's proposal to make government Information, other than that having a bearing on security, available to the public. This decision shall be implemented by suitably empowering NIC to do so. This recommendation addresses the felt need for easy availability and extensive transparency of government information.

85. District Information System (DISNIC) Plan Programme shall be made widespread and databases updated online, shall be made available to the Public and Panchayats, among others. Courts Information System (COURTIS), Parliament Information System (PARLIS), Computerised Rural Information System Programme (CRISP) and other such databases shall be updated online over NICNET and access to public facilitated.

86. A Citizens Charter for effective and responsive administration in terms of time-bound service to the public shall be framed and implemented under the coordination of the Department of Administrative Reforms and Public Grievances and hoisted on the official INTERNET Website 'India Image' of the Government of India.

IT in Government

87. Each Department/Agency in the Central Government and State Governments shall be required to prepare a Five Year IT Plan.

88. 1-3 per cent of the budget of every Ministry/Department shall be earmarked for applying IT in the Department/sector; this investment will include not only the purchase of IT products, IT Software, but also for training and IT services; Reappropriation of the Department's budget for the IT sub-budget head shall be within the delegated powers of the Head of the Department.

89. NIC, at the national level, and technology service organisations at the State level, shall establish 'Framework Contracts' with reputed suppliers to provide a wide range of IT consultancy, specialist services and IT products to Government agencies to reach the benefit of lower costs through bulk purchases.

90. India shall participate in international projects like 'Government Online' Project of G-8 countries so as to not only learn from the experience of others but also to contribute to the global experience in planning and implementing projects to promote IT in Government.

91. Tele-commuting is recognised as a new modality of doing work in an office and labour laws accommodating the same shall be enacted. An option shall be given to employees, where feasible and efficient, to accomplish part of their work through telecommuting in the framework of 'Management by Objectives' (MBO).

92. The Government of India shall set up a central repository of data elements in Government with the NIC and make it accessible through NICNET.

93. The recommendations of the TG-MAP Committee for Map and GIS Data Policy approved by the Committee of Secretaries under the Cabinet Secretary, shall be notified by the Ministry of Defence expeditiously.

94. A computerised National Inventory of Training pertaining to different areas shall be maintained.

95. A computerised Inventory of Government best practices for electronic access shall be maintained.

96. Government shall stipulate IT literacy as an essential requirement for all future Government and public sector employment; in the Annual Confidential Reports of government employees, a column shall be introduced regarding contribution to IT utilisation in the department/organisation.

97. A National Institute of Smart Government shall be set up to focus on all issues concerning IT-supported governance.

98. State Institutes of Public Administrations shall be re-engineered to help bring about IT-responsive State Governments.

99. Suitable floor space in Government buildings, which are not utilised during non-office hours, could be given to private educational institutions for IT training purposes in return for a proportionate number of free nominations of Government employees for IT training.

Data Security Systems and Cyber Laws

100. A National Computerised Records Security Document shall be prepared within three months for enforcing security requirements by consulting similar documents prepared by SAG, JCB, WESEE, etc.

101. An Information Security Agency shall be set up at the National level to play the role of Cyber Cop.

102. A National Policy on Information Security, Privacy and Data Protection Act for handling of computerised data shall be framed by the Government within six months.

103. Cyber infractions shall be addressed within the legal framework by the Ministry of Law, Justice and Company Affairs.

104. The cryptology and Cyber Security knowledge and experience developed by the Defence establishments shall be suitably transferred to the civilian information security agencies for wider dissemination in the country to increase information security, network security and bring about a greater degree of secure use of EFT, Digital Signature, etc.

105. The procedure of keeping records in paper form in public and private STPs shall be restricted to a maximum duration of two months after which the records shall be kept only in the Electronic/Magnetic/Optical media.

106. The Indian Telegraph Act of 1885, the Indian Post Office Act of 1888 and the Indian Wireless Telegraphy Act of 1993 shall be suitably modified in the light of the growing predominance of IT in day-to-day life. Suitable changes will also be made in other Laws/Acts, wherever necessary.

107. The draft set of Cyber Laws prepared by the Cyber Law Committee set up by the Committee of Secretaries, shall be approved by the Government with suitable modifications and implemented, as a first step, within six months.

108. All necessary instructions, notifications and amendements to procedures. Law shall be issued by the respective Ministries/Departments within three months.

ANNEXURE

Notification: Appointment of Task Force
F.No. 360/31/C/10/98-ES.II
Government of India
(Bharat Sarkar)
Prime Minister's Office
(Pradhan Mantri Karyalaya)

New Delhi, dated 22-5-1998

Subject: Appointment of a National Task Force on Information Technology and Software Development

Government has decided to constitute a National Task Force on Information Technology and Software Development to formulate the draft of a National Informatics Policy with the following composition:

Chairperson Shri Jaswant Singh
Deputy Chairperson, Planning Commission

Co-Chairpersons Shri N. Chandrababu Naidu
Chief Minister of Andhra Pradesh

Dr. M.G.K. Menon
Former Union Minister of State,
Science & Technology

Members

Dr. N. Seshagiri Member-Convener — Director General, National Informatics Centre

Shri N. Vittal — Chairman, Public Enterprises Selection Board, Former

	Secretary, Department of Electronics and Chairman, Telecom Commission
Shri A.V. Gokak	Chairman, Telecom Commission
Shri R. Gupta	Secretary, Department of Electronics
Shri P.G. Mankad	Secretary, Ministry of I&B
Shri T.H. Chowdary	Former CMD of VSNL and Information Technology Adviser to the Chief Minister of Andhra Pradesh
Dr. P.V. Indiresan	Former Director, IIT, Chennai
Shri Dewang Mehta	Executive Director, National Association of Software Companies (NASSCOM)
Shri N.R. Narayana Murthy	Chairman & Managing Director, Infosys
Shri Ashok Soota	Group President, WIPRO Info-tech Group
Shri Rajendra Pawar	Vice-Chairman and MD, NIIT
Dr. Y.S. Rajan	Senior Adviser (Technology), CII
Shri Ravi Parthasarathy	Managing Director, Infrastructure Leasing & Finance Services (ILFS)
Shri Anil Bakht	IT professional
Shri Sudheendra Kulkarni	Director (Communications and Research), PMO

The tasks and terms of reference of the Task Force are given in the Annexure.

The Task Force will be guided by an "IT Vision Group" consisting of eminent IT professionals, academics, civil servants (serving or retired), businessmen, political leaders and prominent IT professionals from abroad—both NRIs and foreigners.

The Task Force may with the permission of the Chairperson, co-opt or invite as many persons, including officials of relevant Government departments, as it may deem appropriate in the course of its deliberations.

The Task Force will be covered within the definition/explanation of High Level Commissions/Committees as given in Cabinet Secretariat O.M. No. 105/1/1/75-CF dated 20.11.75.

Secretarial assistance to the Task Force will be provided by the National Informatics Centre (NIC), Planning Commission.

The TA/DA of official members shall be borne by their Parent Departments. The TA/DA of non-official members (as admissible to Grade I officers of the highest category in Government of India) shall be paid by the National Informatics Centre, Planning Commission.

The Task Force will complete its work and submit its final report to the Prime Minister within 90 days.

(T.K.A. Nair)
Secretary to the Prime Minister

Tasks

The various tasks of the National Task Force on Information Technology and Software Development are as follows:

- This Task Force will formulate the draft National Policy on Informatics whose aim will be to enable India to emerge as an Information Technology superpower within the next ten years. It will submit the Draft Policy to the Prime Minister in three months.
- The Task Force will recommend an appropriate empowered institutional mechanism to implement this policy as a national mission with the participation of the Central and State Governments, industry, academic institutions, and the society at large.
- This Task Force will recommend, within one month, immediate steps that the Government needs to take to remove bottlenecks and give a big boost to India's Information Technology industry.
- This Task Force will prepare a Vision Statement that will excite and energize the people of India, creating the faith in them that Information Technology vitally aids personal growth and national growth. It will also suggest a strategy for the effective articulation and dissemination of that Vision, so as to create an ethos, an ambience, a mindset, and a work culture consistent with the needs of the emerging knowledge-driven global civilisation.
- This Task Force will prepare a blue print for making the adoption of Information Technology into a national movement, with a wide network of empowered task forces at all governmental and non-governmental levels.

Terms of Reference

The terms of reference of the National Task Force on Information Technology and Software Development are as follows:

1. Recommend a strategy for the extensive use of Information Technology in all areas of national economy—agriculture, industry, trade and services—as a critical input in making India a global economic power.
2. Prepare the design for building a world-class physical, institutional and regulatory IT infrastructure, which is appropriate for India. This design will embrace the growing convergence of telecommunications, computers, consumer electronics and the media infrastructure (minus its content).
3. Towards this end, determine the means for creating a National Informatics Infrastructure (NII) backbone, bridging it to the Local Informatics Infrastructure (LII) and the Global Informatics Infrastructure (GII). The design of the NII will be dynamic, taking into account the rapidly changing nature of Information Technology.
4. Recommend how NII can be created at an optimal cost by using the existing resources of the various wings of Government such as the Department of Telecommunications, Prasar Bharati, Railways, Power Grid Corporation of India, etc.

5. Suggest measures for achieving a massive expansion in the use of the Internet by all sections of society, especially in business and education, and development of Indian content on the Internet.
6. Recommend a strategy for boosting the learning and use of Information Technology in Indian languages. The policy will suggest measures to promote the development of software, especially educational and commercial software, in Indian languages.
7. Develop a strategy for a twenty-fold increase in India's software and other IT service exports in the next ten years. In particular, the Policy will focus on the development of world-class software products and brands that can quickly establish global dominance.
8. Suggest measures to catalyze the growth of exports through the extensive use of Commerce and EDI (Electronic Data Interchange).
9. Suggest ways in which the use of IT can be maximised in the Government at all levels, so as to make its functioning people-friendly, transparent and accountable.
10. Develop a strategy for dramatically increasing the PC density in the country and, to that end, ensure that every household and commercial establishments that has a telephone also has a computer. The strategy will aim to facilitate the availability of computer hardware, software and connectivity at the lowest possible cost.
11. Device a strategy for establishing a strong and internationally competitive domestic manufacturing base for computers, computer components and peripherals.
12. Design a training and manpower development plan involving Government agencies, private business, voluntary organizations, educational institutions and others to quadruple the number of IT professionals in the country in the next two years. The Task Force will suggest a plan to implement the commitment made in the National Agenda for Governance to ensure universal computer literacy in all secondary schools in the country. The plan will also aim at making available IT education to all those sections of the economy where it serves as a productivity multiplier.
13. Develop a strategic plan to raise the necessary financial resources to realise the objectives of the National Informatics Policy. This plan will rely on innovative means of funding that minimise government outlay.
14. Suggest an appropriate legal framework for the creation of an IT-based society, with due focus on Intellectual Property Rights (IPR), secrecy, security and safety of information.
15. Recommend how India can leverage its global competitiveness in Info-Tech to play a prominent role in the development of IT in other countries, especially those that are underdeveloped.

ANNEXURE
List of Co-opted Members

1. Dr. M.S. Ahluwalia
   Secretary (Finance), Ministry of Finance

2. Shri P.P. Prabhu
   Secretary (Commerce), Ministry of Commerce
3. Shri N.K. Singh
   Secretary (Revenue), Ministry of Finance
4. Lt. Gen. S.S. Mehta
   Dy Chief of Army Staff
5. Commodore Prem Chand
   Additional Director General, WESEE, Navy

NEW TELECOM POLICY

Importance of Telecommunications

The Government of India (Government) recognises that provision of world class telecommunications infrastructure and information is the key to rapid economic and social development of the country.

It is critical not only for the development of the Information Technology industry, but also has widespread ramifications on the entire economy of the country. It is also anticipated that going forward, a major part of the GDP of the country would be contributed by this sector. Accordingly, it is of vital importance to the country that there be a comprehensive and forward looking telecommunications policy which creates an enabling framework for development of this industry.

NTP 1994—Objectives and Achievements

In 1994, the Government announced the National Telecom Policy which defined certain important objectives, including availability of telephone on demand, provision of world class services at reasonable prices, ensuring India's emergence as major manufacturing/ export base of telecom equipment and universal availability of basic telecom services to all villages. It also announced a series of specific targets to be achieved by 1997.

As against the NTP 1994 target of provision of 1 PCO per 500 urban population and coverage of all 6 lac villages, DoT has achieved an urban PCO penetration of 1 PCO per 522 and has been able to provide telephone coverage to only 3.1 lac villages. As regards provision of total telephone lines in the country, DoT has provided 8.73 million telephone lines against the Eighth Plan target of 7.5 million lines.

NTP 1994 also recognised that the required resources for achieving these targets would not be available only out of Government sources and concluded that private investment and involvement of the private sector was required to bridge the resource gap. The Government invited Private Sector participation in a phased manner from the early nineties, initially for value added services such as Paging Services and Cellular Mobile Telephone Services (CMTS) and thereafter for Fixed Telephone Services (FTS). After a competitive bidding process, licenses were awarded to 8 CMTS operators in the four metros, 14 CMTS operators in 18 state circles, 6 BTS operators in 6 state circles and to paging operators in 27 cities and 18 state circles. VSAT services were liberalised for providing data services to closed user groups. Licences were issued to 14 operators in the private sector out of which only nine licencees are operational.

The Government has recently announced the policy for Internet Service Provision (ISP) by private operators and has commenced licensing of the same. The Government has also announced opening up of Global Mobile Personal Communications by Satellite (GMPCS) and has issued one provisional license. Issue of licenses to other prospective GMPCS operators is under consideration.

The Government recognises that the result of the privatisation has so far not been entirely satisfactory. While there has been a rapid rollout of cellular mobile networks in the metros and states with currently over 1 million subscribers, most of the projects today are facing problems. The main reason, according to the cellular and basic operators, has been the fact that the actual revenues realised by these projects have been far short of the projections and the operators are unable to arrange financing for their projects and therefore complete their projects. Basic telecom services by private operators have only just commenced in a limited way in two of the six circles where licenses were awarded. As a result, some of the targets as envisaged in the objectives of the NTP 1994 have remained unfulfilled. The private sector entry has been slower than what was envisaged in the NTP 1994. The Government views the above developments with concern as it would adversely affect the further development of the sector and recognises the need to take a fresh look at the policy framework for this sector.

Need for a New Telecom Policy

In addition to some of the objectives of NTP 1994 not being fulfilled, there have also been far reaching developments in the recent past in the telecom, IT, consumer electronics and media industries world-wide. Convergence of both markets and technologies is a reality that is forcing realignment of the industry. At one level, telephone and broadcasting industries are entering each other's markets, while at another level, technology is blurring the difference between different conduit systems such as wireline and wireless.

As in the case of most countries, separate licences have been issued in our country for basic, cellular, ISP, satellite and cable TV operators each with separate industry structure, terms of entry and varying requirement to create infrastructure. However, this convergence now allows operators to use their facilities to deliver some services reserved for other operators, necessitating a relook into the existing policy framework. The new telecom policy framework is also required to facilitate India's vision of becoming an IT superpower and develop a world class telecom infrastructure in the country.

Objectives and Targets of the New Telecom Policy 1999, the Objectives of the NTP 1999 are as under

Access to telecommunications is of utmost importance for achievement of the country's social and economic goals. Availability of affordable and effective communications for the citizens is at the core of the vision and goal of the telecom policy.

Strive to provide a balance between the provision of universal service to all uncovered areas, including the rural areas, and the provision of high-level services capable of meeting the needs of the country's economy. Encourage development of telecommunication facilities in remote, hilly and tribal areas of the country. Create a modern and efficient telecommunications infrastructure taking into account the convergence of IT, media, telecom and consumer electronics and thereby propel India into becoming an IT superpower. Convert PCO's, wherever justified, into Public Teleinfo centres having multimedia capability like ISDN services, remote database access, government and community information systems etc.

Transform in a time bound manner, the telecommunications sector to a greater competitive environment in both urban and rural areas providing equal opportunities and level playing field for all players. Strengthen research and development efforts in the country and provide an impetus to build world-class manufacturing capabilities. Achieve efficiency and transparency in spectrum management. Protect defence and security interests of the country. Enable Indian Telecom Companies to become truly global players.

In line with the above objectives, the specific targets that the NTP 1999 seeks to achieve would be:

Make available telephone on demand by the year 2002 and sustain it thereafter so as to achieve a teledensity of 7 by the year 2005 and 15 by the year 2010. Encourage development of telecom in rural areas making it more affordable by suitable tariff structure and making rural communication mandatory for all fixed service providers. Increase rural teledensity from the current level of 0.4 to 4 by the year 2010 and provide reliable transmission media in all rural areas. Achieve telecom coverage of all villages in the country and provide reliable media to all exchanges by the year 2002. Provide Internet access to all district headquarters by the year 2000. Provide high speed data and multimedia capability using technologies including ISDN to all towns with a population greater than 2 lac by the year 2002.

New Policy Framework

The New Policy Framework must focus on creating an environment, which enables continued attraction of investment in the sector and allows creation of communication infrastructure by leveraging on technological development. Towards this end, the New Policy Framework would look at the telecom service sector as follows—Cellular Mobile Service Providers, Fixed Service Providers and Cable Service Providers, collectively referred to as 'Access Providers', Radio Paging Service Providers, Public Mobile Radio Trunking Service Providers, National Long Distance Operators, International Long Distance Operators. Other Service Providers, Global Mobile Personal Communication by Satellite (GMPCS) Service Providers, V-SAT based Service Providers.

Access Providers

Cellular Mobile Service Providers (CMSP)

The CMSP shall be permitted to provide mobile telephony services including permission to carry its own long distance traffic within their service area without seeking an additional licence. Direct interconnectivity between licenced CMSP's and any other type of service provider (including another CMSP) in their area of operation including sharing of infrastructure with any other type of service provider shall be permitted. Interconnectivity between service providers in different service areas shall be reviewed in consultation with TRAI and the same would be announced by August 15, 1999 as a part of the structure for opening up national long distance. The CMSP shall be allowed to directly interconnect with the VSNL after opening of national long distance from January 1, 2000. The CMSP shall be free to provide, in its service area of operation, all types of mobile services including voice and non-voice messages, data services and PCOs utilizing any type of network equipment, including circuit and/or packet switches, that meet the relevant International Telecommunication Union (ITU)/Telecommunication Engineering Center (TEC) standards.

CMSP would be granted separate licence, for each service area. Licences would be awarded for an initial period of twenty years and would be extendible by additional periods of ten years thereafter. For this purpose, service areas would be categorized into the four metro circles and Telecom circles as per the existing policy. CMSP would be eligible to obtain licences for any number of service areas.

Availability of adequate frequency spectrum is essential not only for providing optimal bandwidth to every operator but also for entry of additional operators. Based on the immediately available frequency spectrum band, apart from the two private operators already licenced, DoT/MTNL would be licenced to be the third operator in each service area in case they want to enter, in a time-bound manner. In order to ensure level playing field between different service providers in similar situations, licence fee would be payable by DoT also. However, as DoT is the national service provider having immense rural and social obligations, the Government will reimburse full licence fee to the DoT.

It is proposed to review the spectrum utilisation from time to time keeping in view the emerging scenario of spectrum availability, optimal use of spectrum, requirements of market, competition and other interest of public The entry of more operators in a service area shall be based on the recommendation of the TRAI who will review this as required and no later than every two years. CMSP operators would be required to pay a one time entry fee. The basis for determining the entry fee and the basis for selection of additional operators would be recommended by the TRAI.

Apart from the one time entry fee, CMSP operators would also be required to pay licence fee based on a revenue share. It is proposed that the appropriate level of entry fee and percentage of revenue share arrangement for different service areas would be recommended by TRAI in a time-bound manner, keeping in view the objectives of the New Telecom Policy.

Fixed Service Providers (FSP)

FSP shall be freely permitted to establish 'last mile' linkages to provide fixed services and carry long distance traffic within their service area without seeking an additional licence. Direct interconnectivity between FSP's and any other type of service provider (including another FSP) in their area of operation and sharing of infrastructure with any other type of service provider shall be permitted. Interconnectivity between service providers in different service areas shall be reviewed in consultation with TRAI and the same would be announced by August 15, 1999 as a part of the structure for opening up of national long distance. The FSP shall be allowed to directly interconnect with the VSNL after the opening up of national long distance from January 1, 2000.

The FSP may also utilize last mile linkages or transmission links within its service area made available by other service providers. The FSP shall be free to provide, in his service area of operation, all types of fixed services including voice and non-voice messages and data services, utilizing any type of network equipment, including circuit and/or packet switches, that meet the relevant International Telecommunication Union (ITU)/Telecommunication Engineering Center (TEC) standards.

The FSP shall be granted separate licence, on a non-exclusive basis, for each service area of operation. Licences would be awarded for an initial period of twenty years which shall be extended by additional periods of ten years thereafter. The FSPs shall be eligible to obtain licences for any number of service areas. While market forces will ultimately determine the number of fixed service providers, during transition, number of entrants have to be carefully decided to eliminate non-serious players and allow new entrants to establish themselves.

Therefore, the option of entry of multiple operators for a period of five years for the service areas where no licences have been issued is adopted. The number of players and their mode of selection will be recommended by TRAI in a time-bound manner. The FSP licencees would be required to pay a one time entry fee. All FSP licencees shall pay licence fee in the form of a revenue share.

It is proposed that the appropriate level of entry fee and percentage of revenue share and basis for selection of new operators for different service areas of operation would be recommended by TRAI in a time-bound manner, keeping in view the objectives of the New Telecom Policy. As in the case for cellular, for WLL also, availability of appropriate frequency spectrum as required is essential not only for providing optimal bandwidth to every operator but also for entry of additional operators. It is proposed to review the spectrum utilisation from time to time keeping in view the emerging scenario of spectrum availability, optimal use of spectrum, requirements of market, competition and other interest of public.

The WLL frequency shall be awarded to the FSPs requiring the same, based on the payment of an additional one time fee over and above the FSP entry fee. The basis for determining the entry fee and the basis for assigning WLL frequency shall be recommended by the TRAI. All FSP operators utilising WLL shall pay a licence fee in the form of a revenue share for spectrum utilization. This percentage of revenue share shall be over and above the percentage payable for the FSP licence.

It is proposed that the appropriate level of entry fee and percentage of revenue share for WLL for different service areas of operation will be recommended by TRAI in a time-bound manner, keeping in view the objectives of the New Telecom Policy.

Cable Service Providers (CSP)

Under the provisions of the Cable Regulation Act, 1995, Cable Service Providers (CSP) shall continue to be freely permitted to provide 'last mile' linkages and switched services within their service areas of operation and operate media services, which are essentially one-way, entertainment related services.

Direct interconnectivity between CSP's and any other type of service provider in their area of operation and sharing of infrastructure with any other type of service provider shall be permitted. Interconnectivity between service providers in different service areas shall be reviewed in consultation with TRAI and the same would be announced by August 15, 1999 as a part of the structure for opening up national long distance. In view of convergence, it is highly likely that two-way communication (including voice, data and information services) through cable network would emerge in a significant way in future. Offering of these services through the cable network would tantamount to providing fixed services.

Accordingly, in case the above two-way communication services are to be provided by CSPs utilising their network, they would also be required to obtain an FSP licence and be bound by the licence conditions of the FSPs, with a view to ensure level playing field.

Internet Telephony

Internet telephony shall not be permitted at this stage. However, Government will continue to monitor the technological innovations and their impact on national development and review this issue at an appropriate time.

Radio Paging Service Providers (RPSPs)

RPSP shall be permitted to provide paging services within their service area of operation. Direct interconnectivity between licenced RPSPs and any other type of service provider in their area of operation including sharing of infrastructure shall be permitted. Interconnectivity between service providers in different service areas shall be reviewed in consultation with TRAI and the same would be announced by August 15, 1999 as a part of the structure for opening up of national long distance.

The RPSP shall be granted separate licence, on a non-exclusive basis, for each service area of operation. Licences would be awarded for an initial period of twenty years and will be extended by additional periods of ten years thereafter.

For this purpose, the service areas would be categorized as per the existing structure. The RPSP shall be eligible to obtain licences for any number of service areas. Availability of adequate radio frequency spectrum is essential not only for providing optimal bandwidth to every operator but also for entry of additional operators.

It is proposed to review the spectrum utilisation from time to time keeping in view the emerging scenario of spectrum availability, optimal use of spectrum, requirements of market, competition and other interest of public. The entry of more operators in a service area shall be based on the recommendation of the TRAI who would review this as required and no later than every two years.

The radio paging licencees shall pay a one time entry fee. The basis for determining the entry fee and the basis for selection of additional operators will be recommended by the TRAI. All radio paging licencees shall pay licence fee as a revenue share. It is proposed that the appropriate level of entry fee and percentage of revenue share for different service areas of operation will be recommended by TRAI in a time-bound manner, keeping in view the objectives of the New Telecom Policy. Further, TRAI may also examine and recommend the revenue sharing arrangements between RPSP and other access providers, subject to technical feasibility.

Public Mobile Radio Trunking Service Providers (PMRTSP)

PMRTSP shall be permitted to provide mobile radio trunking services within their service area of operation. Direct interconnectivity between licenced PMRTSP's and any other type of service provider in their area of operation shall be permitted after examining the legal implications in view of the CMSP licences. The PMRTSP shall be granted separate licence, on a non-exclusive basis, for each service area of operation. Licences would be awarded for an initial period of twenty years and will be extended by additional periods of ten years thereafter.

For this purpose, the service areas would be categorized as per the existing structure. The PMRTSP shall be eligible to obtain licences for any number of service areas. PMRTSP licencees would be required to pay a one time entry fee. The basis for determining the entry fee and the basis for selection of additional operators will be recommended by the TRAI. Apart from the one time entry fee, PMRTSP licencees would also be required to pay licence fee based on a revenue share. It is proposed that the appropriate level of entry fee and percentage of revenue share arrangement for different service areas would be recommended by TRAI in a time-bound manner, keeping in view the objectives of the New Telecom Policy.

National Long Distance Operator

National long distance service beyond service area to the private operators will be opened for competition with effect from January 1, 2000. To promote setting up long distance bandwidth capacity in the country, provide a choice to consumers and promote competition, all NLDOs should be able to access subscribers. With a view to achieve the above, all access providers shall be mandatorily required to provide interconnection to the NLDOs resulting in choice for subscribers to make long distance calls through any operator.

For this purpose, the terms and conditions and other modalities would be worked out in consultation with TRAI and the same will be announced by August 15, 1999. The terms and conditions would also specify the number of operators, licence conditions on revenue sharing basis and other related issues. Usage of the existing backbone network of public and private power transmission companies/Railways/GAIL, ONGC etc., shall be allowed immediately for national long distance data communication and from January 1, 2000 for national long distance voice communications. Resale would be permitted for domestic telephony, announcement for the modalities thereof to be announced along with the opening up of national long distance by August 15, 1999. Resale on international long distance will not be permitted till the year 2004.

International Long Distance Services

The subject of opening up of international telephony service to competition will be reviewed by the year 2004.

Other Service Providers

For applications like tele-banking, tele-medicine, tele-education, tele-trading, e-commerce, other service providers will be allowed to operate by using infrastructure provided by various access providers. No licence fee will be charged but registration for specific services being offered will be required. These service providers will not infringe on the jurisdiction of other access providers and they will not provide switched telephony.

Global Mobile Personal Communication Services

The Government has opened up the GMPCS market in India and has issued a provisional licence. The terms of the final licence would need to be finalised in consultation with TRAI by June 30, 1999. All the calls originating or terminating in India shall pass through VSNL gateway or in case of bypass, it should be possible to monitor these calls in the Indian gateways. VSNL is also to be compensated in case gateway is bypassed.

The GMPCS operators shall be free to provide voice and non-voice messages, data service and information services utilising any type of network equipment, including circuit and/or packet switches that meet the relevant International Telecommunication Union (ITU)/Telecommunication Engineering Center (TEC) standards. However, the licences be awarded after the proposals are scrutinised from the security angle by the Government. The appropriate entry fee/revenue sharing structure would be recommended by TRAI, keeping in view the objectives of the New Telecom Policy.

SATCOM Policy

The SATCOM Policy shall provide for users to avail of transponder capacity from both domestic/foreign satellites. However, the same has to be in consultation with the Department of Space. Under the existing ISP policy, international long distance communication for data has been opened up. The gateways for this purpose shall be allowed to use SATCOM. It has also been decided that Ku frequency band shall be allowed to be used for communication purposes.

VSAT Service Providers

The VSAT Service Providers shall be granted separate licence, on a non-exclusive basis for an initial period of twenty years and will be extended by additional periods of ten years thereafter. Interconnectivity between service providers in different service areas shall be reviewed in consultation with TRAI and the same would be announced as a part of the structure for opening up national long distance by August 15, 1999. The VSAT service providers shall be granted separate licence, on a non-exclusive basis. Licences would be awarded for an initial period of twenty years and will be extended by additional periods of ten years thereafter.

VSAT licencees would be required to pay a one time entry fee. The basis for determining the entry fee and the basis for selection of additional operators will be recommended by the TRAI. Apart from the one time entry fee, VSAT licencees would also be required to pay licence fee based on a revenue share. It is proposed that the appropriate level of entry fee and percentage of revenue share arrangement would be recommended by TRAI in a time-bound manner, keeping in view the objectives of the New Telecom Policy.

Electronic Commerce

On line Electronic Commerce will be encouraged so that information can be passed seamlessly. The requirement to develop adequate bandwidth of the order of 10 Gb on national routes and even terrabits on certain congested important national routes will be immediately addressed to so that growth of IT as well as electronic commerce will not be hampered.

Resolution of Problems of Existing Operators

The New Policy Framework which seeks to significantly redefine the competitive nature of industry, would be applicable to new licensees. There are, however, multiple licences that have been issued by the Government for cellular mobile services, basic services, radio paging services, internet services etc. It is the Government's intention to satisfactorily resolve the problems being faced by existing operators in a manner which is consistent with their contractual obligations and is legally tenable.

Restructuring of DoT

World-wide, the incumbent, usually the Government owned operator plays a major role in the development of the telecom sector. In India, DoT is responsible for the impressive growth in number of lines from 58.1 lakh on April 1, 1992 to 191 lakh in December 1998, showing a CAGR of 20 per cent. DoT is expected to continue to play an important, and indeed, dominant role in the development of the sector. Currently, the licensing, policy making and the service provision functions are under a single authority. The Government has decided to separate the policy and licensing functions of DoT from the service provision functions as a precursor to corporatisation. The corporatisation of DoT shall be done keeping in mind the interests of all stakeholders by the year 2001. All the future relationship (competition, resource raising etc.) of MTNL/VSNL with the corporatised DoT would be based on best commercial principles.

The synergy of MTNL, VSNL and the coporatised DoT would be utilised to open up new vistas for operations in other countries.

Spectrum Management

With the proliferation of new technologies and the growing demand for telecommunication services, the demand on spectrum has increased manifold. It is, therefore, essential that spectrum be utilized efficiently, economically, rationally and optimally.

There is a need for a transparent process of allocation of frequency spectrum for use by a service and making it available to various users under specific conditions. The National Frequency Allocation Plan (NFAP) was last established in 1981, and has been modified from time to time since. With the proliferation of new technologies it is essential to revise the NFAP in its entirety so that it could become the basis for development, manufacturing and spectrum utilization activities in the country amongst all users.

The NFAP is presently under review and the revised NFAP-2000 would be made public by the end of 1999, detailing information regarding allocation of frequency bands for various services, without including security information. NFAP shall be reviewed no later than every two years and shall be in line with radio regulations of International Telecommunication Union. Relocation of existing Spectrum and Compensation: Considering the growing need of spectrum for communication services, there is a need to make adequate spectrum available. Appropriate frequency bands have historically been assigned to defence and others and efforts would be made towards relocating them so as to have optimal utilisation of spectrum. Compensation for relocation may be provided out of spectrum fee and revenue share levied by Government. There is a need to review the spectrum allocations in a planned manner so that required frequency bands are available to the service providers. There is a need to have a transparent process of allocation of frequency spectrum which is effective and efficient. This would be examined further in the light of ITU guidelines. For the present, the following course of action shall be adopted. Spectrum usage fee shall be charged. Setting up an empowered Inter-Ministerial Group to be called as Wireless Planning Coordination Committee (WPCC) as part of the Ministry of Communications for periodical review of spectrum availability and broad allocation policy. Massive computerisation in the WPC Wing will be started during the next three months' time so as to achieve the objective of making all operations completely computerised by the end of year 2000.

Universal Service Obligation

The Government is committed to provide access to all people for basic telecom services at affordable and reasonable prices. The Government seeks to achieve the following universal service objectives: Provide voice and low speed data service to the balance 2.9 lac uncovered villages in the country by the year 2002. Achieve Internet access to all district headquarters by the year 2000. Achieve telephone on demand in urban and rural areas by 2002. The resources for meeting the USO would be raised through a 'universal access levy' which would be a percentage of the revenue earned by all the operators under various licences. The percentage of revenue share towards universal access levy would be decided by the Government in consultation with TRAI. The implementation of the USO obligation for rural/remote areas would be undertaken by all fixed service providers who shall be reimbursed from the funds from the universal access levy. Other service providers shall also be encouraged to participate in USO provision subject to technical feasibility and shall be reimbursed from the funds from the universal access levy.

Role of Regulator

The Telecom Regulatory Authority of India (TRAI) was formed in January 1997 with a view to provide an effective regulatory framework and adequate safeguards to ensure fair competition and protection of consumer interests. The Government is committed to a strong and independent regulator with comprehensive powers and clear authority to effectively perform its functions. Towards this objective the following approach will be adopted: Section 13 of the TRAI Act gives adequate powers to TRAI to issue directions to service providers. Further, under Section 14 of the Act, the TRAI has full adjudicatory powers to resolve disputes between service providers. To ensure a level playing fields, it will be clarified that the TRAI has the powers to issue directions under Section 13 to Government (in its role as service provider) and further to adjudicate under Section 14 of the Act, all disputes arising between Government (in its role as service provider) and any other service provider. TRAI will be assigned the arbitration function for resolution of disputes between Government (in its role as licensor) and any licensee.

The Government will invariably seek TRAI's recommendations on the number and timing of new licences before taking decision on issue of new licenses in future. The functions of licensor and policy-maker would continue to be discharged by Government in its sovereign capacity. In respect of functions where TRAI has been assigned a recommendatory role, it would not be statutorily mandatory for Government to seek TRAI's recommendations.

Other Issues

Standardisation

To enable the establishment of an integrated telecommunication network, common standards with regard to equipment and services would be specified by the Telecom Engineering Centre (TEC). TEC would also continue to grant interconnect and interface approvals for various service providers.

Telecom Equipment Manufacture

With a view to promoting indigenous telecom equipment manufacture for both domestic use and export, the Government would provide the necessary support and encouragement to the sector, including suitable incentives to the service providers utilising indigenous equipment.

Human Resource Development and Training

Human resources are considered more vital than physical resources. Emphasis would be placed on the development of human resources for all fields related to telecommunications and the dispersal of this expertise to the related fields. Such expertise shall also be made available to other countries.

Telecom Research and Development

Recognising that telecommunications is a prime pre-requisite for the development of other technologies, telecommunications Research and Development (R&D) activities would be encouraged.

Government would take steps to ensure that the industry invests adequately in R&D for service provision as well as manufacturing. Indigenous R&D would be actively encouraged with a view to accelerate local industrial growth and hasten transfer of technology. Premier technical institutions would be encouraged to undertake R&D activities on a contribution basis by the telecom service providers and manufacturers so as to develop multi-dimensional R&D activities in telecommunications and information technology.

Disaster Management

International cooperation in the use of terrestrial and satellite telecommunications technologies in the prediction, monitoring and early warning of disasters, especially in the early dissemination of information would be encouraged. Financial commitment to disaster management telephony and the development of appropriate regulatory framework for unhindered use of trans-boundary telecommunications would be put in place.

Remote Area Telephony

Rural Telephony, areas of North-East, Jammu & Kashmir and other hilly areas, tribal blocks, etc., may be identified as a special thrust areas for accelerated development of telecommunications. The Ministry of Defence shall be assigned a more active role in the development of telecommunications in such remote areas as are identified for accelerated development of telecommunications.

Export of Telecom Equipment and Services

Export of telecom equipment and services would be actively incentivised. Synergies among the various telecom players (manufacturers and service providers) would be exploited and used to provide integrated solutions for exports.

Right of Way

Government recognises that expeditious approvals for right-of-way clearances to all service providers are critical for timely implementation of telecom networks. The Central/State Government/Local bodies/Ministry of Surface Transport etc., shall take necessary steps to facilitate the same.

Changes in Legislation

The Indian telecommunications system continues to be governed by the provisions of the Indian Telegraph Act, 1885 (ITA, 1885) and the Indian Wireless Act, 1933. Substantial changes have taken place in the telecommunications sector since 1992. ITA 1885 needs to be replaced with a more forward looking Act.

TELECOM COMMISSION

Guidelines and General Information For Internet Service Provider (ISP)
No. 845-51/97-VAS

Invitation of application(s)/proposal(s) for award of licence(s) for providing internet service (ISP—Internet Service Provider Licence).

On behalf of President of India proposals are invited from Registered Indian Companies for providing Internet Service on a licence on non-exclusive basis.

General and Commercial Information

Eligibility Criteria

This invitation is open to any Indian Registered Company. A Company registered in India under the Companies Act, 1956 will be eligible to submit proposal. Licence to run the service will be issued to the proposer company if found eligible and complies with all the requirements laid down in the application form. Foreign equity, if any, shall be as per the Government policy and guidelines from time to time. At present, the foreign equity is permitted to the extent of 49 per cent. There is no requirement of the applicant company having any prior experience in information technology or telecommunication services.

Service Area

Separate licences shall be granted to any applicant company for each service area. For this purpose, the country has been divided into separate service areas in three categories as mentioned below—

(*i*) *Category "A"*—This covers the territorial jurisdiction of the Union of India except specified areas that may be notified to be excluded from time to time.

(*ii*) *Category "B"*—Any of the 20 Territorial Telecom Circles, four Metro Telephone Districts of Delhi, Mumbai, Kolkata or Chennai and four major telephone districts of Ahmedabad, Bangalore, Hyderabad or Pune are Category 'B' Service areas. The four Metro Telephone Districts (Delhi, Mumbai, Kolkata and Chennai) are not part of any Telecom Circle, whereas the four major Telephone Districts (Ahmedabad, Bangalore, Hyderabad and Pune) are part of respective Telecom Circle.

(*iii*) *Category "C"*—Any Secondary Switching Area (SSA) of DoT with geographical boundaries as on 1.4.98, will form a separate category "C" Service Area with the exception that each of the four Metro Telephone Districts of Delhi, Mumbai, Kolkata and Chennai and of four major Telephone Districts of Ahmedabad, Bangalore, Hyderabad and Pune of the DoT/MTNL with geographical boundaries as on 1.4.1998, will form a separate Category 'B' service area. Applicants will be required to submit separate application for each service area. The ISP will be required to set up his nodes i.e., Routes/servers within the geographical limits of the service area. An applicant company may be granted any number of licences. Also, there shall be no limit on number of licences that can be granted in a particular service area. The leased line subscribers shall be from within the service area. However, the ISP can offer dial up service from any part of the country. Existing E-Mail and VSAT Service Licensees may also obtain separate ISP Licence for any number of the above mentioned service areas subject to fulfilment of eligibility criteria.

Validity of the Application

Each proposal shall be valid for a minimum period of six months from the date of application.

Processing Fee

The proposer shall enclose a DEMAND DRAFT for Rs. 5,000 (Rupees Five Thousand only) in favour of Pay & Accounts Officer, Headquarters, Department of Telecommunications, Sanchar Bhavan, New Delhi-110 001 in respect of each service area, separately with each application towards processing fee. The processing fee is not refundable.

Issue of Licence

Separate licence will be issued for each service area proposed, under relevant provisions of Indian Telegraph Act, 1885, Indian Wireless Telegraphy Act, 1933 and TRAI Act, 1997 and the licensee shall abide by the provisions of the said Acts and the rules made thereunder.

Interconnection with Other Networks

Direct interconnectivity between two separately licensed ISPs shall be permitted. Authorised Public/Government organisations will be allowed to provide INTERNET

Gateway access including international leased circuits directly without going through VSNL Gateways. Private ISPs are allowed to provide such International Gateways after obtaining Security Clearance for which the Interface of Private ISPs shall only be with the Telecom Authority.

The licensee may obtain the transmission link on lease from DoT, Licensed Basic Service Operators, Railways, State Electricity Boards, National Power Grid Corporation or any other operator specially authorised to lease such lines to the ISPs.

The licensee may also establish its own transmission links within its service area for carrying traffic originated and terminated by his subscribers, provided that such capacities are not available from any other authorised agencies and subject to permission of Telecom Authority. An ISP may provide Internet Service to any VSAT subscriber (who could be served by a shared hub commercial service provider or captive private VSAT network), if the VSAT is located within the service area of the ISP. For this purpose, a direct interconnection of VSAT or VSAT-hub through leased line obtained from an authorised provider to the ISP's node/server shall be permitted only for the flow of Internet traffic.

The existing licence for Closed Users Group Domestic 64 KBPS Data Network via INSAT Satellite Systems does not grant long distance carrier rights to the licensee. The ISP shall provide to the Telecom Authority a monthly statement of VSAT subscribers served with their locations and details of leased line interconnection with the VSAT hub. The VSAT hub, however, need not be located in the service area of the ISP. Resources required for interconnecting the licensee's network to the network of upstream internet access providers (DoT/VSNL etc.) or any other service provider licensed by the Authority including time frame for provision of the same, will be mutually agreed between the parties concerned.

The resources may refer to include but not limited to physical junctions, PCM derived channels, private wires, leased lines, data circuits other network elements. The licensee shall apply for and obtain the network resources from the concerned parties. The tariff of such network is outside the scope of this licence agreement. Licensor will have no obligation for such resources from other parties.

Delivery of the Service

The LICENSEE shall be responsible for installation, testing and commissioning of all the equipment to provide the SERVICE including connectivity to DIAS or GIAS or authorised Public/Government Organisations for delivery of Internet traffic. The licensee shall provide service within 18 months from the date of signing of the licence agreement. Commissioning of service will mean providing commercial service to customers.

Extension of Licence

The validity of licence is initially for a period of fifteen years unless otherwise terminated. If requested by the licensee, extension may be granted by the TELECOM AUTHORITY on suitable terms and conditions for a period of five years or more at a time. The decision of the TELECOM AUTHORITY shall be final in this regard.

Technical Requirements

Private ISPs shall use IP (Internet Protocol) and shall meet the technical requirements of the Internet Service Providers (DoT/MTNL/VSNL/other ISPs) to which it is connected. The equipment used by the Private ISP shall be in conformance with the Interface/ Protocol requirements as applicable of the service provider. Some of the interfaces required are given below:

Interface Requirements

(*i*) Subscriber Dial up Access 2 wire access over PSTN for modem interface. 2 wire dial up access on ISDN Basic and Primary rate interfaces.

(*ii*) Leased Line Interface 64K, N x 64K or 2.048 Mb/s, N x 2.048 Mb/s Leased lines. Frame Relay. X.25 ATM G. 703 Access to internet through authorised Cable Operator shall be permitted without additional licensing subject to applicable Cable Laws [The Cable Television Networks (Regulation) Act, 1995] as modified from time to time. 'Last mile' linkages shall be freely permitted within local area either by fibre optic or radio communication for ISPs. In case of radio links, clearance from WPC wing of the DoT shall be required to be obtained by the ISPs to avoid frequency interference.

Quality of Service

The quality of service over internet is not established and defined as yet. As such, the QUALITY OF SERVICE is not being defined for the time being. However, it may be defined at a later date based on the experience gained and inputs from the Internet Engineering Task Force (IETF).

Telephony on the Internet

Telephony on the Internet is not permitted. The licence will be liable for termination for any violation of this clause of the Licence Agreement. The licensee shall also take measures on his own and as and when directed by the Government at his own cost to bar carriage of Telephone Traffic over Internet.

Obscene Material and Applicability of Cyber Laws

Flow of obscene, objectionable, unauthorised or any other content infringing copy-rights, intellectual property right and international and domestic Cyber Laws in any form over the ISP's network is not permitted and the ISP is supposed to take such measures as to prevent it. Any damages/claim arising out of default on the part of the licensee in this respect shall be the sole responsibility of the licensee.

IP Address, Domain Name

It will be the responsibility of the licensee to obtain IP address, domain name etc., from the competent authority. In case the IP addresses are taken from the Department of Telecommunications, the same are non-portable and have to be returned to DoT at the termination of connectivity contract.

Financial Conditions

Quantum of Licence Fee and Schedule of Payments

(*i*) The Telecom Authority has decided to waive the Licence Fee for a period up to 31.10.2003. For those ISPs also who obtain licences prior to 01.11.2003, a nominal licence fee of One Rupee per annum will become payable from 01.11.2003.

(*ii*) For access and other charges including MODEM charges payable to the DoT/MTNL/VSNL/other service provider at the prescribed rates, bills will be raised directly by the DoT/MTNL/VSNL/other service provider and shall be a matter between the Licensee and such service provider(s).

Performance Bank Guarantee (PBG)

A PBG of Rs. 2.00 crores for category 'A' Service Area, Rs. 20.00 lakhs for each category 'B' Service Area and Rs. 3.00 lakhs for each category 'C' Service Area valid for two years from any Scheduled Bank in the prescribed form (Schedule 'D' of the draft Licence Agreement) shall be submitted along with the application for each service area. The licensee will be liable to extend the validity of Performance Bank Guarantee two months prior to its date of expiry on its own without demand from the Licensor for a further period of one year on year to year basis.

On any failure to do so, the performance bank guarantee will be encashed without giving any notice. This is without prejudice to any other action that may be taken under the terms and conditions of the licence.

TARIFF ISPs

TARIFF ISPs will be free to fix their own tariff. The tariff shall be left open to be decided by market forces. However, the TRAI (Telecom Regulatory Authority of India) may review and fix a tariff at any time during the validity of the licence which shall be binding on the Licensee.

RECENT CHANGES IN SERVICE TAX LAW

The Finance Act, 2001 has extended the purview of service tax to 15 new services with effect from 16 July, 2001. This article aims to give a brief idea of the changes in Service Tax Law introduced by the Finance Act, 2001.

Legislative Changes

Self-Assessment

The most significant legislative change made in service tax law relates to the introduction of self-assessment procedure vide amendment of Section 70 of the Finance Act, 1994. Section 71 has also been amended to provide for verification by the Superintendent for correctness of the tax assessed by the assessee on self-assessment basis.

Assessment to be Done by Assistant Commissioner/Deputy Commissioner

Where service tax on any services provided has escaped assessment or has been under assessed, the Assistant Commissioner/Deputy Commissioner of Central Excise is required to pass an order of assessment. In view of the amended provisions, the

Superintendent of Central Excise is not required to pass any order of assessment. He should only refer the matter to the Assistant Commissioner/Deputy Commissioner concerned along with his observation and report.

Application for Registration

Section 69 has been amended to specify that application for registration shall be made to the "Superintendent of Central Excise".

Recovery of Service Tax Dues

Section 73 has been amended to provide for recovery of service tax in the case of erroneous refunds. Further, the power to initiate action for recovery of service tax has been specifically vested with the Assistant Commissioner/Deputy Commissioner of Central Excise.

Rate of Interest

Section 75 has been amended to provide for charging of interest at the rate of twenty-four per cent per annum (instead of the rate of one and half per cent per month) for delayed payment of service tax.

Penalty for Failure to Apply for Registration

A new Section 75A has been inserted to provide for a fixed (non-discretionary) amount of penalty of five hundred rupees for failure to apply for registration.

Penalty for Failure to File Service Tax Return

Section 77 has been amended to provide for a penalty not exceeding rupees one thousand for the failure to file the service tax return within the due date.

Changes in Service Tax Rules, 1994

Insurance Auxilliary Services

In relation to "insurance auxiliary services" provided by the insurance agents, it has been prescribed that the service tax shall be paid by the Insurance Company (Insurer). Notification No. 5/2001—ST refers.

Amendment in Form ST-1

A new column has been inserted in ST-1 form for furnishing PAN number by the assessee. Wherever PAN number has not been allotted or not applied for, same may be indicated in the ST-1 form. Notification No. 5/2001—ST refers.

Extension of Service Tax to Fifteen More Services

The following are the new services, which will be subject to service tax from 16th July, 2001:

(*i*) Scientific and technical consultancy service.
(*ii*) Photography service.
(*iii*) Convention service.

(*iv*) On-line information and database access and/or retrieval.
(*v*) Broadcasting service.
(*vi*) Insurance auxiliary services.
(*vii*) Banking and other financial services.
(*viii*) Port services.
(*ix*) Authorised service station for service or repair of motor-car and two-wheeled motor vehicle.
(*x*) Video tape production service.
(*xi*) Sound recording service.
(*xii*) Telegraph services.
(*xiii*) Telex service.
(*xiv*) Facsimile service.
(*xv*) Leased circuits.

The following clarifications have been issued vide Letter F.No. B.II./I/2000—TRU, dated 9-7-2001:

Scientific and Technical Consultancy Service

Section 65(60) defines "scientific and technical consultancy" as any advice, consultancy, or scientific or technical assistance, rendered in any manner, by a scientist or a technocrat, or any science or technology institution or organisation, to a client, in one or more discipline of science or technology. The taxable service has been defined in clause 72 (za) of Section 65 as "any service provided to a client, by a scientist or a technocrat, or any science and technology institution or organisation, in relation to scientific or technical consultancy".

The taxable service should be understood in the context of its commonly understood meaning and scope. For instance, it would cover consultation, advice or technical assistance provided by a scientist or a technocrat or a science or technology institution on any issue relating to any branch of science and technology. Such consultation may be in the nature of an expert opinion/advice in regard to scientific or technical feasibility or any other scientific or technical aspect of a project, process or design, recommending an apt technology, suggestion for improvement in existing technology or process, providing consultation on any technical problem or about new technology, etc.

Points for Clarification	*Clarification*
Whether services rendered by doctors, medical colleges, nursing homes, hospitals, diagnostic and pathological labs, etc., would come under the purview of the proposed levy.	In common parlance, these categories of service providers are not known as scientists or technocrats or science or technology institutions or organisations. They will not be covered.
Whether public funded research institutions like CSIR, ICAR, DRDO, IITs and IISc Regional Engineering colleges, etc., which are exempt from payment of income-tax are covered under service tax.	Yes. Service tax is liable to be paid when any scientific or technical consultancy service is rendered, whether by public funded institutions or by private agencies.

(*Contd.*)

Points for Clarification	*Clarification*
Whether testing services will be covered under the proposed levy?	Mere testing will not attract service tax. However, in case testing is an integral part of the consultancy, then such activity is part and parcel of the taxable service and no abatement of any kind admissible.
Many public funded research institutions receive grants or aids from the Government for conducting research/project work. Whether such activities would be covered under the levy?	In the facts of this case, no service is rendered to any one. Hence, the question of payment of service tax does not arise. However, if they render service to anyone on payment basis, service tax will be payable on such services.
Whether the service tax will be leviable on consultancy provided to Government departments, public sector undertakings?	If scientific or technical consultancy is provided to a Government department for which consultation fees are received, then service tax would be applicable.

Photography Service

As per Section 65(47), the term "photography" includes still photography, motion picture photography, laser photography, aerial photography and fluorescent photography. The taxable service, as per Section 65(72)(zb), is any service provided, to a customer, by a photography studio or agency in relation to photography, in any manner. Photography studio or agency has been defined as "any professional photographer or a commercial concern engaged in the business of rendering service relating to photography" vide Section 65(48).

The services which will come within the purview of service tax are still photography such as photographing persons or other subjects in studios or other locations, passport or identification photographs, fashion photos; industrial photographs of machine and buildings, etc., photographic service for advertising display, brochures, newspapers advertisement, catalogues; photography of any live event such as weddings, receptions, conventions, fashion shows, sports and news events (excluding news agency services, that is, press photographers are excluded); aerial photography such as photographs of landscape, structures and other surfaces from aircraft or helicopter with the help of cameras mounted on such aircraft or helicopter; laser photography to create holograms; motion picture photography, also known as cinematography to make films, which involves the general composition of a scene; the lighting of the set or location; the choice of cameras, lenses, filters and film stock; the camera angle and movements; and the integration of any special effects; fluorescence photography using ultra-violet rays to irradicate a surface or substance to identify dyes, stains, and markings, specific chemical substances, and fluorescent components in microscope specimens; and any other kind of special photography service. Also covered are the photography services such as restoration of old photographs, processing and developing of photographic films and printing of photographs, etc.

Photography services are rendered by still photography studios, still film processing laboratories, cinematographic studios/labs who undertake motion picture photography and processing of cine films, holography studios (laser photography) who make holograms, aerial photographers, industrial photographers, etc.

The value of taxable service is the gross amount charged from the customer for the service rendered. However, the cost of unexposed photography films sold to the customer is excluded. The service provider claiming benefit of the cost of film should be advised to show them clearly on the invoices along with description and particulars of the film. Otherwise, the claim will not be considered as admissible. No other cost (such as photographic paper, chemicals, etc.) is excluded from the taxable value.

In regard to still photography, Notification No. 6/2001—ST dated the 9th July, 2001, has been issued. Accordingly, service providers who are registered under various States/Municipal laws relating to Shops and Establishments or any other law of state which is in force for the time being for carrying out commercial activity only are liable to service tax. Individual professional photographers and other providing still photography service, but who do not have fixed place of business as a shop or office and who are not registered under these enactment, will not be liable to pay service tax. In essence, service tax is payable by shops and studios, processing and developing labs, etc., and not by the individual photographers.

A point has been raised as to whether the X-ray or the CT scan done using fluorescence photography technique will fall in the category of taxable service. It is clarified that these are not photography studios or agencies in common parlance; so the service provided by them does not come within the ambit of tax.

Convention Services

As per Section 65(19), "convention" has been defined to mean a formal meeting or assembly which is not open to the general public, and does not include a meeting or assembly the principal purpose of which is to provide any type of amusement, entertainment or recreation. As per Section 65(72)(zc), the taxable service is any service provided, to a customer, by a commercial concern in relation to holding of a convention.

Any service provided for holding a conference, seminar, meetings, etc., by a commercial concern will come under the purview of service tax. The service could be in the nature of providing of room/hall for the convention. The services could also include providing other facilities such as video conferencing equipment such as overhead projectors, video-roma (LCD projector), speakers, microphones, technical staff for operating these equipment and stationery, etc., apart from providing space for holding a convention. The charges for such facilities shall also be included in the value of taxable service. In some cases, it may appear that it is same as the service rendered by a "mandap keeper". Apart from the fact that there is a subtle distinction between the type of events, (official, social or business function in the case of mandap keeper as opposed to formal meeting in the case of convention services) it is clarified that the intention is not to charge the service tax twice on the same service. If a service provider is already registered as a mandap keeper and paying service tax, he is not liable to pay service tax again under the category of convention services. Similarly, a convention service is not liable to tax as mandap keeper service also.

A doubt has been raised whether holding of conventions by Chambers of Commerce and Industry for their members would be liable to service tax. In this regard, it is clarified that service tax, in the case of convention services, is applicable only when the service is provided by a commercial concern. If the Chamber of Commerce and Industry is not a commercial concern, then the tax does not apply. The memorandum and articles of association of a Chamber of Commerce & Industry would indicate whether it is a commercial concern or not. It is informed by the Chambers that generally they are not commercial concerns.

On-line Information and Database Access and/or Retrieval

As per Section 65(19), 1994, the term "On-line information and data base access or retrieval" means providing data or information, retrievable or otherwise, to a customer in electronic form through a computer network. The words "data", "information", "electronic form" and "computer network" have the same meanings assigned to them in the Information Technology Act, 2000. As per Section 65(72)(zh), taxable service means any service provided to a customer, by a commercial concern, in relation to on-line information and database access or retrieval or both in electronics form.

The definitions given in the Information Technology Act, 2000 are as follows: "Data" means a representation of information, knowledge, facts, concepts or instructions which are being prepared or have been prepared in a formalised manner, and is intended to be processed, is being processed or has been processed in a computer system or computer network, and may be in any form (including computer printouts, magnetic or optical storage media, punched cards, punched tapes) or stored internally in the memory of a computer.

"Information" includes data, text, images, sound voice, codes, computer programmes, software and data bases or micro film or computer generated microfiche.

"Electronic form" with reference to information means any information generated, sent, received or stored in media, magnetic, optical computer memory, microfilm, computer generated microfiche or similar device.

"Computer network" means the interconnection of one or more computers through:

(*i*) Use of satellite, microwave, terrestrialline or other communication media.
(*ii*) Terminals or a complex consisting of two or more interconnected computers whether or nor the interconnection is continuously maintained.

In the context of this service, it may be relevant to point out the manner in which on-line information and database access/retrieval is generally made available. First, the function of what is commonly known as Internet Service Providers (ISPs). The ISPs provide telecommunication network or gateways necessary to access messages and databases and other information holdings of content providers. The second element is on-line information provision services which includes database services, provision of information on websites, provision of on-line data retrieval services from data bases and other information, to all or limited number of users and provision of on-line information by content providers.

Internet Service Providers (ISPs) provide access to the websites through the computer network and the websites. Websites, in turn, provide the database or information. Some of the well-known ISPs operating in India are VSNL, MTNL, Satyam on-line, Bharti, Tata, RPG, HCl, Wipro, BPL, Mantra on-line, Dishnet. They normally charge the customers on the basis of usage of time (hours). They also provide dedicated lease lines on lump-sum payment basis. Clearly ISPs provide service in relation to on-line information and database access or retrieval. They are an integral part of the internet operations and without their service, the data or information can neither be accessed nor retrieved. They are, therefore, liable to pay service tax on the amount charged from the customers whether on usage time basis or on lease line basis.

As regards paid websites, a few examples of Indian dot companies are, Indianinformer.com, CIIonline.com, Taxindiaonline.com who charge the customer for certain specific information contained in their website either in advance or credit basis. They shall be also liable to pay service tax on the paid services provided by them. It is obvious that where the information is supplied free of charge, no service tax is payable.

Points for Clarification

A question has been raised as to whether e-commerce transactions (other than providing on-line information and data) are covered in the ambit of service tax. It is clarified that in e-commerce transactions, no service of on-line information and database access/retrieval is involved. Therefore, e-commerce transactions will not ordinarily be covered under the service tax net. Normally, the websites do not charge the surfers for information on sale of goods or services offered by them. If at all they do, service tax will be payable on the amount charged for providing the information.

Another point raised relates to applicability of service tax on inter-connectivity services provided by one ISP to another and the charges recovered for such services. It is understood that this is done to inter connect various networks so as to reach the server where the information is stored. It is informed that interconnection of one ISP to another is a commercial and technical arrangement under which service providers connect their equipment, networks and services to enable their customers to have access to the data or information. Through this arrangement, it is the customer of an ISP who ultimately receives on-line information and database access and/or retrieval service. Service tax on the amount charged from him is payable. Therefore, interconnection charges paid by one ISP to another ISP are not liable to service tax.

A question has also been raised whether the cyber cafes will be subject to service tax. It is clarified that the cyber cafes provide only the infrastructure such as computer terminals and internet connection. It is the ISP or websits who provide on-line access or retrieval of information. Therefore, cyber cafes are not liable to pay service tax. Services provided by ISP to cyber café are taxable and the ISP will pay the tax on charges realised from the cyber café.

Broadcasting Service

As per Section 65(13), 1994, "broadcasting" has been defined to have the meaning assigned to it in clause (c) of Section 2 of the Prasar Bharati (Broadcasting Corporation of India) Act, 1990. As per this definition "broadcasting" means the dissemination of any form of communication like sign, signals, writing, pictures, images, and sound of all kind by transmission of electro-magnetic waves through space or through cables intended to be received by the general public either directly or indirectly through the medium of relay stations and all is grammatical variations and cognate expressions shall be construed accordingly. The taxable service is any service provided to a client, by a broadcasting agency or organisation in relation to broadcasting, in any manner.

The service covers both radio broadcasting and television broadcasting. While radio broadcasting is done by the All India Radio or any private radio channel, television broadcasting is done by Doordarshan as well as by Indian and Foreign TV Channels. The broadcasting may be of advertisement, serials/programmes or live events. The client is the person who wants an advertisement to be broadcast or the sponsor of a serial or programme or event who wants the serial or programme or event to be broad cast. The service provider, that is, broadcasting agency or organisation is the AIR, Doordarshan, other Indian TV Channels and foreign TV channels who broadcast the programme in India.

Broadcasting is done either terrestrially or through satellite links. Most of the private TV channels are using satellite links for broadcasting their programmes. The uplinking of the programmes to the satellite is done through VSNL or other earth stations located in India or through other agencies located abroad. The up-linking agencies are not broadcasting agencies and are not liable to service tax in respect of such service. The signals beamed by satellite are received either by Multi System Operators (MSO) or directly by cable operators. In the latter case the cable operator further retransmits the signals to the public (viewers). However, in the case of MSO, they first retransmit signals to the cable operator who in turn retransmits the same to the viewers. The cable TV operator who merely retransmits the programme is not a broadcasting agency or organisation with respect to such retransmitted programmes. The MSO also is not a broadcasting agency to the extent he merely retransmits signals. However, in case the MSO operates a local cable channel such as Spectranet, Siticable, Incable, Sumangali, etc., and broadcasts a programme or serial or advertisement on his own, he would be liable to pay service tax on the amount he charges for the service rendered to his clients in relation to broadcasting of such programmes. It may be noted that there may be instances when cable TV operators themselves undertake to broadcast advertisements Cable television operators have, however, been exempted from the levy of service tax vide notification No. 8/2001—ST.

Broadcasting service is provided by selling time slots. In the case of advertisements, service charges are recovered based on the duration and frequency of advertisement and the time slot (prime time, non-prime time etc.) provided for the advertisement. In the case of serials/programmes/events, service charges are made on the basis of factors such as duration, time slot, etc. However, some free commercial time is provided to the sponsor, which he can sell the same to others. In the case of broadcasting service, the advertisement charges or the sponsorship charges received by the broadcasting agency or organisation are the consideration for the services rendered and service tax is payable on these charges.

In case of foreign satellite TV Channels, their head office may be located outside India. However, they have their branch offices or subsidiary companies located in India. In some cases, they have appointed agents. These branch offices/subsidiary companies/agents act on behalf of these channels, selling time slots and recovering service charges and remitting the same to their head office/holding company/principals as the case may be. In such cases, these branch offices/subsidiary companies/agents are rendering the service in relation to broadcasting and therefore, they are liable to pay the service tax and comply with all other procedural formalities relating to service tax.

In the case of AIR and Doordarshan, the billing for the service rendered is done by the Regional Stations of AIR or Regional Doordarshan Kendras. These Regional Offices will have to be, therefore, registered for payment of service tax and for complying with other procedural formalities.

A doubt has been raised whether Prasar Bharati (AIR and Doordarshan) is liable to pay service tax since under Section 22 of the Prasar Bharati Act, 1990, they are exempt from any income tax or any other tax in respect of any income, profit or gains, accruing or arising out of the Fund of the corporation or any amount received by them. In this regard, it is clarified that the said Section 22 applies only in respect of taxes on income or profit or gains. The exemption is only in respect of direct tax and not in respect of indirect tax. As such the argument that AIR or Doordarshan are not liable to pay service tax is not correct.

4

National Broadband Policy, Radio Communication Laws, Satellite and Cable TV Guidelines

BROADBAND POLICY

Preamble

Recognising the potential of ubiquitous Broadband service in growth of GDP and enhancement in quality of life through societal applications including tele-education, tele-medicine, e-governance, entertainment as well as employment generation by way of high speed access to information and web-based communication, Government have finalised a policy to accelerate the growth of Broadband services.

Demand for Broadband is primarily conditioned and driven by Internet and PC penetration. It is recognised that the current level of Internet and Broadband access in the country is low as compared to many Asian countries. Penetration of Broadband, Internet and Personal Computer (PC) in the country was 0.02 per cent, 0.4 per cent and 0.8 per cent respectively at the end of December, 2003. Currently, high speed Internet access is available at various speeds from 64 kilobits per second (kbps) onwards and presently an always-on high speed Internet access at 128 kbps is considered as 'Broadband'. There are no uniform standards for Broadband connectivity and various countries follow various standards.

Government envision an accelerated growth in Internet penetration and PC as the success of Broadband would largely be dependent on their spread. It has been decided that following shall be the framework of the policy.

Broadband Connectivity

Keeping in view the present status, Broadband connectivity is defined at present as:

> "An 'always-on' data connection that is able to support interactive services including Internet access and has the capability of the minimum download speed of 256 kilo bits per second (kbps) to an individual subscriber from the Point of Presence (PoP) of the service provider intending to provide Broadband service where multiple such individual Broadband connections are aggregated and the subscriber is able to access these interactive services including the Internet through this PoP. The interactive services will exclude any services for which a separate licence is specifically required, for example, real-time voice transmission, except to the extent that it is presently permitted under ISP licence with Internet Telephony."

The estimated growth for Broadband and Internet subscribers in the country envisaged through various technologies is as follows:

Year Ending	Internet Subscribers	Broadband Subscribers
2005	6 million	3 million
2007	18 million	9 million
2010	40 million	20 million

Technology Options for Broadband Services

The Broadband Policy Framework visualises creation of infrastructure through various access technologies which can contribute to growth and can mutually coexist. Spread of infrastructure is a must for healthy competition and therefore, it would be the endeavour of the Government that the telecommunication infrastructure growth in the country is not compromised in any manner.

Various Access Technologies, Inter-alia, are

Optical Fibre Technologies

The fibre optics technology can provide nearly unlimited bandwidth potential and is steadily replacing copper network specially in intra-city backbone networks. This is being deployed in commercial buildings and complexes and some metros/big cities having high-density potential broadband subscribers. Hybrid Fibre Coaxial (HFC), Fibre to the Curb (FTTC) and Fibre to the Home (FTTH) networks make use of fibre cabling into the last mile. The fibre based models are future proof as they are able to provide huge amounts of bandwidth in the last mile as well as provide a true IP and converged network that can deliver high quality voice, data and video.

There are more than 4.5 lakh route kms of optical fibre laid by BSNL/MTNL and more than 1 lakh route kms laid by private operators. The spread of the networks of private service providers have to play an important role in bringing the fibre to homes as well as the rural areas and they are expected to focus on it.

With the increase in commercial availability of fibre technologies, the cost of fibre rollout is approaching the cost of other wired networks. Spread of optical fibre networks shall be emphasised keeping in view the long-term perspective.

Digital Subscriber Lines (DSL) on Copper Loop

DSL has proved to be an important technology for provisioning of Broadband services through the copper loop. The owners of copper loop have to be given a high priority because their role is critical as key drivers in the Broadband service market using DSL.

Bharat Sanchar Nigam Limited (BSNL) and Mahanagar Telephone Nigam Limited (MTNL) as well as other access providers are expected to aggressively use their copper loop infrastructure for providing Broadband services through this technology.

Recognising that last mile copper loop is not a 'bottleneck facility' for broadband services, access providers shall be free to enter into mutually agreed commercial arrangements for utilization of available copper loop for expansion of broadband services. The owner of local loop shall be free to decide the areas in which investment is to be made to upgrade the infrastructure for Broadband services. The information regarding the areas in which Broadband services are being offered by a service provider shall be available in the public domain.

Further, use of brand-name being treated as a part of the value shall be permitted in such commercial arrangements.

There are more than 40 million copper loops in the country available with BSNL and MTNL out of which 14 million loops are in rural areas. Copper cable network of these operators is a combination of old and new cable and this makes provisioning of Broadband on all the available copper loop technically unfit. Therefore, around 25-30 per cent of the remaining 26 million loops, i.e., approximately 7 million loops can be leveraged for broadband service by BSNL and MTNL taking into account the condition/life of copper cable and demand potential.

Management of BSNL and MTNL has decided to provide 1.5 million connections by the end of 2005. The corporate/work plan of these PSUs have been drawn up for this purpose. Thereafter, annual plan for expansion of Broadband services by BSNL and MTNL will be determined in consultation with them. A quarterly review of their performance by the Government in the Department of Telecommunications (DoT) shall be undertaken to evaluate the achievement and redefine the future roadmap, if necessary.

It is hoped that other access service providers would also provide broadband connections using their copper in a targeted manner. A constructive review of their performance shall also be undertaken.

Cable TV Network

It is noted that cable TV connection as last mile infrastructure reaches more people than even the telephone copper infrastructure and can be leveraged in providing cable operators a new business model while giving a stimulus to Broadband penetration. Therefore, Cable TV network can be used as franchisee network of the service provider for provisioning Broadband services. However, all responsibilities for ensuring compliance of terms and conditions of the licence shall vest with the Licensee. The terms of franchise agreement between Licensee and his franchisee shall be settled mutually by negotiation between the two parties involved.

Satellite Media

Very Small Aperture Terminals (VSAT) and Direct-to-Home (DTH) services would be encouraged for penetration of Broadband and Internet services with the added advantage to serve remote and inaccessible areas.

It is the intention of the Government to make available transponder capacity for VSAT services at competitive rates after taking into consideration the security requirements. Department of Space is already interacting with VSAT service providers. Department of Telecommunications, in consultation with the concerned Ministries, will soon propose measures in the direction of Open Sky Policy for VSAT operators. The role of Department of Space is critical in such an endeavour.

VSAT service providers are permitted to transmit data upto 2Mbps instead of earlier limit of 512 kbps in a Closed User Group domestic VSAT network. The increased data rate allows new applications like bulk data transfer for software industry, high-speed backhaul links, in-house training using audio-visual etc. Reduction in antenna size enables easy installation, lower space occupancy, lower cost of hardware etc. Accordingly, the antenna size has been reduced to 1.2 metres and 2.4 metres for star network and mesh network respectively in extended C-band. In Ku-band also, 1 metre diameter antenna in star network has been permitted. To keep pace with technological advances, this shall be periodically reviewed.

Commercial VSAT service providers having ISP licence shall be permitted use of same hub station and remote station to provide Internet service directly to the subscribers. Further, this remote station shall be permitted to be used as a distribution point to provide Internet services to multiple independent subscribers. Necessary amendments in the licence agreement shall be carried out immediately.

DTH service providers shall be permitted to provide Receive Only Internet Service after obtaining ISP licence from Department of Telecommunications. Further, ISP licensees shall be permitted to allow customers for downloading data through DTH after obtaining necessary permission from the competent authority. DTH Service providers will also be permitted to provide bidirectional Internet services after obtaining VSAT and ISP licence from DoT.

Terrestrial Wireless

Recognising that terrestrial wireless is another upcoming technology platform for Broadband, it has been decided in principle to de-licence 2.40-2.48 GHz band for low-power outdoor use on non-protection, non-interference and non-exclusive basis. Necessary notification shall be issued. Further, notification regarding delicensing 2.40-2.4835 MHz band for low power indoor permitting use of all technologies, which inter-alia include those based on IEEE 802.11b and 802.11g standards, has been issued.

To accelerate penetration of Broadband and Internet, the 5.15-5.35 GHz band shall be delicensed for the indoor use of low power Wi-Fi systems. For outdoor use, the band 5.25-5.35 GHz shall be de-licensed in consultation with DoS and delicensing in the band 5.15-5.25 GHz would be considered after the process of vacation. Alternative spectrum bands which are not in high usage and could be deployed for Broadband services, shall also be explored and identified.

Future Technologies

In the changing technology scenario, there is a possibility of new options being used for provisioning of Broadband services. These technologies can also be utilised for provisioning of such services within the licensing framework of the service provider and the spectrum management policy of DoT.

Quality of Service (QoS)

As per TRAI Act, 1997, TRAI has to prescribe QoS parameters. Government recognises that QoS parameters are extremely important and have an impact on investment and roll-out decisions of operators. TRAI would be requested to prescribe QoS parameters for provisioning of broadband service using various access technologies at an early date.

Simplification of SACFA/WPC Clearance

The VSAT operators shall be allowed to start the installation process for VSAT terminals after a period of one month of submitting all relevant documents to WPC for SACFA/WPC clearance wherever the total height of such installation is less than 5 meters above the rooftop of an authorised building.

In the case of Receive Only VSAT terminals and DTH with Receive Only Internet, no SACFA/WPC clearance will be required wherever the total height of such installation is less than 5 meters above the rooftop of an authorised building.

Government have decided that the reference to WLL in IND49 of NFAP-2002 shall be deleted to promote use of indigenously developed technologies. This would enable service providers, other than basic service operators, to use the 1880-1900 MHz band for provision of various services under their licence.

A transparent scheme is being outlined separately for time-bound frequency allocation, siting clearance and wireless licensing by removing the cumbersome procedures, computerisation and by setting predetermined standards.

Other Issues

Bandwidth availability including international bandwidth is a major driver for broadband services. In a competitive environment, service providers are expected to take appropriate steps for making required bandwidth available in a time bound manner within their licence framework. Cost of bandwidth constitutes a major cost component for Broadband services. Government and TRAI would address this issue on priority. TRAI has already issued a consultation paper for international bandwidth leased line cost and is expected to address the issue shortly.

Government have recently decided to reduce the licence fee for Infrastructure Provider category-II, who provides end to end bandwidth, to 6 per cent of Adjusted Gross Revenue (AGR). Further, the amount of bank guarantee for such service provider has also been reduced to Rs. 5 crores from Rs. 100 crores.

National Internet Exchange of India (NIXI) has been set up by DIT, Government of India to ensure that Internet traffic, originating and destined for India, should be routed within India. It is expected that NIXI will take appropriate steps for increasing the utilization of such facilities.

Role of Other Agencies

PCs, content and applications are important constituents for overall growth of Internet and Broadband services. Broadband services will accelerate decentralised governance at Panchayat level.

The role of other facilitators such as electricity authorities, Departments of ITs of various State Governments, Departments of Local Self-Governments, Panchayats, Department of Health and Family Welfare, Department of Education is very important to carry the advantage of Broadband services to the users particularly in rural areas.

Fiscal Issues

The Department of Telecommunications assigns a very high priority to indigenous manufacture of Broadband related equipments. It shall endeavour to work closely with the concerned Ministries and Manufacturers' Associations so that the equipments are available at an affordable price. The department is conscious of the fact that Broadband services can reach the urban and rural consumers only if services are offered at affordable and easy terms. Department of Telecommunications will work out a package in consultation with Ministry of Finance and related Departments as well as concerned service providers to achieve this.

PRESS INFORMATION BUREAU

ISP Licensing Conditions Amended to Permit VPN Services

New Delhi,
November 10, 2004

The Department of Telecommunications today decided to extend the scope of the Licence conditions of Internet Service Providers (ISP), thereby allowing them to provide managed 'Virtual Private Network' service to corporates and individuals.

In accordance with the decision, the ISP licences (both-Licence without Internet Telephony and with Internet Telephony) will have an enabling provision for VPN services by ISP's of under specified terms and conditions. The annual licence fee will be at 8 per cent of the Gross Revenue generated under the licence. There will be one time non-refundable entry fee of Rs. 10, 2 and 1 crore for Category A, B and C ISP's respectively. 'ISP with VPN' licencee will be permitted to lay optical fibre cable or use radio links for provision of the services under their licence in its Service Area. Further, ISPs shall be free to enter into mutually agreed commercial agreement with infrastructure service providers for sharing of infrastructure. The ISPs shall not engage in reselling bandwidth directly or indirectly. The above decision will help as many 388 ISP Licencees, more particularly 61 all India (Category A) ISP Licencees, to offer VPN services to their customers, thus adding to their revenue stream from Internet Access Services.

VPN is a service where a customer perceivers to have been provided with a private network which actually is configured over a shared public network. Benefits of VPN include secure communication over public network and guaranteed quality of service. A High Level DoT Committee had examined the matter and had observed that while on one hand such VPN services were not under the scope of the present ISP licences, on the other hand, it would be desirable to permit ISPs to provide such services in the present day liberalized telecom environment in the country. The services which are technologically possible should be allowed while at the same time ensuring level playing field to all the service providers. Such VPN services which provide a platform for utilization of bandwidth in a very cost-effective and efficient manner are emerging services internationally. This facility is inter-office connectivity to send/transfer data securely and such services are widely available in telecom sector globally.

INTERNET DOMAIN NAME — POLICY FRAMEWORK AND IMPLEMENTATION

Background

Globally, there are approximately 60 million Internet domain names registered. Of these, about 40 million are in generic top level domain (gtld) category, while the remaining 20 million are in country code top level domain (cctld) category. The administration of gtld rests with the Internet Corporation for Assigned Names and Numbers (ICANN), an internationally organized non-profit corporation, with membership from different countries and experts in the field. The responsibility for administration of cctld, on the other hand, has been entrusted to the individual countries who in general follow the guidelines provided by ICANN. These Internet domain names are used by the user entities to identify them in the networked Internet space. In the gtld category, .com and .net domains are the most popular, and have registered in largest numbers. In recent times, the cctld domain registrations are growing with the countries playing active role in the Internet space.

The system of registration of Internet domain names can facilitate the proliferation of Internet in a country. The number of registrations of Internet domain names in a country is also a measure of its popularity in the Internet space. Many countries have therefore adopted liberal and market friendly policies to register large number of Internet domain names under their country code, broadly consistent with global policy and procedures of domain registration. Recently, some of the countries have brought about significant changes to their registration policies and procedures, which has led to a substantial increase in the number of domains registered in a short period of time.

In India, just under 7000 domains have been registered by the Registry at 2nd and 3rd levels under .IN country code over the past decade or so. In addition, the Internet Service Providers (ISPs) have registered about 500,000 .IN domain names at the 3rd level. This number does not truly represent the penetration of Information Technology (IT) in India when compared with a number of companies and public institutions engaged in IT and IT enabled Services (ITeS). The slow growth of .IN domain has been adjudged to be largely due to the absence of contemporary processes and infrastructure, and an over cautious registration policy followed.

The National Centre for Software Technology (NCST), now merged into the Centre for Development of Advanced Computing (C-DAC), was the de facto Registry for .IN domain up to 1997, and became de jure Registry subsequently.

It is widely recognised that .IN domain name has untapped growth potential. A proactive policy for .IN domain proliferation can establish the .IN as a globally recognized symbol of India's growth and developments in the area of information technology.

Adopting New Policy Framework

Internet domain names have assumed greater significance in the recent times with Internet increasingly being used as an effective medium for commerce, education, governance and communication. In order, therefore, to have a larger presence in the Internet space, a forward looking policy for registration under country code Top Level

Domain (ccTLD) will help in its proliferation as all Indian residents, government entities, public service organizations and businesses will be able to establish their Indian identity in the Internet space with a short and unique domain name.

A policy would mainly determine how conveniently a ccTLD name could be registered and maintained for the large number of Internet subscribers and addresses. It will need to address, among other questions, the following:

- What are the domains available for registration?
- Are there any restrictions in registering domain names?
- Where can domain names be registered—including whether there is a single source or a distributed chain of Registrars?
- What prices are charged for registration, and what services do registrants receive in turn?
- Why a registrant would prefer to register in ccTLD—rather than a GTLD?
- Is the process of registration simple, efficient and reliable?

Apart from the policy, any Registry would also need to meet the following criteria:

- *Security*: Registries should be resistant to hacking, and must also withstand Denial-of-Service (DoS) attacks. The hardware and software requirements for such secure systems are high.
- *Reliability*: Various user entities—government, businesses, citizens—rely on the Websites and e-mail messaging that domain names enable. A Registry should provide reliable service, with 100 per cent uptime.
- *Scalability*: The Registry infrastructure should accommodate growth without interruptions.
- *Adherence to technical standards*: The Internet functions well only when the concerned agencies collaborate to create and maintain interoperable technical standards. Registry should adhere to such standards and practices announced by ICANN.

Other countries of comparable size and exposure to Information and Communication Technologies (ICT) have adopted a decentralized organizational structure, liberal policies, and a comprehensive dispute resolution mechanism, deployed state-of-the-art infrastructure, and used the private-public partnership to market Domain Name Registration Services (DNS), resulting in phenomenal growth of their country code domain name.

In order, therefore, to proliferate .IN domain name, a policy framework is instituted, which is open and market friendly, to help brand .IN in a big way and achieve its rightful place in the Internet space that it deserves.

IN Domain Name Policy Framework and Implementation

The policy under the new framework for implementation of .IN Registry focuses on creating liberal, efficient and market friendly processes and a distributed organizational structure.

The National Internet Exchange of India (NIXI), a not-for-profit company under Section 25 of Indian Companies Act 1956 promoted by the Department of Information

Technology (DIT) in association with the Internet Service Providers Association of India (ISPAI), has been entrusted with the responsibility of setting up the Registry for .IN country code Top Level Domain name (ccTLD). For this the NIXI will create the .IN Network Information Centre (INNIC) to operate as a Registry for .IN domain in India.

With the implementation of the new policy by INNIC under NIXI, a 100,000 .IN domain name registrations at the end of 1st of its operation year has been targeted, with an average annual growth of 50 per cent over a couple of years thereafter.

Major Policy Elements

The major elements of the new policy are as follows:

1. Unlimited generic .IN registration will be open to public at 2nd level.
2. Unlimited generic 3rd level registrations will also be open to public, e.g., in certain popular zones like .co.in, .net.in, .org.in, etc.
3. The zones .gov.in, .mil.in and .ac & .edu.in will be reserved for the Government, Defence and Educational institutions respectively. The registrations at the 3rd level in these zones will be carried out by the Government, or an institution identified by the Government. Taking into account the Internet services offered in their respective sectors, .gov.in registration will be handled by NIC, .ac.in & .edu.in by ERNET and .mil.in by a Defence organization suggested by the Ministry of Defence (MoD), as Registrars in these zones.
4. State Governments and Union Territories can register under .gov.in category. They are also free to register at 2nd level using a two letter nomenclature adopted by the Transport Department. The City administrations will be open to register at 3rd level either with the State or under .gov.in category.
5. One or two character domain registration will not be allowed at the 2nd and 3rd levels for use by the general public.
6. Prior to the opening of registration at 2nd/3rd levels, following category of names will be reserved:
   - Constitutional Authorities
   - States/Union Territories/Cities
   - Specific Names for Registry use
7. Trademark owners, registered companies and owners of intellectual property have a legitimate interest in protecting their brand. In the Internet domain, it is achieved by having a "Sunrise Period". A Sunrise period of 90 days from the opening of registration at 2nd/3rd levels will be announced during which genuine registrations with proper verification will be allowed as per the policy for these registrations, with first preference given to Indian entities. Thereafter, the registrations will be open to public on first come first served basis.
8. The .IN Registry will have authority to deny or suspend the registration to any one if it conflicts with the sovereign national interest or public order.
9. The .IN Registry may also open newly created generic top level zones, e.g., .biz, .info, .coop, .pro, for offering registrations under these categories under .IN domain name.

10. A comprehensive Dispute Resolution Policy (DRP) will be adopted in line with internationally accepted guidelines prescribed by the World Intellectual Property Organization (WIPO) and Universal Dispute Resolution Policy (UDRP) adopted by the ICANN. This will be in line with the relevant provisions of the Indian IT Act, 2000.
11. Any dispute involving the .IN Registry will be considered by a duly appointed Dispute Resolution Committee.
12. The .IN Registry would also appoint Arbitrators, through a process of open selection, who can be approached by any aggrieved party(ies) for redressal of grievance with the Registrars. The decision of the Arbitrator shall be binding on both the parties. A Service Fee will be prescribed which will be required to be paid to the Arbitrator by the aggrieved party for such arbitration.
13. Government of India will be the final authority for .IN domain name policy. This will ensure its administration in accordance with the public interest and relevant laws of the country.

Institutional Framework

The following will be the institutional framework of the .IN Registry:

1. The .IN Registry will be a Not-for-Profit organization, and will function as an autonomous body, accountable to the Government. Its responsibility will be to maintain .IN domain to ensure its operational stability, reliability and security.
2. An executive order through a gazette notification will be issued by the Department of Information Technology (DIT), Government of India according a legal status to the Registry for .IN domain in India. It will also mention the role of National Informatics Centre (NIC), ERNET and the nominated Defence Organization as Registrars for handling .gov.in, .edu.in & .ac.in and .mil.in registrations respectively.
3. The .IN Registry by itself will not carry out registrations. It will do so through a number of Registrars to be appointed by it through an open process of selection on the basis of transparent eligibility criteria.
4. The Registrars will either be an ISP themselves who are connected to the National Internet Exchange of India (NIXI), or use the services of such ISP who is connected to NIXI.

Implementation Mechanism

The implementation mechanism for registration by the .IN Registry will be as under:

1. The Registrars appointed by the Registry will pay a one time non-refundable entry fee of Rs. 50,000.
2. The Registrars will, in addition, deposit a minimum amount of Rs. 25,000 in their account with the Registry based on which they will be authorized to perform domain name transactions and continue to do so as long as they had amount in their account with the Registry. Once the amount deposited is exhausted, they would automatically be disabled to perform transactions until they have

replenished their account. The minimum amount for replenishment will be Rs. 25,000.

3. The Registrars will be charged Rs. 500 per domain name for 2nd level and Rs. 250 for 3rd level domain name by the Registry for registration valid for a period of one year. A Registrar may also register a domain name up to a maximum of 5 years by paying the applicable registration amount of Rs. 2500 or Rs. 1250 respectively to the .IN Registry.
4. The .IN Registry in consultation with the Government will review the .IN domain name pricing structure as and when necessitated.
5. The Registrars, on the basis of their agreement with the Registry, will market and sell the .IN domain name, and provide requisite services to the registrants using competitive pricing policy and best market practices.
6. The entire registration process will be on-line, including any document submission, and payment for registration. The .IN domain name will be registered within 24 hours of the request from the registrant, and the .IN Registry will put in place procedures to ensure that the Registrars do not unduly delay transmission of registration requests from the registrants to the Registrar.
7. The .IN Registry will have a 24/7 state-of-the-art technical infrastructure for .IN domain name registration for maintenance of data bases and providing requisite registration services in conjunction with the Registrars.
8. The .IN Registry will approach Government Departments, service organizations, businesses etc., to progressively adopt .IN domain name by them for their websites and personnel.

RADIO COMMUNICATION LAWS

Consultation on a New Fee and Licensing Regime for Cellular and Incumbent Personal Communications Services (PCS) Licensees

APPENDIX D

Sample PCS Auction Spectrum Licence (existing)
Account No. 07–0XXX000

Spectrum Licence

Issued under the authority of the Minister of Industry in accordance with the Radiocommunication Act and Regulations made thereunder.

Appendix

The following conditions of licence apply to licensees for radio frequency spectrum licensed through the auction of additional PCS spectrum in the 2 GHz frequency range. Please note that under paragraph 5(1)(b) of the Radiocommunication Act the Minister of Industry may amend the terms and conditions of a spectrum licence. Any proposed amendment would be on an exceptional basis, and only following a full consultation.

Licence Term

The term of this licence will be ten years from the date of licence issuance. At the end of this term and any subsequent terms, the licensee will have a high expectation of renewal for a further ten-year term unless a breach of licence condition has occurred, a fundamental reallocation of spectrum to a new service is required, or an overriding policy need arises.

A public consultation regarding the renewal of the licence will commence no later than two years prior to the end of the licence term if the Department foresees the possibility that it will not renew this licence or if renewal fees are contemplated.

It should be noted that the licence is subject to relevant provisions in the Radiocommunication Act and the Radiocommunication Regulations. For example, the Minister continues to have the power to amend the terms and conditions of the spectrum licence (paragraph 5(1)(b) of the Radiocommunication Act). Such powers would be exercised on an exceptional basis, and only after full consultation.

Licence Transferability and Divisibility

The licensee may transfer its licence(s) in whole or in part (divisibility), in both the bandwidth and geographic dimensions. The area transferred in the geographic dimension may be no smaller than a single spectrum grid cell. A spectrum grid cell is a six-sided figure with an area of 25 square kilometres. The grid cells fit together in an interlocking pattern over the geography of Canada. No minimum limit will be imposed on the amount of spectrum transferred in the bandwidth dimension.

For each proposed transfer of this licence, the licensee must provide a written notification to the Department. The transferee(s) must also provide an attestation (or other appropriate documentation) that it meets the eligibility criteria and all other conditions of this licence. The Minister of Industry reserves the right, prior to transferring the licences, to request additional documentation to determine if the transferee(s) complies with the appropriate eligibility requirements. The transferee(s) must also provide an attestation (or other appropriate documentation) that it will meet the appropriate conditions of licence.

For the purposes of this condition, the "transfer" of a licence includes any leasing, subleasing or other disposition of the rights and obligations of the licence.

Spectrum Aggregation Limit

The licensee must comply with the spectrum aggregation limits outlined in Radio Systems Policy 021 (RP-021), *Revision to the PCS Spectrum Cap and Timing for Licensing Additional PCS Spectrum*, published November 5, 1999. The spectrum aggregation limit within a service area consists of spectrum licensed to the licensee and to its affiliates. The licensee must notify the Minister of any change that would have a material effect on its compliance with these spectrum aggregation limits. Such notification must be made in advance for any proposed transactions within its knowledge.

Eligibility Criteria

The licensee will employ the radio frequencies that are the subject of this licence as a radiocommunication carrier in order to operate one or more interconnected radio-based transmission facilities (any radio apparatus that is used for the transmission or reception of intelligence to or from anywhere on a public-switched network) that may be used by the licensee or another person to provide radiocommunication services for compensation.

The licensee acting as a radiocommunication carrier must comply on an ongoing basis with the eligibility criteria in sub-section 10(2) of the *Radiocommunication Regulations*. The licensee must notify the Minister of Industry of any change that would have a material effect on its eligibility. Such notification must be made in advance for any proposed transactions within its knowledge. For more information, refer to Client Procedures Circular 2-0-15 CPC-2-0-15), *Canadian Ownership and Control*, as amended from time to time.

Displacement of Incumbent Microwave Licensee

The licensee must comply with the revised transition policy outlined in Appendix 2 of the *Policy and Licensing Procedures for the Auction of Additional PCS Spectrum in the 2 GHz Frequency Range* issued June 28, 2000, and relocation procedure for the relocation of incumbent microwave stations outlined in Client Procedures Circular 2-1-09 (CPC-2-1-09), *Displacement of Fixed Service Stations Operating in the 2 GHz Frequency Range to Accommodate Licensed Personal Communications Services (PCS).*

Radio Station Installations

For each radio station, the licensee must ensure that:

- radio stations are installed and operated in a manner that complies with Health Canada's limits of human exposure to radiofrequency electromagnetic fields;
- where applicable, antenna structures are marked in accordance with the recommendations of Transport Canada;
- prior to installation of significant antenna structures, consultation with the appropriate landuse authorities has taken place;
- installation of any significant antenna structure must be delayed for a period of time sufficient for departmental review where, after considering reasonable alternatives and consultation options, land-use consultation negotiations remain at an impasse; and
- radio installations are installed and operate in a manner that complies with technical boundary and out-of-band emission conditions as specified by the Department.

Refer to the document *Environmental Process, Radiofrequency Fields and Land-Use Consultation* (CPC-2-0-03), as amended from time to time.

Provision of Technical Information

When the Department requests technical information on a particular station or on a network, the information must be provided by the licensee to the Department according to the definitions and criteria specified by the Department. Refer to Client Procedures Circular 2-1-10 (CPC-2-1-10), *Licensing of Personal Communications Services (PCS) in the 2 GHz Band.*

Laws, Regulations and Other Obligations

The licensee is subject to, and must comply with, the *Radiocommunication Act*, the *Radiocommunication Regulations* and the International Telecommunication Union (ITU) *Radio Regulations* and *Canadian Table of Frequency Allocations* pertaining to its licensed radio frequency bands. The licence(s) is (are) issued on condition that the certifications made in the application materials are all true and complete in every respect.

Technical Considerations

The licensee must comply with the technical requirements set forth in Standard Radio System Plan 510 (SRSP-510), *Technical Requirements for Personal Communications Services in the Bands 1850-1910 MHz and 1930-1990 MHz*, and must deploy equipment certified under Radio Standards Specification 133 (RSS-133), 2 GHz Personal Communications Services. SRSP-510 provides information on channelling plans, out-of-block emission limits, permissible effective isotropic radiated power (EIRPs) and antenna heights. RSS-133 sets out standards for transmitters and receivers for PCS in the 2 GHz band.

International and Domestic Coordination

The licensee must comply with the requirements of cross-border sharing and coordination arrangements established between Canada and the United States, as amended from time to time. While frequency assignments are not subject to site by site licensing, licensees may be required to furnish all necessary technical data to Industry Canada for each relevant site in order for international coordination to be effected with the United States as per the terms of any existing or future sharing arrangement. Should international coordination be required, Industry Canada will identify the appropriate data elements, format and means of submission.

Coordination between licensees within Canada will follow similar procedures as those for international coordination.

Lawful Interception

Licensees using the spectrum for circuit-switched voice telephony systems must, from the inception of service, provide for and maintain lawful interception capabilities as authorized by law:

- The requirements for lawful interception capabilities are provided in the Solicitor General's *Enforcement Standards for Lawful Interception of Telecommunications* (Rev. Nov. 95). These standards may be amended from time to time, following consultation with the Solicitor General of Canada and the licensees.
- Licensees may request the Minister to forbear from enforcing certain assistance capability requirements for a limited period. The Minister, following consultation with the Solicitor General of Canada, may exercise his power to forbear from enforcing a requirement or requirements where, in the opinion of the Minister, the requirement(s) is (are) not reasonably achievable. Request for forbearance must include specific details and dates when compliance to requirement(s) can be expected.

Research and Development

The licensee must invest, as a minimum, 2 per cent of its adjusted gross revenues resulting from its operations in this spectrum, over the term of the licence, in eligible research and development activities related to telecommunications. Eligible research and development activities are those that meet the definition of scientific research and experimental development adopted in the *Income Tax Act*. Adjusted gross revenues are defined as total service revenues, less inter-carrier payments, bad debts, third-party commissions, and provincial and goods and services taxes collected.

If the licence is transferred to any eligible entity prior to the expiration of its term, the condition of licence relating to investment in research and development will continue to apply on the initial transfer of the licence and on any subsequent transfer until the term of this licence expires. Prior to a transfer, in whole or in part, of this licence, the proposed transferee must undertake to ensure that the sum of the investment it will make in eligible research and development activities and all investments made by prior licensees in eligible research and development activities equal, as a minimum, 2 per cent of the aggregated adjusted gross revenues resulting from all operations in this spectrum, over the term of the licence. An attestation signed by the proposed transferee setting out the undertaking must accompany the licence transfer notification to be submitted to the Department by the licensee prior to the transfer being effected.

To facilitate compliance with this condition of licence, the licensee should consult the Department's Guidelines for Compliance with the Radio Authorization Condition of Licence Relating to Research and Development. Further details on the exact administrative procedures for transferring a spectrum licence will be provided in a forthcoming Client Procedures Circular.

PCS Resale

Licensees must offer PCS resale throughout their service area to other PCS licensees on a non-discriminatory basis.

Implementation of Spectrum Usage

Within five years of the auction's close, the licensee must demonstrate to the Department that the spectrum has been put into use. The establishment of coverage to 50 per cent of the population within the licensed service area, or some other indicator of usage that is acceptable to the Department, will be required. Supporting documentation should be submitted to the Manager, Wireless Networks Radiocommunications and Broadcasting Regulatory Branch at the address provided below.

Annual Reporting

The licensee must submit an annual report for each year of the term of the licence indicating continued compliance with all licence conditions, including:

- audited financial statements as required under the licensee's jurisdiction of incorporation, including an audited Statement of Research and Development Expenditures with an accompanying Auditor's Report, prepared in accordance with the same standards of reporting; (to facilitate compliance with this reporting requirement, the licensee should consult the Guidelines for Compliance with the Radio Authorization Condition of Licence Relating to Research and Development published by Industry Canada);

- a copy of any existing corporate annual report for the licensee's fiscal year with respect to the authorization.
- an update on the implementation and spectrum usage within the area covered by the licence.

CITIZEN CHARTER OF RNI

Every citizen publishing, or intending to publish, a newspaper or a periodical, avails the services of the Office of the Registrar of Newspapers for India (RNI). ["Newspaper" means any printed periodical work containing public news or comments on public news.] This Charter is a commitment of RNI to provide to every such person courteous and prompt service in the transparent, equitable and accountable manner.

The following services are provided by RNI:

1. Title verification.
2. Registration of newspapers.
3. Issue of revised/duplicate certificates.
4. Verification of circulation claims.
5. Issue of entitlement certificate for procurement of indigenous newsprint for small/medium newspapers.
6. Authentication of Certificate of Registration for import of newsprint.
7. Issue of essentiality certificate for import of printing machinery/material. Every request for a service shall be acknowledged within seven days of its receipt in the office of RNI.

Receipt of "Ceasing Declarations and Annual Statements will also be acknowledged within the same time limit. Except Registration of a newspaper and verification of circulation claims, all other services shall be provided by RNI within 15 days of receipt of application. With respect to Registration and verification of circulation claims, the time limit shall be 30 days.

In case RNI is not in a position to provide the services within the time limits prescribed a reply indicating reasons therefor shall be given within 15 days of receipt of a request. Every office of RNI will display prominently in its reception area the particulars of officers responsible for various services including redressal of grievances and the time when the public can meet them.

All grievances will be acknowledged within seven days of receipt in RNI. Substantive replies to each grievance will be given within 30 days of its receipt. RNI is always welcome to suggestions for improvement of its services. Suggestions can be sent to the Grievance Officer or dropped in the Suggestion Boxes kept in Reception Areas of its offices.

THE COMMUNICATION CONVERGENCE BILL

A Bill to promote, facilitate and develop in an orderly manner the carriage and content of communications (including broadcasting, telecommunication, and multimedia), for the establishment of an autonomous Commission to regulate all forms of communications, and for establishment of an Appellate Tribunal and to provide for matters connected therewith or incidental thereto.

Whereas it is Considered Necessary

(*i*) to facilitate development of national infrastructure for an information based society, and to enable access thereto;

(*ii*) to provide a choice of services to the people with a view to promoting plurality of news, views and information;

(*iii*) to establish a regulatory framework for carriage and content of communication in the scenario of convergence of telecommunications, broadcasting, data-communication, multimedia and other related technologies and services; and

(*iv*) to provide for the powers, procedures and functions of a single regulatory and licensing authority and of the Appellate Tribunal.

Be it enacted by Parliament in the fifty-second Year of the Republic of India as follows—

CHAPTER I
PRELIMINARY

1. Short Title, Extent and Commencement: (1) This Act may be called the Communication Convergence Act, 2001.

(2) It extends to the whole of India.

(3) It shall come into force on such date as the Central Government may, by notification, appoint and different dates may be appointed for different provisions of this Act and any reference in any such provision of this Act to the commencement of this Act shall be construed as a reference to the commencement of that provision.

2. Definitions: In this Act, unless the context otherwise requires,—

(1) "Adjudicating Officer" means an officer of the Commission appointed as Adjudicating Officer under sub-section (1) of Section 39;

(2) "Appellate Tribunal" means the Communication Appellate Tribunal established under sub-section (1) of Section 43;

(3) "Broadcasting service" means a content application service for providing television programme or radio programme, to persons having equipment appropriate for receiving that service regardless of the means of delivery of that service, but does not include—

(*a*) a service (including a teletext service) that provides only data, or text (with or without associated still images); or

(*b*) a service that makes programmes available on demand on a point-to-point basis, including a dial-up service; or

(*c*) a service, or a class of services, that the Central Government may notify as not being a broadcasting service;

(4) "Chairperson" means the Chairperson appointed under sub-section (4) of Section 7;

(5) "channel" means a set of frequencies used for transmission of a programme;

(6) "Commission" means the Communications Commission of India established under, sub-section (1) of Section 6;

(7) "communication" means the process of conveyance of content through transmission, emission or reception of signals, by wire or other electromagnetic emissions;

(8) "communication service" means a networking service or network application service or value added network application service or a content application service;

(9) "content" means any sound, text, data, picture (still or moving) other audio-visual representation, signal or intelligence of any nature or any combination thereof which is capable of being created, processed, stored, retrieved or communicated electronically".

(10) "content application service" means an application service which provides content meant for the public and includes such other services as may be prescribed;

(11) "frequency" means frequency of electromagnetic waves used for providing a communication service;

(12) "grantee" means a person who has been granted registration under Chapter VII;

(13) "license" means a license granted under Chapter VII or Chapter VIII;

(14) "licensee" means a person who has been granted a license;

(15) "Member" means a Member of the Commission appointed under Section 7 and includes the Chairperson;

(16) "network application service" means the service provided by means of one or more networking services and includes such other services as may be prescribed;

(17) "network infrastructure facilities" means any element or combination of elements of physical infrastructure, which would be utilised by licensees for providing networking services and includes such other facilities as may be prescribed;

(18) "network service" means a service for carrying communications by means of guided or unguided electromagnetic waves and includes such other services as may be prescribed;

(19) "notification" means a notification published in the Official Gazette and the expression "notified", with its cognate meaning and grammatical variation, shall be construed accordingly;

(20) "post" means a post and includes a pole, tower, standard, stay, strut, cabinet, pillar or any above ground contrivance for carrying, suspending or supporting any network infrastructure facility;

(21) "prescribed" means prescribed by rules made by the Central Government under this Act;

(22) "programme" means—television or radio programme including advertising or sponsorship, whether or not of a commercial kind, and broadcast programming shall be construed accordingly;

(23) "programme code" means the code specified under Section 20;

(24) "public authority" means and includes—

(*i*) the Central Government;

(*ii*) a State Government;

(*iii*) any person, agency or organisation engaged in land development for public use, or in roads for public transportation.

(*iv*) any local authorities legally entitled to, or entrusted by the Central or any State Government with, the control or management of any municipal or local fund; and

(*v*) any institution, concern or undertaking or body which is financed wholly or substantially by funds provided directly or indirectly by the Government that may be specified by notification in this behalf by the Central Government.

(25) "public service broadcaster" means any body created by Act of Parliament for the purpose of public service broadcasting;

(26) "registration" means the registration granted under Chapter VII;

(27) "regulations" mean regulations made by the Commission under this Act;

(28) "Secretary-general" means the Secretary-general appointed under sub-section (1) of Section 15.

(29) "service provider" includes any person who provides a communication service;

(30) "spectrum" means a continuous range of continuous electromagnetic wave frequencies upto and including a frequency of 3000 giga hertz;

(31) "Spectrum Manager" means Wireless Advisers to the Government of India notified as Spectrum Manager, Government of India under sub-section (3) of Section 23;

(32) "subscriber of a service" means a person who subscribes to a communication service primarily for his own use;

(33) "Universal Service Obligation"—means obligation as may be prescribed;.

(34) "value added network application service" means the service provided by means of value addition using one or more network application services and includes any article or apparatus as may be prescribed;

(35) "wireless equipment" means any equipment in use or capable of use in wireless communication and includes any article or apparatus as may be prescribed;

(36) "wireless communication" means any communication without the use of wire or cable.

CHAPTER II
REGULATION OF USE OF SPECTRUM, COMMUNICATION SERVICES, NETWORK INFRASTRUCTURE FACILITIES, AND WIRELESS EQUIPMENT

3. Prohibition of Use of Spectrum Without Assignment: No person shall use any part of the spectrum without assignment from the Central Government or the Commission as provided for in this Act.

4. Provision of Services, etc.: (1) No person other than a public service broadcaster shall—

(*a*) own or provide any network infrastructure facility, or

(*b*) provide any networking service, or any network application service or any value added network application service, or any content application service, without a licence or registration:

Provided that all facilities and services exempted from licensing or registration immediately before the commencement of this Act shall continue to be so exempt under this Act, until otherwise notified by the Central Government.

(2) The Central Government may, by notification, exempt any—

(*a*) person, or class of persons; or
(*b*) facility or service, from the provisions of this section.

5. Prohibition of Possession of Wireless Equipment Without a License: (1) No person shall possess any wireless equipment without obtaining a license in accordance with the provisions of this Act:

Provided that the Central Government may, by notification, exempt in the public interest any person or class of persons or any wireless equipment or category of wireless equipment from the provisions of this section.

(2) Nothing contained in sub-section (1) shall apply to—

(*a*) any person or equipment licensed under any law for the time being in force immediately before the commencement of this Act; or
(*b*) any person or equipment exempted from the licensing immediately before the commencement of this Act, until otherwise notified by the Central Government.

CHAPTER III
COMMUNICATIONS COMMISSION OF INDIA

6. Establishment of Commission: (1) With effect from such date as the Central Government may, by notification appoint in this behalf, there shall be established for the purposes of this Act, a Commission, to be known as the Communications Commission of India. The Head Office of the Commission shall be located at Delhi with Regional Offices at Kolkata, Chennai and Mumbai.

(2) The Commission shall be a body corporate by the name aforesaid, having perpetual succession and a common seal with power to acquire, hold and dispose of property, both movable and immovable and to contract, and shall by the said name sue and be sued.

(3) The Commission shall consist of the following Members, namely—

(*a*) a Chairperson;
(*b*) not more than ten persons to be appointed as Members; and
(*c*) the Spectrum Manager, as ex-officio member.

(4) The Chairperson and not less than six Members, (other than the ex-officio Member), shall be whole-time Members and the remaining shall be part time Members.

7. Appointment of Chairperson and Members: (1) The Members (except the ex-officio Member) shall be appointed by the Central Government by notification, from amongst persons recommended by a search committee as may be prescribed.

(2) One-half of the Members shall be appointed from amongst persons of eminence in the fields of literature, performing arts, media, culture, education, films and from persons prominent in social and consumer activities.

(3) One-half of the Members shall be appointed from amongst persons of eminence in the specialized fields such as, telecommunications, broadcasting technology, information technology, finance, management and administration or law.

(4) The Chairperson shall be appointed by the Central Government, by notification, on the recommendation of the search committee referred to in sub-section (1) from amongst persons of eminence in one or more fields enumerated in sub-sections (2) and (3).

(5) Before appointing a person as Chairperson or other Member, the Central Government shall satisfy itself that the person does not have any such financial or other interests as is likely to affect prejudicially his functions as such Member.

(6) A person, who is in the service of Government, shall have to retire or resign from service before entering the office of Chairperson or wholetime Member.

8. Term of Office of Chairperson and Members: (1) The Chairperson and wholetime Members shall hold office for a term of five years from the date on which they enter upon their office or untill they attain age of 65 years whichever is earlier. Provided that the Chairperson and wholetime members shall not be eligible for re-appointment.

(2) The tenure of part time Members shall be such as may be prescribed.

(3) The Chairperson shall have powers of general superintendence and direction in the conduct of affairs of the Commission and shall, in addition to presiding over the meetings of the Commission, exercise and discharge such powers and functions of the Commission as may be assigned to the Chairperson by the Commission.

(4) The Chairperson or any Member of the Communications Commission may resign from his office by giving notice thereof in writing to the Central Government and on such resignation being accepted, the Chairperson or such other Member shall be deemed to have vacated office.

9. Removal from Office of Chairperson and Members: The Central Government may remove from office any member who—

(*a*) has been adjudged insolvent, or

(*b*) has been convicted of any offence, which in the opinion of the Central Government involves moral turpitude; or

(*c*) has become physically or mentally incapable of acting as a Member, or

(*d*) has acquired such financial or other interest as is likely to affect prejudicially his functions as Chairperson or other Member; or

(*e*) has so abused his position as to render his continuance in office prejudicial to the public interest.

No such member shall be removed from his office under clause (d) or clause (e) above unless he has been given a reasonable opportunity of being heard in the matter.

10. Salary and Allowances of Chairperson and Members: The salary and allowances payable to, and the other terms and conditions of service of the Chairperson and Members shall be such as may be prescribed:

Provided that neither the salary and allowances nor the other terms and conditions of service of the chairperson or a member shall be varied to their disadvantage after appointment.

11. Vacancy or Defect not to Invalidate Proceedings: No act or proceeding of the Commission shall be invalidated merely by reason of—

(*a*) any vacancy in, or any defect in the constitution of, the Commission; or

(*b*) any defect in the appointment of a person acting as a Member; or

(*c*) any irregularity in the procedure of the Commission not affecting the merits of the case.

12. Functions of Regional Offices: The Regional Offices of the Commission at Kolkata, Mumbai and Chennai will perform such functions as may be determined by regulation ***.

13. Meetings of Commission: (1) The Commission shall meet at such times and places and shall observe such procedure in regard to the transaction of business at its meetings as may be provided by regulations.

(2) A Member (other than the Chairperson) shall be deemed to have vacated his or her office if he absents himself for three consecutive meetings of the Commission without the leave of the Chairperson.

(3) The Chairperson or, if he is unable to attend a meeting of the Commission, any other Member nominated by the Chairperson in this behalf and, in the absence of such nomination or where there is no Chairperson, any other Member chosen by the Members present from among themselves shall preside at the meeting of the Commission.

14. Power of Commission to Regulate its Procedure: (1) The Commission shall have, for the purposes of discharging its functions under this Act, the same powers as are vested in a civil court under the Code of Civil Procedure, 1908, while trying a suit, in respect of the following matters, namely—

(*a*) summoning and enforcing the attendance of any person and examining him on oath;
(*b*) requiring the discovery and production of documents;
(*c*) receiving evidence on affidavits;
(*d*) issuing commissions for the examination of witnesses or documents;
(*e*) subject to the provisions of Sections 123 and 124 of the Indian Evidence Act, 1972, requisitioning any public record or document or a copy of such record or document, from any office;
(*f*) dismissing an application for default or deciding it, ex-parte;
(*g*) setting aside any order of dismissal of any application for default or any order passed by it, ex-parte; and
(*h*) reviewing its decisions;
(*i*) granting interim relief; and
(*j*) any other matter which may be prescribed.

(2) Every proceeding before the Commission shall be deemed to be judicial proceeding within the meaning of Sections 193 and 228, and for the purposes of Section 196, of the Indian Penal Code and the Commission shall be deemed to be a civil court for the purposes of Section 195 and Chapter XXVI of the Code of Criminal Procedure, 1973.

(3) The Commission shall not be bound by the procedure laid down by the Code of Civil Procedure, 1908, but shall be guided by the principles of natural justice and, subject to the other provisions of this Act and of any rules, the Commission shall have powers to regulate its own procedure, including the fixing of places and times of business.

15. Secretary-General of the Commission: (1) The Secretary-General shall be appointed by the Commission and shall be its Chief Executive Officer and shall exercise and discharge such powers and functions as determined by regulation.

(2) For the purpose of sub-section (1) aforesaid the Commission may seek from the Central Government a panel of not less than three officers who are eligible to be, or are of the rank of, the Secretary to the Government of India for being appointed as Secretary-General.

(3) The terms and conditions, and period of service, of the Secretary-General shall be such as maybe prescribed.

16. Setting up of Panel, Distribution of Business, etc.: (1) The Commission shall set up a Panel from amongst Members appointed under sub-section (2) of Section 7 to deal with matters in relation to the content in content application services, and the Chairperson shall preside over the meetings of the Panel: Provided that wherever necessary the Chairperson may place before the Commission any issue relating to the matters referred to in this section.

(2) Except for the power to make regulations, the Commission may, by general or special order, make provisions for the distribution of its business amongst Members as may be considered appropriate and necessary.

(3) For the discharge of its functions under this Act, the Commission may, if it considers necessary, set up bureaus or divisional organizations on the basis of its principal workload operations and subject to the provisions of Section 53, such bureaus or divisional organizations shall be provided with such officers and other employees as are necessary to perform their functions.

(4) The Commission may, by order in writing, authorize any District Magistrate or Sub-Divisional Magistrate in any area or any other officer of the Central Government or State Government or Union territory Administration to implement and ensure compliance of its directions and orders; and when so directed or authorized, such Magistrate or officer shall be bound to implement and carry out such directions and orders.

CHAPTER IV
OBJECTIVES OF THE COMMISSION

17. Objectives and Guiding Principles: The Communications Commission of India while exercising its functions shall be guided by the following principles governing the administration of this act namely—

(*i*) that the communication sector is developed in a competitive environment and in consumer interest;

(*ii*) that communication services are made available at affordable cost to all especially uncovered areas including the rural, remote, hilly and tribal areas;

(*iii*) that there is increasing access to information for greater empowerment of citizens and towards economic development;

(*iv*) that quality, plurality, diversity and choice of services are promoted;

(*v*) that a modern and effective communication infrastructure is established taking into account the convergence of information technology, media, telecom and consumer electronics;

(*vi*) that defence and security interests of the country are fully protected;

(*vii*) that introduction of new technologies, investment in services and infrastructure, and maximisation of communications facilities and services (including telephone density) are encouraged;

(*viii*) that equitable, non-discriminatory interconnection across various networks are promoted;

(*ix*) that licensing and registration criteria are transparent and made known to the public;

(*x*) that an open licensing policy allowing any number of new entrants (except in specific cases constrained by limited resources such as the spectrum) is promoted; and

(*xi*) that the principle of a level playing field for all operators, including existing operators on the date of commencement of the Act, is promoted so as to serve consumer interest.

CHAPTER V
POWERS, DUTIES AND FUNCTIONS OF THE COMMISSION

18. Powers Duties and Functions of the Commission: (1) It shall be the duty of the Commission to facilitate and regulate all matters relating to carriage and content of communications.

(2) Without prejudice to the generality of the provisions contained in sub-section (1), the Commission shall—

(*i*) carry out management, planning and monitoring of the spectrum for non-strategic/commercial usages subject to the provision of Section 24A;

(*ii*) grant licenses for purposes of the Act, and determine and enforce license conditions and determine fees (including fees for usage of spectrum) wherever required;

(*iii*) determine appropriate tariffs and rates for licensed services, wherever considered necessary and keeping in view the objectives and guiding principles in the Act;

(*iv*) ensure that the grant of licenses will not result in eliminating competition or in one or more service providers becoming dominant to the detriment of other service providers or consumers;

(*v*) promote competition and efficiency in the operation of communication services and network infrastructure facilities;

(*vi*) formulate and determine conditions for fair, equitable and non-discriminatory access to a network infrastructure facility or network service such other related matters in respect thereof;

(*vii*) take measures to protect consumer interests and promote and enforce universal service obligations;

(*viii*) formulate and lay down programme and advertising codes in respect of content application services;

(*ix*) formulate and lay down commercial codes in respect of communication services and network infrastructure facilities;

(*x*) take steps to regulate or curtail the harmful and illegal content on the internet and other communication services;

(*xi*) formulate and lay down codes and technical standards and norms to ensure quality and interoperability of services and network infrastructure facilities (including equipment);

(*xii*) carry out any study and publish findings on matters of importance to the consumers, service providers and the communications industry;

(*xiii*) institutionalise appropriate mechanisms and interact on a continual basis with all sectors of industry and consumers, so as to facilitate and promote the basic objectives of the Act; to encourage self-regulatory codes and standards;

(*xiv*) report and make recommendations on such matters as may be referred to it by the Central Government;

(*xv*) report and make recommedations either suo moto or on such matters as may be referred to by the Central Government in the matter prescribed.

(*xvi*) perform all or any functions in furtherance of the objects of this Act, or such as may be prescribed.

(3) The Commission shall ensure transferancy whilst exercising its powers and discharging its functions.

19. Power to Make Recommendation in Certain Cases: The Commission may at any time make appropriate recommedations to the Central Government with regard to any particular practice or practices that impinges upon or adversely affect the interest of the sovereignty and integrity of India, security of the state, friendly relations with foreign countries or State, public order, decency or morality.

20. Codes and Standards: The Commission shall by regulations from time to time specify programme codes and standards which may include inter alia practices—

(*i*) to ensure that nothing is contained in any programme which is prejudicial to the interests of the sovereignty and integrity of India, the security of State, friendly relations with foreign States, public order or which may constitute contempt of court, defamation or incitement to an offence.

(*ii*) to ensure fairness and impartiality in presentation of news and other programmes.

(*iii*) to ensure emphasis on promotion of Indian culture, values of national integration, religious and communal harmony, and a scientific temper.

(*iv*) to ensure in all programmes decency in portrayal of women, and restraint in portrayal of violence and sexual conduct;

(*v*) to enhance general standards of good taste, decency and morality.

(*vi*) to ensure avoidance of offence to religious views and belief; and

(*vii*) to be followed in connection with the prevention of unjust and unfair treatment in any programme, and unwarrented infringement of privacy in, or in connection with, obtaining of material included in such programme.

21. Hearing of Complaints and Resolution of Disputes by the Commission: (1) The Commission shall—

(*a*) decide any dispute or matter—

(*i*) between two or more service providers on issues relating to spectrum interference, interconnectivity, denial of fair access and practices restrictive of fair competition;

(*ii*) between a service provider and a group of consumers; and

(*iii*) arising out of enforcement of any provision of this Act.

(*b*) hear and determine any complaint from any person regarding contravention of the provisions the Act, rules, regulations or orders made thereunder including contraventions relating to any formulated codes and technical standards, and of other terms and conditions subject to which any license or registration was granted; and if necessary refer the matter for adjudication under Chapter X.

(2) For purposes of sub-section (1) the Commission shall pass such orders and issue such directions as it deems fit.

(3) The Commission shall endeavour to decide disputes and complaints referred to in sub-section (1) as expeditiously as possible.

22. Directives by the Central Government: (1) In exercising its licensing and regulatory functions the Commission shall follow such policy directives as may be communicated to it in writing by the Central Government from time to time. Such directives may include the route and the mode in which any services are to be licensed, whether by way of auction or in any other form.

(2) In framing the policy directives the Central Government shall take into account the objectives and guiding principles governing the administration of the Act.

(3) The decision of the Central Government whether a question is one of policy or not shall be final.

(4) The Commission may request the Central Government by means of a written communication for a review of any policy directive, and if any such request is made the Central Government will respond in writing to such request with all expeditious despatch.

CHAPTER VI
FREQUENCY SPECTRUM MANAGEMENT

23. Spectrum Management Committee: (1) The Central Government shall be responsible for coordination with international agencies in respect of matters relating to Spectrum Management and also for allocation of available spectrum for strategic and non-strategic or commercial purposes.

(2) For the purposes of discharging the responsibility under sub-section (1), the Central Government shall establish, by notification, a Spectrum Management Committee with the Cabinet Secretary as its Chairman and consisting of such other members as may be notified by it from time to time.

(3) The Central Government shall notify Wireless Advisor to the Government of India as Spectrum Manager, Government of India, to act as Member-Secretary of the Spectrum Management Committee.

(4) Subject to general supervision and control of the Spectrum Management Committee, the Spectrum Manager shall, inter-alia, perform the following functions, namely—

(*i*) to coordinate with international agencies, matters relating to overall spectrum planning, use and its management;

(*ii*) to carry out spectrum planning, and assign frequencies to the Central Government and to State Governments to meet their vital needs, including those of defence, national security and of the public service broadcaster;

(*iii*) to allocate frequencies or band of frequencies including frequencies which are to be assigned by the Commission; and reassignment of frequencies from time to time;

(*iv*) to review constantly and make available as much spectrum as possible for assignment by the Commission, in particular by optimising usages;

(*v*) monitoring as appropriate, in consultation with the Commission, the efficiency of the utilisation of the spectrum by all users including investigation and resolution of spectrum interference; and (*vi*) after meeting the requirements of the Central Government and of State Governments for fulfilling their vital needs including those of defence, national security and public service broadcaster, the Spectrum Manager shall make the spectrum available, to the maximum extent possible, for assignment by the Commission, both in the shared as well as in the exclusive bands.

(5) Subject to the general supervision and control of the Spectrum Management Committee, the Spectrum Manager shall assign frequencies on payment of such fee as may be prescribed.

24. Assignment of Spectrum: (1) The Commission shall be responsible for assignment of the non-strategic and commercial spectrum to various users:

Provided that the Commission shall assign such frequencies in case these are not exclusively allocated to it, only with the prior approval of the Spectrum Management Committee.

(2) Whenever the Commission seeks allocation of additional spectrum for assignment, including in the shared bands, a process for mutual consultation between the Commission and the Spectrum Manager shall be initiated in such manner and within time frame as may be prescribed.

25. Commission to Notify Schemes for Assignment of Spectrum: (1) Before assigning any part of spectrum, the Commission shall prepare and notify from time to time one or more schemes or plans for such assignment, after such public hearing as it may consider appropriate.

(2) The Central Government may, by notification, determine the class or classes of persons or services for preferential assignment of any frequency or spectrum by the Commission.

CHAPTER VII
LICENSES FOR REGISTRATION

26. License or Registration of Service Providers: (1) Having regard to the necessity of serving the public interest, ensuring competition and prevention of monopoly in the provision of network infrastructure facilities and communication services, the Commission may, by regulations specify—

(*i*) eligibility conditions for granting of licenses or registrations;

(*ii*) restrictions regarding ownership and control of the media;

(*iii*) restrictions on the number of licenses or extent of accumulation of interest in such licenses by a person; and

(*iv*) such other conditions as may be considered necessary from time to time.

(2)(*a*) The Commission may determine by regulation, the obligations, conditions, restrictions, tariffs and rates subject to which service provider shall provide facilities and services referred to in sub-section (1).

(*b*) The Commission may, by regulations, determine the conditions subject to which a license or registration may be granted or transferred and where a license or registration is transferred, the transferee shall be deemed as licensee or grantees, as the case may be, for the purpose of this Act.

(3) Subject to the provisions of sub-section (1), the Commission may grant license or registration in such manner, and within such time, subject to such terms and conditions,

on payment of such fees and after following such procedure as may be determined by regulations. Provided that the fee for registration shall not exceed thirty thousand rupees.

(4) The Commission shall notify, from time to time, one or more schemes or plans for licensing or registration containing such details as may be specified by regulations:

Provided that the Commission shall, before finalising such schemes or plans, consult the Central Government in order to ensure that the defence and security interests of India are fully protected.

(5) Any scheme or plan referred to in sub-section (4) may provide for eligibility conditions, number, and scope of licenses and registration and such other matters as the Commission may consider necessary.

(6) The Commission may grant license to any person—

(*a*) to provide or own network infrastructure facilities.
Explanation: For the purposes of this clause, network infrastructure facilities shall include earth station, cable infrastructure, wireless equipments, towers, posts, ducts and pits used in conjunction with other communication infrastructure, and distribution facilities including facilities for broadcasting distribution;

(*b*) to provide networking services
Explanation: For the purposes of this clause, networking services shall include band-width services, fixed links and mobile links;

(*c*) to provide application services.
Explanation: For the purposes of this clause, network application services shall include public switched telephony, public cellular telephony, global mobile personal communication by satellite, internet protocol telephony, radio paging services, public mobile radio trunking services, public switched data services and broadcasting (radio or television service excluding continued);

(*d*) to provide content application services.
Explanation: For the purposes of this clause, content application services shall include satellite broadcasting, subscription broadcasting, terrestrial free to air television broadcasting and terrestrial radio broadcasting;

(*e*) to prove value added network application services such as internet services and unified messaging services.
Explanation: For the removal of doubts, it is hereby declared that information technology enabled services such as call centers, electronic-commerce, tele-banking, tele-education, tele-trading, tele-medicine, videotex and video conferencing shall not be licensed under this Act.

(7) The Commission may, while granting a license for any one of the categories under sub-section (6), confine or limit the scope of the facility or service to be provided by the licensee in each category of license, and also specify the conditions for providing that facility or services.

(8) The Commission may, while granting a license under sub-section (6) grant licenses either singly or jointly for one or more of the categories of facilities or services specified therein:

Provided that no license shall be granted under this sub-section, if it conflicts with the objectives and guiding principles set out under this Act particularly in relation to ensuring fair access and promotion of competition.

Explanation: No license shall be required in respect of any person or class of persons, or any facility or service, which has been exempted under the proviso to clause (b) of sub-section (1) of Section 4 unless specifically notified by the Central Government for the purposes of licensing under this Act.

27. Period and Form of License or Registration: (1) A license or registration shall be granted for such period as may be specified by regulations.

(2) A license or registration, granted under this Act, shall be in such form and shall be subject to the payment of such fees as may be determined by regulations:

Provided that the fee for registration shall not exceed the amount referred to in the proviso to sub-section (3) of Section 26:

Provided that the Central Government may, by notification, in the public interest, exempt any person or class of persons from payment of the license fee or registration fee.

28. Duties of Service Providers: (1) Every service provider shall, wherever required or applicable—

(*i*) give effect to Universal Service Obligations;

(*ii*) provide such life saving services as may be prescribed;

(*iii*) provide service to any person on demand within a reasonable period of time and on a non-discriminatory basis; and

(*iv*) follow the codes and standards laid down and specified by the Commission;

(2) Every service provider of a content application service shall, wherever required or applicable—

(*i*) endeavour to provide a suitable proportion of programme of indigenous origin; and

(*ii*) ensure that no programme forming part of its services infringes any copyright.

(3) Without prejudice to the foregoing provisions of this Act, every service provider holding a license for providing distribution of broadcasting services shall, amongst others—

(*i*) provide a specified number and type of broadcasting services, including those of the public service broadcaster, in such manner, as may be prescribed;

(*ii*) include only licensed broadcasting service in his delivery package for the purposes of distribution; and

(*iii*) use not more than such number of channels as specified by regulations, out of the total channel capacity of the system, for providing his own programming.

29. Certain Agreements to be Registered with the Commission: Every agreement entered into or made by any service provider or infrastructure facility provider, falling under one or more of the following classes shall, within sixty days from the making of such agreement, be registered with the Commission namely—

(*a*) shareholders or promoters agreements;

(*b*) interconnectivity agreements; and
(*c*) Such other agreements as may be specified by regulations.

CHAPTER VIII
LICENSING OF POSSESSION OF WIRELESS EQUIPMENT

30. License for Wireless Equipment: (1) Subject to the provisions of sub-section (1) of Section 5, any person who intends to possess any wireless equipment shall make an application to the Commission for the grant of a license.

(2) Every application shall be in such form and shall be accompanied by such fees as may be determined by regulations.

(3) The Commission shall, on receipt of an application under sub-section (1), after making such enquiries as it deems fit, grant the license or reject the application:

Provided that no application shall be rejected unless an opportunity of being heard is given to the applicant:

Provided further that no application for a license shall be rejected except on grounds of security of India or part thereof, public order or other public interest.

(4) Every license granted under this section shall be subject to such conditions and restrictions as may be determined by regulations.

CHAPTER IX
SPECIAL PROVISION IN RESPECT OF CERTAIN SERVICES

31. Provision for Live Broadcasting of Certain Events: (1) For the purpose of ensuring the widest availability of viewing in India of a national or international event of general public interest to be held in India, the Central Government shall notify the same well in advance.

(2) The National or International event of general public interest notified under sub-serction (1) shall have to be carried on the network of a public service broadcaster as well.

(3) In order to strive towards providing a level playing field for bidders for broadcasting rights, or persons interested in receiving broadcasting right for events, notified under sub-section (1), the Commission shall determine, well in advance of such event, the principles and terms for the access to the network of the public service broadcaster.

CHAPTER X
BREACH OF TERMS AND CONDITIONS OF LICENSE OR REGISTRATION, CIVIL LIABILITY AND ADJUDICATION

32. Breach of Terms and Conditions of Licenses, etc.: (1) In any case of breach of any of the terms of the license or registration or failure to comply with any decision, direction or order of the Commission, it may, after providing an opportunity to the party concerned of being heard, do any one or more of the following, namely—

(*a*) direct the licensee or grantee to do or abstain from doing any act or thing to prevent such breach or for such compliance;
(*b*) suspend the license or registration for a specified period;
(*c*) curtail the period of the license or registration;
(*d*) revoke the license or registration; and
(*e*) initiate adjudication proceedings under this chapter.

(2) If the Commission has a reason to believe that the terms and conditions of a license or registration for providing a network infrastructure facility or Communication service under this Act have been or are being breached, the Commission may direct or order the seizure of the equipment being used for provision of such facility or service, and for this purpose the Commission may, by order in writing, authorise any District Magistrate, or Sub-Divisional Magistrate in any area, or any other officer of the Central Goverment or State Government or Union Territory Administration, to implement and ensure compliance of its directions and orders; and when so authorized, such Magistrate or officer shall be bound to carry out the directions and orders of the Commission.

(3) Any person aggrieved by such seizure under sub-section (2), may prefer an appeal to the Appellate Tribunal within thirty days of the seizure and the Appellate Tribunal may pass such orders, as expeditiously as possible as to the disposal of the property so seized as it may deem fit. Provided that no such equipment shall be retained by the Commission or the authorised officer for a period exceeding forty-five days from the date of its seizure, unless the Appellate Tribunal on the report made by the authorised officer, approves such retention for a longer period.

33. Civil Liability for Breach of Terms and Conditions of License etc.: If any licensee or grantee commits breach of, or fails to comply with any terms and conditions subject to which a license or registration, as the case may be, was granted or fails to comply with any rule, regulation or order made under this Act, the licensee or grantee shall be liable to a civil liability under this Chapter.

34. Civil Liability for Contravention of the Provision Relating to Transmission etc.: If any person transmits or distributes any communication or performs any service incidental thereto, by the use of a network infrastructure facility, communication service or wireless equipment which is required to be licensed or registered under this Act and not so licensed or registered, as the case may be, or has been established or maintained or operated in contravention of the provisions of this Act or any rule or regulation made thereunder, such person shall be liable to a civil liability under this chapter.

35. Civil Liability for Delivery of Content Through Facilities, Services or Equipments not Licensed or Registered: If any person delivers any content for transmission or accepts delivery of any content sent by the use of network infrastructure facility, communication service or wireless equipment knowing or having reason to believe that such facility, service or equipment has been established or has been maintained or operated without a license or registration or in contravention of the provisions of this Act or any rules or regulation made thereunder, such person shall be liable to a civil liability under this chapter.

36. Civil Liabilities for Failure to Register Agreements: If a service provider fails without reasonable excuse to register an agreement, which is required to be registered as provided for in Section 29, he shall be liable to civil liability under this chapter.

37. Civil Liability for Failure to Comply with the Decision, Direction or Orders of the Commission: If any person wilfully fails to comply with any decision, direction or order of the Commission, he shall be liable to civil liabilities under this chapter.

38. Filing of Complaint, Reference for Adjudication etc.: (1) A complaint may be filed before the Commission alleging that a service provider or any other person has incurred a liability to a civil liability under this Chapter.

(2) Every complaint under sub-section (1), except a complaint under Section 33, shall be filed within sixty days from the date on which any act or conduct constituting the contravention took place and shall be in such form as may be prescribed:

39. Power to Adjudicate: (1) For the purpose of adjudging whether any person has contravened any of the provisions of this Act, any rules, regulations, made thereunder or directions or orders issued under this Act is liable to a civil liability under this Chapter, the Commission shall, subject to the provision or sub-section (3), appoint by general or special order, an officer of the commission as Adjudicating Officer for holding an inquiry in the manner provided for herein and in the regulations.

(2) The Adjudicating Officer shall give the person referred to in sub-section (l), a reasonable opportunity for making a representation in the matter, and if, on inquiry, the Adjudicating Officer is satisfied that the person has committed any contravention, and is liable to a civil liability, then, such liability as may be determined, by order, shall be imposed by the Adjudicating Officer on such person:

Provided that where the Adjudicating Officer is satisfied that there has been no contravention, he may pass such order as he deems fit.

(3) No person shall be appointed as an Adjudicating Officer unless he possess such experience as may be prescribed.

(4) Where more than one Adjudicating officers are appointed, the Commission shall specify, by order, the matter and places with respect to which such officers shall exercise their jurisdiction.

(5) For the purpose of discharging his powers and functions, every Adjudicating officers shall have the same powers as are vested in a civil court under the Code of Civil Procedure, 1908 in respect of the following matters, namely—

(*a*) summoning and enforcing the attendance of any person and examining him on oath;

(*b*) requiring the discovery and production of documents;

(*c*) receiving evidence on affidavits;

(*d*) subject to the provisions of Sections 123 and 124 of the Indian Evidence Act, 1872, requisitioning any public record or document or a copy of such record or document or a copy of such record or document, from any office;

(*e*) issuing commission for the examination of witness or for production of documents;

(*f*) dismissing an application for default or deciding it ex-parte;

(*g*) setting aside any order of dismissal of any application for default or any order passed by him ex-parte;

(*h*) reviewing his decisions;

(*i*) granting interim relief; and

(*j*) any other matter which may be prescribed.

(6) The Adjudicating Officer shall endeavour to decide disputes and complaints referred to him as expeditiously as possible.

(7) Any proceeding before the Adjudicating Officer shall be deemed to be a judicial proceeding within the meaning of Sections 193 and 228, and for the purpose of Section 196, of the Indian Penal Code and the Adjudicating Officer shall be deemed to be a civil

court for the purpose of Section 195 and Chapter XXXVI of the Code of Criminal Procedure, 1973.

40. (1) If any person damages, displaces or destroys cable or any part of the network infrastructure facility laid, established or place in accordance with the provisions of this Act, or if the communication services by reason of the damage or displacement so caused is interrupted, such person shall be liable—

(*a*) where the act is willful and deliberate, to a civil liability which may extend to rupees five crores and where the actual loss or damage caused is more than rupees five crores then the civil liability up to the extent of damage;

(*b*) where the act is not willful or deliberate, a civil liability not exceeding the actual loss or damage caused.

(2) out of the civil liabilities imposed under sub-section (1), such sum as may be determined by the Adjudicating Officer shall be payable to the licensee or the grantee, as the case may be, as reasonable compensation for damage suffered.

41. If any person contravenes the provision of sub-section (l), such sum as may be liable to a civil liability as determined by the Adjudicating Officer under this chapter.

42. (1) Any penalty imposed under this Chapter shall not exceed fifty crore rupees.

(2) The Adjudicating Officer shall, while adjudging the quantum of civil liability, under this chapter, the Adjudicating Officer, have due regard to the provisions of this Act, and also to the following factors, namely—

(*a*) the amount of revenue loss to the Government;

(*b*) the amount of disproportionate gain or unfair advantage, wherever quantifiable, made as a result of the default;

(*c*) the amount of loss caused to any person as a result of the default;

(*d*) the repetitive nature of the default; and

(*e*) that the amount adjudged shall be such as may act as a deterrent even though no financial loss has been caused by such contravention.

CHAPTER XI
COMMUNICATIONS APPELLATE TRIBUNAL

43. Establishment of Appellate Tribunal: (1) The Central Government shall, by notification, establish an Appellate Tribunal to be known as the Communications Appellate Tribunal, to exercise the jurisdiction, powers and authority conferred on it by or under this Act.

(2) Any person aggrieved by any decision or order of the Commission may prefer an appeal to the Appellate Tribunal.

(3)(*a*) Every appeal under sub-section (2) shall be preferred within a period of sixty days from the date on which a copy of the decision or order made by the Commission is received by the person aggrieved and the appeal shall be in such form, verified in such manner and be accompanied by such fee as may be prescribed;

(*b*) Any person aggrieved by an order of penalty imposed by the Adjudicating Officer may prefer an appeal to the Appellate Tribunal within sixty days from the date on which such order is received and the appeal shall be in such form, verified in such manner and accompanied by such fee as may be prescribed:

Provided that the appellate Tribunal may entertain an appeal under clause (a) or clause (b) after expiry of the said period of sixty days, if it is satisfied that there was sufficient cause for not filing the same within that period.

(4) On receipt of an appeal under sub-section (2), or sub-section (3), the Appellate Tribunal may, after giving the parties to the appeal an opportunity of being heard, pass such orders thereon as it thinks fit.

(5) The Appellate Tribunal shall send a copy of every order made by it to each of the parties to the appeal and to the Commission or to the Adjudicating Officer, as the case may be.

(6) The Appellate Tribunal shall endeavour to deal with and dispose of every appeal preferred under sub-section (2) and sub-section (3) as expeditiously as possible; and all parties appearing before the Appellate Tribunal shall actively assist in ensuring that the appeal is determined and disposed off not later than ninety days from the date of filing of the appeal.

(7) The Appellate Tribunal may, on its own motion or otherwise for the purpose of examining the legality, propriety or correctness of any order or decision of the Commission or of the Adjudicating Officer, call for all relevant records and make such orders as it thinks fit:

Provided that the power under this sub-section shall not be invoked after the expiry of three months from the date of such order or decision. Composition of Appellate Tribunal.

44. (1) The Appellate Tribunal shall consist of a Chairperson and not more than six Members to be appointed, by notification, by the Central Government.

(2) The appointment of Chairperson and Members of the Appellate Tribunal shall be made by the Central Government in consultation with the Chief Justice of India.

(3) The Appointment of Mmembers of the Appellate Tribunal shall be from amongst persons recommended by the search committee as may be prescribed.

(4) Subject to the provisions of this Act—

(*a*) the jurisdiction of the Appellate Tribunal may be exercised by Benches thereof;

(*b*) a bench may be constituted by the Chairperson of the Appellate Tribunal consisting of two or more Members as the Chairperson may deem fit:

Provided that every bench shall be presided over by a Judicial member.

Explanation: For the purposes of this section "Judicial Member" means any member of the Appellate Tribunal who has been a judge of a High Court;

(*c*) the benches of the Appellate Tribunal shall ordinarily sit at Delhi and also at such other places as the Central Government may notify, in consultation with the Chairperson of the Appellate Tribunal.

(*d*) the Central Government shall, on the recommendation of the Appellate Tribunal, notify the areas in relation to which each bench of the Appellate Tribunal may exercise jurisdiction.

(5) The Chairperson of the Appellate Tribunal may, as the exigencies of business may require, request a member of the Appellate Tribunal sitting on one bench of the Appellate Tribunal to sit on another bench thereof.

(6) If at any stage it appears to the Chairperson or a bench of the Appellate Tribunal that the case or matter is of such a nature that it ought to be heard by a bench consisting of more than two members of the Appellate Tribunal, the case or matter may be transferred by the Chairperson to a bench of more than two Members. Qualification, tenure, salary and allowances, vacancy of the Chairperson and Members of the Appellate Tribunal.

45. (1) A person shall not be qualified for appointment as the Chairperson or a Member of the Appellate Tribunal unless—

(*a*) in the case of the Chairperson, he is, or has been, a Judge of the Supreme Court;

(*b*) in the case of a Member, he is or has been a Judge of a High Court, or has held the post of Secretary to the Government of India or any equivalent post in the Central Government or the State Government for a period of not less than two years, or he is a person who is proficient in any of the fields specified in sub-sections (2) and (3) of Section 7.

(2) The Chairperson and every Member of the Appellate Tribunal shall hold office as such for a term of five years from the date on which he enters upon his office:

Provided that no Chairperson or other Member shall hold office as such after he has attained—

(*i*) in the case of Chairperson, the age of seventy years;

(*ii*) in the case of any other Member, the age of sixty-five years.

(3) The salary and allowances payable to and the other terms and conditions of service of the Chairperson and other Members of the Appellate Tribunal shall be such as may be prescribed:

Provided that neither the salary and allowances nor the other terms and conditions of service of the Chairperson or a Member of the Appellate Tribunal shall be varied to his disadvantage after appointment.

(4)(*a*) If, for reason other than temporary absence, any vacancy occurs in the office of the chairperson or a member of the Appellate Tribunal, the Central Government shall appoint another person in accordance with the provisions of this Act to fill the vacancy.

(*b*) When the Chairperson of the Appellate Tribunal is unable to discharge his functions owing to absence, illness or any other cause, any member of the Appellate Tribunal, as authorised so to do by the Central Government, shall discharge the functions of the Chairperson until the day on which the Chairperson resumes charge of his functions.

(5) Before appointing any person as chairperson or member of the Appellate Tribunal, the Central Government shall satisfy itself that the person does not have any such financial or other interests as are likely to affect prejudicially his functions as such member.

(6) A person who is in the service of Government shall have to retire or resign from service before entering the office of chairperson or member of the Appellate Tribunal.

46. Resignation and Removal: (1) The Chairman or a Member of the Appellate tribunal may resign his office by giving notice thereof in writing to the Central Government and on such resignation being accepted, the Chairperson or the Member shall be deemed to have vacated his office.

(2) The Central Government may remove from office, the Chairperson or a Member of the Appellate Tribunal, who—

(*a*) has been adjudged an insolvent; or

(*b*) has been convicted of an offence which, in the opinion of the Central Government, involves moral turpitude; or

(*c*) has become physically or mentally incapable of acting as the Chairperson or a Member; or

(*d*) has acquired such financial or other interest as is likely to affect prejudicially his functions as the chairperson or a member; or

(*e*) has so abused his position as to render his continuance in office prejudicial to the public interest.

(3) Notwithstanding anything contained in sub-section (2), the chairperson or a member of the Appellate Tribunal shall not be removed from his office on the ground specified in clause (d) or clause (e) of that sub-section unless the Supreme Court, on a reference being made to it in this behalf by the Central Government, has, on an inquiry, held by it in accordance with such procedure as it may specify in this behalf, reported that the Chairperson or a Member ought on such ground or grounds to be removed.

(4) The Central Government may suspend from office, the Chairperson or a Member of the Appellate Tribunal in respect of whom a reference has been made to the Supreme Court under sub-section (2), until the Central Government has passed an order on receipt of the report of the Supreme Court on such reference. Distribution of business amongst benches, etc

47. Distribution of Business Amongst Benches, etc.: (1) The Chairperson of the Appellate Tribunal may, from time to time, by order, make provisions as to the distribution of the business of the Appellate Tribunal amongst the Benches and also provide for the matters which may be dealt with by each bench thereof.

(2) On the application of any of the parties and after notice to the parties, and after hearing such of them as may desire to be heard, or suo motu without notice, the Chairperson of the Appellate Tribunal may transfer any case pending before one bench of the Appellate Tribunal for disposal, to any other bench thereof.

(3) If the members of a bench of the Appellate Tribunal consisting of two Members differ in opinion on any point, they shall state the point or points on which they differ, and make a reference to the chairperson of the Appellate Tribunal who shall hear the point or points, and thereafter such point or points shall be decided according to the opinion of the majority who have heard the case, including those who first heard it. Procedure and powers of Appellate Tribunal.

48. Procedure and Powers of Appellate Tribunal: (1) The Appellate Tribunal shall have, for the purpose of discharging its functions under this Act, the same powers as are vested in a civil court under the Code of Civil Procedure, 1908 while trying a suit, in respect of the following matters, namely—

(*a*) summoning and enforcing the attendance of any person and examining him on oath;

(*b*) requiring the discovery and production of documents;

(*c*) receiving evidence on affidavits;

(*d*) subject to the provisions of Sections 123 and 124 of the Indian Evidence Act, 1872, requisitioning any public record or document or a copy of such record or document from any office;

(*e*) issuing Commissions for the examinations of witnesses or documents;

(*f*) dismissing an application for default or deciding it ex-parte;

(*g*) setting aside any order of dismissal of any application for default or any order passed by it, ex-parte;

(*h*) reviewing its decisions;

(*i*) granting interim relief; and

(*j*) any other matter which may be prescribed.

(2) The Appellate Tribunal shall not be bound by the procedure laid down by the Code of Civil Procedure, 1908, but shall be guided by the principles of natural justice and, subject to the other provisions of this Act, the Appellate Tribunal shall have powers to regulate its own procedure.

(3) Every proceeding before the Appellate Tribunal shall be deemed to be a judicial proceeding within the meaning of Sections 193 and 228, and for the purposes of Section 196, of the Indian Penal Code, and the Appellate Tribunal shall be deemed to be a civil court for the purposes of Section 195 and Chapter XXVI of the Code of Criminal Procedure, 1973. Right of application to take assistance of legal practitioner, etc.

49. Rights of Applicant to Take Assistance of Legal Practitioner, etc.: An applicant or appellant may either appear in person or authorise one or more chartered accountants, or company secretaries, cost accountants or legal practitioners, or any of his or its accredited officers to present his or its case before the Appellate Tribunal.

Explanation: For the purpose of this section—

(*a*) "Chartered accountant" means a chartered accountant as defined in clause (b) of sub-section (1) of Section 2 of the Chartered Accountants Act, 1949 and who has obtained a certificate of practice under sub-section (1) of Section 6 of that Act;

(*b*) "company secretary" means a company secretary as defined in clause (c) of sub-section (1) of Section 2 of the Company Secretaries Act, 1980 and who has obtained a certificate of practice under sub-section (1) of Section 6 of that Act;

(*c*) "cost accountant" means a cost accountant as defined in clause (b) of sub-section (1) of Section 2 of the Cost and Works Accountants Act, 1959 and who has obtained a certificate of practice under sub-section (1) of Section 6 of that Act;

(*d*) "legal practitioner" means an advocate, *vakil* or an attorney of any High Court, and includes a pleader.

50. Appeals to Supreme Court: (1) Notwithstanding anything contained in the Code of Civil Procedure, 1908 or in any other law for the time being in force, an appeal shall lie against any order, not being an interlocutory order, passed by the Appellate Tribunal to the Supreme Court on one or more of the grounds specified in Section 100 of that Code.

(2) No appeal shall lie against any decision or order made by the Appellate Tribunal with the consent of the parties.

(3) Every appeal under this section shall be preferred within a period of ninety days from the date of the decision or order appealed against:

Provided that the Supreme Court may entertain the appeal after the expiry of the said period of ninety days, if it is satisfied that the appellant was prevented by sufficient cause from preferring the appeal in time.

51. Execution of Orders: (1) An order passed by the Appellate Tribunal under this Act shall be executable by the Appellate Tribunal as a decree of a civil court, and for this purpose, the Appellate Tribunal shall have all the powers of a civil court.

(2) Notwithstanding anything contained in sub-section (1), the Appellate Tribunal may transmit any order made by it to a civil court having local jurisdiction and such civil court shall execute the order as if it were a decree made by that court.

Explanation: For the purpose of this section, the expression "civil court having local jurisdiction" shall mean, the civil court within whose local limits of jurisdiction, the licensee, grantee, or judgement debtor, as the case may be resides or has a place of office or business and also within whose jurisdiction any property belonging to the licensee, grantee, or judgement debtor is located.

52. Penalty for Failure to Comply with the Orders of Commission and Appellate Tribunal: If any person willfuly fails to comply with any decision, direction or order of Appellate Tribunal such person shall be liable to a penalty to be imposed by the order of Appellate Tribunal which may extend to five crores rupees:

Provided that no such penalty shall be levied without giving any opportunity of being heard to the party concerned.

CHAPTER XII
OFFICERS AND EMPLOYEES OF THE COMMISSION AND THE APPELLATE TRIBUNAL

53. Officers and Employees of Commission of Appellate Tribunal: (1) The Commission or Appellate Tribunal, as the case may be, shall appoint such officers and other employees as the Commission or Appellate Tribunal, as the case may be, considers necessary for the efficient discharge of its functions under this Act subject to such conditions as may be prescribed.

(2) The salaries and allowances payable to and the terms and conditions of service of the officers and employees of the Commission and of the Appellate Tribunal shall be such as may be prescribed.

(3) The officers and employees of the Commission shall discharge their functions under the general superintendence and control of the Chairperson of the Commission and the officers and employees of the Appellate Tribunal shall discharge their functions under the general superintendence and control of the Chairperson of the Appellate Tribunal.

CHAPTER XIII
FINANCE, ACCOUNTS AND AUDIT

54. Proceeds of License Fee, etc.: (1) Subject to the provisions of sub-section (2) of Section 40 and sub-section (2) of Section 23, the proceeds of the license fee, fee paid under sub-section (5) of Section 23, registration fee, amount received by imposition of civil liabilities imposed under this Act and amount of penalties imposed by the Appellate Tribunal shall be credited to the Consolidated Fund of India.

(2) Such portion or percentage of the license fee as may be attributable to the Universal Service Obligation as may be prescribed shall be credited to a separate fund to be called Universal Service Obligation Fund in the public account of India.

55. Communications Commission and Appellate Tribunal Fund: (1) There shall be constituted two separate funds to be called the Communications Commission Fund and the Appellate Tribunal Fund and there shall be credited to these funds sums of money paid or grants made by the Central Government to be utilised for the purposes of this Act.

(2) Subject to the provisions of sub-section (1) of Section 54, fee receivable by the Commission shall be credited to the Communications Commission Fund, and fee receivable by the Appellate Tribunal shall be credited to the Appellate Tribunal Fund.

56. Grants and Application of Funds: After due appropriation made by Parliament by law, the Central Government, shall credit to the funds referred to in sub-section (1) of Section 55 by way of grant, separately for the Commission and for the Appellate Tribunal, adequate sums of money for being utilised for the purpose of this Act, and for meeting the salaries and allowances payable to the Chairperson and Members of the Commission and Chairperson and Members of the Appellate Tribunal and the administrative expenses including the salaries and allowances payable to, or in respect of, officers and other employees of the Commission and of the Appellate Tribunal, as the case may be.

57. Accounts and Audit: (1) The Commission as also the Appellate Tribunal shall maintain proper accounts and other relevant records and prepare an annual statement of accounts in such form and manner as may be prescribed in consultation with the Comptroller and Auditor-General of India.

(2) The accounts of the Commission as certified by the Comptroller and Auditor-General of India or any other person appointed by him in this behalf together with the audit report thereon shall form part of the annual report of the Commission referred to in sub-section (1) of Section 58.

(3) The accounts of the Appellate Tribunal as certified by the Comptroller and Auditor-General of India or any other person appointed by him in this behalf together with the audit report thereon shall be forwarded annually to the Central Government, and that Government shall cause the same to be laid before each House of Parliament.

58. Annual Report: (1) The Commission shall after the end of each financial year, furnish to the Central Government an annual report on its activities during the preceding financial year and containing such information relating to the proceedings and policy as may be prescribed, and such report shall also contain therein the statement of annual accounts of the Commission.

(2) The Central Government shall cause such report to be laid before each house of Parliament.

CHAPTER XIV
RIGHT OF WAY FOR LAYING CABLES AND ERECTION OF POSTS

59. Rights of Facility Providers in Public: (1) Subject to the provisions of this Act, any person entitled under the provisions of this Act, services or facilities (hereinafter referred to as facility provider) may from time to time lay, and establish cables and erect posts under, over, along, across, in or upon any immovable property vested in or under the control or management of a public authority.

(2) Any public authority under whose control or management, any immovable property is vested shall, on receipt of a request from a facility provider permit the facility provider to do all or any of the following acts namely—

(*a*) to place and maintain underground cables or posts; and

(*b*) to enter on the property from time to time, in order to place, examine, repair, alter or remove such cables or posts.

(3) The permission mentioned in sub-section (2) above shall be promptly given and shall not be unreasonably withheld or denied:

Provided that in case of an emergency the facility provider may at any time for the purpose of examining, repairing, altering or removing any cable or post enter upon the property for that purpose without first obtaining such permission.

(4) The facility of right of way under this section for laying underground cables or erecting posts, shall be available to all facility providers without discrimination and subject to the obligation of reinstatement or restoration of the property or payment of reinstatement or restoration charges in resect thereof at the public authority.

(5) Where any shifting or alteration in position of the underground cable or post is required due to compulsive causes like widening of highways and construction of flyovers or bridges, the said facility provider shall shift or alter the same at his own cost within the period indicated by concerned authority.

(6) For the purposes of speedy clearance of requests for laying cables or erecting posts on any property vested in, or under the control or management of any public authority, high powered committees, or other appropriate mechanisms shall be promptly set up by the Central Government or the State Governments in the manner prescribed, they shall in each State act as a single nodal agency to co-ordinate all activities in this regard; and the Central Government may provide appropriate guidelines in this behalf.

60. Rights of Public Authority to Grant Permission: Any permission granted by a public authority under Section 59 may be subject to such reasonable conditions as that authority thinks fit to impose as to the time or mode of execution of any work, or as to any other matter connected with or related to any work undertaken by the facility provider in exercise of those rights.

61. Provision for Removal or Alteration of Cable or Post: When under the foregoing provisions of this Act, any cable or post has been placed by any facility provider under, over, along, across in or upon any property and the public authority having regard to circumstances which have arisen since the cable or post was so placed, considers it necessary and expedient that it should be removed or its position should be altered, it may require the concerned facility provider to remove it or alter its position as the case may be and it shall then be so removed or altered without any delay.

62. Determination of Disputes: (1) If any dispute arises under this Chapter including refusal of permission by the public authority, the district court within whose local limits of jurisdiction the property concerned is situated shall on application determine the same.

(2) Every such determination shall be in accordance with the provisions of this Chapter and such determination will be deemed to be a decree of the district court and be for all purposes treated as such.

(3) The provisions of the Code of Civil Procedure, 1908 shall apply to adjudication of all disputes under this section.

(4) Pending disposal of any application, the district court may pass such interim orders preventive or mandatory for the doing of any act under this Chapter on such terms and conditions as may be provided for in such order.

63. Use of Private Land by Facility Provider: (1) A facility provider may make use of private land for constructing or laying of cables or erecting posts only with the consent in writing of owner of the land or premises, as the case may be:

Provided that where in the opinion of a facility provider consent to the reasonable use of any land is not forthcoming such facility provider, may, on application to and with the approval of the or premises is not forthcoming, such facility provider may, on an application to and with the approval of the Commission, take steps authorized by the Commission for use of the land or premises for constructing or laying cables or erecting posts on such terms as the Commission may deem fit.

(2) Where immediately before the commencement of this Act, a facility provider has made use of private land or premises for constructing or laying of cables or erecting posts without consent of the owner of the land or the premises and despite owner's objection, the facility provider shall, within a period of six months from the date of commencement of this Act, obtain a written consent of the owner, and the proviso to sub-section (1) shall apply *mutates mutandis* to this situation.

64. Power of Commission to Issue Order, Regarding Use of Private Land: (1) The Commission may, by order, require any network infrastructure facility to be provided, constructed, installed, altered, moved operated, used, repaired or maintained on any private land or premises or any system of method to be adopted by any person interested in or affected by the order, and at or within such time subject to such conditions as to compensation or otherwise and under such supervisions as the Commission may determine to be just.

(2) The Commission may, by order, specify by whom, in what proportion and at or within what time the cost of doing anything required or permitted to be done under sub-section (1) shall be paid.

(3) Any orders of the Commission under sub-section (1) or sub-section (2) shall be enforceable under Chapter X of this Act as if such order is the order referred to in Section 37.

65. Right of a Facility Provider: Nothing in this Chapter shall confer any right upon any facility provider other than that of a user for the purpose only of laying cables or erecting posts or maintaining them.

CHAPTER XV
INTERCEPTION OF COMMUNICATION AND PUNISHMENT FOR UNLAWFUL INTERCEPTION

66. Interception of Communication and Safeguards: (1) Subject to the prescribed safeguard, the Central Government or a State Government or any officer specially authorized in this behalf by the Central Government or a State Government, on the occurrence of any public emergency or in the interests of the security, sovereignty and integrity of India, friendly relations with foreign States or public order or for preventing incitement to the commission of an offence, may direct—

(*i*) any agency of that Government to intercept any communication on any network facilities or services;

(*ii*) any service provider that any content brought for communication by or communicated or received by, him shall not be communicated or shall be intercepted or detained or shall be disclosed to that Government or its agency authorized in this behalf.

(2) The service provider shall, when called upon by any agency, which has been directed to carry out interception under sub-section (1), extend all facilities and technical assistance for interception of the content of communication.

(3) Any service provider who fails to assist the agency referred to in sub-section (2) shall be punished with imprisonment for a term, which may extend to seven years.

(4) Save as otherwise provided under this section, any person, who intercepts any communication or causes any communication to be intercepted or discloses to any person, any content shall be punishable with imprisonment which may extend to five years or with fine which may extend up to ten lakh rupees, and, for a second and subsequent offence, with imprisonment which may extend to five years and with fine which may extend up to fifty lakh rupees.

Explanation: For the purposes of this section, "interception" means the aural or other acquisition of the content through the use of such devices or means as may be necessary for such acquisition.

67. Nothing in this Chapter shall affect the provision of Section 69 of the Information Technology Act, 2000.

CHAPTER XVI
CRIMES AND PUNISHMENT

68. (1) Save as otherwise provided in this Act, any person who, without a licence, owns or provides any network infrastructure facility or provides any communication service or knowingly assists in the transmissions or distribution of such service in any manner including—

(*a*) collection of subscription for his principal; or

(*b*) issuing of advertisements to such service; or

(*c*) dealing in, or distribution of, equipment for decoding programme,

shall be punishable with imprisonment which may extend to five years, or with fine which may extend to five crore rupees, or with both, and, for the second offence, with imprisonment which may extend to five years or with fine which may extend to ten crore rupees or with both.

(2) Any person who without the permission of the service provider and with the intent to defraud, diverts any signal or decodes any content or deals in decoding equipment for such purpose shall be punishable with imprisonment which may extend to five years and with fine which may extend to five crore rupees or with both and, for

the second or subsequent offence with imprisonment which may extend to five years and with fine which may extend to ten crore rupees.

(3) Any person who, knowingly benefits from any unauthorised diversion or tampering with any communication service or network infrastructure facility with the knowledge that such service or facility is unauthorized or tampered, shall be punished with imprisonment for a term which may extend to two years, or with fine which may extend to rupees two crores, or with both.

(4) Any person who, abets or induces the making of any unauthorised diversion or tampering with any communication service or network infrastructure facility shall be punished with imprisonment for a term which may extend to two years, or with fine which may extend to rupees two crores or with both

(5) Any person who, having already been convicted of an offence under sub-section (3) or sub-section (4) is again convicted thereunder, shall on every such subsequent conviction, be punished with imprisonment for a term which shall not be less than six months but which may extend to five years, and with fine which may extend to rupees five crores.

69. Punishment for Possession of Wireless Equipment etc., Without Licence: (1) Any person—

(*a*) who possesses any wireless equipment in contravention of the provisions of Section 5; or

(*b*) who uses a radio frequency which he is not authorised to use under this Act,

shall be punishable with imprisonment which may extend to three years or with fine which may extend to rupees two crores, or with both.

Explanation: For the purpose of this sub-section "radio frequencies" means any frequency of electro-magnetic waves upto and including a frequency of 3000 giga hertz.

(2) When any person is convicted for an offence punishable under sub-section (1), all wireless equipments or any part thereof in respect of which the offence has been committed, shall be forfeited to the Central Government.

(3) Any wireless equipment confiscated which has not been claimed by anybody shall vest in the Central Government.

(4) Any officer authorised by the Central Government or the Commission in this behalf may search any building, vehicle, vessel or place in which he has reason to believe that any wireless equipment in respect of which an offence punishable under sub-section (1) has been committed is kept or concealed and take possession thereof.

70. Punishment for Sending Obscene or Offensive Messages: Any person who sends, by means of a communication service or a network infrastructure facility—

(*a*) any content that is grossly offensive or of an indecent obscene or menacing character; or

(*b*) for the purpose of causing annoyance, inconvenience, danger, obstruction, insult, injury, criminal intimidation, enmity, hatred or ill-will, any content that he knows to be false or persistently makes use for that purpose of a communication service or a network infrastructure facility,

shall be punishable with imprisonment which may extend upto three years or with fine which may extend to rupees two crores or with both.

71. Attempt to Commit Offences: Whoever attempts to commit or abets the commission of any offence, under sub-section (3) or sub-sections (4) of Section 66 under this Chapter shall be punished with the punishment provided for that offence.

72. Offences by Companies: (1) Where an offence under this Act has been committed by a Company every person who at the time of the offence was committed was in charge of, and was responsible to, the company, for the conduct of business of the company, as well as the company shall be deemed to be guilty of the offence and shall be liable to be proceeded against and punished accordingly:

Provided that nothing contained in this sub-section shall render any such person liable to any punishment, if he proves that the offence was committed without his knowledge or that he had exercised all due diligence to prevent the commission of such offence.

(2) Notwithstanding anything contained in sub-section (1) where any offence under this Act has been committed by a company and it has proved that the offence has been committed with the consent or connivance of, or is attributable to any neglect on the part of any director, manager, secretary or other officer of the company, such director, manager, secretary or other officer shall be deemed to be guilty of that offence and shall be liable to be proceeded against and punished accordingly.

Explanation: For the purposes of this section—

(*a*) "company" means any body corporate and includes a firm or other association of individuals; and

(*b*) "director" in relation to a firm, means a partner in the firm.

73. Offences Triable by Court of Session: No court inferior to that of a Court of Session shall try an offence under this Act.

74. Offences to be Cognisable: Notwithstanding anything contained in the Code of Criminal Procedure, 1973 every offence punishable under this Act shall be cognisable.

CHAPTER XVII

TRANSFER OF PROCEEDINGS

75. Transfer of Proceedings to Commission: (1) On the date of establishment of the Commission under sub-section (1) of Section 6, all proceedings pending before the Telecom Regulatory Authority of India established under sub-section (1) of Section 3 of the Telecom Regulatory Authority of India Act, 1997 shall be deemed to be pending before the Commission and shall be disposed of in accordance with the provisions of this Act.

76. Transfer of Proceedings to Appellate Tribunal: On the date of establishment of the Appellate Tribunal under sub-section (1) of Section 43 all proceedings pending before the Telecom Disputes Settlement and Appellate Tribunal established under Section 14 of the Telecom Regulatory Authority of India Act, 1997 shall stand transferred to the Appellate Tribunal which shall hear and dispose of such proceedings from the stage at which the proceedings were pending before the first-mentioned Tribunal in accordance with the provisions of this Act.

CHAPTER XVIII

MISCELLANEOUS

77. Taking Over Control and Management of Communication Service or Network Infrastructure Facility in Public Interest: (1) In the event of war or any calamity of national magnitude, the Central Government may by notification for a limited period, in public interest, take over the control and management of any communication service or any network infrastructure facility connected therewith, suspend its operation or entrust any agency of that Government to manage it in the manner directed by the Government for such period as provided for in the notification.

(2) If it appears necessary or expedient to do so, the Central Government may, in public interest, at any time request the Commission to direct any licensee to—

(*a*) transmit in its broadcasting service specific announcements, in such a manner as may be considered necessary;

(*b*) stop any broadcasting service which is prejudicial to sovereignity or integrity of India, security of the State, friendly relations with foreign States, or to public order, decency or morality, or communal harmony.

(3) On the issue of such directions by the Commission it shall be the duty of the licensee to ensure strict observance of such directions.

78. Obligations of Licensees and Grantees: (1) Every licensee or grantee shall—

(*a*) commence operation of his service within such period as may be specified by the Commission;

(*b*) maintain such documentary records and transmission schedules as may be specified by the regulations;

(*c*) allow inspection of such facilities and such documentary records and transmission schedules as may be specified by the Commission or by any person authorised by the Commission.

(2) The Commission may call for any information from the licensee or grantee including information necessary for ensuring transparency or for ascertaining the true ownership of the license or licensee or grantee.

(3) The Commission or any officer authorised in this behalf by the Commission shall have power to inspect and obtain information, wherever necessary, from programme producers, distributors and advertising agents.

(4) For effective enforcement of the terms and conditions of licenses or registration, the Commission or any officer authorized by the Commission for that purpose, shall have all the powers of an officer making inspection for the purpose of inspecting books of account and other books and papers of any licensee or grantee officer as provided under Section 209A of the Companies Act, 1956. 1 of 1956.

(5) It shall be the duty of every licensee to carry out the directions of the Commission given under this section.

79. Licenses to Operate Wireless Equipment on Board Ships and Aircraft: (1) No person shall operate any wireless equipment on board any ship or aircraft registered in India without a license granted by such authority or agency as may be notified by the Central Government.

(2) The Central Government may prescribe the qualification for the authority to be notified under sub-section (1) and the manner for granting the license to operate wireless equipment on board, ships and aircraft.

(3) The Central Government may prescribe qualification for the person to whom a licence for operating wireless equipment referred to in sub-section (1) may be granted

examination, if any to be conducted for granting such a licence the conditions of the licence, the fee to be paid thereof and other connected matters.

80. Recovery of Civil Liabilities: Without prejudice to other modes of recovery, any civil liability imposed under this Act if not paid be recovered as an arrear of land revenue and the Commission shall be empowered to suspend the licence or registration of the person on whom the civil liability is imposed till the same is not paid.

81. Supply of Information to Authorised Officers: Notwithstanding anything contained in any other law for the time being in force, where the Central Government or a State Government is satisfied that any information, document or record in possession or control of any service provider relating to any service availed by any consumer or subscriber is necessary to be furnished in relation to any pending or apprehended civil or criminal proceedings, an officer specially authorised in writing by such Government in this behalf shall direct such service provider to furnish such information, document or record to him and the service provider shall comply with the direction of the officer.

82. Act not to Apply in Certain Cases: Subject to the provisions contained in Chapter VI nothing contained in this Act shall apply to network infrastructure facilities or communication services owned, and operated by the Central Government or any State Government for their own use.

83. Bar of Jurisdiction of Civil Courts: No civil court shall have jurisdiction to entertain any suit or proceeding in respect of any matter which an Adjudicating Officer or the Appellate Tribunal or the Commission is empowered by or under this Act to determine, and no injunction shall be granted by any court or other authority in respect of any action taken or to be taken in pursuance of any power conferred by or under this Act.

84. Chairman, Members etc., to be Public Servants: The Chairperson, Members and other officers and employees of the Commission, and the chairperson, members, officers of the Appellate Tribunal shall be deemed to be public servants within the meaning of Section 21 of the Indian Penal Code.

85. Protection of Action Taken in Good Faith: No suit, prosecution or other legal proceeding shall lie against the Commission, or any member or officer or other employee thereof or against the Appellate Tribunal or the chairperson or member or officer or other employee thereof for anything, which is in, good faith done or intended to be done in pursuance of this Act or of any rules or regulations made thereunder.

86. Exemption from Tax on Wealth and Income: Notwithstanding anything contained in the Wealth Tax Act, 1957 the Income Tax Act, 1961 or any other enactment for the time being in force relating to tax on wealth, income, profits or gains the Commission or Appellate Tribunal shall not be liable to pay wealth tax, income tax or any other tax in respect of its wealth, income, profits or gains derived.

87. Act to have Overriding Effect: The provisions of this Act shall take effect notwithstanding anything inconsistent or contrary therewith contained in any other law for the time being in force or in any instrument having effect by virtue of any law other than this Act.

88. Power to Make Rules: (1) The Central Government may by notification make rules for carrying out provisions of this Act.

(2) In particular and without prejudice to the generality of the foregoing power, such rules may provide for all or any of the following matters, namely—

(*a*) other services relating to content application service under clause (10) of Section 2;

(*b*) other services relating to network application services under clause (16) of Section 2;

(*c*) other facilities relating to network infrastructural facilities under clause (17) of Section 2;

(*d*) other services relating to networking service under clause (18) of Section 2;

(*e*) obligation in respect of services under clause (33) of Section 2;

(*f*) other services relating to value added network application service under clause (34) of Section 2;

(*g*) other article or apparatus relating to wireless equipment under clause (35) of Section 2;

(*h*) the search committee for the purposes of sub-section (1) of Section 7;

(*i*) the tenure of part-time members under sub-section (2) of Section 8;

(*j*) the salary, allowances payable to and other terms of service of the Chairperson and other Members under Section 10;

(*k*) any other matters in respect of which the Commission may exercise the powers of a civil court under clause (j) of sub-section (1) of Section (14);

(*l*) the terms and conditions of service of the Secretary-General under sub-section (3) of Section 18;

(*m*) other matters under clause (vi) of sub-section (2) of Section 18;

(*n*) measure to protect consumer interests under clause (vii) of sub-section (2) of Section 18;

(*o*) other matters under clause (xv) of sub-section (2) of Section 18;

(*p*) fee for assignment of frequencies under sub-section (5) of Section 23;

(*q*) the manner and time frame for consultation between the Spectrum Manager and the Commission for seeking allocation of additional spectrum under sub-section (2) of Section 24;

(*r*) life saving services to be provided by a service provider shall provide under sub-clause (ii) of sub-section (1) of Section 28;

(*s*) the manner in which the number and type of broadcasting services including those of the public service broadcaster is to be provided by every service provider under clause (i) of sub-section (3) of Section 28;

(*t*) the form in which a complaint may be filed under sub-section (2) of Section 38;

(*u*) experience required for the appointment of an adjudicating officer under sub-section (3) of Section 39;

(*v*) any other matters in respect of which an adjudicating officer may exercise the power of the civil court under clause (j) of sub-section (5) of Section 39;

(*w*) the form, the manner of verification and fee to be accompanied with the appeal under clause (a) of sub-section (3) of Section 43;

(*x*) the form, the manner of verification and fee to be accompanied with the appeal under clause (b) of sub-section (3) of Section 43;

(*y*) search committee for the purposes of sub-section (3) of Section 44;

(*z*) the salary and allowance payable to and other terms of conditions of service of, the chairperson and other members of the Appellate Tribunal under sub-section (3) of Section 45;

(*za*) any other matter with respect to which the Appellate Tribunal may exercise powers of a civil court under clause (j) of sub-section (1) of Section 48;

(*zb*) the conditions subject to which the appontment of officers and employees of the Commission or the Appellate Tribunal shall be made under sub-section (1) of Section 53;

(*zc*) the salary and allowances payable to, and the terms and conditions of service of the officers and employees of the Commission or the Appellate Tribunal shall be made under sub-section (2) of Section 53;

(*zd*) the portion or percentage of the licence fee as may be attributable to Universal Service Obligation to be credited to the Universal Service Obligation Fund under sub-section (2) of Section 54;

(*ze*) the form and manner in which the annual statement of accounts shall be prepared under sub-section (1) of Section 57;

(*zf*) the information relating to the proceedings and policy to be contained in the annual report under sub-section (1) of Section 58;

(*zg*) the manner of setting up high powered committees or other appropriate mechanism by the Central Government or a State Government under sub-section (6) of Section 59;

(*zh*) safeguards under sub-section (1) of Section 66;

(*zi*) the qualifications for the authority to be notified under sub-section (1) of Section 79 and the manner for granting licences under sub-section (2) of that section;

(*zj*) the qualifications for the person to whom a licence for operating wireless equipment referred to in sub-section (1) of Section 79 may be granted, examination if any to be conducted for granting such a licence, the conditions of the licence, the fee to be paid thereof and other connected matters under sub-section (3) of that section;

(*zk*) any other matter which is to be or may be prescribed or in respect of which provision is to be made by rules.

89. Power to make Regulations: (1) The Commission may by notification make regulations consistent with this Act and the rules made thereunder to carry out the purposes of this Act.

(2) In particular and without prejudice to the generality of the foregoing power such regulations may provide for all or any of the following matters namely—

(*a*) the function to be performed by the regional offices of the Commission under Section 12;

(*b*) the time and places, and the procedure to be observed in regard to the transaction of business at the meetings of the Commission under sub-section (1) of Section 13;

(*c*) the powers and functions of the Secretary General under sub-section (1) of Section 15;

(*d*) the programmes, codes and standards to be specified under Section 20;

(*e*) the eligibility conditions for grant of licence or registration restriction regarding ownerhip and control of the media, restrictions on the number of licences or extent of accumulation of interest of such licences by a person and other conditions as may be considered necessary under sub-section (1) of Section 26;

(*f*) the obligations, conditions, tariffs and rates subject to which a service provider shall provide facilities and services under clause (a) of sub-section (2) of Section 26;

(*g*) the conditions subject to which a licence or registration may be granted or transferred under clause (b) of sub-section (2) of Section 26;

(*h*) the manner, the time, the terms and conditions, the fee and the procedure for grant of a licence or registration under sub-section (3) of Section 26;

(*i*) the details to be specified under sub-section (4) of Section 26;

(*j*) the period for which licence or registration shall be granted under sub-section (1) of Section 27;

(*k*) the form and the fee payable for granting licence or registration under sub-section (2) of Section 27;

(*l*) the number of channels for providing distribution of broadcasting services under clause (iii) of sub-section (3) of Section 28;

(*m*) other agreements to be registered with the Commission under clause (c) of Section 29;

(*n*) the form of application and the fees to be accompanied therewith under sub-section (2) of Section 30;

(*o*) the conditions and restrictions subject to which the licence may be issued under sub-section (4) of Section 30;

(*p*) the manner of holding inquiry by the Adjudicating Officer under sub-section (1) of Section 39;

(*q*) the documentary records and transmission schedules to be maintained by a licensee under clause (b) of sub-section (1) of Section 78;

(*r*) the eligibility and other terms and conditions for granting licence or registration under sub-section (3) of Section 98;

(*s*) such other regulation as may be required to carry out the purposes of the Act.

90. Laying of Rules and Regulations: Every rule and every regulation made under this Act shall be laid as soon as may be after it is made before each House of Parliament while it is in session for a total period of 30 days which may be comprised in one session or in two or more successive sessions, and if, before the expiry of the session immediately following the session or the successive sessions aforesaid, both Houses agree in making any modification in, the rule or regulation or both Houses agree that the rule or regulation should not be made, the rule or regulation shall thereafter have effect only in such modified form or be of no effect, as the case may be; so, however, that any such modification or annulment shall be without prejudice to the validity of anything previously done under that rule or regulation.

91. Power to Remove Difficulties: (1) If any difficulty arises in giving effect to the provisions of this Act, the Central Government may, by order published in the Official Gazette, make such provisions, not inconsistent with the provisions of this Act, as may appear to it to be necessary or expedient removing the difficulty:

Provided that no such order shall be made after the expiry of a period of three years from the commencement of this Act.

(2) Every order made under this, section shall be laid, as soon as may be, after it is made, before each House of Parliament.

92. Amendment 2 of 1974: In the Code of Criminal Procedure 1973—

(*a*) in Section 91, in sub-section (3), in clause (b) for the words "postal or telegraph authority" the words and figures "postal authority or any other service provider holding a licence or registration granted under the Communication Convergence Act, 2001" shall be substituted;

(*b*) in Section 92, for the words "postal or telegraph authority" wherever, they occur the words and figures "postal authority or any other service provider holding a licence or registration granted under the Communication Convergence Act, 2001" shall be substituted.

CHAPTER XIX
REPEAL AND SAVINGS

93. Repeal of Certain Acts, Saving of Licenses and Dissolution of Certain Authorities: (1) Subject to the other provisions of this sections, the enactments namely, the Indian Telegraph Act, 1885, the Indian Wireless Telegraphy Act, 1933, Telegraph Wire (Unlawful Possession) Act, 1950, and the Telecom Regulatory Authority of India Act, 1997 are hereby repealed.

(2) Notwithstanding such repeal, any person, who has obtained license or registration under the policy of the Central Government in force may continue to provide his services, if he has made an application to the Commission for the grant of a license or registration under this Act within a period of six months from the date of establishment of the Commission under this Act or where he has already made such an application, until the disposal of such application, whichever is later.

(3) The Commission shall, on receipt of an application referred to under sub-section (2), grant a license or registration after taking into consideration the terms and conditions on which such service were licensed or registered under any of the provisions of the repealed Acts, or the policy referred to in sub-sections (2), as the case may be, and keeping in view the objectives of this Act

(4) During the period of six-months mentioned in sub-section (2) or till his application is disposed off, whichever is later, the applicant shall continue to be governed by, and shall comply with, the provision of the Indian Telegraph Act, 1885, the Indian Wireless Telegraphy Act, 1933, Telegraph Wires (Unlawful Possession) Act, 1950 or the Telecom Regulatory Authority of India Act, 1997, as the case may be, as if these Acts had not been repealed, or the policy referred to in sub-section (2).

(5) Save as otherwise provided under this Act, with effect from the date of the establishment of the Commission and the Appellate Tribunal under this Act, as the case may be, the Telecom Regulatory Authority of India established under sub-section (1) of Section 3

of the Telecom Regulatory Authority Act, 1997 and the Telecom Disputes Settlement and the Appellate Tribunal established under Section 14 of that Act, shall stand dissolved.

94. Repeal of Act 7 of 1995 and Transitional Provisions: (1) Subject to the other provisions of this section, the Cable Television Networks (Regulation) Act, 1995 is hereby repealed.

(2) Notwithstanding such repeal, any cable operator registered under the Act so repealed, may continue to provide his cable services, if he has made an application to the Commission for the grant of a license under this Act within a period of six months from the date of the establishment of the Commission under this Act or where he has already made such an application, until the disposal of such application, whichever is later.

(3) The Commission shall, on receipt of an application referred to under sub-section (2), grant a license after taking into consideration the terms and conditions on which such cable operator was registered under the provisions of the repealed Act, and keeping in view the objectives of this Act.

(4) During the period of six-months mentioned in sub-section (2), or till his application is disposed of whichever is later, the applicant cable operator will continue to be governed by, and shall comply with the provisions of the Cable Television Networks (Regulations) Act, 1995 as if that Act had not been repealed.

THE NATIONAL SECURITY ACT

[Act No. 65 of 1980 dated 27th December, 1980]

An Act to provide for preventive detention in certain cases and for matters connected therewith.

BE it enacted by Parliament in the Thirty-first Year of the Republic of India as follows—

1. Short Title and Extent: (1) This Act may be called the National Security Act, 1980.

(2) It extends to the whole of India except the State of Jammu and Kashmir.

2. Definitions: In this Act, unless the context otherwise requires—

(*a*) "appropriate Government" means, as respects a detention order made by the Central Government or a person detained under such order, the Central Government, and as respects a detention order made by a State Government or by an officer subordinate to a State Government or as respects a person detained under such order, the State Government;

(*b*) "detention order" means an order made under Section 3;

(*c*) "foreigner" has the same meaning as in the Foreigners Act, 1946;

(*d*) "person" includes a foreigner;

(*e*) "State Government", in relation to a Union Territory, means the administrator thereof.

3. Power to make Orders Detaining Certain Persons: (1) The Central Government or the State Government may—

(*a*) if satisfied with respect to any person that with a view to preventing him from acting in any manner prejudicial to the defence of India, the relations of India with foreign powers, or the security of India, or

(*b*) if satisfied with respect to any foreigner that with a view to regulating his continued presence in India or with a view to making arrangements for his expulsion from India,

it is necessary so to do, make an order directing that such person be detained.

(2) The Central Government or the State Government may, if satisfied with respect to any person that with a view to preventing him from acting in any manner prejudicial to the security of the State or from acting in any manner prejudicial to the maintenance of Public Order or from acting in any manner prejudicial to the maintenance of supplies and services essential to the community it is necessary so to do, make an order directing that such person be detained.

Explanation: For the purposes of this sub-section, "acting in any manner prejudicial to the maintenance of supplies and services essential to the community" does not include "acting in any manner prejudicial to the maintenance of supplies of commodities essential to the community" as defined in the Explanation to sub-section (1) of Section 3 of the Prevention of Black-marketing and Maintenance of Supplies of Essential Commodities Act, 1980, and accordingly, no order of detention shall be made under this Act on any ground on which an order of detention may be made under that Act.

(3) If, having regard to the circumstances prevailing or likely to prevail in any area within the local limits of the jurisdiction of a District Magistrate or a Commissioner of Police, the State Government is satisfied that it is necessary so to do, it may, by order in writing, direct, that during such period as may be specified in the order, such District Magistrate or Commissioner of Police may also, if satisfied as provided in sub-section (2), exercise the powers conferred by the said sub-section:

Provided that the period specified in an order made by the State Government under this sub-section shall not, in the first instance, exceed three months, but the State Government may, if satisfied as aforesaid that it is necessary so to do, amend such order to extend such period from time to time by any period not exceeding three months at any one time.

(4) When any order is made under this section by an officer mentioned in sub-section (3), he shall forthwith report the fact to the State Government to which he is subordinate together with the grounds on which the order has been made and such other particulars as, in his opinion, have a bearing on the matter, and no such order shall remain in force for more than twelve days after the making thereof unless, in the meantime, it has been approved by the State Government:

Provided that where under Section 8 the grounds of detention are communicated by the officer making the order after five days but not later than ten days from the date of detention, this sub-section shall apply subject to the modification that, for the words "twelve days", the words "fifteen days" shall be substituted.

(5) When any order is made or approved by the State Government under this section, the State Government shall, within seven days, report the fact to the Central Government together with the grounds on which the order has been made and such other particulars as, in the opinion of the State Government, have a bearing on the necessity for the order.

4. Execution of Detention Orders: A detention order may be executed at any place in India in the manner provided for the execution of warrants of arrest under the Code of Criminal Procedure, 1973.

5. Power to Regulate Place and Conditions of Detention: Every person in respect of whom a detention order has been made shall be liable—

(*a*) to be detained in such place and under such conditions, including conditions as to maintenance, discipline and punishment for breaches of discipline, as the appropriate Government may, by general or special order, specify; and

(*b*) to be removed from one place of detention to another place of detention, whether within the same State or in another State, by order of the appropriate Government:

Provided that no order shall be made by a State Government under clause (b) for the removal of a person from one State to another State except with the consent of the Government of that other State.

[1][**5A. Grounds of Detention Severable:** Where a person has been detained in pursuance of an order of detention [whether made before or after the commencement of the National Security (Second Amendment) Act, 1984] under Section 3 which has been made on two or more grounds, such order of detention shall be deemed to have been made separately on each of such grounds and accordingly—

(*a*) such order shall not be deemed to be invalid or inoperative merely because one or some of the grounds is or are—

(*i*) vague,

(*ii*) non-existent,

(*iii*) not relevant,

(*iv*) not connected or not proximately connected with such person, or

and it is not, therefore, possible to hold that the Government or officer making such order would have been satisfied as provided in section with reference to the remaining ground or grounds and made the order of detention;

(*b*) the Government or officer making the order of detention shall be deemed to have made the order of detention under the said section after being satisfied as provided in that section with reference to the remaining ground or grounds.]

6. Detention Orders not to be Invalid or Inoperative on Certain Grounds: No detention order shall be invalid or inoperative merely by reason—

(*a*) that the person to be detained thereunder is outside the limits of the territorial jurisdiction of the Government or officer making the order, or

(*b*) that the place of detention of such person is outside the said limits.

7. Powers in Relation to Absconding Persons: (1) If the Central Government or the State Government or an officer mentioned in sub-section (3) of Section 3, as the case may be, has reason to believe that a person in respect of whom a detention order has been made has absconded or is concealing himself so that the order cannot be executed, that Government or officer may—

(*a*) make a report in writing of the fact to a Metropolitan Magistrate or a Judicial Magistrate of the first class having jurisdiction in the place where the said person ordinarily resides;

---

1. Section 5A inserted by the National Security (Second Amendment) Act, 1984 (Act No. 60 of 1984) w.e.f. 21st June, 1984.

(*b*) by order notified in the Official Gazette direct the said person to appear before such officer, at such place and within such period as may be specified in the order.

(2) Upon the making of a report against any person under clause (a) of sub-section (1), the provisions of Sections 82, 83, 84 and 85 of the Code of Criminal Procedure, 1973, shall apply in respect of such person and his property as if the detention order made against him were a warrant issued by the Magistrate.

(3) If any person fails to comply with an order issued under clause (b) of sub-section (1), he shall, unless he proves that it was not possible for him to comply therewith and that he had, within the period specified in the order, informed the officer mentioned in the order of the reason which rendered compliance therewith impossible and of his whereabouts, be punishable with imprisonment for a term which may extend to one year, or with fine, or with both.

(4) Notwithstanding anything contained in the Code of Criminal Procedure, 1973, every offence under sub-section (3) shall be cognizable.

8. Grounds of Order of Detention to be Disclosed to Persons Affected by the Order: (1) When a person is detained in pursuance of a detention order, the authority making the order shall, as soon as may be, but ordinarily not later than five days and in exceptional circumstances and for reasons to be recorded in writing, not later than ten days from the date of detention, communicate to him the grounds on which the order has been made and shall afford him the earliest opportunity of making a representation against the order to the appropriate Government.

(2) Nothing in sub-section (1) shall require the authority to disclose facts which it considers to be against the public interest to disclose.

9. Constitution of Advisory Boards: (1) The Central Government and each State Government shall, whenever necessary, constitute one or more Advisory Boards for the purposes of this Act.

(2) Every such Board shall consist of three persons who are, or have been, or are qualified to be appointed as, Judges of a High Court, and such persons shall be appointed by the appropriate Government.

(3) The appropriate Government shall appoint one of the members of the Advisory Board who is, or has been, a Judge of a High Court to be its Chairman, and in the case of a Union Territory, the appointment to the Advisory Board of any person who is a Judge of the High Court of a State shall be with the previous approval of the State Government concerned.

10. Reference to Advisory Boards: Save as otherwise expressly provided in this Act, in every case where a detention order has been made under this Act, the appropriate Government shall, within three weeks from the date of detention of a person under the order, place before the Advisory Board constituted by it under Section 9, the grounds on which the order has been made and the representation, if any, made by the person affected by the order, and in case where the order has been made by an officer mentioned in sub-section (3) of Section 3, also the report by such officer under sub-section (4) of that section.

11. Procedure of Advisory Boards: (1) The Advisory Board shall, after considering the materials placed before it and, after calling for such further information as it may deem necessary from the Appropriate Government or from any person called for the purpose through the Appropriate Government or from the person concerned, and if, in any particular case, if considers it essential so to do or if the person concerned desires to be heard, after hearing him in person, submit its report to the appropriate Government within seven weeks from the date of detention of the person concerned.

(2) The report of the Advisory Board shall specify in a separate part thereof the opinion of the Advisory Board as to whether or not there is sufficient cause for the detention of the person concerned.

(3) When there is a difference of opinion among the members forming the Advisory Board, the opinion of the majority of such members shall be deemed to be the opinion of the Board.

(4) Nothing in this section shall entitle any person against whom a detention order has been made to appear by any legal practitioner in any matter connected with the reference to the Advisory Board; and the proceedings of the Advisory Board and its report, excepting that part of the report in which the opinion of the Advisory Board is specified, shall be confidential.

12. Action Upon the Report of the Advisory Board: (1) In any case where the Advisory Board has reported that there is, in its opinion, sufficient cause for the detention of a person, the Appropriate Government may confirm the detention order and continue the detention of the person concerned for such period as it thinks fit.

(2) In any case where the Advisory Board has reported that there is, in its opinion, no sufficient cause for the detention of a person, the Appropriate Government shall revoke the detention order and cause the person concerned to be released forthwith.

13. Maximum Period of Detention: The maximum period for which any person may be detained in pursuance of any detention order which has been confirmed under Section 12 shall be twelve months from the date of detention:

Provided that nothing contained in this section shall affect the power of the Appropriate Government to revoke or modify the detention order at any earlier time.

14. Revocation of Detention Orders: (1) Without prejudice to the provisions of Section 21 of the General Clauses Act, 1897, a detention order may, at any time, be revoked or modified—

(*a*) notwithstanding that the order has been made by an officer mentioned in sub-section (3) of Section 3, by the State Government to which that officer is subordinate or by the Central Government;

(*b*) notwithstanding that the order has been made by a State Government, by the Central Government.

[1][(2) The expiry or revocation of a detention order (hereafter in this sub-section referred to as the earlier detention order) shall not [whether such earlier detention order has been made before or after the commencement of the National Security (Second Amendment) Act, 1984] bar the making of another detention order (hereafter in this sub-section referred to as the subsequent detention order) under Section 3 against the same person:

---

1. Sub-section (2) substituted by Act No. 60 of 1984, w.e.f. 21st June, 1984.

Provided that in a case where no fresh facts have arisen after the expiry or revocation of the earlier detention order made against such person, the maximum period for which such person may be detained in pursuance of the subsequent detention order shall, in no case, extend beyond the expiry of a period of twelve months from the date of detention under the earlier detention order.]

15. Temporary Release of Persons Detained: (1) The appropriate Government may, at any time, direct that any person detained in pursuance of a detention order may be released for any specified period either without conditions or upon such conditions specified in the direction as that person accepts, and may, at any time, cancel his release.

(2) In directing the release of any person under sub-section (1), the appropriate Government may require him to enter into a bond with or without sureties for the due observance of the conditions specified in the direction.

(3) Any person released under sub-section (1) shall surrender himself at the time and place, and to the authority, specified in the order directing his release or cancelling his release, as the case may be.

(4) If any person fails without sufficient cause to surrender himself in the manner specified in sub-section (3), he shall be punishable with imprisonment for a term which may extend to two years, or with fine, or with both.

(5) If any person released under sub-section (1) fails to fulfil any of the conditions imposed upon him under the said sub-section or in the bond entered into by him, the bond shall be declared to be forfeited and any person bound thereby shall be liable to pay the penalty thereof.

16. Protection of Action Taken in Good Faith: No suit or other legal proceeding shall lie against the Central Government or a State Government, and no suit, prosecution or other legal proceeding shall lie against any person, for anything in good faith done or intended to be done in pursuance of this Act.

17. Act not to have Effect with Respect to Detentions under State Laws: (1) Nothing in this Act shall apply or have any effect with respect to orders of detention, made under any State law, which are in force immediately before the Commencement of the National Security Ordinance, 1980, and accordingly every person in respect of whom an order of detention made under any State law is in force immediately before such commencement, shall be governed with respect to such detention by the provisions of such State law or where the State law under which such order of detention is made is an Ordinance (hereinafter referred to as the State Ordinance) promulgated by the Governor of that State and the State Ordinance has been replaced—

(*i*) before such commencement, by an enactment passed by the Legislature of that State, by such enactment; or

(*ii*) after such commencement, by an enactment which is passed by the Legislature of that State and the application of which is confined to orders of detention made before such commencement under the State Ordinance, by such enactment.

as if this Act had not been enacted.

(2) Nothing in this section shall be deemed to bar the making under Section 3, of a detention order against any person referred to in sub-section (1) after the detention order

in force in respect of him as aforesaid immediately before the commencement of the National Security Ordinance, 1980, ceases to have effect for any reason whatsoever.

Explanation: For the purposes of this section, "State law" means any law providing for preventive detention on all or any of the grounds on which an order of detention may be made under sub-section (2) of Section 3 and in force in any State immediately before the commencement of the said Ordinance.

18. Repeal and Saving: (1) The National Security Ordinance, 1980, is hereby repealed.

(2) Notwithstanding such repeal, anything done or any action taken under the said Ordinance shall be deemed to have been done or taken under the corresponding provisions of this Act, as if this Act had come into force on the 23rd day of September, 1980, and, in particular, any reference made under Section 10 of the said Ordinance and pending before any Advisory Board immediately before the date on which this Act receives the assent of the President may continue to be dealt with by that Board after that date as if such Board had been constituted under Section 9 of this Act.

MONOPOLIES AND RESTRICTIVE TRADE PRACTICES

Objective

The Monopolies and Restrictive Trade Practices Act, 1969, was enacted to prevent the concentration of economic power to common detriment, control of monopolies, prohibition of monopolistic and restrictive trade practices and matters connected therewith.

Prevention of concentration of economic power under this enactment, any undertaking producing one-fourth or more of any type of goods and having assets of more than Rupees One Crore, is required to obtain clearance for any scheme of expansion. Initially, for the purpose of computing the total goods produced by the undertaking, goods that were exported were also taken into account. By an amendment in 1980, those goods, which are exported, are no longer taken into account while computing the total goods produced. This was in view of the objective of the enactment to control such practices within India.

Monopolistic trade practices Section 2(i) of the Act defines monopolistic trade practice while Section 31 provides for investigation into such practices by the MRTP Commission, either on reference by the Central Government or on receipt of information as to the carrying on of such activities by any such undertaking. Monopolistic Trade Practices such as maintenance of prices and profits at unreasonable levels, arbitrary price increases, high expenditure on advertisement and high power salesmanship to maintain the undertaking in a monopoly situation, limiting technical detriment to common detriment or allowing quality of goods to deteriorate, are some of the situations which would call for investigation and action under this enactment.

Under Section 32 of the Act, such monopolistic trade practices are deemed to be prejudicial to public interest. Monopolistic trade practices that may be permitted. The Central Government may permit such practice if satisfied that it is necessary for defense purposes, to ensure maintenance of supply of essential goods/services or to give effect to any terms of an agreement to which the Central Government is a party.

Restrictive trade practices Section 2 (o) defines restrictive trade practices, which may be investigated by the MRTP Commission under Section 37 of the Act. Restrictive Trade Practices such as differential or discriminatory incentive based on quantities, stipulation in agreement as to the prices that should be charged on re-sale, territorial restrictions and restricting terms of guarantee, bumper prize contests wherein the prices of goods are increased to cover the cost of prizes, announcing loan facilities without a guarantor while charging guarantor's commission, sale of goods for a particular price and issue of cash memos for a lesser sum, display of price-lists indicating maximum recommended rates and absence of indication that a lower price could be charged thus encouraging consumers to ask for rebates, prohibiting film producers from selling/assigning video rights, fixing prices and discounts in concert, collusive tendering, predatory pricing and cutting prices below cost price, boycott of products of a particular company by traders, or for obtaining higher commission, and such other practices would call for investigation and action under this enactment. Restrictive trade practices that may be permitted. The Act provides for registration of agreements containing clauses that are indicated under Section 33 as a restrictive trade practice. Such practices may be permitted by the Commission under Section 37, on such steps taken by the undertaking to ensure that such practice is not prejudicial to public interest.

This however does not apply in case of restrictive trade practices under Section 2 (o). If any clause in an agreement is a restrictive trade practice as defined in Section 2 (o) the same is void and cannot be permitted.

Advantages

In cases, where it is proved that any undertaking is about to carry on any monopolistic, restrictive or unfair trade practice, which is likely to prejudicially affect public interest, or the interest of any trader of consumer, the Commission may restrain such undertaking from carrying on such activity by way of injunction, which includes the power to grant ex-parte temporary injunction also.

The Commission is also empowered to hold investigation on receipt of a complaint by any trader, consumer or such affected party. Disadvantages. The Monopolies and Restrictive Trade Practices Commission established under Section 5 has its central office in Delhi which makes the remedies available under this Act, inaccessible to other parts of the country and also entails delay.

Unfair Trade Practices Under the MRTP Act, 1969

An Unfair Method or an unfair deceptive practice adopted for the purpose of promoting the sale, use or supply of any goods or for the provision of any services, is an unfair trade practice under the Monopolies and Restrictive Trade Practices Act, 1969.

Unfair Trade Practices under the Act include, practices such as making false statements in relation to the quality, quantity (the statement could either be oral or in writing or even by visible representation), sponsorship, uses or benefits of goods, passing off old goods as new, or giving of warranty/guarantee which is not based on proper test, making public representation that purports to be a guarantee or warranty or a promise to replace or replace articles if there is no reasonable guarantee that the warranty/repair or replacement will not be carried out.

Further practices such as misleading the public concerning the prices at which certain goods are to be sold or giving misleading facts or disparaging the goods or services of the other person, advertising the sale or services at a bargain price which is not intended to be sold at such bargain price, offering gifts or prices that are fully or partly covered by the amount charged, sale or supply of goods knowing fully well that they do not comply with the standards prescribed, hoarding or destruction of goods, etc., are also included in the definition of unfair trade practices.

Remedy

Any trade association, consumer or registered consumers' association aggrieved by such of the practices mentioned above can seek relief by filing a complaint before the Monopolies and Restrictive Trade Practices Commission, which on such complaint has powers to conduct an inquiry into such practices. Any consumer can approach the Commission irrespective of whether such consumer is a member of the consumers' association or not. The Commission can also conduct inquiry on the reference of the Central/State Government, on an application by the Director General or on its own knowledge or information.

Powers of the Commission

The Commission may, on satisfaction that the practice is an unfair trade practice, direct that such practice shall be discontinued, and in cases in which agreements in relation to such practices are made, the Commission may also direct that such agreement shall be void or specify the manner in which it shall be modified. Further, the Commission also has the power to direct that any information relating to such unfair trade practices shall be disclosed, issued or published. Where such party takes such steps to ensure that the trade practice is no longer prejudicial to public interest, or the interest of any consumer or consumers generally, the Commission may permit such party to carry on such trade. Case Laws on Unfair Trade Practices, the following have been held to be unfair trade practices:

Contests

Manufacturer of a cigarette announcing a contest for married couples, provided one of them was a smoker, offering prizes which would be given to three healthy, good looking couples, whose photographs would be used to advertise that brand of cigarette, held amounts to unfair trade practice, as it would give non-smokers an impression that even smokers can be healthy and therefore loss or injury is implicit from such practice. [1985 (1) Comp LJ 235 (MRTPC)].

Contest to which there is no restriction on the number of entry forms that could be sent, on the condition that each entry form should be accompanied by the cash memo for having purchased certain tablets (Panjon), held unfair trade practice and cease and desist order issued. [(1987) 61 Comp Cas 352 (MRTPC)].

Contest with no restriction on the number of entry forms that could be sent, on condition that it should be accompanied by the upper part of two tooth brush covers and in which the participant was required to write a sentence on the why his family used that tooth brush, held unfair trade practice, as it was organised for promoting the sales of the tooth brush directly or indirectly [1991 (2) Comp LJ (MRTPC)], also see 1991 (3) Comp LJ 181 (MRTPC), 1992 (3) Comp LJ 304 (MRTPC)] and 1993 (2) Comp LJ 109 (MRTPC).

Contest to promote tours, announcing Maruti 100 as the highest prize, requiring participant to avail of any of the tours or services for a minimum of Rs. 5,000 or to deposit the sum as a condition to take part in the competition, held unfair trade practice as it was meant for promoting sale/supply of the services rendered. [1992 (3) Comp LJ 301 (MRTPC)].

Lucky Draws

Promoting sales of journals by announcing prizes to be decided by lots. Held unfair trade practice. [(1987) 62 Comp Cas 263, p 264 (MRTPC)].

Announcing lucky draw to persons who purchases goods worth Rs. 250 or more, held unfair trade practice as it was in the nature of lottery and game of chance. [1993 (1) Comp LJ 311 (MRTPC)].

Announcing lucky draw scheme and accordingly increasing the price of bicycles with an intention to partially or fully finance the prizes offered while giving consumers an impression that they were being given for free of cost. [1986 Comp Cas 1036, p. 1041].

Gifts and Exchange

Announcing exchange of old cookers for new and offering prices by way of lucky draw, whose price was fully or partially covered by the overall price of the cooker and resale price maintained by fixing the amounts which were to be paid by consumers on exchange, held amounts to unfair trade practice as it was likely to cause injury to consumers and distorts competition. [1986 (1) Comp LJ 89 (MRTPC)].

Advertising gift of cold coffee shaker on the purchase of instant coffeė, while the price of the shaker was partly covered by the cost of the product and further no providing the same number of shakers as those of the coffee packets resulting in consumers paying a higher price, held prejudicial to public interest, cease and desist order passed. [1993 (3) Comp LJ 229 (MRTPC)].

REPORT ON THE WORKING OF PRASAR BHARATI

Introduction Background

Ministry of Information and Broadcasting, Government of India constituted a Committee comprising the following to carry out a comprehensive review of Prasar Bharati: Shri N.R. Narayanamurthy Chairman & Chief Executive, Infosys Shri Kiran Karnik.

Managing Director, Discovery Communications India, Shri Shunu Sen, Chairman & Chief Executive, Quadra Advisory, Marketing Consultant Shri R.C. Mishra, Jt. Secretary (Broadcasting, Ministry of I&B), Shri Rajeeva Ratna Shah, Chief Executive, Prasar Bharati, Special Invitee.

Mr. Naraynamurthy suggested that Mr. Sen be appointed as the Chairman of the Committee. The Committee unanimously agreed to this suggestion.

A total of nine meetings have been held consequent to the first meeting with Shri Arun Jaitley, Minister of Information and Broadcasting.

The Committee was briefed to study the working of the Prasar Bharati and, keeping in view its responsibility as a public service broadcaster, to make appropriate recommendations with regard to its organisation structure, legal framework, systems and all other relevant areas to ensure quality, credibility and professionalism within the organisation.

Members of the Committee met the Prasar Bharati Board on two occasions and also sent to them a draft of the key recommendations.

The Committee is most indebted to the Prasar Bharati Board for their suggestions and comments.

The Committee was pleased to meet a large cross-section of working groups from within Doordarshan and All India Radio. The meetings were of very considerable help to the Committee. In addition, the Committee is grateful to the large number of persons who have provided useful advice, both, as individuals as well as groups. These include advertisers and advertising agencies, production companies, media specialists and many others.

However, the Committee wishes to state that they are solely responsible for the recommendation made in the report. The members were conscious of its responsibility in providing advice and direction to an organisation, Prasar Bharati, which is concerned with development of media and communication as a public broadcaster within the largest democracy in the world.

Broadcasting as a Public Service

The Need for Public Service Broadcasting

There are three crucial issues relating to Prasar Bharati. These are the identity, funding and functioning of this organisation.

In order to establish the identity of Prasar Bharati it is imperative to seek answers to some basic questions; such as, whether there should be a public service broadcaster and what should it be doing?

A simple answer could be that All India Radio and Doordarshan (the two major constituents of Prasar Bharati) are a historical reality; already in existence, with one of the largest broadcasting networks in the world. Therefore, there is no point in questioning their existence.

Such a proposition, however, does not lend meaning to the existence and identity of an organisation. An organisation cannot grow and excel if it exists only because of historical accident. For any living and vibrant organisation, there must be a larger purpose and mission. It is, therefore, essential to look for the basic purpose behind Prasar Bharati in the context of public service broadcasting.

In order to do this, it is necessary to analyse the characteristics of the broadcasting industry and to determine whether commercial broadcasting can fulfil the objectives of public service broadcasting. In other words, can market forces, alone, meet all the objectives of public service broadcasting.

In the parlance of economics, a good television programme is a "merit" good, similar to education, training and health services. Left to the market forces, it is possible that purely commercial broadcasting will not meet the full needs of public service broadcasting. This is because commercial broadcasting regards the audience as consumers and not as citizens.

In a poor and developing country like India, this distinction has considerable implications, since the market power or purchasing power of a large segment of the population is small. Moreover, the information and education needs of this segment of the population may not be met by commercial broadcasting. Hence, the need for public service broadcasting.

One of the basic objectives of the public broadcasting system should be to strengthen the democratic process by providing information, promoting debate and discussion on all vital issues, and providing a platform for interaction between the common man and the policy maker. Market forces cannot be expected to take care of these objectives. This reinforces the need for a public service broadcaster which would take care of these objectives and also promote a common national outlook by providing shared experiences. In addition, such a broadcasting system is also expected to promote and foster the diverse culture of the country.

Broadcasting has several unique influences on society; such as, on its value systems, social norms, interpersonal behaviour and cultural identity. Given the perceived, if not proven, impact of broadcasting, especially on such important and sensitive issues, governments around the world have sought to regulate broadcasting.

There are two ways to influence a nation's broadcasting. The first is direct regulation; such as, for example, the intent of our proposed Broadcasting Bill. This would prevent broadcasters from offering programmes that (for example) offend certain sections of the community; or, require broadcasters to air certain number of news and education programmes. However, it has been the worldwide experience that such regulations, even if legally permissible, are not good enough to meet the public service objectives. Such regulations are primarily negative in nature and can, at best, prevent the undesirable, but cannot ensure the desirable.

The second, and, perhaps, the only meaningful manner in correcting the market deficiencies is through the strong and dominant presence of a Public Broadcaster. Such a broadcaster would set programming norms and standards; and, provide leadership in this area. Experience shows that commercial broadcasting services follow the lead of such a broadcaster in order to compete for the viewership of such programmes.

Such an approach brings a clear concept of what constitutes public service broadcasting. It is a broadcasting service which does not depend solely on market forces, but must take into account audience needs and requirements. Indeed, a public service broadcaster should primarily focus on influencing the programme quality and content of all broadcasting, including those by the private sector.

However, the broadcaster cannot take the audience for granted. If such programmes lack appeal, they will not have an audience. The challenge is to provide programmes that are meaningful and need-oriented, and yet achieve a reasonably high audience share.

This requires a high degree of commitment to the mission and policy by the public service broadcaster. It also requires access to appropriate funding and an organisation structure which promotes credibility and creativity, while ensuring the efficiency and effectiveness in the entire operation.

Setting Standards: Some International Experiences

A recent survey by McKinsey provides some interesting insights into the operation of public service broadcasting elsewhere in the world. Commercial terrestrial competition in Sweden began in 1991, and, not surprisingly, new competitors such as TV3 and TV4 (commercial broadcasters) quickly gained market share. But SVT (Sweden's PSB) gets its funds from a license fee (a fixed fee charged to every home with a television), so this development did not immediately affect its budget or weaken its commitment to distinctive programming. Indeed, it soon became evident that viewers continued to watch SVT's high-quality programmes, and SVT's market share never fell below 40 per cent. Commercial broadcasters, who might otherwise have wanted to make their standard programmes, had to compete for viewers by increasing the number of factual, cultural and educational programmes on the commercial channels. SVT now has a prime time market share of more than 50 per cent, and Sweden boasts of a high level of public service programming by all television stations.

This is not the only example of the ability of public service broadcasters to influence the behaviour of their commercial rivals. In the United Kingdom, BBC spend large amounts of money and time making landmark natural history programmes. This genre of programming by BBC has created the need for similar programming on other channels; programmes such as Survival and Equinox. It has been found that this type of competition among broadcasters raises the quality of the broadcast and develops the taste of the audience; as a result, ratings for such quality programmes remain comparatively high.

Similarly, when Canada's CBC invested in its French-language news coverage, it forced its main commercial competitor, TVA, to do the same, thus meeting the needs of a minority group and raising overall production standards. In Germany, the high standards of PSBs, ARD and ZDF, in news production prompted their commercial competitor RTL to introduce Spiegel TV news, a programme produced with the help of Der Spiegel, Germany's most respected magazine. The early commitment of ZDF to local production rather than to cheaper foreign imports not only increased their rating but forced its commercial competitors to rethink the use of imports.

The evidence from these claims is not merely anecdotal. The McKinsey survey reveals a strong cause-and-effect link between the distinctiveness of programmes screened by the Public Broadcaster and that of commercial operators in the same market. In the words of Michael Grade, former Managing Director of Channel 4, "The BBC keeps us all honest".

There is one proviso though: the Public Broadcaster must operate from a position of strength. The US Public Broadcasting Service (PBS), which concentrates on education, the arts, and current-events programmes, was never a major broadcaster in terms of audience. With a market share of only 3 per cent today, PBS is hardly a significant rival to commercial operators and cannot meaningfully shape their approach to programming.

The Focus of Public Service Broadcasting

The need for public-service broadcasting was never greater. The proliferation of channels has fuelled many wants and fulfilled some needs, but, has left gaps. These should be filled by a public service broadcaster. This is because commercial television broadcasting conducted by privately owned satellite channels must target the relatively affluent urban market as they can only air their programme through a cable operator. Similarly, the private FM radio stations would target the up market, more urban radio listener. The private channel must primarily deliver an audience; rather than being a vehicle for delivering new ideas, information and education to its viewers and listeners.

A public service broadcaster must be concerned about a broader set of clientele and has a much larger mandate. It has to meet the complete media needs of all, including those of a villager who has very few media options. Such a person is either watching television or listening to radio, on a community set, in an isolated part of the country. The public service broadcaster also needs to take into account the media needs of the minority audience, whether they be ethnic, religious, or linguistic. Such a broadcaster needs to concern itself with developing taste, promoting understanding, spread literacy and development, create informed debate and empower the disadvantaged: major issues that a commercial broadcaster rarely addresses. This, then, is the real raison d'être of a public service broadcaster.

The Indian Context

In India, the process of large-scale commercialisation of broadcasting began in the 80's. Even though Doordarshan and All India Radio enjoyed a monopoly, a reduction in the proportion of budgetary support, combined with pressures to raise more revenues to fund rapid expansion, forced the pace of commercialisation.

As Doordarshan sells airtime on the basis of the size of its viewership, it began to look for ways and means of increasing its share as the media market became increasingly more competitive. This resulted in a reduction in emphasis on public service programmes, as the prime time was reserved for commercial programming which earned the most revenue. Radio underwent a similar process, though to a lesser extent.

A problem has arisen because both services, particularly, Doordarshan, auctioned airtime slots, either by programmes and, more recently, in half-hour segments during the evenings, to private producers in order to maximize revenue. This has led to a quixotic situation that, increasingly, Doordarshan, a public service broadcaster, owns neither the programme content nor the marketing rights to the programme being shown on its channel.

While the above steps have resulted in Doordarshan's income increasing, the overall growth in income since 1995 is significantly less than the industry; be it the national or the regional language channels. This is responsible for the loss in Doordarshan's market share in terms of viewership and revenue, even though the organisation broadcasts the most popular programmes in Hindi and many of the regional languages, and has the largest audience amongst all television channels.

It is within this context—and within the overall role for public service broadcasting—that the Committee would like to make certain specific recommendations on Prasar Bharati.

With regard to the overall aspect of public service broadcasting, the Committee would like to suggest that: Public service broadcasting is essential in India, and must be seen as a right of all citizens. It must provide a platform for free discourse and debate, while its content must empower people. In the present context, it is essential to have Prasar Bharati in the role of a public service broadcaster in India. Prasar Bharati, and its constituents—Doordarshan and All India Radio—must be autonomous and completely free to make their own operational and tactical decisions.

The ensuing sections of this report will look at other important issues which deserve recognition and require discussion; on the basis of which the Committee will make certain firm recommendations and suggest a set of consequent action.

The Mission and Objectives for Prasar Bharati

As outlined earlier, the Committee would like to see Prasar Bharati, as the public broadcaster, playing an important and critical role in determining the direction and thrust of broadcasting in India by setting standards through programmes that are meaningful, absorbing, diverse in content, innovative in design and of the highest quality.

However, the role of Prasar Bharati goes beyond this. The power of the broadcast medium is acknowledged, especially in areas like agenda setting, information transfer, experience sharing, motivation and mobilisation. The Committee believe that Prasar Bharati can play a major role in spreading knowledge and education; in countering superstition and promoting a modern scientific attitude; in fostering social change and in catalysing development.

Of course, the medium must, also, provide entertainment; and, indeed, this is its main strength. However, care should be taken to ensure that, for Prasar Bharati, advertising revenue earned by selling entertainment programming does not become the only yardstick for judging the performance of this organisation. Alternative indices, related to audience size and share, programme content, quality and impact are more meaningful and must be used. Once the vision and framework of Prasar Bharati are clearly defined, then, within these, revenue maximisation should be a goal.

The mission of an organisation defines broadly its purpose to its stakeholders. It helps to set the overall direction and provides a touchstone in deciding what it should do and, importantly, what it should not do. We feel that a clearly articulated mission is of particular importance to Prasar Bharati, in order to steer the organisation on a course that is in line with the key objectives underlying its creation.

The mission and objectives of Prasar Bharati need clear articulation. This is essential so that Prasar Bharati, on one hand, resists the temptation of the commercial market; and, on the other hand, also resists the power of political pressures and patronage

Most important of all, Prasar Bharati must ensure that it meets its central mandate of providing its audience with programmes that inform, educate and entertain.

The mission statement that we would commend for adoption by Prasar Bharati is as follows: Prasar Bharati will aim to provide, in the most efficient manner possible, media content of the highest quality that will empower and enlighten the citizens of India, and audiences outside the country, through original and relevant programmes which inform, educate and entertain whilst ensuring a sizeable audience and reach.

While the vision must necessarily be broad and somewhat general, it is necessary to define, with greater precision, the role of Prasar Bharti as the public service broadcaster in India. This is best done through the enunciation of the key objectives for the organisation.

We recommended that the key objectives be: To create content—textual, graphic, pictures, video and audio—that is absorbing, interesting and enjoyable; and is relevant to the audience is impartial, unbiased and presents all sides of a story; respects and gives due weightage to differing and contrary opinions, beliefs and viewpoints Reflects the diversity and richness of India's culture, Develops specific programmes appropriate for a most important audience: children Addresses the needs of minority audiences: the disadvantaged, linguistic, cultural, ethnic, religious and special interest groups, serves as an input for education, social change and national development is of the highest quality, and sets standards for other broadcasters to serve as a unique platform that: Creates a forum for informed debate and discussion on issues of national or regional importance; particularly those which are agitating people's minds provides space for issues, artists and programmes that private channels are unlikely to air Serves as a means for audience feedback and for people-to-people communication acts as a vital means for empowering and enlightening people through information, education and culture, in an absorbing manner provides entertainment and enjoyment to its large and varied audience. To ensure that transmission provides the best technical signal quality to every receiver in India, in the most efficient and cost-effective manner. In addition, to carry Indian content to its relevant audience worldwide through appropriate means. To create and to utilise the necessary hardware infrastructure so as to fully exploit the potential of new media and technologies for the benefit of its present and potential audience. Restructure and fashion itself to emerge as an efficient, world-class producer and broadcaster of meaningful, entertaining content.

Accountability and Structure

The public service broadcaster plays a key role in any society, especially, in a large and thriving democracy. It must be a part of "civil society", independent of and distinct from the government. In fact, the public service broadcaster must act as one of the bedrocks of society, and seek to continuously enlarge the so-called "public sphere". It must play host to informed debate, provide space for alternative and dissenting viewpoints, be a voice for the voiceless, and give substance to the phrase "participatory democracy".

A key principle of a public service broadcaster is that it must be completely independent. Its structure, financing and personnel policies should be such that it must not be at the mercy of—or amenable to pressures from the government of the day. On the other hand, the public service broadcaster need not give in to the temptation of maximising commercial revenue by providing mindless programming. To maintain this balance may not always be easy. A clear understanding of its own accountability and a good organisation structure can help to facilitate this objective; and a truly professional staff will ensure it.

At the same time, the public service broadcaster must be accountable directly to its "owners", the citizens of India. This means, in practice, Prasar Bharati must be accountable to the body which represents the citizens of the country—the Parliament.

It is within these broad parameters that the Committee examined the structure of Prasar Bharati.

The Sengupta Committee had suggested that the functions of the Chairman and Executive Member be combined. While the suggestion does have some merit, this committee felt that, on balance, the advantage lay in separating these two functions.

The Committee strongly recommends that Prasar Bharati retains the concept of a part-time Chairman and a full-time Executive Member (to be designated as the Chief Executive).

The issue of genuine corporatisation of Prasar Bharati was looked at. This would entail adopting a normal corporate model, having equity and shareholders. The Committee felt that the role of Prasar Bharati is unique, and while the efficiency, flexibility, transparency and responsiveness of a good corporate structure are essential, the organisation of Prasar Bharati has to be somewhat different. The Committee therefore, commend the present concept of Prasar Bharati being a "body corporate" created by an Act of Parliament.

However, it is recommended that the possibility of corporatising certain activities of Prasar Bharati be examined. For example, the transmission activity, the studio and production facilities could be corporatised; as also, in due course, some of the newer areas of such as Internet and DTH.

As mentioned earlier, the role and functions of a public service broadcaster require that must it be autonomous. While Prasar Bharati should be accountable to Parliament for policy and strategic decisions, the organisation would be responsible for its own operational and tactical decisions. The Government of the day must have no hand in its functioning or decision-making, and must remain at arms-length from Prasar Bharati. While the structure and systems can help to promote this, ultimately it is the commitment and professional integrity of the key individuals in Prasar Bharati and in the Government which will ensure that suitable conventions are developed so that this objective is met. At the same time, Prasar Bharati must function in cooperation and in collaboration with the Government; in crucial areas such as education, health, environment and rural development.

The relationship between the Government and Prasar Bharati will always continue to be difficult to define. It will require self-discipline on both sides, and a non-adversarial approach. Once healthy precedents are set, it will be much easier for those who follow.

A crucial manner by which Prasar Bharati can reinforce its independence would be through financial independence. In Committee's view, Prasar Bharati must aim to become self-sufficient within 5 years and must not depend on Government financing in the longer term. The only possible exception could be capital financing to meet strategic or national goals that go beyond public service broadcasting. Indeed, it is vitally important that, for the financing of revenue expenditure, Prasar Bharati does not depend on the Government, as this could lead to some form of political or other pressure.

The second key element of the separation from government is in the area of personnel. The Committee recommends strongly that the entire staff required by Prasar Bharati and its constituents be transferred to that organisation. Further, it is recommend that the Prasar Bharati management be allowed to select only those whom they require. Others could either return to their parent department within the Government, or be given a suitable VRS.

Moreover, in the future, there should be no further deputation of government employees to Prasar Bharati. Such deputations are often counter-productive and go against the principle of autonomy and being at arm's length from both the politician and the bureaucracy. Similarly, deputation from the private sector should also not be considered. This important recommendation should be put into effect as soon as it becomes implementable as a part of the total reform of the personnel policy.

It is important to define the relationship of Prasar Bharati with the Parliament and the Government. In a cabinet form of Government, within a parliamentary democracy, it is perfectly in order for Prasar Bharati to discharge its accountability to the Parliament and its committees through the Minister of Information and Broadcasting.

We consider accountability to the public as being a key area for any public service broadcaster. To ensure this, we recommend that, once a year, on radio and television, the Board of Prasar Bharati and the Chief Executive make a brief, yet comprehensive, presentation as an annual review, highlighting the objectives of the year, major activities of the organisation and key achievements and failures; in addition, provide a perspective and the key objectives for the forthcoming year. The feasibility of adding an interactive element to this presentation by receiving comments and questions on fax, phone or Internet may also be explored.

It is also important that the audience for Doordarshan and All India Radio be able to send their views, air their grievance and raise any question they may have with the organisation. BBC has an excellent programme where viewers and listeners write, phone, fax or e-mail their comments, criticisms and questions. A spokesperson, on behalf of BBC, answers a selected number of queries in an interesting and honest manner on a weekly programme. This programme has celebrated its Silver Jubilee. Perhaps, this example could be adapted by Prasar Bharati for both television and radio.

The composition of the Prasar Bharati Board, which must deal only with overall matters of policy, needs to be modified. The Board should consist of a Chairman and six part time Members, in addition to a representative of Ministry of I&B who should not be below the rank of Joint Secretary. Amongst the full-time Prasar Bharati employees, only the Chief Executive must be a member of the Board. The present structure, as enunciated in the Act, could undermine the authority of the Chief Executive by including other members of the operating management on the Board. However, as and when required, any of the functional or departmental Heads will be invited to a specific Board Meeting by the Chief Executive depending on the need for that person to be present at a particular Board Meeting.

A Management Council should be constituted, chaired by the Chief Executive, Prasar Bharati with the senior executives who are either profit or function responsible, as members. We recommend that the membership comprise: DG: AIR, DG: DD, heads of proposed new Transmission and New Business functions, heads of Strategic Planning and Technology and heads of Personnel and Finance. Thus there will be 8 members. The Management Council should be responsible for all operational and management matters. In addition, the Management Council should discuss and make recommendations to the Board on policy issues, and oversee the implementing of the decisions of the Board and the Council.

There is need for autonomy, decentralisation and devolution of power within Prasar Bharati. For example, within each business—Doordashan, All India Radio and the proposed new business—there should be a body of operating managers responsible for all day to day operations; such as content, marketing, commercial operations and, importantly the regional network.

Financing and Funding Mechanisms

An appropriate funding mechanism is crucial for achieving the mission and objectives of a Public Broadcaster.

There are two major ways to fund such an organisation. The first could be through licence fees, public subsidies and Government grants. Alternatively, the funding could be primarily from commercial revenue such as advertising and sponsorship revenue, pay channels, sale of audio and video programmes, and programming agreements. Indeed, a broadcaster has the choice of several different methods for its financing.

In UK, BBC is funded by license fee and by the sale of its materials and services. BBC does not, in the UK, depend on advertising, sponsorship or subscription revenues.

In some other countries, like Japan and Sweden, Public Broadcasters rely almost entirely on licence fee. Spain's TVE and New Zealand's NZTV are, on the other hand, completely financed by advertising revenue. PSBs in France, Germany, Italy and Ireland combine the licence fee revenue with advertising, while Australia's ABC is entirely funded by Government grants. Canada's CBC combines Governments grants with advertising revenue. In USA, where PBS plays a marginal role, the organisation is funded by Government grants and private donations.

It is difficult to say which funding model is ideal for Prasar Bharati. The success and failure of a model could depend on the national values and traditions of a country; and on the media market opportunities available. No single universal model can be recommended across the globe. Every country, keeping in mind its own strengths and weaknesses, its opportunities and threats to its system, would need to adopt its own model.

Before finalising an appropriate funding model in the context of India, it is important to recognize the advantages and disadvantages of each option. Funding of public service broadcaster by a direct charge on the user (that is, by a licence fee), was earlier considered to be the ideal mechanism for funding such a broadcaster. While a similar system is successfully working in UK and Sweden, the same has been abandoned in Australia and New Zealand. Australia has substituted it by a Government grant and New Zealand is still considering various options to substitute the license fee, which they have abolished recently. In India, the system of Radio and TV receiver licence and associated fee was abolished in 1985 as it was difficult to administer and costly to implement.

To overcome the administrative and other difficulties in collecting the license fee, some countries have substituted the fee by a Government grant from the pool of general taxes levied by the State. However, sole dependence on Government grant runs, in our view, contrary to the basic principle that Prasar Bharati should keep at arms length from the Government. Attempts have been made by countries which have adopted this system of funding, to neutralise the direct influence of the Government by building appropriate institutional mechanisms (through statutes), organisational structures, and by having healthy traditions and conventions.

Funding through advertisement and sponsorship revenue could bring about a much desired efficiency in the utilisation of public resources. However, it may dilute the purpose of a Public Broadcaster. This is because if the organisation has to survive solely by competing in the market, the Public Broadcaster may not be in a position to correct market deficiencies by providing a genre of programming which is necessary for society. Therefore, funding a Public Broadcaster entirely through advertisement and sponsorship revenue is not often recommended.

Similarly, funding entirely through a system of 'pay TV' runs contrary to the basic philosophy of a public broadcaster in a developing economy, as it is required that its basic service should be available universally, irrespective of the viewer's capacity to pay. However, this option certainly merits consideration for the premium products which may be marketed by Prasar Bharati; for example, the specialist channels which are targeted at the upper end of the market or New Media services such as DTH or Internet. Indeed, entering the New Media is a business decision which is difficult to justify conventionally, in terms of Government funding. The Committee believes that it is essential for Prasar Bharati, as a leading player in the ICE category, to exploit this opportunity; which, may be small today, but with the exploitation of convergence technology, is likely to become as important as the traditional service of providing television and radio, in the not-too-distant future.

Opportunities to earn revenues from the sale of television and radio programmes both within and outside the country should also be targeted. We believe that there is considerable scope for the sale of television programmes to channels abroad, which are targeted to the Indian diaspora; and in certain specialised markets which are not of immediate interest to Prasar Bharati. Indeed, a special marketing operation must be developed to fully exploit such opportunities; as such business, if properly conducted, could add a not insignificant amount to the commercial earnings of Prasar Bharati.

Two major commercial opportunities which need to be exploited are Prasar Bharati's transmission capabilities and its studio and production facilities. There is an opportunity to utilise the large transmission capability of the organisation to provide digital terrestrial transmission to private operators in addition to providing uplinking facilities through the satellite network on which Doordarshan currently has excess capacity. Similarly, in the area of Radio, there are transmission, engineering and studio capabilities which All India Radio could profitably sell to private operators.

The Central Studios which belong to Doordarshan and All India Radio along with the regional production capabilities need to be refurbished; indeed, to ensure professional capability, of the desired quality, it is certain that additional investment in equipment would be required. After the internal production requirements needs have been met, the opportunity to rent the available excess capacity should be considered. Not only will this bring in additional revenue, but it will also provide an incentive to these facilities to remain up to date and "top of the line" in their category.

The Committee would like to state that the growing demands on Government financial resources from various competing sectors of the economy which are the Government's prime areas of responsibility (such as, the social and infrastructural sector), would mean that public institutions such as Prasar Bharati will be under pressure to generate their own resources. The Committee believes that this pressure is to the public good. Because a self-sufficient Prasar Bharati, in the area of financing, will not only reduce the pressure on the public exchequer, but would bring about a significant increase in the degree of efficiency in the overall operation of Prasar Bharati.

Channel Positioning

Approach and Strategy

Prasar Bharati operates a large number of radio and TV channels. While some have a clear definition, target audience, and positioning, others seem to have no clear identity. Moreover, some channels are not only serve little purpose, but also cannibalise viewership from other Prasar Bharati channels. It is critical that each channel is positioned clearly and distinct from one another. In terms of its objectives, each channel must be differentiated so that it is preferred viewing/listening for a specific set of customers.

We recommend that each channel, both on radio and TV, have a clearly defined identity and positioning; so that, each channel is the specific choice for a type of viewer (or listener).

As a public broadcaster, Prasar Bharati has multiple responsibilities. Amongst these, a particularly important one is its duty to ensure that, as far as possible, each listener and viewer is able to access relevant information and entertainment in a form, language and idiom which is understandable to the audience. In order to do this, a substantial amount of the transmission must be decentralised with programmes produced locally, in the local language.

Hence, it is important, that in the case of television, each Regional Kendra broadcast for, at least, four hours during the late afternoon and evening, in the relevant regional language, over the terrestrial channel. In the case of radio, it is important that FM radio stations develop themselves as local or city stations and there is significant local programming on the Akashvani stations.

Finally, we must have a set of national channels, both in radio and television, with programmes of broader national content and interest. Such programming may primarily be in Hindi or English, a constraint that we will have, at least till technology is in place to cost-effectively broadcast multiple audio channels.

The division of time between these three different categories (local, regional, national) is not easy, and could vary from State to State, or even within a State. We recommend that two principles must apply: Broadcast by all transmitters of a mandatory, "must-carry" part of the national channel. Beyond this mandatory part, decentralisation of decision-making to the regional TV Kendras and radio stations as to whether or not to carry other programmes of the national channel or to develop adequate high quality local programming.

Each TV Kendra must, in part, act and behave as a local channel. Depending on the location, such programming could take a small, yet significant, portion of time. To benefit from such TV programmes, it is best if the local content is 'actionable'. Therefore, to the extent possible; such programming must be participatory in nature.

Thus, the terrestrial transmitters must carry local, regional and national programmes, with the mix of these being determined locally; except, for the mandatory portion of the national channel.

In addition to having programmes on the DD National channel, each State must have in its Primary channel, programmes catering specifically to the audience and the culture of that State, in the local language. We must recognise the growing mobility of people across the country. Such 'non-residents' desire to retain contact with their own culture and language; hence, each of the major regional languages should have a channel carried via satellite, so as to be available for cable carriage anywhere in this country. These channels will be language and culture specific; and will focus on the needs and interests of the people living in that particular State.

It is important that the local, regional and national programming content is distinct. Overlaps, or even repetition, must be avoided.

Channel Identity

There should be a national channel, DD National, that will broadcast for 24-hours a day. Its primary mode of distribution will be terrestrial, though it will also be transmitted by satellite and cable. The content will cover a whole range of topics and subjects, keeping in mind the mass reach that it will enjoy, and the fact that the "must-carry" programmes of this channels are the only ones to which all viewers in the country will have access. Accordingly, it must seek to inform, enlighten and stimulate; and provide entertainment and enjoyment.

The second national channel, which will be both terrestrial and satellite, will be DD Metro. This channel will be positioned clearly and without any ambiguity as the DD Entertainment Channel. DD Metro will be aimed at the same market as the Hindi satellite channels which broadcast to a large market; currently, about 30 million homes. It is important to perceive this channel not just as a major revenue earner for Prasar Bharati, but as a channel which provides a large audience base amongst the urban middle class. Currently, amongst cable and satellite viewers, Metro in the danger of becoming a minority channel.

A major area of focus will be the news, current affairs and information channel ("DD News"); primarily in Hindi and English. DD News will focus on news, current affairs, discussions and debates on topical issues, and on providing information. The purpose will be to provide a national perspective on matters that are of importance to India. It is, therefore, important that this channel, which, along with DD National, forms the core of public-service broadcasting, has the widest possible reach. Hence, in addition to satellite broadcasting, DD News will also broadcast from the terrestrial transmitters already available in Mumbai, Kolkata, Delhi and Chennai. In the evening hours, when news in Hindi and English is being broadcast on DD National, it is proposed that the terrestrial stations at Mumbai, Kolkata and Chennai will broadcast news or current affairs programme in the local language.

Another satellite channel of DD will be aimed primarily at show-casing quality entertainment, art and culture and fostering their growth. This will be known as DD Prime. This channel will feature classical and folk music concerts, dance, drama, art and quality cinema from India and around the world; in addition to relevant documentaries, book reviews, talk-shows and discussions.

DD Prime will provide an outlet for outstanding and deserving artistes and will seek to meet the needs of an interested audience while simultaneously developing the taste for such quality fare. This channel will include programmes such as plays and cinema in regional languages, with sub-titling where appropriate. It is proposed that DD Prime operate primarily from 7 in the evening till late night.

It is hoped that this channel could be developed into a true multi-purpose channel. While in the evening hours, as mentioned above, the channel will host DD Prime, during the day this channel can offer technical and continuing education, on an interactive format; aimed during the early morning hours, at young professionals and during the afternoon provide programmes which offer suitable vocational, education and training to high school and college students.

During the late afternoon and early evening, this channel should broadcast both instructive and enjoyable children's programming under a suitable brand name. This is important because good children's programmes, particularly in Hindi and regional languages, are just not available on television; and there is little incentive amongst creatives to develop such programmes.

To cater to the immense and widespread interest in sports, and to promote interest and participation in certain games, DD will run a dedicated sports channel ("DD Sports"). This channel will be distributed via satellite and cable.

DD will have an international channel ("DD International") which will pick appropriate programmes from other channels, and also create special programmes aimed to meet the needs and interests of the potential audience for this channel. Its primary audience will be the Indian diaspora, but it should aim to get an audience beyond this, especially for certain programmes on Indian culture, news about South Asia, and our neighbouring countries. This will be distributed via the wide-area beam of INSAT 3C and other platforms appropriate to each country: cable/DTH/MMDS or even terrestrial, where possible. The Committee recognises, as provided in the Prasar Bharati Act, the status of this channel; in the view of its funding by the Government. While the bulk of educational programmes must be in the local language in each region, and must therefore find appropriate and suitable time slot in local/regional channels, we recommend strong support to and strengthening of the newly-started DD Gyan Darshan channel. This must have nation-wide reach, which means that its content will be primarily in Hindi/English and be focussed on higher secondary, tertiary and professional education. It must have linkages with inter-active initiatives like the Training and Development Communication Channel (being operated by ISRO) and the Internet. It must serve as a major vehicle for organised/structured distance-education programmes (such as, those of IGNOU) and for enrichment (for example, UGCs Countrywide Classroom) and aim at a nationwide audience.

At present, DD does not have multiple channels in any regional language. Over time, this should be perceived as a desirable development. When that happens, we would again recommend a clear and distinct identity for each channel, and a clear purpose vis-à-vis Prasar Bharati's mission and objectives.

NORMS, GUIDELINES AND PROCEDURES FOR SATELLITE COMMUNICATIONS

The Government has approved a policy that envisages allocation of INSAT system capacity for non-governmental users, registration of Indian satellite systems by private Indian companies and limited use of foreign satellites in special circumstances.

The Department of Space (DOS) will be the administrative ministry in all matters related to satellite systems in India. As per the policy, the Indian National Satellite System (INSAT) capacity will be made available to non-government (private) Indian Service Providers on a commercial basis subject to availability after meeting the government needs.

The DOS will allocate INSAT capacity for private users. DOS may also build capacity in INSAT system for private users on request on commercial basis. Private Indian companies with a foreign equity less than 74 per cent are now allowed to establish Indian Satellite Systems.

These companies can submit their applications for registering their satellite systems to the Committee for Authorising the establishment and operation of Indian Satellite Systems (CAISS).

The office of CAISS is set up at the SatCom Programmes Office at ISRO Headquarters, Antariksh Bhavan, New BEL Road, Bangalore-560 094. The authorisation to operate the Satellite System and the Orbit spectrum notification/registration will be done by CAISS.

However, operating licenses for services to be provided by the Indian Satellite Systems will be issued only by the concerned administrative departments like Department of Telecommunication for telecom services and Ministry of Information and Broadcasting for TV/Radio broadcasting.

Foreign satellites will also allowed to be used in special circumstances for satellite communication services in India.

The service licensing departments may allow the use of foreign satellites only in consultation with the Department of Space. If suitable capacity/capability is available in INSAT or Indian Satellite Systems, operations with foreign satellites will not be permitted. For the use of foreign satellites for Internet Service Provider (ISP) gateways, the existing procedures established by Telecom Commission will apply.

REPORT CONDITIONAL ACCESS SYSTEM

Introduction

The issue of introduction of an addressability system has been engaging the attention of the Government for sometime, keeping in view the problems being highlighted by sections of the broadcasting industry, including Cable operators, MSO's and Content Providers. A large number of complaints had also been received from subscribers, protesting unwarranted and frequent increase in subscription rates by Cable operators. With almost 38 million cable and satellite households in the country and with a household paying on an average Rs. 125 per month, as subscription charges, the revenue generated in the sector is close to Rs. 5,700 crores. Of this, there have been reports of substantial under reporting by different sections depriving the different players of the industry of their entitled revenue/collection and reportage of transparent viewership figures and the Government tax.

To deliberate and decide upon various issues on this topic, it was decided to set up a Task Force, under Joint Secretary (Broadcasting) in the Ministry of Information and Broadcasting, with representations from the cross-section of the industry. The objective, inter-alia, was to deliberate in the need for introducing a Conditional Access System for viewing channels through the cable network and to determine the modalities for doing so.

Constitution of Task Force and Terms of Reference

The Task Force was constituted by an order dated 25th September, 2001 and it consists of representatives from Indian Broadcasting Federation, MSOs Content Creators, Cable Operators, Broadcasters, Infrastructure Providers, nominee from the Ministry of

Consumer Affairs, representative of Consumer activists and technical experts. The order constituting the committee, with its Terms of Reference, is annexed.

The Committee was empowered to invite experts and to broad base the representation on the Task Force, technical experts were co-opted from the industry. Other participants who desired to contribute were also invited to attend. The primary issue of concern for the Committee was to establish the need for introducing Conditional Access System in order to provide a choice to the consumer and to examine the feasibility of doing so, to protect the interests of the consumer from additional costs on replacement of the TV receiver or on purchase of the Conditional Access System, and to debate technology issues relating to standardization and performance.

Meetings

The Task Force held three meetings, one each in the month of October, November and December 2001. At each meeting specific issues were identified for discussion and deliberation and decisions were taken thereon, at the same meeting. Since the technology issues were more complex and required extensive consultations, a Subcommittee was constituted under Director (BD), I&B with representations from the industry, equipment manufacturers and technical experts to go into those aspects. This Subcommittee held separate meetings and their recommendations were considered by the Task Force in its last meeting held on 26th December, 2001. At each stage the members were encouraged to send further comments/observations in writing for the consideration of the Task Force.

After each meeting of the Task Force, the minutes were circulated to the members by post as well as over Internet. Members of the Task Force as well as other representatives of the industry have provided inputs, which were also considered by the Task Force. This included comments, which were received from National Cable and Telecommunications Associations, Cable Operators etc.

Summary of Discussions

It was acknowledged that Cable Television in India was a technology, which had entered in an unbridled manner and had become a reality totally through private investment. A connectivity of over 35 million homes had been achieved in this syndrome. The MSOs were later entrants. Cable and Satellite Television had gradually become an irresistible force in the process of transformation of communication technology and the perceived potential of Cable TV, DTH, DTT etc., was immense. The Cable Operators observed that since demand of content was driving ad revenue and viewership, the Broadcasters and the Content Creators were whimsically levying exorbitant charges for programmes, channels and for bouquets. Arbitrary increases in subscription rates were creating a problem because Cable Operators were left with no option but to pass on this burden frequently to the subscribers.

The Group discussed the problems and alternatives available and was of the view that the consumer needed to exercise a choice of watching what he chose, and that the viewer should be made aware of what it would cost to view 'Pay' Channels. Addressability is a technique, where signals are sent in an encoded form and an equipment, placed at the subscriber's end, decodes the signals, in accordance with the choice exercised by the consumer and authorized by the Service Provider, specifically on the subscriber's request. The Task Force considered it desirable that the Conditional Access System should be introduced to provide the consumer choice of viewing and an option to pay for what he chose to watch. The consumer should also not be expected to pay unreasonably for the 'Free-to-Air' channels and must be able to receive the 'Free-to-Air' channels without any Set Top Box or any need to change the existing receiver.

The Task Force acknowledged the existence of the value chain starting from the Content Maker, to the Content Provider (Broadcaster) to the main Content Distributor, to the last mile Content Distributor (Cable Operator) and finally the consumer household. In the existing arrangement the consumer was paying for all the channels, irrespective of what he actually watched or desired to watch. There was now need to make the system transparent in respect of the Pay Channels/Pay programmes, which can be watched by selective subscribers. The subscribership of all 'Pay' channels should be fully determinable.

This transparency would allow entitled revenue to accrue to the different links in the chain, permit the consumer to have programming of his choice and watch channels according to their affordability, hopefully at a lower cost, and provide realistic and authentic viewership data. The Task Force was unanimous that the Conditional Access System is necessary to bring transparency at different levels, but that it should not add to the financial burden of the consumer. It was decided that the Government should mandate it by law.

The Set Top Box, allowing addressability, should be required only for 'Pay' channels; for subscribers who opt to view only 'Free-to-Air' channels, there would be no requirement of a Set Top Box. The Set Top Box shall be supported by the MSOs/Cable Operators through installation of necessary infrastructure like Subscriber Management System etc. It was considered desirable that the Government must be empowered to enter and inspect the premises and operations of the MSOs and Cable Operators to ensure enforcement of the requirements of the Set Top Box, of transparent recording of viewership figures, display of channel rates etc.

The Task Force saw a presentation on the system introduced by M/s. Ortel Communications, in Bhubaneshwar, on experimental basis. It is using 'Dalvi', a low cost conditional access scrambling system, which combines security and multi-tiered addressability. It encrypts analogue signals and the system is compatible with any video transmission system. The system has the potential to address 80,000 customers with a subscriber Management System. A total of 4 channels-mix of 'Free-to-Air' and 'Pay'—are presently being routed through the Set Top Box. The cost of the Set Top Box is approximately Rs. 3,500. The system is one way and not interactive. It was informed that the start up costs, for investment in equipment at Head-end Level, was approximately Rs. 50,000 for each channel. The financial implications of introducing the Set Top Box and addressability system, at each level, were discussed against this background. The need to keep the present system intact, at least for those viewers who prefer to watch only 'Free-to-Air' channels, was favoured.

The Task Force felt that the Set Top Box should be mandated only for "Premium Tier"; 'Free-to-Air' channels being taken in a "Basic Tier", receivable by all viewers at a standard subscription rate. The Task Force debated other issues emerging out of the presentation and felt that the price of channels/content for the Cable Operators should be fixed in a transparent manner, by Content Providers and Channel owners, for all operators.

The Task Force was unanimous in its view that there was need for an enabling provision in the legislation for Government to prescribe certain basic minimum standards for the equipment and its performance. In order to consider all issues relating to prescriptions of Standards and Performance Parameters, for the Set Top Box/Conditional Access System, a Sub-Committee made recommendations on the standards and the specifications for Digital Cable TV and Analogue Cable TV, as well as for Digital/Analogue Set Top Boxes.

It also recommended that the Cable Operator/Equipment Provider should declare, in a transparent manner, the capability of the Set Top Box and its inter-operability with other networks. It also recommended that unauthorized viewing/redistribution of the signal should be made a cognizable offence. The packaging of services, including Value Added Services, should be left to the Operators who should be free to choose the middleware/software/hardware provided that it conformed to basic minimum performance standards. It further recommended that the subscriber management system should provide transparent information to all the players.

The Task Force was of a strong view that there was urgent need to educate the subscribers, by all the stakeholders, on the operation of Cable Television and the cost of various services, including the operation and cost of Set Top Boxes. The Task Force accepted the recommendation of the Sub-Committee, for an enabling provision in the Act to prescribe basic minimum technical standards and performance parameters, through the Bureau of Indian Standards (BIS). The manufacturers of the equipment must provide full information on the capability of the hardware.

It was also considered desirable that BIS may invite comments from the industry and examine internationally acceptable standards before prescribing standards for India. The Task Force was of the view that eventually the Set Top Box would permit migration, by the subscriber, across various delivery media-Satellite, Cable and Terrestrial. The user will thus have the capability to migrate to various delivery media, simply by changing the "Network Interface Module".

The members of the Task Force debated the need for a Conditional Access System base on DVB simulcrypt technology or any other currently acceptable technology but eventually felt it appropriate to leave the issue of technological specifications to the Bureau of Indian Standards, who would ensure that the technology is not proprietary in nature. In order to ensure transparency in the interface between MSOs and the Cable operators, it was decided that the Government be empowered to obtain monthly reports from the MSOs, Broadcasters and Cable operators in the manner prescribed.

The Task Force also debated the issue of "must carry" provision for the content of the Public Service Broadcaster and the pricing of the "Basic Tier" of service and the Set Top Box. The Group felt that the consumer should not be burdened with the cost of changing his television sets on purchasing a Set Top Box, if he wanted to view only Free-to-Air channels. The Subscriber should exercise choice of viewing the 'Pay' channels through a Set Top Box. However, there was no need to prescribe the cost price of either the Set Top

Box. However, there was no need to prescribe the cost price of either the Set Top Box or the 'Pay' channels.

It was however, considered desirable that the pricing of various channel bouquets, by the Broadcasters, MSOs should be done in a transparent manner. The Group was unanimous that the Government should fix the price of the 'Basic Tier' and therefore legislation should enable the determination of the 'Basic Tier' price, from time to time by the Government. The Pricing/subsidy of the Set Top Boxes, by any player should be left to market forces, as long as the consumer was made fully aware of the availability and capability of the equipment. The equipment suppliers were confident that with larger volume, market forces would drive down the price of Set Top Boxes. The Group also felt that the Broadcasters, MSOs and Cable Operators should be allowed the freedom to work out their individual business plans to subsidise the Set Top Boxes, in accordance with their own marketing strategy.

The Group acknowledged the fact that with progressive introduction of Digital Video Broadcasting technology, its combination with interactive return path, between the user and the Service Operator, will pave the way for other services, for which the Subscriber should be prepared to pay on the basis of charges fixed.

Recommendations

1. The Conditional Access System and the Supportive Subscriber Management System should be mandated under the Cable Television Networks (Regulation) Act, 1995.
2. The Set Top Box shall be required only for "Pay" Channels and the "Free-to-Air" channels shall be receivable by the subscribers in the current mode, without Set Top Box. The encrypted channel should be defined as "Subscription based Channel".
3. The Technical parameters of the Set Top Box shall conform to the Indian standards, to be prescribed by the Bureau of Indian Standards, in accordance with the provisions of the Bureau of Indian Standards Act, 1986. While doing so, the Bureau of Indian Standards may take into account the internationally acceptable standards and obtain recommendations from technologists and manufacturers of equipment.
4. It shall be mandatory for the Equipment Provider/Manufacturer to declare, in a transparent manner, the capability of the Set Top Box and its interoperability on other networks.
5. In order to ensure transparency in the operations between MSOs, Cable Operators etc., the Government must be empowered to obtain detailed information, on regular basis, from each level of operation. This may include information on total subscriber base, on individual programmers, viewership of independence channels, subscription rates, charges fixed by the Broadcasters, Content Creators for each channel etc. Each subscriber shall be keep informed in a transparent manner of the subscription rates for each individual 'Pay' channel.
6. Unauthorised viewing/distribution/redistribution of the broadcast signal should be made a cognizable offence.

7. The Government should regulate the price of 'Basic Tier' of the 'Free-to-Air' channels. The Government should also be enabled to revise the cost of the 'Basic Tier', from time to time. The Government will also make a special provision for the channels of the Public Services Broadcaster. No government intervention was considered necessary with regard to the cost of the Set Top Box or the rates of the individual 'Pay' channel.
8. There should be no requirement for change of the receiving set, irrespective of whether the consumer chooses to watch 'Free-to-Air' channels and/or 'Pay' channels.
9. There was an immediate need to educate the consumer on the operation of cable television, on the cost of content creation and its distribution upto the households. The Broadcasters, Content Creators and MSOs should not enhance the charges of the 'Pay' channels arbitrarily, it should be done in a transparent manner.
10. The packaging of services, includes Value Added Services, as well as the pricing of the paid bouquets would be left to market forces. However, consumer interest needed to be protected by providing efficient and responsive service and through a transparent and accurate billing and collection system. This will also ensure that the revenue accruable to the Government is determined in a fair manner.

GUIDELINES FOR USE OF SNG/DSNG

Conditions for use of SNG/DSNG in C Band and KU Band

(*i*) The use of SNG/DSNG would be permitted to News and Current Affairs channels uplinked from India for live news/footage collection and point to point transmission.

(*ii*) PIB accredited content provider(s) if any, to the permitted News and Current Affairs channel(s) can use SNG/DSNG for collection/transmission of news/ footage.

(*iii*) Entertainment channels who are uplinking from their own teleport, can use SNG/DSNG for their approved channels, for transfer of video feeds to the permitted teleport.

(*iv*) All Foreign channels, permitted entertainment channels uplinked from India and companies/individuals not covered in (*i*), (*ii*) and (*iii*) as above will be required to seek temporary uplinking permission for using SNG/DSNG for any live coverage/footage collection and transmission on case to case basis.

(*v*) Only permitted teleport operators and Doordarshan may offer/hire out SNG/ DSNG equipments/infrastructures to other broadcasters who are permitted to uplink from India.

(*vi*) The uplinking should be carried in encrypted mode, so as to be receivable only in closed user group. The signal should only be down linked at the permitted teleport of the licensee and uplinked for broadcasting through permitted satellite through that teleport only.

(*vii*) Each company/channel desiring to use SNG/DSNG would have to apply to Ministry of I&B and get permission before doing the same.

(*viii*) Uplinking from SNG/DSNG should be in SCPC mode only (only single feed can be uplinked from the SNG/DSNG at a time).

(*ix*) The channel would also give an undertaking that the feed collected through SNG/DSNG shall conform to Programme and Advertisement Codes.

(*x*) The use of SNG/DSNG would be permitted only in those areas/regions/states which are not specifically prohibited by MHA.

(*xi*) The company would submit the purchase documents of SNG/DSNG terminals and inform Ministry of I&B about placement of these terminals at the various locations.

(*xii*) Period of Permission:

(*a*) For teleport owners-co-terminus with teleport licence.

(*b*) For permitted News and Current Affairs channels—for the period of the Channel permission.

(*c*) For content providers to permitted channels—for the period of the channel permission.

(*d*) For other broadcasters having temporary uplinking permission—for periods as specified in the temporary uplinking permission.

(*xiii*) The company permitted to use SNG/DSNG shall apply to WPC for frequency authorization of WPC. It should be renewed yearly in time and a copy should be submitted to this Ministry by the company every year.

(*xiv*) The permitted company shall maintain a daily record of the location and the events which have been covered and uplinked by SNG/DSNG terminals and down linked at their main satellite earth station and produce the same before the licensing authority or its authorized representative, which will include officers of Ministry of Home Affairs and Ministry of I&B, as and when required.

(*xv*) The permitted company shall not enter defence installations.

(*xvi*) The equipment should not be taken in the areas cordoned off from security point of view.

(*xvii*) The company/channel desiring to use SNG/DSNG would give an undertaking that it would be used for live newsgathering and footage collection for captive use only.

(*xviii*) Violations of any of the aforementioned terms and conditions would lead to revocation/cancellation of the permission to use the SNG/DSNG.

(*xix*) The permitting authority may modify the conditions laid down or incorporate new conditions, as and when considered necessary.

Additional Condition for use of SNG/DSNG in KU Band

(*i*) SNG/DSNG will not be used for DTH operation, directly or indirectly. Any such use would lead to the termination of licence/permission.

(*ii*) Uplinking Dish used for SNG/DSNG operation would not exceed 2 meters.

(*iii*) There would be no turnaround for broadcasting in KU band.

GUIDELINES FOR UPLINKING OF NEWS AND CURRENT AFFAIRS TV CHANNELS FROM INDIA

Eligibility Criteria

The eligibility criteria in the guidelines for uplinking of news and current affairs TV channels from India have been revised as follows. Other provisions in the guidelines issued on 26th March 2003 remain unchanged.

An applicant company desirous of uplinking news and current affairs channel(s) from India will be considered eligible, if it fulfils the following criteria:

(A) It is a registered/incorporated in India under the Companies Act, 1956.

(B) Foreign Direct Investment (FDI) shall not exceed 26 per cent of the Paid-up Equity of the applicant company.

(C) Permission will be granted only in cases where equity held by the largest Indian shareholder is at least 51 per cent of the total equity, excluding the equity held by Public Sector Banks and Public Financial Institutions as defined in Section 4A of the Companies Act, 1956, in the New Entity. The term largest Indian shareholder, used in this clause, will include any or a combination of the following:

1. In the case of an individual shareholder,
   (*a*) The individual shareholder.
   (*b*) A relative of the shareholder within the meaning of Section 6 of the Companies Act, 1956.
   (*c*) A company/group of companies in which the individual shareholder/HUF to which he belongs has management and controlling interest.
2. In the case of an Indian company,
   (*a*) The Indian company
   (*b*) A group of Indian companies under the same management and ownership control.

For the purpose of this Clause, "Indian company" shall be a company, which must have a resident Indian or a relative as defined under Section 6 of the Companies Act, 1956/HUF, either singly or in combination holding at least 51 per cent of the shares.

Provided that in case of a combination of all or any of the entities mentioned in sub-clauses (1) and (2) above, each of the parties shall have entered into a legally binding agreement to act as a single unit in managing the matters of the applicant company.

(D) While calculating the 26 per cent FDI in the equity of the applicant company, the foreign holding component, if any, in the equity of the Indian shareholder companies of the applicant company will be duly reckoned on pro rata basis so as to arrive at the total foreign holding in the applicant company.

(E) The company shall make full disclosure, at the time of application, of Shareholders Agreements, Loan Agreements and such other Agreements that are finalized or are proposed to be entered into. Any subsequent changes in these would be disclosed to the Ministry of Information and Broadcasting, within 15 days of any changes, having a bearing on the foregoing Agreements.

(F) It will be obligatory on the part of the company to take prior permission from the Ministry of Information and Broadcasting before effecting any alteration in the foreign shareholding patterns and the shareholding of the largest Indian shareholders, as indicated in clause (C) above or any alteration in any other Agreements, as indicated in clause (E) above.

(G) The applicant shall be required to intimate the names and details of all persons, not being resident Indians, who are proposed to be inducted in the Board of Directors of the company.

(H) The company shall be liable to intimate the names and details of any foreigners/NRIs to be employed/engaged in the company either as Consultants (or in any other capacity) for more than 60 days in a year, or, as regular employees.

(I) At least 3/4th of the Directors on the Board of Directors of the company and all key Executives and Editorial staff shall be resident Indians.

(J) The representation on the Board of Directors of the company shall as far as possible be proportionate to the shareholding.

(K) All appointments of key personnel (executive and editorial) shall be made by the applicant company without any reference from any other company, Indian or foreign.

(L) The applicant company must have complete management control, operational independence and control over its resources and assets and must have adequate financial strength for running a news and current affairs TV channel.

(M) CEO of the applicant company, known by any designation, and/or Head of the channel, shall be a resident Indian.

GUIDELINES FOR SYNDICATION ARRANGEMENTS BY NEWSPAPERS

All registered newspapers (Indian publications) are authorised to make syndication arrangements for procuring material including photographs, cartoons, crossword puzzles, articles and features from foreign publications (content provider) under automatic approval route subject to the following conditions:

(*i*) The total material so procured and actually printed in an issue of the Indian publication does not exceed 7.5 per cent of the total printed area of that issue,

(*ii*) The syndicated material does not include full copy of the editorial page or the front page of the foreign publication,

(*iii*) The mast head of the content provider publication is not utilised in the Indian publication,

(*iv*) Credit to the content provider is necessarily given prominently as a byline in the Indian publication,

(*v*) The material procured under syndication arrangement is such that has already been published in the content provider publication.

Any case involving relaxation of any of the above conditions would require to be examined by the Ministry of I&B, and, before any material is actually procured under syndication arrangement beyond the above noted conditions, the Indian publication should have applied for and obtained prior approval of the Ministry of I&B.

These guidelines would not apply to the cases where Ministry of I&B has issued its approval/no objection certificate for publication of Indian edition of a foreign magazine/journal/newspaper.

Bibliography

A. O'Brein (1995), *Management Information Systems—A Managerial End Users Perspective*, New Delhi: Galgotia Publications Ltd.

A.M. McDonough, *Information Economics and Management Systems*, New York, McGraw Hill, 1963, p. 5.

Aboba, Bernard (1993), *The Online User's Encyclopedia: Bulletin Boards and Beyond*, Reading. MA: Addison-Wesley.

Aderson, R. (1974), Honorary Director, Medical Information Unit, Wassex Regional Hospital Board, Winchester, U.K.: "Health Information System" in WHO Chronicle, 28, 52-54.

Adorno, T.W. 1996 [1991], *The Culture Industry: Selected Essays on Mass Culture*, in P. Marris and S. Thornham (eds.), *Media Studies: A Reader*, Edinburgh: Edinburgh University Press.

Aggarwala, Dharma Vira (1977), *Handbook of Management Principles and Practices*, Chandigarh: All India Directories Publishers.

Aggerholm, Barbar (1993), *'UW to probe offensive images in computer network'*, Kitchener Waterloo Record Tuesday, 20 July: 1.

Agrawal, Binod C. (1983), *The Socio-political Implications of Communication Technologies in India*, Ahmedabad: Space Applications Center.

AMCB (1984), "Satellite Technology Seminar of Delhi," 14, 3, pp. 8-9.

Annual Report (1983), Government of India, Department of Space, New Delhi: GoI Press.

Anthony, Robert (1965), *Banning and Control Systems: A Framework for Analysis*, Boston, Mass.: Division of Research, Harvard Business School.

Awad, Elias (1977), *Introduction to Computers in Business*, Englewood Cliffs, N.J.: Prentice-Hall, Inc.

Bannerjee, Shampa (1981), *Kheda: An Experiment in Rural* TV, New Delhi: Center for Development of Instruction Technology.

Baroudi, J., Olson, M.H. and Ives B. (1986), "An Empirical Study of the Impact of User Involvement of System Usage and Information Satisfaction," *Communications of ACM*, Vol. 29, pp. 232-238.

Barthes, R. (1981), *Camera Lucida trans*, R. Howard, New York: Hill.

Baudrillard, J. 1996 [1988], *Selected Writing in* P. Marris and S. Thornham (eds.), *Media Studies: A Reader*, Edinburgh: Edinburgh University Press.

Bell, Daniel (1981), "The Social Framework of the Information Society," in Thomas P. Forrester (ed.), *The Microelectronic Revolution: The Complete Guide to New Technology and Its Impacts on Society*, Cambridge, MA: MIT Press.

Bergson, Henri (1978), *Matter and Memory*, New York: Humanities Press, Inc.

Boland, R.J. Jr. (1978), "The Process and Products of System Design," *Management Science*, Vol. 24, pp. 887-898.

Burnside, Scott and Cairns, Alan (1993), 'Cops seize Teale story at border', Ottawa Sun, 29 November.

Burrell, A. (1994), "Media, Muslims and Manipulation", Unpublished MA dissertation, Goldsmiths College, University of London.

Canadian Library Association (1985), *Statement on Intellectual Freedom*, Ottawa: Canadian Library Association.

Canning, "COBOL Aid Packages," *EDP Analyzer*, January 1972.

Canning, "Computer Security: Backup and Recovery Methods," *EDP Analyzer*, January 1972.

Carey. J. (ed.) (1987), *The Faber Book of Reportage*, London: Faber and Faber.

Chapin, N. (1981), Graphic Tools in the Design of Information Systems, in Cotterman, W.W., Conger, N.L. and Harold, F. (Eds.), *Systems Analysis and Design: A Foundation for 1980's*, North Holland, New York.

Chen, Milton and Willian Paisley (Eds.), *Children and Microcomputers: Research on the Newest Medium* (Sage, 1985).

Chowla, N.L. (1983), "TV Networking Through INSAT-1B," *The Times of India*, October 14, p. 7.

Chowla, N.L. (1986), "Business by the Box," *The Statesman*, November 24.

Clarke, Arthur C. (1981), "New Communication Technologies and the Developing World," *Media Asia*, 8, 4, pp. 185-190.

Condensed from M. Kubr (ed.) (1976), *Management Consulting*, Geneva, Switzerland: International Labour Office, pp. 36-41.

Cooper, J.W. (1977), *The Minicomputer in the Laboratory*, New York: John Wiley and Sons.

Cubby, Inc. v. CompuServe, Inc., 776 F. Supp. 135 (S.D.N.Y. 1991).

Cushing, B.E. (1976), "Pricing for Internal Computer Service: The Basic Issues," *Management Accounting*, 57, pp. 47-50.

D.C. McClelland and D.C. Winter (1969), *Motivating Economic Achievement*, Now York: The Free Press.

Darnton, Robert, (1982), *The Literary Underground of the Old Regime*, Cambridge, MA: Harvard University Press.

Dassetto, F. (1988), The Tabligh organisation in Belgium in T. Gerholm and Y.G. Lithman (eds.), *The New Islamic Presence in Western Europe*, London: Mansell.

Davey, Frank (1994), *Karla's Web: a Cultural Investigation of the Mahaffy—French Murders*, New York: Penguin.

Davis (1972), *Human Behaviour at Work*, New York: McGraw-Hill Book Co.

De Grazia, Edward (1993), *Girls Lean Back Everywhere: the Law of Obscenity and the Assault on Genius*, New York: Vintage Books.

De Lacey, Justine (1987), The sexy computer', *Atlantic Monthly*, July: 18-26.

Dean (1971), "A Comparison of Decision Tables Against Conventional COBOL as a Programming Tool for Commercial Applications," *Software World*, Spring.

Dearden, John and F.W. McFarlan (1966), *Management Information Systems*, Homewood, 111.: Richard D. Irwin, Inc.

DECU (1985), Development and Educational Communication Unit: *Evaluation of CLASS*, Ahmedabad.

Deutsch, M. (1969), "Productive and Destructive Conflict," *J. Social Issues*, Vol. 25, pp. 7-42.

Doll, D.R. (1977), Data Communications: Facilities, Network and Systems Design, New York: John Wiley and Sons.

Douglas, Mary (1982), *In the Active Voice*, London; RKP.

DP Auditing Viewed as Art Form Instead of Science," *Computer-world*, July 11, 1977.

Editors (1966), Scientific American Information, San Francisco: W.H. Freeman and Co.

Edstrom, A. (1977), "User Influence and the Success of MIS Projects: A Contingency Approach," *Human Relations*, Vol. 30, No. 7, pp. 589-607.

Ference, T.P. and M. Uretsky (1976), "Computers in Management: Some Insights into the State of the Revolution," *Management Datamatics*, 2, 5, pp. 55-63.

Forrest E. Under (1976), Director, International Programme of Laboratories for Population Statistics, School of Public Health, University of North California at Chapel Hill, NC, USA: "Recent Trends in Health Statistics" in WHO *Chronicle*, 30: 58-63.

Forrester, J.W. (1968), *Industrial Dynamics*, Wright-Allen Press, Cambridge.

Forrester, J.W. (1968), *Principles of Systems*, MIT Press, Cambridge.

Franz, C.R. (1979), "Contingency Factors Affecting the User Involvement Role in the Design of Successful Information Systems" Ph.D. Dissertation, University of Nebraska.

Fudpucker, Orville (1992), 'PC Magnet', *PC Magazine*. 14: 557.

Fuller, Buckminister, R. (1981), "Utopia or Oblivion" in Albert H. Teich (ed.) *Technology and Man's Future*, New York, St. Martin's Press, pp. 63-85.

Fumiss, Maureen (1993), 'Sex with a hard (disk) on: computer bulletin boards and pornography', *Wide Angle*, 15(2): 19-37.

Gallop, Jane (1988), Thinking Through the Body, New York: Columbia University Press.

Game, Ann (1991), *Undoing the Social*, Toronto: University of Toronto Press.

Ghosh, Avik (1983), "T.V., Social Change and Development," Paper presented at the IX International Film Festival, New Delhi.

Gill, S.S. (1986), "Indian Television, Expansion and After," Paper presented to the Namedia Foundation, New Delhi.

Ginzberg, M.J. (1981), "Early Diagnosis of MIS Implementation Failures: Promising Results and Unanswered Questions," *Management Science*, 4, 27, pp. 459-478.

Globe and Mail (1993), 'Public's right to know gains here, loses there', Globe and Mail, 2 December: Al.

Glueck, William F. (1977), *Management*, Homewood-Illinois: The Dryden Press.

Goethals, G. (1981), *The Television Ritual: Worship at the Video Altar*, Boston: Beacon Press.

Goethals, G. (1990), *The Electronic Golden Calf Images, Religion and the Making of Meaning*, Cambridge: Cowley Publications.

Golding, P. and Elliott. P. 1996 [1979], *Making the News* in P. Marris and S. Thornham (eds), *Media Studies: A Reader*, Edinburgh: Edinburgh University Press.

Gunter, B. and Viney, R. (1994), *Seeing is Believing: Religion and Television in the 1990s*, London: John Libbey.

Gupta, M.P. (1990), Modelling and Analysis of Management Information System Architecture at National Level, Ph.D. Dissertation, I.I.T. Delhi.

Gupta, M.P. and Sushil (1989), Towards Designing an Information-flow-Structure of Resource Waste for National Planning, *Int. Jl. Systems Research*, Vol. 3, No. 3, 247-254.

Hadden, J.K. and Shupe, A. (1988), *Televangelism: Power and Politics on God's Frontier*, New York: Henry Holt and Co.

Hadden, J.K. and Swarm, C.E. (1981), *Prime Time Preachers: The Rising Power of Televangelism*, Reading, MA: Addison-Wesley Pub. Co.

Hafner, Katie and Markoff, John (1991), *Cyberpunk: Outlaws and Hackers on the Computer Frontier*, London: Fourth Estate.

Hall, S. (1992), "Encoding/decoding" in S. Hall *et al.* (eds.), *Culture, Media, Language*, London and New York.

Harper Marion, 'A New Profession to Aid Management' Charles Coolidge Parlin Memorial Lecture, p. 13.

Herbert A. Simon, Theories of Decision Making in Economics and Behavioural Science," *The American Economic Review*, 49 (June, 1959), p. 270.

Hersey and Blanchard (1972), *Management of Organisation Behavior*, Englewood Cliffs, NJ.: Prentice-Hall, Inc.

HIPO—A Design Aid and Documentation Technique (1974), International Business Machines, GC 20-1851, White Plains, New York.

Hoffman, Taara Eden (1994), 'Cyberspace cannot be censored: Wired responds to Canadian ban of its April issue', Wired press release, 23 March.

Holoien, Martin (1977), *Computers and Their Societal Impact*, New York: John Wiley and Sons.

Holy, L. and Stuchlik, M. (1983), *Actions, Norms and Representations*, Cambridge: Cambridge University Press.

Hopper, Max.D., 'Rattling SABRE—New Ways to Compete on Information', *Harvard Business Review*, May-June 1990.

Hunt, Lynn (1993), 'Introduction: obscenity and the origins of modernity, 1500-1800', in *The Invention of Pornography: Obscenity and the Origins of Modernity, 1500-1800*, New York: Zone Books, pp. 9-45.

Huntington, S. (1993), "The Clash of Civilisations?" *Foreign Affairs 72*(3): 22-49.

Hussain, Abid (1986), "Television as a Vehicle of Development," Paper presented to the Namedia Foundation, New Delhi.

Industry Canada (1994), 'The Canadian Information Highway: Building Canada's information and communications infrastructure', in *Spectrum, Information Technologies and Telecommunications Sector*, Ottawa: Industry Canada (April).

Irigaray, Luce (1985), *This Sex Which Is Not One*, New York: Cornell University Press.

Ives, B. and Baroudi, J.J. (1983), "The Measurement of User Information Satisfaction" *Communications of ACM*, 10, 26, pp. 785-793.

Ives, B. and Olson, M.H. (1984), "User Involvement and MIS Success: A Review of Research," *Management Science*, Vol. 30, p. 5.

J. Raymond, Coleman and M.J. Rilley (Ed.), *Management Dimensions*, Holden-Day, WC. 500, Samseone, Street, San Francisco, California, p. 15.

J.M.L. Peters, "The Art of Seeing a Film", *The UNESCO Courier*, March, 1962.

Jacqmotte, Benoit and Broadhurst, Michael, (1993), 'Homolka newsgroup suspended', *McGill Tribune*, 16-22 November: 8.

Jenkins, M.A. (1983), Protoyping: A Methodology for the Design and Development of Application Systems, Working Paper, School of Business, Indiana University Bloomington.

Joshi, P.C. (1983), "Doordarshan Needs Personality," Mainstream (July): 4, Kagal, Ayesha (1983) "Caught in the Netword," *The Times of India*, April 3.

Joshi, S.R. and Parmar, K.M. (1992), *International Television and Video Flow in India: A Case Study*, Development and Educational Communication Unit, Indian Space Research Organisation, Ahmedabad.

Joshi, S.R. (1991), Communication Efficiency Study (Gujarat Region), Development and Educational Communication Unit, Indian Space Research Organisation, Ahmedabad.

Keen, Ben (1987), 'Play it again, Sony: the double life of home video technology', *Science as Culture* 1: 7-42.

Keith, Davis (1972), *Human Behavior at Work*, New York: McGraw-Hill Book Co., p. 517.

Kendrick, Walter (1987), *The Secret Museum: Pornography in Modern Culture*, New York: Vintage Books.

Kennedy, Michael and Martin B. Solomon (1975), Ten Statement Fortran with Fortran IV (2nd ed.), Englewood Cliffs, N.J.: Prentice-Hall, Inc.

Kepel, G. (1997), *Allah in the West: Islamic Movements in America and Europe* (trans S. Milner), Cambridge; Polity.

Kharma, K.C., "Mismanagement of Change: Wivadeshi A Cry in the Wildems", *of India*, January 1, 1986.

King, J. (1993), Tablighi Jamaat and the Deobandi Mosques in Britain, Paper presented at conference on Muslims in Britain, King's College London, December.

King, R.W. and Rodriguez, I.J. (1981), "Participative Design of Strategic Decision Support Systems: An Empirical Assessment, *Management Science*, Vol. 27, p. 6.

Kling, Robert (1980), "Social Analysis of Computing: Theoretical Perspectives in Recent Empirical Research," *Computing Surveys*, 121, pp. 61-110.

Kohn, Mervin (1977), *Dynamic Managing Principles, Process and Practices*, California: Cummings Publishing Co.

Koontz, Harold and Donnell, Cyril O. (1976), *Management: A System and Contingency Analysis of Managerial Functions*, New Delhi: McGraw Hill Kogakusha Ltd.

Kubr (ed.) (1976), *Management Consulting*, Geneva, Switzerland: International Labour Office.

Kumar, Keval J. (1981), *Mass Communication in India*, Delhi: Jaico Publishing House.

Kumar, Keval J., "India's Video Boom: Threat or Alternative" in *Media Development*, 1985/1, pp. 18-20.

Kumar, Keval J., *Mass Communication in India* (Bombay: Jaico, 1984).

Lyneis, M.J., *Corporate Planning and Policy Design: A System Dynamics Approach*; MIT Press, Cambridge, MA.

Martin, James (1976), *Telecommunications and the Computer* (2nd ed.), Englewood Cliffs, N.J.: Prentice-Hall, Inc.

Marvin, Carolyn and MarkWinther, "Computer-Ease: A Twentieth Century Literacy Emergent" in *Journal of Communication*, 33 (1), winter 1983, pp. 92-108.

Marvin, Carolyn (1987), *When Old Technologies were New: Thinking about Electric Communication in the Late Nineteenth Century*, New York: Oxford University Press.

Massis, Joseph L. and Douglas John (1975), *Managing A Contemporary Introduction*, New Delhi: Prentice Hall of India Pvt. Ltd.

McDermott, John (1981), "Technology: The Opiate of the Intellectuals", in Albert H. Teich (ed.) *Technology and Man's Future*, New York: St. Martin's Press, pp. 29-39.

McDonnell, J. (1993), "Religion, education and communication of values", in C. arthur (ed.), *Religion and the Media*, Cardiff: University of Wales Press.

Mckinsey and Company (1969), *"Unlocking the Computers Profit Potential,"* New York.

McLaughlin, Margaret L., Osborne, Kerry K. and Smith, Christine B. (1995), 'Standards of conduct on Usenet', in Steven G. Jone (ed.), *Cybersociety: Computer-mediated Communication and Community*, Thousand Oaks, CA: Sage, pp. 90-111.

McLean, "The Human Side of Systems: The User's Perspective," paper presented to the 1976 Western, Systems Conference, Los Angeles.

McLuhan, M. (1962), *The Gutenberg Galaxy: The Making of Typographic Man*, London: University of Toronto Press.

McLuhan, M. (1964), *Understanding Media: The Extensions of Man*, London.

McNardin, B.C. (1989), *Information Systems Management in Practice*, New Jersey: Prentice Hall.

Mercille, Raynald (legal advisor) (1993), 'Memo to Ms. Frances Groen, Associate Director Public Service & Collections re: "Foreign Press Articles—Canadian Ban"', 3 December, Copy available from author.

Mesthene, Emmanuel G. (1981), "The Role of Technology in Society," in Albert H. Tiech (ed.), *Technology and Man's Future*, NY: St Martin's Press, pp. 99-130.

Micelli, Pat (1994), 'Censorship: it's OK to read about Homolka on computer, lawyers say', *McGill Daily*. 24 January: 3.

Ministry of Human Resource Development, Government of India, *Draft National Policy on Education*, 1986.

Ministry of Human Resource Development, Government of India, *The Challenge of Education*, 1985.

Mirams, G., "How the Cinema Affects Children," *The UNESCO Courier*, March, 1961.

Mody, Bella (1979), "Programming of SITE," *Journal of Communication*, 28: 90-98.

Mohan, Dinesh, "Education" Platitudes and Policy' in *The Indian Express*, May 3, 1986.

Monge, P.R. and others (1984), "The Process of Studying Process in Organisation Communication," *Journal of Communication*, 34, 1, pp. 22-43.

Moon, Peter (1992), 'Network sex: is increasingly explicit material on some computer bulletin boards free speech, or obscenity?' *Globe and Mail*, 20 July: 6.

Morton, Michael Scott (1988), 'Strategy Formulation Methodologies and I.T.', *Information Management-the Strategic Dimension*, Oxford University Press, pp. 54-67.

Mumford, E. (1979), "Consensus Systems Design: An Evaluation of this Approach," *Design and Implementation of Computer Based Information Systems*, Cromingen.

Murphy, Brian, "Computer Children: Are they all Alike?" in IDOC *International*, 1985/1, pp. 30-31.

Murphy, Brian (1983), *The World Wired Up: Unscrambling the New Communication Puzzle* (London: Comedia).

Murthy, N. (ed.) (1981), *Experiments in Management Development: Experience of India Population Project-1*, Ahmedabad: (Mimeo).

Narasimhan, R. (1983), "The Socio-economic Significance of Information Technology to Developing Countries" in *The Information Society*, 2(1), pp. 65-79.

Naumann, J.D. Davis, G.B.' and McKeen, J.D. (1980), Determining Information Requirements: A Contingency Method for Selection of Requirement Assurance Strategy, *Jl. of Syst. and Software, 1*.

Norton, M. Bedfold and Mhamed Onsi, "Measuring the Value of Information, An Information Theory Approach," in Max, D. Richards and William A. Nielander *Readings in Management*, D.B. Tarporevala Sons and Co., Bombay, p. 140.

Olson, M.H. and Ives, B. (1981), "User Involvement in System Design: An Empirical Test of Alternative Approaches," *Information and Management*, 4, pp. 183-196.

Opie, Peter and Opie, Iona (1959), *The Lore and Language of Schoolchildren*, Oxford: Oxford University Press.

Orlicky, J. (1969), *"The Successful Computer System"*, New York, McGraw Hill.

Papert, Seymour (1980), *Mindstorms: Children, Computers and Population Ideas* (New York: Basic Books).

Perry and Adams, "SMF—An Untapped Audit Resource," *EDPACS*, September 1974.

Perry and Fitzgerald, "Designing for Audit ability," Datamation, August 1977.

Perry, "Using SMF as an Audit Tool-Accounting Information," *EDPACS*, February 1975.

Petrek, Melissa and St. Jude (1992), 'Putting It On The Line', *Mondo 2000*, 6: 113-15.

Pool Ithiel de Sola. (ed.) (1977), *The Social Impact of the Telephone*, Cambridge, MA: MIT Press.

Porat, Marc U. (1978), "Communication Policy in an Information Society," in Glen O. Robinson (ed.) *Communications for Tomorrow: Policy Perspectives for the 1980s*, New York: Praeger Publishers.

Porter and Perry (1980), *EDP Controls and Auditing*, Third Edition, Belmont, Calif: Wadsworth Publishing Company, Inc.

Porter, Michael E. and Millar, Victor E., How Information Gives you Competitive Advantage, *Harvard Business Review*, July-August, 1985.

Postman, N. (1987), *Amusing Ourselves to Death: Public Discourse in the Age of Show Business*, London: Methuen.

Powers, R.F. and Dickson, G.W. (1973), "MIS Project Management Myths, Opinions and Reality," *California Management Review*, 3, 15, pp. 147-156.

R.V. Bernardo between Her Majesty the Queen, and Karla Bernardo also known us Karia Teale (1993), O.J. No. 2047. Action No. 125/93, Ontario Court of Justice—General Division, St. Catharine's, Ontario, 5 July 1993.

Raymond, Eric (1991), *The New Hacker's Dictionary*, Cambridge, MA: MIT Press.

Rheingbid, Howard (1993), *The Virtual Community*, Reading, MA: Addison-Wesley.

Roberge, Caston (1985), *Another Cinema of Another Society* (Calcutta: Seagull Publications).

Robey, D. and Farrow, D. (1982), "User Involvement, in Information System Development: A Conflict Model and Empirical Test," *Management Science*, Vol. 21, No. 1.

Rockart, John F. and Bullen, C.V., *'A Primer on Critical Success Factors'*, Cambridge, MA.

Roy, O. (1994), *The Failure of Political Islam*, London: I.B. Tauris.

Sarabhai, Vikram (1969), "Mass Media for Developmental Tasks," Paper presented to the Society for International Development, New Delhi, November 1969.

Sardar, Z. and Davies, M.W. (1990), *Distorted Imagination: Lessons from the Rushdie Affair*, London: Grey Seal Books.

Sdorow, Lester (1990), *Psychology*, Iowa: Wm. C. Brown Publishers.

Sharma, A. (1987), *Monitoring Social Components of ICDS: A Pilot Project*, New Delhi: NIPCCD.

Srivastava, A. and Satvir Singh: "The Use of Computers in Education" in *Journal of Indian Education*, 8(2), July 1982.

Srivastava, J.S. (1984), *Rural India is Not in the Picture*, Pune: Film and Television Institute.

Stephenson, Neal (1993), 'Smiley's people', *The New Republic*, 13 September: 26.

Terry, George R. (1958), *Principles of Management*, Homewood—Illinois Richard D. Irwin Inc.

Thompson, J. (1962), "Organisations and Output Transactions," *American Journal of Society*, pp. 309-324.

Thompson, J.B. (1995), *The Media and Modernity: A Social Theory of the Media*, Cambridge: Polity.

Wadsworth (1973), *The Human Side of Data Processing Management*, Englewood Cliffs, NJ.: Prentice-Hall, Inc.

Waltham, M.A. (1981), SADT; *Structured Analysis and Design Technique Overview*, Softech Inc.

Warmer, J.D. (1981), *Logical Construction of Systems*, Van Nostrand Reinhold, New York.

Weinberg, K. Alvin M. (1981), "Can Technology Replace Social Engineering?", In Albert H. Teich (ed.) *Technology and Man's Future*, New York: St. Martin's Press, pp. 29-39.

Yourdan, E. and Constantine, L.C. (1979), *Structured Design*, Prentice-Hall, Englewood Cliffs, N.J.

Zmud, R.W. (1976), "Individual Differences and MIS Success, A Review of Empirical Literature," *Management Science*, 10, 25, pp. 966-979.

Index